UNDERSTANDING ENTERPRISE, ENTREPRENEURSHIP AND SMALL BUSINESS

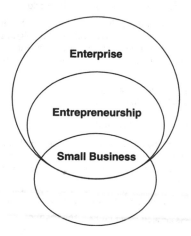

Simon Bridge, Ken O'Neill and Stan Cromie

Second Edition

Chaebols
conglomerate business

palgrave
macmillan

First edition published 1998
This second edition published 2003 by
PALGRAVE MACMILLAN
Houndmills, Basingstoke, Hampshire RG21 6XS and
175 Fifth Avenue, New York, N.Y. 10010
Companies and representatives throughout the world

PALGRAVE MACMILLAN is the global academic imprint of the Palgrave Macmillan division of St. Martin's Press, LLC and of Palgrave Macmillan Ltd. Macmillan® is a registered trademark in the United States, United Kingdom and other countries. Palgrave is a registered trademark in the European Union and other countries.

ISBN-13 987-0-333-98465-9 PAPERBACK
ISBN-10 0-333-98465-X PAPERBACK
ISBN-13 978-0-333-96499-6 HARDBACK
ISBN-10 0-333-96499-3 HARDBACK

This book is printed on paper suitable for recycling and made from fully managed and sustained forest sources. Logging, pulping and manufacturing processes are expected to conform to the environmental regulations of the country of origin.

A catalogue record for this book is available from the British Library.

Library of Congress catalog card number: 2003053568.

10   9   8
12   11   10   09   08   07

Printed and bound in Great Britain by
Creative Print & Design (Wales), Ebbw Vale

CONTENTS

Contents

LIST OF TABLES, FIGURES, ILLUSTRATIONS AND CASES

TABLES

FIGURES

ILLUSTRATIONS

CASES

PREFACE

This is a book about enterprise and its relationship to entrepreneurship and small business. Throughout history many people have been enterprising and small businesses have been with us for many years. Recently however they have been seen as particularly economically beneficial. The world has been changing, and the role of the individual has become increasingly more important, with individual initiative becoming ever more necessary for economic success. This process has been referred to as the development of an enterprise culture and its benefits have been widely sought. Enterprise and its associated concepts of entrepreneurship and small business have therefore all been widely promoted and their development supported.

In many countries in the closing decades of the last century a new industry developed. It was the industry of enterprise promotion and support. It was developed by government departments, by local economic and enterprise agencies, by community initiatives, by private organisations and by academic institutions. This process is also being repeated in other countries, such as those of Central and Eastern Europe, with less well-developed market economies and where enterprise development is seen as a key route to economic growth.

For those working in this field, however, especially when they are new to it, there can be considerable confusion about what is involved. The language used is not clearly defined and many key words, with the word 'enterprise' itself being a prime example, have more than one meaning and are used differently by different people or in different contexts. The new industry has developed theories, policies and practices of its own, and often without a clear objective or strategy. This may be typical of an emerging field but for those unfamiliar with it, and even for many who have some familiarity, it is hard to grasp what is being done and why. Nevertheless the industry will continue to grow and employment in it is already substantial, so that those working in it or close to it need to try to make sense of it.

Comprehensive overviews of the subject have not been available, however. A lot of research has been done, but it has of necessity been rather specialised, often not very widely published and usually of a piecemeal nature. Guides in the form of books and pamphlets that are available on the subject of enterprise and small business often turn out to be mainly on how to start a small business: a relevant subject for those who are thinking of doing just that, but not so useful for those seeking a wider insight into enterprise and its associated concepts in order better to understand, promote or support it. This book therefore attempts to address their needs.

WHO SHOULD READ THIS BOOK

This book is targeted at students of enterprise at universities, business schools and further and higher education establishments; at researchers and teaching staff; at policy-makers and staff of business support organisations; and at the informed public. It provides a foundation text for those who are studying enterprise and want a perspective appropriate both for those who might want to do it by starting a business and for those who might want to work with, but not in, such businesses or with the broader aspects of enterprise. It has been written in the UK but much of its content should be relevant in all countries, where people, for whatever reason, wish to know more about enterprise and its context. It seeks to present them with a sound introduction to the key concepts and issues as a grounding for understanding and work in this area, and as a starting point for further explorations of more specialised elements.

Aspects of the book have been specifically written for students who need a broad introduction to the whole field of enterprise, such as those doing an Enterprise option on a Masters course. It provides students and lecturers with cases and questions, summaries and suggestions for further reading. The three parts of the book, covering different aspects of the subject, may have different relevance to different students. Those wanting an introduction to the subject should read Part One; those wanting also to know about small businesses should use Part Two; and those wanting also to know about the promotion of, and support for, enterprise should study Part Three.

THE STRUCTURE OF THE BOOK

A word about the structure of the book might probably also be helpful. We have tried, in all the main chapters, to start by summarising the contents and the key concepts covered in the chapter together with, for those who are using the book for study, a list of the key learning objectives of the chapter. Where, in addition to text, the chapter contains relevant material in table or figure form this is described as such and separately numbered. Three other types of information are, however, also used. Where additional illustrative material is thought to be relevant as an accompaniment to the text, but not an integral part of it, this has been placed in a box and numbered as an illustration. Where this additional material is in the form of an example of something described in the text which can be used as a case for subsequent questions to test or reinforce understanding, this has also been boxed but separately labelled as a case study. The third type of material is stand alone quotations which we have also used to add examples or emphasis. We hope that in this way we have provided relevant illustrations and examples in a way which gives the reader some choice and variety instead of just more unadorned text.

We have not, however, started with any definitions. Despite a desire by some readers to start with an explanation of the terminology, in this field we are dealing with words which can and do have more than one meaning or use. Because we are looking at enterprise as it is, rather than as we might wish it to be, we should not try to impose our own interpretation on it. Therefore in Chapter Two we explore how the words 'enterprise' and its associated concepts, such as 'entrepreneurship', are used by different people and what they appear to mean in different contexts. Chapter Six offers some of the more commonly found definitions of a small business.

CHANGES IN THE SECOND EDITION

This is the second edition of our book, written some five years after the first edition. In that time there have been new developments in enterprise thinking which we have tried to include. We have also tried to recognise the continuing increase in attention being given to entrepreneurship and the focus now being directed by some people onto the entrepreneur instead of the business (see Chapter Six). We have recognised (for instance in Chapter Eleven) the distinction now being drawn between entrepreneurship strategies, with their focus on more business starts, and small business strategies with their focus on maintaining and growing the existing business stock. We have also included, in Chapter Four, a summary of the findings of the Global Entrepreneurship Monitor (GEM), which has recently been researching differences in the levels of entrepreneurship amongst countries and their implications.

Nevertheless we have not changed our broad conclusions, for instance about the effectiveness of many interventions. We have noted comments that, 'despite an increase in academic knowledge, or even perhaps because of it, there has also been a growth in ignorance about entrepreneurship and small and medium enterprises'.[1] There has therefore been little change to Chapter Fourteen.

THANK YOU

In our work of writing this book we have been conscious of many people who have helped and encouraged us. We owe them considerable thanks. We would like especially to highlight the patience and support shown by our wives, Irene, Jenny and Millicent, who have again had to put up with many evenings and weekends of

[1] A. A. Gibb, 'SME Policy, Academic Research and the Growth of Ignorance, Mythical Concepts, Myths, Assumptions, Rituals and Confusions', *International Small Business Journal* 2000; 18(3) (April–June): 13.

work and many late phone calls and interruptions, which have been as many it seems for the second edition as for the first. We are very grateful to them.

Belfast

SIMON BRIDGE
KEN O'NEILL
STAN CROMIE

ACKNOWLEDGEMENTS

The authors and publisher gratefully acknowledge the following for permission to reproduce copyright material in the second edition of this book.

Chapter 1. The bare facts for the UK, from C. Handy, *The Future of Work* (Oxford: Basil Blackwell, 1984), pp. 16–17; composition of the European business stock 1998, from the Sixth Report of the European Observatory for SMEs, with permission of the Office for Official Publications of the European Communities; Self-Employed and Employers in the UK, from the UK Labour Force Surveys, with the permission of the Controller of HMSO; reasons for the re-emergence of small-scale enterprise, based on D. J. Storey, *Understanding the Small Business Sector* (London: ITBP, 1994), p. 35; an excerpt from T. Peters, 'Travel the Independent Road', *Independent on Sunday* ©, 2 January 1994; A view of Birch, from 'Twenty Years of Job Creation Research: What Have We Learned?' *40th ICSB World Conference, 1995* by B.A. Kirchoff.

Chapter 2. Excerpts from the University of Ulster's material on *Enterprise in Higher Education*; J. B. Cunningham and J. Lischeron, 'Defining Entrepreneurship', *Journal of Small Business Management* (January 1991), p. 47; definitions of the word 'entrepreneur' from A. Lundstrom and L. Stevenson, *Entrepreneurship Policy in the Future* (Stockholm: Swedish Foundation for Small Business Research, 2001); entrepreneurial or enterprising attributes, from A. A. Gibb, 'Enterprise Culture – Its Meaning and Implications for Education and Training', *Journal of European Industrial Training* (1987), p. 6; influences on the development of entrepreneurial ideas and ambitions at different stages of life, from Gibb (1987) *ibid.*, p.13; the components of enterprise culture from Gibb (1987) *ibid.*, p.14; the focus of learning from Gibb (1987) *ibid.*, p.17; entrepreneurial v. corporatist management – some contrasts, from Gibb (1987) *ibid.*, pp. 21–2; 'Hunting the Heffalump in the World of the Enterprise Industry', by F. Coffield, from *The Independent* © 29 August 1990; Pathfinder Initiatives – 2, from *Building a Stronger Economy – The Pathfinder Process* (Belfast: Department of Economic Development, 1987).

Chapter 3. Promotional material used by the Department of Trade and Industry; what makes an entrepreneur, from 'Risky Business' in *Holland Herald*, the in-flight magazine of KLM, with permission from Malcolm Brown and Ken Wilkie; three types of small business owner, from R. W. Hornaday, 'Dropping the E-Words from Small Business Research', *Journal of Small Business Management*, vol. 28 (1990), pp. 22–33; framework for identifying enterprise competency, from S. Caird, 'Problems with the Identification of Enterprise Competencies', *Management Education and Development*, vol. 13 (1992), p. 16, © Sage Publications; change management competencies, from D. Buchanan and D. Boddy, *The Expertise of the Change Agent* (Hemel Hempstead: Prentice-Hall, 1992) pp. 92–3; intentions model of entrepreneurial potential, from N. F. Krueger, *Prescriptions for Opportunity: Communities Can Create Potential for Entrepreneurs* (Washington, DC: Small Business Foundation of America, Working Paper 93-03, 1995); employment and self-employment by occupation – 1998, from the UK Labour Force Survey, with permission of the Controller of HMSO; Ethnic sponsorship as a Sustainable Competitive Advantage (SCA), from P. B. Greene, 'The Resource Based Approach to Ethnic Business Sponsorship – A Consideration of Ismaili-Pakistani Immigrants'; *Journal of Small Business Management* vol. 35 (1997), p. 66, published by Blackwell Publishing.

Chapter 4. Extracts and one diagram from pp. 15, 19 and 67–9 of Research Report 0012/E, *An Eclectic Theory of Entrepreneurship: Policies, Institutions and Culture*, by I. Verheul *et al.* (Zoetermeer, The Netherlands: EIM Business and Policy Research 2001), subsequently published as Chapter Two in D. Audretsch *et al.*, *Entrepreneurship: Determinants and Policy in a European–US Comparison*, published by Kluwer Academic Publishers, 2002 with permission of S. Wennekers and Kluwer; extract from pp. 47–9 of M. Carree *et al.*, *Research Report 9809/E – Business Ownership and Economic Growth* (Zoetermeer, The Netherlands: EIM Business and Policy Research, 2001) – also to be published in a forthcoming issue of *Small Business Economics*, with permission of S. Wennekers and Kluwer; Initiating Entrepreneurship, from p. 106 of S. Carter and D. Jones-Evans (eds), *Enterprise and Small Business*, copyright © Pearson Education Limited, 2000; various short excerpts from pp. 10, 63, 74, 111, 117 and 159 and selections from tables on p. 67 and p. 73, from G. Hofstede, *Cultures and Organisations* (London: HarperCollins Publishers 1994), © G. Hofstede; G. Redding, 'Three Styles of Asian Capitalism'; in 'Mastering Enterprise', no. 7, *Financial Times* ©, 13 January 1997, p. 10; the triangle of enterprise, from O. R. Spelling, 'Enterprise in a Cultural Perspective', *Entrepreneurship and Regional Development*, vol. 3 (1991) p. 39, © Taylor & Francis Publishers; various extracts and diagrams from the *Global Entrepreneurship Monitor: 2000 and 2001 Executive Reports* (Kauffman Centre for Entrepreneurial Leadership, Ewing Marion Kauffman Foundation, Kansas City, MO, USA).

Chapter 5. Network capitalism, from G. Redding, 'Three Styles of Asian Capitalism', in 'Mastering Enterprise', no. 7, *Financial Times* ©, 13 January 1997, p.11; autonomous and community entrepreneurs, adapted from B. Johannisson and A. Nilsson, 'Community Entrepreneurs: Networking for Local Development', *Entrepreneurship and Regional Development*, vol. 1, no. 1 (1989), p. 5; W. Hutton, 'Ethics Man Finds No Place in the Enterprise Era', from *Guardian* ©, 21

March 1994; K. Gold, 'Must We Buy Schooling from Marks and Spencer?', *The Observer* ©, 21 January 1990.

Chapter 6. Three dimensions of habitual entrepreneurs, from P. Rosa, 'Entrepreneurial Process of Business Cluster Formation and Growth by Habitual Entrepreneurs', *Entrepreneurship: Theory and Practice*, vol. 22 (1998), pp. 48–51, reprinted by permission of Baylor University, publishers of *Entrepreneurship: Theory and Practice*; the five stages of business growth, from N. C. Churchill and V. L. Lewis, 'Growing Concerns: The Five Stages of Small Firm Growth', *Harvard Business Review*, May–June (1983), pp. 31, 32, 33 and 34; growth process as reflected in possible growth paths, from E. Garnsey, 'A New Theory of the Growth of the Firm', *41st World Conference of ICSB, Stockholm, June 1996*, p. 4; diverse trajectories of a cohort of businesses, from E. Garnsey (1996) *ibid.*, p. 18; influences on the entrepreneurial decision, from A. C. Cooper, 'Technical Entrepreneurship; What Do We Know?', *R & D Management*, vol. 3 (1973), pp. 59–64; Vickery's model, from B. Garnier and Y. Gasse, *An Experience in Training in the Area of Entrepreneurship and Starting a Business in Quebec: The Project 'Becoming an Entrepreneur'*, October 1986; entrepreneurial success, from R. Peterson and R. Rondstadt, 'A Silent Strength: Entrepreneurial Know Who', *The 16th ESBS, efmd IMD Report* (86/4), p. 11; the self employment spectrum, from R. Lessem, 'Getting Into Self-Employment', *Management Education and Development* Spring (1984), p. 31, © Sage Publications; an analysis of a business start-up, from M. Scott and R. Bruce, 'Five Stages of Growth in Small Business', *Long Range Planning*, vol. 20 (1987), p. 48, © 1987 Elsevier Science Ltd; business survival rates: percentage of enterprises surviving after one, two and five years, from *The 3rd Annual Report of the European Observatory for SMEs* (Zoetermeer, The Netherlands: EIM Small Business Research and Consultancy, 1995), p. 87; advantages and disadvantages of family controlled businesses, reprinted from M. F. R. Kets de Vries, 'The Dynamics of Family Controlled Firms – the Good News and the Bad News', *Organisational Dynamics* vol. 21 (1993), p. 69, copyright © 1993 with permission from Elsevier Science Ltd.; transactions between family and business, from K. Stafford *et al.*, 'A Research Model of Sustainable Family Business', *Family Business Review*, vol. 12 (1999), p.204, reprinted with permission from The Family Firm Institute, Inc., all rights reserved.

Chapter 7. Six phases of reaction to unemployment, from J. Hayes and P. Nutman, *Understanding the Unemployed* (London: Tavistock, 1981); debt structure by country, from P. Burns and O. Whitehouse, *Financing Enterprise in Europe 2* (Milton Keynes: 3i Enterprise Centre, 1995); small business problems, from 'Problems Facing Small Firms', *Nat West/Small Business Research Trust Quarterly Survey of Small Business in Britain*, vol. 17 (2001), p.20; the ingredients of failure, from P. Burns, *Entrepreneurship and Small Business* (London: Palgrave Macmillan 2002), p. 271, reproduced with permission of Palgrave Macmillan; the layers of the small business support network, from A. A. Gibb, 'Towards the Building of Entrepreneurial Models of Support for Small Business', paper presented at the *National Small Firms Policy and Research Conference* (Cambridge, 1988).

Acknowledgements

Chapter 8. Previous academic approaches to understanding small business growth, from A. A. Gibb and L. Davies, 'In Pursuit of Frameworks for the Development of Growth Models for the Small Business', *International Small Business Journal*, vol. 9 (1990), pp. 16–17; managing factors and stages, from N. Churchill, 'The Six Key Phases of Company Growth', in 'Mastering Enterprise', © *Financial Times*, 20 February 1997, p. 3; management weaknesses as a constraint on growth: internal barriers to growth (percentage of respondents citing factor as important), from Binder Hamlyn and the London Business School, 'The Quest for Growth', reprinted from *Managing to Grow* (London: CBI, 1995), p. 11; constraints for small business growth, from ESRC Centre for Business Research, *The State of the British Enterprise* (Cambridge: Cambridge Small Business Research Centre, 1992); constraints on small business growth, from A. Cosh and A. Hughes (eds), *Enterprising Britain: Growth, Innovation and Public Policy in the Small and Medium Sized Enterprise Sector 1994–1997*, (Cambridge: Centre for Business Research, University of Cambridge).

Chapter 9. 'Who is the entrepreneur?', adapted with permission from G. Pinchot III, *Intrapreneuring* (New York: Harper & Row, 1985) pp. 54–6, by Gifford Pinchot III; activities of a sponsor in a change programme, from D. Jones-Evans's chapter on 'Intrapreneurship', in S. Carter and D. Jones-Evans (eds), *Enterprise and Small Business*, copyright © Pearson Education Limited, 2000, reprinted by permission of Pearson Education Limited; slightly modified version of T. Heller, 'Loosely Coupled Systems for Corporate Entrepreneurship', *Entrepreneurship: Theory and Practice*, vol. 24 (1999), pp. 25–31, reprinted by permission of Baylor University, publisher of *Entrepreneurship: Theory and Practice*; the old and new paradigm at Baxi, based on J. Balogun and V. Hope-Hailey, *Exploring Strategic Change*, copyright © Prentice-Hall 1999, reprinted by permission of Pearson Education Limited; manager mindset and behaviour for innovation, from © The ForeSight Group Diagram, S. Hamngatan 37, 41106 Göteborg, Sweden; extract from E. Garnsey, 'Knowledge-Based Enterprise in a New Economy', in *New Economy: New Entrepreneurs* (Zoetermeer, The Netherlands: EIM Business and Policy Research, 2001).

Chapter 10. Objectives of small firm policy, from D. J. Storey, *Understanding the Small Business Sector* (London: ITBP, 1994), p. 260; extracts from a personal communication from members of an OECD Working Party on SMEs called *The Role of SMEs: Findings and Issues*, with recognition to the Organisation for Economic Co-operation and Development, Paris (OECD/DSTI/IND, 2000); A View of Market Imperfections, Their Causes and Actions Taken, developed from D. Keeble and S. Walker, 'New Firms, Small Firms and Dead Firms: Spatial Patterns and Determinants in the United Kingdom', *Regional Studies*, vol. 28 (1994), pp. 411–27 and P. Westhead and A. Moyes, 'Reflections on Thatcher's Britain: Evidence from New Production Firm Registrations 1980–88', *Entrepreneurship and Regional Development*, vol. 4 (1992), pp. 21–36; Small Business Growth Stunted by Reluctance to Seek Advice, from, *Business Link Press Release*, 8 October 2001, with permission from The Small Business Service; Variations in Business Start-up Rates

Across the UK from www.hm-treasury.gov.uk/press/2000, with permission from the Controller of HMSO; Influence Through the Education System from I. Verheul *et al.*, Research Report 0012/E, *An Eclectic Theory of Entrepreneurship: Policies, Institutions and Culture* (Zoetermeer, The Netherlands: EIM Business and Policy Research, 2001), subsequently published as Chapter Two in D. Audretsch *et al.*, *Entrepreneurship: Determinants and Policy in a European–US Comparison*, with the permission of S. Wennekers and Kluwer Academic Publishers; J. Curran, 'What is Small Business Policy in the UK For? Evaluating and Assessing Small Business Policies', *International Small Business Journal*, vol. 18 no. 3 (2000), pp. 43–5, with permission of the journal editor; The Rationale for an Industrial Policy, from *An Address by Mary Harney, Tanaiste and Minister for Enterprise to Dail Eireann on 18 June 1998*, reproduced with the permission of the Department of Enterprise and Employment, Dublin.

Chapter 11. Does Location Matter in Israel and Ireland, from *Does Location Matter for Innovation? A Comparison of High-Tech Firms in Israel and Ireland*, with permission from the Northern Ireland Economic Research Centre, Belfast, 2002; The Start-Up Failure Myth, from A. A. Gibb, 'SME Policy, Academic Research and the Growth of Ignorance: Mythical Concepts, Myths, Assumptions, Rituals and Confusions', *The International Small Business Journal*, vol.18 (2000), pp. 22–3.

Chapter 12. Short extract and table entitled Linking Entrepreneurship and Economic Growth from A. Lundstrom and L. Stephenson, *Entrepreneurship Policy in the Future*, (Stockholm: Swedish Foundation for Small Business Research, 2001); objectives of small firm policy, from D. J. Storey, *Understanding the Small Business Sector* (London: ITBP, 1994), p. 260; confusion and churn amongst support agencies, from L. Perrin, M. Davis and K. Krossin, *Mapping the UK SME Management and Leadership Development Provision* (London: Council For Excellence in Management Leadership, 2001); the training and development of people in SMEs, from L. Perrin and P. Grant, *Management and Leadership in UK SMEs* (London, Council for Excellence in Management Leadership, 2001); The UK Small Business Service, Public Sector Initiatives for High-Tech Business, The Cruickshank Review, The Social Investment Task Force and Government Initiatives for Deprived Areas, all from *Finance for Small Firms: An Eighth Report* (London: Bank of England, 2001), with kind permission of the Bank of England; letter from the Chief Executive of the Small Business Service to the Business Links Network on 20 November 2001 and a letter from the Chief Executive to the Institute of Business Advisers and others on 9 May 2001, with the kind permission of the Small Business Service; SME policy areas, from European Network for SME Research, *The European Observatory for SMEs 2nd Annual Report* (Zoetermeer, The Netherlands: EIM Small Business Research and Consultancy, 1994); UK government SME policies, from D. J. Storey, *Understanding the Small Business Sector* (London: ITBP, 1994), p.269; policy fields and instruments, from K. de Lind van Wijngaarden and R. van der Horst, 'A Comparison of SME Policy in the EU Member States', *Business Growth and Profitability*, vol. 2, no. 1 (March 1996), p. 40; issues relevant to an entrepreneurship policy, from various reports written by the

Acknowledgements

authors of the *Global Entrepreneurship Monitor* (Kauffman Centre for Entrepreneurial Leadership at the Ewing Marion Kauffman Foundation, Kansas City, MO, USA); 'The Dirty Dozen' from Help for Small Firms to Beat Bureaucrats by Claire Oldfield from *The Sunday Times* © Times Newspapers Limited, 14 November 1999; extract from 'Banks Face Price Controls Aimed at Curbing Charges', by James Moore from *The Times* © Times Newspapers Limited, 15 March 2002; extract from 'Brown to End Banks' Abuse of Small Firms', by David Smith from *The Sunday Times* © Times Newspapers Limited, 10 March 2002; extract from 'Police Castigation from the Voice of Small Business Owners', by Harriet Arnold from *The Financial Times* © 13 July 2001; setting up a private limited company, from *Entrepreneurship in the Netherlands. New Economy: New Entrepreneurs* (Zoetermeer, The Netherlands: EIM Business Policy and Research, 2000); the existence of a funding gap for SMEs from, P. Burns, *Entrepreneurship and Small Business* (London: Palgrave Macmillan, 2002), reproduced with permission of Palgrave Macmillan; table on implemented and planned national actions in Europe to support SMEs from 1997 to 1999 and an extract on new developments in SME policy in Europe, from the *Sixth Report of the European Observatory for SMEs* (Luxembourg, 2001), with permission from The Office for Official Publications of the European Communities.

Chapter 13. The difference between evaluation and appraisal, from *Appraisal and Evaluation in Central Government – the Green Book* (London: The Stationery Office, 1997), pp. 96–7, with permission from the Controller of HMSO; monitoring and evaluation, from the work of the late R. Scott based on his work at Northern Ireland's Department of Economic Development; the six steps to heaven from D. J. Storey, 'Six Steps to Heaven: Evaluating the Impact of Public Policies to Support Small Businesses in Developed Countries', in D. L. Sexton and H. Landstrom (eds), *Handbook of Entrepreneurship* (Oxford: Blackwell, 2000), pp. 176–94; why workers in smaller businesses are less likely to receive training, from S. Fraser, D. Storey, J. Frankish and R. Roberts, 'The Relationship Between Training and Small Business Training: An Analysis of the Barclays Bank Small Firms Training Loans Scheme', Paper presented at the *23rd ISBA National Small Firms Policy and Research Conference, Aberdeen, 2000*, pp. 1–2; two types of evaluation, from J. Curran, 'What Is Small Business in the UK For? Evaluating and Assessing Small Business Policies', *International Small Business Journal*, vol. 18 (2000), pp. 38–9; profile of entrepreneurs and enterprises using external advice, from *The Fifth Report of the European Observatory for SMEs* (Luxembourg, 2000), p. 8, with permission of The Office for Official Publications of the European Communities; measuring performance, from A. Lundstrom and L. Stevenson, *Entrepreneurship Policy in the Future* (Stockholm: Swedish Foundation for Small Business Research, 2001), pp. 144–6, with permission from the Swedish Foundation for Small Business Research.

INTRODUCTION

This book seeks to introduce the concepts of enterprise, entrepreneurship and small business and their interrelationships. It is not intended to be a comprehensive theoretical study, but instead tries to provide a practical guide to these subjects for those working in this field, be they students, promotion and support agency staff, civil servants, advisers, counsellors, trainers or academics. It aims to provide a guide to the key facts, ideas, concepts, theories and thinking about enterprise and entrepreneurship, to look at their relationship to small businesses, and to consider the methods that are used to promote them.

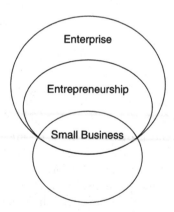

The word 'enterprise' is, at present, much used in a variety of contexts and with a wide range of meanings. Within this range there are narrow meanings of the word specifically related to business, and there are wider meanings indicating a way of behaving that can apply in a variety of contexts, including business. The narrower meanings are closely linked to entrepreneurship, and in turn, the concepts of enterprise and entrepreneurship embrace much that would be considered to be expressions of small business activity. Indeed, the words enterprise, entrepreneurship and small business often appear to be used interchangeably;

but it is also argued that there are many small businesses that do not demonstrate much enterprise.

The variety of uses made of the word 'enterprise' and the variety of contexts in which it is applied are indicative of the appeal of the concept and its various applications. Evidently, the main reason for this appeal of enterprise is jobs. Small businesses are frequently net creators of jobs, more so than big businesses. Those, therefore, who wish to encourage and promote more jobs are interested in small businesses and often in what can be done to develop more of them. It is this process of business formation and development that is often referred to as entrepreneurship, which therefore forms, for many people, an important sub-set of enterprise.

The book consists of three parts. Part One starts with a largely historical examination of why the concept of enterprise has been presented by many people as something desirable and worth pursuing in practice. It then explores the variety of ways in which the word is used and the spectrum of meanings it can have. In particular it refers to the narrow and broad definitions which see enterprise respectively as being just business entrepreneurialism, or as the qualities which enable people to be creative and adaptable in the face of economic and social change. It presents a number of theories about enterprising behaviour in individuals, looking at the external environment in which individuals and groups operate and at the influences that cultural, economic and political conditions can have on enterprise. The link between entrepreneurship and economic success is also explored.

Part Two focuses on the narrow but important view of enterprise as small business formation and development. This is often the reason why people are interested in enterprise. There are many varieties of small business, which differ from each other as much as they differ from larger businesses. Small businesses should not, however, be viewed as smaller versions of large businesses. They have many distinctive features, and those who wish to understand and influence the development of small businesses need to be aware of these distinctions. A popular category of small business is the 'growth' business, because this is frequently seen as offering the best job creation prospects. Therefore small business growth is considered, as is the issue of corporate entrepreneurship, or 'intrapreneurship', which is the application of enterprise inside larger businesses.

If enterprise and small business are beneficial then there will be a wish that there should be more of them. In Part Three the issues of how, and why, to promote enterprise are explored and the distinction made between the concepts of entrepreneurship policy and small business policy, where the former can be said to focus mainly on business formation and the latter on business development. Small businesses are important for a variety of reasons including their contributions to economic diversity, social stability, and support for other businesses.

Attention has been focused on them in particular because of the indicated links between small business and job creation. Governments, especially in times of high unemployment, want more jobs and are therefore prepared to intervene to secure the development of more enterprise.

Part Three starts by considering the reasons for intervention and the benefits sought from it. It then considers a number of theories and assumptions about the nature of the enterprise process in order to see how intervention might work and what interventions might be successful. The possible areas for intervention and the forms it might take are examined; this is followed by a look at the issues of evaluating interventions and the results indicated by some of the relevant research.

An important theme highlighted in the book is the need to look at enterprise and small business formation and development from the perspective of the individual who is the agent of change, instead of using only the business as the main focus of attention. The final chapter in the book therefore attempts to take a wider view of what has been presented on enterprise and its relevance to the economic future of individuals.

THE CONCEPT OF ENTERPRISE

INTRODUCTION

Part One of this book looks at the concept of enterprise, and the concepts of entrepreneurship and small business which are often associated with it, to see why they have been and are the focus of considerable attention, what they are interpreted to mean, and what appear to be the main influences on them.

Chapter One starts with a largely historical examination of why enterprise has been presented by many as something desirable and worth pursuing and why, therefore, it is the subject of considerable interest in government, academic and business circles.

Chapter Two explores the concept of enterprise and the variety of ways in which the word is used, and looks at the spectrum of meanings it can have. In particular it refers to two definitions: a 'narrow' definition, in which enterprise means the same as entrepreneurship and is specifically concerned with the start-up and development of business; and a 'broad' definition, which considers enterprise as the behaviour resulting from the exercise of a set of attributes that can be demonstrated in a variety of different contexts.

Chapters Three and Four look at the factors which have been thought to influence enterprise. There are many factors which can be categorised in a number of ways but here, in order to provide some structure for presenting them, the factors are broadly categorised as internal or external to the individual. Chapter Three considers the internal factors and looks at a number of theories about enterprising behaviour and what it is in individuals that influences them to engage in enterprising acts. Chapter Four considers the environment external to the individual, and to the group, and at the influences that economic, cultural and political conditions can have on his or her behaviour individually and collectively.

In practice, as the boundaries distinguishing internal and external influences are not absolute, there are areas of overlap. Those theories which include aspects of both sets of influences are also reviewed in Chapter Four, thus developing some of the separate ideas presented earlier.

A number of important aspects and perceptions of enterprise do not however fit into the categories of internal and external. They are therefore presented separately in Chapter Five, which looks at some of these perceptions, at some enterprise connotations, at the possible disadvantages of enterprise, and at possible aspects of its future development.

1

WHY TALK ABOUT ENTERPRISE?

CONTENTS

Introduction
The passion for enterprise

KEY CONCEPTS

This chapter covers:
- the expectation people have of employment and the desire of governments to maintain full employment;
- the trends in work, in employment, and in self-employment and the ending of the expectation of a job for life;
- Birch's finding in the USA that small businesses created the majority of net new jobs;
- the extent to which small businesses predominate in the world's economies;
- the attractiveness of enterprise therefore as a source of employment and other economic benefits.

LEARNING OBJECTIVES

By the end of this chapter the reader should:
- understand why the current interest in enterprise has arisen and why enterprise has become a focus of government policy;
- appreciate how many businesses are small businesses and the significance of that;
- be aware of the trends in the structure of employment.

INTRODUCTION

Chapter One introduces the subject of enterprise by considering why it has become a popular subject. It explores how and when the concept of enterprise gained its present desirability and why it has therefore become the subject of considerable interest in government, academic and business circles. This largely historical explanation provides a background for the subsequent chapters, which consider what enterprise is and what factors are thought to influence it.

THE PASSION FOR ENTERPRISE

> This budget puts Britain on course to be the enterprise centre of Europe.
> Kenneth Clarke, UK Chancellor of the Exchequer, 1995
>
> The implementation of this strategy will lead to what the President (of the European Commission) referred to as 'Enterprise Europe'.
> European Commission Working Paper SEC(2000)771, Brussels, 2000
>
> The central economic policy issue will be widening and deepening the enterprise culture.
> Gordon Brown, UK Chancellor of the Exchequer, 2001

There are a number of generally recognised human rights, but the one that probably commands the greatest recognition, if not the greatest observance, is the right to freedom. But can a government ensure freedom for its subjects? Good laws, it has been said, can promote freedom, whereas bad laws can prevent it. Despite its recognition as a right, laws cannot therefore, of themselves, ensure freedom; they can only help to set the conditions in which it can exist.

Another human benefit sometimes recognised as a right is an education. Education, however, differs from freedom in that, whether it is seen as a right or not, a government can take steps to provide at least a basic education for its citizens. An education, it is generally recognised, is within a government's gift.

ILLUSTRATION 1.1
The right to a job
....

The other day one of the authors was having a Saturday morning coffee in his favourite café. He happened to know the two people at the adjacent table. He had said hello to them when they came in before resuming his attempts to solve the crossword in the daily paper. Suddenly something one of them said impinged on his consciousness. 'Everyone' she said, 'has the right to a job'. What are the implications of that, he wondered; how can such a right be ensured and how does it fit into an enterprise culture?

But can the same be said of work, and is the right to work the same as the right to a job? That 'everyone has the right to work' is enshrined in the Universal Declaration of Human Rights signed by the members of the United Nations. The desirability of full employment as a political objective is often debated, however, not so much because people don't want full employment, but because questions are raised about the practicality of achieving it and the implications it might have. Is employment like health or education, where a government can provide a basic level of service or provision for everyone? Or is it more like freedom, in respect of which a government's powers are more negative than positive: where it has the power to deny freedom but cannot itself directly provide freedom for everyone? Can a government provide a basic job for everyone who wants one? Governments do directly create some jobs but, at least in capitalist societies, they are not the main sources of direct employment, and they cannot themselves create enough jobs for everyone who might want one.

It is businesses that create most jobs. Governments can encourage businesses to create jobs, they can try to provide a supportive environment for the creation of jobs and they can legislate for people to have an equal opportunity to get the jobs that do exist, but that is not the same as offering the right to a job. That would mean that everyone who wanted a job could have one, but how can a government maintain that when it can't actually create enough jobs itself? If a government cannot create enough jobs then is it practical to talk about the 'right to a job'?

For many people a key feature of the communist-inspired systems of government was that they guaranteed a job for everyone. Actually, it would seem that that was not really the case and that it might be more accurate to say that they provided everyone with an employment contract and a wage, whether or not they really had a full job to do at their official place of employment. However, to achieve even that required centrally controlled economies, which are now largely deemed to have failed. A job for everyone who wants one nevertheless remains a very desirable aspiration.

Earlier last century, after the upheavals of the Industrial Revolution and the First World War, there did seem to be some prospect that a job for everyone might become the norm. Then, in the Western world at least, there were the traumas of the 1930s. Following the Wall Street crash in 1929 it appeared that there were indeed fundamental problems with the structure of capitalist economies in maintaining full, or nearly full, employment. However, by the end of that decade major job creation initiatives had produced significant reductions in unemployment and John Maynard Keynes had in theory suggested how unemployment might continue to be controlled. In addition, by 1940, there was again a war which increased the demand for armaments and other requirements for the military struggle and brought an end to the remaining unemployment.

After that war, economic prospects seemed to be much better. Keynesian economic theory seemed to be working, the experiences in the 1930s of practical employment creation seemed still to be valid, and in Britain unemployment seemed to be relatively steady at about a quarter of a million. This was a manageable figure, which offered support to the view that full employment was realistically achievable. Alarm bells did not ring loudly when by the end of the 1960s this figure had doubled to about half a million. Although history is lived forwards it is viewed backwards, and it is only in retrospect therefore that it would now seem that this was a turning point. Half a million now looks like a relatively small figure, and it was during the 1970s, when the figure grew to one and a half million, and the 1980s, when it rose again, to three million, that notions about the practicality of achieving full employment were finally shattered (Figure 1.1).

Source: CSO/ONS, Labour Market Statistics

Figure 1.1   UK unemployment (millions), 1950–2000

What was going on? One person who has studied this matter is Charles Handy. He saw that what was happening in the 1970s and 1980s was a fundamental restructuring of work. For millennia of human history the major source of jobs

---

ILLUSTRATION 1.2
The bare facts for the UK, as set down by
Charles Handy in 1984*

....

- There were fewer jobs than there were, but not that many fewer.
- But jobs had been continuously squeezed out of business.
- Jobs had been picked up by the public sector, however – but no longer.
- In general, jobs had continuously moved from manufacturing to service
- Meanwhile the labour force had been expanding ... and was going to go on expanding for the next twenty years.
- Demand for jobs had consistently exceeded supply and looked like continuing to do so.[1]

* In 2003 they are still relevant!

was agriculture. Then, with increases in industrial production and increases in agricultural efficiency, work for many became based in industry through the process which came to be known as the Industrial Revolution. Was that revolution itself, however, now being superseded?

In his introduction to *The Future of Work*[2] Handy points out that it was during the 1970s that visible changes began to appear in what had until then been the normal working life. Large organisations began to decline and concepts such as redundancy and long-term unemployment became more familiar. Britain, along with other countries such as the USA and France, was no longer primarily an industrial nation. Since the early 1970s the aggregate profits from the service sector had exceeded those from manufacturing. Internationally it was the same. Similar changes had taken place throughout the industrialised world. The problem for many, however, was not the change to new jobs but that the generation of the new jobs did not seem to be keeping pace with the reduction in the old ones.

In this situation there was a natural tendency to look back to the 1930s when job creation measures had worked, and to try to repeat that prescription. A number of solutions were proposed. Expanding the business sector was one solution considered, although to an extent business output was already expanding, but through increases in productivity not in jobs. Some businesses were simultaneously increasing output and shedding jobs – a phenomenon referred to as 'jobless growth'. Other suggestions included expanding government employment to take up the slack in jobs – a Keynesian type of solution that suggested increased government spending on infrastructure, health and education. That however looked problematic, because of the numbers who would have to be employed, the cost and the potential impact on inflation. Governments struggled to find something that might work and certainly still hoped that business would make a major contribution. They were not looking however at small businesses. They had been seen as being a 'vanishing breed' and any efforts to preserve them 'had more to do with democratic and political values than with economic efficiency'.[3]

It was in this situation in 1979 that David Birch published the results of his research into employment in the USA. He concluded that it was small firms, defined as those with 100 employees or fewer, which had in the early 1970s created over 80 per cent of net new jobs. Net new jobs is the difference between the total of new jobs created and the total of jobs lost during the same period, and is sometimes used as a reasonable indicator of economic growth. The implication was that, in the USA, it was small firms which were responsible for much of the economic growth and were the prime source of employment creation. Many people discounted Birch's work when it was first published, as his conclusion was contrary to the perceived wisdom of the time. Nevertheless, the issue was important enough to stimulate others to try to replicate his work. (See also Case 1.1 for a more detailed view on Birch, and Chapter Seven for further reference to the validity of Birch's findings.)

While the statistical debate still continues, it can be seen that it was the work of Birch, followed by that of others, that challenged the previously held common belief that economic benefits of business such as jobs and growth came always from big business, and that small business was almost incidental to this. This work led to a recognition that the bulk of the new jobs being created to maintain, or to grow, employment levels was actually coming from small businesses. While it is not all small businesses which create additional jobs and many small businesses are in the service sector, where there may be more part time and low paid work than in the manufacturing sector, that does not detract from the perceived value of the small business sector as an important source of employment. It has also been argued that small businesses can provide other economic benefits, such as a relatively greater rate of innovation.[4]

This process applied not just in America. In Europe (the 15 countries of the EU plus Iceland, Liechtenstein, Norway and Switzerland) for instance, by 1998 the number of enterprises in the non-primary private sector reached almost 20 million, of which 99.8 per cent were SMEs (Small and Medium-sized Enterprises – for definition see Chapter Six). In Europe as a whole 93 per cent of these businesses were micro-businesses and in the UK it was 94 per cent. In Europe the SMEs accounted for nearly 66 per cent of private sector employment and in the UK 56 per cent.[5] Table 1.1 shows the European figures in more detail.

Therefore those looking for an expansion of business employment, or even for a maintenance of existing employment levels, looked increasingly to small businesses to do this. Small businesses became a focus of interest for policy-makers, and they wanted to know more about them. They were seen as a fundamental component of any effort to increase employment. There was a desire to promote more of them and consequently to understand and promote the concept of enterprise that was thought to underlie them. Enterprise was becoming a vogue word, and the number of businesses and the extent of self-employment were increasing, as shown for the UK in Table 1.2 (although part of the increase may have been due to factors such as the tax changes in the 1980s which led to many contract workers being reclassified as self-employed).

Table 1.1 Composition of the European business stock, 1998

Business size (number of employees)	Micro (<10)	Small (10–50)	Medium (50–250)	Large (250+)
Number of enterprises %				
EU	93.1	5.8	0.8	0.2
Non-EU	88.2	9.3	2.1	0.4
Employment %				
EU	33.9	18.8	13.1	34.1
Non-EU	25.9	21.9	20.5	31.7

Source: Sixth Report of the European Observatory for SMEs (Luxembourg, 2001). Reproduced with the permission of the Office for Official Publications of the European Communities.

Table 1.2 Self-employed and employers in the UK, 1951–2001

Year	Total (million)
1951	1.65
1961	1.72
1971	1.79
1981	2.06
1991	3.30
2001	3.15

Source: UK Labour Force Survey. Reproduced with the permission of the Controller of HMSO.

Essentially what Birch had done was to challenge a particular assumption that the future is a continuation of the past, and had shown it to be wrong. He looked at what was already happening and demonstrated that it was not what many experts had assumed. Others have also highlighted aspects of the present and used them to suggest that there are changes that many have not perceived. At the same time as Birch was releasing his work, Alvin Toffler was writing *The Third Wave*[6] in which he described large scale industrial mass production as 'second wave' industry and forecast that both the office and the factory would be revolutionised over the future decades in a way which would affect the structure of industry, the size of work units and even the location of work. In effect, Toffler analysed reasons for the change that gave rise to the developments Birch had recorded. Table 1.3 also indicates some of the reasons for the re-emergence of the small business.

Table 1.3 Reasons for the re-emergence of small scale enterprise

Supply	Demand
Technological changes	*Structural changes*
• New products	• Demand for service
• New industries	• Demand for variety
• Fragmentation/cost advantage	• Uncertainty of demand
• Sub-contracting	• Individual customer requirements
Labour force/unemployment	*Macro-economic conditions*
• Redundancy	• Unemployment
• Education	
Government	*Economic developments*
• Privatisation	• Services
• Deregulation	• Just-in-time
• Tax benefit	• Niches

Source: Based on D. J. Storey, *Understanding the Small Business Sector* (London: Routledge, 1994), p. 35.

Charles Handy also talked about the 'shamrock organisation'.[7] It had been the assumption, he suggested, that an organisation should do as much as possible in-house with its own permanent workforce. Indeed, vertical and horizontal integration was seen as the norm for business development. However organisations in future would most likely have three distinct categories of people working for them, like the three leaves of a shamrock. The first category was the professional core, the second was the contractual fringe and the third was the mostly part-time flexible labour force. The result, he suggested, was that in the UK already by the end of the 1980s about one third of the paid workforce were part-timers or self-employed, and it could be 50 per cent by the end of the century. Subsequent experience has confirmed this trend. The proportion of part-time workers in organisations and self-employed workers contracted to them has increased, with consequent changes in employee loyalty and in length-of-service expectations.

ILLUSTRATION 1.3
Contracting out

'Contract out everything except your soul!', exhorted management expert Tom Peters.

'The airline is going to examine every part of its operation and decide which services it can buy more cheaply elsewhere ... Over the past four years ... it has contracted out its security arrangements, heavy engineering and much of its catering. It has recruited small external 'franchise' airlines to fly several routes on its behalf ... "There is no part of the operation that we are not going to look at", said one source.'

'Rolls-Royce last year signed a deal with EDS to provide all its IT needs for ten years.'

'J P Morgan is paying a consortium of suppliers $7 bn over seven years.'

Source: Excerpts from business articles in *The Observer* © on one Sunday in 1996.[8]

A generation ago, Handy said,[9] we used to work for 47 hours a week, for 47 weeks a year and for 47 years, or about 100,000 hours in a lifetime. Now he suggested this may be down to 50,000 hours for someone just starting work. This may be $37 \times 37 \times 37$, or it could still be 47 hours a week for 47 weeks a year but only for 25 years in an intense professional job, or possibly 22 hours a week for 47 weeks a year for 50 years of part-time work extending well into one's sixties as it is a continuing part, but not the whole, of life.

The 50,000-hour job is just one of the unanticipated outcomes of the shamrock organisation, and there are going to be many more. It was already clear, however, that the employee society had changed fundamentally and would not readily change back. Half as many people in the core of the business, paid twice as much and producing three times as much may make economic sense for a business, but what did it mean for the assumption of secure jobs for life? Other attitudes to employment will be needed. Those not in the core will not have a permanent job but will have 'portfolio' careers moving from job to job or from contract to contract. They will have to find such work, to contract to do it, and to manage its delivery. Such a situation will require behaviour that has been described as enterprising.

Tom Peters also looked at trends in business organisation. He foresaw the time when the organisation as we know it would not exist. Instead there would be smaller, flat and flexible network organisations. To get beyond your own brain-dead management, he said, you must subcontract everything. The future, he went on to suggest, even for larger organisations, is to deconstruct the organisation and to organise work by small teams. Otherwise the responsiveness needed for true competitiveness would be impossible to achieve.

Changes in the organisation of many businesses are already clear. The hands-on management style, flexible structures and consequent fast response times of small firms can be very beneficial in the rapidly changing modern world and bigger businesses have sought to benefit from them. In effect they have been diminishing the disadvantages of bigness by contracting out many production and service functions. As Mintzberg notes,

> This is what NASA did in the 1960s, when its attention was focused on the Apollo project, whose singular goal was to put an American on the moon before 1970. NASA conducted much of its own development work but contracted production out to independent manufacturing firms.[10]

It is also possible to contract in. Self-employed people can take on specific responsibilities 'within' large businesses, working in effect for a price not for a wage. This form of organisation is not new. Clawson[11] shows that it was an important aspect of industrial organisation in textiles, transport and iron and steel in the transition from craft organisations to the fully fledged factory in eighteenth-century Britain.

There is another discernible trend among large organisations: the creation of federal structures. As large organisations divest themselves of their divisions in pursuit of the benefits of smallness, the task of managing all divisions from the centre – and a much reduced centre, at that – becomes increasingly problematic. An example of this has been seen recently in the *chaebols* (conglomerate businesses) such as Hyundai and Daewoo in Korea which have had to divest and restructure as the competitiveness and viability of their parts became confused. The solution can be to create a federation, or network, of connected units in which the core organisation acts on behalf of its constituent parts. This only works when the centre

> genuinely is at the middle of things and is not a polite word for the top ... the centre must cling to its key functions of new people and new money, but its decisions have to be made in consultation with, and on behalf of, the chiefs of the parts.[12]

While such arrangements do provide large organisations with greater flexibility they have potential drawbacks. They mean a lessening of commitment on both sides, with employees and subcontractors having to look out themselves for the best deals and for new opportunities. A lessening of paternalism has been accompanied by a lessening of employee loyalty. It is increasingly a case of everyone for himself or herself.

This trend has been assisted more recently by the application of information and communication technology (ICT) to provide the internet and facilitate the emergence of significant numbers of knowledge-based and internet businesses. They are sometimes referred to as the 'new economy' and are typically small businesses each concentrating on an aspect of the overall process, communicating electronically, and often delivering their products or services the same way. In contrast, in the 'old economy' of traditional businesses such as chemicals and heavy engineering, the technology requires the majority of the process workers to be physically present on the same site. However it could be said that the new economy has precedents such as the clock industry in the nineteenth century when, instead of big manufacturers building complete clocks there were, in places such as Clerkenwell in East London, assemblers of clocks who bought the necessary components from an array of local small manufacturers each specialising in the supply of one sort of component.

These developments have major implications for individuals. If a job for life is no longer either the norm or a realistic aspiration, if even a succession of different jobs may not always be easy, if businesses will contract out work rather than employing people to do it, and if those who do have jobs will be working in smaller more independent business teams or individually, then people themselves will have to be more proactive in arranging and managing their own economic activity. If there will no longer always be an employer to find work, to arrange materials and facilities and to pay wages, then people will have to do it themselves. There will be an increase in the number of people, either from want or necessity, who will be thinking and acting to establish their own smaller work units. That process has also been called 'enterprise', and the changes outlined above stimulated a desire for more of it and an exploration of what it involved.

> People do realise that job security is gone, but many don't realise what it has been replaced by. The driving force of a career must come from the individual, not the organisation.
>
> Professor Homa Babrami[13]

As well as individuals perceiving the advantage of being able to fend more for themselves, there has also been an interest in reversing the apparent tendency of many people to look to government, or at least to someone else, for the provision of whatever seems to be missing in society. Some saw this change as the essence of what in the UK was called Thatcherism, and in the USA Reaganism; but whatever its label, there has been, in many developed countries, a reduction in the perception of government as the universal provider. There have as a result been corresponding moves to make the individual more aware of his or her own ability to do things, to accept responsibility and to foster more communal and social development. This has been called an enterprise culture, and associated with it are views that there are general economic and social benefits to be gained from having a more enterprising culture, society, family or person. 'Enterprise' has in consequence been on many agendas.

The changes mentioned above were not apparent initially, they were not instantaneous, and they did not proceed smoothly. Nevertheless they were, and are still, being felt, and the responses that were perceived as necessary to accommodate them were described as enterprise. Whether it was a move at government level to promote more small business, or an individual response to changed employment market conditions, or something in between, the word 'enterprise' came to be attached to it. Enterprise came to be seen as an important part of the way forward to a stronger economy, to a less dependent society and to a more prosperous future.

> The role of entrepreneurship and small business has evolved considerably since the Second World War. What was once considered to be a perhaps necessary drain on Western economies has become a central strategic instrument for competitiveness in global markets. Just as it has been important to understand how to manage entrepreneurial firms, it has now become at least as important to understand how to achieve an entrepreneurial society. While this emphasis on small entrepreneurial firms as engines of dynamic efficiency may seem startling after decades of looking at the corporate giants as engines of growth and development, it may not be so new. Before the country was even half a century old, Alexis de Tocqueville, in 1835, reported, 'What astonishes me in the United States is not so much the marvellous grandeur of some undertakings as the innumerable multitude of small ones.'
>
> Acs and Audretsch (2001)[14]

For all these reasons enterprise became the thing to explore, to understand, and to promote. This resulted in a growth of research about 'enterprise' topics, a proliferation of courses or programmes with 'enterprise' in their title, and an increased readiness to apply the label 'enterprise' to anything remotely connected to small business or to the attitudes or behaviour perceived to be associated with it. It began to be seen almost as some sort of universal cure-all for economic ills.

What enterprise consisted of was not always clear, however. For some it would appear to have meant simply small business and the activity of starting and running a small business. For others it was a set of personal qualities that made their holders more ready than others to seek their own solutions to economic or other problems. In this wider sense, an enterprising person was one who saw opportunities not problems, who looked to the future and not to the past, who was more creative than analytical and who was more active than passive. There was, however, a spectrum of ways in which the word was used, rather than one narrow definition.

To address only one definition of enterprise would not be relevant to other uses of the word. The first part of this book therefore addresses the question 'What is enterprise?' by looking at the range of contexts in which the word has been used and the spectrum of different meanings that these usages imply. It explores some of the components associated with these concepts and examines the ideas associated with enterprise from a number of different perspectives. It concludes by considering the implications of some current and potential future developments in society for our need for enterprise or for aspects of it.

Those wishing to study enterprise are often interested in one or other of two key aspects. As noted the word 'enterprise' is often used to refer to small business, and for many policy-makers this aspect of enterprise would appear to be of prime importance. In Part Two of this book, therefore, small business is explored from the point of view not of the small business practitioner or the person thinking of starting a business, which is the approach taken by many writers on the subject, but from the point of view of someone who might desire to encourage more of them and might question what constitutes a small business and what particular insights are helpful in understanding small businesses. The issues of small business growth and other associated concepts such as entrepreneurship and innovation are also linked in to this.

The second aspect, covered in Part Three, is the issue of how to promote the growth of enterprise and within that the growth of small businesses in general and in particular. The possible reasons for such external interventions are considered, together with some of the more common or useful theories and assumptions about intervention in enterprise or small business development. Specific intervention categories and methods are then explored, together with some indication of their apparent results. Evaluating the effectiveness of such measures is crucial to determining the efficiency and effectiveness of intervention, and so this part concludes by considering the possibilities, limitations and pitfalls of measuring and evaluating results.

KEY POINTS OF CHAPTER 1

··

- The last 25 years have been a time when a number of parallel developments have become clear.
- Following the relatively successful attempts in some countries such as the UK to address unemployment in the 1930s, and the apparent ease of maintaining virtually full employment after the Second World War, a belief had arisen that permanent full employment was possible and that it was the duty of the government to maintain that position.
- In the 1970s and 1980s, however, unemployment, in particular in the UK, rose considerably, without apparently being susceptible to government attempts to reverse it. Actually employment was not falling, but the number looking for employment was rising.
- Another development was that industry, the traditional main source of employment, was itself changing. It was actually increasing its output, but through increased productivity, not through increased numbers of employees. Expanding output no longer automatically increased employment.
- Birch, however, showed that, at least in the US, the bigger businesses were actually losing jobs, and that the source of the increased number of jobs to maintain employment levels was small businesses. Governments therefore wanted to promote more small business development, in order to maintain economies and to promote more employment.
- Other commentators showed that the structure of employment was itself changing. The mass, long-term employment resulting from the Industrial Revolution was being replaced by a much more flexible employment structure.
- The development of information and communication technology, combined with the increased need for inputs of knowledge rather than physical effort, have facilitated the interactive supply of input from remote locations. This has enabled small suppliers in the 'new economy' to operate remotely from their customers instead of having to be co-located on or close to the same production site.
- The implication of this was that business would be increasingly likely to be offering to people, not jobs, but tasks to undertake. People therefore would need skills and aptitudes for utilising opportunities to be paid a fee for an amount of work done, instead of finding jobs in which they would then be paid for an amount of time spent. They would have to be more flexible themselves, and more prepared and able to find their own sources of such work. In other words, they would have to be more enterprising.
- In addition to the benefits to individuals of being more enterprising, there are also perceived benefits to society of a more enterprising culture in general that would result in less dependence on government to address all society's ills.

CASE 1.1
A view of Birch

Since David Birch first published his research on job creation by size of firm in 1979, a great deal of public attention has focused upon small firms' role in economic growth. His original research provided a measure of job creation in the US from 1969 to 1976 and concluded that small firms created the majority of net new jobs. Subsequently, the US Small Business Administration has built a similar database and has produced job creation statistics from 1976 to 1990. Thus, a continuous series of job creation statistics exists for twenty years.

Other researchers have used different data sources and methods to examine job creation categorised by size of firm. Some have emulated Birch's research data and methodology and have come to the same conclusions as he. Still others have found new data sources that purport to be better than Birch's. Some of these sources show similar results. More recently, others have criticised Birch's sources and methodologies, suggesting that both are incorrect.

Neo-classical economics' theoretical constructs

Birch's 'The Job Generation Process'[15] created quite a stir among economists when it reported that most net new jobs were created by small firms not large corporations. This finding was contrary to all previous economic analyses in the US. Few economists understood Birch's work because he used a new data source, Dun and Bradstreet data files, instead of US Department of Labour or Bureau of the Census data. Furthermore, he analysed the employment history of millions of firms individually rather than using the classified data on which mainstream economists relied.

But no one criticised Birch for violation of theoretical constructs, for there is no economic theory about firm size and job creation activity and little mainstream economic theory that addresses firm size at all. Neo-classical economic theory, the foundation of mainstream economic theory in the US, does not incorporate any constructs about small firms except one. That one is an assumption rooted in the ideas of Adam Smith[16] and well known as the theory of 'economies of scale'. Economies of scale theory simply states that as production volume increases, the cost per unit of output declines. Thus, the larger production organisation will have the lower cost of production. Although it is empirically logical, and can be supported by engineering calculations, the theory is troubled by non-linearity in its structure and has been a consistent source of discord in the ranks of macro- and micro-economists. Nevertheless, it is a theory, and it is violated by Birch's findings since it is illogical that an economy will have most of its new jobs created by small firms when large firms have lower costs of production. In a competitive market, small firms with higher costs will have lower profits and therefore are unlikely (or unable) to expand their operations.

There is a second economic theory construct, Gibrat's Law,[17] that seems to be violated by Birch's findings. Gibrat's Law states that all firms grow at the same rate regardless of their size. If this is true, large firms' job creation must necessarily be greater than small firms' because large firms have a larger employment base at the start of any time period.

Interestingly, neither of these theoretical bases was used to object to Birch's research. It is not clear even today, fifteen years later (at the time of writing), why theoretical critiques have not emerged. It can only be assumed that the absence of debate indicates that Birch's research has been ignored because his results were of minor importance in the minds of most mainstream economists. This is because firm size is of no importance in the neo-classical theory model. Firm size is determined by the operation of markets. Smaller size firms have higher costs of production because of economies of scale and must struggle to survive in a market dominated by large firms. Firm size is not a cause of anything in the neo-classical model. Firm size is considered to be a dependent variable and is simply not a variable of any significance.

Thus, there is an absence of neo-classical theoretical constructs to provide a domain for examining job creation research. In fact, many mainstream economists do not understand why the topic is even being discussed. This has led to misunderstanding and conflict among proponents and opponents of the small firm job creation hypothesis. The motives of both sides seem clear. Small business believers have gained much public attention and some policy initiatives to assist their cause. The large business believers have watched their influence wane within society and have received the brunt of much criticism during the recent years of 'downsizing'. In the US and Canada, a wave of social antagonism is sweeping over large corporations while small business owners have become heroes of job creation. In response, recent job creation research has emerged challenging the appropriateness of all previous research in an effort to regain the long-held view that large firms create the majority of new jobs.

Emergence of dynamic methodologies

Most researchers have been trained in the classical scientific method, which states that a hypothesis must be proposed prior to empirical testing. One reason the classical scientific thinkers have for their view is that theory provides a domain within which empirical methods are designed and applied. Without theory to guide empirical methods, methods become arbitrary. Those who merely 'massage data' to extract meaning are scorned as second-rate researchers by the classical thinkers.

On the other hand, it is argued by some that empirical research results lead theory development. In this manner, the job creation empirical research of the last 20 years has clearly challenged mainstream economic theory but no new theory has emerged. Still, this research is full of differing data sources, research methodologies and procedures. Not surprisingly, it is empirical research without theoretical foundations and, as dictated by classical thought, it is full of conflict without resolution since there is no agreement on what is being tested and why. In other words, the absence of theory leads to confusion in job creation research.

For this reason, determining what we have learned from job creation research requires a theoretical foundation. Adoption of a theoretical domain will provide a basis for evaluating the arguments that are being advanced today. The theoretical domain proposed is Schumpeter's theory of economic development, modified into a typology called 'dynamic capitalism'.

Creative destruction

Schumpeter[18] argues that the main mechanism of economic development in a capitalist economy is creative destruction. Creative destruction occurs when an entrepreneur forms a new firm that uses (an) innovation(s) to enter an existing market dominated by a few large suppliers. The innovative new firm will grow through the dual processes of (1) increasing overall demand for the products (services) offered in the market and (2) taking market share from the existing suppliers. Thus, while the new firm expands overall economic activity, it also redistributes wealth by destroying market structure and shifting market shares from existing large firms to itself. This creation of new wealth combined with destruction of market structures is called 'creative destruction'.

Schumpeter's theory is quite different from the neo-classical model with its equilibrium market structures. In fact the two theories defy comparison. The neo-classical model is built on a static concept – market equilibrium. Creative destruction is build upon dynamic, deliberate entrepreneurship efforts to change market structures. However, dynamics are difficult to model in mathematics and therefore cannot be developed into predictive models useful for policy-making. Since prediction is an attractive component of economic theory, Schumpeter has traditionally been largely ignored in the US and Canada (see also Chapter Two).

Source: From B. A. Kirchhoff, *Twenty Years of Job Creation Research: What Have We Learned?*, paper presented to the 40th International Council for Small Business World Conference, Sydney, 1995.[19]

Points raised

This piece by Bruce Kirchhoff provides some background to Birch's work and highlights how both his methods and findings differed from those of the more traditional economists. It indicates the potential of dynamic theory, such as that advanced by Schumpeter, to explain the strength of small businesses, in contrast to the static neo-classical model which does not.

QUESTIONS, ESSAY AND DISCUSSION TOPICS

- Why is enterprise now a popular subject for study?
- What are the benefits of enterprise?
- Can governments deliver full employment and, if not, what can they do?
- Explain the reason for the rapid growth in the number of SMEs in the latter part of the 20th century.
- Provide examples of large firms downsizing and small firm growth in your local area.
- According to economic theory (see Case 1.1), larger firms should have better economies of scale than smaller ones yet, according to Birch, smaller firms create more jobs than larger ones. Do you think that this is correct and, if so, why?

SUGGESTIONS FOR FURTHER READING AND INFORMATION

Z. J. Acs and D. B. Audretsch, *The Emergence of the Entrepreneurial Society*, Presentation for the acceptance of the 2001 International Award for Entrepreneurship and Small Business Research (Stockholm: Swedish Foundation for Small Business Research, 2001).

R. Gavron, M. Cowling, G. Holtham and A. Westall, *The Entrepreneurial Society* (London: Institute for Public Policy Research, 1998).

C. Handy, *The Future of Work* (Oxford: Basil Blackwell, 1984).

C. Handy, *The Age of Unreason* (London: Arrow, 1990).

J. A. Schumpeter, *The Theory of Economic Development* (Cambridge, MA: Harvard University Press, 1934); *Capitalism, Socialism and Democracy*, fifth edition (London: Allen and Unwin, 1976).

A. Toffler, *The Third Wave* (London: William Collins, 1980).

http://www.smallbusinessportal.co.uk – The Small Business Research Portal 'has been designed to provide links to internet sites that will be helpful to fellow small business researchers, policy-makers and support agencies'.

REFERENCES

1 C. Handy, *The Future of Work* (Oxford: Basil Blackwell, 1984) pp. 16–17.
2 *Ibid.*, p. ix.
3 I. Verheul, S. Wennekers, D. Audretsch and R. Thurik, *Research Report – An Eclectic Theory of Entrepreneurship: Policies, Institutions and Culture* (Zoetermeer, The Netherlands: EIM / Small Business Research and Consultancy, 1999), p. 8.
4 For instance see Z. J. Acs and D. B. Audretsch, *Innovation and Small Firms* (Cambridge, MA: MIT Press, 1990).
5 Bank of England, *Finance for Small Firms: An Eighth Report* (London: Bank of England, 2001), p. 11.
6 A. Toffler, *The Third Wave* (London: William Collins, 1980).
7 C. Handy, *The Age of Unreason* (London: Arrow, 1990).
8 From J. Walters, 'Turbulence Ahead for City's Airline' and S. Caulkin, 'Dismembering the Body Corporate' (both in *The Observer* ©, 15 September 1996).
9 C. Handy, *The Age of Unreason*, pp. 34–5.
10 H. Mintzberg, *The Structuring of Organisations* (Englewood Cliffs, NJ: Prentice-Hall, 1979) p. 131.
11 D. Clawson, *Bureaucracy and the Labour Process: The Transformation of US Industry, 1860–1920* (New York: Monthly Review Press, 1980).
12 C. Handy, *The Age of Unreason*, p. 98.
13 Quoted in T. Peters, 'Travel the Independent Road' (*Independent on Sunday*, 2 January 1994).
14 Z. J. Acs and D. B. Audretsch, *The Emergence of the Entrepreneurial Society*, Presentation for the acceptance of the 2001 International Award for Entrepreneurship and Small Business Research (Stockholm: Swedish Foundation for Small Business Research, 2001), pp. 26–7.
15 D. Birch, *The Job Generation Process* (Cambridge, MA: MIT Programme on Neighborhood and Regional Change, 1979).
16 A. Smith, *An Inquiry into the Nature and Causes of the Wealth of Nations* (New York: Modern Library, 1937) (first published in 1776).
17 R. Gibrat, *Les Inégalités Economiques* (Paris: Editions Sirey, 1931).
18 J. A. Schumpeter, *The Theory of Economic Development* (Cambridge, MA: Harvard University Press, 1951) (first published in 1934); *Capitalism, Socialism and Democracy*, fifth edition (London: Allen and Unwin, 1976).
19 B. A. Kirchhoff, *Twenty Years of Job Creation Research: What Have We Learned*, Paper presented to the 40th International Council for Small Business World Conference, Sydney, 1995.

WHAT DOES ENTERPRISE MEAN?

KEY CONCEPTS

. . . .

This chapter covers:
- the spectrum of meanings of the word enterprise which, judging from the contexts in which it is used, range from the narrow to the very broad;
- its narrow meaning as business entrepreneurialism. In this context it can mean starting a business, being in business or growing and developing a business, or it can even refer to a business itself;
- its broad meaning as referring to attitudes and skills which, when possessed by individuals, lead them to exhibit innovative behaviour, including business entrepreneurialism;

- how these attributes and skills differ often from many of those fostered by traditional education or by larger corporate businesses.

LEARNING OBJECTIVES
....

By the end of this chapter the reader should:
- be aware of how the word 'enterprise' is used, and the range of meanings it can have, including having an understanding of both the 'narrow' and 'broad' meanings;
- understand the meaning of 'entrepreneurship' and its links with 'enterprise';
- understand the differences between enterprise attitudes and skills and those fostered by traditional education or by larger corporate businesses.

INTRODUCTION

Enterprise – Undertaking, esp. bold or difficult one; readiness to engage in such undertakings; enterprising, showing courage or imaginativeness.
The Oxford Handy Dictionary
Mastering Enterprise: all you need to know about starting and developing a successful business.
Trailer for a series of newspaper features[1]

Many things have been described as 'enterprise'. It has been a popular label for a variety of initiatives.

ILLUSTRATION 2.1
Enterprise
....

The British sense of enterprise
DTI: The Department of Enterprise
The Enterprise Initiative for Industry
Scottish Enterprise
The Enterprise Investment Scheme
Enterprise Ireland
Enterprise Directorate General
Local Enterprise Agencies

Enterprise in Higher Education
Young Enterprise
and even
The Starship *Enterprise*

However, like many fashionable labels, it appears sometimes to have been applied more for the cachet it brings with it than for the appropriateness of its application. Dictionary definitions of enterprise are of some help, but language evolves and the meaning of words can change as their usage develops. This book is concerned *inter alia* with understanding what people actually mean when they use the word 'enterprise', and its implications, rather than trying to isolate an abstract concept of enterprise or trying to impose a single uniform meaning for it. In this chapter, therefore, some of the key usages are considered and the meaning, or meanings of their authors extracted or deduced.

EXAMPLES OF 'ENTERPRISE' USAGE

International economic agenda

The word 'enterprise' appears in many international contexts, but mainly in the context of economics and business. Smaller businesses are almost universally referred to as Small and Medium-sized Enterprises, usually abbreviated to SMEs. Many bodies with an economic remit have an enterprise policy which is often focused on the needs of business. The EU and the OECD are examples of this.

The European Union

In his communication to the European Council at Lisbon, the President of the Commission called for the European Union, building on the stability that had been achieved and taking advantage of the favourable economic outlook, to take action to ensure stable economic growth, full employment and social cohesion. The communication pointed to the important role, which has to be played by enterprise policy in fulfilling this ambition and in ensuring that Enterprise Europe meets the challenge of the knowledge economy.

Commission of the European Communities[2]

The European Union's commitment to help create a climate in which enterprise, industry and innovation can thrive is officially stated in EC Article 157 (in Title XVI of the EC Treaty).

EU enterprise policy today is tailored to the needs of the entire business community and its environment. Its history has been shaped by work in three key policy areas: small and medium-sized enterprises (SMEs), innovation and competitiveness, including single market opportunities and benefits.[3]

OECD (Organisation for Economic Cooperation and Development)

'The OECD groups 30 member countries sharing a commitment to democratic government and the market economy.' Its directorates include the Directorate for Financial, Fiscal and Enterprise Affairs which has the objective of 'promoting the efficient functioning of markets and enterprises in a globalised economy'. Among its main activities is 'enterprise development' for which it has established the Enterprise Development Unit 'to focus its work with non-OECD economies in the area of enterprise development and investment promotion'.[4]

UK Government enterprise initiatives

Lord Young, when he was the UK Secretary of State for Employment, said, 'We must have an enterprise culture, not a dependency culture.' When he was asked what he meant by 'enterprise' he described it as: 'Get up and go – not sitting back and accepting it. Think positive and things can happen; if you are passive and think negative then nothing happens. It's a mental attitude.'

Department of Trade and Industry[5]

The DTI (Department of Trade and Industry) launched its Enterprise Initiative in 1988, which brought together many of the schemes of support provided by the DTI for industry and commerce. At its launch the DTI considered whether its plans were 'an industrial policy', but concluded that:

the phrase itself is unfortunate, because it appears to concentrate on industry rather than consider all the factors which affect the ability of industry and commerce to create wealth; it also carries the flavour of the DTI taking responsibility for the fortunes of individual industries and companies. It will be obvious that neither is consistent with the philosophy of this paper ... But the Government has a coherent set of policies towards industry and commerce. That set of policies is better described as an enterprise strategy than an industrial policy.[6]

The DTI described its objectives as follows:

The needs and demands of society can only be met by increasing prosperity. The prime objective of the Department is to assist this process throughout the economy and then to champion all the people who make it happen, rather than just individual sectors, industries or companies ... We seek to:

- produce a more competitive market by encouraging competition and tackling restrictive practices, cartels and monopolies;
- secure a more efficient market by improving the provision of information to business about new methods and opportunities;
- create a larger market by privatisation and deregulation;
- increase confidence in the working of markets by achieving a fair level of protection for the individual consumer and investor.

We will encourage the transfer of technologies and cooperative research, the spread of management education and the growth of links between schools and the world of work. Our objective will be to produce a climate which promotes enterprise and prosperity.[7]

In the 1988 White Paper describing the role of the DTI, encouraging enterprise was described as 'one of the major economic goals of the Government'. 'Enterprise', the DTI said,

is fundamental to a dynamic and growing economy. Lack of enterprise played a major part in the relative decline of the British economy; its return has played a major role in the recent economic revival. The key to continued economic success lies in the further encouragement of the enterprise of our people ... The change of approach is reflected throughout DTI's activities. The DTI will be the department for Enterprise.[8]

CASE 2.1
Pathfinder initiatives: 1
···

In Northern Ireland the former Department of Economic Development (now the Department of Enterprise, Trade and Investment) launched an interim report on the 'Pathfinder' initiative in 1987. Its aim was 'to find new and better ways of building a stronger economy in Northern Ireland ... to find new ways to build on our strengths and to correct our weaknesses'. Among those weaknesses were the 'lack of an enterprising tradition: Northern Ireland is proud of its "work ethic", but this is essentially an employee ethic. As a result there are few role models or mentors for those who wish to enter business and the option of self-employment is novel in many areas.' 'Enterprise' the report defined as: 'the propensity of people to create jobs for themselves and for others by engaging in and creating a legitimate activity which will earn them a living or by developing their existing jobs'.[9]

The Local Enterprise Development Unit in Northern Ireland (then known as LEDU but now subsumed into Invest Northern Ireland) was sponsored by the Department of Economic Development and was tasked with implementing many of the Pathfinder recommendations (see Case 2.3). Its aim was to strengthen the Northern Ireland economy by encouraging enterprise and stimulating improvements in the competitiveness of both new and existing businesses.

Points raised

This example shows a number of uses of the word 'enterprise' in UK government circles and an attempt to define it.

These examples are all taken from UK government initiatives and publications. The major thrust of government industrial policy in the UK under the Conservatives in the 1980s and 1990s was the creation of a climate that stimulated enterprise and thereby sought to increase prosperity. In this context, as the above examples show either explicitly or by implication, the concept of enterprise is concerned with business, with the creation of new businesses or with the development of existing ones. Some reference is made in the DTI literature to the need for links between business and education, and the Northern Ireland Pathfinder proposals (see Case 2.3) included producing a more positive attitude to enterprise. These aspects, however, are in support of the overall aim of economic improvement. This was expected to come from business development which, in turn, was to come from more enterprise.

Enterprise organisations: Local Enterprise Councils, Local Enterprise Agencies and others

The Local Enterprise Companies (LECs) in Scotland, and the former Training and Enterprise Councils (TECs) in England and Wales, were formed as the result of a central government initiative.

CASE 2.2
The 'E' in TEC
....

Although they have now passed into history and their training and enterprise responsibilities have been taken over by other organisations, the Training and Enterprise Councils (TECs) provided many examples of the use and interpretation of the word 'enterprise'.

According to the government's strategic guidance paper, 'Improving the competitiveness of business and people was one of the central purposes of TECs.'[10] Examples of the interpretation individual TECs put on this however included these:

> Birmingham TEC was set up to stimulate Birmingham's economy by investment in both training and career development, and business support.
>> Information leaflet issued by Birmingham TEC[11]

> [To] serve and support the business growth, performance improvements and management development needs of all industry and commerce within the Greater Nottingham area.
>> Aims of Greater Nottingham TEC[12]

> The Leicestershire Training and Enterprise Council is one of a number of similar organisations recently set up in the UK to help stimulate the local economy. In short, the Leicestershire TEC is here to help you build *better* jobs, *better* businesses and a *better* future.
>> *Guide to Services*, Leicestershire TEC[13]

> To improve the economic prosperity and quality of life for all in Sheffield, through a training and enterprise partnership and investment in people.
>> Long-term goal of Sheffield TEC[14]

Points raised
These examples indicate what the former Training and Enterprise Councils took the word 'enterprise' to mean.

Local Enterprise Agencies (LEAs) have been around for longer than TECs and many of them are still operating. Their formation was due, not primarily to a central government policy, but to a series of local initiatives. Their aims are therefore more diverse than were those of the TECs. One example was the London Enterprise Agency (LEntA), which

> exists to enable a group of the UK's leading companies to work together to tackle some of the economic and employment issues facing inner London ... the LEntA member companies aim to foster job and wealth creation, and to improve the economic prospects of the least advantaged among inner London's residents.[15]

Local Enterprise Agencies vary greatly in size and in the range of services offered. But they all have one thing in common, one core activity: counselling of clients looking for advice in starting up or expanding small businesses.
>> Business In the Community booklet[16]

The remit of the TECs, and the way it was put into practice, clearly indicate that in this context enterprise was taken primarily to mean business growth and competitiveness. The LEAs may, between them, encompass broader remits, but again their primary focus tends to be business start-up and development and its contribution to local economies. Little recognition is given to a wider meaning of enterprise.

Enterprise in Higher Education

The UK's Enterprise in Higher Education initiative (EHE) was introduced by the Secretary of State for Employment in December 1987. According to the Training Agency,

the main aim of EHE is to assist institutions of higher education develop enterprising graduates in partnership with employers. There are as many definitions of 'enterprise' as there are people defining the word! However, there is a great deal of common ground, and most people would agree that the enterprising person is resourceful, adaptable, creative, innovative and dynamic. He or she may also be entrepreneurial. However, the qualities of enterprise are as useful in the employee as the employer, and equally important in the public, private and voluntary sectors ... The broad aims of the initiative are that:

- Every person seeking a higher education qualification should be able to develop competencies and aptitudes relevant to enterprise.
- These competencies and aptitudes should be acquired at least through project based work, designed to be undertaken in a real economic setting, which should be jointly assessed by employers and the student's higher education institution.[17]

The aim of the Enterprise in Higher Education programme in one university was described as

to provide the opportunity for all full-time undergraduate students to acquire enterprise competencies, without compromising academic and intellectual standards. Students will be afforded the chance to develop both personal skills, such as leadership, creativity, problem analysis and solving, self awareness and flexibility; and interpersonal skills such as team building, negotiation and persuasion, conflict resolution and all forms of communication including IT.

This was also expanded as

giving all full-time undergraduate students the opportunity to develop their enterprise competencies as an integral part of their academic programme. The university has chosen to adopt a broad definition of enterprise, based on personal transferable skills. These include:

- Communication skills   Written reports, oral presentations, media awareness
- Groupwork skills   Leadership, teamwork, group dynamics
- Personal skills   Self-awareness and self-appraisal

- Organisational skills   Time management, task management, objective-setting
- Interpersonal skills   Listening, negotiation and persuasion, mutual confidence and respect
- Problem-solving   Problem analysis, creative thinking and decision-making
- Social and community awareness   Sensitivity to others, moral and ethical bases of decision-making
- Resource management skills   Economic awareness, costing and budgeting[18]

While the Enterprise in Higher Education initiative was launched by government, it interpreted the enterprise it was promoting as a range of skills. These are not just business and business-related skills, but a range of personal skills that are useful, both in the environment of work and also in a wide range of other contexts. Indeed the Training Agency made a distinction between enterprise and entrepreneurship, the latter being a possible subset of the former.

Young Enterprise

Young Enterprise has its origins in the Junior Achievement programme in the USA. In the UK it is a national educational charity, founded in 1963, with the mission of providing young people from 5 to 25 years of age with an exciting, imaginative and practical business experience, enabling them to develop their personal and interpersonal skills, knowledge and understanding of business objectives and the wealth creation process. It does this primarily by giving young people the chance to learn from setting up and running their own companies during one academic year. By 2001 more than 75,000 students from 2600 schools and colleges were participating each year in the UK, supported by 2000 businesses and 11,500 volunteers. The benefits it delivers to its participating 'Achievers' include improving their business knowledge, influencing their career and study preferences, improving their attitudes and skills, such as the ability to work in a team and self-confidence, and supporting qualifications in business core skills.

Young Enterprise therefore sees enterprise in the context of business, but within that context it is concerned with the acquisition of attitudes and skills that involve discovery, confidence and achievement, as well as the specific business skills of marketing, finance, communication and organisation.

Other examples

An enterprise culture is one in which every individual understands that the world does not owe him or her a living, and so we act together accordingly, all working for the success of UK plc. The gross national product is earned by companies. Successful companies which regularly make profits and grow are the flagships of the enterprise culture. Directors who lead those successful companies are heroes of the enterprise culture. Any of our products or services which lead the world are the pride of the enterprise culture.

In an enterprise culture we expect that some of the wealth will be used for public goods and services, but we believe that wealth creation comes first.

Peter Morgan[19]

How is the 'enterprise culture' to be regarded? Just like some handy little slogan? A simple shorthand way for describing developing small business activity? Some proverbial wisdom about such? Small businesses' new guiding spirit? Or just some well promoted party political trademark? Maybe the latest populist catchphrase? A carefully sanitised euphemism which glosses over something else?

John Ritchie[20]

Other examples of the use of the word 'enterprise' include:

- *The Enterprise Allowance Scheme* was introduced to direct financial support to unemployed people wishing to become self-employed. Its aim was stated as being to encourage unemployed people to create thriving new businesses.
- *Graduate Enterprise* provision is a scheme to raise the awareness and preparedness for self-employment among undergraduate and postgraduate students.
- *Scottish Enterprise* is the successor to the Scottish Development Agency. Its remit is to help to generate jobs and prosperity for the people of Scotland.
- *British Coal Enterprise* was a wholly owned subsidiary of British Coal set up in 1984 to help to create alternative job opportunities in areas associated with coalmining.
- *Enterprising Nottinghamshire* is an initiative designed to promote an awareness and understanding of the creative potential of people. Its aim is 'to develop and encourage an enterprising culture in Nottinghamshire' and a presentation on its achievements indicates that 'an Enterprising Person is someone who displays initiative, makes decisions, manages resources, shows drive and determination, influences others and monitors progress.'[21]
- *Enterprise Northern Ireland* is the association of 31 of Northern Ireland's Local Enterprise Agencies.

One can be **enterprising** both by making a million before one's fortieth birthday and by shepherding passengers out of a burning aeroplane.

Coffield and MacDonald (1991)[22]

Enterprise is having ideas and imagination and using them.

Marks & Spencer[23]

The mission of the **Starship *Enterprise*** is 'to boldly go where no one has gone before'.

These other examples of the word 'enterprise' demonstrate that the word has, in normal usage, a wide variety of meanings. In some cases its meaning is limited to the business context; but in others, for instance when applied to the Starship *Enterprise*, it is an attitude to life, an attitude of exploring, of developing, of leading and of taking initiatives, which, while it may help in the business context, has much wider relevance.

NARROW AND BROAD MEANINGS OF ENTERPRISE

Endeavour to be firm (10 letters)

Crossword clue[24]

In many of the examples examined above the implication is that enterprise is seen, at least primarily, as connected with the promotion of business generally or of small business and/or business starts in particular. The later examples however suggest that, for some people at least, it can have a wider meaning. Writing on enterprise culture the author of an OECD monograph indicated that:

> there are, in effect, two definitions of, or approaches to, the word 'enterprise' and the practice of it. One, which can be termed a 'narrow' one, regards enterprise as business entrepreneurialism, and sees its promotion and development within education and training systems as an issue of curriculum development which enables young people to learn, usually on an experiential basis, about business start-up and management. The second approach, which can be termed the 'broad' one, regards enterprise as a group of qualities and competencies that enable individuals, organisations, communities, societies and cultures to be flexible, creative, and adaptable in the face of, and as contributors to, rapid social and economic change.[25]

In answer to the question, 'What do we mean by enterprise?', another commentator replied:

> Two schools of theory and practice are evident, each based on different although not contradictory answers to the question. They can be called the 'economy school' and the 'education school'. The 'economy school' says that enterprise is what entrepreneurs do and entrepreneurs create business and jobs and wealth and those things all contribute to, indeed they comprise, the economy ... The 'education school' says that enterprise has a broader meaning and application than that ... It says that many types of initiative which need to be taken, many types of responsibility which need to be discharged and many types of problems which need to be resolved require the individual to act in an 'enterprising' manner. Thus this school sees business-type entrepreneurialism as just one context in which people act in 'enterprising' ways. It says that enterprise involves using the imagination, being creative, taking responsibilities, organising, identifying ideas, making decisions, dealing with others in a wide range of contexts. It says that as society becomes more complex and as it changes towards greater complexity, people need to be more and more enterprising. At the heart of this approach is, therefore, personal development and, in particular, the development of self-confidence.[26]

Enterprise is about attitudes and skills in whatever sphere of life.

The narrow view of enterprise: entrepreneurship: business creation and development

> The carrying out of new combinations (of means of production) we call 'enterprise'; and the individuals whose function it is to carry them out we call 'entrepreneurs'.
>
> Joseph Schumpeter[27]

The 'narrow' or 'economy' school view is the one behind many of the examples quoted in the introduction to this chapter. In that context it is not possible to explore enterprise without also examining 'entrepreneurialism' and 'entrepreneurship', because frequently the words are used interchangeably, and do indeed have a common root.

There have been, of course, examples of entrepreneurs and entrepreneurial behaviour from very early times. As Bolton and Thompson point out,[28] one type of entrepreneur who has appeared consistently throughout history has been the merchant entrepreneur, some of whom made the Great Silk Road into the market-driven highway it became. However they did not describe themselves as entrepreneurs nor appear to have had a concept of entrepreneurship.

The evolution of that concept can be traced back to an Irish economist living in France called Richard Cantillon, who introduced the word into economic literature in his '*Essai Sur la Nature du Commerce en Général*', said to have been written in 1734 but not published until 1755, some 21 years after his death. The word is derived from the French *entreprendre* meaning 'to undertake'. Cantillon's implicit concept of the entrepreneur is a broad one, but it is based on the entrepreneur as a person with the foresight and confidence to operate in conditions when costs may be known but rewards are uncertain.

Jean-Baptiste Say (1767–1832), the first professor of economics in Europe, produced a narrower definition of the entrepreneur that involved the combination and coordination of the factors of production to accommodate the unexpected and overcome problems. It was however earlier, in 1776, that the capitalist concept had been first described as a relatively complete theory by Adam Smith in his book *The Wealth of Nations*.[29] This work was the foundation of the classical capitalist economic theory; it identified the capitalist as the owner or manager who, from basic resources of land, labour and capital, constructed successful industrial enterprises. By the middle of the next century the word 'entrepreneur' was being used to indicate the owner-manager of an industrial enterprise.

By the start of the twentieth century a further refinement in the theory of the capitalist economy had been developed by the neo-classical school, in particular by Leon Walras and Alfred Marshall. Its key component is that of market equilibrium, when supply equals demand in a perfectly competitive market. This theory does not, however, have a place for the 'entrepreneur' as a cause of economic activity. Suppliers should instead respond to market pressures: if prices rise they should supply more, and if they fall, less. They should not upset this equilibrium by introducing innovative products or services. Classical economists, however, and in particular a group in Austria, objected to this absence of entrepreneurialism. One of their students was Joseph Schumpeter, who went to the USA early in his career. He believed that the concept of innovation, described as the use of an invention to create a new commercial product or service, was the key force in creating new demand and thus new wealth. Entrepreneurs were the owner-managers who, in this way, started new businesses to exploit invention. If successful they thus created wealth for themselves and employment for others from their ability and ambition, rather than only from ownership of land or capital. (See also Case 1.1 in Chapter One.)

Leibenstein, whose first theoretical observations on entrepreneurship were published in 1968, distinguished between two activities: the activity of the entrepreneur who introduces innovation in product, process or service; and the activity of the manager who establishes or runs a business in traditional ways. Schumpeter argued in 1934, in *The Theory of Economic Development*, that entrepreneurs were different from those who solely managed businesses without innovating, and it was these entrepreneurs who were the key to wealth creation and distribution in capitalism. Innovations create new demand and entrepreneurs bring the innovations to the market. This destroys existing markets and creates new ones, which will in turn be destroyed by even newer products or services. Schumpeter called this process 'creative destruction'. This is a dynamic process, which contrasts sharply with the static, equilibrium theory of the neo-classicists. Nevertheless it was the almost scientific appeal of the latter that remained as the dominant theory for much of the twentieth century.[30]

Willard Whyte, in his book *The Organization Man* (1956) suggests that the American experience of the Depression, followed by the military training of the Second World War, created a belief in or at least an obedience to bureaucracies.[31] America had thus become conditioned to believe in the large corporation as the major, and the preferred, source of employment. In 1967 John Kenneth Galbraith published *The New Industrial State*, in which he highlighted the benefit of economies of scale in production, as evidenced by Henry Ford's assembly lines.[32] As production organisations become larger, the theory went, greater specialisation of labour and machines was possible, which in turn reduced the unit cost of production. Large firms therefore had lower costs of production than small ones and, as there were no theoretical limits to their size, they would dominate society. Galbraith thus believed that large corporations would work with government and large unions and, based on a shared view of organisation life, they could in effect run the state.

The idea of economies of scale fitted in well with neo-classical economic theory and evidence for their existence appeared to be provided by management information and by plant engineers' calculations. The fact that researchers had difficulty in documenting real examples did not impinge on mainstream economic thought. Big business ruled, and the dominant perception of entrepreneurs was summed up in the saying that 'Entrepreneurs are people who start their own business to avoid getting a job.'[33] It was the results of Birch's economic analysis that changed this perception. He concluded that in the USA, in the period between 1969 and 1976, small firms created the majority of the net new jobs, a result that was initially discounted by most economists.[34] While Birch's conclusions have been challenged by some subsequent work, the importance of the entrepreneur and the relevance of Schumpeter's theory were at last established and became accepted by mainstream economists. (See also Case 1.1 in Chapter One.)

Although this central role of the entrepreneur, and therefore of entrepreneurship, in business and economics is now accepted, this does not now mean that there is a single accepted definition of what an entrepreneur is. On the contrary, there are a range of possible meanings, derived from different ways of looking at the entrepreneur and how he or she operates. Table 2.1 summarises the main approaches (some of which are also explored in more detail in Chapter Three).

It is this contribution of entrepreneurship to economic development that is one of the areas of meaning assigned to 'enterprise'. In this context the words 'enterprise' and 'entrepreneurship' can be synonymous. The word 'enterprise' is also used to mean a unit of business, the processes of business start-up, and the process of being in business and of business growth and development. In other words, it is used to refer to the various elements that contribute directly to economic development and to job creation. These are the narrow meanings of enterprise: it is a form of behaviour devoted to the successful development of business.

Table 2.1 Summary of approaches to describing entrepreneurship

Entrepreneurial model	Central focus or purpose	Assumption	Behaviour and skills	Situation
'Great person' school	The entrepreneur has an intuitive ability – a sixth sense – and traits and instincts with which he or she is born	Without this 'inborn' intuition, the individual would be like the rest of us mortals, who 'lack what it akes'	Intuition, vigour, energy, persistence, and self-esteem	Start-up
Psychological characteristics school	Entrepreneurs have unique values, attitudes, and needs that drive them	People behave in accordance with their values; behaviour results from attempts to satisfy needs	Personal values, risk-taking, need for achievement, and others	Start-up
Classical school	The central characteristic of entrepreneurial behaviour is innovation	The critical aspect of entrepreneurship is in the process of doing rather than owning	Innovation, creativity, and discovery	Start-up and early growth
Management school	Entrepreneurs are organisers of an economic venture; they are people who organise, own, manage and assume the risk	Entrepreneurs can be developed or trained in the technical functions of management	Production planning, people organising, capitalisation, and budgeting	Early growth and maturity
Leadership school	Entrepreneurs are leaders of people; they have the ability to adapt their style to the needs of people	An entrepreneur cannot accomplish his or her goals alone, but depends on others	Motivating, directing, and leading	Early growth and maturity
Intrapreneurship school	Entrepreneurial skills can be useful in complex organisations; intrapreneurship is the development of independent units to create, market, and expand services	Organisations need to adapt to survive; entrepreneurial activity leads to organisational building and entrepreneurs becoming managers	Alertness to opportunities, maximising decisions	Maturity and change

Source: J. B. Cunningham and J. Lischeron. 'Defining Entrepreneurship', *Journal of Small Business Management* 1991; 29(1): 47.

35

Enterprise, entrepreneurship and SMEs

As the previous paragraphs indicate, the narrow meaning of enterprise is closely associated with the concept of entrepreneurship and with smaller businesses in particular, often referred to as small and medium-sized enterprises (SMEs). Again, as with enterprise, there is no single generally accepted definition of entrepreneurship but it is not necessarily synonymous with small business, because some small businesses are not thought to be entrepreneurial, and questions are therefore asked about the extent to which 'entrepreneurship and SME agendas relate to each other'.[35] Among the definitions and uses of 'entrepreneurship' are:

> In this paper we will use the terms business ownership and self employment as equivalent to entrepreneurship.[36]

> Entrepreneurship has been defined as 'any attempt to create a new business enterprise or to expand an existing business by an individual, a team of individuals or an established business'.[37]

> Most definitions of the word 'entrepreneur' will take into account the individual aspect, the innovative aspect, the commercial organisation aspect and business behaviour ... However ... (only) a small fraction of new starters are really innovative (and) if such a criterion is used ... the level of entrepreneurial vitality will be fairly low ... We use an approach to define entrepreneurs (as) mainly people in the pre-start-up, start-up and early phases of business ownership.[38]

Therefore if one person or culture uses the word 'enterprise' and another 'entrepreneurship', it should not necessarily be inferred that they are taking about different concepts. It might be that they are just using different language to refer to exactly the same thing.

The broad view of enterprise: attributes and resources

An enterprising individual has a positive, flexible and adaptable disposition towards change, seeing it as normal, and as an opportunity rather than a problem. To see change in this way, an enterprising individual has a security, born of self-confidence, and is at ease when dealing with insecurity, risks, difficulty and the unknown. An enterprising individual has the capacity to initiate creative ideas ... develop them, and see them through into action in a determined manner. An enterprising individual is able, even anxious, to take responsibility and is an effective communicator, negotiator, influencer, planner and organiser. An enterprising individual is active, confident, purposeful, not passive, uncertain and dependent.

OECD/CERI[39]

The makeup of the entrepreneur has been explored by a number of people. McClelland looked at motives, and identified three underlying ones: the need for achievement, the need for affiliation and the need for power (see also Chapter Three). According to him, the person motivated to high achievement has optimism, wants responsibility, enjoys challenges and novelty and is a moderate risk-taker.[40] Others have looked at the need for autonomy and the desire for influence. What however is generally being described is a set of attributes that can be used in a number of situations, although often the starting point for identifying these attributes has been the entrepreneur. (See Table 2.2.)

Enterprise, claims Gibb, is the exercise of such a set of attributes and the entrepreneur, he suggests, is someone who demonstrates a marked use of these attributes in a particular task or context, usually in business or commerce. However, if

entrepreneurship is defined solely in terms of a set of attributes, used in a certain task context, it follows that there are entrepreneurs in all kinds of organisations, for these attributes are displayed and developed by a wide variety of people working in many different circumstances – these are 'enterprising' people. There is for example, much scope for entrepreneurial behaviour within bureaucracies, although when this behaviour is frustrated or cannot be contained within the organisation and is regarded as deviant, then job change, or indeed self-employment, may be pursued as a means of exercising these attributes. This is in line with the idea of the entrepreneur as a 'marginal man': put simply, this is someone who does not fit easily into the conventional organisation. Within the conventional employee role, there may be more or less scope for exercise of entrepreneurial attributes, depending on the structure and purpose of the organisation (or parts of it) and the amount of individual freedom. Motivation to

Table 2.2 Entrepreneurial or enterprising attributes

Typical of the attributes identified by a variety of writers
on the subject of entrepreneurship or enterprise are:

- Autonomy / independence
- Belief in control of one's own destiny
- Creativity
- Determination
- Flexibility
- Goal orientation
- Hard work
- Imagination
- Initiative
- Leadership
- Moderate rather than high risk-taking
- Need for achievement
- Optimism
- Perseverance
- Persuasive powers
- Problem-solving ability

develop and exercise entrepreneurial attributes, whatever the nature of the work or location, is important. It is clear that, in some organisations, the exercise of such attributes will be seen as 'desirable'; in others it will be labelled as 'deviant'. The issue of 'desirability' of entrepreneurial behaviour is an important one not confined only to the culture of the work place, but also clearly of importance in terms of society as a whole.[41]

If enterprise, or entrepreneurship, is the exercise of a set of attributes or behaviours then those attributes can also be illustrated by the process by which they might, or might not, be developed. Gibb has analysed and described the relevant attributes, ideas, ambitions and culture and their development utilising a number of diagrams.

At almost all stages of life there are factors that can influence the development of enterprising/entrepreneurial ideas and some of these are summarised in Table 2.3.

Table 2.3 Influences on the development of entrepreneurial ideas and ambitions at different stages of life

Childhood	Adolescence	Early adulthood	Middle adulthood	Late adulthood
Parental and wider family class and class mobility	Parental / wider family influence on educational choice	Choice of further education / training	Occupational and class mobility	Class attained and income / wealth achieved
Parental and wider family work situation	Parental and wider family influence on vocational preference	Own class ranking	Nature of work	Family situation
Parental and wider family educational choice	Choices of vocational education available	Friendship and community attachment	Own family and friendship	Communal attachments
Parental and wider family values and 'life goals'	Education as provider of values and goals	Residual family influence	Working relationships	Extra work opportunities
		Possible own family	Reward systems and job satisfaction	Job satisfaction
	Friendship and community attachments	Nature of work	Interactions with environment socially and at work	Pensions and early retirement facilities
			Business training and development	

Source: A. A. Gibb, 'Enterprise Culture: Its Meaning and Implications for Education and Training', *Journal of European Industrial Training* 1987; 11(2): 13.

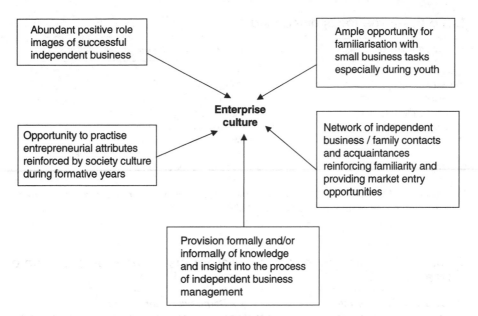

Source: A. A. Gibb, 'Enterprise Culture: Its Meaning and Implications for Education and Training', *Journal of European Industrial Training* 1987; 11(2): 14.

Figure 2.1 The components of enterprise culture

An enterprise culture is generally one in which several influences combine to reinforce the development of enterprise. This is for instance indicated in Figure 2.1 although this example presents enterprise somewhat towards its narrower (business) definition.

Youth is the stage of life when people are possibly most susceptible to the influences of an enterprise culture. Often, however, the focus of formal education is different from that of enterprise, as Table 2.4 shows.

Later in life also people are subject to influences that are not enterprising ones. Gibb, for instance, also contrasts the values and systems embodied by a corporate and/or bureaucratic approach to those of an entrepreneurial management system. (See Table 2.5.)

The issue of enterprise within business relates both to business founding owners, who might be expected to have some enterprise, and business managers, who might be more inclined to take the corporatist approach. In the 1950s and 1960s, when markets seemed more stable, many managers saw the efficient utilisation of resources and the perfecting of performance in marketing and production as their primary tasks. They implemented plans, coordinated disparate activities and controlled behaviour.

In the relatively more turbulent world of the 1980s this behaviour no longer brought continued success. Rapid changes in knowledge, in markets and in education meant that organisations needed to strive for both efficiency and the

Table 2.4 The focus of learning

Education focus on	Entrepreneurial focus on
The past	The future
Critical analysis	Creativity
Knowledge	Insight
Passive understanding	Active learning
Absolute detachment	Emotional involvement
Manipulation of symbols	Manipulation of events
Written communication and neutrality	Personal communication and influence
Concept	Problem or opportunity

Source: A. A. Gibb, 'Enterprise Culture: Its Meaning and Implications for Education and Training', *Journal of European Industrial Training* 1987; 11(2): 17.

Table 2.5 Entrepreneurial vs corporatist management: some contrasts

Entrepreneurial management	Corporatist management
Values, beliefs and goals	
Growth by green field management	Growth by acquisition
Short time horizons	Long time horizons
Informal strategic project planning (policy and practice interlinked and changing and emerging)	Formalised planning systems (policy laid before practice)
Failure means missed opportunity	Failure means resource-centred misdemeanour (variance from standard)
Seeks incremental development as a means to reduce risk	Seeks large scale development with risk reduction by analysis/information
Pursues action strategies with negotiation as and where necessary	Pursues pre-negotiation strategies for decision-making (personal risk reduction)
Management evaluation on task completion	Management evaluation as routine aspect of organisation
Status equals success in the market	Status equals control over resources
Avoidance of overhead and risk of obsolescence by high subcontracting	Seeks ownership of all resources with objective of power and control
Pursues effectiveness in the marketplace	Pursues efficiency information to justify control
Organisational contrasts	
Flat organisational structure	Hierarchical organisation structure
Challenge to owner legitimacy	Clear authority
Need to trust others for reward	Clear reward system defined
Organic relationship emerging	Rational/legal structures

Source: A. A. Gibb, 'Enterprise Culture: Its Meaning and Implications for Education and Training', *Journal of European Industrial Training* 1987; 11(2): 21–2.

customisation of goods or services. Several writers have highlighted the role of managers in energising adaptable employees to use all their skills and knowledge in a flexible manner to provide customers with satisfaction. High quality customised products provide benefits, but they can only be produced by committed flexible employees, not alienated ones maintaining rigid demarcations.[42] Thus, for Salaman the essence of management is the ability to enhance the performance of subordinates by 'doing the right things, doing things right and then better, or learning to do new things'.[43] While new small businesses may play an increasing role in net job creation, increasing enterprise in established businesses is also critical to at least the continuance of existing jobs.

This focus on excellence and continuous improvement was recognised in the Management Charter Initiative in the UK.[44] It was claimed in the mid-1980s that managers in Britain did not possess the education, knowledge and skills required for international competitiveness, and the MCI set about articulating the competencies required for effective management performance, and developing several dimensions of personal competency, one of which highlighted the competency of 'showing concern for excellence'. For effectiveness in this domain managers are required to be adept at setting and expressing high performance goals, doing things better, identifying and overcoming constraints on excellence and being opportunity-oriented in a changing situation. These behaviours are commonly exhibited by all enterprising people, and further confirmation of this link was provided by the then British Institute of Management (now the Institute of Management). It reviewed the literature on key managerial competencies as depicted by a variety of influential writers and concluded that a number of attributes and behaviours underpinned a concern for excellence. These include achievement orientation, efficiency orientation, proactivity, entrepreneurial drive and entrepreneurial skill. Thus enterprising managers are concerned constantly to improve what they and their people do. This is in contrast to bureaucratic managers, who tend to protect the status quo.

This contrast between an entrepreneurial, or enterprise, approach and the one to which we might have been accustomed, particularly in the workplace, has been recognised in other situations also. The attributes and resources required for enterprise in a business context are applicable to enterprise in whatever situation it is manifest. This has been summarised as:

> the change of social policies and practices towards the development of policies that, as in the workplace, make the best use of all available human resources. They are called 'enterprising' policies and practices, in which a new balance of power is being achieved between the institution and the individual ... Because of these changes all organisations and wider society need to be enterprising. The desired results are systems and structures which encourage and enable the individuals who work in them and are served by them to be enterprising. When and where this happens, we have an enterprising culture ... While the changes that are going on in modern societies are complex and manifold, there is a common thread passing through all of them. What they amount to is a change in the balance of power, and a parallel change in roles, between what individuals do for themselves and what others (especially society's

institutions) do for them. As the balance changes, we move towards the creation of an enterprising culture.[45]

Within the debate on enterprising attributes and culture it has been pointed out that the characteristics that are required for the broad application of enterprise are also those needed for the narrow one. It is not possible to develop attributes only in, or for application in, a business context. If someone has these attributes then he or she is liable to use them wherever they appear to be appropriate, whether it be for an economic, a social, a political, an environmental or other purpose. Further, if these attributes are, at least in part, acquired during upbringing and through education then that happens often before career choices are made. To get more enterprise in business it would therefore be necessary to try to develop more enterprise for all contexts.

ILLUSTRATION 2.2
Enterprise and happiness

There appears to be an assumption, in the way in which the desirability of enterprise is sometimes promoted, that being enterprising can somehow be equated with being happier. That association is however rarely overtly stated, and so can be very difficult to pin down.

It can be argued that the results of enterprise can lead to greater happiness. As a result of enterprise a person may have a more rewarding occupation, in terms of financial reward or other benefits such as variety and interest; or it can lead to a person achieving more, which is particularly appropriate for those with a high need for achievement (see Chapter Three). However, being enterprising *per se* does not necessarily directly produce happiness.

OTHER ASPECTS OF ENTERPRISE

A further development of this debate has taken place more specifically in the context of enterprise as applied to business start-up. The more traditional view of enterprise has been largely that it is an attribute that exists and can be measured and encouraged, but which is not evenly distributed among the population. Some have more of it than others, and it is those with more of it who tend to display enterprising activity such as starting businesses. The implication has been that if more of those individual levels of enterprise could be raised above some sort of implicit enterprise threshold, then more enterprise activity and more business start-ups would be the result. This view of enterprise does not however fit with some of its observable aspects. It is not static, yet the threshold theory makes no provision for the dynamic effects that can be observed when enterprise behaviour snowballs by people being influenced by the example of others. Nor is enterprise a one-way activity: people can move out of it as well as into it. Enterprise is complex and there are many influences on whether an individual shows enterprise activity; therefore raising levels of enterprise attributes, if that is possible, may be swamped in its effects by other influences.

An alternative view of enterprise, and of enterprising behaviour, is based on the attributes and resources that an individual may possess at any point in time. It is suggested that it is the interaction between these factors which produces a rational response, on the basis of available information, when the opportunity occurs for a business start-up. This view acknowledges however that there is inertia in individual behaviour and that it may take a discontinuity in work, or in life, to trigger a review of an individual's situation. Whether this review will lead to an individual trying his or her own enterprise will then depend on the attributes and resources they have accumulated and on the perception of environmental factors such as the availability of grants and training. (This and other related concepts are developed further in Chapter Three.)

> A close examination of what is taught under the name of enterprise reveals, however, that instead of the consensus claimed by leading practitioners, the organisations that are teaching this new culture are all working with different lists of the core skills.
>
> Part of the confusion stems from the fact that the word 'enterprise' is used in different ways, sometimes referring to an individual ability considered amenable to improvement and at other times to a form of economic activity, usually in small business.
>
> We are not dealing with a tightly defined, agreed and unitary concept but with a farrago of hurrah words such as creativity, initiative, and leadership.
>
> Professor Frank Coffield[46]

IN CONCLUSION

As indicated earlier there are many different usages, and therefore definitions, of the word 'enterprise'. These different meanings are related to each other, however. There are not just two or three distinct meanings but instead a spectrum: a range of meanings, each one merging with those close to it but perceptibly different from those far from it. It is not possible to indicate that one particular meaning is the correct one. The word is in practice used in these different ways, and those trying to understand it need to be aware of what it means to whomsoever is using it.

The UK government, however, has almost always used it in the context of economic growth through (small) business start-up and growth. That is what its 'enterprise' schemes are aimed at. Training and Enterprise Councils,

Enterprise Agencies and similar organisations have had the same usage. Other initiatives, however, such as Enterprise in Higher Education, have treated enterprise more as a set of attitudes and competencies that may have a wider application than just the world of business. Possibly its most famous application, the Starship *Enterprise*, the spacecraft in the Star Trek series, has nothing to do with business and everything to do with a readiness to explore the new.

One end of the spectrum of meaning could be considered to be the narrow definition of enterprise, which could be summarised as:

Starting up a business,

Enterprise = Entrepreneurship = Being in business, *and*

Growing and developing a business

(or = a business)

The other end of the spectrum could be enterprise as a positive, flexible, and adaptable attitude to change. It is the exercise of enterprising attributes. It is a new balance in power between the institution and the individual. In this context it has a far wider application than just business, as such attributes can be applied in all walks of life. It could be summarised as:

Enterprise = Innovative attributes and behaviour

The spectrum analogy is not perfect, however, because a broad meaning can include a narrow one. To get the enterprise that is sought in business, some believe, it is necessary to promote a culture of enterprise that is much broader than business. For them it is all or nothing: you can't have enterprise only in business and not in other fields – you must have both or neither.

The application of enterprise in practice, however, takes more than just an aspiration to be enterprising. For someone to behave in an enterprising way, he or she may need at least some of the right attributes combined with some of the relevant resources with which to apply the attributes, and then it may take a specific trigger to start it off.

'Enterprise' in the way people apply the word is undoubtedly very varied. Some further aspects of that variety are explored in the rest of Part One of this book.

KEY POINTS OF CHAPTER 2

- In recent years 'enterprise' has been a popular word to attach to a variety of initiatives. However, it has often seemed that it has been used more for the cachet of a supposedly desirable label than because it is the most appropriate word in the particular circumstances.

- The way it is used indicates nevertheless that it has a wide continuum of meanings. In some case its use implies a meaning that is limited to a business context, and it can even be used as a synonym for business. Other uses, however, imply a wider meaning: it is often associated with an attitude to life: of exploring, of developing, of leading and of taking the initiative. Such an attitude can be very helpful in the business context, but it also has much wider applications.

- These different uses have been described as the narrow and broad meanings of enterprise. The narrow meaning regards enterprise as business entrepreneurialism, and in that context the words 'entrepreneurship' and 'enterprise' are usually interchangeable. The broad one, on the other hand, regards it as a set of qualities and competencies that enable individuals and groups that possess them to be flexible, creative and adaptable in the face of change. These two approaches have also been labelled the 'economy school' and the 'education school': at the heart of the latter is the concept of personal development and the development of self-confidence.

- In a business context, the word 'entrepreneurship' is often used in the same way as the word 'enterprise'. Its use can be traced to 18th-century France and, with the development of the concept of capitalism, the entrepreneur came to be seen as essential to the process of wealth creation. When very big businesses developed, the entrepreneur seemed to have been supplanted by the manager in business relevance, but the recent demonstration of the potential and achievements of small businesses has once again highlighted their importance.

- Those who have looked at the makeup of the entrepreneur have identified entrepreneurship, or enterprise, as the exercise of a set of attributes. The possession of at least some of these attributes has been particularly helpful in times of change, but their exercise need not be limited only to a business context. There is however no clear agreement on precisely what these attributes, skills, or attitudes are.

- Further, the possession of such attributes, skills and attitudes is not necessarily sufficient for a person to act in an enterprising manner, especially when that implies taking the initiative in business formation and development. What are also needed may be the resource with which to act and a trigger to start it off. It is also believed that the necessary qualities can be acquired and are not necessarily innate.

- 'Enterprise' therefore is a varied concept, both in its application and in its explanation. It is however the subject of considerable interest.

CASE 2.3
Pathfinder initiatives: 2

An interim discussion document from the Pathfinder Process Proposals from the Enterprise Taskforce

Brief

To examine the level of enterprise in Northern Ireland, attitudes to enterprise and how these might be changed, whether current arrangements for stimulating business start-up are adequate and how the community can be involved more fully in economic development.

Background

- 'Enterprise' was defined as the propensity of people to create jobs, for themselves and others, by engaging in and developing a legitimate activity which will earn them a living or by developing their existing jobs.

Attitudes

- There is a general attitude in Northern Ireland that working for oneself rather than for an established company is somehow second best.
- Self-employment is often seen as impractical or excessively risky: not as legitimate or socially desirable as other employment.

Support currently available

A wide range of support is currently available to those wishing to establish or develop a business:

- Finance, in the form of Enterprise Grants (from the Local Enterprise Development Unit) and Enterprise Allowances (from the Department), supplements commercial and voluntary sources of business finance.
- Training, ranging from brief seminars for Enterprise Allowance participants to courses such as the Graduate Enterprise Programmes, provides information and skills which are important to small business growth and development.
- Advice, ranging from informal counselling to the inputs of professional advisers such as accountants, is also an important part of a small business and enterprise support system.

Conclusions

- There is a need to generate a more positive attitude to enterprise throughout the community.
- We need to generate greater self-confidence and skills among those who may wish to start a business so that they can identify and respond to challenging business opportunities.

- A restructuring of assistance is required to ensure that all types of assistance are made available in a coordinated way, both in terms of those eligible for assistance, and in terms of measures which should be complementary.
- Particular attention should be paid to the development of supportive networks of contacts and advisers.

The way forward

Existing small and enterprise programmes should be critically examined to ensure that they can achieve the following objectives:

- To encourage and increase the propensity of people in Northern Ireland to start their own businesses.
- Within five years to increase the rate of formation of businesses to the UK average.
- To produce a more positive attitude to enterprise.
- To provide more positive 'triggers' for business start-up, aimed particularly at those most likely to be successful (those in their 30s, well educated, widely travelled, currently in employment) and at those groups – in particular women – who at present appear under-represented in the business community and whose skills remain to be tapped.
- To ensure adequate provision of finance for new businesses (not necessarily public money), appropriate training, introduction to adequate networks and suitable premises.
- To monitor the effects of the programme, which would have as a necessary preliminary establishing a benchmark from which to judge improvement.

The main components of such a revised programme would be:

- a campaign aimed at changing attitudes towards enterprise, which could include work within the education sector and the further development of community businesses and use of the media;
- provision of appropriate assistance for those who wish to try to set up or develop businesses;

Step 1: For those who wish to try self-employment

- A small starter grant, paid weekly on a reducing scale for one year
- A preliminary self-assessment module, and basic business training course
- Introduction to potential network contacts

Step 2: For businesses with the potential to contribute more than at the previous step to the development of the economy, normally by employment

- Applicants to have basic business skills and produce business plans
- Grant (or possibly loans) of £4000/5000
- Enhanced training and appropriate network contacts

Step 3: LEDU job-related selective financial assistance with LEDU's normal requirements and conditions

Step 4: IDB (Industrial Development Board) assistance for companies which have successfully grown to more than 50 employees

Businesses would be encouraged to start at the highest step for which they can meet the requirements, but many will climb from the initial step sequentially to the higher level. If this model were adopted, it would ultimately replace the existing Enterprise Allowance and Enterprise Grant arrangements.

Action points

- Establish a Steering Group to develop the programme, and monitor and advise on its execution.
- Develop an enhanced enterprise awareness plan.
- Develop the assistance package, and provide enhanced means of delivering it (perhaps through local communities).
- Enhance arrangements for support to community businesses.
- LEDU should apply further resources to the local enterprise network through its Local Enterprise Programme.
- The new components of the support package should be developed in ways which secure the involvement of enterprise practitioners.
- Initiate measurement and monitoring of performance and refine quantitative measurement of business information.
- A research workshop should be held to identify priorities for research into specific proposals or problems such as barriers to small firm growth.

Source: Department of Economic Development, *Building a Stronger Economy: The Pathfinder Process*, (Belfast: Department of Economic Development, 1987). This material should not be taken to reflect the current policy of the Department of Enterprise, Trade and Investment or of Invest Northern Ireland.

Points raised

This example gives an insight into how a UK government department interpreted an enterprise brief in the 1980s and the range of instruments then considered to address it.

QUESTIONS, EXERCISES, ESSAY AND DISCUSSION TOPICS

- Distinguish between 'enterprise', 'entrepreneurship' and 'small business'. To what extent do these concepts overlap?
- What is an enterprise culture?
- In what ways can education stimulate entrepreneurship?

- Is it possible to promote enterprise only in its narrow sense?
- How did the Northern Ireland Government's interpretation of enterprise (see Cases 2.1 and 2.3) appear to differ from that of the TECs (see Case 2.2)?
- Do you think that the Pathfinder Enterprise proposals (see Cases 2.1 and 2.3) would, if implemented, actually promote more enterprise?
- The Pathfinder Enterprise proposals (see Cases 2.1 and 2.3) were formulated over 15 years ago. How do you think they could now be improved?

SUGGESTIONS FOR FURTHER READING AND INFORMATION

P. Carr, *The Age of Enterprise* (Dublin: Blackhall, 2000).

R. Gavron, M. Cowling, G. Holtham and A. Westall, *The Entrepreneurial Society* (London: Institute for Public Policy Research, 1998).

www.businesslink.org – Business Links have agendas which overlap those of the former TECs.

REFERENCES

1   From the trailer to a twelve part series, 'Mastering Enterprise', *Financial Times*, 18 November 1996.
2   Commission of the European Communities, *Commission Staff Working Paper: Towards Enterprise Europe – Work Programme for Enterprise Policy 2000–2005* (Brussels: The Commission, 2000), p. 3.
3   Taken from www.europa.eu.int.scadplus
4   Taken from www.oecd.org/about
5   In answer to questions during a celebrity lecture in Northern Ireland, May 1993.
6   *DTI: The Department for Enterprise*, White Paper presented to Parliament, Cm 278 (January 1988), p. 41.
7   *Ibid.*, p. ii.
8   *Ibid.*, pp. 1 and 5.
9   Department of Economic Development, *Building a Stronger Economy: The Pathfinder Process* (Belfast: Department of Economic Development, 1987).
10 *Towards 2000*, the government's strategic guidance paper to TECs (May 1994), p. 6.
11 Birmingham TEC, information leaflet.
12 Greater Nottingham TEC, information folder.
13 Leicestershire TEC, *Guide to Services* (1993) p. 1.
14 Sheffield TEC, information booklet.
15 London Enterprise Agency, *Annual Review* (1992), p. 1.
16 Business in the Community, *A Review of the Enterprise Agency Network*, June 1989, p. 5.

17 Training Agency (1990).
18 University of Ulster, *Enterprise in Higher Education*, leaflet.
19 P. Morgan (Director General, Institute of Directors), speech to Institute of Directors' Convention reported in *Director*, March 1990.
20 J. Ritchie, 'Explaining Enterprise Cultures', paper presented at the Tenth National Small Firms Policy and Research Conference, Cranfield Institute (1987).
21 Nottingham Polytechnic, *Enterprising Nottinghamshire Final Evaluation Report* (1991); and personal communication.
22 F. Coffield and R. MacDonald, *Risky Business? Youth and the Enterprise Culture* (Brighton: Falmer Press 1991), p. 29.
23 *Enterprise and Education*: The *Primary Enterprise Package*, sponsored by Marks & Spencer.
24 From the crossword, *Independent*, 8 January 1996.
25 'Towards an 'Enterprising' Culture: A Challenge for Education and Training', *OECD/CERI Educational Monograph* 1989; 4: 6–7.
26 'What Do We Mean by Enterprise?', *Employment Initiatives*, February 1990: 3–4.
27 J. A. Schumpeter, *The Theory of Economic Development* (New York: Oxford University Press/Galaxy, 1961) (first published in 1934), p. 74.
28 W. K. Bolton and J. L. Thompson, *Entrepreneurs: Talent, Temperament, Technique* (Oxford: Butterworth-Heinemann, 2000), p. 261.
29 A. Smith, *An Inquiry into the Nature and Causes of the Wealth of Nations* (New York: Modern Library, 1937) (first published in 1776).
30 Schumpeter, *op. cit.*
31 W. H. Whyte, *The Organization Man* (Garden City, NY: Doubleday Anchor Books, 1957).
32 J. K. Galbraith, *The New Industrial State* (Boston, MA: Houghton Mifflin, 1967).
33 B. A. Kirchhoff, personal communication (1993).
34 D. L. Birch, *The Job Generation Process* (Boston, MA: MIT study on neighbourhood and regional change, 1982).
35 A. Lundström and L. Stevenson, *Entrepreneurship Policy for the Future* (Stockholm: Swedish Foundation for Small Business Research, 2001), p. 15.
36 I. Verheul, S. Wennekers, D. Audretsch and R. Thurik, *Research Report: An Eclectic Theory of Entrepreneurship: Policies, Institutions and Culture* (Zoetermeer, The Netherlands: EIM/Small Business Research and Consultancy, 1999), p. 9.
37 A. L. Zacharakis, W. D. Bygrave and D. A. Shepherd, *Global Entrepreneurship Monitor National Entrepreneurship Assessment: United States of America* (Kansas City, MO: Kauffman Centre for Entrepreneurial Leadership, 2000), p. 5.
38 Lundström and Stevenson, *op.cit.*, pp. 18/19.
39 Taken from *Towards an Enterprising Culture: A Challenge for Education and Training* (Paris: OECD/CERI Educational Monograph No. 4, 1989), quoted in C. Ball, B. Knight and S. Plant, *New Goals For an Enterprise Culture* (London: Training for Enterprise Ltd, 1990), p. 21.
40 D. C. McClelland and D. G. Winter, *'Motivating Economic Achievement'* (New York: Free Press, 1969).
41 A. A. Gibb, 'Enterprise Culture: Its Meaning and Implications for Education and Training', *Journal of European Industrial Training* 1987; 11(1): 10.
42 C. Alter, and J. Hage, *Organisations Working Together* (Newbury Park, CA: Sage, 1993).
43 G. Salaman, *Managing* (Buckingham: Open University Press, 1995), p. 60.

44 MCI Personal Competence Project, *Summary Report* (London: Management Charter Initiative, 1990).
45 C. Ball, B. Knight and S. Plant, 'New Goals for an Enterprise Culture' (London: Training for Enterprise Ltd, 1990) pp. 19 and 21.
46 F. Coffield, 'Hunting a Heffalump in the World of the Enterprise Industry', *Independent*, 29 August 1990.

ENTERPRISE IN INDIVIDUALS

CONTENTS

KEY CONCEPTS

• •

This chapter covers:

- the different theories about people's internal make-up which have been suggested to explain why some people are more enterprising than others;
- the key points and limitations of these theories;
- the significance of gender and ethnicity in enterprise.

> **LEARNING OBJECTIVES**
> ....
>
> By the end of this chapter the reader should:
> - have an appreciation of the different theories about people's internal make-up which have been suggested to explain why some are more enterprising than others;
> - understand the key points and the limitations of each theory;
> - be able to recognise the key personal traits which are claimed to distinguish entrepreneurs and enterprising people from other groups in society;
> - have a view on the usefulness of trait theory;
> - be aware of the main points of cognitive theories of entrepreneurial motivation;
> - understand the possible roles played by gender and ethnicity in the enterprise shown by individuals.

INTRODUCTION

Chapter Two showed that the word 'enterprise', in the way it is actually being used, has a range of meanings. Some of these overlap, some embrace others and some appear to be very different. Within this range there are two main areas of meaning: those reflecting the broad or education approach, in which enterprise is a type of behaviour that can be exhibited in many contexts, and those representing the narrow or economy application, in which enterprise is sometimes used as a synonym for small business or the process of starting one. The latter use is sufficiently common and important to be explored further in Part Two. However there are many aspects of the broad definition to be considered first.

The broad approach to enterprise considers it to be a type of behaviour demonstrated in the actions of a variety of individuals. These actions are taken as the result of individual decisions but the factors which are thought to influence these decisions, and therefore to influence both enterprise and entrepreneurship, are many and varied. They can be categorised in a number of ways but one of the main divisions is probably that between the internal and the external: between those factors which are apparently unique or specific to each individual, whether innate or acquired, and those factors which determine the environment in which individuals operate.

Therefore the internal factors or influences are considered in this chapter and the external influences in Chapter Four. However, it should be pointed out that the boundaries are not rigid and there are areas of overlap. Also, for convenience, those theories which combine both internal and external influences are considered in Chapter Four, after both sets of factors have been presented.

Enterprising acts

The 'broad' or 'education' approach is largely based on the concept of enterprise as something demonstrated in the actions individual people take: actions that can be enterprising in a variety of situations, not just in business. These actions are in turn due to a considerable extent to the make-up of the individuals concerned: to their attributes, competencies, attitudes, skills, ideas and resources. The context in which the individuals operate is also of relevance, because enterprise in some aspects and in some contexts seems to be due more to group and societal dynamics than to individual ones. This chapter, however, explores enterprise largely from the perspective of the individual; the group and societal aspects are considered in Chapter Four.

In looking at the personal aspects of the broad definition of enterprise, it is worth considering how far they apply also to the narrow definition and therefore, by implication, whether the two are inconsistent with each other. The narrow definition regards enterprise as synonymous with business-founding, for which the term entrepreneurship is also often used, while the other sees it as the application of an array of adaptable skills to new, unique or complex tasks. Enterprising individuals often initiate and develop projects; they do not sit around and wait for things to happen but take control and see issues through to their conclusion. Although there is an apparent difference between the two aspects of enterprise, the distinction may be more apparent than real. In reality, founding a business can be just as much an enterprising act as any other, and that aspect of enterprise can be seen as one component of a larger domain. The 'narrow' definition is therefore just an example of the 'broad'.

Consider the act of initiating and developing a business venture. In developing a business idea, many potential proprietors will have a futuristic and opportunistic orientation and think creatively about different ways of satisfying human needs. In locating and marshalling necessary resources and suppliers of funds, they will be imaginative and persistent. In recognising and overcoming unique problems they will display proactivity and flexibility. And in keeping going in the face of innumerable setbacks they will draw on all their self-confidence, perseverance and dynamism. However, numerous acts in other environments can be considered as enterprising, such as those of the university dean who successfully introduces a radical way of teaching graduate students, the nurse who revolutionises post-operative care, the community leader who convinces the local authority to care for the homeless or the missionary who improves the conditions of the underprivileged. It might be considered that such actions are specific to their different situations, but they do appear to have many common features. However, before they can all be described as enterprising, it will be helpful to have some idea of what constitutes an enterprising act.

Entrepreneurship has been described as 'the creative extraction of value from environments',[1] which emphasises the outcome as well as the process and is a starting point in considering enterprising acts as enterprising outcomes. In the

[handwritten margin note: perhaps entrepreneurial characteristics]

context of business, few doubt the often enterprising nature of business formation and development. One possible indicator of the degree of enterprise to be found in individuals in a community or in an economy is therefore the number of small firms in existence there. It is relevant to note, however, that business formation rates fluctuate widely, and that many self-employed people and small firms fail each year. How, then, should business failure be regarded? If the act of starting a small business is enterprising, what is a subsequent failure? Does it negate the enterprise of the original act? There are no obvious answers to these questions but they highlight the complexity of coming to terms with the notion of enterprise.

If it is difficult to say unequivocally whether an action is enterprising in a business context, what are the prospects in other contexts? Consider a welfare officer faced with a serious teenage drugs problem. The officer has ideas about what might be done. She mobilises parents, community groups, doctors, police and others connected with the problem to take action. She communicates with the teenagers and elicits their views on the issue. She lobbies, deals and harangues to obtain the physical and monetary resources to create a day centre manned by advisers with access to medical personnel. One year after her intervention the drug problem has not gone away, but teenage suicides have decreased in the area, fewer teenage pregnancies are reported and large numbers attend group therapy sessions. Was this an enterprising process? The individual concerned displayed many of the qualities usually associated with the business formation process and the outcome of this project would be regarded by many as reasonably successful, even if the original aim was not achieved. Many would therefore describe the individual concerned as enterprising.

There are innumerable undertakings of this nature in business, family and private life that can be described as enterprising and, though it is a relative and not an absolute term, it can be considered appropriate to enumerate the key characteristics of such undertakings. In doing so it can be helpful to distinguish between the nature of the task and the manner in which it is tackled. Broadly, however, the label 'enterprise' might be applied when:

- the task is non-routine;
- the task is somewhat complex;
- the task is goal-directed;
- the goal(s) are demanding but attainable;

and also when:

- the task is tackled in an adventurous manner;
- the task is approached in a determined and dynamic manner;
- the task accomplishes the set goals (or comes near to so doing).

A project has been defined as 'a task requiring considerable or concerted effort'[2] and, in short, it might therefore be considered that an enterprising act is one in which a project is undertaken in an energetic, bold and adaptable manner. This means therefore that there are businesses, and even business start-ups, which would not be considered to be enterprising. This would be the case, for instance, in some family businesses when a second or third generation takes over without making any significant changes.

Defining enterprise in this way can accommodate both the narrow and broad approaches to the subject outlined in Chapter Two, and underpins the importance of newness, change and flexibility for enterprise. This definition also emphasises the relevance of success. Bold, dynamic acts that fail to meet predetermined goals may not always be considered to be enterprising. Those goals, however, need not be economic, and success in enterprise is not just limited to commercial success. In addition, actions that appear to be, or indeed are, initially successful and would be regarded as enterprising, but which then subsequently fail, would usually still be regarded as having been enterprising. Enterprising acts take place within a time-frame, and outside it conditions can change radically.

Enterprise and entrepreneurship

As indicated in Chapter Two, the term entrepreneurship is frequently used in conjunction with issues of business formation and development. Further, the ways in which entrepreneurs are said to act when seeking business opportunities, and in coordinating resources to cope with business problems, are very similar to what has been described as enterprise in looking to the future, initiating projects and managing them in a creative and adaptable manner. Entrepreneurship is in effect the same thing as enterprise in its narrower sense and so, in this chapter, analysis of entrepreneurship has also been included in the discussion of the determinants of enterprise.[3]

Invention and innovation

The concepts of creativity, invention and innovation are also closely associated with enterprising outcomes. They cover part, but not all, of the process of generating those outcomes. Invention, it is generally agreed, is the origination of a new concept or idea as the result of a process of creativity. There is less agreement on what innovation is. For some it is the development or adoption of new concepts or ideas, while for others it is the new or adopted ideas themselves. These approaches are linked, however, and there is general agreement that invention precedes innovation and that the latter can be viewed as the successful exploitation of new ideas, but not the origination of the ideas.[4] Creativity is having the idea, and innovation is its application. Creativity is not itself enterprising and neither is invention, because they do not generate change; that does not happen until the innovator takes the idea and does something with it.

The place of innovation in commercial success has been illustrated in Figure 3.1, and this can be extended to the successful exploitation of new ideas that leads to any form of increased organisational or social benefit.

Source: DTI (UK) promotional material

Figure 3.1   The role of innovation

What skills are needed by successful innovators? Forehand[5] suggests that innovative behaviour 'includes the development and consideration of novel solutions to ... problems, and evaluation of them in terms of criteria broader than conformity to pre-existing practice ...', and argues that self-reliant, enquiring, flexible, original and independent people are most likely to engage in innovative behaviour. It will be seen that there is considerable similarity between these attributes and those linked with enterprising behaviour. However, the inclusion of originality and enquiry underline the importance of uncovering new ways of doing things. Moss Kanter[6] considers that innovators must develop a vision of something new, must generate a power base to progress the idea, and must build commitment and systems to sustain the new endeavour. For Moss Kanter, visions emerge from kaleidoscopic thinking. Some people have the capacity to view existing structures and behaviours from a variety of perspectives and, unrestrained by existing assumptions, are able to see useful new combinations of resources. Once envisioned, this new possibility must be enthusiastically and articulately communicated to others.

This is very similar to the language used to describe successful enterprise, and so it would appear that there are many similarities between innovation and enterprise. Both involve extended and concerted effort; enterprise requires boldness because its steps are often new, while innovation employs novel solutions that may take boldness to implement; implementation of both takes place in uncertain conditions and may require consideration of technical, economic, social and political dimensions; and both are likely to draw on change management skills, including networking, for success. However, enterprise is concerned with initiating and managing tasks and projects, and may not involve many new or unique approaches. On the other hand, innovation is vitally concerned with novel approaches, new ideas, enquiry and originality, and is the means by which ideas are exploited for competitive advantage.

Enterprising individuals

Enterprising acts, whether in business or in a wider context, and whether incorporating original ideas or not, are generally acts initiated, or led, by individuals. Those individuals are said to display enterprise. Thus, to a considerable extent, it can be envisaged that there is something within those individuals that makes them disposed to, and prepared for, such acts. Enterprising acts are defined as such because they have particular characteristics, and certain individuals may be predisposed to pursue such activities. Many therefore have seen the individual as important for enterprise, indeed as key to its success. Lord Young suggested that 'the basis for the enterprise culture lies with the restoration of the age of the individual'.[7] This is not necessarily so, however. The completion of an enterprising project often requires the involvement and cooperation of numerous people, but individuals and small groups are the building blocks for community and society, and it therefore seems unlikely that an enterprise culture will develop in the absence of a critical mass of enterprise in individuals.

Are entrepreneurs born or made?

Underlying much of the debate about entrepreneurship and enterprise in individuals is the question of whether entrepreneurs are born or are made. Many people have assumed that they are born: that is, they have certain inherent characteristics which lead them to be enterprising, and therefore if a person is not born with these characteristics they cannot be induced by subsequent upbringing, experience or training. Those who subscribe to the 'born not made' view thus assume that the internal influences on an individual's behaviour (those covered in this chapter) are the important ones, whereas those who believe that at least a certain amount of 'making' is possible also consider that the external influences (those covered in Chapter Four) can be relevant.

In Chapter Two the broad definition of enterprise was connected to the possession and use of enterprising, or entrepreneurial, attributes. Figure 3.2 illustrates two possible models for the distribution in a population of those attributes. There is a tendency to think that the distribution of entrepreneurial attributes amongst people is like that illustrated in Model A, with two distinct groups: those with few attributes and those with many. Actually it is probably more like Model B. A key difference is that, if the first model were correct, it would imply that making incremental changes in the distribution will not have much effect: there will still be few people with many attributes; whereas in the second model an incremental change will have the effect of a significant increase in the number with many attributes or at least with sufficient attributes to act entrepreneurially.

These models of entrepreneurship also relate to the 'born or made' debate. Model A is consistent with the view that enterprise is essentially innate, whereas Model B supports the contention of many that enterprise can, at least to some

Figure 3.2 Possible models of the distribution of entrepreneurial attributes

extent, be learnt. Individual capacity is of course variable and, while many 'star' entrepreneurs may owe their achievement more to their own innate abilities than to any formal development process they may have been through, that does not mean that enterprise conditioning is inappropriate or will be wasted, in particular for those without the same 'star' capacity.

WHY ARE SOME INDIVIDUALS MORE ENTERPRISING THAN OTHERS?

Identifying what it is that makes some individuals more enterprising than others has been a challenge to a number of researchers. Among the theories explored in the study of this question are the following:

- personality theories;
- behavioural theories;
- economic approaches;
- sociological approaches;
- other approaches, including attributes and resources;
- a number of integrated approaches.

These theories which relate to the make-up of individuals are described in more detail below.

PERSONALITY THEORIES

Personality theories of enterprise consider that it is the personality of individuals that explains their actions. The simplest theory suggests that it is the possession by individuals of a trait, or traits, that predisposes them to enterprising behaviour; the traits most often proposed are achievement motivation, risk-taking propensity and the desire for control. Other personality theories consider combinations of traits. The psychodynamic approach views the enterprising individual as someone who is 'deviant' in society, and the social-psychological approach also views the context in which the individual operates. Then, in the context specifically of enterprise as exemplified by business formation, there are attempts to produce owner/founder typologies to provide a theoretical framework for dealing with different types of business founders/owners.

CASE 3.1
One person's summary of what makes an entrepreneur

It is ironic that one of the biggest academic growth industries in recent years has been the study of what makes entrepreneurs tick. Every university worth its salt has groups of researchers scurrying round the topic. Yet no real entrepreneur actually believes entrepreneurial skills are learnable or transferable. As they see it, you're either an entrepreneur or you're not. It's a state of being, not a trade or a vocation.

That said, the eggheads do occasionally come up with interesting hypotheses about entrepreneurs. Psychoanalyst Abraham Zaleznik, for instance, the Matsushita Professor of Leadership at Harvard Business School, says that if you want to understand entrepreneurs, you have to study the psychology of the juvenile delinquent. 'They don't have the same anxiety triggers that we have', he explains.

Leaving aside the question whether Zaleznik therefore regards entrepreneurship as a good career move for upwardly aspirant juvenile delinquents, maybe the professor has put his finger on something important.

The textbook definition of an entrepreneur is someone who undertakes the risks of establishing and running a new business in return for profit – and risk-takers do tend to be people who, rather than calculating the odds of success or failure in a systematic way, get an adrenaline rush from going out on a limb. They don't avoid anxiety, they embrace it.

Of course, those who go out on a limb often fall off. The ability to do so and survive, according to management writer Charles Handy, is a prime qualification, almost a *sine qua non* for the entrepreneur. Successful entrepreneurs, he calculates, have on average nine failures for every success:

It is only the successes that you will hear about, the failures they credit to experience. Oil companies expect to drill nine empty wells for every one that flows. Getting it wrong is part of getting it right. (Source not given in original)

The corporate trap
Usually the errors are hidden away or airbrushed out of the successful entrepreneur's CV, but occasionally entrepreneurs get things wrong in a

spectacularly public fashion. Often it is when they try to become mainline business people, or rather to become part of the world of corporate business. Sir Terence Conran was an unstoppable success when he was simply reinventing Conran, but encountered disaster in the 1980s when he led the merger of Habitat with other retailers such as Mothercare, Heals and British Home Stores to form the gargantuan Storehouse group. Now that he is back to creative risk-taking – this time reinventing the restaurant – he's as happy as a dog in muck.

It isn't difficult to see why entrepreneurs trying to transform themselves into corporations nearly always come unstuck. Entrepreneurship is about risk-taking; corporate business is about risk management, even risk avoidance. So the entrepreneur in the boardroom really is a fish out of water.

Conran, incidentally, has given what is perhaps the best description of what it feels like to be an entrepreneur. 'I get a tremendous charge out of business', he told the *Daily Express* in 1986. 'I get the same sort of feeling that women must have when their babies pop out.' That is not, one suspects, quite the way that the bosses of ICI or Unilever see the world.

Which isn't to say that entrepreneurs cannot build big, even huge, businesses, but when they do they tend either to dominate them, like Rupert Murdoch astride News Corp, or to embody them, as Richard Branson does Virgin. Murdoch is News Corp just as Branson, for very different reasons, is Virgin.

Murdoch questions whether there are enough real entrepreneurs in the UK. Interviewed about the setting up of Sky Television on the BBC's *The Money Programme* in 1995, Murdoch said that anybody could have done it:

> Anybody. And we started it. And people are still free to start against us. But they'd rather write articles, bitch and moan, lay around and say 'No, we'd rather keep our lazy way of life. We don't want to compete.' You know, it's not until we get people being equally entrepreneurial and really driving at it that Britain is going to get going again.

Sacred mushroom

Richard Branson – Mr Nice to Murdoch's Mr Nasty – has turned his entrepreneurial flair into a multi-million-pound business by the trick of making those who work for him want to emulate him, be him. Yet he isn't quite sure how he does it:

> I never actually set out to see how I could make the most cash [he told Jeffrey Robinson, author of *The Risk Takers*]. I've always merely tried to make the figures fit the ideas I've had rather than the other way around. I guess that's doing it backwards.

Ted Levitt, editor of the *Harvard Business Review*, calls entrepreneurship the 'sacred mushroom of the 1980s' – 'it seemed delusively greater and grander than it was' – but many of his fellow scholars and not a few business people are still mesmerised by it. Finding that entrepreneurs cannot be made, they have come to the conclusion that they can at least be made use of. Hence the advent of the intrapreneur, an entrepreneur who works within a big corporation.

Ignoring the fundamental difference between the entrepreneurial and corporate mind-sets, the academics hypothesise that the intrapreneurs, who are encouraged to do things like working out ways to 'sell' their goods and services to other people within the organisation, will somehow spread the entrepreneurial habit like a benevolent virus.

The idea seems to miss the obvious point that no real entrepreneur would be seen dead inside a big corporation; these are clearly only ersatz ones, A version of intrapreneurship did work in the USA for a short time in the 1980s, when a number of blue-chip corporations set up special enclaves for handfuls of brilliant but anarchic individuals who were encouraged to 'do their own thing' in the hope that they would come up with something marketable. The special units became known as 'skunk works' and, predictably, their inhabitants often behaved like the eponymous animals, hightailing it as soon as they got a good idea.

Maybe the great corporate chieftains could have been taught at least that at business school – that trying to mix the two cultures would be like mixing oil and water.

In his latest book, *Great Myths of Business*, author and self-made millionaire William Davis nominates the idea that entrepreneurship can be taught as one of the great myths of our time. He quotes Anita Roddick, founder of The Body Shop, to reinforce his point. Roddick, as it happens, sounds uncannily like Harvard's Professor Zaleznik when she gets going. How, she asks, do you teach an obsession?

> There is a fine line between the delinquent mind of an entrepreneur and that of a crazy person. The entrepreneur's dream is almost a kind of madness, and it is almost as isolating. When you see something new, your vision usually isn't shared by others. The difference between a crazy person and the successful entrepreneur is that the latter can convince others to share the vision.

Source: Malcolm Brown, 'Risky Business', in *Holland Herald* (the in-flight magazine of KLM). Reproduced with permission of M. Brown and of K. Wilkie, the editor of *Holland Herald*.

Points raised

This is an example of the point of view that entrepreneurs are 'born, not made'. Nevertheless it summarises some views about the entrepreneur's approach and the essence of entrepreneurship, including its ability to flourish in difficult contexts.

Personal qualities: traits and attributes

There is a considerable literature on those factors or traits that purport to predispose individuals to behave in an enterprising, or entrepreneurial, fashion. McKenna points out that traits can relate to motives, temperament, style and ability.[8] Many commentators consider that entrepreneurs have a strong need to achieve and to control their own destiny, and we can readily see why people with these dispositions might be interested in tackling enterprising tasks.[9] The successful accomplishment of an enterprising task would provide individuals with a strong sense of achievement and confirm their capacity to control their lives. Others consider that risk-taking tendencies are characteristic of entrepreneurs, although there is a debate about whether they take high, moderate or calculated risks. Stevenson and Gumpert do not define the degree of risk taken, but note that entrepreneurs continuously seek business opportunities without being concerned about the necessary resources.[10] They take a chance on resources and consider that suitable quantities will be forthcoming. Timmons considers that people with persevering, problem-solving and reliable temperaments will have entrepreneurial tendencies, but his list of traits is long and it is unlikely that many entrepreneurs will exhibit all the traits he mentions.[11]

In addition to these traits there is a plethora of qualities that are purported to predispose people to being enterprising. Such personal qualities include being purposeful, proactive, dynamic, active, positive and able to take the initiative; being able to regard change as an opportunity; being able to identify ideas; being innovative, imaginative, creative, flexible and able to tolerate ambiguity; being adaptable, trusting, moderate risk-takers, at ease with risk; being determined, persistent, capable of seeing ideas through to fruition; and being responsible and self-confident. These qualities may emerge from traits, life's experiences or the structure of organisations and society, but their antecedents are less important than their link with enterprise. There are numerous variables, but we can see that these attributes are clustered, and research[12] on enterprising tendencies reveals that enterprising people tend to have a strong need for achievement and autonomy, an internal locus of control, are strongly proactive and independent, have a creative tendency, and are moderate risk-takers. Others add self-confidence, persistence, an ability to deal with failure, and trust.[13] More recently vision has been added to the list.

Some of the main traits or qualities identified are described below.

Achievement motivation

Enterprising people have a strong need for achievement (usually referred to as NAch), which stimulates them into action. When they accomplish something they consider to be worthwhile, their self-esteem is enhanced and they are encouraged to seek other demanding assignments. Thus enterprising people are constantly on the lookout for challenges.

Content theories of motivation suggest that individuals have basic needs, and from time to time a particular need is not fulfilled. When this happens the person experiences unease and attempts to satisfy the need. He or she does this by attaining goals that have the capacity to meet the need. Once these are satisfied, the unease or tension diminishes and will not motivate an individual until, once again, a need is not realised. Note that achievement is not an innate need like the need for food; it is learned, most probably during childhood. It has been suggested that strong-willed children, with parents who make their expectations known and who provide feedback, become high achievers, although McClelland also argues that NAch can also be developed in adults.[14]

NAch has been widely used as one measure of the entrepreneurial personality but results are not clear-cut. Cromie[15] reviews some recent findings and concludes that whilst NAch shows that entrepreneurs consistently out-score undergraduates, naval officers and civil servants on measures of NAch, other groups such as managers and university professors have equally high scores. However, since professors and managers might also be enterprising, it could be that NAch is a basic attribute of the enterprising.

Some refinement of the concept has also been proposed recently. Cassiday and Lynn[16] suggest that achievement motivation should be regarded as being comprised of four distinct elements: work ethic, pursuit of excellence, mastery, and dominance; whilst Miner and his colleagues feel that the simple achievement motive construct should be replaced by five motive patterns: self-achievement, risk-taking, feedback of results, personal innovation, and planning for the future.[17] In support of this development Delmar argues that Miner *et al.*'s overall scale correlates quite well with indicators of entrepreneurial performance.[18]

An interesting point also arises in connection with causality. It is generally assumed that achievement-oriented people become entrepreneurs or enterprising individuals. However, it is equally plausible that the sense of mastery and achievement that accompanies a successful enterprising project might persuade individuals, and people close to them, to categorise that person as an entrepreneur. Behaviour becomes ingrained in the personality. Some evidence for this social construction of personality along the lines proposed by Hampson was provided recently by Littunen. Her empirical work confirms that 'a change in life (entrepreneurship) shapes to some extent the characteristic of the entrepreneur.'[19]

The importance of NAch for enterprise is not generally in dispute, but how can an individual with a high NAch be recognised? McClelland argues that such a person:

> is more self-confident, enjoys taking carefully calculated risks, researches his environment actively, and is very much interested in concrete measures of how well he is doing. Somewhat surprisingly ... he does not seem to be galvanised into activity by the prospect of profit; ... [he] ... works hard anyway, provided there is an opportunity of achieving something.[20]

High achievers often regard money as a measure of achievement, not an end in itself, but they do need feedback of evidence of their achievement, and money can provide such feedback.

> **CASE 3.2**
> **An achiever**
>
> ....
>
> A business founder, when asked why she created her firm replied: 'The major attraction is self-esteem ... the ah ... carrying a job through from beginning to end ... ah ... I suppose putting my standard on things. I had four children and so all I felt I was good for was being a mum and you don't always get a lot of appreciation for this.'[21]
>
> **Points raised**
> Achievements are not always obvious.

Risk-taking propensity

Proactive achievers break new ground, but there are considerable risks in this behaviour. There are many failures that can spell disaster for an organisation or a career. The outcomes of enterprising events are less certain than those of conservative ones, and therefore enterprising individuals will need to have the capacity to tolerate risks: to have the psychological make-up and resources to cope with any failure.

While they must be able to countenance risk, that is not to say that enterprising people are high risk-takers. Entrepreneurial research suggests that effective entrepreneurs are moderate risk-takers, while others believe that enterprising people take calculated risks. They assess situations thoroughly and do not pursue options which they consider to have a small probability of success. In this vein Drucker argues that successful entrepreneurs 'try to define the risks they have to take and to minimise them as much as possible'.[22] They search for opportunities, give them serious consideration and if promising, capitalise on them. Drucker goes so far as to say that successful entrepreneurs tend to be cautious and are opportunity-focused, as opposed to risk-focused. For them, 'defending yesterday' rather than 'making tomorrow' is really risky.

The debate about the importance of risk-taking for enterprise is ongoing and Cromie[23] reviews some of the recent findings. However, Chell *et al.* point out that there are problems in defining risky behaviour.[24] Risk assessment takes place in context, and behaviour that appears risky to outsiders may not be perceived as risky by those who are fully cognisant of a situation. Enterprising persons may not perceive a course of action as risky because they fully understand the situation, but this can also arise because of cognitive biases. It is argued[25] that entrepreneurs may not perceive a risk in a risky situation because they are overconfident, because they have the illusion that they are in control of a situation and because they tend to associate with optimistic people who do not dwell on failures. They take mental shortcuts when making decisions with the result that '[low] risk perception, rather than [high] risk propensity, might explain why individuals start ventures'.[26] Simon *et al.* present evidence from a recent study which suggests that entrepreneurs do misperceive risk. This occurs not because they are overconfident but because they have the illusion of control over key events in the entrepreneurial process. They also rely on a narrow range of sources of information and are not exposed to disconcerting facts. This is an interesting development in that it moves the debate on entrepreneurial motivation from the innate drives of individuals to their decision-making processes; this issue will be explored later in the chapter.

Locus of control

'Locus of control' refers to the question of where the control of events resides. Enterprising people believe that they personally make things happen in a given situation, and underplay the importance of luck and fate. They make things happen; things do not happen to them. In essence they feel that they exercise considerable control over events in their everyday world. Rotter was instrumental in assessing this aspect of personality, and he designated those who feel in control as 'internals' and those not in control as 'externals'. 'Internal' declarations emphasise the importance of ability, hard work, determination and planning in achieving outcomes, and their outlook is epitomised by the statement 'What happens to me is my own doing.'[27]

Locus of control is often regarded as a crucial indicator of enterprising potential but there are concerns about the construct.[28] The concept was not designed for entrepreneurial settings and has been described as a 'distal' measure:[29] that is, it might explain general behaviour but is of little use in predicting how people will behave in specific situations. In addition, entrepreneurial studies which have used the construct have produced inconclusive results. Some investigations find that entrepreneurs out-score other groups, including managers, whilst others do not. Finally, as Chell *et al.* point out, perceptions of control will be influenced by many variables including experience. If individuals have recent successful experience of completing enterprising projects they might consider themselves to be capable of controlling events. If, however, they have experienced failure they may blame external factors.

'Internals' believe that they are in control and there is some evidence that they become leaders in organisations more often than 'externals', when they can then exercise control over events,[30] but there are those who argue that 'organisations are structures of control'.[31] Individual behaviour can be severely curtailed by rules, norms, and ever-present bosses, and this is something 'internals' dislike. Enterprising people in organisations may well become frustrated, and as a consequence many frustrated individuals leave organisations and set up their own ventures.

Need for autonomy

'Autonomy' refers to independence from other people, being in control of one's own destiny. This can accompany 'locus of control', which involves control of events beyond the individual, but it is not the same thing. Enterprising people have a strong desire to go it alone. In interviews with enterprising people they constantly refer to a need to control their own lives. Phrases such as 'I want to be in control', and 'I do things my way', are used regularly.[32] Individuals in many groups, organisations and societies are expected to adhere to the norms, rules and regulations of collective social organisms. Conformity is the price of membership. However, independent people often resent these constraints and regard them as counterproductive in developing innovative proposals. Enterprising people want to reduce barriers to progress, and though they may see some merit in the stabilising impact of rules and behavioural norms, they see more merit in independent thought and action. They can be regarded as headstrong and disruptive in social settings.[33]

There is however a possibility that apparently independent-minded people may not be negating the forces of conformity in social entities, but merely 'having problems dealing with authority and working for others'.[34] People who do their own thing regardless of others or who disregard with impunity rules that constrain them could be considered as disruptive dissenters. Independence may produce negativity, but enterprising people tend to be freethinkers who need to break away from the shackles imposed by collective social institutions. When asked why they wanted to start their own firm, aspiring entrepreneurs in one study most frequently cited autonomy, and the need to achieve, as the most important factors in their decisions.[35] It should be noted, however, that the experience of entrepreneurship can cause people to want even more autonomy.[36]

Determination

Enterprising people also possess determination. They normally complete projects and a degree of persistence is necessary for success. If individuals wish to exercise their individuality in meeting 'standards of excellence' then they will need to explore alternatives, overcome difficulties and make their plans work. Being in control is important, as is the freedom to exercise ingenuity, but a determination to see a difficult project through is also vital.

Initiative

In addition to the qualities discussed above, the enterprising individual will need to be proactive. A person may have a strong need to achieve, may possess determination, may welcome the chance to do his or her own thing and to exercise control over his or her environment in pursuit of an assigned project, and may, when presented with an opening, exhibit many enterprising qualities. If, however, he or she does not actively take the initiative and seek openings and opportunities, then the enterprise is limited.

Enterprising people take bold steps and have a propensity to seek new opportunities. The search for newness can often lead to uncharted waters, and proactive people generally seize the openings that present themselves and outdo others.[37]

Some recent research by Ardichvili and Cardozo[38] provides detail on the process by which opportunities are recognised. These authors claim that opportunities are uncovered through recognition rather than through organised searches and they believe that certain factors facilitate recognition. They feel that entrepreneurs must be alert to surrounding information. Ray and Cardozo define entrepreneurial alertness as 'a propensity to notice and be sensitive to information about objects, incidents and patterns of behaviour in the environment, with special sensitivity to ... problems, unmet needs and interests, and novel combinations of resources'.[39] People pay attention to information that is connected to information they possess already and it is suggested that prior learning creates a 'knowledge corridor' which allows enterprising people to recognise some opportunities but not others.

Ardichvili and Cardozo argue that the more information entrepreneurs have about markets and customer problems, information that can arise as a result of experience or extended personal networks, the greater the likelihood of opportunity recognition. Alertness and subsequent recognition of an attractive circumstance in the current environment can come about as a result of innate personal qualities and experience. This research points to a less aggressive approach to uncovering opportunities than previous work, but it is unlikely that people who merely react to their environment will uncover opportunities. They will still need to 'act on rather than react to their environments',[40] although they may not go so far as to 'change the environment to create opportunities'.[41]

Creativity

The enterprising person is often concerned with developing new products, processes or markets, but the ability to 'bring something new into being' is not evenly distributed within the population. Such people tend to have more originality than others and are able to produce solutions that fly in the face of established knowledge. They are also inclined to be more adaptable and are prepared to consider a range of alternative approaches. They challenge the status quo, which can sometimes bring them into conflict with their colleagues. They dismiss their detractors and are sometimes regarded as aloof.[42] Creative outcomes seldom emerge in an instant: a recognised process is involved, even if it appears to be rather chaotic. It begins with recognition of a problem or anticipation of an opportunity, and then, through understanding the situation and reflecting on the issues, new linkages are contemplated and possible new combinations of components are aired. From this emerge viable solutions or possibilities that are subjected to evaluation, which may be continuous with judgement being suspended while the search process is prolonged in pursuit of genuine newness.

Enterprising individuals take bold creative steps but situations encourage creativity. Thompson summarises the situational requirements for creativity succinctly. He believes that creativity is enhanced when people have 'some freedom, but not too much; high internal commitment to the task, but not too high a commitment; a high proportion of intrinsic rewards, but some extrinsic rewards as well; some competition but not winner-take-all competition'.[43] It is, however, important to recognise, as indicated earlier, that an enterprising outcome depends on the process of innovation following creativity, not on the creativity alone.

Self-confidence and trust

It has been argued that enterprising individuals seek out demanding tasks that produce the intrinsic rewards of achievement, that they act on their environments in uncovering these opportunities rather than responding to changes and that they impose their independent authority to explore creative risky options for problems or opportunities. It is most unlikely that people who lack self-confidence could undertake these tasks. Proactivity, creativity and achievement are not accomplished without major change and, as Gibb has argued, enterprising persons have 'a security born of self-confidence' in uncertain situations. Self-confidence seems therefore to be indispensable for enterprise.

If, as a result of their endeavours, projects are successfully completed, self-confidence will be reinforced. Success generates more success and may encourage individuals to take on ever more enterprising projects. But what of failure? In such an uncertain environment failure is common and may be viewed as a learning experience, but if failure is repeated then it can dent the confidence of the most self-assured. Continuing enterprise would seem to rely on regular or intermittent success.

Along with self-confidence generally goes trust. Some people consider enterprising individuals, especially in a business context, to be selfish, exploitative and uncaring, with a short-term, get-rich-quick approach to business. In reality, however, successful enterprise requires the coordination of disparate inputs, and a degree of trust. Indeed: 'Studies of entrepreneurs indicate that many are highly ethical and socially responsible compared to the general population.'[44] Successful entrepreneurs have faith in the intentions of those who assist them in their endeavours and do not exploit them.

Critiques of trait theory

Simple trait theory implies that the kind of person you are will influence whether you become an entrepreneur but this short review of some classic traits suggests that the connection between innate qualities and enterprise is not simple. The traits and qualities described do impact on behaviour but it is accepted that most entrepreneurs do not possess all the enterprise traits identified, and many of the traits are also possessed by those who would not be described as entrepreneurs. However, some authors go further and suggest that trait theory is obsolete. Delmar[45] for instance holds that trait theory has serious limitations. He argues that there is little consistency in trait research in that there are a large number of traits linked to entrepreneurship; the same traits are operationalised in different ways and research evidence linking predisposition, enterprise and performance are at variance. The second difficulty relates to the supposed static nature of entrepreneurial traits and the environments in which enterprise is acted out. In practice environments are changeable and traits also change over time. Delmar also claims that the bulk of the research on this matter has been based on US samples and thinks that some entrepreneurial attributes are culture-dependent. For example the drive and desire to achieve is instilled into American children from an early age. Finally, he claims that 'the theory and methods in use are, in relation to modern psychological research, obsolete.'[46] He argues that personality is not a one-dimensional but a multi-dimensional construct comprised of at least five broad dimensions. Furthermore he considers that a much more fruitful direction for research in this area is to examine the cognitive processes which underpin the decision to become an entrepreneur.

However not everyone agrees with Delmar and the trait approach still has its supporters who contend that personality traits play a meaningful role in predicting behaviours.[47] Fagenson[48] argues that it is still important to carry out research 'that can further delineate the fundamental psychological differences between entrepreneurs and non-entrepreneurs' but an examination of some other approaches to the entrepreneurial personality is warranted.

Psychodynamic approaches

Psychodynamic approaches are the product of Freud's psychoanalytic theory of personality. Freud considered that individuals have instinctive drives, and that a part of the personality seeks instant gratification for these desires. However, the pursuit of instant gratification can get people into trouble and as they develop the *ego* emerges to constrain instinctive behaviour. This controlling mechanism protects the individual from the unpleasant consequences of pursuing innate desires. With further development the individual realises that behaviour can meet with the approval or disapproval of significant others and a *superego* develops to limit behaviour to that which is in keeping with the moral code of parents and society. Freud argues that there are many conflicts between these forces, and that the resolution of these conflicts is instrumental in creating the personality. If instinctive behaviour is severely constrained then it can lead to frustration, and psychodynamic approaches to entrepreneurship consider that this frustration is the source of much entrepreneurial motivation.

Psychodynamic approaches are based on three basic premisses: that most behaviour is goal-directed and is caused by a force within the person; that much behaviour originates from the unconscious mind; and that early childhood experiences are crucial in the development of the personality. One of the leading advocates of this approach in the entrepreneurial field is Kets de Vries, who suggests that early frustrations are the product of unhappy family backgrounds.[49] Fathers, in particular, are seen as controllers and manipulators who are remote. In addition they are often seen as deserters who place an unwarranted burden on heroic mothers. These negative images of fathers may have little basis in reality, but perception is all-important. As a result of these experiences or perceptions, these individuals develop an intense dislike of authority figures and develop suppressed aggressive tendencies towards persons in control.

These unconscious motives impact adversely on careers. Rejection of controlling others in organisations leads these individuals to be classified as 'deviant' or 'marginal' people, with the result that they change jobs on a regular basis. While they cannot tolerate direction and control in organisations, the variety of job experiences provides them with a range of skills that are indispensable for running a business. As a consequence of their behaviour these individuals make a determined effort to start their own business. In this milieu they are in control, are answerable to no one and are 'at the centre of action'.

Comments

Psychodynamic theories have, in general, been criticised because of their subjective nature and the lack of empirical evidence. Their ability to explain enterprise, especially in the context of entrepreneurship, has been found wanting because they do not cover all situations, such as a business start prompted through unemployment; because not all deviants start businesses and many characteristics associated with deviancy are not typical of successful entrepreneurs; and because, in addition, entrepreneurs tend to create their ventures in their thirties or later when many of life's experiences, not merely childhood ones, will influence their behaviour.[50]

Delmar[51] supports these general contentions but points out that Kets de Vries' work is useful in that it does not present the entrepreneur as an exceptional person with superhuman capabilities. Entrepreneurs have problems like everyone else and they are not immune to failure when creating an enterprise.

Social-psychological approaches

Trait approaches depict behaviour as being determined by innate qualities but it is widely recognised by social psychologists that behaviour is constrained by contextual factors. Behaviour is influenced by social realities and is also interpreted in a given context. The work of Chell and her colleagues has been mentioned which notes that behaviour which is classified as risky and innovative can only be categorised as such in a given context. Indeed those who observe enterprising individuals, and indeed the individuals themselves, classify given behaviour as enterprising only in certain circumstances.

Chell and her colleagues, following the procedures suggested by Hampson,[52] developed a holistic classification system for business owners. To classify business owners these researchers identified, from the research literature and prior experience, the defining characteristics of prototypical entrepreneurs and their associated behaviours. The entrepreneur was considered to be 'alert to business opportunities, proactive, innovative, a utiliser of a variety of sources of finance, a high profile image-maker, restless, adventurous, an ideas person and an agent of change'. To classify individuals they presented their subjects with certain critical incidents and asked them to describe their likely behaviour in these situations. The researchers noted how often and how consistently behaviours were exhibited before classifying them as prototypically entrepreneurial. They also took into account the growth orientation and stage of development of the subjects' businesses and considered that, compared with other types of business owner, entrepreneurs are more likely to own growth-oriented businesses. Some business owners had all of the characteristics mentioned above, some had none and others were in between. A hierarchical model was therefore conceived with four categories of owner: the entrepreneur, the quasi-entrepreneur, the administrator and the caretaker.

Context is important and some writers[53] argue that individuals who find it difficult to make progress in mainstream careers become marginalised and turn to entrepreneurship as a means of escape. This is an interesting debate and it has been used to explain the emergence of women and ethnic entrepreneurs in Britain – two topics which will be examined later in the chapter.

Comments

Chell *et al.*'s theory is based on quite a narrow sample and does not yet appear to have been validated by other researchers. It is, however, useful in pointing to the influence of context on behaviour, in pointing out that there is not one entrepreneur but several types and that traits 'co-occur' to create an entrepreneurial profile.

Owner typologies

Chell *et al.*'s work has as noted included owner typologies. These classifications look specifically at the small business context of enterprise and have been built on the presumption that small business owners are not all the same. The researchers present a theoretical framework to deal with the differences. Most studies have identified three main types of owner, typically labelled 'craftsman', 'entrepreneur' and 'professional manager'. (See Figure 3.3.)

The model presented in Figure 3.3 bears some similarity to the typology developed by Smith in the 1960s.[54] Smith's typology identified craftsman-owners who ran rigid, stable firms and opportunistic owners who headed growing, adaptive firms. These types resemble the craftsman and entrepreneur types in Figure 3.3. However, in his original work, Smith alluded to the existence of a third type of owner, the inventor-entrepreneur. This person creates and develops a firm, 'not as

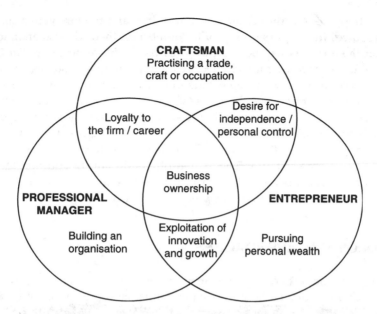

Source: R. W. Hornaday, 'Dropping the E-words from Small Business Research', *Journal of Small Business Management* 1990; 28: 22–33.

Figure 3.3   Three types of small business owner

an end in itself' but as a mechanism to facilitate invention and the presentation of new products. This sort of categorisation also helps to make the point that not all business owners are entrepreneurial. A 'craftsman' practising the same trade as his or her parents in the same way may have a business but may not be enterprising. Interestingly some work in the 1990s by Miner, Smith and Bracker confirms the existence of this tripartite typology.[55]

Comments

There are a number of drawbacks to this approach. There is for instance a problem in maintaining consistent labelling amongst different studies. In addition, the typologies apply only to people in the context of their businesses, which means that they cannot be applied to other examples of enterprise, and the question of whether small business owners can change from one typology to another has not been given much attention.[56]

ECONOMIC APPROACHES

The economic theories of enterprise are also specifically concerned with entrepreneurship and the function that an entrepreneur serves in an economy. They see the entrepreneur as the seeker of opportunities and the innovative coordinator of resources in the pursuit of profit. Equilibrium theories of economics consider that these profits will be short-lived as competition increases, but Casson considers that their foresight and effective judgement about sources and combinations of resources allow entrepreneurs to reap economic rewards.[57] Economic motivation is important, but the successful initiation of a venture could well afford a sense of achievement to individuals. Of all the theories of entrepreneurship, economic theories are of the longest standing, because they go back at least to the time of Cantillon. (See Chapter Two.) However they do not indicate why some people emerge as entrepreneurs and others do not. In addition they consider that entrepreneurs are rational decision-makers and play down the role of perception and interpretation in this process. (See also Chapter Four.)

SOCIOLOGICAL APPROACHES

Psychological and economic approaches to entrepreneurship emphasise the degree of choice exhibited by individual potential entrepreneurs, but some sociologists consider that individuals are seriously constrained in making career choices. They argue that choices are limited by the experience and expectations that individuals face in the social world. Indeed, Roberts[58] goes so far as to say that careers follow patterns that are 'dictated by the opportunity structure to which individuals are exposed first in education, and subsequently in employment'. He contends that ambition is moulded by 'the structures through which' people pass. Others, who would not deny that individual choice plays a part in career decisions, still emphasise contextual awareness. Opportunity structures vary from person to person, and different structures will lead similar individuals towards the development of differing levels of knowledge, skill and drive.

Different opportunity structures expose people not only to different possibilities but also to different expectations from other people. Individuals are socialised to behave in ways that meet with the approval of their role set. To take an example, a young person with a business-owning parent may well be expected to join the family business, and not to do so would create a vacuum in the business. The son of an unemployed labourer will be socialised quite differently. The dominant values of close associates will translate into expectations which strongly influence individual behaviour.

Some sociologists emphasise the importance of entrepreneurial opportunity in the entrepreneurial process. For example, it is suggested that the decision to seize opportunities is made when the opportunities present themselves. It has been argued, however, that enterprising individuals do not just sit around and wait for opportunities to emerge, but if a society does present numerous opportunities this will quite clearly act as a catalyst for entrepreneurship.

If it is accepted that entrepreneurs require ideas, opportunities, resources, skills and motivation for success then the social structures and situations to which they are exposed will impact on the choice process. It could well be, for example, that socio-economic factors such as social class, family composition and background and parental occupation will strongly influence entrepreneurial decision-making. In the UK at least it appears, for instance, that individuals whose parents, or other close relations, have had their own business are generally much more likely to have businesses themselves, and certain social groupings, such as particular ethnic minorities, produce proportionately more entrepreneurs than others. As evidence of parental influence, Stanworth and Gray describe research results for persons employed in selected service sectors:

> Overall some 43.5 per cent ... had fathers and/or mothers who had been self-employed ranging from 56 per cent for the owners of free houses, wine bars and restaurants down to 33.3 per cent for the owners of both advertising, marketing and design companies and computer services business. This finding thus strongly supports the contention that parental experience of self-employment in general, and small business ownership in particular, is the best single predictor of the propensity to enter into small business ownership, although this propensity will clearly differ across different types of small enterprise.[59]

Localities that allow individuals to develop problem-solving and marketing skills, which contain institutions geared to the support of small businesses and that are favourably disposed to the notion of entrepreneurship, are likely to encourage and sustain more entrepreneurship than other regions.[60] Such localities might be said to have an enterprise culture which is defined by Gibb as 'a set of values, attitudes and beliefs supporting the exercise in the community of independent entrepreneurial behaviour in a business context'.[61] Gibb has illustrated (see Table 2.5 in Chapter Two) the difference between 'entrepreneurial management' and the more traditional corporate or bureaucratic management by looking at their respective values, beliefs and goals. The implication of this approach is that enterprising individuals differ from others in at least some of their values and beliefs and these are derived from many sources including the family, peers, community activists and the media.

COGNITIVE APPROACHES

Trait theories are concerned with the innate qualities which motivate individuals to act in certain ways and social-psychological and sociological approaches emphasise the impact of social structures on behaviour. However, another approach has found favour recently: that of cognitive psychology.

Cognitive approaches consider that whilst the personal characteristics of individuals may play a part in determining who becomes an entrepreneur it is more important to examine the decision-making process by which individuals choose to act entrepreneurially. Cognitive theorists argue that decisions are made, not on the basis of reality, but on the basis of perceived reality: entrepreneurs, in other words, perceive things differently. Delmar[62] argues that entrepreneurship, and other career choices, have a major interpretative element and that behaviour 'is heavily based on how individuals perceive the situation or environment and how it is presented to them'. For a person to decide to become an entrepreneur he or she will have to believe that this is a viable career option. The intending entrepreneur will form an opinion about the 'job' – the requisite attributes, knowledge, skills and resources needed for success, and about 'self' – the perceived attributes, knowledge, skills and resources that are possessed by the person before expending energy in the pursuit of this career. The personal background of the prospective entrepreneur will also be an issue. The individual, on the basis of these assessments, which may not be worked out in a precise manner, will decide on his or her level of potential. However, it has been suggested that potential will only be realised if individuals have:

- 'a certain specific ability and sensitivity;
- environmental possibilities;
- social support'.[63]

Delmar has produced a useful analysis of cognitive models of entrepreneurship and his main ideas will be summarised in this section. Delmar first explores *attitude-based models* of motivation. As mentioned above a potential entrepreneur must believe that this 'career' is a viable option and if this is so he or she will tend to adopt a positive attitude towards entrepreneurship. Whilst there is some debate about the impact of attitudes on behaviour, it is suggested that they can be influential in certain circumstances. Furthermore, attitudes are more specific or 'proximal' than 'distal' traits and are more easily influenced than personality traits. However, attitudes can influence choice but they tell us little about how much effort will be expended in pursuing a course of action. [64]

Beliefs and attitudes can influence behaviour but it is suggested that the link between these variables is mediated by intentions. Boyd and Vozikis[65] argue that intentions are indicative of a person's willingness to engage in a behaviour and are influenced by personal factors such as personality, experience and perceived ability and by contextual factors such as social and economic structures. Intentions are moulded further by analytic and holistic thought processes. These ideas lead to the development of a theory of planned behaviour which illustrates how people behave in situations which are not entirely within their control. This is the situation facing the intending entrepreneur who cannot control how external backers and other interested parties will behave.

Behaviour is influenced by intentions which are themselves dependent on attitudes but Delmar argues that more is needed to elicit planned behaviour. A second condition is that perceived social norms must be supportive of the *intended behaviour*. In other words the potential entrepreneur must believe that significant others will approve of the chosen course of action. However, supportive attitudes and societal norms are necessary but not sufficient conditions. Unless individuals feel in control of key factors which can create a successful outcome, intentions will not be converted into actual behaviour. If they are positive about their ability they are said to have *perceived behavioural control*, and this will be influenced by issues such as experience, perceived aptitudes and favourable economic conditions. The belief by a person that he or she has the capability to succeed will strongly influence behaviour; indeed it is suggested that this factor is much more important than either supportive attitudes or encouraging societal norms. Delmar argues that this approach is more useful than trait theories in that it more clearly reflects the complexity of the entrepreneurial decision-making process. It also highlights some factors which are amenable to change through intervention. However, he concedes that the connection 'between intentions and actual behaviour is still an uncharted area'.[66] This link between intentions, norms and actual behaviour is also reflected in Krueger's model shown in Figure 3.6 later in this chapter.

Planned behavioural approaches explain how preferences amongst various courses of action are made but entrepreneurial research has also borrowed from the social cognitive theory of self-regulation.[67] This theory aims to explain goal-directed behaviour and assumes that behaviour has a purpose. The theory proposes that in deciding to behave in a given manner people juggle with notions of what they are able to do, they visualise the results that will flow from their behaviour, they set goals and plan events that can lead to the attainment of proposed outcomes. A central concept in this model is self-efficacy. Boyd and Vozikis[68] define self-efficacy as 'a person's belief in his or her capability to perform a given task'. These authors argue that self-efficacy is crucial in determining whether a person will pursue a goal and is equally important in maintaining motivation once action is taken. In short, if people firmly believe that they have what it takes to set up and complete enterprising projects this will strongly influence their intention to attain this outcome. However, if a person has low self-efficacy, he or she is unlikely to pursue a given goal even if it is regarded as important by self, others and society. Self-efficacy develops over time and may develop into a self-fulfilling prophecy. A probable course of events is: I believe I can do, I aspire to achieve, I achieve, and consequently I believe that I can accomplish more. Failure to achieve may produce negative reinforcement.

Self-efficacy is not dissimilar to perceived behavioural control but it is a specific concept. It explains how a person's beliefs, about their capacity to gather the necessary resources, acquire the knowledge and skill and sustain the motivation to remain in control of a complex project, actually influence behaviour and accomplishment. Unlike locus of control, which is a 'distal' construct, self-efficacy is 'proximal' and there is some evidence that it is a useful predictor of intentions to become an entrepreneur or to expand a business. Recent research on entrepreneurial self-efficacy (ESE) has been carried out by Chen, Gene-Green and Crick and they report that the findings of previous research, which confirm that self-efficacy is an important determinant of career choice, can be extended to entrepreneurship.[69] ESE is a useful construct in predicting who will become an entrepreneur. Furthermore, although self-efficacy is task-specific it can be applied to occupational domains as well as to specific jobs. Whilst every enterprising act may be unique, entrepreneurship has a number of recognisable features and a concept like ESE can be generalised to a range of similar tasks such as entrepreneurship. In Chen *et al.*'s work ESE encompassed such components as capability in innovation, risk-taking, marketing, management and financial control. This broad notion can predict who will become an entrepreneur and the component ESE measures allow interested parties to examine the relative potency of specific sub-domains with regard to particular choices of occupation.

ESE is useful in predicting who becomes an entrepreneur but these authors argue that it is also very useful in explaining why people avoid this occupation. They suggest that certain groups, such as women and ethnic groups, are often discouraged from pursuing an entrepreneurial career by perceptions of inadequate ESE. Efforts at augmenting the perceived ESE of these groups could prove useful in expanding the potential entrepreneurial population.

Favourable attitudes and social support, perceived behavioural control and high self-efficacy can encourage entrepreneurship but Delmar introduces an additional concept to the debate, the notion of *intrinsic motivation*. People are intrinsically motivated when they carry out an act simply because they enjoy it. Activities are undertaken for their innate attractiveness and Bandura[70] points out that intrinsic motivation improves perceived self-efficacy which in turn increases intrinsic motivation. If people are intrinsically motivated they are interested in an activity, whilst their attitudes reflect the importance attributed to events. Taken together these issues influence the manner in which individuals choose between alternatives when making decisions. Interests influence what people pay attention to and consequently have an impact on how they interpret and perceive events. Interests, together with a strong sense of self-efficacy, also play a part in achievement. Achievers are interested in goals which are demanding but attainable and once they achieve them self-efficacy is increased. Interests are also related to other important entrepreneurial concepts such as autonomy and creativity. If a person finds aspects of the entrepreneurial process attractive he or she will set goals which are capable of attaining desired outcomes and strive hard to achieve such goals. An important entrepreneurial goal is business growth and, if individuals find such a goal to be attractive, Delmar argues that there is a strong possibility that they will succeed in expanding their ventures. Furthermore his research reveals that 'job interests have been shown to predict entrepreneurial behaviour (measured as business growth and profitability) and how it is manifested.'[71] In general 'interest leads to higher attention, better decision-making and a feeling of enjoyment.' If interest is accompanied by perceived self-efficacy a mutually reinforcing cycle of behaviour will emerge and enhance entrepreneurship.

The cognitive concepts reviewed by Delmar are useful in understanding the process of business formation and growth. They are less concerned with the way people are and place greater emphasis on how people interpret events, perceive issues and make decisions. They bring the following issues to the forefront of the entrepreneurial debate:

- the role of attitudes in determining what is considered important;
- the impact of attitudes on intentions;
- the role of perceived social support for activities;
- the impact of perceived behavioural control on decision-making and outcomes;
- the specific and important role of perceived self-efficacy on choice and action;
- the way in which interest and the emotional matter of enjoyment impact on attention, perception and achievement.

These models more readily reflect the complexity of the entrepreneurial process than trait theories and they lend themselves to empirical testing. Concepts such as self-efficacy are also more 'proximal' than 'distal' constructs like locus of control and, because they relate to thinking processes, perception and decision-making, they are more amenable to manipulation through intervention.

BEHAVIOURAL THEORIES

Cognitive theories emphasise the individual decision-making process and the impact of perceived competency on the decision to become an entrepreneur. The context, or at least the manner in which it is interpreted, is regarded as important.

The behavioural approach to studying enterprise also views an enterprising act in the context in which it happens, a context that is often complex. The study of the enterprise of individuals should therefore focus on the behaviours they display in this context, rather than on what they themselves are. Two approaches with particular relevance to this theory are the examination of individual 'competencies' relevant to a specific event and the study of the change of behaviour over time, in particular at different 'stages' of business development.

Competencies

Cognitive approaches have been highlighted by psychologists but other writers have also commented on the role played by competencies and attributes and resources: ideas that are closely linked with issues such as perceived behavioural control and self-efficacy in the entrepreneurial decision-making process.

An individual will not be in control of an enterprising event if he or she is not competent and there is now considerable interest in enumerating the key competencies of successful entrepreneurs. Competency has been described as the modern terminology for 'ability'. However, there is still considerable confusion around the concept, in particular with regard to what the term 'competency' actually means. There are two broad approaches to the question. Boyatzis considers that competency relates to the 'personal characteristics' of individuals, while the Management Charter Initiative in the UK adopts a work-functions approach. The former focuses on the person and on the characteristics that make people

Source: Reprinted by permission of Sage Publications from S. Caird, 'Problems With the Identification of Enterprise Competencies and the Implications for Assessment and Development', *Management Education and Development* 1992; 23: 16. © Sage Publications.

Figure 3.4 Framework for identifying enterprise competency

competent, while the latter looks at the job and details those job functions that competent people can perform effectively.[72]

Most work in the area is devoted to managerial competency, but Caird[73] has explored some competencies for enterprise. She concludes that there are four aspects of competency: knowledge, performance, skill and psychological variables, which specifically relate to a field of expertise.[74] Her model is presented in Figure 3.4 and it includes variables examined by both trait and cognitive theorists.

Caird argues that, while the requisite knowledge and skill are contextual, the underlying psychological variables may be more generic. She points out also that it is important to distinguish between the everyday aspects of competency and those aspects that are critical in separating very enterprising people from the only adequately enterprising. The former can cope with complex and variable situations, while the latter may not. In addition, different levels of competency are required in different jobs and business ventures. Caird's work is useful in clarifying concepts, but she notes that there still 'is no clear understanding of what enterprise competency means', with the result that the concept 'runs the risk of meaning everything and nothing'.[75]

There are a number of lists of possible enterprise competencies that overlap but do not coincide, and the lists of enterprise competencies also overlap with lists of enterprise traits or attributes. The following are some of the enterprise competencies frequently cited:

Dedication	Creativity	Technical competencies
Decision-making	Confidence	Sensitivity to changes
Goal-setting	Innovation	Networking and contacts
Planning	Risk-taking	Developing relationships
Responsibility	Insight	Project management

It can be seen that these competencies include personal qualities set alongside skills and individual orientations. It would also seem that they have much in common with the competencies identified by Boddy and Buchanan in relation to the 'perceived effectiveness of change implementation'.[76] This is not surprising because enterprise thrives in a changing environment and therefore requires change management ability. Boddy and Buchanan have, from their empirical work, identified fifteen change management competencies, which they have grouped in five clusters. (See Table 3.1.)

Comments

A major problem with the competency approach, as with some other approaches, is that it is not definitive. There appears to be no competency that is possessed by

Table 3.1 Change management competencies

Goals
1 Sensitivity to changes in key personnel, top management perceptions, and market conditions, and to the way in which these impact [on] the goals of the project in hand.
2 Clarity in specifying goals, in defining the achievable.
3 Flexibility in responding to changes (outside) the control of the project manager, perhaps requiring major shifts in project goals and management style, and risk-taking.

Roles
4 Team-building abilities, to bring together key stakeholders and establish effective working groups, and clearly to define and delegate respective responsibilities.
5 Networking skills in establishing and maintaining appropriate contacts within and outside the organisation.
6 Tolerance of ambiguity, to be able to function comfortably, patiently, and effectively in an uncertain environment.

Communication
7 Communication skills to transmit effectively to colleagues and subordinates the need for changes in project goals and in individual tasks and responsibilities.
8 Interpersonal skills, across the range, including selection, listening, collecting appropriate information, identifying the concerns of others, and managing meetings.
9 Personal enthusiasm, in expressing plans and ideas.
10 Stimulating motivation and commitment in others involved.

Negotiation
11 Selling plans and ideas to others, by creating a desirable and challenging vision of the future.
12 Negotiating with key players for resources, or for changes in procedures, and to resolve conflict.

Managing up
13 Political awareness, in identifying potential coalitions, and in balancing conflicting goals and perceptions.
14 Influencing skills, to gain commitment to project plans and ideas from potential sceptics and resisters.
15 Helicopter perspective, to stand back from the immediate project and take a broader view of priorities.

Source: D. Buchanan and D. Boddy, *The Expertise of the Change Agent* (Hemel Hempstead: Prentice-Hall, 1992), pp. 92–3.

all entrepreneurs, and many examples exist of non-entrepreneurs who appear to possess more entrepreneurial competencies than do some people who clearly are entrepreneurs. Lists of competencies are more general than domain-specific concepts such as self-efficacy. However, if individuals could be convinced of their self-efficacy with respect to key entrepreneurial competencies this would increase their motivation to become entrepreneurs.

Attributes and resources

Perceived self-efficacy is an important aspect of cognitive models, and it corresponds with a view of enterprise, and of enterprising behaviour, that is based on the attributes and resources an individual may possess at any point in time. Attributes may include self-confidence, diligence, perseverance, interpersonal skills and innovative behaviour. Resources may include finance, experience, knowledge, skills, a network and a track record. It is suggested that it is the interaction amongst these factors that produces a rational response, on the basis of available information, when the opportunity occurs for a business start-up.

This view also acknowledges that there is inertia in individual behaviour and that it may take a discontinuity in work, or in life, to trigger a review of an individual's situation. Whether this review will lead to an individual trying to start up his or her own enterprise will then depend on the attributes and resources he or she has accumulated, together with his or her perception of environmental factors such as the availability of encouragement, and support such as advice, grants and training. This is illustrated in Figure 3.5.

The implications of this view are that the start-up decision will be affected by the attributes and resources acquired prior to the trigger for taking the decision, and that there is scope for initiatives to enhance the acquisition of those attributes and resources (for a list of possible attributes and resources, and how they are acquired, see Table 3.2). It does not deny that, at the time of the decision, the availability of support such as grants and training is influential on that decision. It does however indicate that whether or not grants and training are available, more people are likely to decide to try a business start-up, and with more chance of success, if they are in possession of the relevant attributes and resources. There should therefore be economic benefits to be gained from enhancing relevant individual attributes and resources.

Perceived behavioural control, self-efficacy, integrated competencies and attributes and resources models of enterprise and entrepreneurship are extremely useful from a policy perspective. This is because constructs such as self-efficacy, though quite stable, are amenable to change through intervention. Furthermore, interventions can focus on the micro level of the individual or on the macro level of the community. Recent theoretical and empirical contributions by writers such as Boyd and Vozikis, Chen *et al.*, Delmar, Krueger and Brazeal[77] offer pertinent advice on how and when to intervene to promote enterprise and entrepreneurship in communities. However the details of proposed interventions are

Figure 3.5   Attributes and resources model

Table 3.2   Attributes and resources, and how they are acquired

Attributes	*Resources*
Attitude	Ideas
Self-confidence	Technical skills
Enthusiasm	Interpersonal and
Diligence and perseverance	communication skills
Initiative	Information, and access to it
Independence	Network
Persuasiveness	Finance
Positive outlook	Experience, e.g. of small
Perception	business, of marketing and of
Attitude to risk	planning
	Track record and credibility
	Direction

How acquired	
Attributes can be acquired from both nature and nurture. The nurture influences can include family, education, culture, work experience, role models, peers, economic structure lifestyle and stages of life.	Resources are acquired through many of the processes of working and living. They will, however, be more readily acquired if this acquisition is planned and targeted.

considered in Chapters 10 and 11 where intervention in support of entrepreneurship is addressed in detail.

The stage model approach

Those who take a longitudinal view of the progress of businesses have identified a number of stages in the business development process (which are considered further in Chapter Six). This stage model approach can highlight both the types of problem encountered at each stage and the abilities required to deal with them. It can also therefore indicate both how the attributes and resources needed vary from stage to stage and the changes thus required in the behaviour and practices of entrepreneurs if they are to progress successfully from one stage to another.

CASE 3.3
An entrepreneur

Alex Hunter is a young single man who had an interest in having his own business. He had always 'messed about with motors', repairing and tuning them. He took several 'O' levels and joined an engineering firm as an apprentice. However, he did not like the atmosphere in this very large organisation, so he left before his apprenticeship was completed. He joined a small local engineering company and sold their products. He loved his job and worked enthusiastically for the company. After three years' employment he became a manager and began to learn about the administrative as well as the technical side of the business. However, his attitude towards the company changed dramatically after a serious industrial injury. He spent some time in hospital and on returning to work found that the firm had appointed a new sales manager and that he had no 'real' job. As a result he decided to have his own firm.

Alex had had an eye for business and had been running a little part-time firm, which repaired damaged machine tool equipment. On the advice of his bank manager he did considerable market research and established that there appeared to be a big demand for this kind of service. Alex left the engineering industry, joined a business start-up training programme and prepared for the launch of his own business. His principal motives for founding a firm were the desire for autonomy, achievement, increased personal satisfaction and a desire to make lots of money. He felt strongly about the impossibility of ever getting rich working for someone else.

In spite of his youth Alex was quite well prepared for managing a business. He had developed important technical skills, had one year's managerial experience, had always dabbled in small businesses, and had a good business brain which he subsequently used to employ fifty workers.

Points raised

This kind of case, which is typical of start-up entrepreneurs, shows both push (no 'real' job) and pull (a desire for autonomy) influences. It also shows the relevance of attributes (such as self-confidence) and resources (such as technical skills) together with a trigger.

ENTREPRENEURIAL PROFILING AND ENTERPRISE PREDICTION

One particular application to which the different theories of enterprising behaviour have been put has been to try to construct a profile of an enterprising person. This has been done primarily in the field of entrepreneurship with the objective of predicting who is most likely to succeed as an entrepreneur. However, with a lack of consensus on the definition of 'enterprise' and of an 'entrepreneur', and in the absence of a single accepted model of enterprise/entrepreneurship, this approach has so far had little success.

AN INTEGRATED APPROACH

Each of the theories so far considered has drawbacks, in particular because no single theory seems to cover all aspects of enterprise. Therefore attempts have been made to amalgamate parts of two or more theories to produce an integrated approach with more general application. One such attempt is the attributes and resources approach, which has already been discussed, and another is the Krueger model which is considered next.

Krueger's model

Krueger[78] produced a model of entrepreneurial potential (see Figure 3.6) which, in view of the similarity of enterprise and entrepreneurship, would seem to apply also to enterprise in its broad meaning. Krueger argues that intentions to act entrepreneurially are underpinned by the development of potential which is in turn built upon credibility.

Krueger contends that to be credible to oneself and to others, entrepreneurs/enterprising persons must both perceive the probable outcome of their endeavours

Source: N. F. Krueger, *Prescription for Opportunity: How Communities Can Create Potential for Entrepreneurs* (Washington, DC: Small Business Foundation of America, Working Paper 93-03, 1995), p.10.

Figure 3.6   Intentions model of entrepreneurial potential (simplified)

in a favourable light and believe that they have the wherewithal to succeed. Perception is all-important in this process; indeed it may be more important than reality. This favourable light is a product of personal preference and social approval of enterprise/entrepreneurship and the wherewithal comes from experience, from innate and learned attributes that might enhance enterprising propensity, and from skills, knowledge and resources that increase self-efficacy. That light and that wherewithal alone, however, are not necessarily sufficient. A trigger or key event (a situational context) may be necessary to start the individual on an enterprising course of action.

It can be seen that this model draws on ideas from trait, cognitive, sociological, behavioural and attributes and resources approaches and neatly summarises a range of relevant variables.

Delmar has however suggested[79] that what stands out among these sorts of influences is whether people feel that entrepreneurship is a feasible option for themselves. He cites for instance the work of Davidsson[80] who explored intentions to start a business in Sweden and found that, while men and women differed little in their attitudes to enterprise, women were low on perceived behavioural control, which could explain why they were under-represented amongst entrepreneurs there. They do not have enough confidence in their own ability and know-how to start and operate a business and therefore abstain from doing so.

It may also be relevant to point out that just because a person took an enterprising decision at one time it does not necessarily mean that he or she would automatically do it again. For instance an owner's motivation to expand a business may decline once that business produces a satisfactory level of income or if his or her personal circumstances change. This can be explained as a change in personal desirability and shows the need to take into consideration more than just factors such as attributes and traits.[81]

GENDER AND ETHNICITY

Two other prominent aspects of individuals are also perceived, at least in some circumstances, to be relevant to the extent to which people engage in entrepreneurship or in wider aspects of enterprise. They are the individual's gender and ethnicity.

Female enterprise and entrepreneurship

While it might be supposed that gender would have little or no effect on whether a person was enterprising the specific example of gender in the business context shows that this may appear not to be the case. Historically most entrepreneurs have been men and those businesses which have been created by women have generally been in a limited range of business sectors. However, in the 1980s and 1990s, this picture began to change:

- The National Women's Business Council[82] in the USA reported that in 1993 one third of all businesses were owned by women. They also estimated that the number of firms with female proprietors was growing twice as fast as firms in total and that 11 million people were now employed in women-owned businesses. Figures provided by the Small Business Administration on the number of women-owned firms in 1980 and 1993 indicated that the proportion of female-owned firms increased from 26 per cent to 33 per cent of all firms in this period.[83] A more recent study by Carter suggests that the figure now approaches 38 per cent.[84]
- Research in Scandinavia also found that around 20 per cent of new firms are now founded by women and that 25 per cent of all private firms in Sweden are women-owned.[85]
- Figures from Britain are in line with those in Scandinavia and the USA. Sarah Carter reported that between '1979 and 1997 the number of self-employed women in the UK increased by 163 per cent from 319,000 to 840,000. In the same period the number of self-employed men increased by 67 per cent, from 1,449,000 to 2,421,000.' Similarly the Equal Opportunities Commission reported that the 1980s and 1990s had seen a large increase in the percentage of self-employed women from a little 'over 3 per cent of the female workforce in 1979 to nearly 7 per cent in 1997. In 1999, 26 per cent of all those running their own businesses were women.'[86]

Therefore, while the proportion of women entrepreneurs is increasing, it is still in most areas significantly less than the proportion of men. The reasons advanced for this include the patriarchal attitudes that existed until recently in countries like Britain where not so long ago women were required to give up their jobs when they got married or, as exemplified by the airline industry, when they reached the 'advanced' age of 27. Barriers such as this prevented enterprising women from acquiring the essential business knowledge and skills so necessary for a successful business launch. Also the recent increases in the proportion of women entrepreneurs could reflect changes in the labour market. Many more women are economically active nowadays. In Britain between 1984 and 1999 women's economic activity rates increased from 66 to 72 per cent and some of this increased number are likely to have opted for self-employment. However the reasons why entrepreneurship has remained a largely male preserve are probably more complex than that and some of the factors which appear to be involved are presented below.

Motivation to create a venture

Krueger's model of entrepreneurial potential, presented earlier in this chapter, seeks to integrate various theories of entrepreneurial intentions and it therefore seems logical to explore the extent to which the various factors in this model apply differently to women than to men.

Personal desirability

Individuals have needs and they engage in activities which should fulfil those needs. Since women and men have historically had a differential attraction to entrepreneurship it might be that women's and men's needs differ and much of the early research on female entrepreneurs explored their motivation to start a firm.

Chell and Baines[87] argue that some feminist literature depicts women and men as biologically different and this might result in different social and economic roles for the sexes. Others argue that biological differences are small and conclude that different socio-economic roles arise from social constrictions imposed on entrepreneurial choice by factors such as family, cultural, political and industrial structures. These factors create and are reinforced by a strongly segregated labour market and occupational structure. These influences suggest that women's and men's experience of occupational choice are different and may explain women's under-representation amongst entrepreneurs.

Despite these and other factors which could account for different motivations of male and female entrepreneurs, many early studies of female entrepreneurs seemed to depict the male experience as the norm and this may have led to the conclusion that 'women act from similar motivations and look for similar rewards from entrepreneurship as their male counterparts.'[88] In support of this view, Carter notes that early studies of the stated reasons for business founding reported by women were quite similar to those mentioned by men. Men and women were depicting those outcomes of business formation which stimulated them into action and many of the reasons were similar. From an 11-country study of motivations for starting a business three broad categories for both genders were identified: challenge, wealth and autonomy,[89] and those studies which used psychological instruments to assess the personal traits of men and women entrepreneurs also found few differences between the genders.[90] However a study by Goffee and Scase indicated that women entrepreneurs were not a homogeneous group,[91] and could be classified according to their attachment to entrepreneurial ideals and conventional female roles. Those women with a strong attachment to both were called 'conventionals'. They accommodated business aspirations and female roles by using flexible working schedules and locations. 'Innovative' women were strongly committed to entrepreneurial ideas such as autonomy and played down conventional female 'responsibilities'. 'Domestics' organised their business ventures around the needs of the family whilst 'radical' women had low attachments to entrepreneurial and traditional female roles. They rejected conventional business- and gender-related norms and were keen on radical change in society. This model and a similar one developed by Cromie and Hayes[92] were criticised on a number of counts but Carter notes that early research on the female entrepreneur did bring the issue of women entrepreneurs into the public domain and did point to some of the tension experienced by female business founders. However, it should be pointed out that men who own firms also experience tension between meeting economic and family needs.

A recent review of the literature by Ljunggren and Kolvereid[93] suggests that there may well be differences in men's and women's motives. Women seek economic outcomes such as profit and growth but they also seek social and relationship goals. Furthermore, Holmquist and Sundin[94] conclude that women often start a firm to allow them to create their own workplaces. This allows them to meet both business and family demands. Ljunggren and Kolvereid do report however that there is no consistency in findings about the association between gender and motivation across countries. For example in Norway men were more likely than women to be motivated by a desire to continue a family tradition and to remain at the forefront of innovative technological developments.

Perceived social norms

Individuals have different needs and therefore some entrepreneurial outcomes will motivate one person but not another. However, Krueger points out that societal norms can also influence the perceived allure of an outcome. If entrepreneurs are revered in a society and if the perceived outcomes of this process are attractive to individuals, this will encourage entrepreneurship. But does society respect female entrepreneurs? In many parts of the world it is assumed that a woman's role is to manage the household and to raise children. Also it is assumed that this requires the so-called feminine qualities such as tenderness and relatedness and these are respected less than supposed masculine characteristics of material success, competition and ruthlessness.

While society norms may not encourage women to be entrepreneurs to the same extent as men, that does not mean that men are universally encouraged. Indeed there would still seem to be elements of society, even in the enterprise culture of the UK at the start of the 21st century, which say that starting a business is something only done by people who couldn't get 'a proper job'. Also there is some evidence that women entrepreneurs tend to have strong supporters, especially from within their families. Ljunggren and Kolvereid[95] investigated the extent to which close family members, work colleagues, entrepreneurial acquaintances and important contacts in the local community supported male and female entrepreneurs in their decision to start a venture. They also asked their respondents whether they cared about what their families thought about their decision. The results showed that women perceived significantly stronger social support than men but they did not feel any more compelled than men to comply with external pressure to start a firm. Ljunggren and Kolvereid surmise that women are less willing to start a firm until they have a support network in place. This might arise because the life and occupational experiences of women have not equipped them for entrepreneurship. They need to compensate for limited knowledge and experience by marshalling support.

Anna *et al.* have also completed some empirical work on support for female entrepreneurs.[96] They argue that social persuasion can be important in encouraging would-be entrepreneurs to pursue this career. This persuasion can range from positive encouragement from significant others to professional advice from bankers and so forth. Research reveals that women tend to have strong support from a network of contacts who provide pertinent information about markets, sources of finance and likely suppliers.

Strong social support can positively influence the attitudes of prospective entrepreneurs; it can encourage women to have self-confidence. Anna *et al.* studied women entrepreneurs in business areas traditionally associated with women and in 'non-traditional' areas and hypothesised that those in non-traditional areas would find it more difficult to gain access to emotional, financial or operational support systems. The results were inconclusive with respect to operational support but women in non-traditional areas found it more difficult to obtain emotional and financial support than those in traditional sectors and women moving into non-traditional areas perceived that support was harder to come by. The 'non-traditional' women described their frustration in trying to secure loans and venture capital from banks and other organisations.

Perceived self-efficacy

To start and run a business an individual needs to be motivated, needs to have a viable business idea and needs relevant knowledge, experience, skills and resources. That person must believe that he or she has the wherewithal to succeed. This, in Krueger's terms, is self-efficacy which can be described as a contextual judgement by individuals about the appropriateness of their skills and abilities for achieving a given goal.

Anna *et al.* argue that beliefs influence subsequent behaviour through the intervening variable of intentions. People form attitudes about doing things. For example, they might develop a positive attitude towards starting a business but this attitude will be strongly influenced by an individual's belief that by performing certain acts the goal of entrepreneurship can be attained.

Perceived self-efficacy leads to intentions which ultimately lead to behaviour. The notion of self-efficacy has been used since about 1980 in examining occupational choice. If individuals do not have a strong perception of self-efficacy then they will fail to realise their career potential and Hackett and Betz claimed in 1981 that this is why many women 'fail to fully realise their capabilities and talents in career pursuits'.[97]

Successful business formulation and management require multiple competencies and Milne and Lewis[98] suggest that entrepreneurs rapidly develop 'a portfolio of knowledge in two fields: first, the product or service techniques and technologies appropriate to their business, and second the business of being a businessman'. They need technical, business and managerial knowledge and skill and they get these largely through employment experience and/or educational exposure and it is suggested that entrepreneurial learning can be gained most effectively from previous entrepreneurial experience, previous experience in the same or a similar sector as that of a new enterprise, in smaller and entrepreneurial incubator organisations, from a family business and from appropriate educational experience. In the case of the latter, management education used to be a male preserve but in the past twenty years women have increasingly taken courses in business and management studies.

However in the case of employment experience there is a key issue. The labour markets in Britain, the USA and many other countries exhibit pronounced gender segregation. Blau[99] reported in 1978 that the women in the USA who had flocked into the labour force in the 1970s were crowded into an extremely narrow range of industrial sectors and occupations. They were not absorbed 'through an across-the-board expansion of employment opportunities'. Table 3.3 shows the employment pattern for the UK in 1998 and the Equal Opportunities Commission[100] reported in 2001 that in Britain the 'most significant differences between the sexes is the pronounced pattern of gender segregation in different industrial groupings and occupations.'

This gender segregation means that women 'are concentrated in lower-skilled and lower-paid jobs with less access to vocational training and education'.[101] Carter reports that early research from the UK and the USA found that women

Table 3.3 Employment and self-employment by occupation in the UK, 1998

Type of work	Thousands	
	Women	Men
Managers and administrators	1385	2816
Professional	1082	1669
Associate professional & technical	1305	1314
Clerical & secretarial	2892	984
Craft & related	281	2877
Personal & protective services	1906	938
Sales	1299	736
Plant and machine operatives	468	1993
Other	1000	1064
Totals	11,618	14,394

Source: *UK Labour Force Survey, Spring 1998*. Reproduced with the permission of the Controller of HMSO.

were pressurised to start businesses in the service and retail areas and that they often lacked the knowledge and managerial experience needed to start elsewhere. However the relative lack of employment opportunities for women may encourage more of them to take the risks of self-employment. Allen and Truman[102] suggested that quite often 'women enter self-employment because they have no alternative means of earning a living' and a recent study of self-employed women in Northern Ireland by Borooah *et al.* suggests that the precariousness of the female labour market, coupled with low pay, encouraged women to seek self-employment 'to gain some form of economic independence'.[103]

These studies suggest that the employment experience of women may mean that they are relatively less well prepared for entrepreneurship. However studies of perceived self-efficacy, such as that by Ljunggren and Kolvereid,[104] investigated the perceived behavioural control and entrepreneurial ability of emerging male and female entrepreneurs. They found that there were no differences between the genders in their ability to detect entrepreneurial opportunities and surmised that this might occur because women, recognising their lack of skill and the risks involved, engage in considerable self-analysis before starting a firm: they prepare thoroughly. Further information about women in business is included in Chapter Seven.

Enterprise and entrepreneurship in ethnic groups

Issues of ethnicity in enterprise arise, not so much in the ethnic homeland where these are also matters of politics and culture (and which are considered in the next chapter), but where there are minority ethnic groups in other countries. Again, as with women, the studies of enterprise among these groups in a number of countries have tended to look specifically at the practice of enterprise in entrepreneurship. They have found that two issues predominate in the initial decision to create an ethnic business: structural matters such as the inhospitality of the environment in which ethnic groups are embedded and the advantage conferred on ethnic business by the ethnic resources at their disposal. A sub-set of the latter is the cultural issue of the relative propensity of certain ethnic groups to become entrepreneurs.[105]

Inhospitality takes many forms but two broad theoretical approaches to ethnic entrepreneurship, middleman minority and ethnic enclave theories, highlight discrimination in the labour market 'exhibited in a denial of access to majority-controlled paths of economic advancement' as a major cause of business formation.[106] Ram and his colleagues[107] are aware of supposed ethnic resources but place more emphasis on the restricted opportunity structures and plain racism faced by ethnic minorities in Britain. In addition, Phizacklea and Ram argue that social marginalisation due to the absence of satisfactory work in mainstream employment and unemployment were by far the most often-stated reasons 'for creating a business in both Lyon and Birmingham'.[108] Ram recognises that other researchers in Britain have reached different conclusions. Other studies conclude that positive issues, such as the desire to achieve, motivate ethnic entrepreneurs, but it is possible that the upward mobility of second-generation immigrants can account for this outcome.[109]

Resource-based explanations of start-up focus on the advantages accruing to those belonging to and strongly connected to an ethnic group. Greene argues that ethnic entrepreneurs are influenced by the cultural context within which they function. Many ethnic communities have their particular value systems, transactions are often conducted on the basis of reciprocity, groups often have a sense of belonging and solidarity and relationships are based on trust. These values and expectations can be a source of social capital, not merely in the more tangible form of 'protected markets', sources of labour, and financial support, but also in the form of intangibles such as values, traditions, ties to one another, group solidarity and networks of information. For example, group solidarity can provide a source of stability for firms as they are established and develop and those communities with a strong proclivity towards entrepreneurship will have visible role models and an atmosphere generally supportive of business formation. The success of business ventures can be a source of pride throughout the ethnic group. Networks which assist in gaining access to information, capital, support and tradition can also be a source of stability in a difficult world. Not all ethnic communities however use such resources to the same extent. Resources only contribute to value when they are utilised and ethnic communities vary in the extent to which resources are used.

An important resource for business start-up is finance. Many small businesses rely on personal savings and informal financial assistance from friends but Fadahunsi, Smallbone and Supri argue that these sources, with additional help from co-ethnics, are particularly important for ethnic entrepreneurs.[110] Networks of contacts were used by some owners to get introductions to bankers and other providers of finance, although the procedure was used much more by Pakistani and Indian Sikh groups than by Nigerians or West Indians. The latter groups also used informal personal networks to raise money in the form of gifts, but more usually in the form of loans, which were offered on the basis of trust between borrower and lender. Fadahunsi and his colleagues also quote the example of a Somali business owner who borrowed £7000 as an interest-free loan from 25 co-ethnics. Clusters of trusting co-ethnics who provide finance are an important feature of the start-up process amongst several socio-cultural groups. (Further information about ethnic businesses is included in Chapter Seven.)

ILLUSTRATION 3.1
Ethnic community support
....

In the USA Greene[111] compared official and community-sponsored support programmes and concluded that community sponsorship was much more powerful than general sponsorship, using a case study of community support for Ismaili-Pakistani immigrants in South Western USA to support her argument.

Table 3.4 Ethnic sponsorship as a sustainable competitive advantage (SCA)

SCA principles	General sponsorship	Ethnic community	Ismaili/Pakistani community example
Valuable	Valuable over the short term	Valuable indefinitely	Ethnic capital fund Assistance in opportunity search Provision of business information Expressive and instrumental support
Rare	Not particularly rare	Increased rareness for members of minority groups	Found only in certain minority groups
Imperfectly imitable unique historic conditions	Unique historic conditions	Unique historic conditions	Recent immigrants
Causally ambiguous	Causally ambiguous	Causally ambiguous	
Socially complex	Socially complex	Socially complex	Compounded with cultural and religious norms
Lack of strategically equivalent substitutes	May provide unsubstitutable resources over the short term	Provide unsubstitutable resources over the long term	Resource mix available indefinitely to members of the community

Source: P. G. Greene, 'A Resource-Based Approach to Ethnic Business Sponsorship: A Consideration of Ismaili-Pakistani Immigrants', *Journal of Small Business Management* 1997; 35: 66. The table was developed from J. Barney, 'Firm Resources and Sustained Competitive Advantage', *Journal of Management* 1991; 17: 99–120; and D. M. Flynn, 'Sponsorship and the Survival of New Organisations', *Journal of Small Business Management* 1993; 31: 51–62. Reproduced with the permission of Blackwell Publishing Ltd.

She interviewed 82 family members in this community and found that Ismaili groups have a long history of business formation and that religious leaders have long promoted self-help, community involvement and business venturing. She also discovered that there is a recognisable route from entry into the community to business founding. New immigrants are attached to sponsors who arrange employment and tutoring in English and American business practices. In return new entrants are expected to accumulate savings. Once assimilated immigrants are assisted in seeking and evaluating business opportunities and if a suitable prospect emerges they can borrow from a substantial community investment fund. Successful business founders meet regularly with their peers and a variety of support is made available to business associates.

Greene compares this community sponsorship programme with general sponsorship as shown in Table 3.4 and it can be seen that the community programme is likely to offer much more sustained competitive advantage than the general programme.

Community sponsorship is special in that there is a semi-formal process to the sponsorship and it provides both tangible resources such as capital and intangibles like an entrepreneurial culture. Furthermore these resources are only available to insiders. Trust is also an issue. Funds are provided in the expectation of reciprocity and on the assumption that resources will not be used to exploit co-ethnics.

It is unlikely that any official sponsorship programme can compete with a scheme like the Ismaili-Pakistani one but not all community support schemes are so well-endowed or actively utilised.

POSTSCRIPT

This brief review of some of the factors that impel individuals to act, or constrain them from acting, in an enterprising fashion has indicated that there is a broad range of variables in any model of entrepreneurial choice and behaviour. Not all variables will impact on all enterprise, but many of these factors will be considered, implicitly or explicitly, by those taking enterprising actions, and will help to determine whether an individual does or does not become an entrepreneur. It is important, however, to note that enterprising individuals are not homogeneous and that therefore different approaches looking at different groups at different stages of organisational development will result in a complex picture. In general there are many variables that can impact on enterprise but, in spite of calls to develop multidimensional models, few have taken up the challenge to do so. The complexity of such models, and the enormous difficulty of using multivariate analysis with so many variables that are difficult to measure, have daunted researchers.

However, the development of cognitive models of entrepreneurial motivation may offer more promise. They focus on the decision-making process, and whilst they incorporate 'soft' behavioural matters such as perception, the social construction of reality, attitudes and emotions, it has been suggested that they are easier to construct and operationalise than other complex models in this area. It could, therefore, be said that the study of entrepreneurship requires the study of people much more than the study of the businesses they create.

THE KEY POINTS OF CHAPTER 3

- Enterprise is generally recognised in the outcomes of acts by enterprising individuals. They can be called enterprising outcomes. They can be seen in the narrow definition of enterprise synonymous with entrepreneurship, or small business formation, and in the broad approach of enterprise, which applies to any task that is non-routine and goal-directed and is accomplished in a determined and adventurous manner.
- Enterprise activity is dependent on enterprising individuals. There have been many studies and approaches to analysing what makes some individuals more enterprising than others. They include:
  - personality theories considering traits in individuals that predispose them to enterprise, psychodynamic approaches that look at the enterprising personality, social psychological approaches that take into account the context in which an individual operates, and owner typologies that look at different types of small business owner;
  - economic theories – covered in Chapter Four;
  - sociological approaches which consider the opportunities for and constraints on career choices;
  - cognitive approaches which suggest that decisions are made on the basis of perceived reality which is in turn affected by attitudes and behaviour;
  - behavioural theories, including competencies, stage model approaches and attributes and resources;
  - integrated approaches, such as that advanced by Krueger, which combine a number of different factors.
- All of these approaches offer some insight into what makes an individual act in an enterprising way. The integrated approaches offer potentially the most useful models for examining the process of enterprise. None has, however, yet proved to be helpful in predicting future enterprise or entrepreneurial success although recent work on entrepreneurial self-efficacy seems to hold promise.
- Two other aspects of individuals which are perceived to have some influence on their enterprise are their gender and their ethnicity.

CASE 3.4
Two enterprising people?

Helen

Helen was born and reared in a rural community in Scotland by middle class parents who had no connection with any small business. When she left school she was sponsored by a large organisation to take a Business Studies degree and worked for them for a year after graduation.

However, she was not content with the routine nature of the work and left to study for a PhD in Finance. After graduating she worked as a research assistant in a university department but soon left to take up a post in a commercial research team. But the job did not live up to her expectations: she found little challenge in it and did not respond well to taking orders from her boss. She found that she was not in control and disliked being told to do things. It was around this time that she married a university lecturer.

Helen left this job and returned for a short time to a university research post but was head-hunted and offered a senior position in the Small Business Unit of a consultancy firm. She imagined that she would have lots of freedom in this job but much of the job was in running pre-planned courses with little non-recurring, innovative work. She also disagreed with her superiors about the kind of contracts that they sought.

Throughout her work history Helen had always tried to be successful and she discovered that she did not like taking orders from anyone. She also found out that her boredom threshold was low and she was always on the lookout for new challenges. She therefore began to think about having her own enterprise. Then things happened very quickly; she wrote a business plan, contacted bank managers, sought clients and copyrights on some of her material and disengaged from her employment. Her main stimulus for starting the business was a realisation that she was very bad at accepting orders from authority figures and her stated motives were: frustration over not being able to do the things she wanted to do; the desire to do something worthwhile and earn more money at the same time; and the wish to get back to the 'sharp end' of finance where the excitement was.

Helen created an innovative financial services business with clients throughout the British Isles. She had developed both the technical and the managerial skills needed for this business through past experience. However her perception of the entrepreneurial role was not clear and she fully recognised that this might cause a problem. She predicted that her life would be a rather lonely one and she was not looking forward to the isolation. She did have a long discussion with a friend who owned his own enterprise and his advice was not to 'go for all the trimmings; just to have a go and meet the problems as they arise'.

John

John came from a Northern Irish lower middle class family which had a long association with a number of small entrepreneurial ventures. He left school without formal qualifications and trained as a caterer but, due to the awkward hours and poor payment, he soon left. His next job was as a bricklayer, a job he thoroughly enjoyed. He was paid an efficiency bonus and felt that he was rewarded for effort. However he fell and sustained injuries which effectively ended his bricklaying days. Next, he attended college, took some 'O' levels and was offered a place on an HND course in Business Studies, but declined the offer. After this he followed clerical and junior administrative jobs in two engineering companies but he could not settle into the required routine.

Around this time John got involved with a number of part-time entrepreneurial ventures including a disco, window-cleaning, selling fruit and vegetables, and painting and decorating. He always had a desire to have his own business and his first important venture was a small catering enterprise. He was employed by a catering firm for a time but he and a partner started their own firm. The venture did not last; John accused the partner of incompetency and they broke up on acrimonious terms. While working in the catering firm he got married and the lack of security in running a venture concerned him, so for the next six years John got involved in selling. He worked for a number of companies and eventually achieved the position of sales manager. However his final employer 'did the dirty on him' so he left. He was scathing about the whole business of selling.

In reviewing his work history he said that he always was rebellious and thought that he had been held back a lot because he was too young. He felt that his working life had been a failure in that he had numerous goals but none of them were really fulfilled. He had little time for authority figures and often felt that others had let him down. He was resentful about his lack of career progress and saw entrepreneurship as a possible way out of his dilemma.

He wanted to be an entrepreneur but had no business idea. Therefore he searched through various catalogues in pursuit of one. He came across an idea for repairing damaged motor vehicles and, because it was already patented by an American, he spent a long time negotiating over patent rights. He negotiated a deal and then set about building prototypes and conducting market research in an attempt to launch his enterprise.

John's motives for founding a business were above all a desire for autonomy, followed by achievement and a desire to make money. His scores on key entrepreneurial characteristics were all high and this, together with his background and job history, might be thought to mark him out as a 'natural' entrepreneur. However he had no previous experience of the motor trade and no knowledge of the motor insurance business. His prior entrepreneurial experience might help with the running of the business but would that be enough?

Points raised

Like the subject of Case 2.3, these are typical entrepreneurs but the examples suggest that not every entrepreneur is perfectly suited and prepared for that role. The desire to have one's own business does not guarantee success; other attributes and resources are necessary.

QUESTIONS, EXERCISES, ESSAY AND DISCUSSION TOPICS

- Critically evaluate the usefulness of trait theory in predicting who will become an entrepreneur.
- Critically evaluate the usefulness of cognitive theories of motivation for those persons charged with increasing the degree of enterprise in a community.
- Comment on the views expressed in Case 3.1.
- According to Case 3.1, 'enterprise can't be taught'. So what is the role of academic schools of enterprise and entrepreneurship?
- Based on Krueger's model what would you do to encourage more entrepreneurial activity? How would this differ from an approach based on the attributes and resources model?
- Using either Krueger's model or the attributes and resources approach, suggest a programme to help individuals to prepare themselves for eventual self-employment.
- Entrepreneurs need motivation, skills, resources and ideas to start businesses and women are just as capable as men of making a success of a business venture. Discuss.
- Compare the motivations of ethnic entrepreneurs to those of indigenous entrepreneurs.
- If you can run a family, you can run a business. Discuss with reference to Case 3.2.
- Are entrepreneurs 'born' or 'made'? Discuss with reference to Cases 3.1, 3.3 and 3.4.
- Study the short profiles of Helen and John in Case 3.4. Which person is the more likely to run a successful firm? Give reasons for your choice.
- Which theories best explain the examples in Cases 3.3 and 3.4?

SUGGESTIONS FOR FURTHER READING AND INFORMATION

B. Bolton and J. Thompson, *Entrepreneurs: Talent, Temperament, Techniques* (Oxford: Butterworth-Heinnemann, 2000).

R. Branson, *Losing My Virginity* (London: Virgin Publishing, 1999).

S. Carter and D. Jones-Evans (eds), *Enterprise and Small Business* (London: Pearson Education, 2000), Chapters 8, 10 and 11.

E. Chell, *Entrepreneurship: Globalisation, Innovation and Development* (London: Thompson Learning, 2000).

A. Roddick, *Body and Soul* (London: Vermillion, 1991); and *Business As Unusual*, (London: Thorsons, 2000).

www.eoc.org.uk – the website for the Equal Opportunities Commission.

REFERENCES

1   M. Scott, A. Fadahunsi and S. Kodithuwakku, 'Mastering Enterprise', No. 7, *Financial Times*, 13 January 1997, p. 6.
2   *New Collins Dictionary* (Glasgow: HarperCollins, 1992).
3   A. A. Gibb, 'The Enterprise Culture and Education', *International Small Business Journal* 1993; 11: 11–34.
4   W. G. Biemans, *Managing Innovation Within Networks* (London: Routledge, 1992).
5   G. A. Forehand, 'Assessment of Innovative Behaviour: Partial Criteria for the Assessment of Executive Performance', *Journal of Applied Psychology* 1963; 47: 206–13.
6   R. M. Kanter, 'Change Master Skills', in J. Henry and D. Walker (eds), *Managing Innovation* (London: Sage, 1991), pp. 54–61.
7   Lord Young of Graffan, cited in A. Tate, 'A Strategy for Enterprise in the University of Ulster', *Journal of Irish Business and Administrative Research* 1993; 14: 1–11, at 1.
8   E. F. M. McKenna, *Psychology in Business* (London: Lawrence Erlbaum, 1987).
9   D. McClelland, *The Achieving Society* (Princeton, NJ: Van Nostrand, 1961); J. Rotter, 'Generalised Expectancies for Internal Versus External Control of Reinforcement', *Psychological Monographs* 1966; 80: 1–27; McKenna (Reference 8) for a discussion on psychoanalytical approaches to personality.
10 H. H. Stevenson and D. E. Gumpert, 'The Heart of Entrepreneurship', in W. A. Sahlman and H. H. Stevenson (eds), *The Entrepreneurial Venture* (Boston, MA: Harvard Business School Press, 1992).
11 J. A. Timmons, *The Entrepreneurial Mind* (Andover: Brick House, 1989).
12 S. Caird and D. Johnson, *A Review of Methods of Measuring Enterprising Attributes* (Durham University Business School, 1988)
13 Timmons, *op. cit.*
14 D. C. McClelland, 'Achievement Motivation Can be Developed', *Harvard Business Review* 1965; November–December: 6–24.

15 S. Cromie, 'Assessing Entrepreneurial Inclinations: Some Approaches and Empirical Evidence', *European Journal of Work and Organisational Psychology* 2000; 9: 7–30.

16 T. Cassiday and R. Lynn, 'A Multifactoral Approach to Achievement Motivation: The Development of a Comprehensive Measure', *Journal of Occupational Psychology* 1989; 62: 301–12.

17 J. B. Miner, N. R. Smith and J. S. Bracker, 'Predicting Firm Survival From a Knowledge of Entrepreneur Task Motivation', *Entrepreneurship and Regional Development* 1992; 4: 145–53.

18 F. Delmar, 'The Psychology of the Entrepreneur', in S. Carter and D. Jones-Evans (eds), *Enterprise and Small Business* (London: Pearson Education , 2000), pp. 142–3.

19 H. Littunen, 'Entrepreneurship and the Characteristics of the Personality', *International Journal of Entrepreneurial Behaviour and Research* 2000; 6: 295–309, at 301.

20 D. C. McClelland (1965), *op. cit.*, p. 7.

21 See this comment by an interviewee in S. Cromie, 'Motivation of Aspiring Male and Female Entrepreneurs', *Journal of Organisational Behaviour* 1987; 8: 251–61.

22 P. F. Drucker, *Innovation and Entrepreneurship* (London: Heinemann, 1985), p. 128.

23 Cromie (2000), *op. cit.*

24 E. Chell, J. Haworth and S. Brearley, *The Entrepreneurial Personality: Concepts, Cases, and Categories* (London: Routledge, 1991).

25 M. Simon, S. M. Houghton and K. Aquino, 'Cognitive Biases, Risk Perception and Venture Formation: How Individuals Decided to Start Companies', *Journal of Business Venturing* 1999; 15: 113–34.

26 *Ibid.*, p. 116.

27 One of the statements used in a questionnaire designed by Rotter, *op. cit.*

28 See Cromie (2000), *op. cit.* for a recent review of research on locus of control.

29 See Delmar, *op. cit.* for a discussion of this concept.

30 C. R. Anderson, 'Locus of Control, Coping Behaviours and Performance in Stress Settings: A Longitudinal Study', *Journal of Applied Psychology* 1977; 62: 446–51.

31 G. Salaman, *Work Organisations* (London: Longman, 1979).

32 See comments by respondents in Cromie (1987), *op. cit.*

33 I. L. Janis, *Victims of Group Think: A. Psychological Study of Foreign Policy Decisions and Fiascos* (Boston, MA: Houghton Mifflin, 1972).

34 S. Caird, 'The Enterprising Tendency of Occupational Groups', *International Small Business Journal* 1991; 9: 75–81, at 77.

35 Cromie (1987), *op. cit.*

36 Cromie (1987), *op. cit.*

37 D. Miller, 'Strategy Making and Structure: Analysis and Implications for Performance', *Academy of Management Journal* 1987; 38: 7–32, a scale to measure proactivity at 32.

38 A. Ardichvili and R. N. Cardozo, 'A Model of the Entrepreneurial Opportunity Recognition Process', *Journal of Enterprise Culture* 2000; 8: 103–19.

39 S. Roy and R. N. Cardozo, 'Sensitivity and Creativity in Entrepreneurial Opportunity Recognition: A Framework for Empirical Investigation', in *Proceedings of the PDMA Conference, 1995*, p. 105.

40 Miller, *op. cit.*, p. 10.

41 M. D. Ensley, J. W. Carland and J. C. Carland, 'Investigating the Existence of the Lead Entrepreneur', *Journal of Small Business Management* 2000; 38: 59–77, at 61.

42 J. A. F. Stoner and C. Wankel, *Management*, Third edition (Englewood Cliffs, NJ: Prentice-Hall, 1986), p. 397 for a discussion of the nature of innovators.

43 V. Thompson, *Bureaucracy and Innovation* (Tuscaloosa, AL: University of Alabama Press, 1969) for a discussion of creativity. Thompson's quotation is at p. 11.

44 J. B. Cunningham and H. Lischeron, 'Defining Entrepreneurship', *Journal of Small Business Management* 1991; 29: 45–60, at 47.

45 Delmar, *op. cit.*

46 Delmar, *op. cit.*, p. 135.

47 I. J. Deary and G. Matthews, 'Personality Traits Are Alive and Well', *The Psychologist* 1993; July: 299.

48 E. A. Fagenson, 'Personal Value Systems of Men and Women Entrepreneurs Versus Managers', *Journal of Business Venturing* 1993; 8: 409–30, at 424.

49 M. Kets de Vries, 'The Entrepreneurial Personality: A Person at the Crossroads', *Journal of Management Studies* 1977; 14: 34–57.

50 A. MacNabb, *Entrepreneurial Profiling* (Belfast: Institute for Enterprise Strategies, 1993).

51 Delmar, *op. cit.*

52 Chell *et al.*, *op. cit.*; S. E. Hampton, *The Construction of Personality* (London: Routledge, 1988).

53 M. J. K. Stanworth and J. Curran, 'Growth and the Small Firm: An Alternative View', *Journal of Management Studies* 1976; 13: 95–110.

54 N. R. Smith, *The Entrepreneur and His Firm: The Relationship Between the Type of Man and the Type of Company*, Occasional paper, Bureau of Business and Economic Research, Graduate School of Business Administration (East Lansing, MI: Michigan State University, 1967).

55 J. B. Miner, N. R. Smith and J. S. Bracker, 'Defining the Inventor-Entrepreneur in the Context of Established Typologies', *Journal of Business Venturing* 1992; 7: 103–13.

56 R. W. Hornaday, 'Dropping the E-words From Small Business Research', *Journal of Small Business Management* 1990; 28: 22–33.

57 M. Casson, *The Entrepreneurs* (Oxford: Martin Robertson, 1982).

58 A. K. Roberts, 'The Social Conditions, Consequences and Limitations of Careers Guidance', *British Journal of Guidance and Counselling* 1977; 5: 1–9, at 7.

59 J. Stanworth and C. Gray (eds), *Bolton 20 Years On: The Small Firm in the 1990s* (London: Paul Chapman Publishing, 1991), p. 174.

60 J. Curran and R. A. Blackburn, 'Introduction', in J. Curran and R. A. Blackburn, *Paths of Enterprise* (London: Routledge, 1991).

61 A. A. Gibb, 'Enterprise Culture: Its Meaning and Implications for Education and Training', *Journal of European Industrial Training*, vol. 1987; 11: 11.

62 Delmar, *op. cit.*, p. 139.

63 Delmar, *op. cit.*, p. 139.

64 E. A. Locke, 'The Motivation Sequence, the Motivation Hub and Motivation Core', *Organisational Behaviour and Human Decision Processes* 1991; 50: 288–99.

65 N. C. Boyd and G. S. Vozikis, 'The Influence of Self-Efficacy On the Development of Entrepreneurial Intentions and Actions', *Entrepreneurship: Theory and Practice* 1994; 18: 63–78.

66 Delmar, *op. cit.*, p. 147.

67 R. Wood and A. Bandura, 'Social Cognitive Theory of Organisational Management', *Academy of Management Review* 1989; 14: 361–84.

68 Boyd and Vozikis, *op. cit.*, p. 67.

69 C. C. Chen, P. Gene-Greene and A Crick, 'Does Entrepreneurial Self-Efficacy Distinguish Entrepreneurs From Managers?', *Journal of Business Venturing* 1998; 13: 295–316.

70 A. Bandura, 'Perceived Self-Efficacy', in A. S. R. Manstead and M. Hewstone (eds), *The Blackwell Encyclopaedia of Social Psychology* (Oxford: Blackwell Publishers, 1995), pp. 434–6.

71 Delmar, *op. cit.*, p. 152.

72 R. Boyatzis, *The Competent Manager* (New York: Wiley, 1982); Management Charter Initiative, *Management Standards Implementation Pack* (London: MCI, 1991).

73 S. Caird, 'Problems With the Identification of Enterprise Competencies and the Implications for Assessment and Development', *Management Education and Development* 1992; 23: 6–17.

74 *Ibid.*, p. 14.

75 *Ibid.*, p. 16.

76 D. Buchanan and D. Boddy, *The Expertise of the Change Agent* (Hemel Hempstead: Prentice-Hall, 1992), p. 92.

77 N. F. Krueger and D. V. Brazeal, 'Entrepreneurial Potential and Potential Entrepreneurs', *Entrepreneurship: Theory and Practice* 1994; 18: 91–104.

78 N. F. Krueger, *Prescription for Opportunity: How Communities Can Create Potential for Entrepreneurs* (Washington, DC: Small Business Foundation of America, Working Paper 93-03, 1995).

79 Delmar, *op. cit.*, p. 148.

80 P. Davidsson, 'Determinants of Entrepreneurial Intentions', Paper presented at the Rent IX Conference, Piacenza, Italy, November 1995.

81 D. Smallbone and P. Wyer, 'Growth and Development in the Small Firm' in S. Carter and D. Jones-Evans (eds), *op. cit.*, p. 413.

82 National Women's Business Council, *Expanding Business Opportunities for Women* (Washington, DC: National Women's Business Council, 1996).

83 R. K. Z. Heck and E. S. Trent, 'The Prevalence of Family Business from a Household Perspective', *Family Business Review* 1999; 12: 209–20.

84 S. Carter, 'Improving the Number and Performance of Women-Owned Businesses: Some Implications for Training and Advisory Services', *Education and Training* 2001; 42: 326–34.

85 E. Ljunggren and L. Kolvereid, 'New Business Formation: Does Gender Make a Difference?', *Women in Management Review* 1996; 11: 3–12.

86 Equal Opportunities Commission, *The Labour Market: Women and Men in Britain* (London: The Commission, 2001), p. 3.

87 E. Chell and S. Baines, 'Does Gender Affect Business Performance? A Study of Microbusinesses in Business Services in the UK', *Entrepreneurship and Regional Development* 1998; 10: 117–35.

88 S. Marlow and A. Strange, 'Female Entrepreneurs: Success by Whose Standards?', in N. Tanton (ed.), *Women in Management: A Developing Presence* (London: Routledge, 1994), p. 173, cited in Chell and Baines, *op. cit.*

89 S. Scheinberg and I. C. MacMillan, 'An 11-Country Study of Motivations to Start a Business', in B. A. Kirchoff, W. A. Long, W. E. McMullan, K. H. Vesper and W. E. Wetzel (eds), *Frontiers of Entrepreneurship Research* (Wellesley, MA.: Babson College, 1988).

90 Cromie (1987) *op. cit.*, pp. 251–61.

91 R. Goffee and R. Scase, *Women in Charge* (London: Allen and Unwin, 1985).
92 S. Cromie and J. Hayes, 'Towards a Typology of Female Entrepreneurs', *The Sociological Review* 1990; 36: 87–113.
93 Ljunggren and Kolvereid, *op. cit.*
94 C. Holmquist and E. Sundin, 'The Growth of Women's Entrepreneurship: Push or Pull Factors?', Paper presented to the EIASM Conference on Small Business, Durham Business School, 1989.
95 Ljunggren and Kolvereid, *op. cit.*
96 A. L. Anna, G. N. Chandler, E. Jansen and N. P. Mero, 'Women Business Owners in Traditional and Non-Traditional Industries', *Journal of Business Venturing* 1999; 15: 279–303.
97 G. Hackett and N. E. Betz, 'A Self-Efficacy Approach to the Career Development of Women', *Journal of Vocational Behaviour* 1981; 18: 326–39.
98 T. Milne and J. Lewis, 'Models and Approaches to Teaching Entrepreneurship', in T. Webb, T. Quince and D. Watkins (eds), *Small Business Research* (Aldershot: Gower, 1983), p. 69.
99 F. D. Blau, 'The Data On Women Workers, Past, Present and Future', in A. H. Stromberg and S. Harkness (eds), *Women Working* (Palo Alto, CA: Mayfield, 1978), p. 44.
100 Equal Opportunities Commission, *op. cit.*, p. 1.
101 Equal Opportunities Commission, *op. cit.*, p. 1.
102 S. Allen and C. Truman, 'Women in Business', in J. Curran and R. Blackburn (eds), *Paths of Enterprise* (London: Routledge, 1991), p. 117.
103 V. K. Borooah, G. Collins, M. Hart and A. McNabb, 'Women and Self Employment', in D. Deakins, P. Jennings and C. Mason (eds), *Small Firms: Entrepreneurship in the Nineties* (London: Paul Chapman, 1997), p. 78.
104 Ljunggren and Kolvereid, *op. cit.*
105 M. Ram and D. Smallbone, *Ethnic Minority Enterprise: Policy and Practice*, SME Seminar Series (London: DTI, The Small Business Service and Kingston University Small Business Research Centre, 2001).
106 P. G. Greene, 'A Resource Based Approach to Ethnic Business Sponsorship: A Consideration of Ismaili-Pakistani Immigrants', *Journal of Small Business Management* 1997; 35: 57–71, at 58.
107 M. Ram and G. Barrett, 'Ethnicity and Enterprise', in S. Carter and D. Jones-Evans (eds), *op cit.*
108 A. Phizacklea and M. Ram, 'Ethnic Entrepreneurship in Comparative Perspective" *International Journal of Entrepreneurial Behaviour and Research* 1995; 1: 48–58, at 50.
109 Phizacklea and Ram, *op.cit.*, p. 50. For positive motivation among ethnic entrepreneurs see J. Curran and R. Blackburn, *Ethnic Enterprise and the High Street Banks: A Survey of Ethnic Businesses in Two Localities* (Kingston: Kingston-upon-Thames University, Small Business Research Centre, 1993).
110 A. Fadahunsi, D. Smallbone and S. Supri, 'Networking and Ethnic Minority Enterprise Development: Insights from a North London Study', *Journal of Small Business and Enterprise Development* 2000; 7: 228–40.
111 P. G. Greene, *op. cit.*

ENTERPRISE: THE EXTERNAL INFLUENCES

KEY CONCEPTS

This chapter covers:
- the various environmental factors, external to the individual, which have been identified as having some influence on the extent of enterprise and entrepreneurship. They include:
  - cultural, political and economic conditions;
  - demand factors;
  - supply factors;
  - government and other interventions;
  - equilibrium rates;
- theories, and investigations, which attempt to link some or all of these factors, and the internal factors considered in the previous chapter, into one model to explain the different rates of enterprise and entrepreneurship observed in different contexts.

LEARNING OBJECTIVES

....

By the end of this chapter the reader should:
- know what are thought to be the main external sources of influence on the extent of enterprising behaviour and entrepreneurship;
- understand how these factors are thought to influence enterprise and entrepreneurship and the differences they are believed to make;
- be able to describe how these factors, in combination with internal factors, might explain why there are different rates of enterprise in different contexts.

INTRODUCTION

Chapter Three looked at those factors internal to people, or at least with an internal component, which are thought to influence enterprise. Its starting point was that enterprise is recognised in enterprising acts performed by individuals. It therefore considered the attributes possessed by those individuals that dispose them towards acting in an enterprising manner. It also looked at Krueger's model which suggests how the various possible factors might combine to influence an individual to engage in enterprising activity. Amongst the components of Krueger's model are social norms and perceived feasibility, which are not, however, issues only or mainly internal to the individual.

Understanding the linkage between individual attributes which are innate or acquired and societally determined attributes is complex and our knowledge is still evolving. There is undoubtedly considerable feedback between those attributes which are perceived as innate or acquired and developed early in life (those which may therefore be referred to as 'born with') and those perceived to be attributable to environmental 'conditioning' (often referred to as 'made'). Chapter Three concentrated on the issues which are considered to be largely internal to the individual and which can be considered to be part of the push or 'supply' side of enterprise. But there are other influences external to the individual, such as societal culture and the 'pull' or demand factor of opportunity, which are also thought to have an impact. In the search for an explanation of why different individuals, or different groups of individuals, show different levels of enterprise and, in particular, entrepreneurship, many external issues have been suggested. As well as cultural and demand factors, external supply factors, external intervention and equilibrium rates have all been proposed. This list can be presented as in Figure 4.1 and it is these issues which are considered in the chapter.

Showing issues in separate boxes, however, does not mean that the issues themselves can be completely separated. And, just as the various influences on

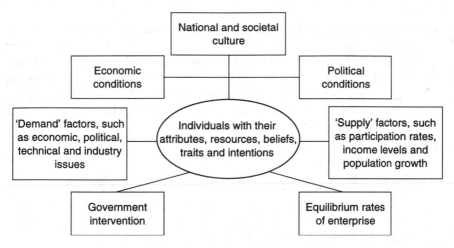

Figure 4.1   Possible influences on the level of enterprising behaviour

enterprise, individual and environmental, are not clearly delineated, so the categories used in this chapter are not absolute and indivisible. They are used as a way of presenting the issues, not as an indication of clear distinctions.

ILLUSTRATION 4.1
The importance of context

The importance of context is highlighted by a study carried out by the University of Groningen, covering nine countries (Brazil, Cameroon, Colombia, Indonesia, Japan, Kenya, Netherlands, UK, and West Germany) and almost 2700 entrepreneurs.[1] It gave some interesting indications of the values and motivations that differ between Western and Eastern countries and the values and motivations that differ between the industrialised and the less developed countries.

Among the findings were:

- Entrepreneurs in the industrialised countries more often started their businesses due to dissatisfaction (push factors) rather than ambition (pull factors). The reverse was the case in less developed countries.
- When determining choice of business activity, personal initiative plays a significant role in the highly individualistic West. Allowing oneself to be guided by the insight and initiative of someone else is very important in highly collectivist countries such as Japan and Indonesia.
- Entrepreneurs in less developed countries ascribe more importance to the business firm as a family institution. In the West, the firm is seen as the institutionalisation of work.

- In collectivist cultures, receptiveness to help and support from the environment is greater.
- Entrepreneurs in European countries are the most individualistic and display self-confidence in their entrepreneurial ability. Japan and Indonesia are the least individualistic (suggesting that individualistic and entrepreneurial behaviours are not, in this context, synonymous).

Other problems of cross-cultural interpretation are revealed by this study, in particular in ascribing variations in entrepreneurship to different cultural, political or economic environments. The authors commented that it is very difficult to disentangle the relative importance of the 'two environments, which, while they may be distinguished from one another, are interdependent'. They went on to say, however, that 'evidence is building' which suggests that entrepreneurship is primarily influenced by the politico-economic environment, which is, 'on the whole', more important than the cultural environment.

This is illustrated by considering the consequences for entrepreneurial behaviour in a less developed country, which may, typically, have an unstable and unpredictable environment. A business functioning successfully one moment can be faced with insurmountable problems the next. Businesses can be viewed as 'temporary projects' with people working on them and earning money in them as long as possible until a more attractive 'project' appears. In more economically stable countries, the continuity of the business, spanning many generations, can be of primary importance to the entrepreneur and the motivation is not just aimed at earning a living. Therefore it is argued that the concept of entrepreneurship acquires an entirely different meaning. 'The term "business" must, under these conditions be interpreted as a 'project', and 'entrepreneur' must be seen as someone who, perhaps temporarily or part-time, provides leadership for a project.'

It is not surprising, therefore, when the studies show that in less developed countries:

- the birth-rate of businesses is higher than in developed countries;
- more businesses are started by entrepreneurs than are bought or inherited;
- more entrepreneurs have had more than one business;
- risk-avoidance behaviour is more pronounced (for example, 'sell out today – who knows what tomorrow holds?').

These are characteristics which might be thought to be culturally determined but in this context can be shown to have their roots in the economic facts of life.

How then does enterprise based on individual attributes and perceptions, as considered in Chapter Three, relate to the idea of the influence of an enterprise culture? Do they offer contradictory or complementary notions? If there is such a thing as an enterprise culture, is it something more than just a collection of individuals who are themselves enterprising, or can the culture of a group, or society, itself be enterprising or influence the enterprise shown by its members? Take for instance the example of the 'tiger' economies of the Pacific Rim. They are thought by many to be very enterprising but they do not in general have a culture based on the individual, and their success is seen to come from aspects of their society as a whole. They therefore provide a prima facie case for saying that an understanding of enterprise must include a view as to its wider context beyond the individual.

In exploring these issues this chapter includes theories which attempt to combine a number of possible influences, both internal and external, to give a more complete view of why enterprise, especially in the context of entrepreneurship, occurs when it does. There is more than one such theory and they do not all include the same factors but that does not mean that some have to be wrong. Essentially these theories are looking at the same issue but from somewhat different perspectives. Therefore they include many of the same components, although not always under the same names, but they present somewhat different aspects, each of which is only one possible view of part of a complex, and not completely understood, whole.

ILLUSTRATION 4.2
From *An Eclectic Theory of Entrepreneurship*

The process by which the actual rate of entrepreneurship is established involves both macro and micro components. On the demand side, entrepreneurial opportunities are created by the market demand for goods and services, whereas the supply side generates (potential) entrepreneurs that can seize the opportunities provided they have the resources, abilities and preferences to do so. Moreover, personality characteristics need to be in line with the entrepreneurial opportunity. The entrepreneurial decision, i.e. occupational choice, is made at the individual level, taking into account entrepreneurial opportunities and resources, abilities, personality traits and preferences of the individual.

An individual's risk-reward profile represents the process of weighing alternative types of employment and is based on opportunities (environmental characteristics, resources, abilities, personality traits, and preferences). The occupational choices of individuals are made on the basis of their risk-reward profile of entrepreneurship versus that of other types of employment.

Source: D. Audretsch, R. Thurik, I. Verheul and S. Wennekers (eds), *Entrepreneurship: Determinants and Policy in a European-US Comparison* (Dordrecht, The Netherlands and Norwell, MA, USA: Kluwer Academic Publishers, 2000), p. 19. Reproduced with the permission of Kluwer Academic Publishers.

CULTURAL, POLITICAL AND ECONOMIC CONDITIONS

Cultural, political and economic conditions are interlinked and there is little doubt that the triggers for enterprise are found along a continuum from inborn attributes of individuals to complex interrelationships amongst often changing cultural, political and economic conditions at national, regional and local levels. Further evidence of these interrelationships is provided by, *inter alia*, Hofstede,[2] Morrison[3] and Garrison[4] as they seek to understand the factors which contribute to or stifle enterprise and entrepreneurship initiation. Hofstede, for example, while concentrating on the importance of cultural influences on development, states the need for a 'market' and a 'political condition' that allow development. He notes that the market circumstances for growth of the 'dragon' economies began only in the mid-1950s as world markets freed up:

> The need for a supportive political context was met in all 'dragon' countries but in very different ways ... with the role of government varying from active support to *laissez-faire*. Labour unions were weak and company-orientated in all the countries and a relatively equalitarian income distribution meant that support for revolutionary social changes was weak.[5]

A representation of these categories of influence on enterprise and their inter-relationship can be seen in Figure 4.2.

National and societal culture

It is argued by some that nations should not be equated to societies as 'societies are organically developed forms of social organisation, and the concept of a common culture applies, strictly speaking, more to societies than to nations'.[6] The nation is a relatively recent phenomenon in human history and can incorporate

Figure 4.2   Impact of external influences on enterprise

plural cultures and layers of sub-cultures. Nevertheless, the nation or country is seen as a feasible proxy for a single organisational unit in 'humanity's organisation of the world today'.[7]

Tayeb[8] defined culture as 'a set of historically evolved learned values, attitudes and meanings shared by the members of a given community that influence their material and non-material way of life'. Members of the community learn these shared characteristics, she claims, 'through different stages of the socialisation processes of their lives in institutions, such as family, religion, formal education and society as a whole'.

Hofstede, noting that 'culture in the form of certain dominant values is a necessary but not a sufficient condition for economic achievement',[9] defined culture similarly. It is the 'shared values that typify a society' and 'the collective programming of the mind which distinguishes the members of one group or category from another'. Hofstede[10] further explains that, as almost everyone belongs to a number of different groups and categories of people at the same time, he or she will unavoidably carry several layers of what he calls 'mental programming' within himself or herself corresponding to different levels of culture.

ILLUSTRATION 4.3
Mental programming

Few will doubt the importance of the formal education system in shaping the attitudes and behaviours of individuals and groups, but in attempting to understand another country or culture it is difficult at times to question one's basic assumptions – deeply ingrained consciously or unconsciously over the years. The purpose of education is perceived differently from society to society. An individualist society aims at preparing the individual for a place in the society of other individuals. This means learning to cope with new, unknown and unforeseen situations … the purpose of learning is less to know how to do as to know how to learn … In the collectivist society there is a stress on adaptation to the skills and virtues necessary to be an acceptable group member. This leads to a premium on the products of tradition … the young have to learn how to do things in order to participate in society.

Hofstede[11]

Culture is recognised as a complex phenomenon. Garrison suggests that:

attempts at definition are problematic due to culture's amorphous, shifting nature. This is further compounded by its multiple representation within such elements as:

- different levels (national, regional, business, individual);
- layers of society (gender, age, social class, occupation, family, religion);
- varying context of life (individual, group, community).[12]

Garrison's categorisations are reflected in those of Hofstede's levels of culture:[13]

- a national level according to one's country (or countries for people who migrated during their lifetime);
- a regional and/or ethnic and/or religious and/or linguistic affiliation level, as most nations are composed of culturally different regions and/or religious and/or language groups;
- a gender level, according to whether a person was born as a girl or as a boy;
- a generation level, which separates grandparents from parents from children;
- a social class level, associated with educational opportunities and with a person's occupation or profession;
- and, for those who are employed, an organisational or corporate level, according to the way employees have been socialised by their work organisation.

Hofstede also identifies and analyses five dimensions by which cultures can be described:

- power distance – expresses dependence relationships in a country. It defines the extent to which the less powerful members of institutions and organisations expect and accept that power will be distributed unequally. For instance, there is only a small power distance in situations where subordinates would expect to participate in decision-making with superiors;
- individualistic/collectivist – reflects the extent to which it is the interest of the individual or the interest of the group that prevails;
- masculinity/femininity tendencies – defines the extent to which social gen-der roles in the society are clearly distinct. In masculine societies, men are supposed to be tough, assertive and focused on material success, and women to be more modest, tender and concerned with the quality of life. Femininity pertains to societies where the social gender roles overlap;
- uncertainty avoidance – defines the extent to which the members of a culture feel threatened by uncertain or unknown situations. This feeling is expressed through nervous stress and in a need for predictability (including a need for written and unwritten rules);
- long-term orientation – defines a country in terms of its trade-off between short-term and long-term gratification of needs. (Long-term orientation emphasises values such as perseverance and thrift.)

Ultimately these dimensions reveal themselves in individual and group values, preferences and behaviour which have been acquired in the context of family, school and occupation. They are a measure of what we call national culture and which many perceive to be a key determinant of the degree of enterprise in a country.

They pose interesting questions such as whether a 'large power-distance' country is likely to be enterprising. In such a country, subordinates in organisations are more likely to accept inequality and hierarchy and, it could be argued, acquire attitudes inimical to entrepreneurial endeavour. Where individualism is counter-cultural, as in Japan (and children think of 'we' not 'I'), is enterprising behaviour inhibited – or can groups be as enterprising as individuals? It has traditionally been common to view attributes of the feminine gender as inherently less likely to lead to enterprising behaviour. Similarly, if a culture is uncomfortable with uncertainty and ambiguity, one might question if it can be as entrepreneurial as one that is comfortable coping in such situations. Equally, taking a long-term view may be felt likely to lead to caution and conservative behaviour. Intriguingly, little is known of how these different dimensions interact to reinforce or negate each other. Hofstede's work reveals that successful nations (in economic terms) can exhibit significantly different scores on each of the dimensions he describes, suggesting that there are no easily defined 'right' or 'wrong' cultural conditions. Positive economic outcomes can emerge from a wide range of contexts.

ILLUSTRATION 4.4
Culture and learning

A Japanese friend once said that he could never ask a question in a class or lecture room unless, by so doing, he was obviously advancing everyone else's knowledge and understanding. Otherwise, he should not waste the teacher's or his fellow students' time. He believed that problems of learning should be handled outside the group.

In the context of modern Western educational practice, such failure to participate and generate teacher feedback would be considered reticent and unenterprising.

Another approach which has been used to develop a model which seeks to identify, categorise and analyse the key features associated with 'entrepreneurship initiation' in society is that of Morrison.[14] Her summary of the influences upon entrepreneurial behaviour as derived from her cross-country research and review of relevant literature is shown in Figure 4.3.

The initiation of entrepreneurship starts, she suggests, at the 'grass roots' level where 'a range of inputs commences the mental and social conditioning of the populace'. These inputs include religion, education, politics, family history, role models and personal characteristics (that is, external and internal influences).

The 'socially developed entrepreneur' is further surrounded by social, economic and institutional constructs within which the entrepreneur may exercise his or her judgment as to whether 'they are sufficiently robust to support the initiation of entrepreneurship'. These constructs include policy, the economy, employment, industry, corporations and networks. They embrace matters such as the extent to which policy frameworks and conditions are encouraged in which

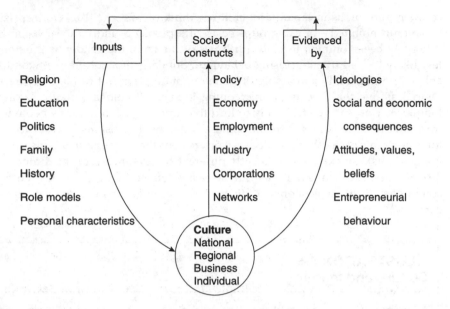

Inputs	Society constructs	Evidenced by
Religion	Policy	Ideologies
Education	Economy	Social and economic
Politics	Employment	consequences
Family	Industry	Attitudes, values,
History	Corporations	beliefs
Role models	Networks	Entrepreneurial
Personal characteristics		behaviour

Culture
National
Regional
Business
Individual

Source: A. Morrison, 'Initiating Entrepreneurship', in S. Carter and D. Jones-Evans (eds), *Enterprise and Small Business: Principles, Practice and Policy* (London: Financial Times/Prentice-Hall, 2000), p. 106. Reproduced with the permission of Pearson Education Ltd.

Figure 4.3 Summary model: key features associated with entrepreneurship initiation

the individual (as opposed to the state) can flourish; the small firm sector is supported; large corporations offer entrepreneurial opportunities through delayering, outsourcing and re-engineering; and strong formal and informal networks exist and grow.

'Inputs' and 'social constructs' combine 'to provide the evidence, negative and/or positive, of entrepreneurial behaviour' and impact upon the extent to which a society values and nurtures or stifles such behaviour.

The outcome is evidenced through a range of factors such as:

- ideologies: particularly in relation to attitudes towards unsuccessful endeavour and a regard for entrepreneurial behaviour generally;
- social consequences: the extent to which it is believed that entrepreneurship has the potential for beneficial outcomes for society as a whole;
- economic consequences: the extent to which entrepreneurial endeavour is seen to be a key driver in generating economic benefits at the level of the individual and business, regionally and nationally;

- attitudes, values and beliefs: whether the dominant value system of a population is communal or individualistic and the extent to which entrepreneurship is consistent with such a value system;
- entrepreneurial behaviour: its development or otherwise will be influenced by a combination of the above factors which react to determine the fertility of the soil for such endeavour and sow the seeds for future propagation.

ILLUSTRATION 4.5
Cultural reinforcement

McClelland provides interesting insights and, as noted in Chapter Three, he links enterprise to the urge to achieve: 'Most people in this world can be divided into two broad groups. There is that minority which is challenged by opportunity and willing to work hard to achieve something, and the majority which really does not care all that much.'[15] He asks, 'Is the need to achieve an accident, or is it hereditary, or is it the result of the environment?' And further, 'is there some technique that could give this will to achieve to people, even whole societies?'[16]

The importance of cultural reinforcement is seen in a study by McClelland in which he attempted to increase the achievement motivation of bright fourteen-year-old boys.

Boys from lower income groups did not maintain their improvements. Possibly it was because they moved back into an environment in which neither parents nor friends encouraged achievement or upward mobility. 'Negroes seeking to improve their condition frequently confront this problem … faced by scepticism at home and suspicion on the job,' claimed McClelland on the basis of his work in the USA.[17]

An interesting contrast to the Negro situation may be the entrepreneurialism displayed by some immigrant groups, such as Hong Kong Chinese or Indians. If, and it is not always the case, immigrants are moving to seek betterment of their condition, it is also likely that entrepreneurial behaviour by members of their community will receive positive reinforcement.

The work of McClelland, who built a reputation for pioneering investigation in the field of achievement motivation, also helps to relate enterprise to culture. His is essentially a Western, individualistic view of motivation, the person being largely his unit of investigation. He points out that persons who are viewed as having engaged in 'outstanding' activities may be motivated by the need for power and/or the need for achievement. He demonstrates that the need for achievement, its frequency in the popular literature of a country, and national economic growth, all correlate:

A nation which is thinking about doing better all the time (as shown in its popular literature), actually does do better economically speaking. Careful quantitative studies have shown this to be true in Ancient Greece, in Spain in the Middle Ages, in England from 1400–1800, as well as among contemporary nations, whether capitalist or communist, developed or underdeveloped.[18]

It is worth noting that it is not a question of some people being motivated and others not being motivated, but that some are motivated by one goal and others by another. Overall, McClelland has found that while it is possible to change an individual's motivation (and performance), motivational change by itself is not enough if the environment in which he or she lives doesn't support, to at least some degree, his or her new efforts. This recognises the influence of the cultural and societal context of values and behaviour. In short enterprise and entrepreneurship happen in all societies. The form in which they happen, however, varies from society to society.

It is appropriate, therefore, to examine societal culture to consider how the concept of enterprise fits into it. Without such understanding, interventions to promote enterprise cross-culturally will, it is reasonable to deduce, be less effective, if not actually counter-productive. Interesting issues are raised by exploring the meaning and nature of enterprise in the context of cultural dimensions.

Redding notes that:

> other features older and deeper than modern policies have helped large Japanese and Korean organisations to ... take a huge chunk of the world market ... These extra features include societal norms supporting acceptance of authority and discipline, a sense of the importance of the organisation in one's life and a consequent wish to belong to it, association of individuals with the collective good of the group, and intense competitiveness on behalf of the nation via the company.[19]

He adds that another societal feature critical to economic efficiency is the 'notion of trust', which explains 'why the Japanese and Koreans can handle very large scale organisations efficiently', the recent and well publicised problems faced by some of Korea's leading conglomerates notwithstanding.

That some nations have achieved significant economic growth without exhibiting preconceived Western notions on the appropriate cultural dimensions should not therefore be surprising. Those Western definitions of entrepreneurial characteristics are themselves culturally biased, as indeed may be the conventional definitions of enterprise and their association with economic success.

ILLUSTRATION 4.6
Entrepreneurship and culture

At the top of Maslow's hierarchy ... there is the motive of self actualisation: realising to the fullest possible extent the creative potential present within the individual. This means 'doing one's own thing' (and) this can only be the supreme motivation in an individualistic society. In a collectivist culture, what will be actualised is the interest and honour of the in-group which may very well ask for self-effacement from many of the in-group members. As the interpreter for a group of American visitors to China remarked, the idea of 'doing your own thing' is not translatable into Chinese ... the Chinese language has no equivalent for 'personality' in the Western sense. Personality in the West is a separate entity, distinct from society and culture: an attribute of the individual. The closest translation into Chinese is *Jen* ... which includes not only the individual but also his or her intimate societal and cultural environment which makes his or her existence meaningful.

Hofstede[20]

The collectivist tradition and culture is about subordinating personal to group interests, sharing, cooperation and group harmony (see Table 4.1). Is

Table 4.1 Key differences between collectivist and individualist societies

Collectivist	Individualist
Collective interests prevail over individual interests	Individual interests prevail over collective interests
Private life is invaded by groups	Everyone has a right to privacy
Opinions are predetermined by group membership	Everyone is expected to have a private opinion
Economy based on collective interests	Economy based on individual interests
Ideologies of equality prevail over ideologies of individual freedom	Ideologies of individual freedom prevail over ideologies of equality
Harmony and consensus in society are ultimate goals	Self-actualisation by every individual is an ultimate goal
People are born into extended families or other in groups which continue to protect them in exchange for loyalty	Everyone grows up to look after him/herself and his/her immediate (nuclear) family only
Identity is based in the social network to which one belongs	Identity is based in the individual
Children learn to think in terms of 'we'	Children learn to think in terms of 'I'
Harmony should always be maintained and direct confrontations avoided	Speaking one's mind is a characteristic of an honest person
Purpose of education is learning how to do	Purpose of education is learning how to learn
Relationships between employer and employee are perceived in moral terms, like a family link	Relationships between employer and employee are a contract supposedly based on mutual advantage
Hiring and promotion decisions take employees' in-group into account	Hiring and promotion decisions are supposed to be based on skills and rules only
Management is management of groups	Management is management of individuals
Relationship prevails over task	Task prevails over relationship

Source: G. Hofstede, *Cultures and Organisations* (London: HarperCollins, 1994) pp. 67 and 73.

entrepreneurial behaviour, therefore, exhibited by the group itself, by individuals working through the group or by breaking group norms? Or does the concept of 'entrepreneurial behaviour' need to be redefined in different cultural contexts?

Given the wide variations in societal understanding, perceptions, attitudes and behaviours, a unicultural interpretation of the meaning of enterprise and its development presents many dangers. Without recognition of such differences, there will be difficulty in gaining global acceptance of enterprise as a positive concept. It will also be more difficult for business leaders to function effectively in other cultures as the drive towards globalisation accelerates. It is however clear that a supportive cultural environment for actions and policies to promote enterprise development and business start-up and growth is important, and that it can take many forms.

CASE 4.1
Different structures for enterprise

Not only are ways of doing business in Asia subtly different from those of the West but they are also different within the region itself ... The past 30 golden years have seen the emergence of three powerful systems of business, each represented by a particular kind of organisation:

- in Japan the large complex networked business, known as the *kaisha*;
- in South Korea the now internationalising *chaebol*;
- elsewhere, in areas where business needs strong local knowledge and connections, the Chinese family business – that most unobtrusive and little understood instrument of wealth creation and progress.

Each of these instruments for bringing together the components of economic behaviour has emerged as a distinct response to its circumstances. They are embedded in the cultures and development histories of their societies. They are not copies of Western forms and their behaviour does not follow Western rules or ideals. In simple terms, they exist for different reasons.

The main reason for the existence and driving logic of the large American corporation is return to shareholders, but that of the *kaisha* is to employ people. The *chaebol* has derived much of its dynamism from its contribution to the national development goals of Korea. The Chinese family business exists primarily to create and sustain family fortunes.

The outcome of these different routes to modern capitalism is that the Japanese firm is a large, professionally managed and highly complex enterprise with wide ownership; the Korean is a huge family business run like a regiment; and the Chinese is a small family business networking to escape the limitations of its size and doing so successfully.

These different organisations compete on equal terms in world markets. Asia today contains some of the world's most competitive forms of enterprise which are able to hammer each other in world markets on equal terms. In doing so however, there is no logic which says they all have to have the same book of rules.

Redding[21]

Points raised

This example shows that the Western model of enterprise is not the only one and that different cultures are likely to produce different working models better suited to their group values and beliefs.

CASE 4.2
A history of regional difference

To understand the reasons for differences in enterprise and economic regeneration between different areas in England, Dodd[22] suggests, it is necessary to examine the relevant social history of the areas over many hundreds of years.

Compared with the North East, the Black Country recovered well from major job losses and still has 50 per cent of its workforce in manufacturing. 'There is still plenty of metal-bashing and lots of foundries and it is still easy to get into all sorts of trades like pickling zinc.' Its history has a number of curious features. It was never conquered by the Romans because it was marshy, inhospitable and easily bypassed. From the 13th century its rich seams of coal near the surface gave it its character. For several centuries mining was carried on by groups of families. By 1665 there were 20,000 smiths within a ten-mile radius of Dudley, and an industrial culture appears to have been in full swing before the Industrial Revolution proper arrived.

It was observed that 'the Black Country was born, not as one area, but as a collection of separate entities of often fierce independence brought together on and about a unique coalfield, heaven-sent complete with an abundance of ironstone, limestone and clay ...'

In contrast, Tyneside in the North East also had coal mining but there that industry had a feudal feel about it, with enormous gaps between owners and workers, a relationship which might have been a carry-over from the employer and employee relationship that had existed in agriculture and tin- and lead-mining. The process of industrialisation in the North gave rise to relatively few small firm operations in manufacturing and engendered attitudes incompatible with entrepreneurial behaviour. The high unemployment of the early 1980s, following the disappearance of many of the big manufacturing operations, was not therefore relieved by smaller operations, as happened in the Black Country, and self-employment is still below the national average.

Points raised

This example too shows that, even within a country, different social histories appear to have an impact on the levels of enterprise.

ILLUSTRATION 4.7
Ethnic or social networks

Mary Waters[23] sheds some light on the issue of ethnic enterprise in a review of five American books on ethnicity and entrepreneurship in the urban USA. The books examine entrepreneurship amongst various ethnic groups in several cities but Waters concludes that they point to the overwhelming importance of social networks and ties in entrepreneurship, and they all explode simple ideas that there are personality characteristics such as risk-taking or rugged individualism that explain specialisation as an entrepreneur.[24] In general the choice of entrepreneurship by specific groups is supported by the existence of 'class resources' such as education and so forth and by 'ethnic resources' such as ties to one another, ethnic solidarity and ethnic connections. More specifically Waters argues that Koreans were channelled into small businesses because they had middle class ambitions and savings, together with 'intact families where members could save some additional capital', and because they were blocked in mainstream jobs. Many ethnic groups collectively enter new industries and occupations but there is widespread gloom about the prospects of African Americans in America entering entrepreneurship in large numbers. This arises in part because of the low level of skills attained by this group but also because of the persistence of a Black Nationalist ideology in American cities which focuses on community and economic control.

Localities that allow individuals to develop problem-solving and marketing skills, which contain institutions geared to the support of small businesses and that are favourably disposed to the notion of entrepreneurship, are likely to encourage and sustain more entrepreneurship than other regions.[25] These and other related matters are important aspects of the cultural dimension of entrepreneurship.

In general, sociological approaches recognise the importance of social structures on individual decision-making and are a counter to those who might extol the virtues of rugged individualism as the sole determinant of entrepreneurship. However, while they do tell us quite a lot about the kind of people who become entrepreneurs, they do not tell us much about the process by which social factors actually influence decision-making.

Community and cultural enterprise

So far in this book, in looking at the influences of culture on enterprise, the enterprise being influenced has primarily been enterprise as it is manifested in private sector business. Therefore the influences on enterprise have been considered in terms of the effects they may have had on business formation and success. This was done primarily because that is the aspect of enterprise that has been most studied and it is therefore the easiest to analyse. However enterprise can be manifest in other ways: for instance in leisure, in cultural activities and in community enterprise.

Even business formation and entrepreneurship need not have profit for individuals as a major motivation. Businesses can be started for other reasons such as family, community or cultural development. Also, businesses need not be started by individuals but can be started by groups. Much enterprise behaviour by groups has been variously known as 'community enterprise', 'social enterprise' or 'social entrepreneurship' and these concepts are explored in more depth in Chapter Five.

Three forms of business enterprise or entrepreneurship have therefore been distinguished: (a) the classical form of private or business entrepreneurship for commercial gain; (b) community enterprise or entrepreneurship for community economic benefit; and (c) cultural entrepreneurship to influence cultural change or improve cultural standards.

It may be obvious that community and cultural enterprise are likely to influence each other. It is also very likely that private entrepreneurship will influence, and be influenced by, the others. Private sector concerns have shown themselves to be responsive to local issues, especially when there has been community action to highlight them, and community and cultural initiatives have benefited from the involvement of the enterprise skills of the private sector. This interrelationship is shown in Figure 4.4.

Community enterprise is of particular interest because, as already noted, Western views of enterprise and entrepreneurship have perceived these as largely the prerogative of individual, as opposed to group, behaviour. Experience, however, suggests that group behaviour can be affected by a community entrepreneur and that, as a result, the actions of a group can be more enterprising than the individual attributes or resources within the group would suggest. Development of community businesses helps those involved to gain business experience, to develop personal knowledge and skills and to acquire a network that enables them to acquire confidence in themselves and to tackle further opportunities. This is done in the relatively safe and low-risk context of group support and participation.

Political and economic conditions

As explained earlier, political and economic conditions are closely linked with cultural conditions and therefore, in considering the cultural influences above,

121

Source: O. R. Spilling, 'Enterprise in a Cultural Perspective', *Entrepreneurship and Regional Development* 1991; 3: 39. Consult: www.tandf.co.uk/journals

Figure 4.4   The triangle of enterprise

political and economic influences have also been introduced. The following paragraphs contain some brief reflections on particular political and economic conditions (the latter in relation to the transition economies of the former Soviet Bloc countries) which demonstrate their influence.

Political conditions

Political conditions are often very hard to separate from economic conditions and therefore their contribution to the total effect is hard to determine. However Case 4.3 presents an example where this seems to be possible and shows that differences in political policies may at least appear to contribute to differences in enterprise behaviour.

CASE 4.3
A study of political conditions

While it is generally impossible to separate the influences of political conditions from the other influences of economics and culture, the island of Saint Martin in the Lesser Antilles does offer one example of a contrast in political styles and of the different effects they appear to have on business enterprise.[26]

The island of Saint Martin is the smallest land mass in the world that is shared by two governments. It is only 37 square miles in area, but it is divided into two legal entities: Dutch Sint Maarten and French Saint Martin. Sint

Maarten is 16 square miles in area and its capital is Philipsburg. It has a Netherlands Antilles constitution and has been self-governing since 1954. Saint Martin is 21 square miles in area; its capital is Marigot but the real administrative centre is Basse Terre on Guadeloupe. Guadeloupe is an overseas department of France and therefore Saint Martin is governed as an integral part of France.

In Sint Maarten there is relatively little government regulation of business. Starting a small business, for instance, is very easy: there is no need for a licence to do so and incorporation is simple, requiring only the assistance of a lawyer specifically appointed to pass deeds. There is no exchange control on currencies imported or exported, and bank accounts may be opened in any currency. There are no import duties and taxes generally are low, with tax holidays and other benefits in certain circumstances. There is an international airport with a 2000-metre runway which accommodates daily international flights and helps to boost the tourist industry. Further, to enhance tourism a number of casinos have been opened. The absence of all customs formalities makes Sint Maarten in essence a free port.

In contrast Saint Martin, the French part of the island, has inherited an abundance of regulations from its mother country. Rules made in France for France must be obeyed in Saint Martin. Some prices, as well as wages, are regulated. A new business venture must involve local participation. Foreigners staying for over 21 days must provide proof of departure as well as proof of citizenship (even though there is no longer any physical barrier, or even a border checkpoint, between the two sides of the island). The airport is tiny, virtually deserted and, because of red tape, there are no casinos.

The contrast between the two parts of the island is striking. Dutch Sint Maarten is a thriving business community with significant entrepreneurial activity, while French Saint Martin is largely rural and agricultural. Sint Maarten has not only achieved full employment for itself, but employs many workers from French Saint Martin and from other neighbouring islands such as the Dominican Republic.

These differences have been ascribed to the different government policies applied to the two parts of the island. On the Dutch side the attitude taken appears to be that it is dangerous to have the government in business and that government can best help business by staying out of it and by being a facilitator rather than a regulator. On the French side the attitude appears to be that government should intervene in the business sector for the purpose of keeping out potential danger. Rules are therefore established to protect business even if to some extent they hinder entrepreneurial activity.

Both sides of the island share a common history. The island was originally populated by Arawak Indians, who survived on local vegetation and seafood. They were then invaded by the more violent Carib tribes migrating from the Amazon basin, who were in turn followed by conquests from Spain, France,

Britain and the Netherlands. As the Indians were wiped out the island was populated by slaves imported from areas such as Togo and Ghana in Africa.

Now, however, there are distinct differences in enterprise and economic performance between the two parts of the island. The reason for this appears to be the different political agendas: one side follows a policy of minimal economic intervention and minimal regulation, while the other has a policy of relatively heavy intervention and rules designed to protect business.

Points raised

In this example it is the different political approaches that appear to explain the difference in the level of enterprise.

Economic conditions

For examples of the differences that economic conditions can make it may be illustrative to look at the transition economic conditions of the former Warsaw Pact or communist countries in Europe.

From the 1950s to the late 1980s these countries shared an economic system: one of central planning based on a communist ideal. Before that system was imposed, however, there had been considerable differences amongst their economies. A number of them had been quite enterprising, with countries like the former Czechoslovakia and Hungary being fully part of Central European economic life.

When they became part of the Soviet Bloc and its economic system the attitude to enterprise and entrepreneurship in all these countries changed. To a greater or lesser extent entrepreneurial behaviour was viewed with considerable suspicion; successful entrepreneurs were seen as antisocial, self-seeking and frequently as acting unethically, if not illegally. Disparities in income and wealth (and so behaviour likely to generate such disparities) made many reasonable people feel uncomfortable about enterprise and see it as a destabilising force in society, once they had grown accustomed to, and comfortable with, an equality that is unusual in non-socialist countries.

ILLUSTRATION 4.8
Employment: the system and the individual

To comprehend the nature of the employment contract in 'communist' Eastern Europe it was claimed by some that you had to understand two 'facts'. The first 'fact' was that the system owed the individual a job. It was the system's clear obligation to provide paid employment for everyone. The second 'fact' was that it was the individual's duty to better him or herself, not by hard work which would return no direct benefits, but by doing as little as possible for the salary which was his or her right.

It has been argued that the collapse of the Iron Curtain came, at least in part, because the disparity between the economic benefits of the 'market' economies on one side and the central 'socialist' economies on the other could no longer be disguised. When it went, there was a desire by many on its former Eastern side to catch up with the West. Based on the perception that enterprise and an enterprise culture were preconditions for a successful market economy, attempts were made to introduce and encourage them. The political imperative of creating wealth in these transition economies, not least through attempts to inculcate such enterprise into them, has however had another effect. It has brought into greater focus the issue of the cultural context of enterprise. Given the different nature of these nations after almost two generations of a particular political and economic system, one cannot ignore the differences in individual and group values, priorities and goals as compared with those in countries with different histories.

The Western cultural traditions they are trying to emulate have been rooted in individualism and, as Chapter Three and Table 4.1 above indicate, definitions of entrepreneurial characteristics emphasise individuality – founding by a single person, personal innovation, risk-taking, proactivity, persistence, and creativity. Individualism is concerned with self-sufficiency; difficulty in coping with a structured pursuit of goals; personal goals that may conflict with those of one's group; a willingness to confront members of the group one belongs to; a suspicion of the world around. It is a culture where a person derives pride from his or her own achievements coupled with a desire for recognition. In contrast, as already noted, the more collectivist tradition and culture involve subordination of personal to group interests, sharing, cooperation and group harmony and, to that extent, an emphasis on the individual is counter-cultural.

ILLUSTRATION 4.9
The unwelcome entrepreneur

When the Central and Eastern European system was beginning to change in the early 1990s it was asked if this meant that the entrepreneur was now in the economic driver's seat. One reply from Poland, one of the first of these countries to move towards a market economy, said that the answer was 'yes, the entrepreneur was driving'; however, he or she had no driving licence, had no brakes, had no airbag, had not enough petrol to complete the journey and found the road ahead was filled by a big empty truck driven by a blindfolded union legislator.

To many people entrepreneurs were still not welcome. Neither politicians nor societies liked having to be grateful to anybody except possibly to God, and certainly not to bright and successful entrepreneurs. (It was wryly commented that this was surprising because God himself was surely an entrepreneur. After all had he not lost control of his enterprise shortly after he launched it?) Indeed ten or more years on, the entrepreneur still struggles somewhat for acceptance, not least because of the doubtful activities of prominent and financially successful Mafiosi.

Although there were and are considerable differences amongst countries in Central and Eastern Europe, and although they had not all been centralised, socialised or collectivised to the same extent, it would seem that the economic system did affect enterprise and the attitudes it engendered are themselves now affecting attempts to reintroduce enterprise. The extent to which an economy has an enterprise culture has assumed a particular importance in understanding the prospects for the development of that economy. However, attempts to understand what an enterprise culture means and the process by which a culture develops has to be done in the context of the socio-economic conditions of the region under investigation. In short, we may speak of the 'cultural context of enterprise'.

DEMAND FACTORS

Supply and demand factors, as the use of economic terminology implies, are most easily identified in entrepreneurship, rather than in the wider non-business aspects of enterprise. The demand factors are those aspects which create entrepreneurial opportunities through the market demand for goods and services, whereas the supply factors stimulate a supply of entrepreneurs to take advantage of those opportunities. The demand for entrepreneurship is affected by issues such as the stage of economic development, globalisation and the stage of technological development, as illustrated in Figure 4.5.

Economic development

The impact of economic development on entrepreneurship has not been clear. For instance economic development tends to raise wage rates and higher wages can discourage people from trying self-employment as there is more for them to lose. However 'it is an observed fact that, since the 1970s, per capita income has had a positive impact on the self-employment rate, at least in developed countries.'[27]

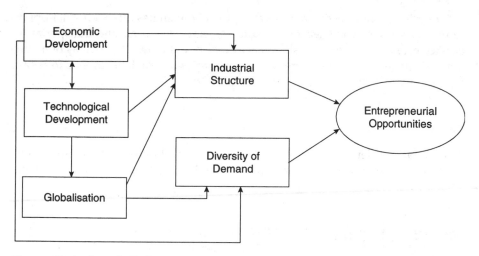

Source: D. Audretsch, R. Thurik, I. Verheul and S. Wennekers, (eds) *Entrepreneurship: Determinants and Policy in a European-US Comparison* (Dordrecht, The Netherlands and Norwell, MA, USA: Kluwer Academic Publishers, 2000), p. 23. Reproduced with the permission of Kluwer Academic Publishers.

Figure 4.5 Demand side determinants of entrepreneurship

Technological development

Technology led to the Industrial Revolution but technology does not always favour the bigger business. In recent years the speed of technological development, which places a premium on responsiveness, and in particular developments such as information and communications technology, which reduces the advantages of scale, have enhanced the opportunities for entrepreneurs.

Globalisation

Globalisation, involving as it does the integration of world markets, favours the larger business able to supply world markets. At the same time, it makes people more aware of the diverse range of goods and services available elsewhere and stimulates a demand for them, a demand which can often be satisfied locally by small businesses able to compete in niche markets. For instance the wider awareness across the world of the cuisine of other countries has stimulated a demand for local ethnic restaurants, many of which are small businesses.

Industrial structure and clustering

Different stages of economic development have been characterised by different levels of self-employment. Agricultural economies have high levels of self-employment but industrial economies favour bigger businesses. The break-up of monopolies, monopolistic practices and protectionism has offered further opportunities, for instance in telecommunications, pharmaceuticals and transportation. Service economies favour small businesses also. Other trends, such as outsourcing and clustering, have also created opportunities for small businesses to service bigger ones.

Other

A summary of demand side influences on the development of the SME Sector (including entrepreneurship generally) is contained in Table 1.3 in Chapter One.

SUPPLY FACTORS

Various factors have, as indicated below, had the effect of either increasing, or decreasing, the supply of entrepreneurs.

Population growth and density

Expanding populations do not just mean extra demand for goods and services but also more people looking for employment. Especially in conditions of population density, such as in urban areas, the local availability of markets and business role models means that many people are likely to consider self-employment as a means of securing an income.

Age structure

Entrepreneurial attitudes, skills and resources are acquired over time and consequently age has an impact on entrepreneurship. It has been suggested, for example, that many people aged 30 or less may not have acquired sufficient organisational experience while those aged 45 or more may no longer possess the required energy. The age structure of a population will affect how many people there are in the 'age-launch-window' band.

Immigration

Immigrants need work but are not in established job networks or may lack the communication skills needed to access existing jobs. Therefore they may, perforce, try self-employment. However, in some cases the identification of immigrants with self-employment is sufficiently well established to suggest to many that their indigenous culture suits them specifically for it. This is especially the case when the immigrants are ethnically different from the native population when issues of ethnicity, which were considered at the end of Chapter Three, will also apply.

Participation

Increased participation in the labour market, especially by women, has also increased the number of people seeking economic activity and who are prepared to consider self-employment. If they are not the sole income earners in their families it also means that they can afford to be relatively less risk-averse, which can also help when contemplating self-employment.

Income levels and unemployment

High income levels can, as suggested above, mean that people have more to lose when they leave jobs. Unemployment, on the other hand, or very low income, mean that there is no job or little to lose and therefore, apart from benefit entitlement, little to risk and an income to gain in trying a self-employment venture. It has also been argued that low levels of unemployment mean a thriving economy which can be a stimulant to entrepreneurship.

Other

A summary of supply-side influences on the development of the SME sector (including entrepreneurship generally) is contained in Table 1.3 in Chapter One.

Comment on supply and demand factors

In looking at the possible supply and demand factors identified it would appear that in many cases the result of the influence is uncertain as the factors in question have both positive and negative features in respect of enterprise. However the issue is whether or not there is an influence to be considered and in all cases it is suggested that there is. The uncertainty of the direction of the effect is not a reason for denying the effect; it just adds to the complexity of the subject. (For further discussion of the influences on entrepreneurship see the summary of the Global Entrepreneurship Monitor project later in this chapter.)

GOVERNMENT OR OTHER INTERVENTIONS

Governments, and sometimes other organisations such as enterprise agencies, intervene to promote more enterprise. They do so on the presumption that they will have an effect. Their interventions must therefore be considered among the factors which influence enterprise. Their motivations, methods and effectiveness are considered further in Part Three of this book.

EQUILIBRIUM RATES

It was noted above, under 'Industrial structure', that different stages of economic development are characterised by different levels of self-employment. This has led to the suggestion that there will be an equilibrium level of entrepreneurship, determined by the stage of development of an economy. That has the implication that deviations in practice from that equilibrium level might, other things being equal, tend to be accompanied by a correcting influence.

In 1999 Carree, van Stel, Thurik and Wennekers produced a report[28] of an empirical investigation into the relationship between the extent of business ownership and economic growth. They investigated:

- 'Whether there is a long-term relationship between the numbers of business owners and the stage of economic development. This arises from scrutinising empirical and theoretical work in this area. The relation is hypothesised to be a decreasing function of economic development in that the self-employment rate is high in low-developed economies whereas there is a later phase where mass production and scale economies thrive. A vast literature points at a still later phase of economic development where the business ownership rate is increasing again. This phase is characterised by 'the reversal of the trend' towards increasing economies of scale and scope. However, it is still unclear to what extent this reversal will be structural. Therefore both a U-shaped as well and an L-shaped equilibrium relation were tested.
- Whether there exists a correction mechanism when the rate of business ownership is out of equilibrium and what the speed of convergence is. Out of equilibrium situations can occur due to exogenous shocks and institutional divergences, (for instance, from government regulation of market activity).
- Whether deviating from the equilibrium rate of business ownership leads to lower economic growth.'

These three aspects were tested using a data panel of 23 OECD countries. The investigations showed that:

both the U-shaped and the L-shaped relation between the number of business owners and the stage of economic development produce satisfactory results, that a statistical discrimination cannot be made since 'the reversal of the trend' is of a recent date only and that the minimum of the U-shaped equilibrium relation is within the range of observations of economic development. The assumption of a U-shaped curve would imply that modern economies are now in a phase where the rate of business ownership is likely to increase structurally. The rate of business ownership is shown to influence economic growth through deviations from the equilibrium rate. As a consequence, economies can have both too few or too many business owners and both situations lead to lower growth rates. By and large, a five per cent point deviation generates a growth loss of between one and three per cent over a period of four years. In particular, the fact that economic development may be hampered by a number of business owners being too high considering an economy's stage of development may come as a surprise for European politicians who see self-employment as a forceful weapon when fighting unemployment and stagnating growth. Different economic stages call for different development and stimulation programs. An error-correcting mechanism exists between the real rate of business ownership and the equilibrium rate. Lagged unemployment appears to be a significant push factor of business ownership whereas a high lagged labour income quota appears to decrease business ownership rates indicating the effect of low business profitability.

INTEGRATED THEORY

As well as the theories which relate entrepreneurship to various demand or supply factors, some of which have been described above, there are also some theories which have been advanced that attempt to link together some or all of these factors, and the internal factors considered in Chapter Three, into a single model. Such a model seeks to explain the different rates of entrepreneurship found in different contexts. Verheul *et al.*,[29] for instance, postulate a theory of entrepreneurship which brings together the multiplicity of influences identified in Figure 4.1 and elsewhere and reflect upon the different levels of entrepreneurship: macro, meso and micro, each of which needs to be understood in its own right as well as in its interaction with the other two levels.

CASE 4.4
From *An Eclectic Theory of Entrepreneurship*
....

The level of entrepreneurship differs considerably across countries and periods. Entrepreneurship is a multidimensional concept, the definition of which depends largely on the focus of the research undertaken. The present study deals with the factors determining the level of entrepreneurship. A broad range of determinants explains the level of entrepreneurship, including economic and social factors. Moreover, it is generally accepted that policy measures can influence the level of entrepreneurship. The government can exert influence on entrepreneurship in different ways; directly through specific measures and indirectly through generic measures. For example, when stipulating a competition policy, the government can influence the market structure and (indirectly) the number and type of entrepreneurial opportunities.

The level of entrepreneurship in a particular country can be explained by making a distinction between the supply side (labour market perspective) and the demand side (product market perspective; carrying capacity of the market) of entrepreneurship. This distinction is sometimes referred to as that between push and pull factors. The determinants of entrepreneurship can also be studied according to level of analysis. A distinction can be made between the micro, meso and macro level of entrepreneurship. The objects of study tied to these levels of analysis, are the individual entrepreneur or business, sectors of industry and the national economy, respectively. Studies at the micro level focus on the decision-making process by individuals and the motives of people to become self-employed. Research into the decisions of individuals to become either wage- or self-employed focuses primarily on personal factors, such as psychological traits, formal education and other skills, financial assets, family background and previous work experience. Studies at the meso level of entrepreneurship often focus on market-specific determinants of entrepreneurship, such as profit opportunities and opportunities for entry and exit. The macro perspective focuses on a range of environmental factors, such as technological, economic and cultural variables as well as government regulation.

The occupational choices of individuals are made on the basis of their risk-reward profile of entrepreneurship versus that of other types of employment, such as wage employment or unemployment ... The process of occupational choice is also embedded in an institutional and cultural environment. First, opportunities for entrepreneurial activity depend upon the development of the private service sector versus the public provision of services and the evolution of the household and the so-called informal sector. Since the late 1980s the balance has shifted towards commercial provision of many services due to privatisation, deregulation and a decreasing tax and social security wedge in many countries. Additionally, entrepreneurial opportunities also depend upon competition and establishment legislation. Second, the government can influence resources and abilities of individuals through subsidised information and advice services, loan guarantees and other direct support schemes. Third, personal attitudes towards entrepreneurship are a 'product' of the current cultural environment. These cultural patterns are however stable and path-dependent, and are reinforced by education and legislation that again are products of the cultural system. Nonetheless, once policies promoting entrepreneurial opportunities, the availability of resources and entrepreneurial ability bear some success, emerging entrepreneurial activity will provide new role models triggering cultural change.

... Entrepreneurship is a multi-faceted phenomenon. This may explain why research on entrepreneurship spans so many academic fields under many disparate guises. At its best, the subject has generated a diversity of approaches and perspectives. At its worst, it has a Tower of Babel nature, where each academic discipline speaks its own distinct language with its own methodology, impenetrable by outsiders.

This paper has tried to build on the positive challenges of entrepreneurship research by drawing on the rich traditions and findings spanning a broad spectrum of academic disciplines to develop an integrated eclectic theory of entrepreneurship. This eclectic theory incorporates multi-level units of analysis – micro (individuals) as well as macro (countries). In addition, it draws on the perspectives and traditions of a number of disciplines, including sociology, management, psychology, regional science, and economics. The resulting eclectic theory ought to provide a conceptual framework for analysing both the determinants of entrepreneurship as well as the consequences or impact of entrepreneurship across a broad array of industry, national, spatial and temporal settings.

Points raised

This is an example of an attempt to link different lines of research and different disciplines to produce a single model for analysing the determinants of entrepreneurship.

Source: D. Audretsch, R. Thurik, I. Verheul and S. Wennekers (eds), *Entrepreneurship: Determinants and Policy in a European-US Comparison* (Dordrecht, The Netherlands and Norwell, MA, USA: Kluwer Academic Publishers 2000), Chapter 2. Reproduced with the permission of Kluwer Academic Publishers.

The Global Entrepreneurship Monitor

A significant development in the field of entrepreneurship research was the creation in 1999 of the Global Entrepreneurship Monitor (GEM). It was a joint initiative by Babson College, Massachusetts, USA and the London Business School, UK and has as its central focus the study of the complex relationship between entrepreneurship and economic growth. GEM was designed as a long-term longitudinal research study involving international comparisons between the G7 countries (Canada, France, Germany, Italy, Japan, UK and USA) and initially three others (Denmark, Finland and Israel). Further additions had raised the total number of countries involved to 38 by the year 2002.

For the purposes of the GEM study, entrepreneurship was defined as 'any attempt to create a new business enterprise or to expand an existing business by an individual, a team of individuals or an established business' and three questions about it were to be explored:[30]

1 Does the level of entrepreneurial activity vary amongst countries and, if so, to what extent?
2 Does the level of entrepreneurial activity affect a country's rate of economic growth and prosperity?
3 What makes a country entrepreneurial?

At the time of writing (in 2002) GEM's answers to these questions might be summarised as follows:

Question 1: Does the level of entrepreneurial activity vary amongst countries?

To illustrate the variation in entrepreneurial activity amongst countries, GEM has used a measure called the Total Entrepreneurial Activity (TEA) index. The index value shows for each country the percentage of the adult population who are trying to start a new firm or are the owner/managers of an active business less than 42 months old. This value is therefore made up of two measures:

- the nascent start-up rate (those in the process of creating a business);
- the new firm rate (those actually running early stage businesses).

The TEA index is therefore a measurement of indigenous entrepreneurial activity. Figure 4.6 shows the TEAs for the countries in the GEM survey, grouped by geographic region. National performance on this measure extends from approximately five per cent in Belgium, Japan and Singapore to approximately 18 per cent in Mexico. It would be expected that countries with substantial international trade (such as the Netherlands, Belgium, Ireland and Singapore) would tend to be less dependent on internal development for national economic growth and this is reflected in their TEA scores.

In 2001 the study was widened to explore two sub-sets within entrepreneurship. Again the levels of these sub-sets varied across countries. This revealed that:

> about 54 per cent ... of those involved in creating and growing new firms claimed they were pursuing a business opportunity for personal interest, often at the same time as they were working in a regular job. These efforts were referred to as 'opportunity entrepreneurship', reflecting the voluntary nature of participation. In contrast, about 43 per cent ... reported they were involved because they had 'no better choices for work'. Such efforts are referred to in the study as 'necessity entrepreneurship', reflecting the individual's perception that such actions presented the best option available for employment but not necessarily the preferred option ... The remaining 3 per cent involved in new business activity reflect other motivations.[31]

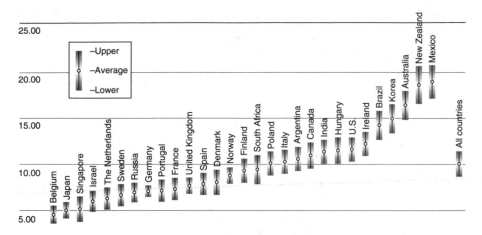

Source: P. R. Reynolds, S. M. Camp, W. D. Bygrave, E. Autio and M. Hay, *Global Entrepreneurship Monitor: 2001 Executive Report* (Kansas City, MO: Kauffman Centre for Entrepreneurial Leadership at the Ewing Marion Kauffman Foundation, 2001), p. 7.

Figure 4.6 Total Entrepreneurial Activity (TEA) by country

GEM has therefore shown that the level of entrepreneurship, and that of two of its sub-sets, does vary significantly amongst countries. This conclusion may not be surprising but GEM has indicated the extent and distribution of that variation.

Question 2: Does the level of entrepreneurial activity affect a country's rate of economic growth and prosperity?

In the first three years of its work (up to the time of writing) the GEM study had indicated a statistically significant association between entrepreneurial activity and national economic growth (as indicated by a growth in GDP) although 'the strength of the association tends to vary depending on the countries included ... and the nature of the entrepreneurial activity.'[32] In 2001, when GEM for the first time looked separately at opportunity and necessity entrepreneurship, it found that 'the prevalence rate of necessity entrepreneurship was positively associated with national economic growth [see Figure 4.7] and that this association was strongest when countries highly dependent on international trade (Belgium, Hungary, Ireland, the Netherlands, and Singapore) were excluded', but that 'the prevalence rate of opportunity entrepreneurship was not associated with any measure of national economic growth.'[33]

The association between the specific measures of entrepreneurial activity and growth in GDP is also presented in Table 4.2 which reveals that none of the measures of entrepreneurship have a negative relationship with actual (and, with one exception, predicted) growth in GDP. The highest correlation (0.73) is between necessity entrepreneurship and 2002 projected growth in GDP.

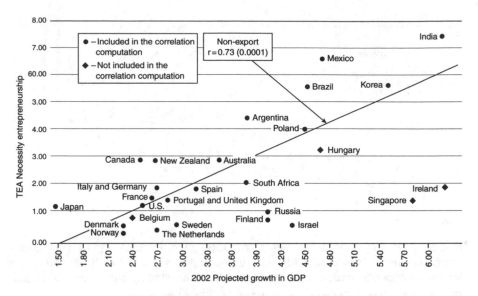

Source: P. R. Reynolds, S. M. Camp, W. D. Bygrave, E. Autio and M. Hay, *Global Entrepreneurship Monitor: 2001 Executive Report* (Kansas City, MO: Kauffman Centre for Entrepreneurial Leadership at the Ewing Marion Kauffman Foundation, 2001), p. 7.

Figure 4.7   Necessity entrepreneurship and 2002 projected growth in GDP

Table 4.2   Correlations between measures of entrepreneurial activity and economic growth

Measure	Real GDP growth 2000	Real GDP growth 2001 (projected)	Real GDP growth 2002 (projected)
Total Entrepreneurial Activity (TEA) 2001	0.31	0.28	0.39
Nascent (start-up) firm prevalence rate 2001	0.09	0.028	0.27
New business prevalence rate 2001	0.51	0.19	0.44
Total opportunity entrepreneurship rate 2001	0.12	0.00	−0.01
Total necessity entrepreneurship rate 2001	0.31	0.58	0.73

Note: GEM 2001, countries without export emphasis (excludes Belgium, Hungary, Ireland, the Netherlands, and Singapore)
Source: Based on P. R. Reynolds, S. M. Camp, W. D. Bygrave, E. Autio and M. Hay, *Global Entrepreneurship Monitor: 2001 Executive Report* (Kansas City, MO: Kauffman Centre for Entrepreneurial Leadership at the Ewing Marion Kauffman Foundation, 2001), p. 12.

Interestingly, while very few GEM countries have high levels of necessity entrepreneurship and low levels of economic growth, the countries with the highest levels of necessity entrepreneurship are also the most underdeveloped. GEM therefore announced its intention to track, over time, this strong association between necessity entrepreneurship and economic growth, to try to unravel 'the causal mechanisms that account for this relationship'.[34]

So, although GEM has to date made no claims about causality, it has reported that 'entrepreneurship is strongly associated with economic growth'[35] and, while it appears to be the necessity entrepreneurship component in particular which is most positively associated with growth, no entrepreneurially active countries have low levels of economic growth. However this relationship is a complex one and longitudinal data will be needed if the mystery of causality is to be unravelled.

Question 3: What makes a country entrepreneurial?

The GEM research programme was derived from a conceptual model summarising the major casual mechanisms affecting national economies. This model is illustrated by Figure 4.8.

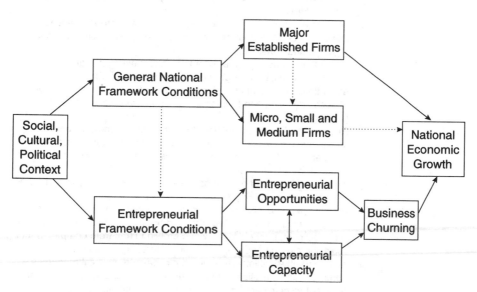

Source: A. L. Zacharakis, W. D. Bygrave and D. A. Shepherd, *Global Entrepreneurship Monitor National Entrepreneurship Assessment: United States of America, 2000 Executive Report* (Kansas City, MO: Kauffman Centre for Entrepreneurial Leadership, 2000), p. 5.

Figure 4.8   GEM conceptual model (the total process)

The components of the model are interpreted in Table 4.3.

The 'Social, Cultural and Political Context', the 'General National Framework Conditions' and the 'Entrepreneurial Framework Conditions' are 'all assumed to have an impact on the national entrepreneurial sector. In turn the national

Table 4.3 Interpretation of components of the GEM conceptual model

Variable	Interpretation
Social cultural and political context	Factors shown to play an important role in shaping a country's national framework conditions, such as demographics, investment in education, social norms and attitudes as they relate to, for example, independence and entrepreneurs
General national framework (GNF) conditions	Role of government institutions, R & D, physical infrastructure, labour market efficiency, legal and social institutions
Entrepreneurial framework (EF) conditions	Comprise factors believed to be more volatile than GNF conditions and reflect intermediate variables in the overall causal sequence. They include: • financial support: the availability of financial resources, equity and debt, for new and growing firms including grants and subsidies; • government policies: the extent to which government policies concerning taxes, regulations and their application are size neutral and/or whether these policies discourage or encourage new and growing firms; • government programmes: the presence of direct programmes to assist new and growing firms at all levels of government – national, regional, and municipal; • education and training: the extent to which training in starting or managing small, new, or growing businesses features in the educational and training system, and the quality, relevance and depth of such education and training in creating or managing small, new or growing businesses; • Research and development transfer: the extent to which national research and development leads to new commercial opportunities, and whether or not R & D is available for new, small and growing firms; • commercial and professional infrastructure: the influence of commercial, accounting, and other legal services and institutions that allow or promote new, small or growing businesses; • market openness / barriers to entry: the extent to which commercial arrangements are prevented from undergoing constant change and redeployment, preventing new and growing firms from competing and replacing existing suppliers, subcontractors, and consultants; • access to physical infrastructure: the access to physical resources – communication, utilities, transportation, land or space, at a price that does not discriminate against new, small, or growing firms; • cultural and social norms: the extent to which existing social and cultural norms encourage, or do not discourage, individual actions that may lead to new ways of conducting business or economic activities and, in turn, lead to greater dispersion in wealth and income.
Entrepreneurial opportunities	The perception as well as the reality of market opportunities
Entrepreneurial capacity	Attitudes and resources of potential entrepreneurs
Business churning	The processes which lead to birth, death, expansion and contraction of businesses
National economic growth	Subsumes a variety of common economic measures such as growth in GDP, employment and per capita income

entrepreneurial sector is considered to have several major features: the perception of opportunity, the presence of entrepreneurial capacity and the motivation to pursue a new firm start-up.'[36]

All three of these features must be present before a viable effort to launch a new firm can begin. A summary of the comparisons of them made in 2000 is shown in Figure 4.9. It graphically illustrates the role of the TEA index and uses the pre-eminent position of the USA in the perceptions of survey respondents as a benchmark. They believe, in general, that Americans perceive opportunities and are capable and motivated to pursue them to a much greater degree than even the others in the high TEA group.

As in previous years the 2001 GEM study also included face-to-face interviews with experts on entrepreneurship within most of the participating countries. Their interviews were based on the GEM model and they indicated that across the countries the three most important issues affecting entrepreneurship were cultural and social norms, financial support, and government policies. For each issue the experts indicated differences between the most and the least entrepreneurially active countries. However describing differences is not the same as prescribing how to change them.

These comments show that the GEM initiative has started to look at what it is that makes some countries more entrepreneurial than others and has highlighted differences in a number of factors which could be relevant.

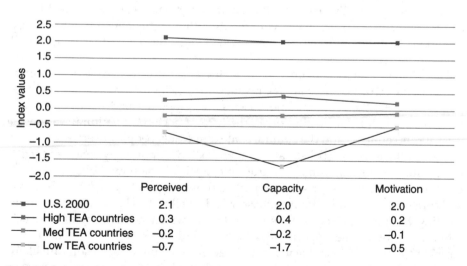

	Perceived	Capacity	Motivation
U.S. 2000	2.1	2.0	2.0
High TEA countries	0.3	0.4	0.2
Med TEA countries	−0.2	−0.2	−0.1
Low TEA countries	−0.7	−1.7	−0.5

Source: A. L. Zacharakis, W. D. Bygrave and D. A. Shepherd, *Global Entrepreneurship Monitor National Entrepreneurship Assessment: United States of America, 2000 Executive Report* (Kansas City, MO: Kauffman Centre for Entrepreneurial Leadership, 2000), p. 18.

Figure 4.9 Perceived opportunities, capacity and motivation indices

GEM conclusions

It may therefore be concluded from the GEM studies to date that the level of entre-preneurship does differ considerably across countries. Further, a high level of entre-preneurial activity, and possibly of necessity entrepreneurship in particular, does seem to correlate to some extent with economic growth. However the determinants of entrepreneurship appear to be many and complex and issues of causality will need to be resolved before clear policy implications can be drawn from them.

CONCLUSION

It has been said that, when decisions about potential actions have to be taken, a number of influences are at work. Krueger's model of these influences (see Chapter Three) includes:

- the perception of the attractiveness of the outcome of an action;
- the perceived opinion of family, friends and peer group;
- the individual's or group's views of their own competency;
- the perception of the environment in which they operate, especially its sup-port for and receptiveness to the proposed actions and their likely outcomes.

Some of these influences are due to internal factors but others are due to exter-nal conditions. Broadly speaking, the external influences can be ascribed to the cultural, political or economic environments, although the effects of all three are interlinked. Studies of enterprise in different countries show that they can all have an impact on enterprise.

This chapter seeks to identify some of the key features necessary in under-standing the intricate and complex manner 'in which entrepreneurship, culture, politics, society, the economy and business development and management are interwoven within the institutional structure of society'.[37] Cultural variations exist across countries and the cultural context in which people are embedded and develop influences their beliefs, attitudes and behaviour in many spheres of activ-ity including their disposition towards enterprising behaviour. Policy-makers in many countries actively strive to strengthen those cultural factors which facilitate enterprising intent and minimise those which inhibit it, while at the same time creating the political and economic conditions which not only reinforce such intent but provide the opportunities for it to find expression. Efforts have had variable success within and across countries and such imperfect results are likely to continue until there is a better understanding of the wide range of factors at work in society and the economy which influence enterprising behaviour.

Indeed it is likely that there is no single economic, political or cultural condi-tion that universally best promotes and supports enterprise. Methods of increas-ing enterprise that work in one situation may not therefore transfer successfully to other situations and to other societies. The link between enterprise and society is not easy to predict.

ILLUSTRATION 4.10
Variations in start-up rates
....

The OECD concluded that, in relation to self-employment rates in various countries, 'there is no unique set of causes'.[38] Mason suggests that the observed differences in business start-up rates even within the UK are because:

> the most important determinants of small business start-up rates are complex, interdependent and likely to vary intra-regionally, inter-regionally and internationally. Nevertheless the determinants will include an industrial structure biased towards small, independent economic units; employees engaged in problem-solving who have close contact with customers (so possessing technical and market knowledge); a concentration of technically progressive small firms; a high awareness of past small business activities; supportive banks and other financial institutions; the availability of help and advice; an affluent population and a social climate which favours individualism.[39]

A study[40] analysing regional variations in business births and deaths in the USA supports Mason's UK findings. Businesses showed significantly higher birth rates in regions that possessed greater economic diversity, more volatile industries, greater personal wealth, and more experienced mid-career people, as well as greater employment flexibility and population growth. Therefore, while the enterprise shown by individuals is influenced by their own internal attributes and resources, it is also subject to external influences. Culture and political and economic conditions have an important part to play.

THE KEY POINTS OF CHAPTER 4
....

- Chapter Three looked at the factors internal to people which are thought to influence enterprise. This chapter has looked at various factors external to the individual which have been identified as having some influence on the extent of enterprise practice both in its broad sense and, particularly, in the context of entrepreneurship.
- There are considerable variations in the levels of enterprise and the rate of emergence of entrepreneurs found in different countries and cultures.

This chapter also looked at theories which attempt to combine a number of possible influences, both internal and external, to provide a more complete view of why enterprise, especially in the context of entrepreneurship, occurs when it does.

- Among the factors which have been identified as influencing enterprise are:
  - national and societal culture;
  - economic conditions, such as a 'market' economy;
  - political conditions, such as government administrative and regulatory regimes;
  - demand-side factors, such as technological development, globalisation, economic development and industrial structure;
  - supply-side factors, such as population growth and density, age structure, immigration, participation rates, income levels and unemployment;
  - interventions by government, or other agencies;
  - equilibrium rates of enterprise;
  - other influences, including social and cultural enterprise.
- Integrated theories are being advanced to explain the influence of such factors, and those 'internal' factors considered in the previous chapter.
- A significant development has also been the work of the Global Enterprise Monitor which has explored the extent of entrepreneurship in many different countries and its relationship with national economic development and growth. One of its findings has been that, in the countries surveyed, there appears to be a strong correlation between the level of entrepreneurship activity and GDP growth.

CASE 4.5
Enterprise in Wales

Research conducted in 2000 for a regional enterprise strategy for Wales[41] found that:
- Wales had the second lowest weekly earnings of any region in the UK;
- only one third of the growth in the national income of Wales was due to entrepreneurial activity;
- the birth rate of new businesses in Wales as a proportion of the existing stock was at least 30 per cent behind the UK average and was lower than it was two decades previously;

- Wales was losing businesses at a faster rate than the UK average. Between 1994 and 1998 Wales lost 4700 businesses while the UK gained 51,100 overall;
- only four per cent of adults in a recent poll described themselves as entrepreneurs;
- only one in eight adults in Wales knew an entrepreneur personally, and only one per cent, when asked to name famous entrepreneurs, named a Welsh person;
- one in five Welsh people said that they would like to be an entrepreneur. The reasons the others gave for not wanting to be an entrepreneur included 'I'm too old', 'It's too stressful', and 'I'm not made that way';
- groups such as Welsh speakers, women, young people and third age people are under-represented in enterprise creation;
- many entrepreneurs leave Wales to become successful, and do not return;
- Wales is too heavily dependent on slow growth markets and has too small a share of fast growth sectors.

Points raised
This example quotes some findings which might help to present a more complete picture of the level of entrepreneurial potential in Wales than merely using business start-up rates.

QUESTIONS, EXERCISES, ESSAY AND DISCUSSION TOPICS

- Are entrepreneurs born or made?
- Which is the more important influence on enterprise in individuals: their attributes and resources or the environment in which they operate?
- To what extent is a person's cultural background likely to affect his or her entrepreneurial behaviour?
- Using examples from your own experience (family, friends and so on) illustrate which of the factors described have had an influence on your disposition towards starting your own business.
- If the factors in Figure 4.1 explain the extent of enterprise, what role does personal choice play?
- Describe the main demand- and supply-side factors which influence the level of entrepreneurship in GEM participating countries.
- To what extent are any of the models of the influences on enterprise consistent with the reported facts on Welsh enterprise?
- How would you rate your own region on a scale of entrepreneurial activity?

SUGGESTIONS FOR FURTHER READING AND INFORMATION

R. Burrows (ed.), *Deciphering the Enterprise Culture: Entrepreneurship, Petty Capitalism and the Re-Structuring of Britain* (London: Routledge, 1991).

B. Deacon, *The New Eastern Europe* (London: Sage, 1992).

T. Garrison, *International Business Culture* (Huntingdon: ELM Publications, 1996).

G. Hofstede, *Cultures and Organisations* (London: HarperCollins, 2001).

A. Lundström and L. Stevenson, *Entrepreneurship Policy for the Future*, Volume 1 of the Entrepreneurship for the Future series, (Stockholm: Swedish Foundation for Small Business Research, 2000).

For more information on the Global Entrepreneurship Monitor look in www.entreworld.org

REFERENCES

1   H. Pompe, M. Bruyn and J. Koek, 'Entrepreneurs in Small Business in International Comparative Perspective', Paper presented at the 13th International Small Business Congress, London, 1986.
2   G. Hofstede, *Cultures and Organisations* (London: HarperCollins, 1994).
3   A. Morrison (ed.), *Entrepreneurship: An International Perspective* (Oxford: Butterworth-Heinemann 1998).
4   T. Garrison, *International Business Culture* (Huntingdon: ELM Publications, 1996).
5   *Ibid.*, p. 169.
6   S. Carter and D. Jones-Evans (eds), *Enterprise and Small Business: Principles, Practice and Policy* (London: Financial Times/Prentice-Hall, 2000), p. 105.
7   Hofstede (1994), *op. cit.*, p. 105.
8   M. H. Tayeb, *Organisations and National Culture* (London: Sage 1988), quoted in S. Carter and D. Jones-Evans (eds), *op. cit.*, p. 99.
9   *Ibid.*, p. 169.
10 G. Hofstede, *Culture and Organisations: Software of the Mind* (London: McGraw-Hill, 1991), p. 5.
11 Hofstede (1994), *op. cit.*, p. 63.
12 T. Garrison, *International Business Culture* (Huntingdon: ELM Publications, 1996), quoted in S. Carter and D. Jones-Evans (eds), *op. cit.*, p. 99.
13 *Ibid.*, p. 10.
14 A. Morrison, 'Initiating Entrepreneurship', in S. Carter and D. Jones-Evans (eds), *op. cit.*, pp. 105–13.
15 D. McClelland, 'That Urge to Achieve', *THINK* (IBM, 1966), p. 111.
16 *Ibid.*, p. 111.
17 *Ibid.*, p. 117.
18 *Ibid.*, p. 114.

19 G. Redding, 'Three Styles of Asian Capitalism', in 'Mastering Enterprise', No. 7, *Financial Times*, January 1997, p. 10.

20 Hofstede (1994), *op. cit.*, pp. 73, 74.

21 Redding, *op. cit.*, p. 10.

22 P. Dodd, *The Influence of Culture on Enterprise*, Theme pamphlet (London: Industrial Christian Fellowship, 1990), pp. 2–5.

23 M. C. Waters, 'Immigrant Dreams and American Realities: The Causes and Consequences of the Ethnic Labour Market in American Cities', *Work and Occupations* 1999; 26: 352–64.

24 Waters (1999), *op. cit.*: 352.

25 J. Curran and R. A. Blackburn, 'Introduction', in J. Curran and R. A. Blackburn, *Paths of Enterprise* (London: Routledge, 1991).

26 Excerpts from L. Dane, *Contrasting Models of Policy Governing Small Business: Does Heavy Regulation Really Hinder the Small Business Sector?* Unpublished paper.

27 I. Verheul, S. Wennekers, D. Audretsch and R. Thurik, *Research Report: An Eclectic Theory of Entrepreneurship: Policies, Institutions and Culture* (Zoetermeer, The Netherlands: EIM Small Business Research and Consultancy, 1999), p. 22. Subsequently published as Chapter Two in D. Audretsch, R. Thurik, I. Verheul and S. Wennekers (eds), *Entrepreneurship: Determinants and Policy in a European–US Comparison* (Boston, MA and Dordrecht: Kluwer, 2002).

28 M. Carree, A. van Stel, R. Thurik and S. Wennekers, Research Report 9809/E-Business Ownership and Economic Growth, (Zoetermeer, The Netherlands: EIM Small Business Research and Consultancy, 1999), pp. 47–9. Subsequently published in *Small Business Economics* 2002; 18.

29 I. Verheul *et al.*, *op. cit.*, pp. 67–9.

30 A. L. Zacharakis, W. D. Bygrave and D. A. Shepherd, *Global Entrepreneurship Monitor United States of America 2000 Executive Report* (Kansas City, MO: Kauffman Centre for Entrepreneurial Leadership at the Ewing Marion Kauffmann Foundation, 2000), p. 5.

31 P. R. Reynolds, S. M Camp, W. D. Bygrave, E. Autio and M. Hay, *Global Entrepreneurship Monitor: 2001 Executive Report* (Kansas City, MO: Kauffman Centre for Entrepreneurial Leadership at the Ewing Marion Kauffmann Foundation, 2001), p. 8.

32 *Ibid.*, p. 12.

33 *Ibid.*, p. 5.

34 *Ibid.*, p. 13.

35 Zacharakis *et al.*, *op. cit.*, p. 4.

36 *Ibid.*, p. 29.

37 S. Carter and D. Jones-Evans (eds), *op. cit.*, p. 113.

38 *OECD Employment Outlook* (Paris: OECD, 2000).

39 R. Burrows (ed.), *Deciphering the Enterprise Culture: Entrepreneurship, Petty Capitalism and the Restructuring of Britain* (London: Routledge, 1991), p. 4.

40 P. O. Reynolds, B. Miller and W. R. Maki, 'Explaining Regional Variations in Business Births and Deaths: US 1976–88', *Small Business Economics* 1995; 7: 389–407.

41 D. Jones-Evans, *Creating a Regional Enterprise Strategy for Wales*, Paper prepared for the European Small Business Seminar, Dublin, September 2001.

OTHER ASPECTS OF ENTERPRISE

CONTENTS

KEY CONCEPTS
....

This chapter covers:
- some of the other agendas, perceptions and connotations which have been associated with enterprise;

- the social economy: social and community enterprises and social capital;
- the potential disadvantages associated with enterprise;
- future trends which may have an impact on enterprise.

LEARNING OBJECTIVES

By the end of this chapter the reader should:
- recognise that enterprise is a value-laden concept;
- have an understanding of the agendas sometimes associated with enterprise;
- understand the concept of a social enterprise and of the social economy;
- have an appreciation of the disadvantages sometimes ascribed to enterprise;
- understand some of the issues which may impact on the future of enterprise.

INTRODUCTION

So far Part One of this book has looked at the ways in which the term 'enterprise' is used in order to ascertain what people actually mean when they use the word, rather than just what a dictionary suggests it should mean. It has also looked at the link with entrepreneurship, which is usually taken to be the practice of enterprise in a business context. This exploration has shown that, rather than having a single narrow definition, the word 'enterprise' can have a whole range of meanings, although these can often be grouped either into a narrow definitional range in which enterprise basically means business and especially small business, or into a broader meaning of enterprise as the set of attributes that enable those who possess them to be creative, adaptable, proactive, innovative and responsive to change.

Such individual attributes were explored further in Chapter Three, which examined those factors largely internal to people which influence the extent to which they are enterprising. Enterprise, however, is also influenced by the external environment in which individuals operate, and these influences were considered in Chapter Four.

There are some other factors moreover which might be considered to relate to these chapters and some other aspects of enterprise and implications of the ways in which the term is used, which have not yet been covered. Therefore before Part Two, in which enterprise is considered specifically in the context of business, this chapter attempts to complete the picture by looking at some of these other aspects. In particular it considers some of the perceptions people may have about enterprise and the connotations it can have; it looks at social, or community, enterprise; it examines the potential and real disadvantages of enterprise; and it reviews some of the forces that may influence its future.

SOME PERCEPTIONS OF ENTERPRISE

A number of judgements are sometimes made about enterprise. While many people might agree with them they should not go unexplored. They include:

- enterprise is a relative concept;
- enterprise is a good thing;
- enterprise is essential for economic advancement;
- enterprise has strong political and social connotations.

Enterprise is a relative concept

At any particular time some societies and some individuals are seen as more enterprising than others. For much of the second half of the 20th century, the 'tiger' economies of the Pacific Rim were seen to be more enterprising than most Western economies, and they in turn were more enterprising than the communist bloc countries. Whether the Western economies were considered to be enterprising therefore depended upon that with which they were compared. Thus the assessment of their level of enterprise was relative.

Comparisons of relative enterprise are still frequently made. For example it is claimed that 'Britain is not as enterprising as it was in the 19th century'; that 'the European Union countries demonstrate much less enterprise than the USA'; and that 'more enterprise is to be found in the informal (black) economy than in the formal economy'. Whether such statements are true is a different matter. As indicated in the previous chapter, this relative nature of enterprise has also been given clear expression in the reporting of the Global Entrepreneurship Monitor[1] which positions countries in league tables according to assumed indicators of entrepreneurial activity.

Individuals can be judged to be enterprising or not be enterprising, which implies some sort of absolute judgement, depending on whether or not they engage in enterprising acts. In reality, we are making comparisons of one individual against another or against some notion of a 'standard' level of enterprise activity, although that standard will change over time and place. However, even in a so-called enterprising society, not every individual will be considered enterprising, yet the society as a whole may be judged to be so. Although as more individuals demonstrate enterprise then the society could be said to be more enterprising.

In short there are no objective benchmarks for what constitutes a high, low or normal level of enterprise.

Enterprise is a good thing

More enterprise is deemed to be preferable to less. This perception is based on certain assumptions: such as that a more enterprising person is happier than a less enterprising one, or that the enterprising person's state of self-actualisation is inherently more satisfying than self-actualisation by a non-enterprising one, or that a more enterprising person creates more utility, pleasure, or social welfare than a less enterprising one, or any combination of these.

The same views exist in respect of nations and societies. Enterprising nations are often viewed as being in a superior condition or moving towards a superior condition (however defined) than less enterprising ones. Why that should be is not always clear, but it appears to be connected with the view that enterprise leads to a higher standard of living or to a greater ability to influence one's own destiny. Indeed, enterprising people and enterprising economies have become synonymous with successful people and successful economies.

The link between enterprise and material reward is one which is often presented. If however happiness is perceived to be more reliant on spiritual or emotional fulfilment than material possessions then there might be a lesser association between enterprise and the success on which happiness depends.

CASE 5.1
However...
•••

A visitor to a Mediterranean country, impressed by the climate and its potential, got into a discussion with a local farmer who was sitting at the side of the road enjoying the sunshine and admiring the view. 'Why', he asked the local, 'are you sitting here, when, with a little effort, this farm could be so much more successful? You could grow such a variety of crops here'. 'Why', the farmer replied, 'should I want to do that?' 'Because you could invest in more land, grow even more crops and soon you could afford a large house with lots of features such as a terrace and swimming pool.' 'Why would I want that?' 'Because you could then relax and enjoy yourself sitting on the terrace and enjoying the sun and the view.' 'And what do you think I am doing now?'

Points raised
Sometimes we can forget why we engage in enterprise. There may be other ways to achieve the same fulfilment.

Enterprise is essential for economic advancement

Enterprise may create happiness or a superior condition, but the means or process whereby this happens is rarely clearly articulated. It would appear that what is envisaged is that enterprise leads to economic growth, which in turn engenders more happiness. Whether economic growth does produce more happiness can be debated, but is beyond the scope of this book. It is however worth considering here the link between enterprise and economic growth.

There is a correlation between the nations that are generally regarded as enterprising and those that achieve significant growth (albeit often at a social cost). Hong Kong has demonstrated a capacity for economic growth, and is regarded as being enterprising by virtue of its thriving business activity, international trading links and considerable entrepreneurial activity. But what is the process by which enterprising behaviour leads to enhanced economic growth? One possible route is that enterprise generates entrepreneurialism, which produces new and growing businesses, which in turn lead to economic growth.

It is possible, presumably, for a nation to be enterprising but not to achieve economic growth, if that enterprise finds outlets that are independent of economic achievement. It is also presumably possible to achieve economic growth without enterprise, at least in the short term, through for example the exploitation of mineral and other natural resources or inward investment. Neither of these two conditions appears to be common. That leads to the conclusion that enterprise and economic growth are linked, and that the mechanism for this is that enterprise produces entrepreneurship, which in turn expands the economy. The link between entrepreneurialism and economic development has been assessed by the Global Entrepreneurship Monitor (see Chapter Four) and the additional link to enterprise also needs to be considered when the creation of an enterprise culture, or the promotion of enterprise and an enterprising society, become part of public policy. This is so, not least when the concept is perceived as ideologically based. All are agreed, however, that the concept of enterprise has a variety of connotations – not just political and economic, but also social and cultural.

Enterprise has strong political and social connotations

The term 'enterprise' has been applied and used to indicate aspects of a wider culture or value system as well as to describe the way an individual performs. Within Europe, for much of the 20th century, the governments of the Central and Eastern countries have been called communist. The economies of these countries were centrally planned in contrast to the market economies of the rest of Europe. The latter economies, with those of many other countries (most notably the USA), were often referred to as 'free enterprise' (see also next section) and in this way the word 'enterprise' has acquired a political association. Such references to enterprise convey notions of freedom, liberalism, the dominance of markets and individual action and choice, for good or ill. Indeed, the concept of the 'enterprise culture' has been used politically in Britain (like 'Thatcherism') as a sort of independent variable which 'has had a considerable impact upon a range of other dependent variables: small business, self-employment, trade unions, manufacturing industry, the public sector, education, welfare and so on'.[2]

This may be a gross distortion of cause and effect, and an unduly simplified political analysis, but it is a view nevertheless propagated, at least in part, by some people. But the restructuring of Britain in the 1970s and 1980s has been attributable to changes to which it has been convenient to attach such a handy label or slogan. In the process, the concept of an enterprise culture has assumed meanings incorporating dimensions such as 'individualism, independence, flexibility, anti-collectivism, privatism, self-help and so on'.[3] Consequently, it has been argued that the former communist countries, if they wish to achieve economic growth, should restructure and develop these characteristics, which have social as well as politico-economic implications.

ILLUSTRATION 5.1
Devalued enterprise
....

This is what angers people about the highly simplistic and distorted ways in which enterprise and the enterprise culture have sometimes been promoted and practised. They miss the human and social justice imperatives entirely. They turn 'enterprise' into a good-for-some part of a political and economic philosophy which is uncaring and divisive, synonymous with greed and self-interest, and a subtle justification of the seeming inevitability of the coexistence of success and failure, richness and poverty, privilege and under-privilege. Others abhor this, and would point out that without social care, justice and cohesiveness, there can be no truly enterprising culture.

'Enterprise' has become one of the most devalued terms in the English language. A word that should embody all the complexities of risk-taking has come to stand as the legitimator of tax cuts, breaking trade unions and denying there is any case for examining how companies are owned and managed.

By this definition, the genius of enterprise is essentially about individuals pitting their wits against the market. It is an individual who develops a new product, grows a company or cuts a deal. The structure and culture of the organisations in which these individuals strut their stuff are ignored. It is low-taxed, lightly-regulated, have-won-the-right-to-manage individuals who make the capitalist system tick ...

Enterprise is in part an economic, in part an individual and in part a moral act. Companies have to reconcile the claims of individuals as social beings as much as assert the iron laws of the balance sheet – and these iron laws themselves change in different cultures and value systems. Enterprise is culturally determined.

Enterprise is as much a social and moral act as economic – but, until this is widely understood, economic success will be elusive. Early accounts of the

> rise of capitalism ... stressed the congruence between Protestant values and those of successful capitalism. Religious non-conformism compelled the early capitalists to invest and not to dissipate their profits in consumption. The early Protestant sects were earning a place in heaven by their acts in the world, and so launching early capitalism.
>
> Will Hutton[4]

OTHER ENTERPRISE CONNOTATIONS

The word 'enterprise' has a number of other connotations. People talk of free enterprise, of enterprise as being the opposite of dependency and of enterprise occurring in clusters.

Free enterprise

Economic enterprise is said to thrive in a free, or market, economy. It was Adam Smith in *The Wealth of Nations* in 1776 who argued that the enormously complex task of deciding which goods and services to produce in an economy should be not be carried out by a central authority but should be delegated to individual buyers and sellers.[5] He did recognise that government nevertheless had a role in such a free market. It had the responsibility for the framework of laws to protect the right of individuals involved in the market and for mechanisms to maintain social stability.

Others more recently have been equally enthusiastic about the workings of the free market. Hayek[6] argues persuasively in *The Road to Serfdom* that socialist planning restricts individual decision-making and is invariably inefficient. Neither innovative technological changes nor changes in consumer preferences can be predicted with any accuracy, and consequently attempts to plan such matters are doomed to failure. The free market is the most flexible and responsive of economic systems and is always more efficient than deliberate economic decision-making by the state. Free enterprise systems can lead to inequality, but it is argued that those with the best economic judgements of events reap the greatest rewards. Hayek deplores any attempt by centralised decision-makers to legislate for equality, because it would restrict liberty and ultimately be ineffective.

These are the principal proponents of the line of economic thought that puts the emphasis on the individual in a system that is regarded as highly flexible and responsive to change and that provides the freedom to choose. This free enterprise economy, with its market-driven changes, is thus an attractive milieu for enterprising individuals to spot economic opportunities and exercise skill and judgement in the pursuit of economic rewards. By way of contrast, it can be seen that individual enterprise would be severely constrained in a command economy.

Much of the rivalry in the last century between the so-called 'East' and 'West', between the first two 'worlds', can therefore be seen in terms of a conflict between the relative advantages of a market versus a command economy. Capitalism, as practised in the 19th century, had been thought by Marx and others to promote the advance of the few and the economic enslavement of the many. Communism was the alternative that promised to end this inequality and to promote the benefit of the many. 'Bourgeois and Proletarians' is the heading of the first section of the *Communist Manifesto* and a note by Engels explains that by 'bourgeoisie' is meant the class of modern capitalists, owners of the means of social production and employers of wage labour, and by 'proletariat' is meant the class of modern wage-labourers who, having no means of production of their own, are reduced to selling their labour power in order to live. The *Communist Manifesto* specifically advocates the ending of the capitalist market and those states that have subsequently claimed to be based on a Marxist ideal have, by and large, had centrally planned, rather than market, economies. The apparent failure of this approach, and the abandonment of central planning in favour of the reintroduction of market forces, have been seen as a victory of 'free enterprise' over communism and as proof therefore of the superiority and rightness of the market approach.

That superiority may not always be so obvious, however, and it is not always so easy to replace a command economy with a free one. The recent apparent degeneration of the Russian economy into a 'mafia'-dominated confusion indicates that the much heralded victory of Western market-dominated economics is not everywhere so clearly beneficial as may have been claimed initially.

The market approach has been identified with enterprise in this way and criticisms of a market economy approach have been portrayed as attacks on the ideas of enterprise. However, there are many variations of the market economy and much of the criticism of one variation is also intended to promote another. Nevertheless, some of this debate has been seen to be anti-enterprise. To see whether it is or not, it is necessary to distinguish between some different models of the market economy and their advantages and disadvantages.

The outward micro-economic manifestation of free-market thinking and behaviour is the perfectly competitive model. In this economic model there are very many firms in each industry producing largely homogeneous goods. No firm is large enough to influence the industry's price; firms and consumers have perfect knowledge; and firms will expand production until the cost of producing an additional item equals the revenue obtained from selling it. Under these conditions there is an optimal distribution of resources among competing ends. When markets are not in equilibrium, the price mechanism comes into play to restore equilibrium.

Among the criticisms of this model are the claims that in reality there are many matters that create and sustain imperfections in the model. Advertising allows firms to differentiate products; monopolistic firms dominate markets; labour markets do not 'clear' the unemployed, and inflation persists. According to one commentator, 'the major tenet of free market economics – that unregulated markets will of their own accord find unimprovable results for all participants – is now proved to be nonsense. It does not hold in theory. It is not true.'[7]

In spite of the claims that economic development in the USA is the 'product of the initiative and drive of individuals cooperating through the free market',[8] governments (the Kennedy and Johnson administrations in the USA are examples) have intervened to produce variations on the capitalist theme. Thomas cites Keegan in concluding that there are at least three versions of capitalism: the American or liberal model, which draws heavily on the views of Smith and Hayek; continental European capitalism, which has active government involvement and embraces important interest groups that run the economy conjointly; and Japanese capitalism, with strong state involvement, partnership and a focus on manufacturing prowess. In the European and Japanese versions, Keegan reports, the notion of 'community' is not seen as injurious to creativity or to the 'incentive to work'. He considers that the Japanese model, which emphasises loyalty and 'the value of long-term relationships between companies, their customers and suppliers, and *within* companies between the organisation, the employees, and the senior executives', is worthy of consideration.[9] Enterprise, in or through a more collaborative German or Japanese model, can indeed flourish in non-liberal (in the US sense) capitalist economies.

The economically sensitive, responsive, American-style capitalism presents many opportunities for enterprising individuals, but setting up and managing projects requires collaboration. Therefore the European and Japanese versions of capitalism can offer opportunities to do new things and to do so with the assistance of others. 'Markets, whether we like it or not', says Hutton, 'are embedded in a country's social system and values.'[10] Thus deviations from the perfectly competitive model of 'free enterprise' are not necessarily inherently contrary to enterprise. They may simply be adjustments to produce a system that promotes the benefits of enterprise in a way that works in reality.

Enterprise and dependency

It has not been only under communism that economic systems have discouraged enterprise, or at least discouraged what are perceived as some of the more beneficial sorts of enterprise. One way of defining enterprise is to describe it as the opposite of dependency; and yet dependency, it is argued, has been the result of some well-meaning attempts at economic stimulation. While governments have naturally been keen to ensure that their efforts benefit the worst-off in society, as well as, if not even more than, those who are more advantaged, their efforts have not always been as effective as they might have wished.

One reason for this is encapsulated in the saying, 'Give people fishes and you feed them for a day; teach them to fish and they can be fed for life.' In economic terms, however, it is often argued that teaching someone to fish is no help if there are no fish in the immediate area and that, in any case, it is a long-term strategy. What is often first needed is short-term relief, and governments often seem to have the resources to buy in fish in the short term. However, economies are said to work when they create wealth and, if poorer regions are not creating wealth, then just putting in money, which is often the main resource to which governments can resort, is unlikely to change things.

Although governments do not like admitting to wasting resources, there is evidence that, even if economic development assistance appears to be carefully used, the result can be to build an attitude of dependency, not of enterprise. In Northern Ireland, for instance, studies in the late 1980s showed that the effect of years of grant support for businesses, ostensibly to help those businesses offset a variety of factors reducing their competitiveness, had had the effect instead of making them 'at least as profitable as their (foreign) counterparts'[11] while remaining less productive. In other words an overall effect of the grants was to underwrite a lack of competitiveness. What could be said to be happening was that individual business owners were learning to be enterprising, not in improving business worth by superior competitiveness, but in improving business worth by becoming better at accessing grants. That is enterprise, but like the stories of individuals in the so-called communist systems who became expert at getting the most out of the system while putting in the least, it is not the sort of enterprise that helps an economy to grow.

It can also be argued that strong government support of that kind can do more than just promote the rise of opportunistic 'grantrepreneurship'. It can also build a real dependency on that support. If there is a feeling that the economic situation is poor and that government ought to do something, and government then does intervene to do something, it reinforces the belief that sorting out the problem is the duty of government and should be left to it. Often the solution sought is inward investment: the attracting into the poorer regions of large industrial projects from elsewhere to provide employment. That employment, however, is then dependent on the continuation of those projects and they are often the first to be closed by their parent companies in periods of economic retrenchment, particularly if they do not include any 'head office' functions such as R&D or marketing. Meanwhile, established local businesses and prospective new businesses, having become used to the availability of grants, tend to develop the attitude that if there isn't a grant for something then they won't do it. And even in local economic development initiatives local businesses and organisations become dependent on government for ideas and drive. It can be like a patient being put on a life-support machine who, if the basic illness is not treated, becomes dependent on that machine for continued life. Enterprise, it could be argued, should be about taking your own initiative to improve your circumstances, not being dependent on others to do it for you.

ILLUSTRATION 5.2
Learned helplessness

....

Learned helplessness is a recognised health care problem in which patients learn to become dependent on external assistance and cannot do without it even when their original complaint is cured. Businesses, it would seem, can suffer from similar problems.

Clusters and competitiveness

What then does actually promote industrial competitiveness? One answer comes from Michael Porter who, in his book *The Competitive Advantage of Nations*, seeks to overturn the traditional view on this subject. The prevailing theory, he suggests, had been that economies of scale, labour costs and interest and exchange rates were the strongest factors in determining competitiveness. He argues, however, that it is domestic rivalry and geographic concentration that provide the conditions necessary to build the expertise and innovation that really produce competitiveness. 'The presence of strong local rivals is a ... powerful stimulus to the creation and persistence of competitive advantage,'[12] and again, 'Nations succeed in particular industries because their home environment is the most forward-looking, dynamic, and challenging.'[13]

Companies achieve competitive advantage through innovation, including innovation in technology, in new ways of doing things, and in perceiving new markets or new opportunities in existing markets. Innovation is, however, linked to change and change is often unnatural. Conventional wisdom had argued that domestic competition was wasteful: that it led to duplication of effort and reduced the potential for economies of scale. Porter suggests, on the contrary, that it is domestic competition that provides the stimulus for innovation and that it is domestic competition that ultimately both forces domestic companies to look at export markets for their expansion and toughens them to succeed in them. When that domestic environment includes demanding customers and strong competition, together with appropriate support industries and the factors of production, there is the basis for international competitiveness. This is the cluster theory, and it has much in common with Mason's suggestions (see Chapter Four) for the determinants of higher business start-up rates. (See also Chapter Eight for the growth implications of clusters.)

Porter's views are not primarily about the promotion of enterprise per se, but they argue against the once conventional wisdom that economic prosperity is linked primarily to big businesses. If he is right then the conditions and attitudes that will give a nation a competitive advantage are those of an enterprise culture. National competitiveness and enterprise will be linked.

ILLUSTRATION 5.3
Network capitalism

While the examples of 'Third Italy' and Silicon Valley in the USA are often quoted as classic examples of clusters, equally impressive are the achievements of ethnic Chinese family businesses in many countries of the Association of South East Asian Nations (ASEAN). The ethnic Chinese have developed a formula for business which appears to have turned them into strong competitors on a world stage. Redding, writing of 'network capitalism', claims that:

> their domains are OEM (original equipment manufacture) production, property, services, retailing, trading ... This network capitalism of the ethnic Chinese is designed to respond to markets which companies from advanced economies would consider disorderly, volatile and very difficult to cope with.[14]

SOCIAL ENTERPRISE

Social enterprises, and the social economy to which they contribute, are concepts that challenge the traditional division of organisational activity into the separate categories of economic or social purpose. The social economy includes those organisations whose aims include both. The term 'social enterprise' may be a relatively new one but the concept which it conveys is not. Some of the oldest non-governmental institutions, such as churches and university colleges, can be included in this category.

There is however no single accepted definition of either a social enterprise or the social economy. In the UK a Treasury report on *Enterprise and Social Exclusion* admits that the social economy is an imprecise term but describes it in general as 'those organisations who are independent of the state and provide services, goods and trade for a social purpose and are non-profit distributing'.[15] These are the three key features that are usually thought of as defining social enterprise: a social purpose; trading or at least supplying goods or services and in return receiving the money needed to pay the operating costs; and not distributing to individuals any profits made. Actually that last point is sometimes omitted on the grounds that there are some organisations (such as cooperatives) with social purposes which do distribute profits. In France the *économie sociale*, from which the term 'social economy' itself probably derives, has been recognised as enjoying an equal role alongside the traditional forms of enterprise and it is often categorised under three forms: associations, mutuals and cooperatives.

Another term used has been the 'third system' which sits

between declining public service provision and a private sector which will supply services strictly where their activities can offer a reasonable return on investment. Its most recent shape has emerged from a variety of national attempts to address two long standing problems: (i) a rising demand for social, personal and community services; (ii) a need to find ways to meet these demands while constraining levels of direct state expenditure and rates of taxation.[16]

The essence of those organisations referred to as social enterprises is that they have all been established for social purposes and not, or not primarily, to maximise financial returns to their investors. However they all survive by securing income for the services they provide. Describing these organisations as 'not-for-profit' can, though, be misleading. Many of them are actually 'not for profit distribution to individuals', although cooperatives can remit profits to their members. But they need to make a profit, or at least to break even over the longer term, to survive and the widespread use of the term 'not-for-profit' may have encouraged some groups to forget this and to concentrate instead on the social purpose: a strategy which has on occasion been fatal to the organisation, as the resultant losses meant that it collapsed. On the other hand there are some organisations in which so much emphasis is placed on achieving financial viability that the overall purpose for which the financial viability is sought gets neglected. However the longevity of some social enterprises shows that problems of viability can be overcome.

There is really no definitive boundary between many social enterprises and other small businesses. Small businesses are not all driven principally or exclusively by the desire to maximise profits; often they are started to provide benefits to their founders and those benefits can include social as well as financial returns. Running social enterprises is however not without its problems, and is frequently a more complex task than that of running other businesses. There is the same need to secure income, without which even survival is not possible, but the income generation is not the end in itself and has to be balanced with achieving the delivery of the social purpose. Then there are issues like motivation. At least some of the staff of these organisations are usually paid, although some rely, at least in part, on volunteers. Board members, unless they are also employees, are generally unpaid and cannot of course receive any share of profits. There can therefore be a tendency for the unpaid contributors to give priority to other activities which help to secure a personal income. Nevertheless having to balance conflicting priorities is not unique

---

ILLUSTRATION 5.4
The contributions of social enterprises
••

As the name 'social economy' suggests, the benefits of its component enterprises are both social and economic. The 'social' benefits can include religious, educational, cultural and charitable benefits, depending on what sort of organisation it is. The economic benefits include employment, which is generally seen as the main one, but can also include the promotion of enterprise (by Local Enterprise Agencies), the provision of financial support (by credit unions), the development of business skills (by community businesses) and the reduction of long-term unemployment (by many back-to-work schemes).

to this sort of business and many do it well, with the result that the people concerned derive considerable satisfaction from the contributions they make.

One reason why social enterprise has not received greater recognition may be that the full extent of its contribution has not been assessed. A possible analogy here is the small business sector and the way it has been viewed by governments. There has always been a small business sector but it was the work of David Birch in America that brought the economic contribution of small businesses into prominence. Before that it was big businesses which were thought to be the principal source of economic benefits such as jobs and growth. It was Birch (see Chapters Two and Seven) who highlighted for the first time the fact that the major portion of new jobs was actually coming from small businesses. It is only since then that they have featured in economic strategies, that steps have been taken to survey them and to quantify their significance, and that significant resources have been put into strategies to support them. Could it be that the social economy is another sector whose economic importance has been overlooked because it has not been highlighted?

One contribution which social enterprises can nevertheless make, which is receiving greater recognition, is the creation of social capital which has been identified as a key factor in community success. It has been described as the networks, norms and trust which facilitate coordination and cooperation for mutual benefit and which may explain why some communities facing similar economic, social and demographic issues cope better than others. For those who are trying to address the needs of disadvantaged communities, the concept of social capital can explain why earlier

CASE 5.2
Sustainable livelihoods
··

The 'sustainable livelihoods' model was developed as a guide to poverty alleviation. It is intended to provide an analytical structure for examining the complexity of community livelihoods. It identifies five types of capital asset upon which people can draw: social, human, natural, physical and financial; which have limited substitution potential and all of which are considered to be important for building a strong community. Whereas it had been thought that providing money, the financial capital, had been an answer to many problems, this model shows that a wider approach is needed.

These capitals have been described as:

Social capital

Social capital is taken to mean the social resources upon which people draw in pursuit of their livelihood objectives and which are developed through networks and connectedness, either vertical or horizontal, that increase people's trust and ability to work together and expand their access; membership of more formalised groups which often entails adherence to mutually agreed or commonly accepted rules, norms and sanctions; and relationships of trust, reciprocity and exchanges that facilitate cooperation.

Human capital

Human capital represents the skills, knowledge, ability to work, and good health that together enable people to pursue different livelihood strategies.

Natural capital

Natural capital is the term used for the natural resources and resource stocks used for livelihoods. These include the air breathed, the land farmed and the trees used.

Physical capital

Physical capital is comprised of the basic infrastructure and producer goods needed to support livelihoods. The infrastructure consists of changes to the physical environment that help people to meet their needs and to be more productive, and includes affordable transport, secure buildings, adequate water supply, affordable energy and access to information (communications). Producer goods are the tools and equipment that people use to function more productively.

Financial capital

Financial capital denotes the financial resources that people use to achieve their livelihood objectives, and which can be exchanged for some of the other 'capitals'.

Source: Based on extracts from the Department for International Development, *Sustainable Livelihoods Guidance Sheets*, October 2001, obtained from www.dfid.gov.uk and www.ids.ac.uk/livelihoods

Points raised

Community welfare needs more than just a financial input. Here we have a list which suggests that five main capitals are necessary.

attempts based largely on financial support have not produced the results required, and focuses attention instead on social enterprises which can build social capital.

One criticism sometimes made of the benefits provided by social enterprises is that the employment they provide is often of 'low quality'. While this may be true in some cases, in others it is a judgement which is itself open to question. Often it seems to be based on the concept of a quality job as one which contributes most to economic development and which is therefore probably full-time, export-based, high value-added (and therefore highly remunerated), and in a new technology area (which is therefore likely to last longer than an old one). However a high level of remuneration may not be all that people want from a job. They may also want their jobs to be locally-based, to be at convenient hours, to have attractive working conditions and to fit the rest of their lives. Some jobs which satisfy these requirements may not be the jobs which suit the economic dimension. In assessing job quality it would seem therefore that there is more than one dimension to be considered and a compromise often has to be made.

Community enterprise

A term which has been used in the context of social enterprise is community enterprise (see also Chapter Four). The creation of new enterprises or the taking of new initiatives is perceived as a vital activity for any community hoping to have a thriving social and economic life. Some communities, however, appear to lack sufficient individual enterprising action to generate and develop new ideas that lead to improvement. Krueger notes that:

> Economically disadvantaged communities often suffer from low self-efficacy. Communities suffering from poverty often reflect the symptoms of learned helplessness, a perceived inability to help themselves. People cannot lift themselves up by their boot straps if they perceive themselves as having no boots.[17]

The low levels of economic activity they have experienced, associated with high rates of unemployment, often result in a lack of confidence, a lack of relevant skills, a lack of resources and a lack of infrastructure. This can be a vicious circle of deprivation: there is a lack of business tradition, little enterprise, and an absence of entrepreneurs. There are therefore no role models and a lack of confidence is reinforced. That is the antithesis of an enterprise culture.

Community enterprise, if it is distinguished from social enterprise, seems generally to be considered to be enterprise which, while fitting a social enterprise definition, is specifically run for the benefit of a particular community, often by a group of people from that community. Sometimes individuals acting together as a team or group can demonstrate qualities, command resources and engage in enterprising behaviour in a way that acting individually they would not. The reasons why group action occurs when individual action does not are an interesting subject of surmise. No doubt issues of motivation, knowledge, skills (as well as of access to resources) and networks all contribute (and a greater readiness to take risks when part of a group). Community enterprise is particularly recognised in community businesses, which have been defined in various ways, but generally are business ventures that not only return to the community any surplus they create but also benefit the community in other ways, such as by working on projects that enhance the environment or by developing skills of community members in their workforces.

Quite often the catalyst for effective community group action is an outsider or enterprising community member who mobilises, and releases, the latent enterprise in others. Such an individual is often referred to as a community entrepreneur. Such enterprises need not have an economic purpose; the purpose can also be social, such as to establish a refuge for victims of domestic violence or for drug users, leading to the term 'social entrepreneurship'. There is evidence, however, that the process of nurturing community or social entrepreneurship is little different from that of individual entrepreneurs. According to Krueger, 'Communities need to create a climate that enhances perceptions of feasibility and desirability.'[18]

Communities have also shown that they increasingly want other things as well as wealth, things which are not themselves wealth-creating, or at least not in the short term. Environmental worries are a case in point, and the rising perception of the importance of 'green' issues testifies to the strength of this concern. Many of the initiatives taken in this area, even if they are not business initiatives, are nevertheless also enterprising. They are also examples of community enterprise and can be the work of community entrepreneurs.

Various attempts have been made to define the concept of the community entrepreneur, and there is general agreement that it is about the use of personal networking, facilitation and resource accessing skills (that is to say enterprise skills) so as to improve a local community in both social and economic areas. Community entrepreneurs facilitate community enterprise in the way that the more traditional entrepreneurs facilitate business development, although, while enterprise in the context of business is often seen in the start-up of new businesses, community enterprise is generally not applied to the start-up of new communities but to the revitalisation of old ones.

Communities are affected by many forces, including structural change, and they can, if action is not taken to counter the effects of those forces, die as a result. Often that structural change has an economic content, such as shifts in the pattern of industry or agriculture, but that does not mean that all the community needs is economic assistance. Community decline, for instance, can often be seen in rural communities where changing patterns of agriculture have reduced both the absolute and the relative wages of agricultural employment. The result can be a move of some people, often the more able ones, to areas where there are more employment opportunities. Their departure in turn takes demand out of the local community, which loses the critical mass it needs to support local shops, schools and other facilities. A vicious spiral results.

Correcting this is not simply a matter of providing an alternative to the lost agricultural employment. It often requires a combination of local economic

Table 5.1 Autonomous and community entrepreneurs compared

Autonomous entrepreneurs	Community entrepreneurs
Aim for the growth of personal resources as the main personal goal	Aim for the development of the community as the main personal goal
Enhance own self-competence	Help to build the self-respect and competence of others
Mobilise resources to build their own enterprises	Inspire others to start their own enterprises
Put themselves at the top of the organisation	Regard themselves as the coordinator in a loose federation
See authority and society interest groups as hindrances	See authority and society interest groups as potential supporters and resource providers

Source: Adapted from B. Johannisson and A. Nilsson, 'Community Entrepreneurs: Networking for Local Development', *Entrepreneurship and Regional Development* 1989; 1: 5. Reproduced by kind permission of Taylor & Francis, Publishers. Consult www.tandf.co.uk/journals

initiatives, of direct action to secure local services, of improvements to the local environment, of local cultural development and of local confidence-raising. Community decline is not irreversible, and there are now many examples of successful community entrepreneurship in which the application of enterprise has built a better community.

There is therefore much in common between community and business enterprise. They both need a vision of what is possible, they both require the application of resources to achieve that vision, they both involve the acceptance of a level of risk and they both generally need personal drive to make them work. There are however some differences, as Table 5.1 shows.

THE ADVANTAGES AND DISADVANTAGES OF ENTERPRISE

> All that glisters is not gold.
>
> Shakespeare, *The Merchant of Venice*

There is, in many places, a prevailing desire to promote enterprise which is in turn based on the assumption that enterprise is essentially something of value and that it is a good thing. It may therefore be necessary to temper this implication by looking at some of the disadvantages of enterprise as well as its advantages and by pointing out some of the problems and the downside of enterprise. These can lie in the results of the practice of enterprising behaviour, in the way that a label of enterprise can appear to justify otherwise undesirable practices, and in the assumption that true enterprising behaviour is what should always be encouraged.

Enterprise can get things done, it can change things, it can give rein to creativity and innovation. In the context of business it can provide people with financial returns, with greater freedom, with a greater sense of achievement and with more enjoyment. However enterprise, it has been said, is spelt R-I-S-K. It is important therefore, when promoting enterprise, to remember that, inherent in enterprise and especially in enterprise in the business context, is risk: the risk of loss of career and of livelihood, of loss of money and resource, and of loss of reputation. While in an enterprising culture it may be expected that many new ventures will work and that as a result, on average, things will progress, it must be remembered that individual initiatives, and the individual people behind them, will not all follow that average path. Some will fail. If however no one is prepared to risk that failure, which is a necessary condition for any venture, then little will progress. An economy is like an ecosystem in nature: organisms in it cannot stand still and survive, at least not for long. In a healthy environment there are both births and deaths. If a living organisation does not continue to renew itself it will die, but not all renewal initiatives will work.

Just as enterprise does not ensure success, neither is it a magic cure-all. It can be an important element in economic, or other, improvement. However, the ways in which it is promoted can be both highly distorting and distorted. They can suggest that it is itself sufficient and can highlight selfish aspects only, as if they alone were what mattered.

If enterprise can be misused in this way, do we want it at all? Is it a force for good, or for bad, or is it actually neutral with the potential goodness, or badness, lying in the way it is used? Some resist it because they see it as replacing clearer positive values with something that is at best only neutral. Attempts to introduce enterprise education into schools have been seen by its proponents as a long-needed attempt to help schools educate their students for a life in the 'real world'. Others, however, have resisted these attempts as propaganda and as a preparation only for the 'nasty' commercial world of business without introducing any positive elements such as consideration, tolerance or generosity. 'Do we really want our nine-year-olds to be adopting such a hard-nosed attitude – shouldn't they, during their ever-shrinking childhood, be thinking about saving the whale, rather than contracting to sell apples in the school tuck shop?'[19] While it can be pointed out that attempting to save the whale will itself require enterprise, there is still the potential danger that the application of commercial considerations will have the opposite effect.

Business failure

One area in which the drawbacks of enterprise are most obvious is that of business failure. In the world of business, failure is not uncommon, but it is often not possible to quantify it. Storey[20] points out that, in the UK, statistics on business failure are bedevilled with problems over definitions and the choice of variables to be used in their measurement. Terms such as bankruptcy, insolvency, failure, ceasing to trade and closure are used at the level of the individual, the plant and the company; and in any case, ceasing to trade and closure may not actually be failures. (See also 'Termination' in Chapter Six.) Storey concludes that we do not really know how many firms go out of business each year because failure is measured by recording compulsory liquidations; individual bankruptcies; company deregistrations; self-employment termination; and VAT deregistrations, and we do not know how many of these might actually be for positive reasons.

Differences in failure rates amongst different types of ownership have been explored and, for instance, there is some a priori evidence that businesses run by women do not survive as long as male-owned firms. In the USA Boden and Nucci[21] argue that women, because of their work and life experiences, do not accumulate as much human and financial capital as men. They are less likely than men to acquire the knowledge, skill and financial resources needed to run a viable business. In contrast some recent work in Britain by Chell and Baines[22] points to numerous contradictions in research findings in this area and to the lack of sophistication in research methods. Furthermore, empirical research by Chell and Baines on the performance of micro-businesses shows that there are no significant differences between that of male-owned and female-owned firms.

However, in spite of the lack of clarity over the extent of failure rates, businesses do fail and indications of this in the UK are to be found in the following types of statistics.

Insolvency figures

A company or person with debts which they cannot pay is said to be insolvent, and it is reported that over 40,000 businesses collapsed in Great Britain in 2001. This figure was made up of 16,724 company liquidations and 23,790 business bankruptcies. In France approximately 50,000 firms and in Europe approximately 150,000 businesses collapsed in the same year.[23]

VAT deregistrations

Burns[24] considers that VAT data offer the best guide to the changing structure of the SME sector and notes that in the UK, during 1999, there were 178,500 VAT registrations and 172,000 deregistrations, leaving 1,658,100 VAT-registered firms at the end of the year.

Movement out of self-employment

There was a considerable increase in the number of self-employed persons in the UK in the 1980s (see Figure 1.1 in Chapter One) with over three million people registered as self-employed in 1986. A similar trend is evident in Canada where Lin, Picot and Compton[25] report that in the 20 years between 1977 and 1997 the number of self-employed persons more than doubled to a total of approximately two and a half million. However, while entries to self-employment outnumbered exits in every year between 1982 and 1994 and led to a gain of almost 30,000 new workers per year, 'over 200,000 self-employed workers ended their entrepreneurial pursuits every year between 1981 and 1994'.

The consequences of failure

If a business fails employees lose their jobs, shareholders lose their investments, 'creditors must suffer through exceedingly long and potentially expensive legal avenues of debt collection; and managers may lose credibility and reputation, effectively precluding them from future jobs'.[26] Since liquidations are most common among firms which have large capital requirements, the potential financial losses can be severe. Furthermore, the stigma attached to failure can be powerful and may limit the likelihood of failed owners getting another chance.

Being an owner-manager is a risky form of enterprise and if an individual is forced out of business the costs can be considerable. Self-employed people in particular tend to create ventures in sectors with few barriers to entry, and competition in these crowded areas is severe. Even if they do not actually fail, they may make little money. They may not accumulate pension funds or savings, with the result they have little financial security, and if they do lose their businesses, their financial prospects can be bleak,[27] especially if they become bankrupt as a consequence. They (and possibly their families) may lose all their assets and they may not be in a position to avail themselves of the protection afforded to bankrupts.[28] Self-employment for some can therefore be the route to impoverishment, not to success.

Learning from failure

Wisdom is meaningless until our own experience has given it meaning.
Bergen Evans

Despite its harmful consequences an element of failure is an inevitable and even an essential ingredient of an enterprising economy. Indeed a high start-up rate and a consequent high rate of mortality among firms are often seen as indicative of a vibrant economy. Attempting a business formation which fails can also be a very useful learning experience. Entrepreneurship is a multi-skilled job and it is difficult to learn all about it only through education and training. Learning from experience is vital and much can be learned from 'intelligent failure'. Indeed it has been shown[29] that an impressive array of British entrepreneurs, including Mike Gooley, owner of Trailfinders travel firm, Katherine Hamnet, the designer of clothes for the trendy, and Theo Fennell, bespoke jeweller, have all had their business failures. Fennell's jewellery firm went into voluntary liquidation in 1986 and the mistake cost him almost everything. However, he learned a lot and this helped him to do things differently with his other ventures.

Failure can be a good learning experience, particularly if the individual who fails is motivated to find out why, prior to trying again. McGrath[30] considers that an intelligent analysis of the cause(s) of failure is necessary if learning is to occur and suggests that entrepreneurs should adopt some of the procedures adopted by academic researchers when seeking explanations for failure. Entrepreneurship is a complex task and action does not always produce expected outcomes. Therefore entrepreneurs should develop hypotheses or sets of assumptions about the likelihood of achieving specific outcomes. If actual outcomes are at variance with expected ones this information can be used to reformulate assumptions. A mindset which considers deviations between actual and expected outcomes as 'vehicles for testing assumptions rather than as failures'[31] can facilitate the discontinuance of, or the alteration of resource flows to, an entrepreneurial project. McGrath suggests that an experimental approach to entrepreneurial action and the conduct of intelligent post-mortems can help promote a step-by-step approach to the development of entrepreneurial projects. In this way entrepreneurs learn from experience and only commit resources when assumptions have been tested. This helps avoid the financial losses that can occur when 'huge, irreversible investments' are made 'as single attempts at innovation'.[32] Wisdom, it has been said, comes from the sum of our failures.

THE FUTURE OF ENTERPRISE

> Forecasting is difficult – especially when it concerns the future.
>
> Groucho Marx

This book was written in response to an increasing emphasis in recent years on enterprise in many areas of life but especially in the economic field. It is therefore relevant to consider whether that emphasis is likely to continue and whether the concept of enterprise, as described here, is likely to continue to be relevant. The following are some of the trends, ideas and concepts which may influence the future of enterprise.

Technology

The rate of development of technology shows no sign of slowing. One obvious result is to make older technologies obsolete and the industries dependent on them expendable. If technology changes, then businesses dependent on it must change too in order to remain competitive. Nowhere is this more so than in the computer and telecommunications industries. The technological changes have been profound, and this has assisted firms in their search for ever more flexible but cost-effective production methods. However, the impact of computers, assisted by fibre-optic capability, has been even more profound in revolutionising information-processing. Personal computers, electronic mail, fax machines, mobile telephones and the internet have transformed the provision of services such as market research, industrial design and advertising. Knowledge-based industries rely on information-processing ability to confer competitive advantage. Therefore, the combination of computing capacity, a focus on knowledge, and fibre optics has, and will continue to have, a marked impact on the way we work.

No longer is it necessary to work in a fixed location under the direct supervision of a manager. The communications revolution has brought the possibility of global teleworking, reducing the problems of distance and the need for sales premises within easy reach of the customer. Even small businesses can join in and offer something on a worldwide basis. Improved communications provide the opportunity for improved services with faster turnround times, but faster responses also require more flexible organisations. Small businesses are then not only able to join in but can do so at an advantage with respect to their bigger rivals. While many of the initial dot.com ventures which tried to take advantage of enhanced information and communication technology (ICT) may have failed because they were far too optimistic in their projections, nevertheless e-business, with its advantages for small businesses, is a reality and is continuing to grow.

Advances in biotechnology are also having a major impact on our daily lives. Not only can food now be grown in formerly inhospitable areas, but microbes are being developed that destroy waste and toxins and medical advances are taking place on many fronts. Consequently people will be able to live longer in most parts of the world, which will have profound social and economic consequences.

Flexibility and service

The possibility of, and the demand for, flexible production and service are increasing. Large, inflexible production lines with their economies of scale, but also with their associated limitation that 'you can have any colour you like as long as it's black', are no longer the only way to meet customer demands. Customers can have, and now expect, variety as well as relative cheapness. Production must change to provide what customers want to buy, not what the business wants to supply. Businesses compete on flexibility and speed of response as well as on price.

Smaller businesses can be more flexible in their approach and quicker to change to meet new conditions. Service industry, where flexibility, quality and speed of response are of primary importance, has a high proportion of small businesses. These combine organic, flexible structures with the decentralisation of decision-making to those with knowledge and expertise. In addition, the need to solve specific client problems, or to customise products for market niches, will entail the use of temporary project groups to meet customer needs. The equipment used by problem-solving work groups will tend to be sophisticated, but employees will exercise a good deal of discretion in utilising it effectively. The organisations doing this will therefore tend to be smaller, more responsive, quality-conscious and much less bureaucratic than formerly. They may well employ a small number of core professional staff and contract out work that is very specialised or for which demand is uneven. They will both be enterprising themselves and also create the opportunity for the enterprise of others.

Changing lifestyles

It is not only the demands of the world of work that are changing, but also the way people feel that they can live their lives. It used to be the case that people expected to work for as long as they could and not to survive very long after that. Now, however, changed work expectations, combined with longer lifespans, mean that more people are planning for what amount to second lives in which their styles of living will be significantly different from those of their first lives. They are no longer planning on the basis of lifetime careers in one organisation, but are increasingly likely to have a second career in which they will be dependent on their own enterprise for their work and income.

Market changes

Markets are also changing. Consumers want not only improved products and services but also improved by-products from those processes. This is particularly noticeable, for instance, in the field of environmental issues. Businesses now have to consider the social, as well as the economic, consequence of their actions. Those that can't adapt will fail. Consequently there will be openings for new businesses that can adapt and for service businesses to help the others to address, reduce or deal with the unwanted consequences of their actions.

Markets are also becoming more international. In a global environment in which businesses increasingly seek, and are encouraged, to establish overseas subsidiaries, who should adapt to whose culture? Should it be the business which wants to sell or the host country which wants the inward investment? There will be a need to think globally but act locally. That too will require enterprise.

Results

The result of all these, and of other, developments is change. Charles Handy among others has pointed out that organisations can normally cope effectively with rapid change so long as the change is incremental and developmental.[33] Organisations have much more difficulty in coping with discontinuous change, but this, according to Handy, is precisely what is happening in today's world. With this type of change, old ways of thinking and functioning are inappropriate and radical new reasoning is required.

In the economic sphere many of the more developed countries will continue to reduce their reliance on the mass production of consumer durables in favour of high-quality, high-volume, customised goods and services. In essence they can no longer compete in labour-intensive or skill-intensive sectors and must move to knowledge-intensive business. Added value will come from the innovation and knowledge base of people in organisations, not from their physical labour. Changes in markets require firms nowadays to offer 'quality, flexibility and inno-vativeness' along with the 'customisation of products' rather than low-cost, high-volume, standard products.[34]

For these reasons, and for others possibly including the management fashion for 'downsizing', many larger businesses have been actively reducing their direct manpower requirements. Charles Handy has spoken of the 'shamrock organisation' (see also Chapter One): a structure with three parts, each of which has different expectations, management systems and methods of pay-ment. One part is the professional core essential to the survival of the organi-sation; the second part consists of the subcontractors who will actually do much of the work; and the third leaf is the growing number of flexible and tem-porary workers and consultants who are hired for specific jobs as the need arises.

As a consequence, the traditional notion of the career is increasingly a thing of the past. Those in the core, with a 'normal' full-time career, will have to work very hard indeed and face the likelihood of burnout by their 40s. Most will retire in their early 50s and leave their intensive brainwork to a younger generation. They can expect to live for thirty more years, but their source of income will have to change. A large number of people will have job histories characterised by part-time or temporary work assignments. Their earning power will be less than full-time careerists, and they will lack job security.

Other changes may incidentally help with the process of mid-career readjust-ment. There will be the subcontracting opportunities for those who want to take them up and, if individuals have the right mental preparation, then some of them may find that the necessary resources are provided by others. Redundancy pay-ments are one obvious source of investment for new business ventures, and, in countries that have enjoyed a high standard of living for a period, inheritance of the assets accumulated by parents is an increasing factor. Also, it has been suggested that a contributory factor in the recent considerable increase in the number of businesses started by women in some parts of the United States is the life-change occasioned by divorce, combined with the opportunity provided by the alimony payments.

Rapid and discontinuous change therefore seems likely to go on having a major impact on the lives of people, organisations and society. Successful individuals in the world of tomorrow will need to be flexible in their attitudes, their acquisition of skills, and their knowledge base. Faced with ever faster environmental changes, organisations must respond, and people, their most flexible of resources, must be equally responsive. Specific knowledge is important for specific roles, but problem-solving, information search and analysis, and decision-making will be crucial skills. People must be adaptable and be able to learn continuously. They must espouse a 'spirit of inquiry' and develop value systems that encourage 'inquiry, examination, diagnosis and experimentation'.[35] In short, they must be enterprising.

In a situation of discontinuous change individuals, organisations and nations must develop the capacity to cope. In doing this, people who display enterprising attitudes, attributes and behaviours will be particularly useful. Individuals, organisations and countries must become more flexible, responsive, knowledgeable, mobile and proactive; and people who possess enterprising attributes such as boldness, innovation and confidence will not only profit themselves but will lead society in its drive to make necessary changes. The future, or at least a significant part of it, is therefore likely to be made by and to belong to the enterprising.

THE KEY POINTS OF CHAPTER 5

- A number of judgements are sometime made about enterprise. While many people might agree with them they should not go unexplored. They include:
  - enterprise is a relative concept. Whether an individual or society is enterprising or not may depend on with what it is compared;
  - enterprise is a good thing. Enterprising people and economies have become synonymous with successful people and economies;
  - enterprise is essential for economic advancement. There appears to be a correlation between enterprise and economic growth, but the mechanism may need to be understood better;
  - enterprise has strong political and social connotations. Enterprise has come to convey notions of freedom, of market choice and of liberalism and has been used as a label for political changes.
- A number of concepts have been attached in some situations to the word 'enterprise'. These associations include:
  - Free enterprise: Capitalism, and particularly American-style capitalism, has been given the title 'free enterprise', and it has been hailed as the

victor in the economic side of the 'cold war' between the Western Alliance and the Communist Bloc. However, there are other forms of capitalism than the American one, and enterprise flourishes in many of them.

– Dependency: There is a danger that, in trying to promote enterprise, initiatives which use means such as grants have instead promoted dependency. Learned helplessness is a recognised medical problem in which patients learn to become dependent on external assistance and cannot do without it even when their original complaint is cured. Business can suffer from similar problems.

– Clusters and competitiveness: Michael Porter has shown that clusters of strong competing domestic rivals can develop strong international competitiveness. It is a truly enterprising culture that gives the clusters their effectiveness.

• Social enterprises are organisations whose aims include both economic and social purposes. They, and the social economy to which they contribute, are concepts that challenge the traditional division of organisational activity into either economic or social categories. Social enterprises include community enterprises in which enterprise is applied specifically for community benefit.

• Enterprise is frequently promoted as something positive. It does however have a number of real or potential drawbacks. Enterprise involves risk; there can be no guarantee that an enterprising act will succeed and, when it doesn't, there will be some loss. Enterprise is not the magic cure-all some people seem to want it to be. In the business context in particular some failure is to be expected. It can be minimised and it can produce useful lessons, but it can have unfortunate consequences for those involved. Enterprise can be an important element in economic improvement, but a distorted view of it and its benefits is sometimes presented, with the result that enterprise promotion is seen by some as just propaganda for a nasty world of shady commercial dealing.

• Enterprise does however have a future. The pattern of work and business is changing. More or different people will be working in and/or establishing their own small businesses. The reasons for this include technological developments, an increasing demand for flexibility and service, changing life styles and changes in markets. The result is that the future, or at least a significant part of it, is likely to belong to the enterprising.

QUESTIONS, EXERCISES, ESSAY AND DISCUSSION TOPICS

- Do we need more enterprise?
- Can enterprise flourish only under capitalism and, if so, what sort of capitalism?
- 'A social enterprise is not a real enterprise and does not require the same discipline and purpose.' Discuss.
- In enterprise the risk of failure is often underrated. For many people the potential rewards are too few and the risks too great to justify entry into business. Is this true?
- Should we intervene to help failing businesses or failed entrepreneurs?
- Is small business the wealth-creating model for the future?
- Where would you strike the balance between earning and living (see Case 5.1)?
- Where do you think enterprise fits into the sustainable livelihoods model (see Case 5.2)?

SUGGESTIONS FOR FURTHER READING

S. Carter and D. Jones-Evans (eds), *Enterprise and Small Business Development* (London: Financial Times/Prentice-Hall, 2000), Chapter Three.

B. Bolton and J. Thompson, *Entrepreneurs: Talent, Temperament, Techniques* (Oxford: Butterworth-Heinemann, 2000), Chapter Ten.

C. Handy, 'Tocqueville Revisited: The Meaning of American Prosperity', *Harvard Business Review* 2001; 79: 57–63.

C. Whyley, *Risky Business: The Personal and Financial Costs of Small Business Failure* (London: Policy Studies Institute, 1998).

Policy Action Team 3, *Enterprise and Social Exclusion* (London: HM Treasury, 1999): www.hm-treasury.gov.uk/docs/1999/pat3.html

REFERENCES

1 P. D. Reynolds, M. Hay, W. D. Bygrave, S. M. Compand and E. Autio, *Global Entrepreneurship Monitor 2000 Executive Report* (Kansas City, MO: Kauffman Centre for Entrepreneurial Leadership at the Ewing Marion Kauffmann Foundation, 2001).
2 R. Burrows, *Deciphering the Enterprise Culture: Entrepreneurship, Petty Capitalism and the Restructuring of Britain* (London: Routledge, 1991), p. 5.

3   *Ibid.*, p. 9.
4   W. Hutton, 'Ethics Man Finds No Place In the New Enterprise Era', *The Guardian* ©, 21 March 1994.
5   A. Smith, *An Enquiry into the Nature and Causes of the Wealth of Nations* (Edinburgh: Adam and Charles Black, 1882, first published in 1776).
6   For a discussion of Smith's and Hayek's contribution to economic theory, see D. King, *The New Right* (Basingstoke: Macmillan (now Palgrave Macmillan), 1987), pp. 70–90.
7   W. Hutton, *The State We're In* (London: Vintage, 1996), p. 237.
8   M. Friedman, *Capitalism and Freedom* (Chicago: University of Chicago Press, 1962), p. 200.
9   W. Keegan, *The Spectre of Capitalism* (London: Random House, 1992), p. 106, cited in M. Thomas, 'Marketing: In Chaos or Transition?', *European Journal of Marketing* 1994; 28: 55–62.
10 Hutton (1996), *op. cit.*, p. xxviii.
11 Department of Economic Development, *Competing in the 1990s: The Key to Growth* (Belfast: Department of Economic Development), p. 44.
12 M. Porter, 'The Competitive Advantage of Nations', *Harvard Business Review* 1990; March–April: 82.
13 *Ibid.*: 74.
14 G. Redding, 'Three Styles of Asian Capitalism', in 'Mastering Enterprise', No. 7, *Financial Times* ©, 13 January 1997, p. 11.
15 *Enterprise and Social Exclusion*, HM Treasury Policy Action Team Report 3 (London: HMSO, 1999), p. 101.
16 *The Third System, Employment and Local Development*, a report prepared for DG-V of the European Commission in respect of the Capitalisation Project on the Role of the Third System in Employment and Local Development (Brussels: Office of Official Publications of the European Communities, 2000).
17 N. F. Krueger, *Prescription for Opportunity: How Communities can Create Potential for Entrepreneurs*, Working paper 93-03 (Washington, DC: Small Business Foundation of America, 1995), p. 16.
18 *Ibid.*, 'Executive summary'.
19 K. Gold, 'Must We Buy Schooling from Marks and Spencer?', *The Observer* ©, 21 January 1990.
20 D. Storey, *Understanding the Small Business Sector* (London: Routledge, 1994).
21 R. T. Boden and A. R. Nucci, 'On the Survival Prospects of Men's and Women's New Business Ventures', *Journal of Business Venturing* 2000; 15: 347–62.
22 E. Chell and S. Baines, 'Does Gender Affect Business Performance? A Study of Micro-Businesses in Business Services in the UK', *Entrepreneurship and Regional Development* 1998; 10: 117–35.
23 Statistics reported by *Credit Control Journal* 1999; 20: 1. The figures are based on data provided by Dun and Bradstreet.
24 P Burns, *Entrepreneurship and Small Business* (London: Palgrave (now Palgrave Macmillan), 2001).
25 Z. Lin, G. Picot and J. Compton, 'The Entry and Exit Dynamics of Self-Employment in Canada', *Small Business Economics* 2000; 15: 105–25, at 108.
26 Z. J. Acs and D. A. Gerlowski, *Managerial Economics and Organization* (Englewood Cliffs, NJ: Prentice-Hall, 1996), p. 249.
27 N. Meager, 'Does Unemployment Lead to Self-Employment?', *Small Business Economics* 1992; 4: 87–103.

28 D. Brooksbank, 'Self-Employment and Small Firms', in S. Carter and D. Jones-Evans (eds), *Enterprise and Small Business* (London: Financial Times/Prentice-Hall, 2000), pp. 7–31.

29 R. Rigby, 'There's No Disgrace in an Honest Business Failure', *Management Today* 2001; July: 74–6.

30 R. G. McGrath, 'Falling Forward : Real Options Reasoning and Entrepreneurial Failure', *Academy of Management Review* 1999; 24: 13–31.

31 McGrath, *op. cit.*: 23.

32 McGrath, *op. cit.*: 24.

33 C. Handy, *The Age of Unreason* (London: Arrow, 1990).

34 C. Alter and J. Hage, *Organizations Working Together* (Newbury Park, CA: Sage, 1993), p. 14.

35 E. H. Schein and W. G. Bennis, *Personal and Organization Change Through Group Methods* (New York: Wiley, 1965), p. 7.

ENTERPRISE AND SMALL BUSINESS

INTRODUCTION

Part One of this book explores the concept of enterprise, what it is and why it is the subject of interest. It shows that the word 'enterprise' has a range of meanings: from the narrow meaning of enterprise, referring to small businesses and the act of starting them, to the broad meaning of enterprise as a set of personal attributes and behaviours that can be demonstrated in a wide variety of different situations and contexts.

The use of the word 'enterprise' to relate specifically to small business is, however, very widespread, and it is the economic and social benefits that small businesses are adjudged to bring that are the prime reasons for the wide interest in enterprise. Part Two therefore looks at this aspect of enterprise in more detail.

The specific aspect of small businesses that distinguishes them from other businesses is obviously their size. Because of this they tend to have some features in common, but they are by no means all identical. There are many varieties of small business, which differ for instance in their stage of development, in their business sector or in the attitudes and aptitudes of their owners. These characteristics and variations are explored in Chapter Six.

Small businesses are not however just smaller versions of big businesses. They have a number of distinctive features that are not always obvious to the untutored observer. Those who wish to understand small businesses therefore need insight into the specific nature of such organisations. This is indicated in Chapter Seven.

If small businesses are popular because they provide employment potential, growth businesses are particularly desirable because they are fewer in number and create disproportionately more jobs. Targeting them may therefore seem to be attractive, but it is not necessarily feasible or desirable. Chapter Eight looks at business growth: its meanings, components, driving forces, motivations and contextual influences.

Although the aim of small business growth policy has been to encourage small businesses to get bigger, the terms 'enterprise' and 'small business' still tend to be used synonymously and, from the perspective of the bigger business, some aspects of 'small' can still seem to be 'beautiful'. Chapter Nine therefore looks at the advantages of small size from this perspective. It considers attempts by bigger organisations to continue to be entrepreneurial, a process known as 'corporate entrepreneurship' or 'intrapreneurship', and at situations where it really does seem to be an advantage to be small.

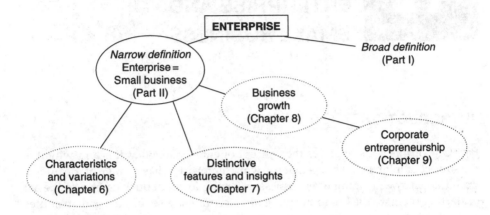

CHAPTER 6

SMALL BUSINESS: DEFINITIONS, CHARACTERISTICS AND NEEDS

CONTENTS

KEY CONCEPTS
··

This chapter covers:
- the definitions of a small business;
- the different perspectives provided by taking the entrepreneur and the business as the core unit of study;
- the stage model approach, its variations and limitations, and the main issues at each stage;
- other variations in small businesses, including family firms, and the different issues relevant to them;
- the variations in the people who start businesses and in their motivations.

LEARNING OBJECTIVES
··

By the end of this chapter the reader should:
- know the main definitions of a small business;
- understand the different perspectives produced by taking the business and the entrepreneur as the unit of study;
- understand the stage model, and its limitations;
- appreciate the different managerial and other issues at different stages of business development;
- understand other variations in small businesses and the different issues relevant to them.

INTRODUCTION

This chapter seeks to explore further what is meant by the term 'small business'. Although small businesses have their size in common, and other features associated with, or dependent on, size, they are in many other respects heterogeneous rather than homogeneous. This chapter therefore considers some of the many different definitions of a small business. It considers small businesses at different stages of their development, in different sectors and under different types of ownership. It seeks to establish what they have in common, as well as the range of their diversity.

DEFINITIONS

ILLUSTRATION 6.1
Some official definitions of a small business*
....

United Kingdom
In the UK for statistical purposes the DTI (The Department for Trade and Industry) usually uses the following definitions:
- Micro firm   Up to nine employees
- Small firm   Up to 49 employees (includes micro)
- Medium firm   50–249 employees
- Large firm   250 employees and over

Companies Act
Section 249 of the Companies Act of 1985 states that a company is 'small' if it satisfies at least two of the following criteria:
- a turnover of not more than £2.8 million;
- a balance sheet total of not more than £1.4 million;
- not more than 50 employees.

A medium-sized company must satisfy at least two of the following criteria:
- a turnover of not more than £11.2 million;
- a balance sheet total of not more than £5.6 million;
- not more than 250 employees.

Value added tax
In the UK the VAT registration threshold is a turnover of £55,000 and the deregistration limit is a turnover of £53,000.

Small Firms Loan Guarantee Scheme
The scheme applies to businesses with fewer than 200 employees and with a turnover of not more than £3 million (manufacturing) or £1.5 million (other eligible businesses).

Corporation tax
The Small Companies Rates of corporation tax apply to businesses with taxable profits of up to £300,000 and a marginal rate applied to profits between £300,000 and £1,500,000. Over that the full rate applies.

British Bankers' Association (BBA)
For BBA statistical purposes, small businesses are defined as those having an annual account turnover of up to £1 million per year.

* At the time of writing (June 2002)

European Commission

In 1996 the European Commission adopted the following definitions of SMEs:

Maximum	Micro-enterprise	Small	Medium-sized
Number of employees	10	50	250
Turnover (million Euro)	N/a	7	40
Balance sheet total (million Euro)	N/a	5	27
Independence criterion[a]	N/a	25%	25%

[a] The independence criterion refers to the maximum percentage that may be owned by one, or jointly owned by several, enterprises not satisfying the same criteria.

To qualify as an SME both the number of employees and the independence criteria must be met, and either of the turnover or the balance sheet total criteria.

The Bolton Report in 1971[1] was very significant in developing the understanding of small businesses in the UK. It defined a small business by reference to an ideal type:

First, in economic terms, a small firm is one that has a relatively small share of its market. Secondly an essential characteristic of a small firm is that it is managed by its owners or part-owners in a personalised way, and not through the medium of a formalised management structure. Thirdly, it is also independent in the sense that it does not form part of a larger enterprise and that the owner-managers should be free from outside control in taking their principal decisions.

However the report also acknowledged the weakness of a qualitative definition and offered the following quantification for different sectors:

Manufacturing	200 employees or fewer
Retailing	Turnover of £50,000 pa or less
Wholesale trades	Turnover of £200,000 pa or less
Construction	25 employees or fewer
Mining/quarrying	25 employees or fewer
Motor trades	Turnover of £100,000 pa or less
Miscellaneous services	Turnover of £50,000 pa or less
Road transport	Five vehicles or fewer
Catering	All excluding multiples and brewery-managed pubs

This rather arbitrary approach gave rise to problems, for instance in respect of businesses which were across sectors. But still today there is no single, clear, precise and widely accepted definition of what is a small business. Different definitions exist, often for different purposes: such as the application of support policy, taxation or legislation. Many people, however, feel that they know what is meant by a 'small business'. It is one that has few employees, a low turnover, little or no formal structure and is usually managed by one person, who is also the business owner. It is these characteristics that make a small business behave in the way it does, and many feel that the key point at which a growing business ceases to be small is when it has to change its organisational and control system, from the loose and informal to the structured and formal, if it is to continue to be effective. However, most definitions use the size of the business as its distinguishing feature, presumably because that is easier to measure. Definitions vary widely in the way they measure the size of a small business. Some use turnover, which can however change over time with inflation; but most go for employment, which, as already indicated, also happens to be the benefit which very often provides the rationale for small business support. Even when employment is used there are different definitions. The EU definition of an SME[†] used to be one that had fewer than 500 employees, but the limit is now 250. (See Illustration 6.1.) The USA Small Business Administration uses 500 as the limit for its remit. Elsewhere the limit is often set at 200, which many take as being closer to the size that forces a change in organisational structure. Some use 100 as the limit, and there are some small business agencies which use 50.

There are also definitions that seek to subdivide the category that others describe as small, by separating those businesses that are merely 'small' from those that are even smaller. As well as the EU definitions quoted above there are others such as:

- self-employed   one person in the business;
- micro-business   up to 19 employees, or up to nine;
- small business   20 to 99 employees, or ten to 99;
- medium-sized business 100 to 499 employees.

'Small' may also be employed as a relative term, rather than an absolute one. A 200-person business may not be small in terms of the absolute definitions given above, but if it is a shipyard then it would be very small compared with the average for its industry sector. One definition of a small business is therefore simply a business with a scale of operations significantly below the average, or below the minimum size usually necessary for efficient operations in its sector.

The above definitions are almost entirely quantitative, but there are qualitative ones. Small businesses tend to share a number of qualities. They are generally businesses that serve only local customers and have only a very limited share of the available market; that are owned by one person, or by a small group of people; and are managed by their owners, who deal with all management issues usually with little other help; and they are independent businesses, not parts of, or owned by, larger companies.

[†] The term 'small business' is, on occasion, used to embrace medium-sized businesses also. To avoid confusion, however, the now ubiquitous term 'SME' (small and/or medium-sized enterprise) has now entered the language, particularly that of policy-makers.

A definition based on only one of these qualities would be in danger of excluding some businesses that others would regard as small. A number of qualitative characteristics should therefore be included. One attempt to do so has been to define a small business as one which possesses at least two of the following four characteristics:

- management of the business is independent. Usually the managers are also the owners;
- capital and ownership are provided by an individual or a small group;
- the areas of operation are mainly local, with the workers and owners living in one home community. However the market need not be local;
- the relative size of the business within its industry must be small when compared with the biggest units in the field. This measure can be in terms of sales volume, number of employees or other significant comparisons.[2]

Most of the definitions of a small business given above are, however, in effect only attempts to provide a proxy for what is the essence of 'smallness' in business units. Smallness is about being autonomous yet having limited resources of manpower, time, skills, expertise and finance, and therefore having to be dependent on external support. It is about having to cope with greater uncertainty and about carrying greater risk while having few opportunities for risk-spreading. It is also about:

- the influence of ownership on entrepreneurial behaviour; having greater individual authority;
- managing a total activity and carrying total responsibility; being closer to customers, and being potentially more flexible and adaptable; managing networks of suppliers, customers, and financiers;
- paying greater attention to business opportunities;
- taking a strategic approach while also having close and informal control structures and communication channels;
- embracing a 'can-do' culture.

These are the things that being small means and that present challenges and opportunities different from those in larger businesses.

THE ENTREPRENEUR OR THE BUSINESS

The previous section gives some definitions of a small business but, before going on to explore other aspects of the concept of a small business, another issue should be highlighted. So far the emphasis has been on the firm, on the enterprise or business created, and that tends to imply that it is that entity which is the primary unit of analysis. It is easy to see why there should be such a focus. It is the business which can be seen to start or to end, it is the business which has the turnover or employment which can be measured, and it is the business which delivers things people want such as jobs and economic growth.

This existence of the business as a potential subject for consideration is clearest when the business is a separate legal entity, such as a limited company, and is least clear when the business is the activity of an individual operating as a 'sole trader'. The assumption may have been that the sole trader should be seen as an embryonic limited company which has not yet made it, but nevertheless the lack of a clear distinction between a sole trader and his or her business points to an important consideration. The business is not only the creation of the person but is also the expression of the person, even when the business is legally separate from that person. A person may start up and close down a business but the person will still continue to exist. The closure of the business is not therefore the end of the matter. It might, as in the case of a 'habitual entrepreneur' (see below), be followed by the start-up of another business and the reason for the closure may lie with the entrepreneur rather than with the business. To make sense of the totality of the entrepreneurial process it is therefore necessary to take the entrepreneur as the focus and unit of investigation, not the business.

Analysing the small business process from this different perspective also reveals another potentially useful focus: that of the group, or cluster,[3] of businesses linked together in some way through common ownership and management by an entrepreneur or entrepreneurial team. Measured on the performance of their latest venture, habitual entrepreneurs may seem to perform no better than novice entrepreneurs, whereas if the performance is measured across the cluster it has been found to be considerably better. Indeed is it quite likely that new firm formation within a cluster is a growth mechanism and therefore that, while individual firms in a cluster may not grow, the cluster does.[4] It may also be relevant to realise that the individual businesses in such a cluster may not, at least under the EU definition, be considered to be SMEs because they do not satisfy the ownership criterion.

Another relatively common form of very small business is the part-time business. Here, looked at from the perspective of the business, a part-time business may seem to indicate a lack of seriousness, but from the point of view of the person it may be a very sensible arrangement. Therefore exploring many aspects of the subject of business development, the fundamental unit should be the entrepreneur, not the firm.

Novice and habitual entrepreneurs, serial and portfolio entrepreneurs

There are entrepreneurs who start just one business and those who start more than one. The term 'habitual entrepreneur' was coined to describe a person who is not satisfied with starting just one business but who goes on to start others also, either in sequence or simultaneously. He or she was considered to be a special type of entrepreneur, different from the supposedly more common 'novice entrepreneur'. However research, for instance by Scott and Rosa,[5] has indicated that multiple business ownership is more common than had been suspected and has more variety. Habitual entrepreneurs have therefore been subdivided into 'serial entrepreneurs', who start a succession of businesses but only manage one at a time, and 'portfolio entrepreneurs', who start a succession of businesses and keep some or all of them going at the same time.[6]

Scott and Rosa have studied the process of multiple business ownership, considering it to be 'fundamental to understanding the process of capital accumulation in a free enterprise capitalist economy'.[7] Their work on the diversity of business foundations revealed many differences between entrepreneurs as regards the kind of ventures started, the strategies followed and the management practices adopted which, due to the considerable heterogeneity of individual entrepreneurs, could only be categorised on very broad criteria (see Table 6.1).

Owners' motivation

As Elizabeth Chell and her colleagues reported (see Chapter Three) there are different types of entrepreneur with different clusters of traits and behaviours. Different types will have different motivations and these can affect their businesses. There will be a lot of difference between a business developed by a sole owner who wants enough income to support his or her lifestyle and a business currently of the same size developed by a group of investors with a view to maximising its future value.

Owners' motivations (see also Chapter Eight) have been divided into three broad categories:

- *Lifestyle.* This is the description often given to a business run by an individual because it not only facilitates, but is also part of, the lifestyle that individual wants to have. Examples of lifestyle businesses are frequently to be found in art or craft businesses where the owner lives to practise that craft rather than only practising that craft in order to live.
- *Comfort-zone.* A comfort-zone business is typically one that provides its owner with sufficient returns for the level of comfort he or she wants in life. Unlike in the case of the lifestyle business, the basis of the business is less important than the level of benefit it can provide in return for a reasonable amount of effort. In some places the comfort-zone business has been characterised as the 'BMW syndrome'. This is where the level of comfort desired includes the possession of recognised symbols of success. Once that level of comfort is reached, however, there is little incentive to build the business further.
- *Growth.* The 'growth' business is the one that approaches closest to what to many is the ideal business, namely one where the owner wishes to manage the business to maximise its earning potential, especially for the future.

Table 6.1   Three dimensions of habitual entrepreneurship

Dimension 1: The background and nature of the habitual entrepreneur
- Multiple venture founders from corporate backgrounds, who tended to be more deliberate in their formation of business clusters and who used more formal management practices in their new ventures
- Multiple venture founders from financial and consultancy backgrounds, who tended to start their careers as management consultants or financial advisers, as well as high-technology engineers founding new firms with limited managerial experience
- Multiple venture founders from non-corporate backgrounds (mostly associated with traditional family businesses), who were especially creative in reacting to new opportunities but who often lacked the resources or capability to take full advantage of them
- Non-entrepreneurial habitual founders, who were involved in several businesses but as a partner of the true driving entrepreneur

Dimension 2: The nature of ventures founded
- Related diversifications: by far the most common form of new venture
- New types of mainstream venture: a complete change of direction (rare)
- Pilot businesses: 'suck-it-and-see' experimental businesses
- Phantom businesses: non-trading ventures set up to trade but which never got off the ground
- Financial management businesses: businesses set up to manage the funds flowing from other businesses
- Buyouts, mergers and acquisitions
- Holding companies

Dimension 3: The strategies used to create and manage ventures
- Competitive efficiency: many new ventures did appear to some respondents to have resulted in some operational advantage
- Serendipity: entrepreneurial opportunism can appear to be an unplanned and serendipitous process
- Strategic accommodation of serendipity: small business owners can have a high degree of strategic awareness
- Strategic management of adversity: the tendency of most entrepreneurs when faced with recession or financial difficulty is to 'pull in their horns' and reduce or eliminate the formation of new ventures

Source: Based on P. Rosa, 'Entrepreneurial Process of Business Cluster Formation and Growth by "Habitual Entrepreneurs" ', *Entrepreneurship Theory and Practice* 1998; 22: 48–51. Reprinted with the permission of Baylor University, the publisher of *Entrepreneurship Theory and Practice*.

It is the influence of the owner, in whatever category his or her motivations may fall, that is a major determinant of how a business behaves. This is therefore considered further in the next chapter which looks at the particular ways in which small businesses behave.

However, the more traditional approach, and the one used in most research and writing about enterprise, has been to take the business as the key unit of analysis. Therefore this chapter, reflecting that study, now takes the same approach.

THE STAGES OF (SMALL) BUSINESS DEVELOPMENT

Despite the relevance of the entrepreneur's viewpoint, small businesses continue to be the focus of much attention. However they are defined, small businesses exhibit considerable variety. In considering them, and in particular in trying to establish their needs and the issues facing them, it can be helpful to try to distinguish groups or categories of them with common characteristics. One of the usual ways of categorising businesses has been by the stage of their development. However, it is important to recognise that the use of the term 'stage' in relation to the business development process does not mean that businesses develop in discrete phases with clear boundaries between them. Separating the development process into stages is rather like dividing the spectrum of visible light into colours. Traditionally there are said to be seven, but in reality there are not seven distinct colours but a continuing gradation through the colours. We can say that one area is green compared with another area which is yellow, but we cannot say precisely where one changes to the other. Dividing the business development process into stages is helpful, in that there are issues at the heart of each stage that differ from the issues central to other stages; but, while we can indicate broadly the stage of development of a business, we cannot say precisely when it moves from one stage to another.

Like distinguishing colours in the colour spectrum, the number of areas ascribed to the process is a matter of interpretation. However, unlike the colour spectrum, the order of the areas is not necessarily fixed. While a 'pre-start' stage cannot follow 'start-up', and 'termination' has to be the end, businesses do not have to progress through every possible stage between; they can be static, they can grow and they can decline in any order, they can do these things more than once, and they can reverse their steps. There are many models of the different stages and the sequence in which they occur, but the reality is that very few businesses actually follow the models. Many of the models, in the way they are presented, imply steady growth, for instance by presenting a steadily rising line on a plot with axes of size and time. Growth, however, is not the norm, and where there is growth it is generally achieved through a number of discrete steps, rather than by a steady, even progression. It is also important to recognise that these models do not explain what is happening inside a business: they only describe its situation, and they present symptoms not causes. Therefore they do not help in predicting what will happen next to a business.

The stage model

Because the development process is not divided by natural boundaries, there is no single, generally accepted development model. Many different ways have been suggested of segmenting the development of a business. One of the most used is the Churchill and Lewis model. (See Table 6.2.)[8]

Table 6.2   The five stages of business growth

- Existence: staying alive by finding products or services and customers
- Survival: establishing the customer base, demonstrating viability
- Success: confidence in its market position, options for further growth
- Take-off: opting to go for growth
- Maturity: the characteristics of a larger, stable company

Source: N. C. Churchill and V. L. Lewis, 'Growing Concerns: The Five Stages of Small Firm Growth', *Harvard Business Review* 1983; May–June: 31, 32, 34, 40.

Other models, however, have additional stages that come either prior to or after the Churchill and Lewis stages. A model proposed by the Forum of Private Business, for instance, does not stop at maturity, but includes the stages of 'decline' and 'termination', while the Krueger model (see Chapter Three) recognises that the commencement of trading is not itself the beginning of the process but that there are stages before the formation of a business which, while not strictly stages in the development of that particular business, are nevertheless relevant to the development of the entrepreneur and to an understanding of the inception of the business. These prior-to-business-start stages can include the following.

- *Culture.* People are more likely to think of starting a business, and that business is more likely to survive, if the underlying culture is one that will help to nurture awareness and interest as well as ideas and embryonic businesses.
- *The idea.* Before they can proceed to start-up, people need to have the idea that they can start a business and have a product or service idea around which the business can be formed. This is the stage where they are not only aware that business start is possible, but must feel that it might be appropriate for them and that they can do it.
- *The pre-start phase.* This is the process whereby those thinking of starting a business progress from the business idea to the stage of actually starting the business.

A fuller list of stages might therefore include the following: (These stages are described in more detail later in this chapter.)

- culture and awareness;
- idea – both the idea that a business is possible and a product/service idea for it;
- intention;
- pre-start/preparation;
- start-up/inception;
- growth and expansion;
- static – including survival, consolidation, comfort and maturity;
- decline;
- termination.

To show the possible sequences of these stages, this model ('Model X') can be presented diagrammatically, as in Figure 6.1.

Figure 6.1 Small business paths from conception to death

As well as showing both pre-start and termination phases, the model also recognises the dynamics of business development. Despite the straight lines of most models, businesses very rarely progress steadily onwards and upwards. The diagram in Figure 6.2 recognises this by showing possible paths for a business, not only in steady growth, but also in a phase of growth reversal, in stability with possible oscillation, in a merger with another business and in early failure. This model also shows the dominant problems that have to be addressed by a business. It is therefore, in effect, presenting the precursors or stimulators of change, rather than the change itself. These precursors or stimulators are, however, very hard to measure, compared with qualities such as turnover or numbers of employees, and are therefore much harder in practice to use to describe a business. Nevertheless, their presentation can provide useful insights.

The diagram in Figure 6.2 can be extended to show a cohort of firms, for which, at any stage, there are possibilities of closure, steady state, merger or independent growth. The presentation in Figure 6.3 gives some impression of the number of different paths that can be followed in reality, and is very different from the single development line of some models.

Another variation is to draw a parallel between Maslow's hierarchy of needs and the stages of business development:

Maslow's hierarchy	Business stage	Related role
Self-actualisation	Maturity	Leader
Recognition	Expansion	↑
Belonging	Growth	Manager
Security	Survival	↑
Survival	Start-up	Entrepreneur

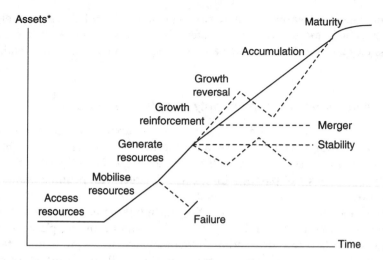

* Firms, as they grow, accumulate assets, both tangible 'fixed' assets and intangible assets such as expertise and reputation. Assets are therefore used here as an indicator of growth.

Source: E. Garnsey, 'A New Theory of the Growth of the Firm', Paper presented to the ICSB 41st World Conference, Stockholm, June 1996, p. 4.

Figure 6.2 Growth process as reflected in possible growth paths

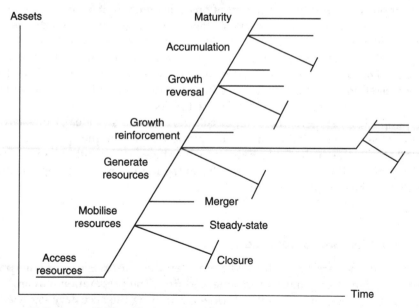

Source: E. Garnsey, 'A New Theory of the Growth of the Firm', Paper presented to the ICSB 41st World Conference, Stockholm, June 1996, p. 18.

Figure 6.3 Diverse trajectories of a cohort of businesses

While the stage model approach may have its drawbacks, it helps nevertheless to divide small businesses into different categories to make them easier to examine. The possible stages in this approach are therefore considered in more detail.

Culture and awareness: the supply of entrepreneurs

What all the listed stages of business development, apart from 'culture / awareness', have in common is that they are all concerned with people who might be or already are, in business. To use a horticultural analogy, they all deal with plants: with sowing the seeds of plants, with growing plants, with pruning plants, with plants flowering and even with plants dying. The 'culture' or 'awareness' stage, however, deals with the preparation of the ground: the preparation of a medium which will encourage, feed and support the seeds and growing plants. Chapter Four has shown that the surrounding human society or culture is important for business growth, just as the condition and type of the soil are important for plants.

The influences on new firm formation can be many and varied. Krueger's model of entrepreneurial potential, described in Chapter Three, and other cognitive approaches illustrate some of the antecedent influences on enterprise. An alternative presentation, which represents the same framework but also highlights some of the specific factors that may be influential in a business context, is shown in Figure 6.4.

This approach illustrates the variety of possible antecedent factors that may be relevant to the 'culture' or 'awareness' stage. This stage can be sub-divided to show the progression from no particular interest in enterprise, through awareness and potential interest, to actual new business formation. This is illustrated in Figure 6.5. Both Figures 6.4 and 6.5 also show the link between enterprise culture in a business sense, and the broad or 'education' definition of enterprise, in that the latter is a necessary precondition for the former.

This approach goes beyond the simple culture/awareness → idea → pre-start → new business model by indicating further gradations within the spectrum.

Another model, which also includes possible stages within culture and awareness, is presented in Figure 6.6. It also shows the importance of the opportunity provided by the education system.

Pre-start: idea and preparation

Businesses do not arise fully fledged from even the most positive of enterprise cultures. A time of preparation is still needed first. The preparation may include identifying a suitable opportunity (the idea), acquiring the necessary knowledge and skills, and locating the contacts who will help. Continuing the horticultural analogy, it is the stage of planting and germination of seeds. The growing medium is important, but seeds are also needed to produce plants and those

Influences upon the entrepreneurial decision

Antecedent influences upon entrepreneur

1 Family and religious background

2 Educational background

3 Psychological makeup

4 Age at time(s) of maximum external opportunity and
   organisational 'push'

5 Earlier career experience

6 Opportunity to form entrepreneurial groups

Incubator organisation

1 Geographic location

2 Nature of skills and knowledge acquired

3 Motivation to stay with or leave organisation

4 Experience in 'small business' setting

External factors

1 Examples of entrepreneurial action and availability of knowledge about
   entrepreneurship

2 Societal attitudes toward entrepreneurship

3 Ability to save 'seed capital'

4 Accessibility and availability of venture capital

5 Availability of personnel and supporting services; accessibility to customers;
   accessibility to university

6 Opportunities for interim consulting

7 Economic conditions

Entrepreneur's
decision

Source: Arnold C. Cooper, 'Technical Entrepreneurship', *R & D Management* 1973;
3: 59–64.

Figure 6.4   Model of new enterprise formation

seeds have to have the ability to take root and to put out leaves. In business terms, negotiating this stage requires both a willingness to start it and some ideas about what might best be done in it.

Krueger (see Chapter Three) has argued that a willingness to start comes from the credibility gained for the proposed action because of its perceived desirability and perceived feasibility; in other words from a recognition that there are rewards

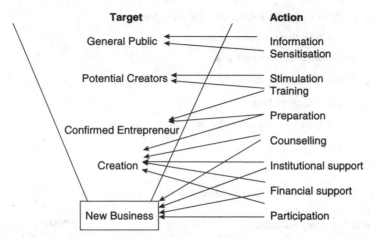

Source: B. Garnier and Y. Gasse, 'An Experience In Training In the Area of Entrepreneurship and Starting a Business in Quebec: The Project "Become an Entrepreneur" ', October 1986.

Figure 6.5 Vickery's model

Stage	What	Where
Stage	*What*	*Where*
Stage 1	Basics ↓	Primary school
Stage 2	Awareness ↓	Secondary school
Stage 3	Creativity	Third level (college / university)
Break for job experience, training, gaining experience, contacts, etc.		
Stage 4	Start-up ↓	In business
Stage 5	Growth	In business

Figure 6.6 Another stages model

that can be gained from starting a business and a desire for those rewards, together with a belief that the rewards can be achieved. It may also be relevant to add that this presupposes that the possibility of engaging in the action in question has already occurred to the person concerned.

If these conditions are met and there is a desire to proceed then it is important to know how. Various suggestions have been made about the key components of the ideal pre-start process. The formula produced by Peterson and Rondstadt (Figure 6.7) summarises some of the key components that are needed for start-up success, components that by implication might then be assembled in the pre-start stage.[9] It is also important to recognise that the pre-start process can be very long.

> **Entrepreneurial success = New venture idea**
>
> **+ Entrepreneurial know-how**
>
> **+ Entrepreneurial know-who**

Source: R. Peterson and R. Rondstadt, 'A Silent Strength: Entrepreneurial Know-Who', *The 16th ESBS/EFMD/IMD Report* (86/4), p. 11.

Figure 6.7   Entrepreneurial success

The pre-start stage can be defined as ending when a business starts, and beginning when there is an intention at some time to prepare for that eventuality.

A traditional view of enterprise has been based on the assumption that some individuals are inherently more enterprising than others. Because of that predisposition towards enterprise, it was assumed that, given the right stimulus, such individuals were more likely to try starting a business. There could then be virtually no pre-start stage in the sense defined above. Another view of enterprise, and of enterprising behaviour, is considered in Chapter Three. It is based on the attributes and resources that an individual may possess, or may believe that he or she possesses. Attributes may include self-confidence, diligence, perseverance, interpersonal skills and innovative behaviour. Resources may include finance, experience, knowledge, skills, a network and a track record. It is suggested then that it is the interaction amongst these factors that produces a rational response, on the basis of available information, when the possibility occurs of a business start-up.

ILLUSTRATION 6.2
Starting a business
....

Given a suitable trigger, the likelihood of start-up is a function of the perceived attributes and resources possessed by the individual, or individuals, concerned, plus the perceived opportunity and the availability of assistance.

It is acknowledged that there is inertia in individual behaviour and that it may take a discontinuity in work, or in life, to trigger a review of an individual's situation. Whether this review will lead to an individual trying his or her own enterprise will then depend on the attributes and resources he or she has accumulated and his or her perception of the opportunity and of environmental factors such as the availability of grants. The acquisition of those attributes and resources, if it is done with a view to a possible business start, is the pre-start stage. It is generally perceived as a stage of individual, or small team, preparation. If the culture stage can be seen to relate to the concepts covered in Chapter Four, the pre-start stage relates to the concepts in Chapter Three.

An individual, or a team, can be helped to acquire the components for a start-up. There are many ways in which this can be done, but the following paragraphs illustrate some of the possibilities.

The idea

The 'idea' can cover both the idea of starting a business and the product or service idea for a particular business. The former comes from the issues just explored. The latter can come from a number of sources, but usually from one's own experience. Table 6.3 is one list of sources of ideas common in small businesses.

Know-how

Know-how covers a number of areas of knowledge and skill, all of which may be needed by the owner-manager of a small business if that business is to be successful. This know-how has been shown to have (at least) four dimensions (see Table 6.4).

Small business training is often the means offered for increasing small business know-how. Despite the plethora of courses sometimes offered, it is important to recognise the potential barriers that can make small business owners averse to conventional forms of training, and some of the possible counterbalancing incentives (see Table 6.5).

One skill often overlooked is communication – the ability to relate to and exchange appropriate information with the people who matter to the business, including staff, suppliers, customers, funders and advisers. It has been suggested

Table 6.3 The self-employment spectrum

Form or approach	Platform	Springboard
Turning a hobby into a business	Long-standing passion	Personal connections
Becoming a professional consultant/trainer	Specialised knowledge	Professional contacts
Acquiring an existing business	Managerial and marketing skills	Financial resources
Taking on a franchise	Organisational ability	Financial and marketing resources
Creating a business of your own	Enterprising spirit	Marketplace
Matching personal and market potential	Personal knowledge and potential	Knowledge and potential of yourself and others
Developing your vision	Personal charisma and inspiration	Economic and social need/potential

Source: Reprinted by permission of Sage Publications Ltd © from R. Lessem, 'Getting Into Self-Employment', *Management Education and Development* 1984; Spring: 31.

Table 6.4   The four dimensions of management development

Functional knowledge and skills	*Generic management knowledge and skills*
The technical knowledge and abilities appropriate to the business. The main know-how typically of 'the butcher, the baker and the candlestick maker'	Planning, organising, managing time, negotiating, coordinating resources, solving problems (not functionally specific)
Business and strategic awareness	*Personal competencies*
Understanding the bigger picture, conceptual skills, analysis, synthesis, creativity, opportunity-spotting	Results orientation, initiative, interpersonal skills, enthusiasm, perseverance, commitment, leadership

Source: Based on R. E. Boyatzis, *The Competent Manager: A Model for Effective Performance* (New York: Wiley, 1982).

Table 6.5   Barriers and incentives to training

Barriers	*Incentives*
Cost implications	*Value*
• Time is the most valuable and precious resource and time spent on training is considered to be a cost not an investment	• Courses of real current relevance that require minimal time off the job, and have identified early benefits
• Time training is time not working	*Funding available*
• Much training is not relevant	• Grant assistance available to help with the cost
• Much training is not effective	*Content*
Attitudes	• Trainers with business credibility
• Bad experiences of formal training, e.g. at school	• Training itself promotes further training
• Failure to perceive the need and the potential benefits	• Process counselling will be accepted but not expert consultancy
• A belief that the benefits will not last	*Promotion*
Lack of relevance	• Peer business managers will be believed
• No desire to improve or grow the business	• Influencers will be listened to, but not 'officials'
• Want solutions to yesterday's problems today	• Mail shots don't work
• Not prepared to look ahead	• 'It's about increasing profits'
Promotion of training	• Through networks of contacts
• The word 'training' is a turn-off	
• Suggestions of paternalism	
• Government initiatives are distrusted	
Apprehension	
• Too many courses on offer	
• Too many agencies	
• They may be sold something they don't need	
• It's an admission of defeat	
• Exposes oneself and one's business	

that the traditional components of pre-start training, namely finance, accounting/ book-keeping, marketing/selling and so forth are secondary skills and that the core skill is communication. Communication is necessary in all aspects of small business development and is of particular relevance in building up and using an appropriate personal network of contacts.

Know-who

The expressions, 'it's not what you know, but whom you know' and 'the old boy network' reflect a sometimes popular, but essentially negative, perception of certain social networks. Yet those who have examined small firm networking are convinced of its importance for the success of enterprise.

> Credibility is established through personal contact and knowledge of the skills, motivation and past performance of the individual – the bankers call this the 'track record'. Since for an embryonic business there is no trading track record, investors must look to their previous relationship with the individual, whether it be commercial or personal. Thus, for example, a previous employer may agree to be the first customer, a friend may allow use of spare office space, or a relative may be prepared to lend money with little real hope of a return in the short or even the medium term.[10]

Advice and guidance are often seen as the benefits of a network, and they may be the traditional base upon which many small firms support agencies have been built. But while they may be important characteristics of an active network they are not the only ones:[11]

- *Information*. Entrepreneurs use their social networks to signal their intentions, and to gather information about potential opportunities.
- *Sponsorship and support*. Family and friends will not only provide introductions into appropriate networks, but will also offer emotional and tangible support.
- *Credibility*. Membership of the network gives added weight to the evaluation of skills. Family and friends can provide credibility in areas unfamiliar to the entrepreneur.
- *Control*. Membership of the network, and assistance from it, require certain standards of behaviour. Owner-managers who do not conduct their business in a way that is acceptable to the community will quickly find themselves, and their businesses, isolated.
- *Business*. There are market networks of customers, suppliers and partners as well as production networks of sub-contractors, consultants and service suppliers. In addition, there are networks of firms that may work together on projects on a basis of collaboration. This structure can provide all the components necessary for a project without the need for 'vertical integration'.
- *Resources*. Friends and family can also be sources of resources for a new small business, and many businesses are assisted by the informal venture capital market that their owners access through their networks.

These networks are complex but relatively user-friendly and informal systems for the exchange of information. They have been described as 'creative communication in the business milieu'. They are not rigidly bounded and exclusive, and individuals often belong to more than one network. In general they facilitate the economic cooperation that is a feature present to at least some extent in all markets.

Networks involving small firms have a number of particular features. They are usually based on personal contacts, not official links, they are informal and are not openly advertised. They are flexible, being built up and maintained specifically to suit the purposes of their members. It is often these networks that give their member entrepreneurs the potential to react quickly to new developments. Having 'know-who' competency or networking skills can therefore be essential for success in dynamic environments.

And the result

Possessing or acquiring some or all of the possible components of the pre-start stage does not guarantee however that a business will be started. The decision still has to be made actually to do it although this is often triggered by an external event. It has been suggested that the decision is essentially a choice about the balance of risk. While the chances of success increase as relevant attributes and resources are built up, the costs of failure can also increase as personal financial commitments accumulate. It has therefore been suggested that there is a window of opportunity when the balance between benefits and costs is at the optimum, typically when people are in their thirties or early forties.

Start-up/inception

The typical small business start-up is:

> a new business venture; in temporary, small or unusual premises; nearly always financed from within, plus bank borrowings and with little or no long-term borrowing. Usually small in terms of employment, often with only family members involved.[12]

Table 6.6 presents an analysis of a start-up business. The reasons for starting the business may vary, but the main values driving the firm will be those of the founder(s). The basic skills of the founder will also determine the functional emphasis and management will be by direct supervision. The main efforts will hinge around developing a commercially acceptable product or service and establishing a niche for it in the marketplace.

The result will normally be one working unit, operating in a single market with limited channels of distribution. Sources of funds will be haphazard, and will place heavy demands on the founder, his/her partner(s) and friends and relatives. With the high level of uncertainty the level of forward planning is low.[13]

Table 6.6   An analysis of a start-up business

Aspect of the business	Description
Key issues	Obtaining customers Economic production
Top management role	Direct supervision
Organisational structure	Unstructured
Product and market research	None
Systems and controls	Simple book-keeping Eyeball contact
Major sources of finance	Owner's savings Owner's friends and relatives Suppliers and leasing
Cash generation	Negative
Major investments	Premises, plant and equipment
Product/market	Single line, limited channels and market

Source: Reprinted from M. Scott and R. Bruce, 'Five Stages of Growth in Small Business', *Long Range Planning* 1987; 20(3): 48. © 1987, with kind permission from Elsevier Science Ltd, The Boulevard, Langford Lane, Kidlington, OX5 1GB, UK.

Needs

At the stage of starting up a business, the entrepreneur doing it and/or the business can have many needs. This is one list:

- Capital
- Family support
- Customers
- Suppliers
- Employees
- Premises
- Company formation: a business name, stationery, management procedures
- Infrastructure
- Management skills: provided externally (consultants), or internally (training)
- Information and advice
- Confidence[14]

Barriers

As well as facing the start-up needs of businesses, which are in the main an inevitable aspect of the process in which they are engaged, entrepreneurs can, at this stage, also face a number of distinct barriers:

- The resource/credibility merry-go-round; this refers to the problem of how to acquire credibility in order to get the resources necessary to prove what you can do. (See Figure 6.8.)

Source: S. Birley, personal communication (1987).

Figure 6.8   The resource/credibility merry-go-round

- High entry or survival barriers. The barriers to entry into business will depend on the amount of investment, technology, and labour skills required or on the availability of niches or of growing markets. Then, once started, the business may find that there may also be barriers to survival. High survival barriers occur when there is intense competition, saturated markets, excess capacity and changing technology or product quality requirements.
- The burden of government bureaucracy. Ignorance is no defence when dealing with the legal requirements of officialdom. There are penalties if forms are not returned, or are returned incorrectly, but full and proper compliance can be costly, even if only in the time it requires, and this is proportionally more costly for small businesses than for large ones.
- The business plan: business plans are often not appropriate. When asked for a plan the new entrepreneur feels irritated, because producing it takes him or her away from the real work, frightened because he or she is not sure what it means, and confused about how to plan at all when things change daily.[15] (See also Chapter Seven.)

Growth or expansion

For some people the growth or expansion of a small business is its most important aspect, because it is that which produces the economic returns of significantly increased turnover, exports and jobs. Indeed a distinction is often made in policy terms between an entrepreneurship policy, which can cover one or more of the preceding stages, and a small business policy which covers this and the subsequent stages, when a small business actually exists.

Growth certainly has its problems, but is not necessarily quite as fraught or as taxing as start-up. Many of the issues of start-up can be the same for growth, such as knowing who are the most influential people, and the risk involved in moving from a known state to an unknown one, but growing also creates its particular and distinctive needs.

Definitions

Growth or expansion has been defined as characterised by the movement of the business into bigger premises, taking on more staff, significant increases of turnover, taking on a new product line or lines, buying another business, and so on. The growth stage can itself take different forms or be sub-divided into different phases:

- *Growth*. Where a distinction is made between growth and expansion, the growth stage is defined as the first significant increase in sales, in revenue and/or in employees after start-up. The business is likely to be established, but still small. It should be profitable, but all the cash generated will be used to finance the increases in working capital needed for growth.
- *Expansion*. Expansion has been seen as the more controlled increase in market share, and business size, after the first growth phase. One difference will be in the rate of increase in size. For a two-person business to 'grow' by taking on two more employees there will be a 100 per cent increase in size and complexity, even if the absolute increase is small. For a ten-person business to 'expand' by taking on two the absolute increase is the same, but it is only a 20 per cent change, which is much more easily absorbed.
- *Gazelles*. Birch noted that a small proportion of any cohort of new businesses creates a disproportionately large share of jobs. He called these job-creating businesses 'gazelles', possibly because of their propensity for sudden leaps upwards that outpace the rest.

Needs

The needs at this stage include courage by the owner to take the risk again, capital to do it, customers, suppliers, employees, space, transport and infrastructure, and management skills and tolerance by his or her family.[16] To these can be added the possible need for a transition in the business, for ensuring product quality, for managing the risks of growth, and for continued product and/or process innovation. If growth and expansion are seen as separate stages, their needs and possible crises, in more detail, can be described:

Growth needs

- Ensuring resources
- Delegation and coordination by top management
- A more formal and deliberate management style
- A functional and centralised structure
- Possibly some new product development

Growth crises

Crises are likely to be caused by the reaction of other, larger competitors and the demands on time and resources made by expansion into new markets or products. Liquidity can be a major problem, especially if the business overtrades and growth gets out of hand. Optimism may be high and businesses can be unaware that there are risks in growing, as well as rewards, and that care is therefore still needed, especially in controlling the flows of money.

Expansion needs

- Financing growth
- Maintaining control
- Delegation by top management
- A professional and administrative management style
- New product innovation and market research
- Moving beyond simple control and accounting systems to budgeting, monthly sales and production reports for delegated control

Expansion crises

Good management is necessary to maintain expansion, and internal politics can be an important issue when the demands of expansion may indicate the need for professional 'middle' management, who may not have the same commitment or outlook as the owner. Top management must then adjust to a new role, and can become distant from the detail of the business, which can be a source of crisis. (See also Figure 8.3 in Chapter Eight.) Another possible source of crisis is the failure to look outside the business to maintain a competitive advantage through a differentiated product, instead of just concentrating on production and selling, as may have been the case at earlier stages. Longer-term funds may be necessary, possibly through new equity partners, so that the founder may lose absolute control, which can be a painful process.

The longer term

It is traditional to see growth/expansion as coming after the stage of start-up. However, it is probably more normal for it to come after a static period or even after a decline. Although it is often portrayed as the natural progression from start-up, growth is not actually the norm for small businesses. Similarly, it is often hoped that growth will be followed by more growth, but the trend of business development is rarely a steady consistent increase in size. If there is a period of growth in a business then it is realistic to expect it to be followed by a time of consolidation before growth may be resumed. However, if the growth is mismanaged then it can be followed by decline and even termination.

Backing winners

Recent research has indicated that it is the relatively small proportion of small businesses that do grow that are responsible for much of the long-term job creation in the small business sector. Therefore many people would like to be able to pick those businesses that are going to succeed in this way and to devote resources to them to speed up and enhance that success. This aspect of growth businesses is therefore considered further in Chapter Eight.

Static: survival, consolidation, comfort and maturity

A static stage in small business development may not sound very exciting, but it characterises the state of most small businesses. Once they have started their own business, many electricians, plumbers, chimney sweeps and consultants, for instance, rarely grow, and many other one-person businesses are the same: static is the normal state for them.

Because, by definition, the static stage is not one that produces results in terms of more start-ups, more jobs or more other benefits, it is often ignored. Growth is a much more attractive stage in those terms, but in many cases it is in the static stage that the growth businesses of the future are to be found. Growth does not often follow immediately after start-up. But even if a static business is not a growth business of the future it can still perform a useful function. Together, static businesses provide significant employment. They also can be an essential part of the social fabric, they can provide choice and diversity, they can provide the necessary infrastructure support for other growth businesses and they can be useful role models. They should not be ignored.

Like the separation of growth and expansion it is possible to distinguish more than one type of stage during which a business, once started, does not grow. Survival has been the name given to that period following start-up during which a business may not grow but is nevertheless working hard to stay still and struggling to establish itself as a viable business. Once established, a business may then have a period of building resources, of consolidation, before the next move. Just because a business shows few signs of growth for a relatively long period, this does not mean that it will never grow. In many cases the growth of a business has been likened to that of bamboo, which can lie dormant for many years before suddenly shooting up in one season.

There is a large group of businesses whose growth is limited by their owners' ambitions or by their market niche. This stage has been labelled comfort or maturity. There may be many reasons why a business does not expand, such as the desired lifestyle of the owner-manager, the limits of his or her management capability, or even peer pressure not to get too far ahead. In general, however, this phase of development is characterised by a business which has taken up its share of the markets, has filled its capacity, or for any other managerial, political or social reason remains at the same size either in physical or economic terms.

A categorisation of static businesses can now be summarised:

- *Survival.* This is the stage which comes after start-up. Typically, a 'surviving' business has the potential to be a viable entity, but needs to work at it. It is probably a one-product or one-service business, but is concentrating on short-term issues of survival rather than the longer-term ones of future growth potential.
- *Consolidation.* After winning the struggle to survive or to grow, most businesses need a period of rest to build up the reserves they need to move forward. This may not be a conscious decision or a deliberate strategy. What was happening may only be obvious in retrospect, when subsequent growth can be seen to have been built on the contacts, the credibility and the expertise accumulated at this stage. A period of consolidation following a period of survival may be one during which even businesses that do eventually grow show few indications of their potential.
- *Comfort.* For a business that does not move on to growth, 'consolidation' can easily merge into 'comfort': the stage at which a business is doing enough to survive at least into the medium term and is providing enough profits to maintain the owner's desired standard of living. There may be little incentive to do anything different.
- *Maturity.* Maturity is generally seen as coming after some growth, and indeed there may still be slow continued growth. The businesses concerned, however, are no longer in the first stages of their existence. They may be passing the peak of their products' life cycles, or they may be on the verge of moving out of the definition of a small business because their management structure is facing a transition phase in which personal contact and word of mouth have to be replaced by more formal systems to cope with a larger organisation and more decentralisation. The onset of maturity may therefore be a transition, either onwards to bigger and better things, or sideways towards an eventual decline.

The issues

In general, the needs at this stage are for encouragement and incentive, either to prevent decline or to encourage expansion. The motivation of the owner is critical. A firm can be adapting and changing while staying still in terms of turnover or employment, but in the long term staying static is not a good strategy. It must always be presumed that competition will change or increase and in that case not to try to grow is to invite decline.

The needs of these businesses include:

Needs of survival businesses

- Control of the business
- Generating revenues sufficient to cover all expenses

- Supervision of the work
- Both entrepreneurial and administrative management
- Simple structures, systems and controls
- Product and/or market research

Needs of mature businesses

- Expense control
- Increased productivity
- Niche marketing, especially if the industry is declining
- Watchdog top management, taking a leadership role
- Product innovation, to replace products towards the end of their life cycle
- Formal systems for objectives and budgets
- Further long-term debt or bridging finance
- Succession planning

The succession planning issue possibly summarises one of the key dilemmas at this stage of the business. The entrepreneur behind the business has probably built it up from its inception, and has a keen sense of achievement and ownership. Now it is being suggested that he or she consider who should succeed to the management of the business. This might be advisable because the business needs it but for the owner concerned it means contemplating giving up the thing that may be the most important part of his or her life.

The longer term

As already explained, the static or survival stage can be seen as the norm for most small businesses. It is not therefore usually a stage on the way to something else, but an end in its own right. It can be preceded by start-up, growth or decline, and be succeeded eventually by growth, decline or termination. It is important to realise that, while this stage is described as static, it may only be so in the short term, and that often in the longer term not to move forward is to risk moving into decline, when others take the market as a result of one's passivity. Survival is not compulsory and there is a natural tendency towards regression. There is no superior power that will intervene to force all businesses to survive and so, ultimately, they must progress or die.

Decline

Decline is another of those stages of business development sometimes ignored by government agencies or support organisations when planning assistance.

However, decline need not always lead to termination if the problems of the business can be addressed. Helping in the decline stage may therefore result in more surviving businesses or jobs than would otherwise be the case.

Definition

The business is losing its market share, profitability, management skills and the ability to sustain itself at a previous high level.

Where from and what next

Decline can come after any stage from start-up onwards. If nothing is done then it will in all probability be followed by termination. If it is arrested then it can be followed by a 'static' stage. If it is cured then a 'static' or even a 'growth' stage is possible.

The issues

The needs of the business are:

- Confidence
- Finance
- Tolerance by the family
- Customers
- Suppliers
- Employees
- New management and leadership
- A strategic review and plan for a new direction, because the decline may be as a direct result of a market or other relevant business environmental change

Termination

Businesses, as Table 6.7 shows, do terminate. In any healthy, living ecosystem there are both births and deaths. Individual business deaths may be deemed regrettable, but some are to be expected in the best of economies. It would be unhealthy to have none, and the policy should therefore to be to avoid the unnecessary ones but not to prevent them completely.

The terminology of termination requires care. The word 'failure' is often ascribed to the termination of a business. A business may cease to exist or otherwise change its identification for a number of reasons. A business can terminate if it is sold and its operations are absorbed into another: the operations of the business continue but its separate legal existence disappears. It can terminate

Table 6.7 Business survival rates: percentage of enterprises surviving after one, two and five years, by country

Country	Surviving after		
	One year	*Two years*	*Five years*
France	84	62	48
Germany	86	70	63
Ireland	91	70	57
Italy	87	66	54
Portugal	76	56	47
United Kingdom	87	62	47

Sources: France: INSEE and ANCE; Germany: IfM; Ireland: Department of Enterprise and Employment; Italy: INPS Data Bank; Portugal: MESS-Portuguese Enterprise's Demography; United Kingdom: Department of Trade and Industry. Reproduced from the *Third Annual Report of the European Observatory for SMEs* (Zoetermeer, The Netherlands: EIM Small Business Research and Consultancy, 1995), p. 87.

when it chooses to cease to trade because those concerned see a better opportunity elsewhere, or it can terminate if it is closed when the owner retires. These are all terminations but they are not all failures. If VAT statistics are taken as guide, a business decline and subsequent VAT deregistration may be treated as a termination, and even as a failure, even if the business is actually still trading. The implication of this for small business statistics is considered further in Chapter Seven. Some of the varieties of termination are shown in Figure 6.9.

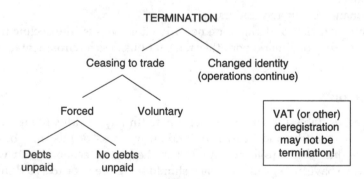

Figure 6.9 Types of business termination

Definition

Termination can be any closure of a business, but the term 'closure' can be ambiguous. It might therefore be more accurate to define it as the ending of the separate legal identity of a business and its ceasing to trade as a separate entity.

The issues

The need is for excellent legal advice to indicate the best way to handle employees, customers, suppliers and finances.

Intervention

It is not necessarily a waste of resources to help a business to terminate. Compared with a bad termination, too late and with many debts, a properly conducted and orderly termination can save resources. It can avoid unpaid creditors with the consequent risk to other businesses. It can save ideas for adoption elsewhere. It can help people to learn and try again instead of being put off ever running their own business again. Assistance can be in the form of advice on how to do it well.

Summary

Many of the aspects of the 'stages' model are summarised in Table 6.8 which lists key stages in the commercialisation process together with some of their actions, priorities and challenges.

THE VARIETIES OF SMALL BUSINESSES

The stage of development of the business may be the consideration most used for distinguishing different types of business, but there are many others that, although sometimes bewildering in their variety, can help to define the distinctions between different types of businesses and their characteristics.

Industry sector

The average size of businesses can differ widely in different industry sectors. Where the purpose of classifying a business as small or large is in relation to its place in its industry, and the influence it might have on that industry, it is important to pick a definition that recognises the average size of businesses in the relevant sector. For instance, in relation to other businesses in the same sector, a ten-person window cleaning business would be very large, while a 100-person

Table 6.8 The actions, priorities and challenges in the commercialisation process

Stage	Actions	Priorities	Challenges
1 Idea	• Develop ideas for innovation • Determine their commercial application	• R&D • IPR protection	• Technical
2 Pre-start	• Research the market • Acquire skills • Decide on the business strategy • Prepare the business plan	• Feasibility • Facilitate partnering • The 'business case'	• Forecasting
3 Start-up	• Raise finance • Put the components in place and • Launch the business	• Management • Finance • Marketing and sales	• Development
4 Survival	• Run the business and • Ensure its survival	• Early growth • Production • Distribution	• Operational
5 Expansion (and rewards?)	• Develop the business and (eventually?) • Find an exit route	• Growth • Planning system • Procedures • Management team	• Planning and strategic

car manufacturer would be very small. Examples from Europe show some of the ranges: thus in 1995 the average employment in a coalmining business was 924, in a railway business 996, and in a communications business 376; but in a travel agency 12, in a retail business four and in an estate agency two.[17]

Legal structure

In the UK a number of terms are encountered describing possible forms of business structure:

- *Sole trader.* Operating as a sole trader is the simplest form of business. An individual can start a business in this way with the minimum of fuss. In this situation, however, there is no legal distinction between the assets of the business and those of its owner. Such people are 'self-employed' and subject to income tax.
- *Partnership.* A business can be established as a partnership of a group of individuals doing business together. However, the business does not have a separate legal identity, and each partner is jointly and severally liable for any

liability incurred by the partners acting for the business. The liability of the partners in unlimited, except in the case of the less common (in the UK) 'limited partnership'.

- *Company.* A business can be established as a company. The company then has its own separate legal existence independent of that of its owners. If it is a limited company, this limits the liability of its owners. This limit can be achieved by shares, in which case the business has shareholders who together own the business and can receive dividends from its profits in proportion to the number and type of shares they hold, or the limit can be by guarantee. A business limited by guarantee is controlled by its members, who each agree to guarantee its liabilities up to an agreed amount (often £1 each) but who cannot benefit from the distribution of the profits of the business. A company limited by shares can be a public or a private company depending on whether the invitation to subscribe for the shares is open to the public or restricted in certain ways.

- *Cooperative.* Cooperative businesses are governed by different legislation from companies. They have to be registered as cooperatives and they have the benefit of limited liability. A cooperative is owned and controlled by its members, who may for instance be a group of workers or people living in a local community, who want to use the business for the benefit of themselves and/or the community. This can be reflected in the memorandum and articles of association of the business. A workers' cooperative is a business owned and controlled by the people working in it, an approach which can lead to greater involvement and responsibility.

- *Community business.* A form of business also sometimes encountered is the community business, which is often set up specifically to assist disadvantaged communities. This, however, is not a distinct legal form of business but an intention of the owners of the business to use the returns from the business for the benefit of the community in which the business operates. Many cooperatives are community businesses. (See also 'social enterprise' in Chapter Five.)

Family business

One distinct type of business that is often small is the family business. In the days when craft businesses and farms were virtually the only businesses in existence it was almost the universal practice for them to be passed on through generations of the same family. It is now widely accepted that family businesses still make a major contribution to many economies and their particular characteristics are therefore worth considering.[18] Recent research[19] suggests that in the USA one household in ten has a family business. Of the 22 million firms in America, between four million and 20 million of them (depending on the definition used and the survey carried out) are said to be family businesses,[20] making a contribution to GDP of between 12 and 49 per cent. Most of them are small, with more than 90 per cent of them employing fewer than 20 people; they operate mainly in the service, retail, construction and agricultural sectors; 55 per cent had a turnover of less than $100,000, and three-quarters are run by men. One of the early studies of family businesses in the UK[21] found that, of its sample, 52 per cent operated in the service sector, 44 per cent employed one hundred or fewer people, 83 per cent had a turnover in the range £2 million to £50 million, and only 25 per cent of family firms achieve growth rates exceeding 20 per cent per annum. In general family businesses are smaller and less likely to grow than non-family businesses. However, the UK study was based on the top 6000 UK private companies and all 2000 companies quoted on the London Stock Exchange, and consequently they represent the larger and more prosperous stock of UK family firms. A more realistic representation of the typical British family business is presented by Cromie *et al.*[22] They found that approximately 45 per cent of their sample traded in the service sector and a similar proportion in manufacturing; that 31 per cent had fewer than ten full-time employees and 81 per cent had fewer than 50; that annual turnover was less than £1 million for half of the sample and less than £5 million for almost 90 per cent. These businesses were therefore typically small; but there are some very large firms amongst them.

One of the problems of identifying and describing family businesses is the variety of definitions. One researcher identified more than 20 different definitions[23] but there are a number of common themes. Table 6.9 is an attempt to summarise a recent review of definitions used in American research on the matter[24] which shows that ownership and control by family members, the degree of family involvement in a business, and the intention or practice of transferring ownership and/or control from generation to generation are for many people the key issues in characterising family businesses.

Table 6.9 Different criteria by which family businesses have been defined

Ownership and management	Family involvement in the business	Generational transfer
Ownership and control by a family unit	Transactions and interaction between two systems: the business and the family	The actual transfer of ownership and control from one generation to another
One family member has to own and manage the business	Interactions involve lots of family members	The intentions to continue transfers between generations
Two or more family members must own and manage the business	Specific family involvement in business decisions and actions	

Source: Based on R. K. Z. Heck and E. Scannell-Trent, 'The Prevalence of Family Businesses from a Household Sample', *Family Business Review* 1999; 12: 210–11.

Some of the confusion arises because there are various types of family business.[25] It is unlikely, for example, that a micro-business run just by a husband and wife and the Ahlstrom Corporation in Finland, which has 200 family members, will display similar characteristics of ownership, control, family-to-business interaction and intergenerational transfers. Issues of age, size and numbers of founders and whether family involvement is increasing, stable or declining will influence the business and they way it behaves.

Broader definitions allow for a developmental, flexible approach to family businesses, but most family business research seems to have focused on the firm and to have considered that family matters are merely an adjunct to that.[26] In line with the suggestion above that often a focus on the entrepreneur provides a better perspective on business development, it has been argued that for family businesses the focus of interest should be on households[27] and that the two-way interaction between business and family dynamics has been neglected in family business research.

Much of the traditional research into the family firm has, however, often been based on a frame of reference in which the family business was regarded as the core system and the family itself was viewed 'only as a component of the business environment'.[28] Other models however recognise that businesses and families are independent systems with each having resources, processes and goals. In a family business context there are interactions between these systems but 'family issues are seen as disabling the effective working of the (business) system'.[29] As a result it is often argued that it is good practice to keep family and business affairs separate. Family business researchers have often used a model of family businesses which sees them as rational units which pursue economic goals. The assumption is then made that family feelings, values and dynamics have a detrimental influence on the business.[30]

This line of reasoning leads to conclusions that family businesses are less efficient than non-family business. Nevertheless, family businesses are reported to be relatively long-lived, with 60 per cent of the family firms in one survey[31] having been established for over 30 years, compared with only 35 per cent of their non-family counterparts. And their managements had longer tenure: over two-thirds of the family businesses had been under the same management for eight years compared with only one third of non-family businesses.

The problems of family firms

Cromie *et al.* found that families are very keen to control the issue of shares and are not keen on selling shares to raise finance for growth; that family members dominate boards and senior management positions, and that families are not keen on using outside advisers. In addition conflicts often arise between parents and their offspring, between siblings and between family and non-family personnel. Furthermore, managerial succession is fraught with difficulties with the result that, while there is an impression of stable, conservative, family-dominated institutions, they are often riddled with conflict. The stereotypical image of the family firm is of a rather dismal working environment which offers little opportunity to non-family personnel and which 'becomes sterile and eventually fails'.[32]

The pre-eminence of the controlling family, centralised decision-making and long-standing management teams can also result in static thinking. It can make it less likely that new ideas which are essential for long-term development will emerge, and family businesses are often reluctant to use outside advisers, preferring instead the counsel of the family when exploring business matters.

Another difficulty in family businesses can be the conflict that often emerges between family members, in particular fathers and their children. The father often recognises that he has to let go of the reins and develop his successor, but the business is such an important feature of his life that he fears that the 'loss' of it will damage his self-image and bring his competency into question. Such behaviour can be resented, and tension can build as a result.

Rivalry between siblings is another common source of difficulties. This conflict can reach such a level of seriousness that it has an impact on 'every management decision and magnifies the jockeying for power that goes on in all organisations'.[33] Where multiple family members have an interest in the business they may all expect equal treatment but, in the nature of things, this is rarely possible. Also, they may have different expectations such as short-term riches or long-term growth. As a consequence, various family members may set about gaining power and influence by means of internecine warfare that is often to the detriment of the business.

Conflict is inevitable in organisations, and it must be managed, but its management presents special problems for family-run businesses. Because the conflict can be intense, and because it is transposed from the business to the personal or family arena, it is often suppressed and not resolved. Therefore open discussion and the challenge of ideas, which can help progress in a changing world, may be avoided. In addition, when disputes do occur, the anger and resentment that occurs may also be transferred to family life, and this makes it difficult for family members to break out of a self-defeating cycle of conflict. All this can make rational business decision-making exceedingly difficult. In family businesses there are often family concerns that override business sensibilities. Incompetent family members may be retained in post as a favour to shore up deteriorating family relationships, and promotion for otherwise eligible non-family managers may be blocked as a result. Business logic and rationale may thus take a back seat in favour of family preference. There is some evidence that this is especially likely in second-generation family businesses. Attempts to improve the business by recruiting professional managers bring other problems: such managers may find that they can never achieve the measure of recognition and control, such as promotion to the board, that their expertise and contribution merit.

Managing the transition of power and control can often be a difficulty in family businesses, especially the transition from one chief executive to another.

There is evidence that this is rarely planned in family firms, and that the transition is, as a result, frequently traumatic. This may contribute to the failure of many family businesses to survive to the second or third generation. This seemingly unprofessional behaviour can come about because owners:

- will not face up to their limited lifespan;
- may unconsciously care little about what happens when they are gone;
- may resent their successor;
- may have an aversion to planning.[34]

Many of the difficulties found in family businesses can be attributed to non-rational behaviour and this view is supported by the traditional approach to family business research. However it has been pointed out that values and perceptions play a key part in the succession process and that concepts from behavioural economics can offer insights into the process. The 'endowment effect' can mean that the person handing over control in a family firm's transition 'is likely to place greater value on the business than is the new leader'.[35] This may well explain why succeeding generations sometimes take risks with, or dispose of, a business they inherit and not much can be done about it. However, drawing on notions of 'sunk costs' and 'windfall gains', it is suggested that the more it costs a successor in terms of money, time and effort to buy into a new business, the more highly he or she will value the business and the more likely he or she is to behave in a conservative manner.

It is argued that when people gain assets easily they will not value them highly and will be prepared to gamble with them. In a family business context if a successor is required to display superior performance before succeeding to a position of control, the business will be highly valued and will be treated with discernment. If the succession process is structured in a way which requires successors to invest money and time in the business and to prove themselves before they are handed the reins they will assume that the business is worth having. Decision-making is influenced by rational considerations but values also play an important part.

Advantages of family businesses

There may be drawbacks to family businesses but there are advantages too. When a family group strongly influences management and control, a permanent, solid atmosphere and an *esprit de corps* can develop. This can often encourage both a closeness among staff and long-lasting relationships with customers, suppliers and other contacts. Family businesses can as a result often build a reputation for dependability and for excellent service.

Staff in family businesses can have a sense of belonging and strong commitment to the goals of the organisation. When the owning family are justly proud of their venture, their enthusiasm and commitment can enthuse non-family staff.

This sense of togetherness is a powerful asset in that it can focus the energies of all involved on customers and on the need to serve them.

This commitment can produce a flexibility in terms of working practices, working hours and remuneration. Family members do what is necessary to get a job done. There is little demarcation of duties, and many family members are reluctant to take money out of the business. Some of this flexibility rubs off on non-family members, and this can allow the family business to respond rapidly to changing technological, sociological and economic conditions.

Family businesses are normally free from stock market pressure to produce quick results, because they are not quoted on the market and have no institutional shareholders. They can, as a result, often take a longer-term view. They are not forced to vacillate, and can pursue a consistent long-term strategy. This long view is reinforced by the permanent nature of their management teams. Permanence of management tends to allow behavioural norms to emerge and a recognised way of doing things to develop.

Family businesses therefore have both advantages and disadvantages and these are summarised by Kets de Vries in Table 6.10.

Table 6.10 Advantages and disadvantages of family-controlled businesses

Advantages	Disadvantages
• Long-term orientation	• Less access to capital markets may curtail growth

• Greater independence of action
   – Less (or no) pressure from stock market
   – Less (or no) takeover risk
	• Confusing organisation
	   – Messy structure
	   – No clear division of tasks

• Family culture as a source of pride
   – Stability
   – Strong identification/ commitment/motivation
   – Continuity in leadership
	• Nepotism
	   – Tolerance of inept family members as managers
	   – Inequitable reward systems
	   – Greater difficulties in attracting professional management

• Greater resilience in hard times – Willing to plough back profits	• Spoiled kid syndrome

• Less bureaucratic and impersonal
   – Greater flexibility
   – Quicker decision-making
	• Internecine strife
	   – Family disputes overflow into business

• Financial benefits
   – Possibility of great success
	• Paternalistic/autocratic rule
	   – Resistance to change
	   – Secrecy
	   – Attraction of dependent personalities

• Knowing the business
   – Early training for family members
	• Financial strain
	   – Family members milking the business
	   – Disequilibrium between contribution and compensation

	• Succession dramas

Source: Reprinted from M. F. R. Kets de Vries, 'The Dynamics of Family Controlled Firms: The Good News and the Bad News', *Organisational Dynamics* 1993; 21: 69. © 1993 With permission from Elsevier Science.

Family business performance

The result of this combination of advantages and disadvantages can be a business that has staying potential, but which does not usually last beyond the tenure of the founder. For instance, UK data[36] suggest that:

- only 30 per cent of family businesses reach the second generation;
- less than two-thirds of those survive through the second generation;
- only 13 per cent of family businesses survive through the third generation.

There is however no conclusive evidence about the performance of family versus non-family businesses. Barbara Dunn,[37] drawing on work in the UK and in the USA, argued that publicly quoted family firms were more profitable than non-family businesses in the 1970s and 1980s. Anecdotal evidence from Finland supports this point of view, where it has been suggested that the $3.3 billion Ahlstrom Corporation prospered by combining the benefits of family involvement with the pursuit of sound business principles.[38] However other British researchers have reported no differences 'in the performance and effectiveness of family and non-family firms'.[39] Inconclusive results can emerge for many reasons but problems with definitions have been alluded to. Definitions are sometimes the product of the working model employed by researchers, and it is noted above that some alternatives to the traditional approach have been proposed recently.

Family business models

It has been suggested that traditional models play down the role of the family in family businesses by considering family interpersonal and intergenerational relations and processes to be an aspect of the business environment, not of the business. In contrast, Stafford *et al.* combine a model of family functioning with one of business prosperity to 'yield a model of family business sustainability'.[40] The latter is the product of family and business attainments together with transactions between the two entities. In this model the family is afforded much more prominence than formerly. It is regarded as a goal-directed system which utilises resources and manages constraints in making transactions which contribute towards desirable goals. If goals are attained a strong sense of achievement results. The achievements can be objective and include such variables as the standard of living. They can also be subjective as represented by such outcomes as satisfaction and successful socialisation. Family resources include physical capital such as property and money and human capital such as knowledge and effective cooperation. Constraints include such variables as the law, economic realities and societal norms. Families use and combine resources by means of various transactions to achieve desirable goals. Like businesses, families structure their relationships and tasks in various ways to attain their goals.

Stafford *et al.* present a similar model for businesses. Systems models of organisations are quite common and that of Stafford *et al.* contains many commonly reported elements but they do point out that the criteria by which success is measured include both objective matters and more subjective issues such as providing a way of life for the family. Business transactions include both resource and interpersonal transformations to reflect both the task-related and emotional transactions in a business.

In a family business there will be regular transactions from family to business and vice versa. Family labour and money might be used by the business, business decisions will reflect the needs of the family, business resources and assets may be used by the family in the pursuit of their objectives, and business managers might allocate time to family needs while at work. In addition to the normal transactions the model includes responses and adjustments by both the family and the business to major changes within either system. In the model, which is reproduced in Figure 6.10, the business and family systems overlap and a

Source: K. Stafford, K. A. Duncan, S. Dane and M. Winter, 'A Research Model of Sustainable Family Business', *Family Business Review* 1999; 12: 197–208. Reprinted with permission from The Family Firm Institute Inc. All rights reserved.

Figure 6.10   Sustainable family business model

sustainable family business is one in which consideration is given to 'the ability of the family and business to cooperate in responding to disruptions in a way that does not impede the success of both'.[41]

The model supports the view that there are different kinds of family business. In some cases the overlap between the systems will be small and business and family issues will be kept separate. In others there will be a large overlap with lots of transactions and responses between the two systems. An important feature of the model is the attention it devotes to the family, the interaction between family and business, and the introduction of the issue of family firm sustainability and its adaptability. It is suggested that the family business is a continuous concept with completely separate and completely embroiled systems only to be found at the extremities of a continuum. However, even where the spheres are kept separate, the family still exerts an influence on the business. The family element makes family businesses unique. To accommodate this reality some American researchers advocate using a household sampling frame rather than a sample composed of firms and they have produced some interesting work on the adjustments that families and businesses make in turbulent times. Both make adjustments but the family accommodates the business more often than conversely.

Other categorisations of small business

In a population as heterogeneous as that of small businesses there will be many different ways in which firms can be categorised and it is neither practicable nor appropriate to try to list them all here. However there are some which get quite frequent mention, even if only by policy-makers seeking to target assistance appropriately. Among them are the following.

High-tech/low-tech

High-tech is a category of businesses often favoured by those promoting small business because of an assumption that high-tech businesses contribute most to an economy. This depends however on what is meant by a high-tech business. Often the definition used seems to be that of a business based on a new and relatively hard-to-acquire technology and which is, as a consequence, likely to be less vulnerable to competition and therefore able to earn more, to export more and to survive longer than businesses based on older technologies. However there is more to business success than the technology on which it is based and therefore, while high-tech businesses may have the newness of their technology in common, there is no guarantee that they share the same level of profitability, of exports or of success. They are nevertheless studied as a category because of issues that they are perceived to have in common such as longer lead times to market, greater difficulty in communicating their potential to other people and needing greater financial resources in order to get started.

Urban/rural

In places like England and Wales, where only seven per cent of the population live in completely rural areas it might be expected that the urban business is the norm. Yet there is evidence that in recent years many people have left the city and moved to the country, sometimes to start small businesses. Those businesses are often set up in rural areas for environmental and lifestyle reasons[42] and they would be classed as rural businesses because they are located in a rural area. However that is often in practice the only rural thing about the businesses: they benefit from cheaper property costs and overheads and they have greater distances to go to market but in other aspects they are just urban businesses which happen to be in a rural setting. Businesses which would have better claims to be rural would be farms and farm diversifications, other primary food producers and rural tourism initiatives.

A distinction which is sometimes made is that between 'accessible' and 'remote' rural areas. Storey[43] points out that 'accessible' rural areas have generally been amongst the most prosperous parts of the United Kingdom and quotes research showing that many businesses there are arts- and craft-based and are started by relatively highly educated individuals who are in-migrants to the area seeking a higher quality of life. It is businesses in the 'accessible' areas which out-perform comparable firms in urban areas, whereas firms set up in 'remote' rural areas do not appear to perform as well.

Apart from these distinctions there seems to be little evidence that rural businesses are in general significantly distinct from urban businesses, although some research has indicated that a few differences may be discernible. Storey reports one finding that owners of rural businesses are more reluctant to move out of their existing town or village than urban owners and have a commitment to a particular location, even though the opportunities for expansion there might be limited.[44] Another survey in England which was conducted in 1991[45] found that:

- rural and small town firms were younger than conurbation firms and that southern firms were frequently young, new enterprises set up in the 1980s;
- there were differences in workforce skill composition between northern and rural firms on the one hand and southern and conurbation firms on the other. The former employed significantly higher proportions of semi-skilled, unskilled and skilled manual workers while the latter had higher proportions of clerical and administrative staff, higher professionals and technologists, and managers;
- urban / rural differences in innovation activity were striking, with higher innovation rates in rural firms compared with conurbation firms;
- and also that there is a consistent urban / rural gradient in employment growth, with the most rapid employment expansion reported in rural firms and the least rapid in conurbation firms.

Female-/male-owned and ethnic businesses

The issue of female entrepreneurship and its implications are discussed in Chapter Three and the difference that this might make between female- and male-owned businesses is considered at the end of Chapter Seven. Ethnic businesses are also discussed in these chapters.

'Third age' businesses

Age distributions of self-employed people generally show that self-employment becomes increasingly common as middle age approaches and that it does not cease at the normal retirement age. The reasons given for these features are that middle age may be a time when capital or knowledge assets have been accumulated, and commitments may be reducing, so a start-up can be attempted. Alternatively it might be a time when people are particularly vulnerable to redundancy or attracted by early retirement offers. Self-employment may persist into the 60s and longer because of a reluctance to let go, although hours can be adjusted to allow for age, and there is no statutory retirement age for the self-employed. Alternatively it may continue because some of those in self-employment may not have adequate pension arrangements.[46]

Craft businesses

A further classification often used to distinguish among categories of business is that of craft, manufacture, service, technology, or agricultural. However, while these categories are in common use, there are no fixed definitions of them. Confusion can therefore arise in their use. For instance the distinction between 'craft' and 'manufacturing' is not clear, and there would appear to be some overlap. Indeed in mainland Europe the category 'craft business' depends more on size and ownership than on the type of handcrafted manufacturing associated with the concept of a UK craft business.

THE IMPLICATIONS OF BEING SMALL

Small businesses have assumed an importance in many people's minds, largely, it would seem, because of their employment creation potential. They are classified as small by their size, whether that is measured in terms of their worth, their turnover or their employment. There are, however, many differences amongst the businesses in those size categories, but there are many aspects, apart from just their size, that small businesses tend to have in common and where they differ from big businesses. It is for these reasons that they often need to be treated differently.

Some aspects of small businesses that require particular insight if misunderstandings are not to occur are considered in the next chapter. It is, however, relevant to consider here some of the aspects of small businesses that make them different. These differences can be grouped under the headings of culture, influence, resources and ambition. They encompass some of the crucial differences between small and big businesses for which distinctions by size are only a proxy. They are the reason for a separate analysis and consideration of small businesses as a category distinct from big business.

Culture

The culture of a small business is tied in with the needs, desires and abilities of its owner. He or she tends to focus on independence; flexibility, both from preference and necessity; closeness to the customer and supplier; individual and personal, rather than system, control; working with networks of contractors; tolerating uncertainty; and the shorter-term view rather than the longer one. There can be different types of owner with different needs and desires. (See also Figure 3.2 in Chapter Three.)

For many people however the culture of a small business epitomises enterprise. It can, nevertheless, be argued that, while starting a small business may be enterprising, running it need not be. In the case, for instance, of an inherited family business, running it may be what the person concerned has been expecting and preparing to do possibly from a young age, and involves little that is new or innovatory. Nevertheless, businesses, and particularly small businesses, are frequently referred to as enterprises, which emphasises this aspect of their culture.

Influence

Small businesses have very little influence over their environments or their markets. Their small size may enable them to respond more quickly to changes in those environments or markets but, unlike their bigger counterparts, they have little influence that would enable them to change them. Their job creation potential, especially when combined with groupings to promote combined lobbying, may give them some political influence, but it is unrealistic to assume that they will individually be able to change their markets in the ways they might wish.

As well as their final markets, the intermediate markets or distribution channels of small businesses are also beyond their control. Again, bigger businesses may be able to dictate terms to distributors, or may be able to acquire their own distribution channels through 'vertical integration'. But not the small businesses: they are at the mercy of their distributors, and also their suppliers, to a very considerable extent.

Resources

It is almost invariably the case that small businesses lack sufficient resources. Most of them are started on a financial shoestring and few get cash-rich subsequently.

Most therefore do not have easy access to the financial reserves necessary to carry them through a lean period or to utilise a sudden opportunity for expansion.

But it is not just finance which they lack. They are usually short of management, both management time and management skills. As has already been mentioned, there is often only one person, the owner, in a management role, and this role will embrace all aspects of managing the business. This means both that the amount of management time that can be focused on a problem is very limited and that aspects of management expertise are also likely to be missing, because the single manager is unlikely to be fully conversant with marketing, production, financial, technical, legal and human resource aspects of business.

In the business world, therefore, small may mean poor, but not always. There are examples of small businesses that do make very large profits, and others that, if not wealthy in themselves, have, by virtue of their technology, markets or other intangible assets, been very attractive propositions for prospective investors.

Ambition

In terms of their behaviour, however, the biggest difference between small and big businesses is likely to be that which results from the ambition and goals of their owners and managers. As indicated above, the larger the business, the more likely it is to be run by a professional management trying to maximise its value. The converse is that the smaller the business, the more likely it is that it will be run by an owner-manager with an aim based on personal values.

IN CONCLUSION

Small businesses are very diverse, and this chapter has looked at their variety by examining a number of different classifications. There is no one best way of classifying the different types of small business. Which is most appropriate in a particular circumstance will depend on what form of analysis or prescription one is engaged in.

THE KEY POINTS OF CHAPTER 6

- There is no single definition of what is a small business. Most definitions use the size of the business as the distinguishing feature, as indicated by either asset value or turnover, or, more commonly, by employment. The upper limit in employment terms can however vary from 50 people to, in the case of SMEs, 500. It is, however, important to remember that 'small' is often used as a relative term, and what is relatively small in one industry may be relatively large in another.

- In examining small businesses the focus of the analysis has often been the business. If though the primary unit of analysis is instead taken as the entrepreneur, a different perspective often emerges, which can explain many features of small businesses and which throws light on the process of capital accumulation and entrepreneurship.
- In whatever way they are defined or viewed, small businesses exhibit considerable variety. One of the commonest ways of categorising businesses has been by the 'stage' of their development, even though there are no clear boundaries between the stages. There are many models of the different stages of business development. These can help in identifying the different issues, such as needs, barriers and crises, that businesses face at different stages of their development, but they do not help in predicting what will happen to the businesses.
- The variety of small businesses is not just due to their different stages of development. Different industry sectors and different legal structures, family ownership and other considerations can all make a difference.
- There is also variety between entrepreneurs, who can, for instance, be categorised as novice or habitual and, if habitual, as serial or portfolio.
- Nevertheless, despite the many differences between different types, stages or ownership of small businesses, they do have a number of key aspects in common, and many of these aspects distinguish them from big businesses. These aspects include issues of culture, influence, resources and ambition. For many commentators it is these aspects that represent the crucial difference associated with size, and even the description 'small' is only a convenient distinction to serve as a proxy for these real differences.

QUESTIONS, EXERCISES, ESSAY AND DISCUSSION TOPICS

- Are definitions based on size meaningful when there is such a variety of small businesses?
- Why can the stage model not be used to predict what will happen next to a small business?
- In the absence of a single universally accepted definition how would you summarise the essence of a small business?
- Is the entrepreneur or the business the more enlightening unit of study in seeking to understand business development and wealth creation?

- In what ways do family businesses differ from non-family businesses?
- What are the implications of studying family businesses from the perspective of the family instead of focussing just on the business?

SUGGESTIONS FOR FURTHER READING

P. Burns, *Entrepreneurship and Small Business* (Basingstoke: Palgrave (now Palgrave Macmillan), 2001).

P. Leach, *The BDO Stoy Hayward Guide to the Family Business* (London: Kogan Page, 1996).

Global Entrepreneurship Monitor: www.entreworld.org

Stoy Hayward's Centre For Family Business: www.fbn-i.org

REFERENCES

1 *The Report of the Committee of Enquiry on Small Firms* (The Bolton Report), (London: HMSO, 1971).
2 D. Carson and S. Cromie, 'Marketing Planning in Small Enterprises: A Model and Some Empirical Evidence', *Journal of Marketing Management* 1989; 5: 33–50.
3 P. Rosa and M. Scott, 'Entrepreneurial Diversification, Business-Cluster Formation, and Growth', *Government and Policy* 1999; 17: 527–47, at 530.
4 P. Rosa and M. Scott, 'The Prevalence of Multiple Owners and Directors in the SME Sector: Implications For Our Understanding of Start-Up and Growth', *Entrepreneurship and Regional Development* 1999; 11: 21–37, at 34.
5 M. Scott and P. Rosa, 'Has Firm Level Analysis Reached its Limits? Time for a Rethink', *International Small Business Journal* 1996; 14: 81–9.
6 P. Westhead and M. Wright, 'Novice, Portfolio and Serial Founders: Are They Different?', *Journal of Business Venturing* 1998; 13: 173–204.
7 Scott and Rosa, *op. cit.*: 81.
8 N. C. Churchill and V. L. Lewis, 'Growing Concerns: The Five Stages of Small Firm Growth', *Harvard Business Review* 1983; May–June: 31, 32, 34, 40.
9 R. Peterson and R. Rondstadt, 'A Silent Strength: Entrepreneurial Know-Who', *The 16th ESBS/EFMD/IMD Report* (86/4), p. 11.
10 S. Birley, 'The Start-Up', in P. Burns and J. Dewhurst (eds), *Small Business and Entrepreneurship* (Basingstoke: Macmillan (now Palgrave Macmillan), 1989), p. 16.
11 S. Birley and S. Cromie, 'Social Networks and Entrepreneurship in Northern Ireland', Paper presented at the Enterprise in Action Conference, Belfast, September 1988.
12 Forum of Private Business, 'The Internal and External Problems That Face Small Businesses', Paper presented at the Sixteenth ISBC Annual Conference, October 1989, p. 6.

13   M. Scott and R. Bruce, 'Five Stages of Growth In Small Business', *Long Range Planning* 1987; 20(3): 45–52, at 49.

14   Forum of Private Business, *op. cit.*, p. 6.

15   S. Birley, 'The Way Ahead for Local Enterprise Centres', Presentation at Enniskillen, Northern Ireland, January 1988.

16   Forum of Private Business, *op. cit.*, p. 7.

17   *The Third Annual Report of the European Observatory for SMEs* (Zoetermeer, The Netherlands: EIM Small Business Research and Consultancy, 1995), pp. 50–1.

18   Stoy Hayward, *The Stoy Hayward / BBC Family Business Index* (London: Stoy Hayward, 1992).

19   R. K. Z. Heck and E. Scannell-Trent, 'The Prevalence of Family Business From a Household Sample', *Family Business Review* 1999; 12: 209–24.

20   M. C. Shanker and J. H. Astrachan, 'Myths and Realities: Family Business Contributions to the US Economy: A Framework for Assessing Family Business Statistics', *Family Business Review* 1996; 9: 107–23.

21   Stoy Hayward, *Managing the Family Business in the UK* (London: Stoy Hayward, 1990).

22   S. Cromie, B. Stephenson and D. Monteith, 'Managing Family Firms: An Empirical Investigation', *International Small Business Journal* 1995; 13: 11–34.

23   M. S. Wortman, 'Critical Issues in Family Business: An International Perspective of Practice and Research', *Proceedings of the ICSB 40th World Conference*, (1995), pp. 53–76.

24   Heck and Scannell-Trent, *op. cit.*: 209-20, base their model of family firms definitions on W. C. Handler, 'Methodological Issues and Considerations in Studying Family Businesses,' *Family Business Review* 1989; 2: 257–76.

25   D. Fletcher, 'Family and Enterprise' in S. Carter and D. Jones-Evans (eds), *Enterprise and Small Business* (London: Financial Times/Prentice-Hall, 2000), pp. 155–65.

26   K. Stafford, K. A. Duncan, S. Dane and M. Winter, 'A Research Model of Sustainable Family Business', *Family Business Review* 1999; 12: 197–208.

27   Heck and Scannell-Trent, *op. cit.*: 212.

28   Stafford *et al.*, *op. cit.*: 203.

29   Fletcher, *op. cit.*, p. 160.

30   S. Birley, D. Ng and A. Godfrey, 'The Family and the Business', *Long Range Planning* 1999; 32: 598–608.

31   Stoy Hayward (1990), *op. cit.*

32   Birley *et al.*, *op. cit.*: 598.

33   H. Levinson, 'Conflicts That Plague the Family Business', *Harvard Business Review* 1971; March–April: 53–62.

34   H. Levinson, 'Don't Choose Your Own Successor', *Harvard Business Review* 1974; November–December: 53–62.

35   D. A. Shepherd and A. Zacharakis, 'Structuring Family Business Succession: An Analysis of the Future Leader's Decision Making', *Entrepreneurship Theory and Practice* 2000; 25: 25–39.

36   Stoy Hayward (1990), *op. cit.*

37   B. Dunn, 'Success Themes in Scottish Family Enterprises: Philosophies and Practices Through the Generations', *Family Business Review* 1995; 8: 17–28.

38   J. Magretta, 'Governing the Family-Owned Enterprise: An Interview With Finland's Krister Ahlstrom', *Harvard Business Review* 1998; January–February: 113–23.

39   Fletcher, *op. cit.*, p. 157.

40   Stafford et al, *op. cit.*: 203.

41   *Ibid.*: 205.
42   Economic and Social Research Council, *Characteristics of the Founders of Small Rural Businesses* (Swindon: The Council, 1989).
43   D. Storey, *Understanding the Small Business Sector* (London: Routledge, 1994), pp. 272–3.
44   Storey, *op.cit.*, p. 273 quoting D. Smallbone, D. North and R. Leigh, 'The Use of External Assistance by Mature SMEs in the UK: Some Policy Implications', *Entrepreneurship and Regional Development* 1993; 5: 279–95.
45   Economic and Social Research Council, *The State of British Enterprise* (Swindon: The Council, 1992).
46   D. Brooksbank, 'Self-Employment and Small Firms', in S. Carter and D. Jones-Evans (eds), *Enterprise and Small Business* (London: Financial Times/Prentice-Hall, 2000), pp. 15–16.

DISTINCTIVE FEATURES
OF SMALL BUSINESSES

CONTENTS

KEY CONCEPTS

This chapter covers:
- the different behaviours of small and large businesses and the ways in which small businesses do not behave like little big businesses;
- the distinctive characteristics of small businesses;
- differences amongst small businesses;
- interpreting small business statistics;
- the importance of looking at small businesses from the viewpoint of the owner;
- the influence of personal relationships on small businesses.

LEARNING OBJECTIVES

....

By the end of this chapter the reader should:
- have an understanding of the distinctive characteristics of small businesses;
- have an appreciation of specific small business issues, including the relevance of the business plan;
- have an appreciation of the difficulties in interpreting small business statistics;
- have an understanding of the possible influences on a small business;
- have an understanding of what constitutes small business success and failure.

INTRODUCTION

The differences in the administrative structure of the very small and the very large firms are so great that in many ways it is hard to see that the two species are of the same genus .... We cannot define a caterpillar and then use the same definition for a butterfly.

Dame Edith Penrose[1]

In seeking to understand how small businesses behave, it is easy to fall into one of two traps by comparing them to big businesses. Small businesses are not big businesses writ small, and concepts, theories, practices, forms of behaviour and interventions that apply to big businesses and their management will not necessarily apply on a small scale to them. As it has been put: 'small business is not big business seen through the wrong end of a telescope'. Neither is every one an embryonic big business that, as a caterpillar turns into a butterfly, will eventually metamorphose into a big business. Many will always remain small.

Understanding both small businesses and their place in an economy requires therefore more than an understanding of business in general. It requires an appreciation of the significant differences between small and big businesses, a knowledge of specific small business issues, and an insight into the ways of small business. It also requires an understanding of the entrepreneurs who start and run small businesses. This understanding is needed by those who have not had the experience of running a small business themselves, and by those who have experienced little else. The former may see the economic wood, but they may also fail to appreciate the nature of at least some of the trees of which it is composed. The latter have been accustomed to the small business milieu and may find it hard to see the larger picture. The difference can be especially important for those who might wish to intervene in the field of small business by offering direct or indirect support. Failure to comprehend crucial aspects of small business behaviour, constraints and issues can often be the cause of much misunderstanding.

This chapter therefore looks at some of these key areas of difference between small and big businesses and some of the pitfalls that those without insight may stumble into. Traditionally the approach taken to this, and the one used in most research and writing about enterprise, has been to look primarily at the business but, as explained in Chapter Six, it can be more helpful to take the entrepreneur as the fundamental unit of analysis. This chapter therefore looks, in the first section, at the areas of difference between small and large businesses, first from the perspective of the business; but then, in the second section, it also looks at the entrepreneurs behind small businesses and how they may behave differently from the owners and managers of bigger businesses.

SECTION A – THE FEATURES OF SMALL BUSINESSES

The distinctive characteristics of small businesses

Many commentators, including Gibb,[2] have identified differences between the behaviour of small and big businesses, differences manifest in a range of characteristics. Some of these have already been indicated in Chapter Two, where the meaning of 'enterprise' was explored. Others significant differences include the following.

An absence of functional managers

Often the management of a small business resides with one person. The advantage of this can be that an overall view of management, including production, finance and marketing, is taken instead of there being a conflict between the different functions. On the other hand, knowledge of such functions may not be evenly developed and in some areas may be severely lacking.

On-the-job learning

Many small business owner-managers have acquired most of their business knowledge on the job. They will often have been in the job a long time and may therefore have a deep experience, but not necessarily a broad one, or an objective and informed view. The business systems employed are likely to be of their own devising, based on experience, and are unlikely to be changed unless experience also suggests it is necessary.

Investment and resources

Money invested in the business is often personal money, not that of impersonal investors. There can therefore be a reluctance to spend this money on anything except the bare essentials, for short-term obvious returns. More formal investment appraisal methods are not seen as being as useful as a 'feel' for what is right. Similarly, the time needed for formal 'training' or review is seen as both an unaffordable distraction from the real work of the business and as earning a return that is more theoretical than practical. Change, where it occurs, is likely to be the response to short-term need rather than the result of long-term strategy.

Discontinuities

There are thresholds and discontinuities in a small business that do not occur in a bigger business. In a bigger business, for instance, increasing capacity by ten per cent in a key department to cope with a ten per cent increase in turnover may be relatively straightforward. In a small business however there may be only two people in the department, who are already fully loaded. Extra capacity is still needed, but taking on an extra person would be a 50 per cent increase and may not be justified by the likely extra return. This same is also true of getting a second machine when one is just unable to cope.

Informal systems and procedures

Many businesses start with one person, for whom formal systems and procedures will seem unnecessary. They will grow by taking on new employees in ones and twos and, again, it would seem strange to introduce formal systems for just a few people, who will learn what is going on quickly enough through their direct involvement in the small team. In any case the owner-manager is probably too busy to introduce more formal systems for running the business. This state of affairs is likely to continue until a crisis arises because the business has grown too big to be run informally. As many small businesses never get to that stage, informality in systems and procedures is a characteristic that they share.

Control, management and organisation in small businesses

Top-down

In a small business the dominant position of the entrepreneur can create a person-centred culture. Consequently the strategy, or absence of one, of the business will correspond to that of the entrepreneur. This top-down approach can be attractive in a stable environment, if the entrepreneur articulates a vision that motivates others. Increasingly, however, even in small businesses, it is intelligent employees, more than the entrepreneur, who are in touch with the latest technological, economic and sociological developments. Considerable decision-making discretion, even at the strategic level, may have to be delegated to these individuals, but entrepreneurs are notoriously reluctant to share their power. In a world of discontinuous change that is a drawback.[3]

Decision-making

In general, the decision-making process in small businesses will be less formal and more personalised than in larger ventures. In a rational approach, objectives are set, alternatives are investigated and economic evaluations are made of alternatives. In a large business the distance from top to bottom, and the consequent number of layers and communication steps, may mean that the message, and the rationale behind it, can be distorted. In small businesses the omnipresence of the owners can mean that everyone in the business can hear a clear articulation of the goals and objectives. However, the smallness of the business, and the lack of managerial skills of its owner, can also mean that goals are not articulated at all. Clear objectives facilitate rationality, but rational economic decisions often depend on having access to large amounts of information and the employment of sophisticated quantitative techniques to make sense of it. The lack of resource in small businesses, and their heavy reliance on information gleaned from personal contacts, are unlikely to encourage rational evaluations of alternatives. The information available to decision-makers in small businesses will be even more inaccurate, incomplete and time-bounded than in other organisations.[4] In the same way, time horizons for planning, whether formal or informal, will tend to be much shorter than in larger businesses. Moreover, decisions are much more likely to be influenced by an owner-manager's emotions and personal interests than by objective analysis.

Organisational structures

Most work in large organisations is highly specialised, and much of the brainwork is removed from operational tasks. However, an extensive division of tasks, especially at management level, only makes sense when there is a large volume of work; it is no use employing experts if they are underemployed. By definition, a small business does not have a large volume of output and work perforce must be done by generalists. Furthermore, organisations tend to perpetuate the fruits of their learning and standardise regularly recurring activities; however, this is sensible only when environmental conditions are stable. In the turbulent environment so characteristic of the small business, change is the order of the day and problem-solving is a higher requirement of organisations than efficiency.[5] As a result of these factors, small firms tend to have simple, flexible, non-differentiated structures and flexible work practices, to possess general-purpose rather than specialised machines and to exhibit few of the features so characteristic of bureaucracies. The general nature of employee skills and flexible production capabilities means that much more of the creative aspects of production can be easily delegated to operators. Faced with an order from a customer, operators and their managers are more likely to plan operations jointly.

Control

If the all-pervasive control mechanisms of large organisations are absent, how do managers in small businesses exercise control? Decision-making can be considered to take place at three levels: strategic, administrative and operational. In the bigger business these will each happen at different levels of the organisation and involve different people. In small businesses they are, as often as not, all done by the same person with no formal or recognised boundaries or hierarchical split amongst them. There is therefore a lack of clarity about the type of decision being taken, with little distinction in thought between strategic and tactical decisions. Once a decision is taken, control through standardisation, performance measurement and bureaucratic structures is often absent in small businesses. Instead the presence of the owners, or their representatives, will mean that control is exercised by direct supervision. These individuals are never far away, and the numerous work-related discussions that take place will confirm the position of managers in an overseeing role. Yet this often leads to much speedier decision-making and shorter reaction times, which in turn can mean an improved competitive edge.[6]

A lack of objectivity

Another key feature of small businesses is the inability, or unwillingness, of their owners to be objective about them. Instead they frequently identify closely with their businesses, seeing them almost as extensions of themselves. This, and its implications, are considered in more detail later in the chapter.

Understanding specific small business issues

Business planning

> Before launching any new venture, the first step is to draw up a business plan.
>
> Introduction to a factsheet on business plans

Business plans are another area in which the appropriate approach for larger businesses is not necessarily also appropriate for small ones. The orthodox view that a business plan is essential for anyone starting a small business is, to some people, so obvious that it does not need to be proved. Others however believe that, at least for some businesses, a formal written business plan in the recommended format would be a waste of time. To understand each point of view it is necessary to look more closely into the limitations of plans and what benefits business planning and plans can offer.

> I only did it for the bank, and a year later it was obvious that the bank had not looked at it.
>
> A successful businessman describing his first business plan

> I had to present a business plan for my grant application and now, actually, I find it very useful. At the end of each week, if the sales are above the projected levels, I get a lot of comfort because it means that the business is actually succeeding. If I didn't have that reassurance I would have a lot of sleepless nights worrying whether the business was a good idea.
>
> Owner of a newly opened small shop

Owing, at least in part, to the way it has been presented, many people starting a business often see the business plan primarily as an obstacle – one that they have to address somehow, because it seems to be a compulsory part of the process. Professional advisers have told them that they should do it and may have indicated that its completion is a precondition for further help. They may have been provided with some guidance on how to do it and given examples of suggested layouts. They may not, however, have been persuaded that it is anything but an unnecessary chore and they don't see it as a helpful tool for the venture they are about to undertake. This is especially so if all a potential funder appears to require in a plan, apart from a CV, are some financial projections (cash flow, profit and loss, and balance sheet) and he or she cannot see how they can possibly make meaningful forecasts of what they can achieve before they have the experience of actually being in business to guide them. Of course often what the funder really needs is the assumptions underlying the projected figures, but that is rarely apparent.

Therefore, for the person starting a small business, the basic question to be answered in relation to the business plan is not how to do it, but why. Of what real use is a business plan to a small business? Only when this is understood may the question of 'how' be relevant.

If the question 'why' is honestly addressed, it will appear that there are some new business starts for which a formal written business plan may not actually be essential. To some advisers that is heresy, which may be why the concept of business plans can get a bad reputation. If the assumption is made that they are essential then there is a temptation to assume that others share this view, and so the reason for it does not have to be explained. Advisers then address the question of how to do it, while those being advised still do not see why. If there is no good reason why then the result is unlikely to be helpful. This is compounded when it is the possession of a business plan, rather than the process of its preparation, which is seen to be the key.

It is generally accepted that there are two ways in which the preparation of a good business plan can be of very real and direct help to a new business.

Funding the business

The simplest application of the business plan to understand may be its role in 'selling' the business, in other words, putting across its merits. Potential funders of the business often need to be persuaded of its worth. A business gets financial support because the providers of that support think that they will themselves benefit from its provision. Banks seek to get paid for an overdraft or loan (interest) and grant-givers seek a contribution to the achievement of their aims (often improvements in the economy). They don't have to help a business. It is like a supplier-customer relationship: both have to benefit for it to work. In this case, however, the funds have to be provided some time before the benefits can be delivered, and the funders have to be able to trust the recipients to do that. In such circumstances, the business plan can be an essential tool for persuading funders that if they provide the funds then the business will be able to deliver the benefits and will survive long enough to do so.

The business plan is in effect the sales document for the business, and an understanding of the benefits the funders seek can be helpful in its preparation, for the following reasons:

- government agencies want a lasting contribution to the economy, by means such as increased business and exports and more jobs. They may use terms such as 'viability', 'additionality' and 'admissibility', so that is what the plan or sales document has to convey;

- banks want interest on their capital, and eventually their capital back, so they will want to see how the business will be able to afford this;
- venture capitalists want to see that their investment in the business will increase in value and can ultimately be realised.

Managing the venture

> The plan is nothing: planning is everything.
>
> Napoleon

Advice about business plans may vary but it is generally agreed that one of the most important uses of a business plan, or rather of the process of preparing it, is that it can help the business owner to see that all relevant aspects of the potential business are addressed and allowed for. Further, the subsequent monitoring of events against the projections can show where action is needed, if any, to keep the business on course. Can someone, in a new business, in a venture and in a field that is to some extent new or novel, allow for everything without thinking it through, and probably putting it on paper? Is he or she prepared to invest savings in the business without analysing the risk? Can he or she do that without going through the analysis needed for a plan? The answer to these questions may be yes, but it may require some thought. The process of producing the plan can assist in focusing strategic thinking; and the plan, when completed, can provide a benchmark against which to measure subsequent performance.

When a business plan does not help

From the above it will appear that if someone starting a business does not need to raise funds, and understands what he or she is about to do, and the process of doing it, then a written business plan may not be needed. That at least is the view of some small business commentators, although it is a controversial one. They believe that strategy is often in the head of the small business owner, and he or she may see no need to write it down. All that is required is that the person starting a business has some idea of the goal and the route to be taken to it. In these circumstances, asking an aspiring entrepreneur for a formal business plan can actually be detrimental to the business. In deference to the apparent expertise, and therefore presumed superior knowledge, of the person making the request for the plan, the emerging entrepreneur may try to produce one in line with a prescribed format. If he or she does not understand what a business plan means, or the logic behind the format, then the plan may be a bad one and the time wasted on it may be considerable.

Demystifying the business plan

> Whereas anyone can make a plan it takes something quite out of the ordinary to carry it out.
>
> General Sir Frederick Morgan

It may help to understand what a plan is and what it is not:

- *What a plan is.* Planning is an essential part of the process of getting positive results. It is the working out of how those results can best be obtained. It is a means of communicating your thoughts on this to others.
- *What plan is not.* A plan is not holy or magical, it is not a forecast, a means in itself, a pious hope or fixed and absolute.

Professional help: a word of caution

Why don't businesses get someone else to prepare plans for them? Others can help, but they should not do it all, unless the sole reason is to get a grant. Getting someone else to prepare it all will not give the business an insight into the issues to watch for and an understanding of what will make the business work best. Apart from possibly securing a grant or a loan, a plan someone else prepares, without the owner-manager and his or her involvement, will at best probably give the business nothing and could actually do worse. Generally, the process of preparing the plan is much more valuable than the plan itself. What, however, if all the business wants is a grant or a loan? The business should invest the minimum of resources required to produce a plan with acceptable content.

ILLUSTRATION 7.1
The failed plan
....

Sue and Mary were two partners who started a clothing design business with financial backing from their parents, who put up their houses as security. Because they were too busy setting up the business, an adviser prepared most of their business plan for them, including the financial projections. The business looked attractive and the bank supported them. Probably because of their personal appeal and enthusiasm they even won a small business start-up award. Unfortunately, however, the partners had never understood cash flow forecasts and the adviser's business plan only served to disguise this. Almost inevitably they lost control of their cash flow, and the business collapsed. The parents of one of them lost their house as a result.

Summary

Everyone plans in some way or other, but not always on paper. Properly used, a business plan is a help, not an obstacle. A lot of nonsense has been talked about it and it has in some cases been promoted as the answer to almost every business ill. A formal written plan is not the essential starting point for every successful business but there have nevertheless been many businesses that suffered because they were not planned properly, and plans are often essential for securing the support of others.

Small business finance

To some extent small business financing issues vary from country to country. In many former communist countries in Central and Eastern Europe, the banking system has been very undeveloped and unreliable and, especially when this is combined with the need to charge very high interest rates in times of high inflation, the result had been that businesses there rarely used bank financing. Even in Western Europe the use of bank financing varies from country to country. This is shown by a survey that produced the results shown in Table 7.1. The majority of small businesses however rely on internally generated funds to finance new activities. According to one survey[7] between 70 and 80 per cent use retained profit and cash flow to fund activities and it has been reported that in the UK one third of small businesses do not borrow at all from banks, another third regularly move into and out of an overdraft, and one third are consistent borrowers.[8]

In many countries there are claims that small businesses are particularly disadvantaged because finding appropriate sources of funding for them is harder than it is elsewhere. In almost every country there are claims of disadvantage because finding funding is harder for small businesses than it is for bigger ones. There is no doubt that the difficulty of financing small businesses is one of the most

Table 7.1 Debt structure by country (percentage of total borrowings)

Type of facility	Britain	France	Germany	Italy	Spain	Overall
Overdraft	42	23	17	32	14	29
Short-term loans (under two years)	9	18	20	20	45	20
Medium-term loans (two to five years)	13	32	20	15	19	18
Long-term loans (over five years)	19	11	36	19	20	21
Leasing and hire purchase	17	14	7	13	3	12
Total	100	100	100	100	100	100

Source: P. Burns and O. Whitehouse, *Financing Enterprise in Europe 2*, (Milton Keynes: 3i Enterprise Centre, 1995).

frequently heard complaints. The reasons why there is this difficulty include the following.

Small businesses are not a good risk. Suppliers of business finance, when they exist, want something in return for their money. Usually this is a financial return, either interest or dividends, plus some way eventually of getting back the initial investment, or a multiple of it. If the finance sought is a development grant then returning it may not be an issue, but there will nevertheless still be an expectation that some benefits will be delivered, such as job creation or other economic bene-fits. In all cases, if the money is to be provided in advance of the returns, which is inevitably the case, then there needs to be some indication that the return will come, and that the business will survive to deliver it. Although the often quoted very high failure rates especially for young businesses are not always what they seem to be (see later in this chapter), a significant proportion of small businesses do fail soon after start-up. Small businesses are therefore more vulnerable than larger ones, and will need to provide potential investors with some evidence that in their particular cases they will not fail.

New small businesses do not have a track record. It is said that business financiers generally assess a business on three aspects: the management, the management and the management. For a new business with no trading history, and often with untried management, it is very difficult to provide satisfactory evidence that they will not only survive but will also do well enough to provide investors with the returns they seek.

It is not cost-effective to provide small amounts of money. Any commercial source of funds will want to check the business, its backers and its proposals before invest-ing and will want to monitor its investment on a regular basis. This is sometimes known as 'due diligence'. The cost of these checks will have to be recouped from any eventual income from the investments made. It is therefore not cost-effective to check requests for small amounts of money, because the cost of checking will not be significantly lower than for larger amounts yet there will be less interest out of which to recoup it. (However some steps can be taken to reduce the costs of small amounts of assistance. One example in the USA is the Wells Fargo Bank which has stopped monitoring many of the small businesses to which it has advanced loans because the cost of monitoring was more than the bad debts it incurred.)

Small businesses lack security for loans. Small businesses often lack the security needed to secure loans, having few or no significant realisable assets in the business.

Small businesses can be equity-averse. There is evidence that many owners of small businesses can be averse to sharing the equity, and therefore the ownership, of the businesses with anyone else. Investors, however, often like to take some equity because it gives them some control over their investments and an oppor-tunity to make greater returns.

Grants produce dependency. Because of their potential contribution to economic development, grants are sometimes considered to assist small business develop-ment and in particular to fill the so-called funding gaps that are perceived.

Source: Based on personal contacts relaying US experience.

Figure 7.1   Early stage small business finance

Without care in their use, however, grants can easily freeze out whatever other sources of funding there are and can build a culture of dependency on 'free' money.

The sources of finance that are generally used by small businesses, especially when they are very small and are in the early stages of development, are the owners' own savings or the resources of family and friends. The result is that a typical pattern of small business funding can be as depicted in Figure 7.1, which is based on American experience.

Small business growth

The growth patterns of small businesses differ from those of big ones. Small size means growth is more likely to be discontinuous than steady, because taking on an extra unit of capacity is a much more significant increase. Not all small businesses grow, and even for those that do, growth can be slow. It has been pointed out that 'seven lean years' between start-up and growth is not at all unusual. Despite this, however, small business growth is the subject of considerable interest because, by definition, it is those small firms that do grow that create the employment that many want to see. It is because of this interest that the next chapter has been devoted specifically to growth issues.

Small business support networks

Many small business owners are inherently suspicious of others who seem to want to interfere in their businesses, including those who may be doing it for the best of motives. (See Figure 7.3 later in this chapter.) Government small business advice centres for instance can be under suspicion in case anything said to them might find its way to other arms of government such as the tax and regulatory authorities. This means that government support initiatives have to find ways of overcoming such reservations if they are to be effective. Support organisations run by businesses or business people are more likely to win clients' confidences. (See also Chapter 12 for more on specific support interventions.)

Small business and social engineering

Small businesses are sometimes seen as having the potential, through their existence, to address issues of disadvantage, such as unemployment or underemployment, and as being a possible source of development for potential community leadership. Small businesses are not however primarily about addressing social problems, but nevertheless this potential is an important dimension for some interested parties, and social engineering and targeting social need can provide the justification for interventions such as the provision of grants. This can lead to a confusion in objectives between funders and business owners, unless the basis for the relationship is clear from the start. In the context of social issues it is also sometimes relevant to recognise that small business is much more compatible with the black economy than big business. A thriving black economy can be prima facie evidence for the existence of at least some elements of an enterprise economy. Moves to legalise unofficial small business can therefore help to reduce the negative effects of illegal trading (see also Chapter Ten).

> We cannot stress enough the importance of individuals making the most of their talents and contributing to their community around them. The Government's aim is to help people to help themselves. That is why I can announce that in the spending review, we will make it possible for anyone anywhere who seriously wants to start a business to get a free package of advice, information and access to mentoring ... And in the high unemployment areas of the country we will support intensive programmes of help ... Our priority in the spending review will be to extend enterprise to all and finance new measures in the poorest areas.
>
> Gordon Brown, UK Chancellor of the Exchequer, June 2000[9]

Why many start-ups fail

According to Storey,[10] the fundamental characteristic, other than size *per se*, which distinguishes small businesses from larger ones is their higher probability of ceasing to trade. As already noted ceasing to trade does not necessarily mean failure, but in many cases that is probably the reason for it. Why small businesses fail however is less easy to state with certainty, both because failure itself is not clearly defined and because the precise causes of it are hard to diagnose.

Table 7.2 Small business problems

Problems cited by a sample of 726 businesses	Proportion of all citings
Low turnover	31.8%
Regulation and paperwork	14.4%
Lack of skilled employees	10.9%
Cash flow/debtors	9.0%
Total tax burden	6.7%
Competition from big business	6.2%
Premises/rent/rates	2.9%
Internal management difficulties	1.9%
Access to finance	1.8%
High rates of pay	0.8%
Interest rates	0.4%
Shortage of supplies	0.4%
Inflation	0.1%
Other	11.0%
No response	1.8%
Total	100.0%

Source: Based on the Nat West/SBRT *Quarterly Survey of Small Business in Britain*, Vol. 17 (March 2001), p. 20. Reproduced with permission from the Small Business Research Trust.

In theory post-mortems could be carried out on individual business failures but this is rarely done. What is more common is to ask small businesses which have not yet failed (and therefore still exist to be asked) to indicate what their problems are. This produces lists such as that in Table 7.2. But the problems are inevitably linked and it is hard to say which problems are causes and which are symptoms.

Another approach is to look at the businesses which have failed and to try to establish correlations with other factors. Storey[11] presents the following useful summary of factors which appear to influence the probability of failure of a business:

- *Age*. As firms get older their chances of survival increase and this is sometimes attributed to the liability of newness. There is a great deal to learn about running a business and expertise grows with time. Other researchers talk about the 'liability of adolescence'.[12] However most firms when they start have a stock of resources and energy, which sees them through their early months or years. When this stock is used up many firms will fail. Thereafter the usual liability of newness arguments apply.
- *Size*. Failure rates are inversely related to the size of the firm at start-up. It has been suggested that larger firms are less likely to fail because, if a firm is relatively large at start-up then it will quickly benefit from economies of scale.

Furthermore, it will probably have sufficient financial resources to see it through its teething problems and it may also be in a good position to raise additional capital.

- *Sector*. Firms in different sectors of the economy exhibit different failure rates. In Britain, for example, failure rates in manufacturing are greater than in various service sectors although Storey notes that variations across sectors are not as great as economists would expect. Indeed, differences in failure rates within sectors are greater than across sectors.
- *Past performance*. Those firms which are able to grow are less likely to fail than those which maintain the status quo. Growth signifies development and learning, which are crucial ingredients for survival. Interestingly survival rates are not linked to the rate of growth. Achieving some growth is the determining factor.

These are the more important factors connected with survival but there are others such as:

- *Ownership*. There is some evidence that the form of ownership can reverse the finding that, other things being equal, smaller firms have higher failure rates than larger firms. It has been argued that larger firms with less personal ownership will more readily leave an industry if demand is falling whilst smaller firms will struggle on. This might arise because larger firms have several plants and they may well close their non-economic plants promptly. In addition, larger firms may have multiple interests and they will divert their resources from an area of declining demand to more profitable sectors.
- *People/management*. It is likely that the kind of managers and non-managerial personnel who work in a firm will influence performance. At the very least there would seem to be a link between competence and success. Storey reviewed a number of studies which attempted to assess how work history with particular reference to previous business ownership and management experience, education, family background and personal characteristics such as gender, age and ethnic background influenced business performance. He concluded that whilst there is much speculation on the impact of these variables 'it is difficult to draw clear patterns from the results so far'.[13]
- *Location*. Research reveals that there are *pro rata* many more business failures in urban as opposed to rural areas in the United Kingdom. However, urban areas also have the greatest number of business formations and since young firms are vulnerable it is not surprising that high start-up and failure rates are connected. Another finding in this area is that those locations which provide support for SMEs in the form of loans or business advice are likely to have lower failure rates than other areas. Support could be vital for success if crucial resources were being provided but it might also be that the existence of support agencies is indicative of a supportive climate for business formation. Sometimes support is in essence a subsidy for the SME and it is interesting

to note that there is little association between subsidy and success. A subsidy is no substitute for a lack of ability or motivation.

- *Firm type.* The final issue investigated by Storey is the connection between the type of business and propensity to fail. Franchise businesses have been found to be less risky ventures than VAT-registered businesses in general and limited companies are less risky than sole proprietorships or partnerships. Cooperatives however have similar failure rates to VAT-registered businesses in general.

- *Macro-economic conditions.* It would seem logical to expect that macro-economic conditions would have an influence on failure rates and some studies have attempted to explore this. For instance the influence of interest rates, which might be thought to be a condition with a very direct influence, has been examined. However there the evidence seems to be inconclusive and it has been suggested that this may be because SMEs do not experience credit squeezes in the way that larger firms do. So too with other conditions and so, while there is some evidence that macro-economic conditions affect failure rates, overall it may not be as strong as might be expected.

An understanding of the connection between these factors and failures is very useful for economic planners but few of the factors are amenable to manipulation by owner-managers. To identify things that owner-managers can do to minimise the chances of failure it is necessary to appreciate the everyday problems that they experience. An analysis carried out in Australia[14] indicated that sales and marketing difficulties were the most common problems encountered. Owners had little appreciation of the marketing concept, had few marketing skills and considered that marketing was synonymous with public relations and advertising. More specifically they had considerable difficulty with market research and promotion. In view of the importance of developing markets for continued business success, interventions to increase marketing awareness and skill seem appropriate.

The survey also found that the businesses were deficient in general management skills. They found it difficult to produce business plans and manage growth but one particular area of concern at the time of the study was the need to have appropriate quality assurance systems. With respect to human resources the biggest problems by far concerned training and development but recruitment and selection also created dilemmas. Some attempt was made to discover if personnel-type problems varied with the size of the firms but for all categories paying wages and benefits, obtaining good people and training were critical issues.

Several firms were attempting to grow and product development difficulties arose. A range of difficulties including pricing and promotion were raised but the biggest concern was over intellectual property protection. There is legislation in Australia for the protection of these rights but the high cost of the service means that many new product ideas are not exploited commercially. The firms also had difficulty in raising start-up finance and in managing cash flows.

Results from this study are largely in keeping with the findings from previous research in the UK and elsewhere, and provide a useful guideline for those whose aim is to support the owners and managers of small firms. It is possible to develop marketing, management, people and financial skills as well as the technical skills which are specific to a particular business enterprise and improving competencies in these areas should improve business performance.

An understanding of the problems that small firms face and the environmental forces that put pressure on them is useful but problems can be overcome. Smallbone, North and Leigh[15] argue that a key factor in survival is the adjustments that firms make to overcome their difficulties. Adjustment requires diagnosis, decision-making and action and depends on effective change management. However, it can be argued that the very characteristics which are needed by entrepreneurs can prevent proper managerial adjustment. For example, high achievers can undertake high-profile but unprofitable projects to feed their egos; independent entrepreneurs can reject the advice proffered by outsiders, and self-confidence can border on the delusional. These ingredients are present within many firms but failure does not always occur. However, small firms often do not have the financial resources to absorb environmental shocks, their owners and management teams are often deficient in managerial knowledge and skill, company structures are often weak and the dominant position of the owner-manager means that any of his or her character flaws cannot easily be offset even by a strong management team. Consequently, any or all of these factors can prevent adjustment and trigger a decline and subsequent failure.

There is therefore no simple solution to the problem of failure. Enterprise does have an inherent element of risk and failure might be reduced but will never be

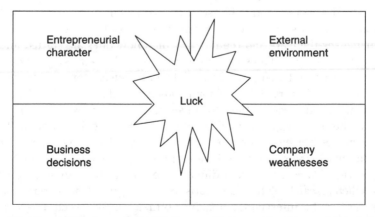

Source: Slightly modified version of P. Burns, *Entrepreneurship and Small Business*, (Basingstoke: Palgrave (now Palgrave Macmillan), 2001), p. 271. Reproduced with the permission of Palgrave Macmillan.

Figure 7.2 The ingredients of failure

eliminated. The recipe for failure will vary from situation to situation but the ingredients for it are at least known. They are summarised by Burns in Figure 7.2.

Small businesses and job creation

There has been considerable interest in recent years in small business statistics, largely because of the work of Birch and others in highlighting the contribution small businesses make to employment and to economic development. Two questions in particular have been raised: first, what is the extent of the overall contribution of small businesses to job creation; and second, does this contribution come, in the main, from all small businesses or from only a few of them? The questions are very relevant to the targeting of government intervention to promote employment, but the answers are not always clear. The first is about the validity of Birch's work and its application to other countries such as the UK, and the second is about which small businesses create most jobs. Exploring issues such as these highlights a number of problems in small business statistics, which may require some insight if they are to be interpreted properly.

A note of caution

Before looking at these questions in more detail it is important to emphasise that a key problem in studying entrepreneurship and small businesses quantitatively is the availability of appropriate data. There is often a distinct difference between the data which are desired and those that are available. Frequently therefore the data used are borrowed from other sources. For instance, in order to explore the issue of entrepreneurship in the UK, many people would like to know how many small businesses there are and the rate at which new ones are started and others terminate. However the data source often used to indicate this is that of business VAT registrations and many businesses do not register for VAT because their turnover is below the threshold; and many businesses de-register, not because they are terminating, but because their turnover has fallen below the threshold. VAT statistics do not provide good small business data because they cover neither only small businesses nor every small business. Nevertheless they are used because they are the best that are available. Another problem is that the data borrowed may record the right subject but use a different definition in a different context. For instance when researching the characteristics of fast-growth small business, which is a popular area for intervention, making comparisons between different studies is often problematic because of significant variations in the definitions of 'fast growth'. The terms 'small businesses', 'start-ups', 'self-employment', 'owner-managers', 'entrepreneurs' and 'SMEs' are all frequently used, often apparently interchangeably, but they are not the same and to explore each fully would require different datasets in each case. Often however these are not readily available and therefore in many cases the distinction is lost in those data which are used.

The validity of Birch

Birch first indicated in 1979 the significant role that small businesses play in the creation of employment. His original work concluded that 81.5 per cent of all net new jobs formed in the USA between 1969 and 1976 were formed by firms with fewer than a hundred employees. Armington and Odle, on the other hand, subsequently looked at job creation results for 1978–1980 using a database specially created by the US Small Business Administration (SBA) and found that less than 40 per cent of net new jobs were created by businesses with fewer than a hundred employees. They had no explanation for the difference as against Birch's figures, but speculated that Birch may have made errors. Subsequently, Armington and Odle have been cited as experts who found Birch to be in error, but, according to Kirchhoff, what is less commented on is that their subsequent research validated Birch and showed that percentages calculated in their way were cyclical.[16]

Sixteen years after Birch, Kirchhoff stated that, 'It seems safe to say that, on average, firms with less than 100 employees create the majority of net new jobs in the US economy.'[17] Others however still disagree. Davis, Haltiwanger and Schuh, in their book *Job Creation and Destruction*, based on the Longitudinal Research Database constructed by the US Census Bureau, state that they 'found no strong, systematic relationship between employer size and net job growth rates'.[18] There is therefore no single agreed verdict on the validity of Birch, who was in any case only looking at the situation in the USA. Nevertheless, right or not, his work was, to a very large extent, the trigger for much current interest in small businesses. Subsequent careful work in both improving and examining the SBA's database appears to have shown that fluctuations in the economy of the USA reveal themselves mainly through job changes in larger firms and that small businesses are consistent net creators of jobs. Taking the period 1976–1988 as a whole, it is now estimated that businesses with fewer than twenty employees provided 19.4 per cent of total employment, but about 37 per cent of net new jobs. In the UK a similar analysis has been carried out with broadly similar results. One analysis indicated 'that during the 1987–9 period, 54 per cent of the increase in employment was in firms with fewer than 20 workers'.[19] In the UK, however, all components of employment change are of lower magnitude than in the USA, and job change in the latter is more strongly influenced by births and deaths, especially of large businesses, whereas in the UK job change 'is more influenced by expansions and contractions'.[20] Nevertheless in both countries there are arguments that small businesses do indeed make a disproportionately large contribution to net job creation. Studies of European, Japanese and Australian businesses, as well as American ones, have also found that firms with fewer than 100 employees are net contributors to employment growth, contributing as much as 75 per cent of new jobs.[21]

Which small businesses create jobs?

If small businesses create significant proportions of net new jobs then govern-ments and others trying to increase employment will be particularly interested in them. However, there are very many small businesses, and support would be spread thinly if it went to all of them. Indications that within the small business population it is a relatively small proportion of each year's cohort of businesses that create a disproportionate share of the jobs over time have had a particular appeal. In the UK, Storey has frequently asserted that 'out of every 100 small firms, the fastest growing four firms will create 50 per cent of the jobs in the group over a decade'.[22] The implication of this was that, if support could be focused on those four businesses, or on the few businesses that had the potential for such growth, it would be applied much more effectively than if all 100 businesses were to be supported. These high-growth businesses are the sort of businesses that Birch called 'gazelles'.

Storey's statement needs to be examined with some care, however. He himself points out that the data it is based on are rather old, but he does indicate that other data, in particular from Northern Ireland, produce fairly close results. He also acknowledges that the data refer only to manufacturing businesses and then only to new ones.

There is also another issue. Despite the way it is sometimes interpreted, Storey's statement does not mean that four per cent of small businesses create 50 per cent of the jobs. What Storey says is that if 100 businesses are started in year t, in the year $t + 10$ only 40 of those businesses may have survived and just 4 of those sur-viving businesses will between them employ as many people as are employed by all the other survivors put together. However, that also means that half of the employment in the survivors will not be in those four businesses, nor will the employment during the intervening ten years in the 60 businesses that did not survive to the end of the period. Storey's own table[23] indicates that all of the four high-growth businesses at the end of ten years employ more than 25 people (one employs 25 to 49, two employ 50 to 99, and one employs over 100); yet he also indicates that businesses with fewer than 20 employees created 'between 78 per cent (1985–7) and 85 per cent of total new employment' from small businesses.[24] It is very hard to compare these figures directly with the ten-year cohort figures and to say how many of them are due to the early stages of growth of the four-per-cent high-growth businesses. For instance in any one year there will be the following:

Jobs in Storey's four per cent of the businesses which started ten years earlier

---

plus

An equal number of jobs in the other surviving businesses which started ten years earlier

---

plus

Jobs in businesses which started fewer than ten years earlier (not all of which will survive the ten years but are nevertheless employing people in the interim)

---

plus

Jobs in businesses started more than ten years ago (some of which will be the four per cent businesses from the earlier cohorts but some of which will also be the other businesses which are nevertheless growing)

Without comparable figures for all these groups, comparisons cannot be made. It would be expected from a Pareto analysis that a relatively small proportion of small businesses that grow significantly would have a disproportionate share of the total employment over time. Nevertheless, the major part of the employment in small businesses appears to come from the other small businesses employing fewer than 20 people, not from the fastest-growing four per cent.

Recent analysis has also confirmed a link between small business start-up rates and employment. A model produced by van Stel, Dielbandhoesing, van den Heuvel and Storey using data for the period 1980 to 1998 shows that in Britain business start-up activity in the late 1980s had a direct positive effect on subsequent employment change, whereas in the early 1980s start-up activity contributed to growth only after a number of years.[25]

A further factor in small business employment which should not be ignored is that most small businesses are in the service sector, which is labour-intensive and for which output can often only be increased by taking on new staff. These staff frequently come from the secondary labour market and may be prepared to work for relatively low wages. Expansion of these businesses will therefore increase employment, and consequently reduce unemployment payments, without causing inflation. This is very attractive to governments.

Dynamic versus static analysis

One of the reasons why Birch's original findings were surprising was that they were contrary to previous research and thinking on job creation. They were also based on a dynamic analysis, while the previous research was carried out using static analysis. Such static analysis is carried out using classified data in the form published by government statistics agencies. Those publications will, for instance, list the number of businesses in given size ranges and the number of jobs in them at the end of each period. However, for a given business size range, the difference between the number of jobs at the end of one period and the number at the end of the previous period does not give the number of jobs created in that period by businesses in that size range. The reason may be illustrated by considering a business employing 70 people which over a period grows by 50 per cent and therefore at the end employs 105 people. At the beginning it would have been classified in the 1 to 100 employee size range, but at the end it is in the 100-plus size range. The effect is thus to reduce by 70 the number of jobs in businesses in the 1 to 100 size range, and increase by 105 the number of jobs in businesses in the higher size range. The static statistics will therefore show a reduction of jobs in businesses in the lower size range and an increase in the higher size range. The reality however is that the net increase came from a business that was in the lower size range. In the reverse situation, however, the shrinkage of a business initially in a higher size range will appear at the end of the period as a reduction in that size range, because *either* the business will still be in the size range but with fewer jobs *or* it will have left the size range and all its jobs will appear to have gone. A lower size range will then correspondingly appear to have grown. Static analysis assumes implicitly that the net inter-class movement of businesses is negligible, which may not be the case.

Cohort analysis

Cohort, or dynamic, analysis, in which a class of subjects is tracked as it changes over time, will avoid the problem of static research analysis. It will also reveal other interesting features of growth. Dynamic analysis of US small businesses has, for instance, indicated that survival rates of businesses improve exponentially with, for a group founded at the same time, a smaller proportion of the original number terminating in each successive year. It has also shown that less than half of the surviving businesses show any growth in the first six years, but that at between six and eight years of age the number of businesses that show growth leaps increases significantly: a result that confirms suggestions of the 'seven lean years' of business development and indicates that observing business survival and growth over a lesser period may be misleading. In taking only new business starts and looking at their employment after ten years, Storey may therefore be missing from his 'high-growth' business those businesses that do not start to grow until after seven years or more.

Another factor which might usefully be taken into consideration when looking for growth is highlighted in the work of Rosa and Scott, already mentioned in Chapter Six, on multiple business ownership. They suggest that if the unit of analysis is the business, which it often is, then this will not provide a full picture. Instead they suggest that the unit of analysis should be the entrepreneur, or team of entrepreneurs, who may start several businesses. They talk of clusters of businesses with linked ownership in which 'diversifying into additional businesses may not only be common but may also be associated with positive growth strategies'.[26] This means that growth from an entrepreneur already in business can occur through new business creation rather than through the growth of already established businesses and that would not be picked up by an analysis with a business unit focus.

Summary

It would appear that there is now clear evidence that small businesses do create a disproportionate amount of new employment. However different researchers vary in their estimates of how much, and there do appear to be variations over time and across countries. It is not yet clear whether this employment is mainly due to only a small proportion of that small business population or to all of it. This lack of clarity may be due to different researchers measuring differ-ent things and to their findings being misinterpreted or misrepresented, but overall it would appear that most of those new jobs at a particular point in time come from the very small businesses in the smallest size ranges and not from Birch's 'gazelles'. The impact of the 'gazelles' is seen when following the job-creation activity of a cohort of businesses over time. It is also important to be aware that, while on average net new jobs may come from small businesses, the performance of the large firms sector and the fluctuations in its employment will also have a significant impact on the overall employment position.

SECTION B – THE FEATURES OF 'SMALL' ENTREPRENEURS

In Chapter Six and above the point was made that, in exploring the subject of enterprise, the fundamental unit to consider should be the entrepreneur, not the firm. So far in this chapter, however, features of small firms have been considered, but many of these are related to the ways that the entrepreneurs behind them think and behave. The issues considered next, while manifest in small businesses, are nevertheless specifically concerned with the owner-managers of those businesses and how they can differ in their attitudes and actions from the owners and managers of larger businesses.

The transition out of employment

The pre-start-up stage of small business development has been described in Chapter Six, and it has its own particular issues to be understood. Despite the emphasis that has been put on the benefits of small business, the predictions of increasing numbers of people who will not have the option of lifetime employment, and the varieties of help available to ease the business start-up process, moving from employment to self-employment can be traumatic. Business planning can help to indicate the physical and financial provisions necessary to establish a business, but not the mental changes necessary.

Especially if the change is an enforced one, such as when it is occasioned by redundancy, the range of mental adjustments that have to be made can be considerable. One study[27] identified six phases in the process of leaving employment in this way:

Immobilisation	The change in status shocks and overwhelms to the extent that understanding, reasoning and planning are not possible.
Minimising change	The first reaction to change is to try to minimise it and to try to carry on as if it hadn't happened.
Depression	When the reality of change can no longer be avoided depression sets in; change has happened, but is neither desired nor understood.
Acceptance	Eventually however the reality of change is accepted, the turning point has been reached.
Testing	Previous attitudes and assumptions are relinquished; new concepts, methods and ways of coping are tested.
Meaning	As this progresses, stereotypes are abandoned, new possibilities emerge and success can be possible in the search for a new meaning.

If the process of leaving employment is continued into starting one's own business, then other changes have to be made. Lessem[28] suggests that they include:

Employee to employer	You become the giver, not just a receiver. You set the standards, not just adhere to them. You accept responsibility for other people's jobs. Money becomes important.
Salary to profit	You need to spend before you receive. Income becomes uncertain. Your family cannot be kept at arm's length.

| Evaluator to decision-maker | You need to consider the options, evaluate them, and then make tough choices. |
| Specialist to generalist | You need to call on technical, marketing, financial, administrative, people and management skills, and possibly all of them from yourself. |

Identification with the business

Once the business has started, the founding entrepreneur is likely to identify with it closely. No matter how dedicated he or she may be, a professional manager brought in to run a business is unlikely to identify with that business to the extent many business founders do. 'The business is the ego', as Gibb points out,[29] 'and therefore even objective criticism of the business is taken personally'. The implications of this include the facts that:

- a business 'consulting' approach, which attempts to analyse and list what is wrong with a business before suggesting corrective actions, will be rejected because it is perceived as a personal criticism. Instead, a 'counselling' approach, which seeks to help the owner himself or herself to identify some of the issues, stands a better chance of being accepted and producing change;
- perceived social status or acceptability may be linked to business success. Indications of business problems will therefore be played down, hidden or even denied, not just in public but also in private, in case they might have an impact on social status.

The values embodied in the business will often be those of the owner-founder and can be revealed in the products or services supplied, growth orientation, quality standards and employee relations. Where these values of the owner differ from those of business advisers, the input of the latter is likely to be rejected and, indeed, small business owners often lack the confidence to discuss problems with professionals. For these reasons, an owner's support network is likely to be based on personal friendships and contacts, rather than on the formal support network.

The influences on a small business

In seeking to understand the behaviour of a small business what matters is often not so much the influences on the business as the influences on its owner. It is not always obvious however what these influences will be or what will be the interplay between the different influences. The relative strengths of the influences of different groups of people are indicated in a diagram produced by Gibb to indicate the layers of small business support networks (see Figure 7.3). One implication of this is that the closer, and more personal, layers may always have a much stronger influence than the outer, and more official, layers.

Source: A. A. Gibb, 'Towards the Building of Entrepreneurial Models of Support for Small Business', Paper presented at the 11th (UK) National Small Firms Policy and Research Conference, Cardiff, 1988, p. 17.

Figure 7.3   The layers of the small business support network

The totality of influences on a small business is often not appreciated. For instance, if assistance is made available to encourage small business development, it may be designed to add a positive influence, but it is unlikely to work if it does not outweigh other existing negative influences. If friends when consulted are negative in their advice then it is likely that it will be far more influential than any positive input from government agencies. It can be helpful to portray the possible influences on a business as being of three types: those that may influence the business to be more competitive; those that may influence it to be less competitive; and those that may influence it to stay where it is. The latter can be the most powerful. Trying to make a business more competitive can be likened to trying to move a heavy weight uphill. Gravity may tend to drag it back, friction and inertia tend to keep it where it is, and only the push applied uphill will tend to move it in the desired direction. This analogy is pursued further in Chapter Eight.

It may also be relevant to compare the prime influences on, and sources of advice for, small businesses with those relating to big businesses. The most powerful influence in a small business often comes from the ownership. This is often one person or a small group who take an active role in the business. They are much more influential on the business than the shareholder owners of a bigger business who, because they are external and disparate, have less immediate impact. In contrast, however, suppliers and customers, although they are external, can have a much bigger influence on a small business than a big business. Some reasons for this are that a small business generally has less market influence in pricing or advertising than a big business, and is likely to have fewer customers and to work more closely with them. Other external influences on big businesses can include trades unions, public bodies and pressure groups. Small businesses, in contrast, are less likely to be unionised, are more likely to try to ignore regulations, and are a less rewarding target for campaigns.

Inside a small firm the owner-manager is often all-powerful. While in a big business the chief executive can be very powerful, he or she still has to answer to a chairman and board, and to work with professional senior managers who often have expert knowledge relevant to their particular functions. In big businesses a unionised workforce can have the influence of its combined strength exercised through the union structure. Also, generally, in big businesses professional sources of advice are used. The small business owner-manager, in contrast, has fewer such sources of influence and will instead be more likely to listen to his or her own inclinations, to rely on his or her own experience and to seek advice, if that is needed, from a network of personal contacts. The small business owner-manager, in comparison with the manager of a larger business, often has less general professionalism but more flexibility and knowledge of his or her particular niche.[30]

Women-owned businesses

Another aspect of business ownership which might be expected to have an influence on the business is the gender of the owner. Female entrepreneurs are considered in Chapter Three and there are some aspects of female entrepreneurship which may be reflected in their businesses. Cromie[31] however examined the problems experienced by male- and female-owned young businesses and discovered that the problems experienced did not really vary by gender. His sample faced a diverse set of personal problems, including lack of time; having to perform a myriad of duties; working too hard; selling oneself; being too conservative; lacking interpersonal skills; and not being taken seriously. Men and women both experienced personal problems but women recorded more difficulties. This is especially true with respect to a lack of self-confidence and not being taken seriously which, when applied by providers of funds, has led to the under-capitalisation of their businesses. However, women respondents did say that once it was clear that they were committed to making a success of their businesses these problems disappeared.

Similarly, Carter argues that certain problems were perceived by women to be gender-related. These include the 'late payment of bills; a tendency to undercharge; getting business and finding clients; and…the effect of proprietorship upon personal and domestic circumstances'.[32]

Business finance

In Britain, Carter reviewed recent work on the financing of women-owned firms and suggested that there have been four recurring problems:[33]

- They have difficulty in obtaining start-up finance.
- They are required to provide guarantees when seeking external finance and they are sometimes unable to provide the requisite collateral.

- They find it more difficult to obtain ongoing finance.
- Bankers tend to have negative stereotypes of women entrepreneurs and discriminate against them.

Results from a recent study by Carter and Rosa[34] indicate that there is support for some of these propositions but some differences are accounted for by factors such as firm size and industrial sector. Women do have less start-up finance than men but they use the same sources: personal money, overdrafts and bank loans. There are also gender differences in the use of ongoing finance: women are more likely to use loans while men are more likely to use overdrafts and supplier credit. Carter and Rosa found no support for the propositions about the need for guarantees nor the supposed negative stereotypical images of women by bankers. In general there appears to be little evidence of deliberate discrimination against women.

The survival of female-owned businesses

There is *prima facie* evidence that female-owned businesses do not survive as long as male-owned businesses, which might be because of the under-capitalisation of female firms at start-up. A recent British study investigated this issue but argued that research on the performance of women-owned firms is complicated by the different theoretical stances adopted by various authors; by the fact that only sole business owners are investigated; by assumptions that male and female entrepreneurs are homogeneous, and by conflicting ideas on whether biological differences between men and women cause them to adopt different socio-economic roles.[35] It was also pointed out that there were lots of contradictions in quantitative studies of the performance of male- and female-owned firms and that some studies do not allow for the fact that women tend to set up businesses in sectors which traditionally have higher failure rates.

It has also been argued that women's life experiences are very different from men's, with the consequence that women do business differently from men.[36] Men are said to aim for profit and growth whilst women focus on relationships and integrate business relationships into their lives. Others however do not feel that such conclusions can be drawn from the evidence.

Ethnic businesses

Another type of small business ownership with distinctive features is the ethnic-owned business. Immigrants come to their adopted country for a number of reasons. In Britain after the Second World War, immigrants came from the Caribbean, South Asia and other areas to work in various industries which were short of labour, but their intention was to earn money to send back home and eventually to return home themselves. However, in 1962 entry to the UK from the British Commonwealth was severely restricted and immigrant workers already in Britain's urban areas decided to remain and to bring their families there as well. This led to the development of large ethnic enclaves in inner city areas where, it has been suggested, due to the decline in large scale industrial employment, to the racism and discrimination they faced in the labour market, and to the revival of the SME sector in the 1980s, people were encouraged to create their own firms.[37]

Ethnic entrepreneurs are considered in Chapter Three, but what, if anything, distinguishes an ethnic business from a small business which happens to be run by someone from an immigrant community? Among the answers suggested are the following:

- A business which draws heavily on a group 'that is socially distinguished (by others or itself) by characteristics of cultural or national origin'[38] for tangible and intangible resources, markets and support constitutes a special kind of small business. Ethnic businesses also develop 'connections and regular patterns of interaction' among people from particular cultural backgrounds.[39] Such ethnic enterprises are commonplace in many parts of the world but problems with definitions and the sheer diversity of these ventures present difficulties for those who try to quantify the phenomenon.
- Ethnic entrepreneurs in different countries may be from different backgrounds. In Britain, Pakistanis, Indian Sikhs, Nigerians, West Indians and East African refugees are common whereas in the USA, Koreans, Mexicans, and Vietnamese are found. Neverthless there is some uniformity in their choice of business activity. For example in North America studies[40] have revealed that ethnic businesses predominate in the wholesale, retail, and service sectors with some presence in light manufacturing, and a recent study in Britain of 82 ethnic minority businesses supports the American finding.[41] However, there were variations amongst the different groups of ethnic business and these can be explained partly by the cultural backgrounds of the respondents, their educational backgrounds and the length of time they have been in the country.
- Two aspects of business in which ethnic businesses rely particularly heavily on others from the same ethnic group are in finding customers and in obtaining labour. Successful businesses must find customers and it is sometimes argued that firms which fully understand the special needs of ethnic groups, and can thus deliver more appropriate benefits, are at a competitive advantage. In addition, co-ethnic customers may patronise a particular firm because of a sense of ethnic solidarity with the owner. These factors may confer initial competitive advantage but it has been argued[42] that sustained competitive advantage will only arise when a business has a strategy which no other business is following and when other businesses cannot duplicate the benefits on offer. However, for ethnic businesses located in service and retail areas where barriers to entry

are low, there are many competitors who can follow the same strategy and offer similar benefits. In Britain therefore, where large scale immigration has ceased and ethnic populations are displaying a degree of social and geographical mobility, the outcome is increasingly 'a mass of ethnic small business owners trapped in a hostile trading milieu'.[43]

- Labour requirements for small ethnic businesses also come largely from co-ethnics in the community and from the extended family. At start-up having a supply of part-time labour allows firms to adjust to the ebb and flow of initial workloads and is cheap and easy to organise. Many of the jobs on offer in the start-up phase are offered to co-ethnics on an informal basis. Indeed, the most noticeable feature of the labour force amongst ethnic businesses is the widespread use of family labour. It is argued[44] that family labour seems attractive in that it helps avoid obstacles to recruitment in the open market, it is flexible and cheap and problems with the supervision of staff can be avoided. Family members can be loyal and committed to the firm and consequently confer advantages on the firm. There is, however, another side to the employment of family members which is more contentious. In many ethnic businesses women manage the production processes as well as attending to the administrative and financial aspects of the business. Men tend to handle external relationships whilst women manage the workflow. This division of labour by gender could be a source of competitive advantage but there is often an exploitative element in the hiring of women. Women manage the work processes and domestic affairs but get little financial or social reward for their endeavours. Men are the official managers, even though women often play 'critical *de facto* managerial roles in running the business'.[45] The domestic subordination of women is reinforced in the workplace in many ethnic businesses.

The lack of prestige afforded to women who manage ethnic family businesses could well have a detrimental effect on economic performance. Another feature of family involvement which is also problematic is the reluctance, also found in non-ethnic family businesses, to recruit non-family managers even when incumbent family managers are less than competent. Family members can be important to ethnic businesses as a means of overcoming the disadvantages of racism and of providing a flexible source of labour, but their over-reliance on the family can also be a source of disadvantage.

Models of success and failure

Another factor which is only perceived when a business in considered from the point of view of its owner is that there can be different models of what constitutes business success or failure. When looking from a business perspective it might be thought that success or failure should be obvious, but a failure to appreciate the owner's perspective can lead to a misunderstanding of what is actually happening.

Models of small business success

What constitutes business success is an aspect of thinking about small business that has not been much commented upon, but which nevertheless probably affects many people's thinking on the subject. The model of success that people have in mind when they talk about small businesses and consider how well they are doing probably falls into one of two categories, depending on whether they are looking primarily at the business or at the person behind it:

- *The business professionals' model.* Many business professionals (which term could include the professional managers of larger businesses, as well as business commentators, advisers, institutional shareholders and academics) look primarily at the business and have as their model of the successful, or 'perfect', business one that is achieving its highest potential in terms of growth, market share, productivity, profitability, return on capital invested or other measures of the performance of the business itself. Professionals may not be conscious that they are adopting this model, because they may fail to see that there is an alternative but, whether it is consciously adopted or not, the result is that a business is often judged by how close it comes to what a 'perfect' business might do in particular circumstances. Small businesses often score badly in such comparisons.
- *The small business proprietors' model.* Many owner-managers of small businesses however do not have the same model as the one just described. Their main concern is whether the business is supplying the benefits they want from it. These benefits are often associated with a lifestyle and an income level to maintain it. If, as already noted, that is achieved satisfactorily then there is no need to grow the business further. Business success for them is being able to reach a level of comfort ('satisficing') rather than achieving the business's maximum potential.

This difference of appreciation may be linked to the different ways in which persons making the appreciation are linked to the business concerned. Even if the 'professional' is employed as the chief executive of a business, he or she probably still sees the business simply as a business, and can compare it therefore with an ideal. It, and its success or failure, may be very important to such persons, but they can and do see those aspects of their life that are not involved with the business as being completely separate. For the small business owner, however, the business is such a crucial and integral part of his or her life that the business and non-business parts of life are not considered separately. Thus the business is seen in terms of life as a whole, including family life, and is subject to more than purely business considerations. The model of a 'perfect' business that the owner has is therefore one that best fits with desired personal goals and values. The stress of further business improvement may be too high a price to pay for a better business if it detracts from other aspects of life, and continuity of employment for well known employees may be more important than increased efficiency.

The implications of having these two different models is that the professionals may see a business as under-performing in terms of its potential as a business, while the owner may see it as successful in terms of what he or she expects from it. In such cases the owners will not automatically share a professional's agenda of pursuing continued business improvement if that involves more effort but has no commensurate increase in benefits.[46]

That does not mean that there will not be scope for further improvement, but it will have to be improvement that also increases the returns desired by the owner from the business. Professionals advising small businesses will be puzzled and ineffective unless they understand this. There is room for their assistance, but they must look at both the negative impact of business improvement on the owner's requirements as well as the positive impact, and ensure that the positive outweighs the negative. The professionals' business model assumes that growth in a business is almost always automatically positive in its effect: the owners' model may not share that assumption. This means that in the extreme case, which is not uncommon, it may be in the owner's perceived best interests to close the business completely, and that obviously doesn't lead to the business performing better. Such a closure is not a failure, but would be counted as such on the professionals' model.

One area where this lack of appreciation of two models is very significant is in business accounting. Traditional accounting focuses on money and therefore has a key place in businesses, because a lack of money is the final symptom of business failure. Thus it needs to be watched closely, and traditional accounting provides the methods of doing this. However, traditional accounting is often linked to business audits and then to reporting on business success or failure. Here the traditional approach is based on the professionals' model or at least on a similar way of thinking. It appraises a business in terms of its financial or other tangible returns and not on any other requirements a business owner may have. Provided that is realised and accepted by the appraisers no problems should emerge. Nevertheless, its very universality of usage means that the traditional method is usually taken as the whole picture, which leaves many business owners feeling that they may be perceived as having failed but not understanding why.

If this two-model concept is correct then it suggests that relatively low productivity in small businesses may sometimes be due, not to a failure of management, but to a different vision of management and of what management should be trying to achieve. The 'may' is because there is undoubtedly a considerable amount of management failure in small business, and by no means all of it is due just to differing agendas being pursued by the various stakeholders. It may be hard however initially to distinguish between 'satisficing' and a mere lack of competence.

Models of small business failure

Just as caution is needed in evaluating the success of a small business, care must also be taken when considering so-called small business failures. Again the problem is one of interpretation and of a propensity to assume that a business closure and a business failure are the same thing.

Most people studying small business will at some time have heard of statements such as 'one in three small firms *go out of business* during the first twelve months' or 'three out of five new businesses *cease trading* within three to five years of starting'. Although statistics, such as those quoted in Table 6.6 in Chapter Six, indicate that such statements are misleading, some claims go further and say that 'one small business in three *fails* in the first three years' or that 'three fifths of businesses *fail* within three to five years'. Those are different things and appear to be quite wrong. The reason that the two sets of statements are different is that there is a difference between business closure and business failure.

Just as there are different models of what constitutes the success of a business, so too there are different models of what constitutes its failure. It may seem that the closure, or termination, of a business and it ceasing to exist as a trading entity is *prima facie* evidence that the business has failed, but that assumption presupposes that the purpose of the business could only be achieved if it continued to exist. That would be the case if the purpose of the business was to maximise the returns from its activities but would not necessarily be so if its owner had other aims in mind for it. If for instance a business is started to provide an income for someone until a pre-planned retirement, and if it does so and is then closed when that retirement time arrives, then the business will both have succeeded in its purpose and been closed. Alternatively, if a business is started as an investment and is then sold for a profit, but the new owner transfers the process to an existing business and closes down the bought business, then again the business has achieved its purpose despite being closed.

This issue was considered in Chapter Six. It is, however, relevant to point out here that instances of business closure are often wrongly described as business failure. Statistics on business failure should therefore be treated warily. The corollary of this is that there are some businesses that do fail, as least in terms of failing to meet their owner-founder's objectives for them, but which don't close. Such a business may still be kept in existence, for instance, either for possible revival in the future, or because it continues to fulfil at least some needs, or to deliver at least some benefit to its owner. The benefit may only be a sop to the owner's pride, but it may be enough to prevent the termination of the business's existence. In such cases, business failure may not lead automatically to business closure.

Working to live

Another category of small business with its own particular issues is the portfolio or part-time business. This is not the same as portfolio entrepreneurship (see Chapter Six), in which one entrepreneur simultaneously has a portfolio of businesses each of which may employ other people. Instead it is when one person engages in more than one activity, which may be a combination, or 'portfolio', of self-employment activities, or a combination of part-time work and part-time self-employment.

Like other aspects of small business, portfolio or part-time businesses can seem different when viewed from different perspectives. From the perspective of the business they can seem to be incomplete, and a less-than-whole-hearted dabbling in business, which may be why business support agencies often refuse to support them. Alternatively, from the point of view of the person concerned, they can be parts of a complete life, and can both be complementary and together provide a balance and diversity which might otherwise be lacking. Thus there are many artists who teach part-time and produce art part-time, some of whom find that the combination of working with people and producing their own work is more rewarding than doing either alone. Also, in rural areas, many people combine part-time farming with another form of income generation, often a part-time business. Without the part-time off-farm income they might have to give up farming completely, which they do not want to do. Both these cases illustrate cases where small businesses are part of the life of the owner, not the ends in themselves, and therefore need to be understood from that perspective.

IN CONCLUSION

Without insight into what is happening, objective observation, it has been suggested, might lead us to conclude that revision causes exams. Without some understanding of the way small businesses behave, and of the factors that influence them, the actions they take may be misunderstood and the wrong conclusions may be drawn about the way they will respond to a stimulus. People who work with small businesses generally do so to achieve a change, either in individual businesses or in groups of them. It is therefore important that they treat them as small businesses, and recognise that they will behave in ways that will not only differ from large businesses but will also differ from one small business to another. Assuming that all small businesses are homogeneous and that they will behave in the same way as big businesses is a recipe for failure in both policy and practice.

THE KEY POINTS OF CHAPTER 7
....

- Small businesses are not big businesses writ small, and concepts, theories and practices that apply to big businesses will not necessarily apply, even on a small scale, to small ones. Neither are small businesses all embryonic big businesses that, as caterpillars turn into butterflies, will eventually metamorphose into big businesses. Many of them will always remain small. Understanding small businesses therefore requires not only an understanding of businesses in general but also an insight into the ways of small ones.

- The characteristics of small businesses that differ from those of big businesses include limited investment and resources, little functional management, and on-the-job learning. Small businesses do however, have many benefits such as meeting many of their owners' needs and the ability to survive market changes by rapidly responding to new customer requirements.

- Just as it is wrong to assume that small businesses will behave and respond like big businesses, it is also very wrong to assume that all small businesses will behave and respond identically. Small businesses in different sectors have their own particular characteristics, as do businesses of different ages and different sizes. Family, ethnic, cooperative and community businesses also have their special features.

- Other particular small business issues include the problems of the transition by an individual out of employment into self-employment; the difference between the view that a business plan is essential for starting a successful small business and the reality that many businesses start without formal plans; the problems of small business finance; small business growth and small businesses as an instrument of social engineering.

- A further potential minefield is the area of small business statistics, where again insight may be needed if they are to be interpreted properly. The original work of Birch, which indicated the job creation benefit of small business, has been challenged but has subsequently been found to be largely correct in both the US and the UK. This has highlighted problems in the completeness of the data, the different relative impact of cyclical fluctuations on large and small businesses, and the research method difference between dynamic and static analysis as well as problems of misunderstanding and misrepresentation.

- Another difference between small and big businesses is the views of their owners. The owner of a small business often identifies closely with it. The implications of this include the necessity for a business 'counselling' approach rather than a 'consulting' one, and the recognition that social status or acceptability may be linked to the success of the business. Also, the values embodied in the business will be those of the owner-founder.

- The influences on a small business are often much clearer if viewed with a focus on the owner rather than on the business. It is not always obvious however who or what will influence a small business or what the interplay will be between different influences. Often at an early stage close families and friends can have more influence than professional business advisers.

As well as positive and negative influences on a business there will also be influences that encourage a business not to change. A positive influence may therefore have no effect if there is a stronger contrary influence.

- Other businesses may also have their particular unique sets of issues to consider. This is the case, for instance, with female- and ethnic-owned businesses.
- In considering small business success there are two main models. Many business professionals have as their model of business success one that involves the business achieving its highest potential. On the other hand, many small business owners have as their main concern whether the business is supplying the benefits they want from it, such as a lifestyle and an adequate income level. Care must also be taken when considering so-called small business failures. Not all business terminations are necessarily due to business failure, nor do all businesses that in reality have failed necessarily close, yet the statistics sometimes presented do not recognise this.

QUESTIONS, EXERCISES, ESSAY AND DISCUSSION TOPICS

- How appropriate is the caterpillar/butterfly analogy to the difference between small and big businesses?
- Producing a business plan is the key to a small business's success. Discuss.
- Small businesses are so varied that it is not practical to have a small business policy. Discuss.
- Is it only those small businesses which grow that contribute to economic benefit?
- Do small businesses create the majority of jobs in your economy?
- What are the main categorisations of small business types? Are these categorisations useful?
- Summarise the problems involved in measuring the employment contributions of businesses of different sizes.
- Are businesses owned by women or by individuals from ethnic minorities at a disadvantage compared to those owned by indigenous males, and what could be done to help them?

SUGGESTIONS FOR FURTHER READING

S. Carter and D. Jones-Evans (eds), *Enterprise and Small Business* (Harlow: Pearson Education, 2000).

D. Storey, *Understanding the Small Business Sector* (London: Routledge, 1994).

REFERENCES

1   E. T. Penrose, *The Theory of the Growth of the Firm* (Oxford: Basil Blackwell, 1959).
2   A. A. Gibb, 'Towards the Building of Entrepreneurial Models of Support for Small Business', *The 11th (UK) National Small Firms Policy and Research Conference* (Cardiff, 1988), pp. 12–15.
3   C. Handy, *The Age of Unreason* (London: Arrow Books, 1990).
4   A. Minkes, *The Entrepreneurial Manager* (Harmondsworth: Penguin, 1987) for a discussion of entrepreneurial decision-making.
5   H. Mintzberg, *The Structuring of Organisations* (Englewood Cliffs, NJ: Prentice-Hall, 1979), pp. 305–13.
6   R. Goffee and R. Scase, 'Proprietorial Control In Family Firms', *Journal of Management Studies* 1985; 22: 53–68.
7   Bank of England, *Finance for Small Firms*, Third Report, January 1998.
8   P. Burns, *Entrepreneurship and Small Business* (Basingstoke: Palgrave (now Palgrave Macmillan), 2001).
9   H M Treasury News Release, 23 June 2000.
10 D. Storey, *Understanding the Small Business Sector* (London: Routledge, 1994), p. 78.
11 Storey, *op. cit.*, pp. 91–104.
12 T. Mahmood, 'Survival of Newly Founded Business: A Log-Logistic Model Approach, *Small Business Economics* 2000; 14: 223–37, at 313.
13 Storey, *op. cit.*, p. 100.
14 X. Huang and A. Brown, 'An Analysis and Classification of Problems In Small Business', *International Small Business Journal* 1999; 18: 73–85.
15 D. Smallbone, D. North and R. Leigh, *Managing Change for Growth and Survival: A Study of Mature Manufacturing Firms in London During the 1980s*, Working paper No. 3 (London: Middlesex Polytechnic, Planning Research Centre, 1992).
16 B. Kirchhoff, 'Twenty Years of Job Creation Research: What Have We Learned?', *The 40th Conference of the International Council for Small Business*, 1995, pp. 201–2.
17 *Ibid.*, p. 202.
18 S. J. Davis, J. C. Haltiwanger and S. Schuh, *Job Creation and Destruction* (Cambridge, MA: MIT Press, 1996), p. 170.
19 Storey, *op.cit.*, p. 165.
20 *Ibid.*, p. 168.
21 OECD, *Globalisation and Small and Medium Enterprises*, Synthesis Report, Vol. 1 (Paris: OECD, 1997), p. 122.
22 *Ibid.*, p. 113.
23 *Ibid.*, p. 114.
24 *Ibid.*, p. 168.
25 A. van Stel, S. Dielbandhoesing, W. van den Heuvel and D. Storey, 'Entrepreneurial Growth in Great Britain: British Regions In the Period 1980–1998', personal correspondence relating to a not yet published paper.
26 P. Rosa and M. Scott, 'Entrepreneurial Diversification, Business-Cluster Formation and Growth', *Government and Policy* 1999; 17: 527–47, at 527.
27 J. Hayes and P. Nutman, *Understanding the Unemployed* (London: Tavistock, 1981).
28 R. Lessem, 'Getting into Self Employment', *Management Education and Development* 1984; Spring: 44.

29 Gibb (1988), *op. cit.*, p. 14.
30 For a discussion on the various sources of influence on organisations, see H. Mintzberg, *Power In and Around Organizations* (Englewood Cliffs, NJ: Prentice-Hall, 1983), pp. 32–46.
31 S. Cromie, 'The Problems Experienced by Young Firms', *International Small Business Journal* 1991; 9: 43–67.
32 S. Carter, 'Gender and Enterprise', in S. Carter and D. Jones-Evans (eds), *Enterprise and Small Business*, (Harlow: Pearson Education, 2000), p. 172.
33 *Ibid.*, p. 167.
34 S. Carter and P. Rosa, 'The Financing of Male- and Female-Owned Businesses', *Entrepreneurship and Regional Development* 1998; 10: 225–41.
35 E. Chell and S. Baines, 'Does Gender Affect Business Performance? A Study of Microbusinesses In Business Services In the UK', *Entrepreneurship and Regional Development* 1998; 10: 117–35.
36 C. G. Brush, S. Marlow and A. Strange, 'Female Entrepreneurs: Success by Whose Standards?', in M Taunton (ed.), *Women in Management: A Developing Presence* (London: Routledge, 1994).
37 A. Phizacklea and M. Ram, 'Ethnic Entrepreneurship In Comparative Perspective', *International Journal of Entrepreneurial Behaviour and Research* 1995; 1: 48–58.
38 L. M. Dyer and C. A. Ross, 'Ethnic Enterprises and their Clientele', *Journal of Small Business Management* 2000; 38: 48–60.
39 R. Waldinger, H. E. Aldrich and R. Ward, *Ethnic Entrepreneurs: Immigrant Businesses in Industrial Societies* (Newbury Park: CA: Sage, 1990), p. 33.
40 V. C. Vincent, 'Decision-Making Policies Among Mexican-American Small Business Entrepreneurs', *Journal of Small Business Management* 1996; 34: 1–13; Dyer and Ross, *op.cit.*; P. G. Greene, 'A Resource Based Approach to Ethnic Business Sponsorship: A Consideration of Ismaili-Pakistani Immigrants', *Journal of Small Business Management* 1997; 35: 57–71.
41 A. Fadahunsi, D. Smallbone and S. Supri, 'Networking and Ethnic Minority Enterprise Development: Insights From a North London Study', *Journal of Small Business and Enterprise Development* 2000; 7: 228–40.
42 D. M. Flynn, 'Sponsorship and Survival of New Organisations', *Journal of Small Business Management* 1993; 31: 51–62.
43 M. Ram, 'Ethnic Minority Enterprise: An Overview and Research Agenda', *International Journal of Entrepreneurial Behaviour and Research*, 1997; 3: 149–56, at 150.
44 M. Ram, 'Unravelling Social Networks In Ethnic Minority Firms', *International Small Business Journal*, Vol. 1994; 12(3): 42–53, at 44.
45 *Ibid.*, at 51.
46 For a discussion on the overlap between personal goals and business goals in SMEs, see R. Goffee and R. Scase, *Corporate Realities* (London: Routledge, 1995), pp. 1–21.

CHAPTER 8

BUSINESS GROWTH

CONTENTS

KEY CONCEPTS

This chapter covers:
- the reason why government policies have focused on growth businesses;
- how business growth can be interpreted;

- the internal and external influences on business growth;
- the arguments for and against targeting growth businesses.

LEARNING OBJECTIVES
....

By the end of this chapter the reader should:
- understand the rationale for a focus on growth;
- understand what growth can mean;
- understand the range of possible influences on growth;
- understand why so few businesses grow to be large;
- understand the case for and against a policy of 'picking winners'.

INTRODUCTION—WHY GROWTH?

In the 1990s there was a substantial shift in focus and emphasis in the field of small business towards the growing business. This shift in the UK and elsewhere was evident in policy-making, in the application of small business support, and in related research and commentaries. Fast growing small firms have been described as 'gazelles', 'fliers', 'growers' and 'winners', and the targeting of effort towards them has been described as 'picking', 'stimulating', or 'backing' winners.

While more recently there has been a further shift back towards support for the start-up process, it is reasonable to ask why the interest in growth developed. It is likely that, just as the earlier emphasis on small businesses in general arose from a recognition of their contribution to the economy, this focus came from a similar desire to maximise that contribution. Birch's study, and other subsequent studies, had claimed to show that the major proportion of net new jobs is created by small businesses. Governments and others saw that there could be economic benefit in supporting small businesses. More detailed analysis showed that many small businesses did not grow and therefore, once established, did not create more jobs. It was suggested that it was a relatively small proportion of small business starts that did subsequently show significant growth and were responsible for much of the main employment benefits over time. The argument, therefore, was that if small business support resources were limited, which was invariably the case, then the way to maximise results was to apply those resources where they would be most effective. The small business sector is huge and varied, and if support has to be rationed, and if growth businesses produce a disproportionately large share of the desired jobs, then the logical thing to do is to concentrate that support on growth businesses in order to secure the best return. (But see also the contrary indications in Chapter Seven, under 'Small Business Statistics'.)

Associated with this line of argument have been other reasons to look favourably on growth businesses (and there is a further discussion of this at the end of the chapter):

- There is a belief that to base support primarily on employment creation can be distorting. Instead, support should try to promote competitiveness in the economy, which should then in turn lead to jobs. Competitiveness embraces notions of innovation, dynamism, efficiency and the winning of greater market share, in particular in export markets. All these are associated with growth firms, which presumably grow because they are competitive. Promoting growth businesses therefore promotes competitiveness and ultimately wealth creation. According to the OECD, SMEs are directly producing about 26 per cent of OECD exports and about 35 per cent of Asia's exports.[1]

- There is a recognition that simply increasing numbers of small businesses may not increase total employment because of displacement effects. Those businesses that do survive may only do so at the expense of others.

- There is also a realisation that new businesses have high casualty rates. Many of those that do start do not survive, and so do not contribute anything lasting to the economy. Effort applied to helping them is therefore wasted.

- Indigenous businesses are seen as crucial for regional development because they have the local roots that inward investments do not have. If a suitable indigenous business base does not exist then it has to be created from growing small firms; and there are considerable differences in the ability of certain regions to generate sufficient numbers of successful small firms.

- The UK economy is thought to suffer from the absence of a population of efficient and resilient medium-sized businesses that could provide a backbone in the manner of the German *Mittelstand*—globally competitive, usually family owned, medium-sized businesses, often quoted as key to the success of the German economy. If such a 'backbone' is to emerge then it must come from small growth businesses. (Views on this vary, however. Levy notes that the 'distribution of manufacturing employees between small, medium and large firms' is not greatly different between the UK and Germany.[2] An alternative analysis contends that within the UK population of businesses there are more 'make-weights' and 'punchbags'. A recent study of 600 manufacturing companies in the UK, Germany, the Netherlands and Finland concluded that the UK had as many world class firms as the other countries, but a significantly higher proportion of companies that lagged badly in many key aspects of performance.[3] It has also been claimed that 15,000 medium-sized businesses in the USA, while being only 1 per cent of all businesses, account for 25 per cent of all sales and 20 per cent of all private sector employment.[4])

- Growth businesses are inherently attractive to suppliers of funding and other business services, because the prospects for financial returns are greatest and because of the feeling of success through association.

We have also begun to recognise the importance of the 'gazelle' (rapidly growing businesses) phenomenon within the small business, as well as the middle size and large company universe. In fact, mobility across firm size is almost more interesting than firm size per se. I would say the number [of gazelles] is somewhere between five and ten per cent. In my last look, four per cent of the firms were doing seventy per cent of the growth. So it's four, five, six seven per cent. You can take it as far as you want. Rank all firms by the growth index we have developed and start peeling them off the top. Four per cent at 70; five per cent at 77; ten per cent at 87.

David Birch[5]

The trend towards concentrating support on growth businesses, pursued by the UK government among others, does not command universal support. Inevitably it results in relatively less support for small business creation. Many would see new businesses as potentially a vital element in a vibrant economy, even if they don't grow, since they produce a variety of products and services on which the economy and the growth businesses in it depend. It is also argued that new businesses are the seedbed for future growth businesses, and even if only a small proportion of the businesses in the seedbed do grow, the bigger the seedbed, the more seedlings that may grow. Indeed, as noted in Chapter Four, a high level of volatility or business churn (the percentage of new firms born added to the percentage of older firms that die) is considered to be the rate at which an economy rejuvenates itself on a regular basis. Moreover there is evidence that the size category of businesses in which net job creation is greatest, over a given period of time, is the employment of up-to-20-people category, because it contains the greatest number of businesses, including almost all new starts.

This debate, and its implications, is an important one for those who seek to enhance the small business contribution to economic development. It is therefore the subject of this chapter.

SOME STATISTICS ON GROWTH

Overall, small businesses can be divided into three broad groupings. First, there is a high proportion of small businesses that have a short life. Then there is a second large group of businesses that, although surviving, remain small. The third group is by far the smallest: it consists of those businesses that achieve rapid growth. These groups have been referred to by Storey respectively as 'failures', 'trundlers' and 'fliers' and by Birch as 'failures', 'mice' and 'gazelles'. The following empirical data help to put the last, the fliers or gazelles, into context (and can also be read in conjunction with the section in Chapter Seven on 'Small businesses and job creation').

On the basis of a study of manufacturing firms in the UK, Storey[6] claims that 'over a decade, four per cent of those businesses which start would be expected to create 50 per cent of employment generated'. The Northern Ireland Economic Research Centre (NIERC)[7] studied the performance of manufacturing firms from 1973 to 1986 and also found that almost ten per cent of surviving firms created 43 per cent of employment. (Applying Storey's assumption that 40 per cent of firms survive ten years, one can again conclude that four per cent of the original firms generated 43 per cent of employment.)

Other findings help to confirm the view that in the UK a small number of businesses have a disproportionate impact on job creation. The US experience is broadly similar. For example, a study of new firm growth in Minnesota found that nine per cent of new firms formed in the 1980s provided over 50 per cent of employment after two to seven years.[8] While there are particular criticisms that can be made of these findings, the general picture is probably reasonably accurate: it is that a relatively small proportion of all small businesses account for the major part of the small business contribution to new jobs. But this is scarcely surprising because it is consistent with Pareto's law (or the 80/20 rule), and of course not all small businesses aspire to or are capable of growth. Their owners form and grow the business to a point where they are satisfied or from where they can go no further.

However it is important to note that demonstrating that, in any cohort of businesses, a few will create most jobs, is not the same as demonstrating that, in any one year or combination of years, the greatest overall net job creation comes from the fastest growing businesses. Indeed the up-to-20-employees size range appears to be the category that generates absolutely and relatively the greatest number of net new jobs.

THE DIMENSIONS OF GROWTH

Before examining growth issues further it is logical to consider the possible dimensions, or meanings, of growth in the context of small businesses, and what observers or business owners interpret as the desirable aspects of growth. Storey, in presenting the statistics given above, makes it clear that, in common with others, he is using increases in employment as a measure of growth. Growth in a business can also be defined as greater turnover or increased profitability but, while these measures may all be seen as desirable, they may not even be positively correlated. As noted by Smallbone and Wyer,[9] 'a number of studies have demonstrated the close correlation that exists between employment growth and sales growth in small firms over a long period of time... although increased employment is less clearly related to a growth in profitability'. Some analysts may in addition interpret growth in the context of a broader product range, or an increased number of patents or of customers, none of which necessarily imply greater turnover, profitability or employment.

People with a financial interest in small businesses often want to increase the value of their investments by growth in shareholder value, which implies a growth in business earnings and net assets, which themselves may be achieved by growth in turnover and/or profitability (or the potential for it). Employment, therefore, for them, is not necessarily a growth goal, but may be a by-product of it. For government support agencies a straightforward growth in employment may however be the requirement, or at least an overall improvement in the economy, that is most likely to come from a growth in exports, or a replacement of imports, and which may lead to a growth in employment.

It is important therefore to realise that, while many people may want to see growth, it will mean different things to different people. For most people, growth in employment will generally be the primary goal. For those managing economies and balances of payments, growth in export turnover, or in import substitution, is critical. For shareholders, profitability as a means to enhance dividends and share value is likely to be predominant. The individual small business owner, however, as noted previously, may have one or more of a number of aspirations. These might include being a major local employer, creating wealth, building a large income, being seen as innovative or providing jobs for the family. Many of these will be derived from, or be facilitated by, growth in aspects of the business.

While researchers frequently measure growth in terms of employment, its potential to signify different things to different people means that care must be taken in describing it. Unless its meaning in a particular situation is clear, misunderstandings may arise. It may also be necessary sometimes to remember the distinction made between growth and expansion that was described in Chapter Six. Some of the yardsticks used for measuring growth are indicated in Table 8.1.

Table 8.1   Yardsticks for business growth

Share value	Return on investment	Market share
Net worth	Size of premises	Exports/imports substitution
Profit	Standard of service	New products/services
Employment	Profile/image	Innovations, patents, etc.
Turnover	Number of customers	Added value

THE COMPONENTS OF GROWTH

Growing a business is not easy. The natural tendency of a business, like any other system subject to natural decay, is to regress. It takes energy and effort to prevent that and instead to grow. The easiest way to understand the effort needed is to look at the needs of a growing business and the things that must be done to address them.

Under almost every definition of growth, growing a small business needs resources, for which it needs money; it needs management delegation, coordination, systems and control; and it needs more sales, which may in turn come from new products or markets. These issues have already been described in Chapter Six but they are repeated here as the starting point for a wider look at the implications of growth.

Understanding growth however requires a regard not just for these internal needs of a business, but also for the totality of the influences on a business. Such influences can be external as well as internal and can hinder or help growth. They are illustrated in Figures 8.1 and 8.2 and see also Table 8.2.

Figure 8.1 Influences on a business

Figure 8.2 Nature of the path to growth

One benefit of establishing the totality of influences on a business is that it helps to put any single influence in perspective. Without this there is a tendency to overestimate the effect of any particular influence. If, for instance, it is considered that R&D can help to build competitiveness and that a grant scheme would encourage R&D, then it might be thought that such a grant scheme would be a positive influence on a business. However, it is important to recognise the strength of the influences keeping the business where it is; they are likely to be much stronger than the more dubious incentive of a grant. This has been likened to pushing a heavy object: friction tends to keep it where it is, unless the pushing force is sufficiently large, and attempts to reduce the frictional resistance might be more effective than attempts to increase the amount of external push.

Table 8.2 Some of the influences on a business

Type of influence	Internal	External
Positive	Owner's desire to increase profitability and/or to prove him or herself Impetus of earlier growth	Stimulus of competition Encouragement of others Favourable tax incentives Encouragement and support from small business agencies
Negative	Bounce back from earlier uncontrolled growth Lack of ability of the owner and/or management team	Adverse tax, interest and exchange rates Improvements in the competition Product obsolescence
Those which can encourage a business not to change	Owner's lifestyle and the consequent need for the present level of return but not for more Inertia and the difficulty of mobilising the resources needed to do more Limits on internal capacity to plan, coordinate and supervise	Peer group pressure

Growth, or its absence, can however be attributable to a wide variety of factors. There is no comprehensive theory to explain which firms will grow or how they grow, but various explanatory approaches have been used. Of course, whatever approach or combination of approaches one favours, seeking to distinguish between what is necessary and what is sufficient for growth has been and is likely to remain an unattainable goal. Indeed most of the research work in this area 'fails to provide convincing evidence of the determinants of small firm growth as a basis for informing policy-makers';[10] and again, 'Given the significance of employment created in rapidly growing small firms, it is surprising that theoretical and empirical understanding of the characteristics of these firms remains somewhat sketchy.'[11]

ILLUSTRATION 8.1
Previous academic approaches to understanding
small business growth
....

[There] has been a considerable body of literature embracing very different approaches to understanding the growth process. This can be broadly divided into four categories as follows:

- Approaches exploring the impact of the entrepreneurial personality and capability on growth including the owner-manager's personal goals and/or strategic vision.
- Approaches seeking to characterise the way the small organisation develops and influences, and is influenced by, the owner-manager. These approaches address issues of management style and models of stages of growth.
- Approaches broadly embraced under the term 'business' which focus upon the importance of business skills and the role of functional management, planning, control and formal strategic orientations.
- Approaches which are more macro in scope and which usually have their academic base in industrial economics. These include sectoral approaches pertaining to regional development, a focus upon specific industry sectors or sub-sectors, for example, high-technology firms.[12]

There are obvious overlaps among these approaches. It is interesting to note however that much recent economics literature on small firm growth has tended to focus on a combination of a life cycle effect (young firms grow faster than older firms) and economic variables, especially financial variables, for an explanation of growth. Indeed in modern micro-economic theory there has been allegiance to a model of small firm growth which has led to the 'removal' of the 'human elements'.[13] Thus within economics there is a failing in empirical enquiry to address 'the key questions of entrepreneurial characteristics and motivations and how they may be translated into business strategy'.[14] Interesting studies by, for example, Barkham, Hanvey and Hart[15] and Storey[16] have adopted a more comprehensive approach, seeking to bring together research in economics, geography, organisational studies and business strategy to examine the link between entrepreneurial characteristics, business strategy and small firm growth across a wide variety of types of small firm. Traditionally, however, the unit of study has often been the business, not the entrepreneur. The needs, aspirations and other characteristics of habitual entrepreneurs have been largely ignored by researchers, policy-makers and support agencies. 'The process of ownership diversification may shed new light on the way we can conceptualise start-up and growth dynamics.'[17]

In the context of small businesses, what are the main influences? Three types in particular are examined here: first the influences of the entrepreneur linked to his or her personality, behaviour, attitude and capability; then the influences due to the business itself, related to its structure and goals and to the performance of its management; and finally the influences of the external environment such as the business's sector, region and other strategic issues.

THE ENTREPRENEUR—MOTIVATION AND ASPIRATION

The first approach focuses on the entrepreneur himself or herself. Personality and behaviour are believed to be causal factors for or against growth-orientated achievement. This is understandable. It is a characteristic of small business that powers of decision are centralised at the level of the owner-manager, so his or her personality, skills, responsibilities, attitude and behaviour will have a decisive influence on business strategy.

Typical of the analysts using this approach is Kirchhoff, who develops a 'dynamic capitalism typology'[18] to explain the relationship between innovation and firm growth. The typology divides firms into four categories: economic core; ambitious; glamorous, and constrained growth. Each category has its own broad growth profile.

'Economic core' businesses are low on innovation and on growth. They are the largest single category, but fast growing firms can leap out from the core; an example is Wal-Mart, the world's largest retailer, where the most significant growth came after over thirty years of operations. 'Ambitious' firms achieve high rates of growth with one, or a few, initial innovations. Growth comes from a gradual build-up of market share. However, growth cannot be sustained without additional innovations (usually in the product or service or in its marketing). With additional innovations, firms become 'glamorous'. Microsoft is a good example. Glamorous businesses, according to Kirchhoff, can have experienced periods of 'constrained growth'[19] for two broad reasons. First, growth may be self-constrained growth owing to the owner's reluctance to relinquish ownership and control to generate the necessary resources for growth; and second, it may be constrained where businesses are genuinely limited by a lack of resources. They can often be highly innovative, but still unable to secure early stage capital.

Kirchhoff concludes that 'what is interesting about these four classes of firms is that they do not depend upon industrial sector, business size, age nor location'.[20] This typology, he continues, 'identifies the firms' behaviours that indicate the true ambitions and goals of the owners and defines their contribution to economic growth. Aspiring entrepreneurs need to realistically assess their personal ambitions and where *they wish to be* in this typology.'[21]

This is a clear attribution of business growth to entrepreneurial motivation and competency, as exhibited in a willingness to innovate. It is probably reasonable to assume that the motivation to grow is likely to be the *sine qua non* of growth.

Yet for many business owners the growth of their businesses is not an objective. Growth is associated with many unattractive circumstances. These may include having to find work for others, loss of management control, reliance on others, sharing responsibilities and decision-making, perhaps relinquishing some ownership stake, and unnecessary risk (although there is evidence from the UK and USA that survival and growth are positively correlated).

A desire to spend more time with one's family or to engage in other forms of social and leisure activity are also valid reasons. Professional and social issues combine very often, as is noted in the significant amount of literature on the family business, which recognises the influence of family in respect of growth and issues of ownership. Often growth is rejected where it might lead to a conflict of interests.

Businesses exist that have a no-growth aspiration. They were described in Chapter Six as 'lifestyle' businesses, and in almost every case they are established solely to provide a satisfactory level of income. They are very often home-based, sole trader operations employing no more than one additional person. Statistics[22] reveal that well over half of all UK business owners in the late 1980s had no plans to grow. In addition there is a clear association between firm size and the desire to grow.

Even among those entrepreneurs who seek growth, significant numbers would appear to seek only moderate or limited growth. They may reach a stage or plateau, described as a 'comfort zone', at which the owner is satisfied with his or her condition and the costs of pursuing continued growth exceed the expected benefits. These perceived costs will dominate over any material or psychological gains that might be expected from growth. As more than one owner has remarked, 'The problems grow geometrically while the firm grows arithmetically.'

With reference to the owner typologies mentioned in Chapter Three, the 'lifestyle' owners would be classified as craftsmen/shopkeepers but some may grow sufficiently to assume the status of Hornaday's 'professional managers'. Carree *et al.*[23] claim that their 'managerial' business owners are to be found in the majority of small firms. They include many franchisees, shopkeepers and people in professional occupations belonging to Kirchhoff's economic core. Indeed they further note that Audretsch and Thurik,[24] in their analysis of how and why entrepreneurship has contributed to economic and social development, assume that their two types have different economic roles in relation to unemployment. They contend that the number of (what they call) 'shopkeepers' is likely to go up if the level of unemployment rises but that that same level is expected to go down if the number of Schumpeterians ('real' entrepreneurs) increases. In reality, of course, it can be difficult to distinguish one type of owner from another since most owners 'share attitudes associated with these extremes in a varying degree'.[25]

The motivation of the owner is undoubtedly a very important ingredient in the (no-)growth process and, of course, the motivation can change over time as the business develops and events external and internal to the business occur. It is a dynamic situation. Firms can appear to be in a steady state for many years and then begin to grow rapidly. Growth is not necessarily a continuous process for many firms, which is an important consideration for those who rely on recent past performance as a predictor of future performance. One possible reason is a need to establish the business—to build strong roots—before moving on and upwards. Similarly, as noted in Chapter Seven, it has been revealed that the majority of firms show no growth for their first six years, while more than 50 per cent of surviving firms show growth after six years. Indeed, rapid growth, when it happens, appears to begin after six to eight years of trading.[26]

It is also worth noting that a significant number of entrepreneurs, instead of managing their established businesses whether in a growth phase or not, may be much more stimulated by, or capable of, generating new business ideas and converting them into new ventures. The excitement and fulfilment for such people may be in creating something new, not in managing an existing operation. In fact while their businesses may essentially be in the early stages of business development, the entrepreneurs themselves can become obstacles to the further development of the business as neither their interest nor competency may be at the appropriate levels. Such people may favour multiple business ownership as habitual entrepreneurs. (See Chapter Six.)

Other entrepreneurial characteristics

It will also be apparent that the will or motivation to grow by no means guarantees growth. So a growth model that focuses on the individual entrepreneur as the key to the growth process must also take into account aspects of the individual other than motivation, such as traits, behaviour and resources. These factors will influence the entrepreneur's ability to achieve growth, as well as his or her will to do so.

Storey[27] has reviewed a number of empirical studies that examine which characteristics of the entrepreneur, including motivation, are related to growth. The conclusions drawn however do not permit the development of a profile or model of the growth-achieving entrepreneur in terms of the subsequent performance of the firm. There is some suggestion that the more significant variables, in addition to motivation, are education, age and management experience, all of which are positively correlated. (Motivation, in this instance, however, refers only to why the business was established—not motivation to grow.) Barkham *et al.*[28] found that the entrepreneurs associated with faster growing manufacturing firms were relatively young and members of professional organisations; that they had worked as part of a larger entrepreneurial team; and that they had a network of other business interests which were mainly legally independent and separate small firms. In some cases the existence of other businesses was advantageous; in others this was not so. Interestingly, there appears to be some evidence that businesses founded by groups are also likely to grow faster than those founded by single individuals, although no definite conclusions can yet be drawn. Indeed the focus on teams of enterprising persons rather than on individuals is commanding greater interest and research in recent times. It is becoming increasingly recognised that the 'lone wolf' entrepreneur, no matter how charismatic or how enterprising, limits the growth potential of the enterprise simply because of his or her personality and the physical limitations of individuality in practising entrepreneurial management.

Another characteristic of the entrepreneur that has also been studied is his or her willingness to accept external equity. As finance from an external source is usually needed to permit rapid business expansion, accepting equity involvement and sharing ownership removes a growth constraint (and of course equity is more likely to be available to growth businesses as they will be more attractive to investors). Alternative funding sources can be used, but usually not without increasing the business's gearing. It is reasonable to infer, therefore, that a willingness by the entrepreneur to share ownership and so decision-making and control is key to the growth of some businesses. When the concept of the entrepreneur is extended to embrace his or her management style and strategic management practices, including the development and use of networks, conclusions are no simpler to reach. For example, there is an increasing tendency to link the business's growth with the quality and quantity of the personal and organisational networks that the entrepreneur develops.

Some studies support the contention that a greater use of external sources of information, advice and other resources results in faster growth, particularly for a high-technology business. It is logical to assume that, as the entrepreneur's resources are often limited and he or she has to gain some control over his or her socio-economic environment, networks play a more crucial role for the small business that seeks growth. Moreover the nature of networks appears to change as the business develops, which is also to be expected.

However, work on management style and networks is subject to criticisms which are frequently mentioned. To be useful, such studies need to distinguish cause and effect and also to distinguish whether the factors being studied actually cause growth or merely facilitate (or hinder) processes determined by other influences.

Conclusion

The findings revealed by one Third World study[29] are instructive. It tested three groups of personal entrepreneurial competencies: first, those perceived to pertain to basic personality, such as assertiveness, determination, initiative; second, those relating to business management styles, such as efficiency orientation; third, those classified as business skill indicators, such as systematic planning. It was concluded from this however that personality variables are not useful predictors of business performance. The personality-orientated competency measures represented in the data did not relate consistently, it was claimed, to the various measures of business performance for the respondents.

It is reasonable to conclude, therefore, that what the entrepreneur 'is' (traits) is less important than what he or she 'does' (behaviour), because the latter effects change. The link between what one 'is' and what one 'does' is clearly largely undetermined. Moreover Gibb and Davies contend that 'Different types of entrepreneurial behaviour are required in different marketplaces to achieve growth and different traits, skills and competencies will be needed depending upon levels of uncertainty and complexity in the market.'[30]

In conclusion, it is reasonable to deduce that the entrepreneur's (or business leader's) ambition and desire to grow are critical. In addition, the skills of the entrepreneur are particularly important in the early stages of growth. The ability to broaden and adapt to changing circumstances is likely to be of major importance in removing obstacles to growth. Different types of behaviour may be required in different market situations and different personal competencies are likely to be needed to deal with the different levels of complexity and uncertainty in the business environment. It is important that entrepreneurs are willing to delegate and, by implication, that employees must be capable and willing to accept that responsibility. It is also a truism to say that an inability to manage growth, despite a motivation to do so, will prevent growth. It is undoubtedly the case that many firms fail to grow because of a variety of barriers, including those of a technical, marketing, and financial nature, but not least those which are managerial (which may in fact be at the root of most of the other barriers). How some management factors can help or hinder growth at different stages is captured in Figure 8.3.

Storey's research stresses the critical importance of the attitude and quality of the initial manager(s) whom the entrepreneur recruits. Such a finding would reinforce the importance of the management team to growth achievement and of the owner's ability to build such a team. These issues of management are explored further in the next section.

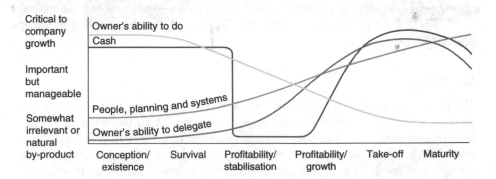

Source: N. C. Churchill, 'The Six Key Phases of Company Growth', 'Mastering Enterprise', *Financial Times* February 1997: 3.

Figure 8.3   Management factors and stages

THE BUSINESS

A second approach to explaining growth is to look at the characteristics of the business itself. These characteristics can be divided into two categories, chosen because they are firm specific:

- the firm's structure: ownership, legal form, age and size;
- the firm's management skills and performance, including its access to resources.

Structure

Storey[31] reviewed research from 11 studies on one or more of the elements in this category. His conclusion was that little is known about the impact of ownership. It is not known, for example, whether a second or subsequent owner is more likely grow a business nor is it known if an individual with more than one business is more likely to succeed in growing one or more of them, nor whether a business begun by a team is more likely to grow.

On the legal form of the business, it would appear that a limited company is more likely to grow as compared with a sole trader or partnership. This should not be surprising because most businesses convert to limited company status at some stage in their development and are frequently under various pressures to convert as they grow.

Most studies also conclude that younger and smaller firms grow more quickly than older and larger ones. It is important to note, however, that one reason for a correlation between size and growth is that it is easier to achieve a doubling in any growth parameter if the business is smaller to start with. Few large businesses would try a 100 per cent increase in employment at one stroke, but that is just what a previously one-person business does when it recruits its first employee. Additionally, many businesses will grow rapidly initially to reach the 'critical mass' needed to service their market efficiently, but subsequently 'plateau'.

In general findings about the firm's characteristics and growth are of very limited value for policy purposes. As with information about the entrepreneur, either the causal relationship is unclear or no meaningful basis for policy intervention has been identified. Indeed none of the structural factors identified indicates, with adequate clarity, anything about the ambitions or goals exhibited by a business's owners and managers.

Management

The second category of firm-specific characteristics relates to management performance. Many would argue that the motivation and ability of a firm to grow rests with the owner and his or her management team. Such an approach recognises that growth is related to a business's performance in the marketplace, and in particular to its ability to make rational (profitable) decisions about its products and/or services in the context of market development.

In short, a condition of growth is the ability of management to plan and implement the firm's growth in both strategic and operational terms. It is instructive to note that a European Observatory for SMEs annual report[32] identifies four weaknesses of smaller businesses:

- high mortality rates;
- weak market orientation due to lack of strategic marketing approaches and to operating in small segmented markets;
- low productivity of labour leading to high unit wage costs;
- low equity/debt ratio and difficult and costly access to financial markets.

All of these weaknesses can be related to management inadequacy (as indeed can almost all aspects of small business performance). Even difficulty in raising finance can be attributed to a 'failure' of management adequately to search for sources, build networks, prepare suitable business plans or share ownership and control.

Evidence concerning the impact of a selection of firm-specific factors attributable to the performance of the management team is summarised by Storey.[33] These factors are: management recruitment and training; workforce training; technological sophistication; market positioning; market adjustments; planning; new product introduction; customer concentration; exporting (information and advice); and external equity. The list of factors reflects research that has been done, and is not necessarily an exhaustive list of management-related issues.

Unfortunately, as before, the findings are not conclusive. It seems to be counter-intuitive that proper practice in many of these factors, which conventionally constitute good management, are as yet not found to be correlated with growth in businesses. It is, however, suggested that three aspects of management do appear to be the most closely linked with growth, as opposed to size (an important distinction): these are market positioning, new products, and management recruitment.

Market positioning

A key decision for any business is the definition of its market and where it perceives itself to be in relation to its competitors. While it is difficult to define precisely, market positioning has to do with notions of who the customers are, competitive advantage, product and service range and the role of quality, service and price. These are important issues for management to clarify—otherwise, the business's ability to take corrective action if things go wrong will be limited. It would appear that the ability to know of and take advantage of market positioning (in other words, to determine one's niche) is related to growth success.

Barkham *et al.*[34] found that undertaking formal market research had strong associations with growth, while the use of agents (as opposed to in-house sales staff) to sell products had the reverse effect.

ILLUSTRATION 8.2
Breakout by ethnic entrepreneurs

It is contended that effective market definition and positioning and the appropriate introduction of new products can allow firms to grow but this may not be so easy for ethnic businesses. These firms can benefit from a deep understanding of the needs of their co-ethnic clients and an ability to meet them, but Ram points out that many ethnic markets are static and fiercely competitive. Growth depends on breaking into non-ethnic markets but this is predicated on the development of an effective marketing strategy. Ram notes that not many ethnic firms are sophisticated marketers and that problems with under-funding, inadequate premises and equipment, labour-intensive production methods and inadequate insurance make breakout difficult. However, some firms with innovative products, differentiated market contacts and willpower do manage to enter new markets and achieve sustainable growth.

Source: M. Ram, 'Ethnic Minority Enterprise: An Overview and Research Agenda', *Journal of Entrepreneurial Behaviour and Research* 1997; 3: 145–56.

New products

Related to market positioning is the development and introduction of new products. There is some evidence, but it is by no means conclusive, that new product introductions are associated with faster growth. Introducing new products is usually seen as part of the process of innovation, which is itself in much of the literature seen as the engine driving continued growth. Innovation is often limited however to development by absorption of new techniques. Indeed, definite conclusions in this area are difficult to draw from empirical studies, although the OECD expresses a commonplace view in suggesting that 'A businessman's attitude to using new technologies to ensure or increase competitiveness...appears extremely significant. His attitude will be determined by his experience and training but also by those of his management team.'[35]

Management recruitment

Common sense dictates that as a firm grows it becomes more dependent on its management team. A CBI report revealed that there is a 'greater awareness of

Table 8.3 Management weakness as a constraint on growth: internal barriers to growth (percentage of respondents citing factor as important)

Management team too small/too stretched	65
Reluctance to dilute ownership	57
Reluctance to take on new debt	55
Lack of successful innovation	40
Preference for maintaining the manageability of small size	40

Note: Respondents were 667 private companies with turnover between £2.5 and £25 m.

Source: Binder Hamlyn and London Business School (1994), 'The Quest for Growth', reprinted from *Managing to Grow* (London: CBI, 1995), p. 11.

management weaknesses among growth firms ...', and that 'recruitment of outside managers also tends to increase with growth'. Table 8.3 taken from this report, highlights the perceived importance of management.[36] There is much other research evidence to show that not acquiring the right management expertise and not building the appropriate structure are amongst the main reasons why growth-orientated firms fail to achieve their objective of growth.

Other factors

Overall, one cannot deduce that other firm specific factors are not important for growth: there is merely an absence of strong evidence to demonstrate the causal relationship. Indeed, even for the factors highlighted in this section, the evidence presented remains open to challenge. Controversially, neither workforce nor management training is shown to be a causal factor influencing the growth of the business. Their association is with larger but not necessarily growing firms, and they are as likely to be a consequence as a cause.

What research there is confirms the importance of management development in a growing business, and demonstrates individual examples of its impact on performance. It does not, however, isolate the impact of different approaches to management development (such as training, mentoring, counselling, presence of non-executive directors) across a group of small businesses.

This emphasis on rational business management approaches to growth has led to an increasing flow of literature that attempts to link not only the personal characteristics of the entrepreneur but also those of the management team to planning and performance.

As with many factors studied, definitional problems make comparability of findings difficult, not least in the area of planning. Despite this, few studies demonstrate a convincing link between formalised planning and improved performance of the small firm. Planning seems to be related to size, not growth.

Many familiar with micro- and small-firm behaviour will recognise that the 'informal and intuitive' dominates over formal planning procedures and is at least equally effective. Nor should the existence of a business plan be confused with planning! The OECD reports in its study on globalising SMEs that 'Successful small firms often do not rely on formal strategic planning although they are very conscious of what they want to achieve.'[37] Overall however it might be foolish to deny the significance of product- and/or market-related decisions, cost/price decisions, and constraint decisions (including time and finance) taken by a strategically aware management team as critical to business growth, despite the absence of conclusive evidence. Barkham *et al.*[38] found that four business aims stated by owner-managers were significantly associated with growth: those of expansion of profits; improving margins; having a marketing strategy; and improving the production process. It is interesting to note that a study of 179 super-growth companies in the US resulted in the identification of five factors leading to a 'winning performance'.[39] These were:

- competing on quality not prices;
- domination of a market niche;
- competing in an area of strength;
- having tight financial and operating controls;
- frequent product or service innovation (particularly important in manufacturing).

Barkham *et al.*[40] reinforce this view in that their results reveal that it is the characteristics of the entrepreneur and the strategies he or she adopts which largely determine the growth of the small enterprise. Company characteristics including size, location and sector appear to be influential but in a relatively minor way. To a large extent growth in small firms derives from the skills, values and motivations of the entrepreneur and the strategies adopted with regard to innovation, marketing and market research.

This approach to explaining small business growth reflects what Gibb and Davies[41] described as a business or 'organisational' approach, emphasising the development sequence of a firm as it passes through a series of stages in its life cycle. (Some of these 'stages of growth' models are described in Chapter Six.)

THE EXTERNAL ENVIRONMENT

Yet another approach to understanding and explaining growth lies in examining the impact of factors or constraints external to the entrepreneur or the business. These include macro-economic variables such as aggregate demand, taxation, regulations, labour market skills and labour relations, but also embrace sector and region specific matters such as product/service and/or market, competition, government assistance, location, and the availability (and use) of information.

Macro-economic variables

Looking first at macro-economic variables, it is clear that policies on demand, taxation, interest rates and public spending will affect the fortunes of small firms. Indeed government policies in these areas are intended to induce behavioural change by individuals and organisations. It is indisputable that these policies have a major impact on the trading performance of small firms.

Despite the continuing calls by small firm representative bodies for reduced regulations ('less red tape') it is not clear to what extent administrative and legislative burdens hinder business growth. It is reasonable to assume, however, that anything that absorbs time and resources that would otherwise be devoted to business development is likely to have a deleterious effect.

Studies in many OECD member countries, including the UK, highlight the constraining effect of small business being unable to obtain good quality or skilled labour even in a relatively slack overall labour market. At any given time, how much the problem is on the supply side (recruitment processes, remuneration, employment rights and conditions), as opposed to the demand side, is not clear.

In general, governments' macro-economic policies are geared to all enterprises and not just smaller businesses. Moreover, while the impact of governments' macro policies can fall unevenly on different sectors and/or markets (and labour markets are partially differentiated), the specific effect on the growth of an individual business is likely to be much less than the effect on business in general and not least on international competitive comparisons. It is unlikely, therefore, that macro-economic and national policies will explain differential growth rates within different sectors, whatever the effects across sectors.

Sector

A number of studies[42] in recent years indicate that the average growth rate of firms is higher in some sectors than in others. Particular attention has been paid in numerous studies to businesses in the high-tech sector where, for example, Westhead and Storey[43] conclude that high-technology small firms in the UK not only have higher growth rates but also have lower failure rates than small businesses in other sectors. Kirchhoff,[44] examining US data, only partially agrees: 'The chances of achieving high growth are almost twice as great for high-tech firms as for low-tech firms. Still, among high-tech firms terminations take a greater toll as low-growth firms are unable to hang on for as long as low-tech firms.' Kirchhoff attributes their superior growth performance to the high cost of innovation, which requires growth if the firm is to survive. However high-tech sectors can suffer reverses as was shown in the 'winter of technology' in 2000 and subsequently when many ICT businesses collapsed.

Sectoral studies serve the purpose of highlighting the particular constraints and opportunities of sectors (such as financing problems for the high-tech sector).

They do not typically offer a basis for predicting the extent to which growth businesses will emerge or in what conditions, however. They also encourage analysis of the structure of an industry, and especially the role of large firms and their interaction with smaller ones. Large–small firm linkages may play an important role in influencing small firm growth. Growth can occur on the basis of servicing the needs of large firms; large firms can spin out numbers of small ones; strategic partnerships across a variety of functions can develop; large firms can provide management and technological support and advice. On the other hand, large firms through their power in the marketplace can hinder or eliminate small business growth through acquisition, control over intellectual property, slow payment and quasi-monopolistic practices.

It is misleading however to place too much reliance on sectoral performance from a policy perspective. As research[45] has indicated, performance within sectors varies to a much greater extent than across sectors.

Competition

It may appear *prima facie* that for a given market size, the smaller the number of competitors the greater the likelihood of any given business capturing a large share of the market. However, many influences may be operating, such as (dis)economies of scale; product or market differentiation; the relative importance of large and small firms in the market; and transportation costs, which make it very difficult to define the 'competitiveness' of a market or sector. It is not surprising, therefore, that no correlation appears to exist between growth and competition. Porter argues however that greater competitiveness in an industry's home market can lead to stronger export performance and growth. (See the subsection 'The cluster effect' later in this section.)

Location

The concept of location is more complex than it first seems. Locational attributes such as those of being urban, rural, peripheral or central can mean differences in many of the other factors such as competition, labour market, and government support. It then becomes difficult to determine which of the influences is at work.

However, it is safe to say, once again, that there is not yet enough evidence to suggest that growth is location-determined. Possible exceptions to this conclusion are businesses (usually service or service-related firms) serving local markets, because these are likely to be small, although the benefits of larger markets may well be offset by greater numbers of competitors. A review of lists of UK fast-growth firms (such as the Sunday Times/Virgin Fast-Track 100) suggests that they are disproportionately concentrated in the South of England. Findings by Vaessen and Keeble[46] in a recent analysis of small business by regional location, on the other hand, suggest a different link between growth and location. Peripheral regions are found to contain proportionately more growing small businesses than what they call the 'core' region (South East England). A partial explanation is that greater R&D and training inputs are generated in the peripheral locations. These findings can only be tentative however: their counter-intuitive nature may suggest that differences in external environments are not sufficient to explain growth differentials. Indeed, to assume otherwise would be to suggest that the entrepreneur's and the business's behaviour are largely constrained by their location, an assumption that does not allow significant scope for variable responses. Either way, the policy implications are unclear.

Information and advice

The provision of information and advice by government agencies is itself a growth sector in many countries seeking to support their small businesses. This form of support can also come from private sector sources (such as bankers, accountants, non-executive directors and consultants); and the use made of accountants and bankers, at least in developed economies, would appear to be much higher than that made of public information and advice services. Indeed the uptake of public sector provision seems generally to be very low (less than ten per cent of potential users). However, satisfaction with information and advice, from both public and private sources, appears generally to be high. Importantly, despite the significant investment being made in these services in the USA, the UK and the European Union generally, there appears to be no convincing evidence that their uptake improves business performance and growth, although growing businesses would appear to make greater use of information and advisory networks.

Government support

Government support can take a wide variety of forms, but usually consists of grant aid, subsidised loans and/or the provision of subsidised services such as consultancy, training and the provision of information and advice.

The impact of direct financial support from government or its agencies is the issue most often studied. Such support normally comes from local or regional agencies. The small business community generally expresses dissatisfaction with the grants regime, or at least with its administration. It is reported[47] that it feels that grants go to large or foreign firms; that application procedures are too complicated and lengthy; and that not enough information is available on how to access grants. Notwithstanding these views, significant sums across many regions have been provided to small business. Once again, research findings are incon-clusive in determining whether financial support generates further growth, improved profitability or less efficient performance. (See also Chapter 13.)

The cluster effect

There is however one theory that links issues such as location, competition and government support to the competitiveness, and hence to the potential growth, of businesses. This theory is propounded by Porter[48] (see also Chapter Five) who, following a four-year study of ten important trading nations, ultimately con-cluded that nations succeed in particular industries because their home environ-ment is the most forward-looking, dynamic and challenging. These conclusions, he suggests, contradict the conventional wisdom that labour costs, interest rates, exchange rates and economies of scale are the most potent determinants of com-petitiveness. It is too easy, he says, for governments to adopt policies, such as joint projects for R&D, that operate on the belief that independent research by domes-tic rivals is wasteful and duplicative, that collaborative efforts achieve economies of scale, and that individual companies are likely to under-invest in R&D because they cannot reap all the benefits. That view, he claims, is flawed and fundamen-tally misperceives the true sources of competitive advantage.

Porter argues that, while successful businesses will each employ their own strategy, they achieve competitive advantage through acts of innovation. Further, he believes that it is demanding buyers in the domestic market who pressure companies to innovate faster. Why is it, he asks, that certain companies based in certain countries are capable of consistent innovation? The answer lies in four broad attributes of a region. These are: *factor conditions* (labour force quality, infra-structure); *demand conditions* (the nature of home market demand); *related and sup-porting industries* (the presence of supplier industries and other related industries which are internationally competitive); and *firm strategy, structure and rivalry* (the conditions in the nation affecting how businesses are created, organised and man-aged and the nature of domestic competition). These four determinants form the points on Porter's 'diamond', and the diamond is itself a system. Together they affect the key elements that beget international competitiveness and, by implica-tion, firm and industry growth.

How these determinants combine to produce a successful industry is complex, but Porter notes that internationally competitive businesses are usually found in geographically concentrated clusters of related businesses. 'Among all the points on the diamond, domestic rivalry is arguably the most important because of the powerfully stimulating effect it has on all the others,' asserts Porter, adding that 'Geographic concentration magnifies the power of domestic rivalry.'[49] One of the most commonly quoted such examples is that of 'The Third Italy': a prolifer-ation of concentrations of various industrial sectors benefiting from a variety of effects that include pools of skilled workers and technicians; related input from maintenance, service and design businesses; supporting companies that offer materials, supplies and other services including subcontracting; and specialist businesses offering consultancy and advice on logistics, advertising, finance and general support. Support agency services develop that are geared to meet a cluster's needs in the form of education and training, research and development, and fiscal and legal advice. In Italy these interrelationships are reinforced by family connections and traditional links that significantly strengthen the power of the network. Such inbuilt cultural ties however complicate the situation for those who might otherwise think that they could merely 'import' the cluster effect. Despite this, efforts continue to create clusters of mainly high-technology companies. For example in the UK in 1999 a research team under Lord Sainsbury highlighted the importance of public sector encouragement of clustering, while a joint Department of Trade and Industry and Department for Education and Employment (now Department for Education and Skills) White Paper *Opportunity for All in a World of Change* (February 2001) encouraged regional development agencies to continue developing existing and embryonic clusters.[50] On the wider front the OECD notes that smaller firms are increasingly going global, 'building on local networks and inter-firm clusters to derive scale economies in international markets'.[51]

General

This brief review covers only some of the factors that have been considered as possible influences on the growth performance of small businesses. This chapter has classified the range of factors into three broad categories: the entrepreneur, the firm and the external environment. Other classifications exist. The OECD,[52] for instance, categorises the key factors in the *competitiveness* of SMEs as:

- the owner's/manager's basic role (drive);
- intangible investment ('intelligence management'), including:
  - the ability to obtain information through environmental scanning and search;
  - at least an intermittent R&D capability;
  - the quality of the firm's organisation;
  - the quality of its training;
- tangible investment (based on new management and production technologies);
- the business's strategic capabilities (innovation and flexibility).

However, as already noted, the research on these, and on other, classifications and their components has produced no conclusive results and no firm evidence to support interventions, either to increase the pace of growth or to increase the number of growing businesses.

Table 8.4   Constraints on small business growth

Constraint	Ranking	
	1997	*1990*
Increased competition	1	4
Availability and cost of finance for expansion	2	1
Marketing and sales skills	3	5
Availability and cost of overdraft finance	4	2
Growth of market demand	5	3
Management skills	6	6
Skilled labour	7	7
Acquisition of new technology	8	8
Difficulty of implementing new technology	9	9
Availability of appropriate premises	10	10
Access to overseas markets	11	11

Sources: 1997: adapted from A. Cosh and A. Hughes (eds), *Enterprising Britain; Growth, Innovation and Public Policy in the Small and Medium Sized Enterprise Sector 1994–1997* (Cambridge: ESRC Centre for Business Research, 1998) (originally appeared in P. Burns, *Entrepreneurship and Small Business* (Basingstoke: Palgrave (now Palgrave Macmillan), 2001), p. 274); 1990: ESRC Small Business Research Centre, *The State of British Enterprise: Growth, Innovation and Competitive Advantage in Small and Medium-Sized Firms* (Cambridge: ESRC Small Business Research Centre, 1992).

Nevertheless, it would be foolish to set aside a pragmatic approach to this problem, such as to note what businesses themselves have been saying. Table 8.4 shows the barriers to growth reported in a small firm survey of 2500 businesses in the UK in 1997[53] carried out by Cambridge University's Centre for Business Research, the results of whose 1990 study[54] are also shown for comparison. The top issues in both studies revolve around market demand and competition, the availability and cost of finance, and the firm's ability to deal with them, with the scores being sufficiently close together to highlight these issues as the key to growth. In addition, medium-sized firms reported inadequate management skills, and to a lesser extent marketing and sales skills, as greater constraints than did smaller firms. Younger and faster growing firms stressed financial constraints while faster growing ones also placed management skills shortages higher. Manufacturing firms revealed generally more constraints than service firms, and innovating firms reported more than non-innovating ones.

It may be reasonable to accept these rather typical results (albeit no mention is made of administrative and regulatory burdens!) at face value, subject to two caveats: first, businesses may tend to blame external, and therefore uncontrollable, factors before internal, controllable, factors; and second, there is a tendency to confuse causes and effects. In the latter case, financial constraints may become apparent because of a lack of demand or, in the case of a growing business, because of a reluctance to dilute ownership or control or because of poor financial management skills.

A second commonsense approach is to recognise that growth is likely to be dependent upon the interaction of a number of influences, and that these influences may be important in different combinations for different businesses. This makes generalisations very imprecise and of limited use as guides to action. Growth is likely to occur when a number of the key factors in each category combine, although it is most unlikely that there is only one or a few successful combinations, and the combinations for success could change as the business develops and market circumstances alter. The dynamic process implied in this interpretation of how growth is generated through the interaction of the entrepreneur, the firm and its environment, local and regional as well as national and international, is at the heart of understanding the growth process itself. However, given the heterogeneity of entrepreneurs and of small businesses, and the complexity and diversity of the markets in which they operate, any attempt to produce a comprehensive theory or any meaningful analysis of growth may be unrealistic, at least in the short term. One may also add that there is no single correct management of a business for growth and that growth itself, as has been noted, is not a simple linear process: rather, businesses are growing, contracting and growing again several times and at different rates.

TARGETING GROWTH

As has been explained earlier in this chapter, much of the interest in growth businesses arises because they represent employment potential and there is therefore a wish to target them for support to enhance that employment potential. Such a policy of targeting growth has its proponents as well as its opponents. The arguments often used by each are set out below.

Arguments for targeting growth businesses

Five arguments are presented here (and see also the list at the beginning of this chapter):

1 *Targeting increases the effectiveness of support measures.* As explained earlier, statistical evidence has been presented that, over time, a proportionately small number of firms out of any cohort of businesses will create a large proportion of new jobs. It is consequently argued that targeted support for these 'growth' businesses should be more effective in promoting jobs than more generalised support, because it has a clear focus and concentrates resources where they are most needed and where they can produce the best results.

2 *It minimises support requirements.* By applying support only to growth businesses, the total support requirement, and its cost, is reduced. Indeed with
   many hundreds of thousands of businesses starting each year, it is not feasible
   to deal with them all and make a sufficient impact with limited resources.

3 *It encourages a clearer strategic focus on the needs of such businesses.* Targeting
   growth businesses forces small business support organisations to identify more
   clearly how to support such businesses and to develop appropriate strategies
   for such support. It also helps agencies to develop a better understanding of the
   processes of growth in the target market and how best to assist such processes.
   High levels of expertise are thus more likely to be developed.

4 *More business starts are not needed.* There are situations, such as that pertaining
   in the UK in the 1970s and 1980s, where it has been argued that the rate of
   business starts was higher than that in some competitor economies. More
   business starts were not therefore needed and attention should instead have
   been focused on promoting business growth, which was needed.

5 *Supporting start-ups distorts the market.* The market mechanism serves as the most
   efficient means of allocating scarce resources and supporting start-up businesses
   will distort this. This argument however only has validity if the assumptions
   underlying the neo-classical approach to economic theory always hold.

Arguments against targeting growth businesses

Four arguments are presented here:

1 *It is difficult.* The process of picking winners has been likened to selecting a
   potentially good wine. It is viewed as more of an art than a science and is the
   preserve of a tiny group of *cognoscenti* with exceptional 'noses' and 'palates';
   it is a skill that takes years of training and experience to acquire, and not
   everyone can do it even then. (Even the wine *cognoscenti* generally only make
   predictions for wines with a good pedigree, with the result that most of them
   missed the potential of the 'New World' wines.) It is not therefore something
   that can be systemised in business agencies.

2 *It is not the same as providing venture capital.* The venture capital industry would
   pride itself on picking winners, and needs to pick them to survive. However it
   only needs to select a few winners that would be enough for its own purposes,
   and it would acknowledge that it still selects a majority of 'dogs' that have to
   be compensated for by the occasional correctly chosen 'star'. Public support
   policy, in contrast, would seek to back all the winners and avoid any losers.

3 *It is misguided.* Those who regard targeting, or 'picking winners', as a misguided policy do so for the following reasons:
   • *The structure of business.* It is argued that the quality, volume and viability
     of new business starts can influence the strength and competitiveness of
     the small business sector. This in turn is at the root of the creation of an

economy which not only generates job creation, but also contributes to the achievement of wider economic and social goals, including productivity, living standards, price stability, diversity, choice and personal opportunity. It is suggested that three key questions need to be asked when considering the part that start-ups play in an economy:

- Are there enough of them?
- Is the quality of the stock of new and small businesses adequate?
- Are start-up rates, and net additions to the business stock, rising or falling?

Answers to these questions will help prioritise the importance of start-up support.

- *The policy rationale for support of start-ups.* The key policy arguments for support are:
  - Start-ups are the seedbed for growth. This argument is summarised in the view that, without a healthy and quality stock of new businesses, the future supply of 'winners' or growth businesses will be curtailed. Not to support them, therefore, would be to reduce the pool of potential 'winners'.
  - Market failures constrain start-up rates. This argument seeks to highlight barriers to start-up which are attributable to organisational or institutional deficiencies. These 'market failures' are seen as impacting disproportionately on new and small businesses, disadvantaging them. These barriers include cultural/social values, difficulties in financing, legislative and administrative burdens including reporting requirements, and access to information.
  - More employment creation. A 'picking winners' policy ignores the fact that most of the jobs in the small business sector still come from businesses with fewer than 20 employees: so not only are non-growth businesses and start-ups the source of future growth businesses, they provide employment now (between one third and two thirds of all new jobs in the UK). The assertion is not contrary to the findings that out of any group of existing firms measured over a discrete time period a small number will create a disproportionate number of jobs (see Chapters Seven and Eight).
  - Lower costs per job. Job creation costs are lower for start-ups than for many existing businesses. This argument is based on a perception that the costs associated with new jobs in start-ups are lower than for existing businesses including inward investment.
  - The impact of start-up rates. High start-up rates have a positive impact on regional prosperity. There appears to be a positive relationship between start-up levels and regional prosperity—including a positive correlation between levels of new venture creation and employment generation (see also Chapter 13).

4 *What is needed is an enterprising culture.* This set of arguments revolves around the view, explored in Chapter Four, that cultural values supportive of

entrepreneurial activity and entrepreneurs can be considered a major influence on the level and success of start-up activity. In consequence it is argued that an investment needs to be made in building support and stakeholder networks positively disposed towards start-ups and growth rather than in direct intervention in growing businesses.

> I haven't figured out a way [to anticipate which firms will be the gazelles and which will end up the mice]. In fact, one of the fascinating things about the gazelles is that they sometimes appear to be mice for long periods of time.
>
> David Birch[55]

IN CONCLUSION

The targeting debate is not over, however. The search for the Holy Grail, the formula for creating and/or picking winners, will no doubt continue. Growth businesses may still be desirable, even if they can't be spotted in advance. To quote Storey again, 'It is the failure of UK small enterprises to grow into large enterprises that may be at the heart of the country's long-term poor economic performance.'[56]

THE KEY POINTS OF CHAPTER 8

- When it was suggested that the major proportion of net new jobs was created by small businesses, governments and others saw that there could be economic benefit in supporting small businesses. More detailed analysis appears to have shown that it is a relatively small proportion of small businesses which grow. 'Over a decade, four per cent of those businesses which start would be expected to create 50 per cent of employment generated.'[57] However businesses with fewer than 20 employees still generate most employment.
- If small business support resources are limited, which is invariably the case, then it has been suggested that the way to maximise results is to apply those resources only to growth businesses, and in the most appropriate way so that they can be most effective. Therefore there has been considerable interest in learning what makes businesses grow and how such businesses can be spotted.
- It is important to realise that growth in a business context can have many meanings. For the investor it may be growth in shareholder value. For the business it may be growth in sales and in profits, and for government it may be growth in employment. These forms of growth may not all coincide.

- In the context of small businesses, three main areas of influence are examined. It is reasonable to deduce that the entrepreneur's (or leader's) ambition and desire to grow is critical and, in addition, the skills of the entrepreneur are particularly important in the early stages of growth. It can also be said that many firm specific factors may be important for growth, but there is an absence of strong evidence to demonstrate the causal relationship. Yet another approach to understanding and explaining growth lies in examining the impact of factors or constraints external to the firm. These include macro-economic variables such as aggregate demand, taxation, regulations, labour market skills and labour relations, but also embrace sector and region specific issues and factors such as sector/market, competition, government assistance, location, and the availability (and use) of information. All these are seen as having some impact, not least those concerned with the characteristics of the entrepreneur and his/her choice of business strategy, but none are useful as predictors.
- In the context of the external environment, 'cluster' theory is of interest. It is based on research that shows that internationally successful businesses are often found in geographic clusters where the environment is most advantageous to them; that it is innovation that makes businesses competitive, and thus provides the potential for growth; and that it is demanding buyers in the domestic market that can pressure companies to innovate faster.
- Ultimately growth is likely to be dependent upon the interaction of a number of influences, each of which may be important in different combinations for different businesses.
- As for the issue of whether to target growth businesses or not, the debate is not over. The search for the Holy Grail, the formula for creating and/or picking winners, will no doubt continue. Growth businesses may still be desirable even if they can't be spotted in advance.

QUESTIONS, EXERCISES, ESSAY AND DISCUSSION TOPICS

- How could more small business growth be encouraged?
- How might growth as an indicator of business success be measured?
- Is the natural tendency for a business to grow or decline? Explain your reasoning.
- Describe some broad academic approaches taken to analysing the influences on the growth of the firm.

- Which of the following influences on the growth of the firm are likely to be the strongest in their impact: the entrepreneur(s), the firm's strategic positioning and operational procedures, or the external environment?
- The real barriers to growth are attributable only to managerial weaknesses, everything else being an excuse. Discuss.
- Is it reasonable to expect that a comprehensive theory of business growth will ultimately be developed? Explain your thinking.
- Trying to 'pick winners' is either like the search for the Holy Grail or is akin to looking for a needle in a haystack. It is, therefore, no basis for policy. Discuss.
- What are the arguments for and against implementing a business birth-rate strategy in your region?

SUGGESTIONS FOR FURTHER READING

A. Atherton, A. Gibb and L. Sear, *Reviewing the Case for Supporting Business Start-Ups: A Policy Overview of Current Thinking on Business Start-Ups* (Durham: Durham University Business School, 1997).

R. Barkham, E. Hanvey and M. Hart, *The Role of the Entrepreneur in Small Firm Growth* (Belfast: NIERC, 1995).

P. Burns, *Entrepreneurship and Small Business* (Basingstoke: Palgrave (now Palgrave Macmillan), 2001), Chapters 9, 10, 11.

D. F. Kuratko, J. S. Hornsby and D. W. Nattziger, 'An Examination of Owners' Goals in Sustaining Entrepreneurship', *Journal of Small Business Management* 1997; 35(1): 24–33.

M. E. Porter, 'From Competitive Advantage to Competitive Strategy', *Harvard Business Review* 1987; 65(3): 43–59.

D. Smallbone, R. Leigh and D. North, 'The Characteristics and Strategies of High Growth SMEs', *International Journal of Entrepreneurial Behavior and Research* 1995; 1(3): 44–62.

D. J. Storey, 'Symposium on Harrison: Lean and Mean: A Job Generation Perspective', *Small Business Economics* 1995; 7(5): 337–40.

D. J. Storey, *Understanding the Small Business Sector* (London: Routledge, 1994), Chapter 5.

G. Timmons, *New Venture Creation: Entrepreneurship for the 21st Century*, Fifth edition (Singapore: Irwin/McGraw-Hill, 1999), Chapter 16.

REFERENCES

1   OECD, *Globalization and Small and Medium Enterprises (SMEs)*, Vol. 1, Synthesis Report, (Paris: OECD, 1997), p. 7.
2   J. Levy, *Small and Medium Sized Enterprises: A Recipe for Success* (London: Institution of Electrical Engineers) as cited in D. J. Storey, *Understanding the Small Business Sector* (London: Routledge, 1994), p. 24.
3   DTI, *Competitiveness: Helping the Smaller Firm* (London: DTI, May 1995), p. 2.
4   OECD (1997), *op. cit.*, p. 17.
5   Extract from an interview in: 'The Job Generation Process Revisited', *ICSB Bulletin*, Spring 1995.
6   D. J. Storey, *Understanding the Small Business Sector* (London: Routledge, 1994), p. 115.
7   NIERC, *Job Generation and Manufacturing Industry 1973–86* (Belfast: Northern Ireland Economic Research Centre, 1989).
8   E. Garnsey, 'A New Theory of the Growth of the Firm', in *Proceedings of the 41st ICSB World Conference*, Stockholm 1996, p. 126.
9   D. Smallbone and P. Wyer, 'Growth and Development in the Small Firm', in S. Carter and D. Jones-Evans (eds), *Enterprise and Small Business: Principles, Practice and Policy* (London: Financial Times/Prentice-Hall, 2000), p. 410.
10 A. Gibb and L. Davies, 'In Pursuit of Frameworks for the Development of Growth Models of the Small Business', *International Small Business Journal*, Vol. 1990; 9(1): 26.
11 Storey, *op. cit.*, p. 121.
12 Gibb and Davies, *op. cit.*, pp. 16–17.
13 H. Barreto, *Entrepreneurship in Micro-economic Theory* (London: Routledge, 1989).
14 R. Barkham, E. Hanvey and M. Hart, *The Role of the Entrepreneur in Small Firm Growth* (Belfast: NIERC, 1995), p. 2.
15 Barkham *et al.*, *op. cit.*, p. 2.
16 Storey, *op. cit.*, pp. 137–43.
17 M. Scott and P. Rosa, 'Has Firm Level Analysis Reached its Limits? Time For a Rethink', *International Small Business Journal* 1996; 14: 81–9.
18 B Kirchhoff, personal communication.
19 *Ibid.*
20 *Ibid.*
21 *Ibid.*
22 C. Hakim, 'Identifying Fast Growth Small Firms', *Employment Gazette*, January 1989.
23 Quoted in M. Carree, A. van Stel, R. Thurik and S. Wennekers, *Business Ownership and Economic Growth: An Empirical Investigation*, Research Report 9809/E (Zoetermeer, The Netherlands: EIM Small Business Research and Consultancy, 1999), p. 11.
24 D. B. Audretsch and A. R. Thurik, *The Knowledge Society, Entrepreneuship and Unemployment*, Research Report 9801/E (Zoetermeer, The Netherlands: EIM Small Business Research and Consultancy, 1998), p. 11.
25 Carree *et al.*, *op. cit.*, p. 1.
26 B. Kirchhoff, 'Twenty Years of Job Creation Research: What have We Learned?', *Proceedings of the 40th ICSB World Conference*, Stockholm, 1995, pp. 195–219, at p. 210.

27 Storey, *op. cit.*, pp. 126–37.
28 Barkham *et al.*, *op. cit.*, p. 15.
29 Gibb and Davies, *op. cit.*, p. 18.
30 *Ibid.*, p. 20.
31 Storey, *op. cit.*, pp. 137–43.
32 European Network for SME Research, *The European Observatory for SMEs: First Annual Report* (Zoetermeer, The Netherlands: EIM Small Business Research and Consultancy, 1993), p. 24.
33 Storey, *op. cit.*, pp. 144–54.
34 Barkham *et al.*, *op. cit.*, p. 16.
35 OECD, *Small and Medium Sized Enterprises: Technology and Competitiveness* (Paris: OECD, 1993), p. 21.
36 CBI, *Managing to Grow* (London: CBI, December 1995), p. 11.
37 OECD (1993), *op. cit.*, p. 9.
38 Barkham *et al.*, *op. cit.*, p. 16.
39 Quoted in P. Burns, *Entrepreneurship and Small Business* (Basingstoke: Palgrave (now Palgrave Macmillan), 2001), p. 272.
40 Barkham *et al.*, *op. cit.*, pp. 15–18.
41 Gibb and Davies, *op. cit.*, pp. 15–31.
42 Storey, *op. cit.*, pp. 138–40.
43 P. Westhead and D. Storey, *An Assessment of Firms Located On and Off Science Parks in the UK* (London: HMSO, 1994).
44 B. Kirchhoff, personal communication.
45 D. Smallbone, R. Leigh and D. North, 'Characteristics and Strategies of High Growth SMEs', *International Journal of Entrepreneurial Behaviour and Research* 1995; 1(3): 44–62.
46 P. Vaessen and D. Keeble, *Growth Oriented SMEs in Unfavourable Regional Environments*, Working paper (Cambridge: ESRC Centre for Business Research, 1995).
47 Institute of Directors, *Your Business Matters: Report from the Regional Conference* (London: Institute of Directors, 1996), pp. 6–7.
48 M. E. Porter, 'The Competitive Advantage of Nations', *Harvard Business Review*, 1990: March–April: 73–93.
49 *Ibid.*: 82.
50 Quoted in Bank of England, *Finance for Small Firms: An Eighth Report* (London: Bank of England, March 2001), p. 60.
51 OECD, Directorate for Science, Technology and Industry, Industry Committee, *The Role of SMEs: Findings and Issues*, DSTI/IND(2000)15/REV1 (Paris: OECD, December 2000), p. 3.
52 OECD (1993), *op.cit.*, p. 21.
53 A. Cosh and A. Hughes (eds), *Enterprising Britain: Growth, Innovation and Public Policy in the Small and Medium Sized Enterprise Sector 1994–1997* (Cambridge: ESRC Centre for Business Research).
54 Cambridge Small Business Research Centre, *The State of British Enterprise* (Cambridge: Department of Applied Economics, University of Cambridge, 1992).
55 Extract from an interview in 'The Job Generation Process Revisited', *ICSB Bulletin*, Spring 1995.
56 Storey, *op. cit.*, p. 159.
57 *Ibid.*, p. 115.

SMALL IS BEAUTIFUL: ENTREPRENEURSHIP IN THE BIGGER BUSINESS

CONTENTS

KEY CONCEPTS

This chapter covers:
- why corporate entrepreneurship, and innovation, are desirable in big businesses;
- different approaches to the practice of corporate entrepreneurship;
- why corporate entrepreneurship may need to be encouraged, the barriers to it and what can be done to promote its manifestation in strategic entrepreneurship, innovation and an entrepreneurial culture;
- areas where there appear to be disadvantages of size and where being small can be an advantage;
- some of the implications of ICT and e-business.

LEARNING OBJECTIVES

By the end of this chapter the reader should:
- understand the concept of corporate entrepreneurship;
- appreciate the need for, and the possible barriers to, corporate entrepreneurship and innovation;
- appreciate some of the circumstances in which being small can be an advantage;
- understand some of the issues relevant to businesses' ability to capitalise on the opportunities offered by ICT and e-business.

INTRODUCTION

The last chapter considered the growth of small businesses because much small business policy and support have been focused on them in particular. However growth, or at least the maturity and size which come from growth, can be a disadvantage because it can be harder for the business then to remain entrepreneurial. Even for big businesses, some aspects of 'small' can still seem to be 'beautiful'.

This chapter therefore looks at two aspects of 'small is beautiful' from the perspective of the bigger business. It looks at attempts by established businesses to continue to be entrepreneurial, a process which is often referred to as 'corporate entrepreneurship' or 'intrapreneurship', and it looks at situations where it really does seem to be an advantage to be small.

ENTREPRENEURSHIP IN BIGGER BUSINESSES

Growth in the early stages of a small business can be seen as a natural extension of its original formation, and at least to some extent it requires the same sense of adventure, of initiative and of opportunity. However, as has been pointed out in previous chapters, many organisations have developmental stages and different priorities and practices prevail at different stages of development. For example, Greiner[1] suggests that after the start-up or entrepreneurial phase, many organisations focus on the efficient division of labour and the elaboration of structure, which increases the need to formalise procedures and control behaviour. Management effort focuses on efficiency and the maintenance of the *status quo* and change becomes something to be resisted or avoided. Yet in a dynamic business environment, where competition is severe and where market developments present new opportunities, to stand still is to court regression.[2]

Standing still and maintaining order are appropriate reactions in a stable environment but the modern business environment is extremely dynamic, and standing still is not an advisable managerial option. A turbulent business environment is commonplace nowadays but it is worth emphasising why such a state of affairs exists.

Genus[3] and Jones-Evans[4] argue that many organisational contexts are now characterised by:

- a decline in stable mass consumer markets and an increase in fragmented markets in which product life cycles are much shorter than formerly;
- a significant increase in the size of the service sector;
- a marked reduction in labour market rigidities with major consequences for the employment patterns of individuals and the utilisation of labour by firms;
- major technological and information revolutions which have transformed industries and organisations;
- the deregulation of industrial sectors and the privatisation of nationalised industries;
- intense international competition and the development of global production capabilities and markets;
- the glorification of entrepreneurship and the enterprise culture.

Basically 'old certainties have been superseded by new and continuing uncertainties'[5] and consequently organisations must innovate and differentiate products and services while improving quality. They must do this by modifying their internal arrangements and their association with external parties.

Innovative responses to the modern organisational world are necessary for large and small firms but the approach is somewhat different in the more mature business. Business formation and early growth, which frequently depend on the ideas, drive and personality of the founder, are seen as the essence of entrepreneurship. Growth in a mature business also requires enterprise, ideas, drive and culture, but these must come at least in part from those working in the business as well as from an owner-manager.

> Today's businesses, especially the large ones, simply will not survive in this period of rapid change and innovation unless they acquire entrepreneurial competence.
>
> Peter Drucker[6]

It was an American, Pinchot, who invented the word 'intrapreneurship'[7] to describe the practice of entrepreneurship within mature businesses, a necessary practice if those organisations are to continue to develop indefinitely. Organisational development implies change and improvement; it means doing new and more productive things that can sustain or enhance profit. This development requires the application of enterprise in the mature organisation; the process which has been described as intrapreneurship or, more recently, as corporate entrepreneurship.[8] Corporate entrepreneurship has been defined in a number of ways and some of the approaches used to develop it are considered in more detail later in this chapter. But before presenting them, the connection between entrepreneurship, innovation, and enterprise is summarised in order to provide a context for corporate entrepreneurship.

Entrepreneurship

Entrepreneurship has been described in terms of:

> the ability to create something from practically nothing. It is initiating ... and building an enterprise rather than ... watching one. It is the knack for sensing opportunities where others see chaos, contradiction and confusion. It is the ability to build a 'founding team' to complement your own skills and talents. It is the know-how to find, marshal and control resources. Finally it is a willingness to take calculated risks.[9]

This definition is consistent with that used in Chapter Three but it emphasises the range of activities that are needed to initiate and to launch the development of a new business venture. It does not dwell however on the nature of the business that is then created. A great deal of entrepreneurship, or enterprise, must still be exercised, even in a mundane small business, if that business is to survive. The interactions 'between smallness, exposure to the environment, ownership and personal control, condition the culture of the business'.[10] The task environment is complex and changeable, and the continuing exercise of enterprise is essential for success. Problems have to be solved for which there is little or no precedent.

Learning and problem-solving are common activities in many working environments nowadays, but some people consider that true entrepreneurship occurs when individuals 'ignore the established ways of thinking and action' and seek novel ideas and solutions that can meet customer needs. Entrepreneurship is therefore:

> the innovatory process involved in the creation of an economic enterprise based on a new product or service which differs significantly from products or services offered by other suppliers in content or in the way its production is organised or in its marketing.[11]

In this approach entrepreneurship is therefore concerned with newness: new ideas, products, services or combinations of resources aimed at meeting the needs of consumers more efficiently.

Innovation

Innovation has also been considered in Chapter Three, but it is appropriate to mention it again. It has been described as the successful development of competitive advantage and, as such, it is the key to corporate entrepreneurship. For example, Pinchot, in his seminal work, *Intrapreneuring*, argues that entrepreneurs in businesses are 'the dreamers who do: those who take hands-on responsibility for creating innovation of any kind within an organisation. The intrapreneur may be a creator or inventor but is always a dreamer who figures out how to turn an idea into a profitable reality.'[12] More recently Kuratko and Hodgetts have argued that 'the major thrust of corporate entrepreneurship is to develop the entrepreneurial spirit within organisational boundaries, thus allowing an atmosphere of innovation to prosper';[13] the corporate entrepreneur therefore is an individual who initiates innovative change in mature firms.

It is also argued that it is the presence of innovation that distinguishes the entrepreneurial organisation from others. Covin and Miles go so far as to say that 'the label "entrepreneurial" should not be applied to firms that are not innovative'.[14] For them, innovation is necessary for corporate entrepreneurship and that means being innovative in relation to the competition. They suggest, for example, that firms which replace their basic technologies with new methods which are being disseminated throughout an industry can be regarded as innovative from an internal perspective but will hardly be considered innovative by outsiders. For Covin and Miles innovation must 'increase competitiveness through efforts aimed at the rejuvenation, renewal, and redefinition of organisations, their markets or industries' if businesses are to be deemed entrepreneurial.[15]

Inventors are usually individuals, but corporate entrepreneurship is frequently carried out by groups or teams. Caird points out that there are leading innovators who are frequently the driving force behind innovations. They are 'the project champions', and the project 'has no chance of being realised without their belief and commitment'.[16] However, while the lead innovator may have inventing or managerial skill or both, many of Caird's innovators lacked marketing and general management skills, which were provided by members of the project team.

Innovation itself can take several forms, all relevant to corporate entrepreneurship:[17]

- innovation in processes, including changes and improvements to methods. These contribute to increases in productivity, which lowers costs and helps to increase demand;
- innovation in products, or services. While progressive innovation is predominant, radical innovation opens up new markets. These lead to increases in effective demand which encourage increases in investment and employment;
- innovation in management and work organisation, and the exploitation of human resources, together with the capacity to anticipate techniques.

It is important in this context to recognise that innovation is not confined to the manufacturing sector. Today the service sector plays a dominant role in enterprise and economic development in mature economies.

ILLUSTRATION 9.1
The Ten Commandments of innovation

....

1 Take risks – adopt a 'can do' philosophy
2 Stimulate creativity and seek out new ideas
3 Reward success and tolerate failure
4 Set realistic targets and review
5 Adopt an open management style
6 Focus on the customer – cultivate partnerships
7 Actively manage investors
8 Know what your competition is up to
9 Work with other companies and academics
10 Patent/protect

DTI presentation

Enterprise

If corporate entrepreneurship is the continuing generation of innovation by applying entrepreneurship within established businesses then it is, in turn, an example of the broad meaning of 'enterprise'. As a result the terms 'entrepreneurship', 'enterprise', 'innovation', 'change', 'intrapreneurship' and 'corporate entrepreneurship' are frequently used interchangeably and, while this is sometimes due to a looseness in writing style, it is clear that there are many similarities amongst the terms.

Innovation and enterprise are known to be important in the private sector in most economies but Borins[18] points out that they can also be commonplace in the public sector. This occurs despite deterrents such as the close political management of the executive aimed at securing a consistent implementation of policy, tight controls and checks aimed at preventing corruption, and the keenness of the media to expose any errors and mistakes that may be made. It is also part of the conventional wisdom that, because public services are generally not exposed to market forces, they are liable to operate inefficiently and that this will continue until they are forced by a public crisis to innovate. However Borins reveals that public servants often initiate external innovation to solve problems before they become crises and that other innovations emerge in response to perceived opportunities, sometimes as a result of initiatives by politicians.

CORPORATE ENTREPRENEURSHIP

The importance of corporate entrepreneurship

Before discussing corporate entrepreneurship in detail we should establish the importance of this activity for business development. Management writers, such as Peter Drucker, have for a long time argued that entrepreneurial competency is essential for continued success. However Wiklund reviewed the literature on the connection between an entrepreneurial strategic orientation and business performance in established smaller companies and concluded that there is no simple link between them. He also raised a point about the timescale of any correlation and wondered if corporate entrepreneurship was a quick fix for firms in trouble or whether it did indeed produce long-term results.

It is recognised that size as well as maturity has an impact on corporate entrepreneurial activity, so Wiklund carried out research on Swedish businesses with between ten and fifty employees. This is one of the few studies which utilises large longitudinal datasets in investigating the link between entrepreneurial orientation and business performance and therefore, although these were not large businesses, this research is relevant to the issues covered in this chapter.

Wiklund argues that, in the short run, proactive firms pay attention to environmental trends and can respond quickly to opportunities by introducing innovations. Their alertness allows them to target markets and charge premium prices. It also allows them to stay ahead of the competition and gain a competitive advantage. Wiklund believes that this alertness provides established smaller firms with a strategic advantage which compensates for their lack of resources. He also believes that firm-level entrepreneurship confers advantage in the longer term. Their early movement into markets allows entrepreneurial firms to dominate distribution channels and establish industry standards which consolidates their advantage.

There is some research support for the long-term benefit of entrepreneurship but, in view of the inconclusive evidence in support of the entrepreneurship-performance link, Wiklund carried out his longitudinal study to discover if performance was enhanced as a result of entrepreneurial strategy in both the short and long run. Results indicate that there is a positive association between entrepreneurship and performance in both the short and longer term, thus offering support for those who argue in favour of entrepreneurship.[19] However, it should be pointed out that the link is not a simple one. Wiklund found that availability of finance, which can be considered to be a 'pull' factor, had a stronger impact on performance than entrepreneurship, which is a 'push' factor. Having the money to complete requisite activities is very important. In another recent article Chandler, Keller and Lyon[20] indicate that an innovation-supportive organisational culture does have a positive impact on revenue in many firms but only under conditions of rapid environmental change.

Defining corporate entrepreneurship

Corporate entrepreneurship may lead to superior performance but, as we have found with several of the issues raised in this book, there are various definitions of key concepts in this field. For example Miller, in the early 1980s, began to distinguish between conservatism and entrepreneurialism in established firms and for him entrepreneurial businesses are proactive initiators who try to outdo the competition. They also have a proclivity for bold, risky acts and are highly innovative. In short they are innovative, proactive risk-takers.[21] Recently Lumpkin and Dess[22] have added autonomy and competitive aggressiveness to Miller's list of entrepreneurial attributes but it has been pointed out that Miller's instrument measures entrepreneurial disposition rather than entrepreneurial action. Vesper[23] has added to the debate on corporate entrepreneurship by suggesting that it is characterised by three activities:

- the creation of a new business unit by an established firm;
- the development and implementation of entrepreneurial strategic thrusts;
- the emergence of new ideas from various levels within an organisation.

Vesper's last point is supported by Covin and Miles[24] who believe that in some businesses an entrepreneurial philosophy impregnates the entire organisation. Zahra, Jennings and Kuratko[25] suggest that there are many facets of firm-level entrepreneurship which reflect different combinations of:

- the content of the entrepreneurship, which can be activities such as corporate venturing, innovation and proactivity;
- the source of the entrepreneurship, which can be internal to the firm or external;
- the focus of the entrepreneurship, which can be formal or informal.

These views cover a wide range of entrepreneurship but from them three main ways can be identified in which larger and more mature businesses can seek to promote entrepreneurship within the business. These are the promotion of entrepreneurship through formal strategic decision-making, which will sometimes require the creation of a separate corporate venture; the formal and informal development of innovative ideas by middle managers and professional staff, which often entails the creation of a new project; and the creation of an entrepreneurial philosophy throughout the organisation. Various terms have been used in the literature to describe these activities but in this chapter they are referred to as 'strategic entrepreneurship', 'developing innovation within organisations' and 'entrepreneurial culture' respectively.

Strategic entrepreneurship

In a start-up the entrepreneur is regarded as the key actor in developing a business idea, marshalling resources and creating an organisation to bring a new product or service to the market. In a competitive business environment it is clear that mature and larger organisations should continue to seek out new opportunities and make the necessary arrangements to convert them into new goods and services. At a strategic level this requires an effective plan and the proper positioning of the organisation to respond effectively to its environment.[26] Porter argues that strategic decision-makers must appreciate the competitive dynamics of their chosen industry.[27] The current and predicted industrial structure strongly influence the rules of the competitive game and offer certain strategic choices for organisations. He suggests that strategic planners should analyse the current and expected state of competitive rivalry by paying attention to such matters as the threat from new entrants, the availability of substitutes and the power of suppliers and customers. Industries can be classified as attractive or unattractive and Porter argues that the profit potential of an industry is a function of industry attractiveness coupled with an appropriate competitive strategy. He recognises that competitive forces within an industry can drive down profits but contends that organisations must position themselves properly in the industry. Strategic choice in pursuit of specific goals is more important than environment or structure in promoting innovation.

There are many criticisms of Porter's approach to strategic change but it is representative of a body of managerial thought which associates organisational development with rational, logical, strategic decision-making by managerial elites in both the private and public sectors. In general this approach to corporate entrepreneurship is akin to what Heller[28] calls strategic forcing. The innovation is 'forcibly fitted into the resisting organisation [whilst] the "champion" project leader uses a mix of political power, organisational savvy, and technical powers to get the innovation past organisational roadblocks to implementation'.

This is a top-down approach to corporate entrepreneurship. Top managers are strategically aware and see the need for change but they often forget that there are powerful individual, managerial, organisational and cultural reasons why innovative changes are resisted. Faced with resistance, managerial elites will attempt to overcome it at individual and organisational levels, so it seems sensible for powerful elites to understand how individuals react to change.

Resistance to change by individuals

Individuals in many organisations will resist change if they feel that their skills, status, power and relationships have to be altered significantly to meet the needs of the new order.[29] They will also want to understand why change is necessary. In this context it should be realised that people from different parts of an organisation interpret events in different ways and the need for change clearly perceived by senior managers may not be shared by other individuals and interest groups.[30] Sometimes they do not 'see' a problem, and therefore see no reason to change. Senior managers must also understand that individuals proceed through recognised phases often typified by denial, resistance, exploration and commitment as they experience a change in their situation, and that people therefore need time to digest changes.[31] Forcing change through is a dangerous approach; it must be managed effectively if people are to commit themselves to the new order.[32]

Independent versus corporate venturing

This view of strategic entrepreneurship in established firms indicates that new strategic directions may often require the creation of a separate corporate venture to deliver results. It might be argued that a separate corporate venture developed by an established business would bear a strong resemblance to other non-corporate new business ventures. However, Jones-Evans[33] points out that major differences exist between corporate and non-corporate ventures, not least in that with a new venture the ground rules for running it emerge as it develops, whereas the leaders of corporate ventures must conform to general corporate procedures from the start. Such constraints may reduce flexibility in the corporate venture and inhibit development. Jones-Evans also argues that an existing firm will have an established product-market portfolio and the new corporate venture can expect to experience serious resistance if it attempts to compete in the same markets.

Another difference will be in financing. An independent new venture will have several potential sources of funding and lenders will normally have considerable experience of assessing the potential of a new business. In contrast, new corporate ventures are likely to have only one source of funding, namely the corporate body; its financial custodians will seldom review more than a handful of corporate venture proposals per year and may not have the experience of evaluating emerging business proposals. In any event, evaluations will tend to be based on standard financial decision-making procedures and these may be inappropriate for evolving ventures. In addition, the initiators of rejected corporate venture proposals do not have alternative sources of funding to which they can go. In general non-corporate venture leaders are in control of financial and other decisions whilst corporate venture leaders must work within the constraints imposed by the established organisation.

Jones-Evans also points out that funding for a corporate venture will most likely be allocated at an early stage of a project's development. A return on investment will then be expected fairly quickly and if this fails to materialise all supplies of funds may dry up. In contrast the early funding of new independent ventures may be rather limited and this may be quite appropriate. Even though new businesses tend to be under-capitalised they often obtain additional funding on a step-by-step basis. As new products or developments come on-line additional funding is sought and this means that there may be no acquisition of major funding until it is warranted by developments.

As well as different sources of funding for new corporate and non-corporate ventures there are also likely to be different sources of human resources. In a new venture, staff will be recruited in the labour market according to their skills and commitment to the entrepreneur's vision. In contrast corporate ventures may be staffed by existing corporate employees with more interest in developing their careers. They may see their transfer to a corporate venture as a promotion and a reward for their overall contribution to the firm. Further rewards for corporate venture staff will probably be in line with corporate remuneration procedures whereas staff in a non-corporate venture can more easily be rewarded in line with the profitability of the venture.

Jones-Evans considers that new ventures sometimes benefit substantially from having expert advice from a board of directors. Directors often have diverse backgrounds and can advise on financial, market and technical matters. Corporate ventures may not have this resource; indeed project leaders usually report to the board of the controlling firm and must compete with other shareholders to have their interests addressed.

In general there are significant differences in the strategic resource management and organisational processes in corporate as opposed to new ventures and these differences will have an impact on the potential profitability of these dichotomous units. The differences will also impact on the likelihood of continued innovation.

Developing innovation within organisations

Aggressively and proactively seeking innovative opportunities outside the organisation is the essence of strategic entrepreneurship but entrepreneurship is not the sole preserve of CEOs and managerial elites. Mintzberg[34] contends that all managers, and many support staff and others, take on an entrepreneurial role as part of their work. These individuals are in unique positions to understand what is happening within organisations and some of them are able to develop an inter-departmental perspective. Many will also be in touch with peers, customers, suppliers and others outside the organisation and can spot external opportunities. Many business founders are keen to retain strategic decision-making themselves but as organisations grow they are rarely able to develop the skills and know-how, nor have access to all the resources needed to continuously expand the business. Continued growth occurs when owners involve others, and not just those at the strategic apex of the business, in the entrepreneurial process. Indeed some people argue that strategy can emerge from various levels in the organisation; however the creation and development of innovatory strategic thrusts by people other than those in the top management group can only occur if appropriate managerial and organisational systems, structures, styles and cultures are in place. Not all management styles and organisational arrangements facilitate innovatory development and therefore organisational barriers to, and assistance for, innovation need to be considered.

Managerial barriers to entrepreneurship

Managers can and do act entrepreneurially as they proliferate in growing organisations and as they acquire more decision-making authority with the dispersal of company ownership amongst shareholders. It is incumbent on managers to look to the future but management is a multi-faceted job and attentions can focus on stewardship and control rather than on entrepreneurship. Stevenson and Gumpert[35] argue that managers frequently regard themselves as trustees, and this engenders caution. They are responsible for expensive human and material resources, and they feel duty-bound to use these resources wisely. They are concerned to earn an acceptable rate of return on their resources in the shorter term and to protect the lives and livelihoods of their employees.

Managers have numerous constituents who must be at least partially satisfied. Consequently, decision-making and change are a cautious process of negotiating with major players, and pursuing a less risky, middle-of-the-road strategy is preferred. Caution is also necessary, because larger organisations typically commit large amounts of resource to important projects at one time. A lot of analysis is usually done before a project is supported, but once the decision is made the organisation is committed. Entrepreneurs, on the other hand, evaluate many projects simultaneously and quickly drop those that do not look promising. Stevenson and Gumpert also point out that there is a connection between managerial power and the resources that managers control. This being so, they are reluctant to take risks and often therefore reinforce the *status quo*. Managers also tend to have a narrower focus than entrepreneurs and to be concerned with building the power and reputation of their departments. However the process of new product development should be holistic and a narrow departmental focus can inhibit innovatory thinking.

Support staff are often technical experts who are keen to prove their worth to organisations by introducing as many innovative ideas as possible. By so doing they can increase the reliance of others on their expertise and consequently increase their power and status. While they are generally keen on newness and change, there are often conflicts between individual staff as they endeavour to extol to the organisation the virtues of their particular speciality. They are also likely to come into conflict with line managers who are keen to maintain the *status quo* as they seek efficiency gains.[36]

Barriers to innovation are commonplace in many organisations but Borins[37] shows that in public sector organisations there are additional obstacles. His research reveals that many of the barriers emanate not only from the bureaucratic nature of public sector organisations but also from the inherent caution of various internal actors. The barriers to innovation come from 'attitudes within the bureaucracy itself, turf wars, difficulties in coordinating organisations, logistical problems, the difficulty of maintaining the enthusiasm of programme staff, difficulties in implementing a new technology, opposition by unions, opposition by middle management, and opposition to entrepreneurial action within the public sector'. In addition, many initiatives are opposed by politicians because they require additional resources, because of legislative constraints and because of direct political opposition. Furthermore, various external interest groups, including private sector organisations who would have to compete with the public sector, resist many innovations.

Organisational barriers

Managerial roles and responsibilities can induce caution but managers and professionals work in an organisational context and the realities of this environment can also encourage conservatism. This occurs because organisations as they grow and mature tend to install standard operating procedures and rules that constrain initiative. The first time a new job is tackled there is a time-consuming learning process, but after it has been repeated several times a satisfactory method will be identified, remembered and used again. If the task is done continuously then recommended methods will be written down and employees told to follow them as the correct procedures.[38] As the volume of output increases there is more division of labour and specialisation, which leads to the creation of functional departments. Behaviour of individuals must be predictable, and this is achieved by introducing standard work practices. To make sure that individual and group tasks coalesce, schedules, process plans and control mechanisms are introduced.

However, as the complexity of the task increases, people lose sight of the ends they are serving. 'Management must find the means to make behaviour lower down more predictable and so it turns to rules, procedures, job descriptions, and the like, all devices that formalise behaviour.'[39] Organisations, as they develop, introduce standard practices, but also develop less tangible but equally powerful cultures. They develop characteristic ways of doing things that are guided by a set of shared norms and values. Organisations are infused with values, and this culture transmits to people in the organisation what they should be doing, what they ought to believe in or what the organisation is really about. Standard procedures and culture are powerful controlling mechanisms, and can easily defeat innovatory initiatives.[40]

As mentioned above, strategic planning can assist entrepreneurship. Some writers suggest that, with sufficient will and skill, organisations can become almost anything they want to be. However, in practice this rarely happens. Organisations specialise, which can mean that a huge investment in plant, machinery and manpower may have to be written off if the specialisation changes.[41]

Drucker recognises that many of these factors affect organisations but considers that size, *per se*, is not 'an impediment to entrepreneurship and innovation; (the main impediment) is the existing operation itself and especially the existing *successful* operation'. Total commitment to the existing operation is needed to ensure continued success and to manage 'the daily crises' that normally occur. The current activity requires priority attention 'and deserves it'. Drucker goes on to argue that most successful firms of today will in ten years' time derive a significant proportion of their income from a similar product range to their present one, but for long-term survival they must also look for a new range. This is not easy. 'The temptation in the existing business is always to feed yesterday and starve tomorrow. The current business is not in trouble, and there does not seem to be any pressure to innovate.'[42] It is evident that even leading organisations such as Royal Dutch Shell, IBM and Xerox, which have been very innovative businesses, can lose their competitive edge. Conditions change and the very procedures which proved very effective in one era are the source of disadvantage in another.[43]

Facilitating innovation

Porter has pointed out that continuous innovation is essential for organisational survival in competitive markets but, in view of the barriers, achieving it requires hard work, appropriate attitudes and proper structures. However, just as there is no single agreed route to developing enterprise, there are a number of suggestions as to what constitute the innovatory aspects of corporate entrepreneurship.

In considering policies, procedures, structures and cultures which help sustain corporate entrepreneurship it is possible to differentiate between those activities which encourage the development of new thinking and new projects by decentralising innovation to middle managers and professional staff, and those activities which extend the enterprising culture to every person in the organisation. In some cases it may prove difficult to locate a procedure in one or the other of these categories but it seems that there are differences in the mindsets required for extending the formal and informal development of new projects to middle levels of an organisation and for creating a wider enterprise philosophy. Also, while the policies and procedures which support strategic entrepreneurship by top managers have already been discussed, some of the discussion which follows, especially that in connection with Lessem's work, is relevant to the encouragement of strategic entrepreneurship.

Roles

Lessem in particular has highlighted the importance of managerial roles and behaviour in supporting corporate entrepreneurship, although he uses the older term 'intrapreneur' which will therefore also be used here in discussing his work. He identifies the key to intrapreneurship as the intrapreneurs themselves and the roles they perform.[44] For him, the intrapreneur combines many of the qualities of the entrepreneur and the manager. The impatience of the entrepreneur with the constraints imposed by the organisation produces too much conflict with the desire of managers to control events. For Lessem, the concept of intrapreneur is important for two reasons. 'Firstly, it cuts across the division between management and enterprise. But secondly, it forms a bridge between enterprise and development.'[45]

For Lessem, there are several roles or archetypes that can elicit effective development in differing business contexts. Some support strategic entrepreneurship while others support innovation from below. In some situations rugged entrepreneurs are needed. They have an instinctive approach to opportunities and impatience when faced with obstacles. They seldom let a real or perceived lack of resources inhibit their search for new profitable opportunities. However, in a mature venture their impatience and aggression can create conflict.

It is recognised that large and mature companies may not be attractive to entrepreneurial types unless they can find opportunities in areas such as sales and new product development. The organisation should offer them the chance to take on risky projects, however. Their success should be rewarded, but failure must not lead to censure. Mature organisational entrepreneurs can develop the capacity to focus on business renewal as a goal.

In some instances entrepreneurial activity is not enough for development; what is needed is an *adventurer*. The latter is a major risk-taker who enters uncharted waters in search of opportunity. There are difficulties in making huge changes in strategy, but in some instances this is required and the courage and forcefulness of the adventurer is indispensable. In an increasingly global economy, organisations need the drive and audaciousness of the adventurer to enter new and difficult markets.

Innovators are needed also. They are the first or early users of new ideas and are the essential link between research and accomplishment. They must create structures and a climate conducive to the generation of, experimentation with and realisation of new ideas. They encourage creativity, but they also have a strong commitment to the commercial exploitation of ideas. Innovators get their rewards from seeing the successful transformation of an idea into a successful good or service, but there can be a tendency to marginalise adventurers and innovators in successful businesses. Firms must find mechanisms to allow innovation to coexist with current product efficiency.

Exploring random innovative ideas may be exciting but firms also need a sense of direction and discipline. There must be some pattern in a firm's strategy and *leaders* ensure that new projects are aligned with their vision for the business. Leaders stand back from the intensive competition in firms and act as somewhat impartial arbitrators, coordinators and conflict-handlers. The leader takes an overview, reconciles differing perspectives, and creates a climate of cooperation, but also exercises authority when needed to keep the business on the rails. Like the leader of an orchestra, the business leader has concern for the final product and for the people, and uses a range of methods of influence to make sure that all play in tune.

In addition, the role of effective *change agents* can be crucial. They effectively bring new products to market, implement new management systems and reorganise working arrangements. Change agents like freedom from controls and are not bound by convention, but they also possess the managerial and political skill to manage change programmes. They appreciate the importance of creating a general awareness that the *status quo* will not do in a turbulent era and in creating an image of the future and letting key players know what it will look like. Further, using change management theory, they can design and implement the practical first steps to bringing about change. They also recognise and can deal with resistance to change. Change agents are keen to do new things and get their motivation from the mental excitement that accompanies change.

Change agents are important, but they cannot function on their own. Another key intrapreneurial type therefore is the *enabler*. Many authors point out the importance of creating a climate or culture for enterprise and innovation and the lack of appropriate cultures in many organisations. Therefore a facilitator or enabler aims to:

> develop self-renewing, self-correcting systems of people who learn to organise themselves in a variety of ways according to the nature of their tasks, and who continue to expand the choice available to the organisation as it copes with the changing demands of a changing environment.[46]

Enablers use 'soft' behavioural skills to encourage people to question ideas, challenge conventions and seek, through collaboration with insiders and outsiders, to come up with forward-looking ideas.

Lessem also describes one more intrapreneurial type: the *animateur*. Organisations are technical and economic tools, but they are also living social systems, which need to be humanised and enlivened. An *esprit de corps* or sense of community is vital for a developing organisation, and this is where the animateur assists. The emphasis is on teams and on development through cooperation, problem-solving and concern for the organisational community. Enablers and animators develop the supportive atmosphere and trust that is essential for individual and group risk-taking in pursuit of better options.

Lessem's approach is useful in that it recognises the importance of numerous roles, from the aggressive and competitive adventurer and entrepreneur to the people-oriented enabler and animateur, in the continued development of mature organisations. Several of these intrapreneurial types can deliver innovation in appropriate situations, but others provide the change leadership skills to guide a project to fulfilment and create the flexible structures to sustain change.

ILLUSTRATION 9.2
Who is the intrapreneur?

Primary motives: the intrapreneur wants freedom and access to corporate resources and is self-motivated, but responds to corporate rewards.

Time orientation: the intrapreneur has end goals of three to 15 years, depending on the nature of the project, and strives to meet self-imposed and corporate timetables.

Action: the intrapreneur does whatever is needed to accomplish tasks and is not interested in status.

Skills: the intrapreneur knows the business intimately, but recognises the importance of managerial and political skill.

Confidence: the intrapreneur is self-confident and courageous and, if necessary, will outwit the organisational system.

Focus: the intrapreneur focuses both inside and outside the business. The intrapreneur pays attention to customers and gets insiders to do the same.

Risk: the intrapreneur likes moderate risk and undertakes market research in order to understand the risks.

Failure and mistakes: the intrapreneur regards mistakes as a learning experience, but is sensitive to the needs of the organisation for stability and hence may hide risky projects from view.

Decisions: the intrapreneur is adept at communicating his or her own private vision to others and is willing to compromise to make progress with this vision.

Attitude towards the system: the intrapreneur dislikes the system, but learns to manipulate it.

Background: the intrapreneur is often from an entrepreneurial, small business, professional or farm background and is often middle class and highly educated, particularly in technical fields.

Source: 'Who Is the Intrapreneur?', adapted from G. Pinchot III, *Intrapreneuring* (New York: Harper & Row, 1985) pp. 54–6. Copyright © by Gifford Pinchot III. Reprinted by permission of the author.

Systems and structures that support innovation

Peter Drucker, in writing about innovation and entrepreneurship, like Lessem, highlights the importance of managerial decision-making but considers also that appropriate policies and procedures are needed. He considers that the essence of innovation and corporate entrepreneurship is the development of new or different processes, products or services that utilise resources more productively than before. He contends that innovators must systematically review the changes taking place in society to identify and exploit business opportunities. Entrepreneurial managers must also scan the environment to become aware of changes in those management principles and practices, production processes, and market structures and requirements that can conceivably have an impact on their organisations. They must also be aware of changes in knowledge, but are warned against an overemphasis on knowledge-based innovations. Some are spectacular and transform markets, but although the vast majority of innovations are more mundane they have a much greater cumulative impact on profits and employment.

It is important to emphasise the weight that Drucker attaches to solid, systematic investigation in the process of modernisation. This is seldom the result of genius or high-technology discoveries; more often it is the application of systematic search and logic to a host of organisational procedures and practices. Instalment credit or hire purchase, for instance, had a much greater impact on the business sector than more novel and spectacular changes. There are barriers to successful organisational innovation but, if the right managerial policies and practices are put in place, then innovation can become normal.

Many managers protect what they have currently, but if they are to change they must become aware that it is company policy systematically to give up those products and practices that are unproductive. They must therefore place all activities periodically 'on trial' for their lives. Managers should answer critical questions on the contribution products make to productivity and should be encouraged not to shore up the obsolete. Obsolete or declining products absorb scarce resources at the expense of the new. The best people tend to be charged with overcoming the problems associated with old products, whereas they should be encouraged to develop the new. Entrepreneurial business 'management must take the lead in making obsolete its own products and services rather than waiting for a competitor to do so'.[47]

Another approach is to use successful innovators as role models. They are asked to make presentations to their peers to explain their actions: to outline those factors that lead to success and those that cause difficulties. The fact that senior managers encourage this activity sends a clear message that innovative behaviour is appreciated. Then, if innovation is to become an important business function, mechanisms must be initiated to assess innovative performance. It is important to know what the expected outcomes of the innovation are likely to be, what resources are necessary and when results are to be achieved. Innovation concerns the new and largely unknown, but serious attempts must be made to gain feedback on progress to assess performance.

Policies, practices and appraisals assist innovation, but innovative ideas and their commercialisation are generated by people. Since behaviour is influenced by context, the organisational context must support innovative behaviour. Successful innovation emerges when organisations have appropriate personnel in post, when management systems support change and when a suitable climate obtains. The complexity of large organisations can stifle classic entrepreneurs, even if they are the company founders. Without appropriate policies the organisation is likely to become performance-oriented rather than innovation-oriented. 'Companies that have built entrepreneurial management into their structure ... continue to be innovators ... irrespective of changes in chief executives or economic conditions.'[48]

Just what is meant by entrepreneurial management and the creation of an appropriate climate? Jones-Evans[49] argues that managers cannot tell people to engage in innovation: they self-select and will only continue to develop their ideas if appropriate organisational arrangements are in place. An important requirement is to have clearly defined roles for those involved in the change process. In change management projects Jaffe[50] argues that it is important to identify:

- the top executive team of the whole organisation in which the innovation will develop;
- the project sponsor – the person who makes the decision to make the change;

- the project leader, who is often the person who has developed the new ideas;
- the change navigator – the person with knowledge of and skill in implementing change programmes.

Innovatory change will not succeed unless the top management group supports it, and it will be problematic if there is not a skilled change agent in the entrepreneurial group. The leader has the detailed knowledge and enthusiasm to energise people but the sponsor must also be active in:

- overcoming the financial concerns of other managers regarding risky ventures, in both initial review and follow-up evaluations;
- curing the need for resources by defending proposals in evaluation meetings, allocating initial exploration funding to new ideas and permitting flexibility in budgets in terms of money, people and equipment;
- ensuring that corporate venturing develops quickly within an organisation by putting the rewards and initiatives in place for intrapreneurs;
- fighting internal departmental issues, such as the hoarding of resources in one division, and empire-building.[51]

Jones-Evans also argues that it is important to retain those who initiate innovations in the corporate entrepreneurial team even if they lack managerial or organisational skill. If they are removed their strong motivational drive will be lost. Quite often the initial innovator does lack certain skills but this can be accommodated by creating a project team, which includes those with technical, economic, managerial and change management skills. It is also important for the project team to be kept intact even after the initial completion of the project. The team may have to respond to outsiders who develop new variants of the idea.

Corporate entrepreneurship is not easily confined within an organisational department. Bringing an idea to market will involve lots of knowledge which is located within functional departments. It is important therefore that corporate entrepreneurs and their associates have the power to make decisions and the political skill to obtain the level of cooperation they require. To avoid the damaging conflicts that can arise between departments it may also be sensible to define innovation as a crucial business process and reorganise the business along business process lines (where a process is 'a specific ordering of work activities across time and place with a beginning, an end, and clearly identified inputs and outputs: a structure for action'.[52])

Corporate entrepreneurs have a strong proclivity for advancing risky projects, but as we have already seen, organisational policies and procedures often discourage managers and others from taking risks. Indeed failure is often seen as a barrier to career advancement. A mature business which wants to encourage corporate entrepreneurship must find ways of encouraging risky initiatives without damaging the careers of those individuals who lead these projects.

Resources must also be provided for corporate entrepreneurs. In the early stages of project development, time is a vital resource and those with an interest in developing new ideas must get away from regular duties. If a new idea looks promising then adequate funds must be made available. In general, there must be a degree of surplus or slack in organisations, which can be allocated to the generation and development of new business ideas.

If mature organisations are to continue to encourage entrepreneurship then corporate entrepreneurs must be appropriately rewarded. Organisations have been devising reward systems to motivate staff for a long time but in view of the recent emergence of corporate entrepreneurship this presents a new challenge. Jones-Evans reports that Balkin and Logan[53] have examined this issue and concluded that corporate entrepreneurs should be paid at or below market rate but that a significant bonus should be linked to the success of an innovative project. In the short run, new venture personnel could be offered a profit-sharing option where profits from the new venture are paid to individuals in line with their current salaries. In the longer term, personnel could be offered shares in the new venture in proportion to their basic salaries.

Reward packages, in encouraging corporate entrepreneurship, are frequently out of line with traditional remuneration arrangements. Indeed, it can be difficult to combine conservative and entrepreneurial reward packages within the same organisation and Jones-Evans notes how firms like 3M and Johnson & Johnson manage to handle this problem. In 3M a 'dual promotion system' is in place where successful entrepreneurs can choose to advance within the administrative or the technical hierarchy. Those who choose the latter attain appropriate status and remuneration without becoming burdened with managerial matters. Corporate entrepreneurs can also be rewarded by being offered more autonomy or by becoming the heads of semi-independent business units within the corporation.

CASE 9.1
New products at 3M

The Minnesota Mining Company (3M) has a reputation as one of the most innovative companies in the world. In the late 1980s it had developed more than 60,000 products and almost one third of sales in 1988 came from products developed in the previous five years. Sales exceeded $10 billion in 1988 yet it was exceedingly entrepreneurial.

A major mistake by the founders around 1900 forced the company to innovate or go under and it has remained innovative for most of its subsequent existence. One early innovation was in the company's approach to selling. Rather than selling to purchasing officers, salesmen tried to meet their ultimate customers in the operating core of firms. They talked to production people and tailored their products to their needs.

These days 3M encourages innovative behaviour amongst all of its staff. They realise that many ideas will not reach fruition or become commercially successful but they work on the principle that the more attempts at innovation the more 'hits' they will have. Things that get in the way of innovation, like company politics or over-zealous planning, are stamped out. Cooperation, sharing information and informal communication are encouraged. Divisions are kept small, there were 42 in 1988, and functional structures are discouraged. A product or process approach to departmental structures is favoured, individuals are multi-skilled and they are expected to accept responsibility. There is also a strong focus on teamwork. When an individual has a new idea he or she forms an action team drawn from manufacturing, technical and commercial staff. The team design and develop the idea and they are rewarded as the project passes important hurdles. Furthermore, the initiator of a successful development is given the chance to manage it as a founding entrepreneur. He or she runs a micro-company within 3M.

At 3M innovative thinking is encouraged and systems and structures are put in place to support it. However, resources are also made available. For example, there is a 15-per-cent rule which allows anyone to spend up to 15 per cent of their time on what they want to do so long as it is production-related. 'Genesis grants' of $50,000 are also available to allow people to progress projects beyond the ideas stage.

3M empowers its staff but there are guidelines and behavioural controls. The 25-per-cent rule is important and bonuses are based on achieving it. The rule states that 25 per cent of annual sales must emanate from products introduced during the previous five years. 3M is also keen on cost control. When Jake Jacobson became CEO in 1985 he said that manufacturing costs had to be reduced by 35 per cent by 1990 and the company initiated an innovative programme to achieve this goal. People are free to debate and discuss issues but they are subject to rigorous questioning by their peers. In effect individuals are controlled by means of peer review and feedback.

3M has a focus on innovation and the company philosophy and culture are instrumental in sustaining this. Innovation as a means of getting close to customers and their needs is the philosophical bedrock on which the company is built. Another basic belief is that managers must support and facilitate innovation and be constructive in their dealings with others. 3M's values seem to build loyalty. Staff turnover is low and the company seldom hires from outside.

Source: Based on R. Mitchell, 'Masters of Innovation: How 3M Keeps Its New Products Coming', *Business Week* 1989; 10 April: 58–63.

Points raised

This is an example of the sort of deliberate steps taken by a company to ensure that innovation continues at a high level.

Adhocracies

A theme of this chapter is that enterprise is both necessary and possible in organisations which, once established, need to continue to develop by introducing new products, processes or services while maintaining the efficiency of their existing portfolios.

There are organisations where innovation is the norm and which will continue to innovate boldly unless and until evidence emerges that there are dangers from excessive innovation. Miller and Friesen[54] point out that in these organisations the impetus for innovation comes primarily from the goals espoused by senior managers and associated strategies, but Covin and Slevin suggest that appropriate structural arrangements are also necessary.[55] Organisations in the computer, biomedical and film industries are constant innovators and require appropriate structures if they are to remain successful.

Mintzberg indicates that *ad hoc* flexibility is the key to this type of organisation.[56] This flexibility extends to the domain of strategy. Since these are innovative, problem-solving ventures, and individuals and teams are constantly working on new projects, no one can be sure how things will work out. So long as they fit in with the broad vision of the firm, successful projects which emerge from below will strongly influence strategy. Their structures are also highly flexible. There is no extensive division of labour or departmental specialisation, and little reliance on procedures, rules and plans. The reason is clear: as innovators they do not follow standard operating procedures and must devise new ways of tackling new jobs.

Because they are refined and complex innovators, these firms rely heavily on the knowledge of their expert staff, and quite often senior managers do not fully understand the intricate details of the work done by these staff. The power of knowledge becomes important and managers must delegate and have confidence in the ability of their experts. In addition, the experts will come together in *ad hoc* project teams to work on client problems. Teamwork is not easy, but the managers of project teams must be skilled in group dynamics, facilitation and motivation. The intrapreneurial roles of enabling and animation are vitally important, and, because the work can only be done well in small groups, managerial spans of control are limited.

These structural arrangements are the antithesis of bureaucratic principles. Bureaucracies are control-oriented organisations, adhocracies are freedom seekers, and if both are housed in the same location then the culture of one will adversely impact on the effectiveness of the other. Drucker therefore argues for a physical separation of the innovative from the performance parts of businesses.

Coupling innovative projects and host organisations

Calls for the separation of innovative projects from mature organisations are common from popular management writers like Drucker, but Heller argues that two contrasting models of the link between host organisations and projects are common. In some cases an innovative project is developed by a 'product champion' who then, using his or her political skills, foists it upon and embeds it into a reluctant host organisation. Alternatively projects are 'imbued with the values and strategies of the firm and thereby channel their creations to be consistent with established consistencies'.[57] In this mode of development managerial elites monitor and encourage the alignment of new projects and corporate strategy. Heller believes, however, that it is more sensible to look at the link between host organisation and innovative project as a 'relationship of mutual influence between innovation and host organisational systems'. Loosening the link can allow the innovative unit to be creative in an atmosphere of psychological safety. It can also allow the innovators to deviate from the legitimate behaviour of the host organisation and can prevent problems in the innovative unit from percolating into the host organisation. Conversely, tight coupling can allow the innovative unit to benefit from the technical, human and financial expertise of the host organisation. Heller's research reveals that there are eight devices for coupling routine with innovating systems, as shown in Table 9.1.

It seems likely that in practice there will be less separation, forcing and assimilation of projects and hosts and more management of a dynamic interface between the two through everyday decisions. There are some additional points of interest emerging from this research. Heller points out that coupling occurs at different levels and may lead to pseudo-looseness. This occurs when a project is given considerable flexibility at a total level but is expected to conform to senior management's decision-making parameters. She also argues that the oft-claimed motivational benefits of decentralisation may be more to do with changes in

Table 9.1   Categories of loosening and coupling mechanisms

There are three mechanisms which rely heavily on assumptions about what the organisation does with respect to:

• 'strategy, • existent technology, • and established markets.'	Projects which conform to the established understandings are closely coupled with the host while those which do not are unshackled.

and an additional five devices which connect projects by means of:

• 'funding, • senior management attention, • structural location of the new product development activities, • standard operating procedures, • and human resources deployments.'[58]	Decisions on these variables determine the extent of the coupling between host and project. Coupling brings advantages such as legitimacy and funding and drawbacks such as interference and rejection.

Source: Modified version of Table 1, p. 28 of T. Heller, 'Loosely Coupled Systems for Corporate Entrepreneurship: Imagining and Managing the Innovative Project/Host Organisation Interface', *Entrepreneurship: Theory and Practice* 1999; 24: 25–31. Reprinted by permission of Baylor University, publisher of *Entrepreneurship: Theory and Practice*.

delegation than with an outcome of a particular structure. Tightly coupled projects which are set loose engender exhilaration. Nevertheless, while it might be attractive to separate innovative projects and host organisational systems completely, management of the interface is a more common occurrence.

Entrepreneurial competencies

It has been suggested that some business strategies, such as downsizing, have actually caused organisations to reduce their capacity to innovate and to identify and build on new opportunities. To offset such tendencies, and in recognition of their need to continue to develop opportunities, businesses are adopting specific strategies to build entrepreneurial competencies.

There are several strands to this approach in the strategic change literature but their primary focus is on the effective management of internal resources and the emergence of special competencies as a result of the intelligent utilisation of resources.[59] The creation of unique competencies allows organisations to rid themselves of outmoded procedures and develop new routines which allow the organisation to meet the changing needs of customers. Competencies also assist in altering the nature of competition in industries. Organisations redefine the nature of competition in a way which allows them to use their special combinations of production, service and information provision skills. Competent organisations provide customers with both tangible and intangible benefits. Some writers in this area concentrate on combining product and process technologies to afford competitive advantage, while others focus on the structural and cultural changes needed to create advantage.

A variant on this theme is provided by the 'capabilities school' promoted by authors such as Nonaka.[60] They take a more holistic approach to the effective leverage of resources and emphasise the importance of values in promoting special capacities. They recommend the use of language, metaphor and analogy in enhancing the creation of knowledge, which can lead to improved customer related capabilities.

Entrepreneurial culture

Mention of values leads into the final area for consideration in the corporate entrepreneurship debate. The ideology and values of senior managers are important determinants of entrepreneurialism in mature ventures but this must be supported by entrepreneurial management, organisational systems and structures.

Managers and professional staff at all levels will be expected to look to the future on occasions but there are those who argue that everyone in organisations must be entrepreneurial, including first line supervisors, staff in the operating core, clerical workers and security personnel. Senior managers and others can create an environment which is conducive to entrepreneurship but they cannot order it. If the dominant organisational form for most of the 20th century was a bureaucracy which relied on standardisation, specialisation, rules and procedures, and obedient service by operators,[61] then the inculcation of an all-pervasive entrepreneurial orientation in bureaucratic businesses represents a huge shift in the organisational paradigm. It implies a shift in the culture and many of the elements of the cultural web that sustain the paradigm.

Table 9.2 illustrates some of the changes that emerged when the Baxi Heating company changed from a 'solid, slow manufacturing organisation to a more dynamic, market-focused organisation' (extract from same source as Table 9.1). It can be seen that the structures, behaviours and assumptions needed to support the new paradigm are very different from those underpinning the old.

There are many contributors to the organisational culture debate but Peters and Waterman were early and influential protagonists. They[62] believe that managers should not aim to control individual behaviour by issuing directives but should try to influence the way people think. The goals are to win their hearts, to engender absolute commitment to the organisation, and to encourage them to challenge the *status quo* and try out new solutions to problems. This is a very different mindset than that which pertains in a bureaucratic organisation, and is brought about by various mechanisms, as shown in Table 9.3.

Genus[63] argues that, while the proponents of the 'excellence school' are wary of concentrating too much on structural form, they believe that certain structures are crucial in promoting innovation and entrepreneurship. To support an entrepreneurial culture it is essential that the structure be simple, non-hierarchical, decentralised, flat, team-oriented and flexible.

Managers, especially senior managers, play a key role in articulating and creating the culture of entrepreneurship but they will only be successful to the extent that individuals identify with this ideology. Some individuals will identify naturally with managerial values, some will be selected to important teams because they so identify, many others will be successfully socialised and indoctrinated by

Table 9.2   The old and new paradigms at Baxi Heating

Old	New
Solid	Dynamic and responsive
Stable/safe	Market-focused
Excellence	Continuous learning
Proud	Proud and profitable
Lifetime employment	Open communication and trust
Slow	Continuous improvement

Source: Based on J. Balogun and V. Hope-Hailey, *Exploring Strategic Change* (London: Prentice-Hall, 1999), pp. 50–1. Copyright © Prentice-Hall, 1999. Reprinted by permission of Pearson Education Ltd.

Table 9.3 A motivational framework

Feature	Remarks
Value-driven	It is vital that basic beliefs and values concerning what the organisation stands for should be communicated to all employees by managers who speak with one voice. Managers take the process of inculcating values seriously and preach it using analogy and metaphor rather than more direct methods.
Simultaneous loose–tight properties	Individuals are encouraged to challenge, debate and engage in innovation and entrepreneurship but these activities are the means. The ends are highly prescribed through adherence to basic beliefs, which are strongly reinforced by the cultural web. Workers are empowered but within tight confines.
People-orientated	People, who have the capacity to be extremely creative and flexible, are regarded as the greatest asset of excellent companies and a family atmosphere is frequently engendered. People are treated with respect and are well trained but are expected to perform.
Entrepreneurship	A critical feature of excellent companies is their ability to create an entrepreneurial orientation. This state of affairs is promoted by granting autonomy to the individual and 'product champions' are encouraged to run their own 'independent businesses' under the corporate umbrella. Entrepreneurship is also fostered by intense, open and informal communication facilitated by the provision of flip charts, whiteboards and tables in many locations throughout the organisation.
Customer- and action-focused	Excellent organisations believe that the customer is king and that customers can be a fine source of new ideas. Excellent firms have a bias for action rather than analysis. Complex jobs are broken down into manageable bits and small is beautiful: it assists the management of units and creates a sense of ownership.
'Stick to the knitting'	Excellent firms stick to what they know well. They do not move readily into uncharted industrial sectors and, if they do, they first test the water adequately.

Source: Based on T. Peters and R. H. Waterman, *In Search of Excellence* (London: Harper and Row, 1982).

management endeavour; but some will merely identify because they calculate that it is in their best interest to do so. Peters and Waterman give the impression that the modification of culture and its assimilation by all participants is a practical possibility for many organisations but many other authors are less sure about the possibility of changing culture to order.[64] Even those authors who consider that cultural change is important and feasible believe that it is a long-term endeavour which requires leadership backed up by the other elements of the cultural web.

A new mindset

It is important for managers to set the tone and adopt a new mindset if they want all employees to act entrepreneurially, but as with culture, it is unlikely that they can produce innovation to order. In a real sense they must empower their innovative personnel rather than exercise power over them. Hales notes that much endeavour by managers is geared towards overcoming resistance to their authority and, in spite of a host of techniques such as participative management, quality circles and incentive schemes, many managers still exercise an autocratic form of power over others. However, he notes that many organisations are recognising that power in the sense of 'transformative capacity' or 'power to ...' now resides in the interdependence which is characteristic of work organisations.[65] For innovation and enterprise, 'power to ...' is more important than 'power over'.

Many of the attitudes, behaviours and organisational arrangements which support innovation are presented by Sven Atterhed and his colleagues, from the ForeSight Group, as in Figure 9.1.

Flexibility, experimentation, empowerment and risk-taking are crucial in engendering an innovative spirit and capacity in mature organisations. Imported

Source: Slightly modified from © The ForeSight Group Diagram, S Hamngatan 37, 41106 Göteborg, Sweden.

Figure 9.1 Manager mindset and behaviour for innovation

techniques can assist, but Atterhed argues that such mechanisms will achieve little if managers still try to reduce uncertainty and protect existing practices. He suggests that it is important to have a 'managerial mindset and behaviour that encourages enterprise and innovation and equips people to be open to the new'.[66] The new mindset 'requests and requires' that innovation be the responsibility of all. For Atterhed this will not happen unless management develops a new mindset.

A modern study of entrepreneurial culture

Hornsby, Kuratko and Montagno note the increasing interest in entrepreneurial culture in recent years but argue that very few studies have empirically tested the existence of factors thought to be important in creating such a culture.[67] They reviewed the literature on those factors in the corporate environment which are conducive to corporate entrepreneurship and conclude that five are important:

- management support;
- work discretion;
- rewards/reinforcement;
- time availability;
- permeable organisational boundaries.

In view of some claims in the literature that the managerial culture is different in Canadian and US firms, the authors looked at the initiatives coming from 353 mid-level managerial workers from 12 Canadian firms and from 174 managers from six US firms. They asked respondents to complete a Corporate Entrepreneurship Assessment Instrument to discover if the five supporting mechanisms were present in the two countries. They also asked six open ended questions to assess the extent of entrepreneurial behaviour. The questions referred to:

- the number of ideas suggested in the last six months;
- the number of ideas which were implemented;
- the number of ideas implemented without official organisational approval;
- the amount of time spent thinking about new work-related ideas;
- the number of times managers talked outside their own departments about new ideas;
- the number of times managers bypassed normal channels to pursue an innovative idea.

The results revealed that there were no differences between the perceived entrepreneurial cultures in US and Canadian firms. Furthermore, there were no significant differences between the reported entrepreneurial behaviours of the US and Canadian managers, although the former had greater absolute scores on all six indicators of behaviour. There was a positive connection between work discretion, managerial support, rewards and low organisational boundaries. Results also indicated that, while there was no difference in the overall level of innovative behaviour in US and Canadian firms, US managers were more likely to respond to an encouraging corporate culture than Canadians. The authors speculated that the more security-conscious Canadian managers did not respond very positively to expressions of support for innovation from senior managers. This study is useful for its timely review of the literature but even more so for its operationalisation of key variables and the introduction of a cross-cultural perspective on this subject.

Networks

So far, corporate entrepreneurship has been described as largely an intra-organisational process, as that is the original essence of the concept. However, there are situations where inter-firm contact and cooperation can help the process, especially that of innovation. Firms can search for opportunities and try to realise them by developing products to meet market needs. If, however, having seen an opportunity, a business does not have the wherewithal to address it, it may help if they collaborate with one that can supply the missing component(s). This can also bring benefits of shared knowledge, reduced development and process costs, reduced risks of failure and knowledge of key benchmarks. In some markets it is also common for customers to initiate innovations.[68] Users are often the first to recognise a need and may then pass such information on to manufacturers, or use it in cooperation with them to develop an appropriate new product.

A level of collaboration has long characterised innovation, but it has been argued that inter-organisational cooperation is much more common in today's world. One reason argued for by Alter and Hage is that, with the pace of change in technology and markets, the risks in carrying out innovation have increased considerably.[69] Innovators need time to recoup development costs but, in current conditions, product life cycles may be too short to guarantee recovery. They also argue that the state plays an increasing role in much industrial innovation. Often it encourages lots of players to get involved and promotes collaborative practices to let many of the players share in the benefits. Porter argues against encouraging joint ventures between domestic competitors, because this reduces the incentive to maintain a competitive advantage. However collaboration and the development of long-term relationships with customers and suppliers can help to reduce costs and enhance competitiveness.

Such inter-organisational relationships, however, are unlikely to develop instantaneously. Parties must be sensitive to one another and feel that the others have something of use to them. They must also communicate to explain their needs and examine possibilities for exchange. A degree of consensus is also important. They must have reasonably compatible values and be able to work problems through by means of 'adjustment and compromise: a process that entails negotiating and bargaining'.[70]

Market uncertainties, experience in developing long-term relationships, and the complexity of the innovation process have led many firms to form links with a number of outside organisations when generating ideas, developing prototypes and testing markets. As James notes, 'The significant change in the business environment...has changed the focus of alliance strategies (for innovation) to the point where they are now becoming the rule rather than the exception.'[71]

WHEN SMALLER IS AN ADVANTAGE

Introducing corporate entrepreneurship into bigger businesses, and making them more entrepreneurial and innovative and thus more like small businesses in their market responses, is not however always the best way to take advantage of new business opportunities. As Charles Handy argues in his most recent book,[72] economic prosperity needs both elephants and fleas. Sometimes it is better to be a flea. Examples of that can be found with high technology businesses and in the 'new economy'.

ILLUSTRATION 9.3
The rules of the new economy

The rules as applied to our economies by traditional economists have changed. In the old economies, convergence within and across countries was possible as, in the longer-term, capital migrated to lower wage areas. But there is no such convergence in a knowledge economy. Knowledge doesn't spread so easily. It tends to stay 'regional' as evidenced by what some have alluded to as the knowledge 'black holes' of Silicon Valley, Route 128, Atlanta and Austin in the USA and of Cambridge in the UK. Knowledge develops within and through close personal networks which are facilitated by geographical proximity. Indeed it is also now well known that 'business angels', who are important to high-growth start-ups, concentrate their investments within easily accessible distances. It is an apparent paradox that in an era in which data and information can be transmitted globally in fractions of a second, knowledge is relatively immobile and still requires geographic proximity for its spread.

Factor	Old economy	New economy
Unit of analysis	The plant/business	The entrepreneur
Policy instrument	Interest rates	Knowledge infrastructure
Entry criteria	Financial capital (available to a few)	Knowledge (available to all)

Factor	Old economy	New economy
Growth drivers	Managers	Entrepreneurs
Source of competitiveness	Economies of scale and cost reduction	Knowledge and value added
Infrastructure required	Transport infrastructure Labour supply	Knowledge infrastructure

It is interesting to note that in this context countries can be placed within one of three categories:

- *creators of knowledge*: about 30 countries are, according to the number of patents filed, significant creators of knowledge;
- *users of knowledge*: many countries, such as the former Soviet Bloc countries, use knowledge but do not appear to create it;
- *others*: those countries which are neither creators nor users of knowledge, such as parts of Africa and Latin America.

To convert from a 'user' to a 'creator' it is necessary to have an infrastructure that both generates and applies knowledge. As well as universities and research institutes, that also requires, for example, market researchers and marketing organisations as well as knowledge-based businesses.

ICT and e-business

The 'new economy' has also been described as the knowledge economy. The term 'new economy' is used to encompass issues of the globalisation of business, the expansion of information and communication technology (ICT) and the increasing importance and pervasiveness of knowledge.[73] Indeed many now see the availability of appropriate knowledge as a key driver of competitiveness, superseding the availability of raw materials, or of energy, or of labour, which had been predominant. Information technologies, which facilitate the application of knowledge, promote new business methods and new specialisations. The new economic conditions promote new opportunities for enterprise.

Although ICT may have received particular attention, particularly in the news media, there are other technologies which depend on knowledge and which have the potential to transform the way in which their users operate. They include biotechnology, new materials and new environmental technologies and the firms producing them are known as high-tech enterprises.[74] They often spin out from universities or research institutes and cluster around such centres of knowledge. Knowledge, although it can be applied at a distance, in particular through ICT, is more easily shared, developed and grown through local networks and it is the proximity of the components of a knowledge economy which have facilitated its development in places such as Silicon Valley and around Atlanta, Austin and MIT in the USA, and around Cambridge in the UK.

Knowledge, in comparison with other products of business, is also strange stuff. It can be sold, and yet still be retained by the seller after it has been sold. It can be shared indefinitely but not diluted. It can be valuable and, as intellectual property, its ownership can be protected, yet it is of most use when it is fresh, and it is hard to keep because if it is retained for too long it tends to leak out. It can belong to a company but it resides in the employees and, if they leave, it can go too.

The emergence of these new forms of economic activity creates new opportunities which are often taken up by small businesses, rather than through innovation in bigger businesses. As already noted, small businesses, especially at the time of their start-up, are often more flexible than big businesses and their speed of response is generally quicker. They can therefore occupy, and capitalise on, a niche opportunity more quickly than their bigger rivals. Their owner-managers do not have other operations to distract them and typically are fully committed to the new venture depending, as they often do, on it alone for their future. One analogy that has been used for this sort of economy is an ecology, in which it is new seeds which colonise new spaces first and in which biodiversity facilitates transition. It is not the case that all new organisations will survive, but that the wider the diversity of new organisations and the larger the number of them, the more likely it is that some of them will occupy the available niches and prosper. However it is not just small businesses which have made use of the internet. Home shopping and airline booking are examples used by many people of bigger businesses using the technology to gain or maintain their market positions.

One response to the new economy has been a drive by governments to monitor and promote ICT on the assumption that this will be crucial to maintaining international competitiveness. Businesses do seem to be increasing their 'connectivity', although to what extent this is a result of these initiatives is not clear. In the UK, a DTI international benchmarking study is expected to indicate that 1.7 million SMEs were online in 2000, compared to only 1.1 million a year earlier, exceeding the Government's target of 1.5 million by 2002. However, while the new technology is a powerful business tool which can strongly influence competitive performance, it has to be recognised that it is just a tool. What matters is not the possession of the tool but how businesses conceive of and use the tool and how they respond to the changes which the use of the tool is occasioning in their marketplaces. It is a tool which can be very effective in assisting communication and marketing and in providing a global shop window through which good and services can be supplied, but that is not of equal value to all businesses.

The introduction of ICT has been likened to the earlier introduction of the telephone or of the railways in the opportunities it offers and in its potential to change business. First there are opportunities to produce the technology on which communications depend. While many of the computer companies are relatively large, there are small businesses in niches such as designing silicon chip hardware and software for the very demanding requirements of battery-operated low-power hand-held equipment, but there are not many like this and they are often spin-offs from university research. For other businesses the opportunities, Paul Burns suggests,[75] lie in the following areas:

- the opportunity to establish the network through which other traders can gain access to the new marketplace. Businesses doing this can be likened to the railway companies which built and operated the early railways and may, like them, find that it is not in reality a source of long-term profit;
- the opportunity to use the technology to do business by becoming a trader in the e-marketplace, like the businesses which used the facilities provided by the railway companies to do their work better. These opportunities can in turn be of two sorts:
  - the opportunity to establish innovative trading businesses which exploit the unique characteristics of the internet. These are businesses which could not exist without the internet;
  - the opportunity to use the internet to reach a global market and to compete there on price, on the differentiated qualities of the product or service, or by focusing even more effectively on particular market segments. This is done by businesses which could probably operate without the internet but which use it to reach a wider market.

It is the last of these areas of opportunity which will in particular have implications for businesses which are not themselves e-businesses. While they may not be using the internet, many of their customers are, and by doing so they are finding other suppliers. Almost all businesses therefore need to see what ICT is doing to their market and to take appropriate steps to respond. Those steps may involve the businesses concerned using the internet themselves, by becoming 'connected'. However in some cases it might be appropriate to change, or even end, the business. The growth of low-cost airlines with online direct booking of flights has taken business away from travel agents and they will not get it back just by using the internet themselves.

CASE 9.2
The dot.com phenomenon
....

One area in which small businesses have recently shown some of their advantages has been that of information and communication technology (ICT). The proliferation of this technology, also sometimes referred to as the internet age, has provided businesses with the means of communicating from a distance an amount of information which had previously needed a face-to-face meeting or the physical exchange of many sheets of paper. This has in turn reduced the need for teams of people to work in the same office, or for impressive premises in which to receive customers. It has also helped to put a premium on the supply of knowledge. It has therefore been possible for small businesses to contribute to a venture, without having to be organically part of the same entity. In this way some aspects of the internet age are rather like the clock manufacturing industry which existed in Clerkenwell in North East London in the 18th and 19th centuries. That was an industry which employed over 7000 people[76] yet did not have big manufacturers but instead consisted of clock 'assemblers' who ordered and then assembled components supplied from a wide range of independent specialist component producers.

However the internet age has been marked particularly by the development of a whole new language of business: e-commerce, e-business, B2B (business to business), B2C (business to consumer) and the dot.com. Millions of pounds were pumped into online business applications, not least in the information technology and telecommunications sectors. Many entrepreneurs in this sector, a lot of whom were very young, became millionaires through public offerings of shares, takeovers, buy-ins and buy-outs. Suddenly it was the era of the instant entrepreneur and the apparent opportunity for immense wealth, which could be achieved just by sitting in front of a keyboard and screen with an internet connection. Valuations of 150 times their future revenue streams were accorded to some businesses.

But the bubble burst. The 'dot.com hype' was revealed as a sideshow, driven by greed, ignorance and, no doubt, wishful thinking. Telecommunication companies, the favourites of fund managers, saw their market valuations plummet as analysts and investors reassessed future revenue streams and profitability potential. Large and small businesses cut staff or closed down.

The highly publicised collapse of companies like Boo.com and eToys.com was matched by the countless collapses of smaller companies whose failures did not make headlines. Too often these businesses had at least one thing in common: an ability to leak millions of cash made available by investors. The digital downturn, also referred to as 'The Winter of Technology' had global repercussions following, as it did, the over-optimism of the late 1990s and early 2000s. Economies slowed down and communities that rode the 'new economy' faltered. In the USA, high-tech communities felt the pain of shutdowns, lay-offs, commercial property vacancies, evaporating venture funding and slower growth and jobs. In the 18 months between January 2000 and June 2001, '555 dot.coms closed and there were 127,000 internet-related layoffs'.[77] Nortel Networks shares fell from a 52-week high of $86 to a low of $12.50 (end of March 2001), Lucent Technologies similarly fell from $63 to $6.75. The NASDAQ composite stock exchange index (comprised of technology-related shares) fell from just over 5000 in April 2000 to around 1800 in March 2001, while the German Neuer market dropped 75 per cent: its worst drop in 100 years.

This catalogue of disaster does not mean that ICT has no potential for small businesses; it just reinforces the point that any new venture requires a degree of care and that no technology or market will guarantee success however it is approached. Many internet ventures seized on new ideas without any great in-depth analyses of the possible markets for them:

They sped through the search and select phase and hit upon an idea that enabled them to build on the timeliness of their business concept. They took advantage of IT infrastructure and reached a state of critical maturity and entry opportunity. Many of them failed to follow up their opportune timing with effective resource mobilisation and revenues to sustain success. Hence the disappointed hopes of the dot.com ventures. There is often a predictable failure to generate revenue early enough to satisfy investor expectations. Management of expectations is critical.[78]

Points raised

Because innovations are new it is hard to know how to treat them. Many innovations are treated with too much caution. ICT however was often hailed as the technology of the future which every business had to use if it was to survive, almost as some sort of magic route to success. This summary is a reminder that there are no such magic routes. It shows that, while there were and are real business opportunities in ICT, this has been a situation in which many people may have treated an innovation with too little caution.

The new economy is nevertheless an area in which it can help to be small, where there do appear to be disadvantages of scale, and there are other areas where this applies also. As a result some entrepreneurs prefer to grow the totality of their portfolio, not by growing their existing business or businesses, but by forming new businesses. Richard Branson is an example of someone who has grown Virgin by new ventures united, not by organisational control, but by his interest and the Virgin label. However not all of this 'growth' would be seen from a business-centred perspective because it arises not only from growth in the businesses themselves but from new business formations.

IN CONCLUSION

Innovation is at the heart of the spirit of enterprise. Practically all firms are born from a development which is innovative, at least in comparison with their existing competitors in the marketplace. If they are subsequently to survive and develop, however, firms must constantly innovate – even if only gradually. In this respect, technical advances are not themselves sufficient to ensure success. Innovation also means anticipating the needs of the market, offering additional quality or services, organising efficiently, mastering details and keeping costs under control.

EU Green Paper on Innovation[79]

Small businesses are a reservoir, a source, both for the creation of jobs and for the development of diversity within economies. Capitalising on this reservoir means growing those small businesses and maintaining the attitudes of enterprise in the business upon which that growth will depend. That internal enterprise, in larger businesses, requires some different approaches from the enterprise which typically starts a small business. It has been called corporate entrepreneurship.

THE KEY POINTS OF CHAPTER 9

- Growth in the early stages of a small business can be seen as a natural extension of its original formation, but when a business reaches a steady state different attitudes can prevail and further change can be resisted. Maintaining growth in a more mature business can therefore require a different approach, a process of internal enterprise, which has been called 'intrapreneurship' or more recently 'corporate entrepreneurship'.
- Corporate entrepreneurship is therefore connected to the concepts of entrepreneurship, enterprise, and innovation. Entrepreneurship has typically described the drive that starts a business, and a similar drive is needed to maintain its advance. Innovation is the successful development of competitive advantage and, as such, can be said to be the key to corporate entrepreneurship. That innovation can take several forms: innovation in processes and methods; innovation in products or services; and innovation in work organisation. Entrepreneurship and innovation, applied to the continued development of a business, are still enterprise even if the business is a larger one.
- There are however inherent difficulties in corporate entrepreneurship. These are such that some writers on corporate entrepreneurship, or formerly on intrapreneurship, have contended that many large corporations will in practice survive only by restructuring their businesses as confederations of small businesses. There are barriers of human resistance to change, barriers of management roles and motivation, and barriers of organisational structures and systems. Size, *per se*, is not an impediment to entrepreneurship and innovation, but the attitude and methods that size can bring are.

- The process of corporate entrepreneurship itself has been analysed in terms of the roles a corporate entrepreneur must play, including those of entrepreneur, adventurer, innovator, leader, change agent, animateur, and enabler, many of which do not fit in easily with a large company ethos. The structures that best support the processes of corporate entrepreneurship have also been considered, with recommendations for solid systematic investigations into the relevance of current products and procedures and into the process of modernisation.
- Some organisations, in industries such as computers, biomedical products, and management consulting, are constant problem-solvers and innovators. Flexibility is the key to their success. They are also frequently knowledge-based and have structural arrangements that are the antithesis of bureaucracy. Empowerment is important, as well as having the right mindset.
- Corporate entrepreneurship can be seen as a response by bigger businesses to some of the perceived advantages of small businesses. However, despite this, there are areas of business, such as in the 'new economy', where sometimes small businesses really do seem to have an advantage. In that situation some entrepreneurs, instead of trying to grow their existing businesses by making them behave like small ones, increase their portfolios by starting new separate small businesses.

QUESTIONS, EXERCISES, ESSAY AND DISCUSSION TOPICS

- What can enterprise add to big business?
- What are the differences between the practices and processes of creating a new independent venture and the launching of a subsidiary venture by an established firm?
- How would you define the terms 'corporate entrepreneurship' and 'intrapreneurship'?
- Identify and describe three broad approaches which encourage the development of innovative projects within large organisations.
- Describe the types of managerial role which are conducive to innovation in an organisation.
- What might be done to create an entrepreneurial ethos throughout an established organisation?
- What might be done to make 3M even more innovative than it is (see Case 9.1)?
- 'Size really matters: the bigger you are, the smaller you need to be.' Discuss.
- Dot.coms: are they a temporary aberration or the start of a trend? Discuss with reference to Case 9.2.

- What caused the demise of many dot.com businesses?
- What is the future for e-businesses?

SUGGESTIONS FOR FURTHER READING

C. Handy, *The Elephant and the Flea* (London: Hutchinson, 2001).
For more on corporate entrepreneurship see:

S. Carter and D. Jones-Evans (eds), *Enterprise and Small Business* (Harlow: Financial Times/Prentice-Hall, 2000), Chapter 13.

P. Drucker, Innovation and Entrepreneurship (London: Heinemann, 1985).

D. F. Kuratko and R.M. Hodgetts, *Entrepreneurship: A Contemporary Approach* (Orlando, FLA: Harcourt College Publishers, 2001), Chapter 6.

Special Issues in Volumes 23 and 24, 1999 of *Entrepreneurship: Theory and Practice*.

For more about e-business see:

P. Burns, *Entrepreneurship and Small Business* (Basingstoke: Palgrave (now Palgrave Macmillan), 2001), Chapter 7.

Among the various public sector supported initiatives is the provision of an online business adviser on: www.ukonlineforbusiness.gov.uk

REFERENCES

1   L. E. Greiner, 'Evolution and Revolution as Organizations Grow', *Harvard Business Review* 1972; July–August: 40–7.
2   P. Drucker, 'Our Entrepreneurial Economy', *Harvard Business Review* 1984; January–February: 59–64.
3   A. Genus, *The Management of Change* (London: Thomson Business Press, 1998).
4   D. Jones-Evans, 'Intrapreneurship', in S. Carter and D. Jones-Evans (eds), *Enterprise and Small Business* (Harlow: Financial Times/Prentice-Hall, 2000).
5   Genus, *op cit.*, p. 5.
6   P. Drucker, *Innovation and Entrepreneurship* (London: Heinemann, 1985), p. 132.
7   G. Pinchot III, *Intrapreneuring: Why You Don't Have to Leave the Organization to Become an Entrepreneur* (New York: Harper & Row, 1985).
8   See for example S. A. Zahra and J. G. Covin, 'Contextual Influences On the Corporate Entrepreneurship-Performance Relationship' *Journal of Business Venturing* 1995; 10: 43–58.
9   J. A. Timmons, *The Entrepreneurial Mind* (Andover: Brick House, 1989), p. 1.
10 A. A. Gibb, 'The Enterprise Culture and Education', *International Small Business Journal* 1993; 11: 11–34, at 16.

11 J. Curran and R. Burroughs, 'The Sociology of Petit Capitalism: A Trend Report', *Sociology* 1986; 20: 265–79, at 269.
12 Pinchot, *op. cit.*, p. 46.
13 D. F. Kuratko and R. M. Hodgetts, *Entrepreneurship* (Fort Worth: Dryden Press, 1995), p. 95.
14 J. G. Covin and M. P. Miles 'Corporate Entrepreneurship and the Pursuit of Competitive Advantage', *Entrepreneurship: Theory and Practice* 1999; 23: 47–66, at 51.
15 Covin and Miles, *op cit.*: 52.
16 S. Caird, 'How Important Is the Innovator for the Commercial Success of Innovative Products in SMEs?', *Technovation* 1994; 14: 71–83, at 81.
17 'Green Paper on Innovation', *Bulletin of the European Union Supplement* 5/95 (Brussels: ECSC-EC-EAEC, 1996).
18 S Borins, 'Loose Cannons and Rule Breakers, or Enterprising Leaders? Some Evidence About Innovative Public Managers', *Public Administration Review* 2000; 60: 498–507.
19 J Wiklund, 'The Sustainability of the Entrepreneurial Orientation-Performance Relationship', *Entrepreneurship: Theory and Practice* 1999; 24: 37–48, at 41.
20 G. N. Chandler, C. Keller and D. W. Lyon, 'Unravelling the Determinants and Consequences of an Innovation-Supportive Organisational Culture', *Entrepreneurship: Theory and Practice* 2000; 24: 59–76.
21 D. Miller and P. H. Friesen, 'Innovation In Conservative and Entrepreneurial Firms: Two Models of Strategic Momentum', *Strategic Management Journal* 1982; 3: 1–25.
22 G. T. Lumpkin and G. G. Dess, 'Clarifying the Entrepreneurial Orientation Construct and Linking It To Performance', *Academy of Management Review* 1996; 21: 135–72.
23 K. H. Vesper, 'The Three Faces of Corporate Entrepreneurship: A Pilot Study', in J. A. Hornaday *et al.* (eds), *Frontiers of Entrepreneurial Research* (Wellesley, MA: Babson Colleges, 1984), pp. 294–320.
24 Covin and Miles, *op. cit.*: 52.
25 S. A. Zahra, D. F. Jennings and D. F. Kuratko, ' The Antecedents and Consequences of Firm Level Entrepreneurship: The State of the Field', *Entrepreneurship: Theory and Practice* 1999; 24: 45–63.
26 For a short critical review of the strategic planning approach to change see Genus, *op cit.*, pp 15–25.
27 M. Porter, *Competitive Strategy* (New York: Free Press, 1980).
28 T. Heller, 'Loosely Coupled Systems for Corporate Entrepreneurship: Imagining and Managing the Innovation Project/Host Organisation Interface, *Entrepreneurship: Theory and Practice* 1999; 24: 25–31, at 25–6.
29 L. Clarke, *The Essence of Change* (Hemel Hempstead: Prentice-Hall, 1994).
30 G. Zaltman and R. Duncan, *Strategies for Planned Change* (New York: Wiley, 1977).
31 D. Jaffe, *Leading Change* (Washington, DC: NTL Workshop, 1999).
32 C. Handy, *The Age of Unreason* (London: Arrow, 1990).
33 Jones-Evans, *op. cit.*, pp. 244–6.
34 H. Mintzberg, *The Structuring of Organizations* (Englewood Cliffs, NJ: Prentice-Hall, 1979).
35 H. H. Stevenson and D. E. Gumpert, 'The Heart of Entrepreneurship', in W. A. Sahlman and H. H. Stevenson (eds), *The Entrepreneurial Venture* (Boston, MA: Harvard Business School Press, 1993), pp. 9–25.
36 H. Mintzberg, *Power in and Around Organisations* (Englewood Cliffs, NJ: Prentice-Hall, 1983).

37 Borins, *op. cit.*: 504.
38 Mintzberg (1979), *op. cit.*, p. 233.
39 *Ibid.*, p. 233.
40 P. Selznick, *Leadership in Administration* (New York: Harper & Row, 1957).
41 W. Starbuck, *Organisational Growth and Development* (Harmondsworth: Penguin, 1971).
42 Drucker (1985), *op. cit.*, p. 137.
43 D. Miller, *The Icarus Paradox* (New York: Harper Business, 1992).
44 R. Lessem, *Intrapreneurship* (Aldershot: Gower, 1987).
45 *Ibid.*, p. 7.
46 J. Sherwood, 'An Introduction to Organizational Development', in R. T. Golembiewski and A. Blumberg (eds), *Sensitivity Training and the Laboratory Approach* (New York: Peacock, 1973), at p. 431.
47 Drucker (1985), *op. cit.*, p. 142.
48 *Ibid.*, p. 156.
49 Jones-Evans, *op. cit.*, pp. 247–51.
50 Jaffe, *op. cit.*
51 Jones-Evans, *op. cit.*, p. 247. Copyright © Pearson Education Limited 2000. Published with the permission of Pearson Education Limited.
52 T. Davenport, *Process Innovations: Reengineering Work Through Information Technology* (Boston, MA: Harvard Business School Press, 1993), p. 5.
53 D. B. Balkin and J. W. Logan, 'Reward Policies That Support Entrepreneurship', *Compensation and Benefit Review* 1988; 20: 18–25.
54 Miller and Friesen, *op. cit.*: 6.
55 J. D. Covin and D. P. Slevin, 'The Influence of Organisational Structure In the Utility of an Entrepreneurial Top Management Style', *Journal of Management Studies* 1988; 25: 217–34, at 222.
56 Mintzberg (1979), *op. cit.*, p. 433.
57 Heller, *op. cit.*: 26.
58 *Ibid.*: 28.
59 See Genus, *op. cit.*, pp. 28–33 for a critique of the organisational capabilities school.
60 I. Nonaka, 'The Knowledge-Creating Company', *Harvard Business Review* 1991; November–December: 96–104.
61 See J. Balogun and V. Hope-Hailey, *Exploring Strategic Change* (London: Prentice-Hall, 1999), pp. 48–52 for a discussion of the paradigm.
62 T. Peters and R. H. Waterman, *In Search of Excellence* (London: Harper and Row, 1982).
63 Genus, *op. cit.*, p. 35.
64 See Genus, *op. cit.*, pp. 36–8; C. Mabey, G. Salaman and J. Storey, *Strategic Human Resource Management* (Oxford: Blackwell, 1998), Chapters 15, 16 for a discussion of culture.
65 C. Hales, *Managing Through Organisation* (London: Routledge, 1993), p. 44.
66 G. Haskins, 'Entrepreneurship Inside Corporations', *efmd Forum* 1994; 2: 12–15. The ForeSight Group, 1990; diagram and quotation at p. 15.
67 J. S. Hornsby, D. F. Kuratko and R. V. Montagno, 'Perceptions of Internal Factors for Corporate Entrepreneurship: A Comparison of Canadian and US Managers', *Entrepreneurship: Theory and Practice* 1999; 24: 9–29.
68 See W. G. Biemans, *Managing Innovation Within Networks* (London: Routledge, 1993) for a discussion of networks and innovation.
69 C. Alter and J. Hage, *Organizations Working Together* (Newbury Park, CA: Sage, 1993).

70   A. H. Van de Ven and D. Ferry, *Measuring and Assessing Organisations* (New York, NY: Wiley, 1980), p. 312.

71   B. G. James, 'Alliance: The New Strategic Focus', *Long Range Planning* 1985; 18: 76–81, at 76.

72   C. Handy, *The Elephant and the Flea* (London: Hutchinson, 2001).

73   E. Garnsey, 'Knowledge-Based Enterprise In A New Economy', *in New Economy: New Entrepreneurs* (Zoetermeer, The Netherlands: EIM Business and Policy Research, January 2001), pp. 51–69, at p. 51.

74   *Ibid.*, p. 52.

75   Based on P. Burns, *Entrepreneurship and Small Business* (Basingstoke: Palgrave (now Palgrave Macmillan), 2001), pp. 177, 178.

76   P. Ackroyd, *London, The Biography* (London: Chatto and Windus, 2000), p. 663.

77   *USA Today*, Section B, 'Money', "Cover Story", 10 July 2001.

78   Garnsey (2001), *op. cit.*: 61.

79   'Green Paper on Innovation', *Bulletin of the European Union, op. cit.*, p. 19.

PART III

PROMOTING ENTERPRISE

INTRODUCTION

Part One of this book looked at the concept of enterprise and showed that the word 'enterprise' has a range of meanings. It includes what has been described as the narrow meaning, referring specifically to the development of small business, which was the prime focus of Part Two. Small businesses are important for reasons of innovation, diversity and social stability, and for supporting the competitiveness of other businesses. Particular attention has been focused on them because of the indicated links between small businesses and job creation. Governments, especially in times of high unemployment, want more jobs. For these reasons they are prepared to intervene in the economic process to secure the development of more enterprise.

Part Three therefore looks at this intervention: intervention which cannot of itself create enterprise but, at least in theory, can promote it. It is people who can act in an enterprising way and it is people who can start and develop small businesses, and intervention can seek to encourage them to do it more and to make it easier or more rewarding for them. That is what is meant by promoting enterprise.

Chapter Ten, therefore, after first reviewing the concept of intervention, examines the motivation for intervention and the justification for it, which may not be the same thing. It considers the pressure that sometimes exists for intervention, even if only to appear to be doing something. It looks at the benefits sought and the arguments that there are barriers to enterprise and its benefits which might be addressed by intervention.

The forms of intervention to be used will, at least in part, depend on theories and assumptions about the nature of the enterprise process and about the barriers it faces. It is necessary to have some understanding of the process, from culture through to growth business, in order to see how intervention might work and what intervention might be successful. These issues are examined in Chapter 11.

As well as ideally having a sound theoretical and practical basis, intervention, if it is to succeed, should also be based on clear objectives, be delivered through appropriate structures and use relevant approaches. Chapter 12 therefore builds on Chapter 11 and looks at these issues, at the possible areas for intervention and the forms it might take.

The variety of interventions that are practised raises the question of how successful they are. Evaluating enterprise intervention is not easy. The requirements for it can be complex and there are many difficulties in doing it. These issues are covered in Chapter 13, which also looks at the findings of some of the evaluation research to date and at the current state of knowledge about the effectiveness of intervention.

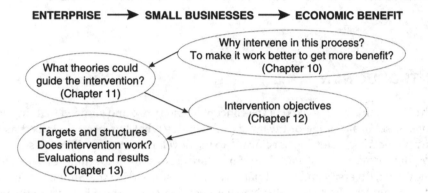

WHY INTERVENE?

CONTENTS

KEY CONCEPTS
· ·

This chapter covers:
- what is meant by intervention;
- the motivations for intervention and the benefits it is expected to deliver, including the creation of employment and other economic and social benefits;
- the justification advanced for intervention including the arguments that there are failures in markets, governance and economic systems which adversely affect entrepreneurship and small business development and which it would be beneficial to correct;
- barriers to enterprise development at the cultural and educational levels;
- some of the arguments against intervention;
- why governmental intervention is nevertheless still likely.

LEARNING OBJECTIVES

By the end of this chapter the reader should:
- have an understanding of what is meant by intervention;
- be aware of the benefits enterprise, entrepreneurship and/or small businesses are supposed to deliver and why governments therefore consider intervening to promote them;
- understand the conceptual case for intervention based on market, governmental or systemic failure;
- have an understanding of the arguments against intervention;
- appreciate the pressures that can exist for intervention.

INTRODUCTION – WHAT IS INTERVENTION?

Throughout the world governments and governmental organisations, national, regional and local, intervene in the economies of their countries, regions or localities. In the context of this chapter intervention is taken to be the attempt by a governmental or other body to affect the behaviour of an economy, or to improve an input to an economy, in a way which is intended to produce an increase in economic benefit which would not have happened had it been left solely to market forces.

However much market forces may be praised, and *laissez-faire* economics promoted, no government, it seems, can resist the pressure to intervene in some way to promote, or protect, the economy for which it is perceived to be responsible. That intervention may not always be effective, or may have effects contrary to what was intended, but there is still always a pressure to do something, and often to be seen to do something.

Much of this economic intervention is intended to have the effect of promoting more enterprise, usually in the form of business and not least of small business. Before looking at the methods that might be employed in such interventions, however, it may be relevant to consider why intervention to promote enterprise and/or small business development may be desired, and why it might be justified.

WHY INTERVENE? — THE MOTIVATIONS

Small firms were the source of the majority of net new jobs created between 1969 and 1976 in the USA.

David Birch[1]

The UK results are broadly similar to those of the United States ... indicating that smaller firms provide a disproportionate share of new job creation.

Colin Gallagher[2]

Small firms play an important role in the economy, in creating jobs, in innovation and in regenerating regions.

Andrea Westall and Marc Cowling[3]

Faced with a serious unemployment problem, such as that in the UK in the 1980s and 1990s, and persuasive evidence that small businesses are effective as job creators and are particularly resilient in an economic recession, there would seem to be a strong *prima facie* case for government intervention in support of small businesses.

Jobs are the usual, and apparently obvious, argument for intervention to promote enterprise. To prevent or reduce unemployment, jobs are required and, if small businesses provide jobs, it might be assumed that more small businesses will provide more jobs. Therefore, if intervention can mean that there will be more, and faster-growing, small businesses, intervention can achieve the desired benefit of more jobs.

There are however other factors at work which may affect this reasoning and which are not always considered. For instance:

- Some jobs in small businesses may be the result of transfers of work from bigger businesses, which in turn may have resulted in efficiency gains but may not lead to net job creation. Productivity gains in bigger businesses can result in greater output but fewer jobs. Therefore the existence of figures showing net job creation in smaller businesses does not necessarily mean that they are better wealth creators.
- The creation and growth of new small businesses can result in considerable displacement of jobs from existing businesses, although there can still be benefits in wealth creation if more efficient businesses replace the less efficient.
- A strong emphasis on jobs in economic interventions may result in a bias against improvements in productivity, because such improvements, which can benefit an economy, may actually result in net job losses.

These are not criticisms of small businesses, and do not mean that they are not important. It is just a caution that small business development need not inevitably result in net economic growth, and that increases in employment in some small businesses do not necessarily mean more jobs overall. However the indications from the Global Entrepreneurship Monitor (GEM) (summarised in Chapter Four), and other research (see Chapter Seven), appear to suggest that there is a strong correlation between the level of entrepreneurial activity and growth in GDP, at least in the GEM countries, and possibly between the level of entrepreneurship and increases in employment.

However, the 'more small businesses equals more jobs' approach would seem to be so obvious that it would appear that it is often followed without further exploration or consideration. Storey points out that in Europe there is a wide range of policy initiatives to assist small businesses, but that the governments concerned have yet to formulate a coherent policy towards the sector:

> In no country, as far as we are aware, is there the equivalent of a 'White Paper' which articulates the range of public policies towards smaller firms which currently exist, which provides a justification for the existing configuration of policies, and which provides criteria for judging whether or not policies are successful.[4]

If policies are to be successful, it will be helpful if the argument for the policies is correct. For the employment argument to hold, small businesses must provide jobs, more and/or faster-growing small businesses must provide more jobs, and intervention must promote more and/or faster-growing small businesses. The evidence that small businesses create jobs has been considered earlier, in Chapter Seven. Whether intervention is actually effective however is a different issue and depends on whether intervention can have a positive effect on small businesses and whether the cost of that effect, in terms of both the cost of the intervention and the cost of any side-effects, is less than the benefit gained and less than the cost of alternative interventions to produce the same benefit. Intervention must not just make the recipient businesses better off, it must overall make a positive net contribution to the economy, and a better contribution than might be achieved from any alternative interventions. As well as employment, that economic contribution might also include wealth creation, choice, variety and innovation (see Chapter 13 for further elaboration of this issue).

There are arguments that intervention is only justified if it will achieve a net economic benefit and that, if there is to be such a net benefit, then there must be a market or other 'failure' to be addressed (see later in this chapter), and addressing it must increase the economic welfare of society as a whole. There are reasons however to think that intervention in some form is inevitable because it is politically desirable. This obviously introduces into the argument a political element based on the perceived attractiveness of the benefits to be gained. Consideration of the justification for intervention therefore requires a look at the range of benefits that might be derived from intervention (including political benefits); at the barriers or obstacles preventing, or hindering, those benefits which intervention may help to overcome; and at the overall balance between costs and benefits.

The benefits sought

Intervention has a cost and should be considered only if it is likely to result in a net benefit. Therefore, if there is to be intervention to promote more enterprise, then it should be because of the benefits more enterprise can provide.

The economic benefits of small business

> Entrepreneurship and innovation are central to the creative process in the economy and to promoting growth, increasing productivity and creating jobs.
> UK Department of Trade and Industry 1998[5]

Some of the economic benefits of enterprise have been considered in earlier chapters. However, because they are also relevant here, a summary is provided:

- Enterprise, in its narrow definition of small business, can create wealth (but so also can larger businesses).
- Small businesses can provide jobs (see Chapter Seven).
- It has also been argued that small businesses have a greater proclivity to innovate than their larger counterparts and are therefore crucial in helping a country respond to the myriad changes in the economic, technological and social environment.[6] For instance, the OECD points out that small firms are innovative in different ways and are especially active in developing new approaches to management and marketing.[7]
- Small businesses can make an important contribution to the infrastructure needed to support larger competitive businesses (see Chapter Five for cluster theory). Particularly today, when 'downsizing' has been more common than vertical integration, it is almost impossible to find a business that does not in some way depend to a considerable extent on small business subcontractors as an integral part of its supply chain.
- Small businesses can help to counter regional economic decline. This assertion is sometimes made but finding evidence to support it is harder. It seems to be based on the view that, in relatively deprived areas, it would be easier to start smaller businesses than bigger ones or that small businesses could survive in limited markets when bigger businesses could not. That might be so but it does not mean that starting a small business in such an area will be easy or, from the perspective of the entrepreneur, sensible. On the contrary, it would seem preferable to start a small business, if that is what someone wanted to do, in a more prosperous area where there might be more niche opportunities; where it would be closer to a larger market; and/or where disposable income and price expectations might be higher.
- Other benefits provided by small businesses are increased competition, choice and diversity; regeneration and revitalisation of sectors; and political stability and social cohesion.

Whether actual interventions are based on all these benefits is a different issue. In many cases the objectives of the interventions are not clearly stated, and have to be deduced from other information. Storey has inferred objectives from observing public policy in the UK. His list is presented in Table 10.1.

Table 10.1 Objectives of small firm policy

Intermediate	Final
1 Increase employment	Increase employment
	Reduce unemployment
2 Increase number of start-ups	Increase number of start-ups
	Increase stock of firms
3 Promote use of consultants	Promote use of consultants
	Faster growth of firms
4 Increase competition	Increase competition
	Increase wealth
5 Promote 'efficient' markets	Promote 'efficient' markets
	Increase wealth
6 Promote technology diffusion	Promote technology diffusion
	Increase wealth
7 Increase wealth	Votes

Source: D. J. Storey, *Understanding the Small Business Sector* (London: Routledge, 1994), p. 260.

The social and wider benefits of enterprise

As noted above, small businesses can provide a range of social benefits. They can provide jobs in areas where few big businesses can operate, such as very rural areas, and in this way they can distribute jobs more widely. Small businesses can supply a range of personal and community services, such as those of restaurants, window cleaning, household repairs, and local corner shops. Most artists are, in effect, small businesses, as also are legal and medical practices. Small businesses are therefore essential to the way of life many people enjoy.

Enterprise in its broad sense also provides many benefits. People who have been successfully encouraged to be more enterprising will be more confident and self-reliant. They are a good illustration of the change principle which states that successful people who are experiencing problems are the most likely to enthusiastically embrace change.[8] Such people may suffer less from social exclusion and from deprivation. This is not to say that enterprise will solve all their problems, but that it can help them to start to overcome some of them. Many immigrant communities often seem to thrive because they are enterprising, even if that enterprise has been born of necessity; although it may be that it is mainly the more enterprising who leave their original countries and become immigrants. Enterprise sustains change and encourages new approaches that allow individuals, organisations and societies to adjust effectively to changing environments. Whether it is in business, in politics, in the arts or in community work, enterprise in its broad sense is beneficial in responding to change, which, in all except the short term, is inevitable.

WHY INTERVENE?—THE JUSTIFICATION

Intervention to promote more enterprise, more entrepreneurship and/or more growth in small businesses is considered because these are thought to be beneficial. However, intervention should only be considered if it will indeed enhance the level of enterprise, entrepreneurship and/or growth of small businesses and thus actually deliver the benefits sought. The argument that it will do so is generally that there are obstacles and barriers preventing their development; that these obstacles and barriers occur because there has been failure of some sort; and that intervention can correct this failure. Whether that failure is in the market, in governance or in economic systems will determine what sort of intervention should be considered but, the argument goes, if there is no failure there is no justification for intervention.

Market failure

It is argued that SMEs face particular challenges compared to larger businesses. They face discriminatory barriers that prevent a 'level playing field', and these are generally classified as 'market failures'.[9] According to neo-classical economic theory there is a tendency towards perfect markets. Attempting to intervene in a perfect market would not result in any improvement in that market. The value of any apparent benefits in one area would be outweighed by the cost of displacement effects elsewhere, and there would be no net economic benefit. However, after a disruption in the market, there may be some factors that delay the return of the market to perfection. Intervening to address these inherently temporary factors could therefore produce benefits. Such factors are market failures in that they represent a failure of the market to perform perfectly. The term 'market failure' therefore can mean different things to different people. To the neo-classical economist, if it exists, it is only a temporary phenomenon that will eventually go. If it is not temporary, it is not a market failure, and trying to address it will not result in a net benefit. To others, however, a market failure is potentially a permanent feature, which will continue to disrupt unless addressed.

They point out that the neo-classical perfect market is a myth and that many of the assumptions about markets made by neo-classical economists do not hold true. There are always imperfections in markets. Many organisations have the power to dominate markets, and use it. Large corporations dominate them, product differentiations by means of marketing manipulations are manifold, and predatory practices are commonplace. The result is many 'market failures' which place small businesses at a disadvantage and are likely to be permanent unless steps are taken to address them.[10] (See also Table 10.2.)

The advantages of big business

There are multinational firms with turnovers that exceed the gross national product of most nations. The sheer size and economic power of such firms allow them to

---

ILLUSTRATION 10.1
Policy rationale 1: an OECD view

....

'It is often argued that governments should promote SMEs because they face special challenges, as well as special opportunities, compared to larger firms. SMEs have been shown to be important for the economy, particularly for job creation. But is this sufficient justification for special treatment or schemes for smaller firms? Policies and measures targeted on SMEs should be adopted only to the extent that there is a clear rationale for doing so, particularly in terms of market and other failures [governmental or systemic – see Illustration 10.3]. In addition, there is a broader, wide-ranging set of government policies (competition, fiscal, and so on) which affect SME performance, and these must also be reviewed in terms of their implications for smaller firms.

'Traditional market failure arguments, when cited in the case of SMEs, usually concern problems related to economies of scale, asymmetric information and imperfect appropriation of returns. Smaller firms generally have fewer financial, human and technical resources which constrain their ability to take advantage of given opportunities, particularly those associated with economies of scale. Small firms also suffer more from information gaps and have difficulty evaluating the benefits of, for instance, adopting new technologies or entering distant markets. SMEs may be at a disadvantage in adopting new technology due for example to greater dependence on external sources of scientific and technological information and the need for tailored technical responses. With regard to financing, small firms have more problems obtaining bank loans and other capital due to a lack of collateral, unproven track record and risk-adverse investors; at the same time, they may lack information on alternative financing sources. In general, the social returns of SME activities are higher than the expected private returns, but more difficult to appropriate, resulting in under-investment by the market.'

Source: OECD, *Working Paper On the Role of SMEs: Findings and Issues* (Paris: OECD/DSTI/IND, 2000), p. 7. Personal communication from members of The Working Party on SMEs.

---

dominate consumer and factor markets. They can use huge advertising and marketing expenditure to make it very difficult for new entrants to gain a foothold in their markets. They can benefit from economies of scale. In the procurement field, large firms can secure discounts and organise just-in-time contracts that shift the burden of stockholding to their suppliers. In the labour market they can attract the best staff with their competitive remunerative packages and career prospects for employees.

Table 10.2 A view of market imperfections, their causes and the actions needed

Market gap	Cause of market gap	Action needed
Supply of entrepreneurs	Social and economic bias in favour of employment rather than self-employment	Social security system Education Tax system
Supply of innovations	Inadequate R&D	Education and research policy R&D expenditure Tax system
Lack of capital	Distortions in capital markets	Tax system Subsidised lending Monopoly policy Credit guarantees
Labour shortage	Imperfections in the labour market	Social security system Social environment Housing policy Training and education Monopoly policy Labour relations policy
Lack of premises	Imperfections in property market	Urban redevelopment Planning regulations Infrastructure investment Tax system
Bureaucracy and compliance costs	Growth of government	Simplification, exemption, changes in local taxation Reorganisation of central and local government
Purchasing Marketing	Imperfections in supplier markets Imperfections in seller markets	Monopoly policy, tax system, government 'crowding out'

Sources: Developed from D. Keeble and S. Walker, 'New Firms, Small Firms and Dead Firms: Spatial Patterns and Determinants in the United Kingdom', *Regional Studies* 1994; 28(4): 411–27; and P. Westhead and A. Moyes, 'Reflections on Thatcher's Britain: Evidence from New Production Firm Registrations 1980–88', *Entrepreneurship and Regional Development* 1992; 4(1): 21–36.

Some of the reasons for their advantages are as follows:

- Their ability to spread fixed overhead costs over a larger output confers significant advantages on large businesses. Larger businesses may have higher fixed costs than small ones, but such costs tend to increase in discontinuous steps that are proportionately higher for small producers than for larger ones.[11]
- Large businesses use their size and power to advantage in other areas. When they need finance they can use the capital market with greater facility than small

businesses, and they can benefit from considerable economies of scale. Indeed, it has long been argued that an equity gap exists for small businesses which cannot find market sources for the type and amount of capital they need.[12] (This is explored in more detail in Chapter 12.) This gap exists in part because of the inefficiency of the capital market with respect to small businesses. In an efficient market, buyers and sellers of finance act through intermediaries and legal remedies are available in cases of dispute. However, many small businesses are unquoted companies and the divestment and exchange of information between the parties is less than perfect. Firms are reluctant to divulge sensitive data and investors are reluctant to lend in the absence of detailed information. In this situation an effective working relationship must be built up between the principals before business can be done, but this is time-consuming and costly for both the small businesses and the venture capitalists involved.[13]

- It is also argued[14] that small firms are at a relative disadvantage when complying with a range of statutory and administrative regulations imposed by government. Governments introduce all manner of regulations, and compliance with them can impose relatively heavier fixed costs on individual SMEs. Regulatory systems are often characterised by delays and poor implementation, and compliance with them can reduce flexibility and diminish some of the competitive advantages of SMEs. Compliance with regulations on the collection and disclosure of information can also prevent the development of efficient information networks.[15]

- Entrepreneurialism is concerned with spotting and realising opportunities but small firms rarely have sufficient resources to exploit them, particularly those openings which offer economies of scale. Small firms also suffer from a lack of information on environmental trends and they often have insufficient data to evaluate new developments.

A counter to this is the argument that in many cases large firms have earned these cost advantages. Developing a business can require considerable skill and capital, and cost advantages are the reward for this endeavour. In this sense these are not market failures. It can also be pointed out that large firms are currently breaking themselves up into smaller strategic business units and are reducing the size of these units by outsourcing services. If this trend continues then some of the benefits of size may no longer be available to large firms.

However, despite these arguments, supporters of small firms feel that large ventures do have real advantages and that the perpetuation of those advantages will damage the prospects for the small business sector to realise its maximum economic benefit. Therefore intervention to reduce the relative advantages is justified.

The need for support

Businesses, if they are to develop, need access to a range of skills and abilities in areas such as organisation, management, production, marketing, selling, strategy, finance and law. Bigger businesses can have all of these competencies in-house, but smaller businesses must inevitably depend on external agencies to provide at least some of them. They need such support but are often reluctant to seek it.

It has been argued that if the felt need for services is great enough then small businesses will seek out the services on offer and pay the market price for them. This economic argument for the free functioning of markets is persuasive but it has been pointed out that small businesses frequently do not seek out the providers of services, even when the need is great, and that they give a variety of explanations for this:

- The need for support is not appreciated. It can be difficult to analyse fully the complexities of a business organisation and identify needs precisely.
- Owners fear that exposing their efforts to others may lead to their ideas being stolen.
- There is a reluctance to approach experts because owners fear that the experts may despise their efforts and because they believe that they do not have the interpersonal and technical skills to deal with sophisticated advisors.
- The traditional approach to consultancy is off-putting to many small businesses.
- They do not have sufficient information about the availability and cost of services to make a rational choice.
- They feel that the available support is not appropriate to their needs.
- They might also be discouraged by the price of advice.

ILLUSTRATION 10.2
A low take-up of small business support

Specific government-funded programmes have been provided to try to provide services in a way which avoids or minimises some of these issues, but they too suffer from low levels of take-up. Curran[16] suggests that there are three reasons in particular for this:
- Owner-managers frequently claim that the support provider 'does not understand' the business. So common is this response that it suggests it does not simply refer to an external adviser's lack of close knowledge of the business, nor to a lack of understanding of problems in particular sectors. Instead Lightfoot[17] suggests that this extreme reluctance to accept external advice has its roots in small business owners' psychology, which shows a strong commitment to independence resulting in a stubborn 'I did it my way' individualism.
- The content of the support appears to be 'top down' in character. Providers see what they offer as the know-how for business success and distil that know-how from standard texts and large firm practice. But small businesses are not large businesses scaled down (see Chapter

> Seven), and good practice in a large business may be poorly suited to the needs of a small business.
> - Government departments favour standardised approaches which are easy to cost, administer and monitor, but which ignore the heterogeneity of small firms or the special characteristics of localities.

A counter-argument might be that making a special case for small business support is a paternalistic approach. Business founders have to learn to stand on their own feet and in doing so will develop an invaluable set of skills and contacts. Gibb[18] argues that the development of transactions with the suppliers of needed services is a crucial aspect of entrepreneurial learning. Owners must understand their environments and learn how to acquire resources on favourable terms. Services from accountants, market researchers and consultants are commercial offerings and there are adequately developed markets in these areas. It could also be pointed out that there is no overwhelming demand for the services of small business support agency services and that this might well arise because there is little need for the services.

Another argument against the provision of support is that large firms have gone through a learning phase and have survived, so why should emerging small businesses now be pampered? However a view put forward by Bannock is that large firms are disproportionately represented in the British economy to the detriment of economic development. He argues that the percentage of small businesses should be increased, and contends that 'We cannot leave it to the market.'[19] If small businesses face temporary market or managerial problems then financial and other means of support could provide a vital breathing-space until circumstances improve. If we want small firms to make the maximum contribution to the economy then it makes sense to assist businesses that are basically viable until their expertise and experience improve and allow them to reap the benefits which size and age confer on organisations. Of course such a policy will not add overall to the economy if the supported small businesses, by virtue of that support, force out of the market existing businesses that are fundamentally no less competitive. The displacement effect must always be considered.

In addition to the usual arguments for support there are additional reasons for supporting embryonic small businesses. Economists extol the virtues of small businesses in facilitating structural changes in industries. As old and inefficient firms expire, new, more productive small businesses fill the gap. But numerous studies have pointed to the vulnerability of small businesses, especially in their formative years. If individuals are to be encouraged to set up in business then they might warrant assistance in the dangerous early years. Many small business people are in need of help as they struggle with the multiple and complex tasks of business formation, launch and early development; and it seems sensible to offer them assistance, especially if the assistance is based on a deep understanding of the 'world' of the entrepreneur.

CASE 10.1
'Small business growth stunted by reluctance to seek advice'

Survey finds biggest barrier to advice is a psychological one

'The vast majority of the UK's small businesses do not ask for business advice because they don't think they need it. According to leading psychologist, Dr. Peter Collett, entrepreneurs are less likely to ask for advice due to their psychological make-up.

A survey of small businesses conducted by NOP and commissioned by Business Link, the information and advice service for small businesses, found that 82 per cent of businesses said the reason they do not seek business advice was because they don't need it. Surprisingly this ranked way above other barriers to advice like cost, which was stated by five per cent of respondents, and lack of time which was cited by only one per cent of the sample.

'Dr. Peter Collett, a psychologist specialising in culture and management style, believes that attitudes have to be changed to encourage people to ask for advice. He explains:

> "People who run their own business are usually extremely confident and self-assured: they need to be in order to survive. But they sometimes feel hesitant about asking for help, particularly if they feel they ought to know the answer. What makes them so effective up to now often prevents them from being even more successful in the future."

'David Irwin, Chief Executive of the Small Business Service, the agency within Government tasked with managing Business Link, said:

> "There is a common misconception that you only need to ask for advice when your business is in trouble. It is our job to challenge this view and ensure that UK businesses benefit from the wealth of expertise that Business Link has to offer."

'During his analysis of the results Dr. Peter Collett identified the following types of business that appear to be most in need of advice:

1 Small businesses that have just started up and which need to learn the ropes.
2 Those that have been in existence for a long time and which have become set in their ways.
3 Small businesses with a small turnover, which are particularly vulnerable.
4 Those that don't have many employees, and which therefore have less internal expertise and diversity of opinion.
5 Those that don't get a lot of advice from institutions like banks.

'On this basis one would expect to find that these five types of business ask for advice more often. The survey results indicate that the opposite is true – those that are most in need of advice are least likely to ask for it.'

Source: Business Link Press Release, 8 October 2001.

Points raised
This report is a reminder that meeting an apparent need is not always a straightforward process.

Government and systemic failures

Much attention has been given to market failure as a justification for intervention but, it would seem, there has been less recognition of the problems of relevant 'failure' in areas such as government and economic systems. Initiatives have been introduced to try to correct market failures but, the Organisation for Economic Cooperation and Development (OECD) argues, this has often been a piecemeal development of policy measures and that 'Insufficient coordination between different government bodies and policies has reduced the efficiency of SME policies and thus limited their potential to fuel economic growth.'[20]

ILLUSTRATION 10.3
Policy rationale 2: an OECD view

Government failures occur when government intervenes where markets would have worked better if they had been left alone. SMEs tend to shoulder a relatively heavy burden in terms of regulation since overly bureaucratic administrative practices can impose high fixed costs on individual firms. For example, when implemented inadequately, standardisation can prevent flexibility, which is an important source of competitiveness for SMEs, especially in the case of new, technology-based firms. Another example relates to networks which are proving to be instrumental in increasing SME performance: their development is often confronted with various information and regulatory barriers, which may prevent them from taking shape spontaneously or, at least, significantly slow their development. Also, lags and deficiencies in information, complexity of regulatory measures, delays in their implementation and poor quality delivery limit the scope for successful government involvement in rapidly evolving fields. These problems led to OECD recommendations on easing the regulatory burden on smaller enterprises, such as:
- The regulatory reform process should be based on an explicit understanding of the overall economic importance of the SME sector.

- Regulatory policy should be forward-looking, part of a broader strategy to foster a large and healthy community of SMEs, and needs to be considered in the context of structural reforms which include other factors such as taxation.
- Regulatory reform for SMEs should not take a 'good or bad' regulation approach but a 'better' regulation approach in all policy areas.
- Regulations should ensure an economic structure within which SMEs, and in particular micro-enterprises, are given a fair opportunity to compete.
- Mechanisms should be established to ensure that SME concerns are considered and debated in the regulatory process.
- Attention should be given to the cumulative effects of regulations on SMEs, particularly micro-enterprises, for both regulatory and economic reasons.
- Special attention should be given to regulations that affect flexibility for entrepreneurial activities, which is a major SME advantage.
- All types of SMEs, including those which are not technology-based, innovative or high-growth, should be considered when vetting regulations and reviewing regulatory effects.

Systemic failures, which are related to institutional interactions in the economy, occur partly because SME policies remain the concern of specific ministries and/or government agencies directly in charge of SME development, even though responsibilities in areas affecting SMEs are scattered among different ministries and agencies. In the past, SME policies were viewed as having a distinctive role, targeting a specific and disadvantaged group of firms, and as different from other economic policies in that they were serving not only economic but also social objectives. In many countries, there has been a lack of understanding among government officials not directly in charge of SMEs of the importance and special economic issues relating to SME performance. There has been insufficient attention to SMEs in the broader economic context, reflecting an outdated perception that SMEs are of limited importance to technology development or growth despite their potential for job creation. This has resulted in a piecemeal development of policy measures, aiming to deal with specific problems at a given time and often protecting small firms from normal business pressures. Insufficient coordination between different government bodies and policies has reduced the efficiency of SME policies and thus limited their potential to fuel economic growth.

Systemic failures also exist on an international scale as national policies regarding SMEs sometimes contradict and cancel each other. National policy measures may lead to unintended impacts on smaller firms in other countries, in particular smaller countries. Various factors may interact to cause discrimination against newcomers (such as registration procedures, norms and standards, labour and product market regulations, and so forth) which are particularly disadvantageous for smaller firms trying to bridge national borders. National competition policies also vary widely across countries in their treatment of SMEs, for which the abuse of market power is a formidable problem. Such cross-boundary effects raise the question of how countries can take advantage of the opportunities created by the trend towards globalisation and how together they can alleviate unnecessary obstacles to the international activities of smaller firms.

Source: OECD, *The Role of SMEs: Findings and Issues* (Paris: OECD/DSTI/ IND, 2000); personal communication from members of The Working Party on SMEs.

Other barriers to enterprise development

Government and economic system failures do exist, but they apply across wide areas and do not explain, for example, the variations in business start-up between different regions in the same jurisdiction (see Table 10.3). Market failure may explain part of this variation but that applies to the narrow aspect of enterprise as small business. There are other barriers that are more apparent when the development of enterprise in its broad sense of an enterprise culture is considered, and these will be relevant when an 'entrepreneurship' as opposed to a 'small business' policy is being considered. Barriers of culture or of education exist that prevent people from starting businesses, or even thinking of starting them, as well as from being enterprising in the broad sense, and intervention might be considered to address these also.

Table 10.3 Variations in business start-up rates across the UK (as indicated by VAT registrations per 10,000 resident adult population in 2000)

UK overall	**40**	Cornwall	33
City of London	2893	Cardiff	31
Borough of Islington, London	106	Northern Ireland	31
Shetland Islands	59	Glasgow	30
Bristol	49	Dover	29
Aberdeen	42	Oxford	29
Cambridge	41	Liverpool	27
Edinburgh	39	Fife	22
Highland Scotland	37	Merthyr Tydfil	16
Leeds	34	South Tyneside	15

Sources: H. M. Treasury website (www.hm-treasury.gov.uk/press/2000) and Northern Ireland Economic Research Centre. Crown copyright material is reproduced with the permission of the Controller of HMSO.

Cultural barriers

One way of identifying the presence of other barriers is to look at the variations between levels of enterprise in different regions and countries. The UK has been described as the enterprise centre of Europe, yet even within the UK there are variations in the level of enterprise, as has been pointed out in Chapter Four and as is indicated in the variations in VAT registration rates, which may be seen as an observable proxy for the levels of enterprise. It has been argued that some societies have economic and social structures that encourage and facilitate enterprise while others do not. For example, within the UK, Northern Ireland's recent economic history is characterised by a reliance on a self-sufficient agricultural sector, large employing organisations in declining industries; and a dominant public sector. Its social and political problems are severe and some suggest that it has a dependency culture. It therefore lacks a strong non-agricultural small business tradition and the culture that might support one. That is an obstacle to enterprise.

In this situation social conditions are such that the option of entrepreneurship as a form of employment is not commonly recognised. There are very successful entrepreneurial ventures in Northern Ireland, but most individuals lack the knowledge, skills and mindset to pursue this career option successfully. They see two economic possibilities: if they are lucky they can have a job working for someone else, or if they are unlucky they will be unemployed and reliant on social security benefit payments. In this, and in other situations of economic and social deprivation with second- and third-generation unemployment, the facilitation of the entrepreneurial process could be viewed as one means of overcoming social disadvantage. However it is not easy: the problems are long-term ones that are likely to require long-term solutions, and many government activities in this sphere are viewed with suspicion because they can have strong political overtones.

The typical Northern Ireland view of a market economy may not be very close to the American or liberal model of capitalism, but markets do exist there. In some areas of Eastern Europe, however, markets have been poorly developed. Under the so-called communist system the state determined what was to be produced and how, and many employees aimed to extract the greatest benefit from the state at minimum effort to themselves. This was a situation where the entrepreneurship option, far from not being recognised, often simply did not exist, or was not developed. Under these conditions the removal of state controls has in some cases tended to lead not straight to a market economy but instead to chaos and opportunities for the criminal fraternity. These countries want a market economy, and enterprise is no longer actively discouraged. Possibly the neo-classical economists might be proved correct and perfect markets might evolve, given enough time. However, the countries concerned want improvements quickly and are willing to consider intervention to get them.

Thus certain countries appear to be more enterprising and entrepreneurial than others. Many factors create an enterprise culture and the values, beliefs and assumptions that are widely shared by members of a community will not be the same in Britain, in Scandinavia and in Eastern Europe. The discussion in Chapter Three of cognitive approaches to entrepreneurship by individuals indicated that more people are likely to become entrepreneurs when attitudes and general opinion support the notion of entrepreneurship. If the government, media and popular opinion are supportive of entrepreneurship it is likely that individuals will develop positive attitudes towards this form of work and it will be regarded as important.

Nevertheless, attitudes alone are unlikely to produce entrepreneurs. What has however been identified as important is whether individuals have perceived behavioural control and 'whether people feel that entrepreneurship is a feasible option for themselves'.[21] People with strong attitudes seek out people who share their point of view and in an entrepreneurially rich locality there will be opportunities to meet or observe people who could well act as positive role models. The lack of role models and the formerly strong anti-capitalist attitudes in Eastern Europe will have done little to encourage entrepreneurship there.

Within countries, certain regions also appear to be more enterprising and entrepreneurial. Economic theory suggests that a market-driven reduction in wage rates and other costs plus the exit of firms from certain industries would provide opportunities for profit in some areas and therefore encourage an influx of entrepreneurial firms. However, economic forces alone are unlikely to redress the balance between regions.[22] That implies that if an imbalance is to be redressed then intervention of some sort will be necessary.

Education

Intervention may be considered, either to promote small businesses specifically, or to promote enterprise in its broad sense, or both. Enterprise in its broad sense is about the development of certain types of attitudes and behaviours in individuals. Gibb argues that enterprising people are adventurous go-getters who have a self-reliant approach to life and who exhibit behaviours ranging from persuasion and problem-solving to independent action, and that these are supported by a collection of skills and attributes.[23] He contends further that some aspects of enterprise are learned, and as such are amenable to development by education and training. He questions nevertheless whether some traditional approaches to education, with their reliance on teacher-led passivity, are what are required to promote the spread of enterprise. If his model of education is accepted then there could well be grounds for state-led interventions to redirect aspects of the educational system towards the use of new materials, contents and teaching approaches to promote more enterprise in students. Gibb[24] has also been critical of interventions and initiatives which purport to develop enterprise or entrepreneurial skills but which, instead, develop skills which are useful for careers in the corporate world.

It is often argued that competencies must be task-specific if they are to be useful for entrepreneurs. Some literature which adopts a role-task approach to entrepreneurship is reviewed by Chen *et al*.[25] They identified six entrepreneurial roles: 'innovator, risk-taker and bearer, executive manager, relation-builder, risk-reducer and goal-achiever'.[26] If these are crucial entrepreneurial roles then educational interventions should aim to develop the behaviours which are associated with them. Enhanced behaviours would go some way towards increasing the perceived self-efficacy of potential entrepreneurs, which is an important determinant of the intention to pursue an entrepreneurial career.

ILLUSTRATION 10.4
Influence through the educational system

Education (in its broadest sense) is important for stimulating entrepreneurship because:

- education provides individuals with a sense of autonomy, independence and self-confidence and these qualities are important when starting a business;
- education makes people aware of alternative career choices;
- education broadens the horizons of individuals, thereby making people better equipped to perceive opportunities;
- education provides knowledge that can be used by individuals to develop new entrepreneurial opportunities.

One can distinguish between this general education and more specific education focusing on the promotion of entrepreneurship and stimulating entrepreneurial skills and knowledge. The educational system can be used for:

- creating an awareness of the role of the entrepreneur in the economy;
- encouraging commercial awareness;
- raising the social standing of the entrepreneur;
- creating an awareness of entrepreneurship as a career option;
- developing the necessary entrepreneurial skills;
- stimulating the application of entrepreneurial knowledge and qualities in an entrepreneurial context.

Source: I. Verheul, S, Wennekers, D. Audretsch and R. Thurik, *An Eclectic Theory of Entrepreneurship: Policies, Institutions And Culture*, Research report 0012/E (Zoetermeer, The Netherlands: EIM Business and Policy Research, 2001), pp. 56–7. Also published in D. Audretsch, R. Thurik, I. Verheul and S. Wennekers (eds), *Entrepreneurship: Determinants and Policy in a European–US Comparison* (Boston, MA / Dordrecht: Kluwer, 2002), Chapter Two.

Support for ethnic and women-owned ventures

It is argued by some that ethnic business firms and those owned by women face discrimination and that special support should be offered to help them overcome their disadvantages. Although many people from immigrant communities do start businesses this may, at least in part, be because they have little choice as they perceive that language problems, a lack of recognised qualifications, glass ceilings or just racism reduce their chances of finding suitable employment, and not because they find it a particularly easy thing to do. It was a cultural norm in many Western societies until recently that women and ethnic groups played subordinate roles and in recent years enterprise agencies in Britain have been keen to assist where possible in the formation and development of ethnic business enterprises. Interestingly, Phizacklea and Ram[27] report that, when the director of a business start-up agency in Venisseux, France visited England, he was impressed by the 'proliferation of business agencies which specifically target ethnic minority populations, not just at the inception but by providing business support services as well'. Help is offered but there is a low take-up of support and recent studies[28] of ethnic firms in Britain give the following reasons for the reluctance to use formal support services:

- language difficulties;
- 'I started on my own therefore I don't need help';
- agencies are only interested in larger firms;
- 'I can't afford the time to attend meetings and courses';
- West Indians are stereotyped as incapable of running a firm;
- 'we are discriminated against for being Nigerian'.

Ram[29] approached the topic of under-use from the perspective of providers and concluded that problems arose because:

- there were no precise data about ethnic entrepreneurs;
- providers were unsure of the rationale for intervention;
- there was competition between the agencies;
- it was more important to meet 'targets' than specific needs;
- providers perceived themselves as marginal.

Curran has mentioned that the take-up of support services by small firms is patchy and in the case of ethnic businesses this might occur because there is a network of local support for embryonic firms. It is mentioned in Chapter Three that Ismaili-Pakistani immigrants in South Western USA have their own self-help community support programme and that this has many advantages compared to officially sponsored aid programmes.

Just as some people feel that it is important to assist ethnic entrepreneurs, others feel that women entrepreneurs face discrimination and should be assisted.

Additional business barriers may exist for women entrepreneurs if they cannot acquire resources as easily as men, if their work and life experiences have not allowed them to develop entrepreneurial competence, or if they face gender discrimination. We should note, however, that some recent studies on discrimination against women in acquiring start-up capital, for example, point to the complexity of the topic.[30] Evidence in this area suggests that discrimination against women arises for economic reasons. Women tend to operate riskier firms than men and are less well prepared for management. Consequently lenders are reluctant to divert funds to these ventures.

Walker and Joyner[31] argue that women's difficulties in getting business finance can arise because of pure gender discrimination, institutionalised gender discrimination, statistical gender discrimination, or economic gender discrimination. Gender discrimination occurs when women are offered different financial terms simply because they are women. Institutional discrimination occurs when it is presumed that a woman is less likely to operate a firm successfully. Statistical discrimination occurs when women as a group are less well qualified as borrowers and economic discrimination occurs when a woman does not meet the criteria for financing and that the latter arises from the fact that she is a woman. These authors point out that various forms of government assistance have different impacts on these four kinds of discrimination. For example government procurement programmes in the USA, which ration contracts on the basis of gender, can remove pure and institutional discrimination but not statistical and economic discrimination. On the other hand business counselling and training can reduce all four kinds of discrimination. Walker and Joyner argue that care should be exercised when developing special support programmes. Specific policies impact on specific kinds of discrimination and policies in support of women or other groups can create resentment and actually increase discrimination. Furthermore, support can discourage those who are supported from seeking 'new and creative ways of overcoming obstacles'. Entrepreneurs must use their own skills to overcome obstacles. Support in the form of grants or loan guarantees can also cause women to enter more risky ventures than they ought to and this may lead to the subsequent failure of the business. Loans can cloud economic judgement. It seems attractive to offer support to disadvantaged groups but Walker and Joyner show that caution should be exercised when advocating such policies.

WHY NOT?—THE ARGUMENTS AGAINST INTERVENTION

It is almost universally accepted among politicians that more small enterprise is unquestionably beneficial to the economy. Yet this can be questioned ... Several frequently offered justifications for policies appear dubious.

> For example, the alleged existence of shortages of start-up finance or the negative impact of employment legislation on small business expansion and job creation have been overwhelmingly rejected by research. Yet Conservative and Labour administrations [in the UK] have continued to cling to these assumptions and policy continues to be influenced by them strongly.
>
> James Curran[32]

Economic arguments justify intervention in a market economy when there is market failure. Some economists, however, maintain that market failure, although a necessary condition, is not alone a sufficient condition for intervention. There must in addition be evidence that the overall welfare improvements resulting from the intervention will be sufficient to justify the cost of that intervention, and that there is no better way of achieving the same improvements.

It might be expected that attempts to promote enterprise and entrepreneurship would find favour in most quarters, but this is not necessarily the case. It is said that enterprise thrives in a free enterprise economy, and many advocates of this economic system caution against interference with market forces. These people argue that the laws of supply and demand, operating through the price system, send signals to interested parties, who respond to market opportunities and threats. Those persons who are able to interpret market forces accurately will reap economic rewards, and this pursuit of self-interest leads to the most efficient utilisation of economic resources. Enterprising individuals are inclined to be energetic, forward-looking people who take bold steps to realise opportunities, and it can be seen that free enterprise economic systems are an attractive milieu for enterprising individuals to display their skills. It is therefore argued that there is no point in promoting entrepreneurship and enterprise: the enterprising will avail themselves of opportunities, and the aggregate outcome of their decisions will produce greater welfare than decisions made by central authorities.

This argument assumes perfectly competitive markets, yet many maintain that markets are far from competitive. Nevertheless, it is still contended that there is no generalised market failure in the small business sector. Bennett, like Gibb, points to the size and growth of the sector as evidence of advance. He argues that, when asked about those factors that inhibit development of small businesses, owners comment on general economic and regulatory factors such as the condition of the economy and the inhibiting impact of statutory regulations. Where specific needs are highlighted they arise in areas such as venture capital, marketing advice, training and cash flow problems: 'areas where well developed markets already exist'.[33]

Two comments in particular may be made in response to these views. First, many small businesses may be unaware of the immense power of large corporations and their subtle ability to inhibit competition. Those small businesses may occupy niche markets where, unless they threaten industrial giants directly, they may be tolerated or, with the advent of strategic outsourcing, they may be positively welcomed by some large businesses. Second, the methods used by those who seek to identify the problems experienced by small firms rarely delve, in a detailed way, into the problems small firms experience. Researchers commonly present entrepreneurs with lengthy lists of problems and ask them to say which of the problems apply to them. Just as Bennett argues that it is only by means of in-depth discussion with small business owners that the effectiveness of policy initiatives can be judged, so it can be argued that quantitative studies of the problems faced by small businesses will merely elicit pre-programmed responses. It is important to understand how entrepreneurs perceive and construct problems and there may also be a tendency for small business owners to project their problems away from themselves towards more distant perceived impediments such as the government or the European Commission.

On the issue of the provision of needed services, such as information, advice and training, Bennett argues that if the felt need of businesses is great enough then they will pay the market price for the consultancy services on offer. As mentioned above, however, economic reasoning ignores many of the personal and interpersonal aspects of seeking external advice, whether it is from consultants, counsellors or mentors. Many owners have a real need for such assistance, but lack the information and confidence needed to identify, approach, and if necessary negotiate terms for suitable help.

ILLUSTRATION 10.5
An analogy?

In some respects classical economic theory is like the theory of natural selection in nature. According to that theory, in the long term the fittest for survival will survive and nature itself is an effective way of ensuring that this happens. However, in a system in which natural selection rules, what then is the role of selective breeding and intensive farming, both of which are much practised in agriculture? The answer may be that the question is to some extent itself misleading. Left to itself nature has produced a very wide variety of life forms, all of which thrive in their own niches. However, for our own purposes we want to encourage the growth of some of these life forms and to make them better suited to our requirements. That is what agriculture does: it intervenes to create circumstances in which those that survive and grow are those that we want to harvest.

May it not be that markets, left to themselves, will also produce a variety of businesses? However, if we specifically seek to influence the course of development in the population of SMEs, may we not also have to intervene to create the conditions that specifically encourage their development?

INTERVENTION EXISTS

Small-businesses have had a key role in UK government strategies since the early 1980s. Already by 1983, the Department of Trade and Industry (DTI) listed 93 small business support measures and a House of Commons Library Paper estimated that between 1980 and 1985 government assistance for small business totalled over £1.1 billion ... Up-to-date estimates are harder to come by but one source reports that the almost 200 government initiatives had an overall cost of £632 million in 1995–6.

James Curran[34]

A pragmatic view of intervention is to recognise that it exists and will, in some form or another, continue to exist. One form of existing intervention is laws and regulations to control business: laws that require businesses to be registered, laws that seek to control monopolies, and laws that stipulate permitted labour practices, are all interventions.

In addition to this precedent there is an almost irresistible temptation for governments to intervene. If it is understood that small businesses create jobs, and if significant numbers of people are unemployed and want jobs, then government will find that intervention to promote small business will be a popular option. Politically motivated behaviour is also prevalent in conditions of uncertainty. The SME area is complex and there is limited knowledge about the connection between policy and its outcomes. In this context few governments will wish to irritate electorates with subtle arguments on the pros and cons of intervention.

There are many advocates of a *laissez-faire* economic policy, but no government, even among those that purport to champion liberal capitalist economics, appears to have adhered strictly to such a policy. Governments intervene in numerous ways to manage their economies and redistribute wealth. As the editors of *Business Week* note, the most successful economies, in spite of huge differences among them, all have 'broad support throughout their societies for basic national economic goals and for measures of industrial policy to achieve them'.[35] In many respects the debate about intervention is not therefore about the principle of intervention but about the means that are to be used.

There is debate about the wisdom and efficacy of state intervention in support of enterprise and entrepreneurship, but the sheer size of the small business sector makes it very difficult for governments to ignore the real or perceived needs of the sector. In addition the variety of the goals pursued by small business policy-makers and the lack of measurement of their success, create ideal conditions for the political manipulation of policy. There are many people in the 'small business support industry', and any apparent willingness to promote small businesses,

---

ILLUSTRATION 10.6
Four main objectives in SME policy pursued by EU
member states[36]
....

- Creation of employment
- Competition
- Strengthening the production chain
- Diversification

However, these objectives have had to be inferred from observing policies in operation. Only a few countries overtly select employment creation as an objective. None of them emphasises competition, strengthening of the production chain or diversification explicitly as an objective.

---

especially when combined with any uncertainty surrounding policy objectives, provides them with ample opportunity to use their creativity in providing and developing small business support services. The great difficulty in conducting scientific evaluations of policy measures only adds to this confusion.

Part of the debate should be about the effectiveness of those means, yet, as a number of writers have pointed out, there have been no sophisticated, systematic evaluations of specific interventions to enhance the achievements of small businesses in creating new jobs. The result is that many uncertainties arise in connection with the usefulness of various policies. These uncertainties permit, or even encourage, a political dimension of policy to develop. If actions appear to look good and there is no clear evidence for what they achieve, or fail to achieve, then the actions may be pursued, not for the results they bring, but for the credit that applying them will earn for those responsible.[37]

This is politically motivated behaviour, and it is particularly prevalent when an objective is desired but its achievement cannot easily be measured. These conditions apply in small business support. There is a considerable willingness to support small businesses, combined with a lack of information on what really works. In these circumstances, intervention, if at least superficially justified, may actually be engaged in for political reasons, connected with the desire for recognition or advancement by the people involved, rather than because of any real desire to promote enterprise.

Requirements

If interventions are to happen then they should be evaluated to see if they produce useful benefits in terms of their intended purpose. Evaluating interventions is not however always straightforward (a subject developed further in Chapter 13), and there are also problems in establishing what intervention is required in the first place. This arises because it is difficult to find out what help businesses need. Established firms may not request specific assistance from government in overcoming their difficulties because they are more concerned with aggregate demand and general labour market issues. However, this does not mean that they do not have problems which could be overcome with help.

THE KEY POINTS OF CHAPTER 10

- Intervention is the attempt by a governmental or other body to affect the behaviour of an economy, or to improve an input to an economy, in a way which produces an increase in economic benefit which would not have happened had it been left to market forces.
- The purpose of small business intervention is not often made clear, but it would appear to be to promote economic and/or social welfare benefits, of which the most obvious is employment. Small businesses can create jobs, but they can also provide more innovation, which is needed for future competitiveness, and they can provide essential support for other businesses. Enterprise in its broad manifestation can also provide social and political benefits.
- The rationale for intervention is that there are barriers to the development of enterprise, entrepreneurship and/or small businesses due to failures in markets, governance or economic systems and that intervention can correct them.
- To be justified, intervention must be based on a valid way of achieving the outcomes sought. Usually that way is by addressing obstacles and barriers to enterprise, of which there are many. Some of these are classified as market failures, and there are economic welfare arguments about the value of intervening to address these. Classical theory may suggest that the market will make its own adjustments, but others maintain that there are real and lasting imperfections which will only be corrected by external intervention. These problems include the power of big businesses, the imperfections of the capital market, the impossibility of small businesses employing directly all the skills and expertise they need, the excessive regulatory regimes that governments impose on SMEs, and a reluctance by small businesses to seek the help they need.
- There can also be barriers of culture and education to the development of enterprise. In the former communist countries of Eastern Europe and the Soviet Union, for instance, there had for many years been no tradition of enterprise nor role models for it.

- While there seems to be very wide acceptance of the rationale for intervention, there are arguments that several of the justifications offered, especially those for providing small business assistance, do not stand up well to close scrutiny.
- To be justified, intervention must make a positive change, the value of which exceeds the cost of the intervention. Classical theory suggests that, while the direct results of intervention may be positive, the indirect results, such as displacement, can negate the direct benefits. Others argue that imperfections exist, and that if more enterprise is required, and if there are barriers to its development, then intervening to reduce the barriers will be beneficial.
- However, whatever the arguments, intervention is practised. Governments are subject to political pressures as well as economic ones, and the political pressures for supporting enterprise seem irresistible. Governments do intervene therefore to promote enterprise, even if the objectives of their interventions, and their results, are often unclear.

CASE 10.2
The rationale for an industrial policy

From an address by Mary Harney, Tánaiste and Minister For Enterprise, Trade and Employment, to Dail Eireann on the second stage of the Industrial Development (Enterprise Ireland) Bill on 18 June 1998:

'The Bill before you today provides for the creation of a new support structure for enterprise development. First and foremost, that structure entails the creation of a new agency, "Enterprise Ireland", through the amalgamation and restructuring of Forbairt, An Bord Tráchtála and relevant elements of the Services to Business function of FÁS. But this Bill is about much more than a technical change in agency configuration – it is also about a fundamental reappraisal of industrial policy.

'I believe that industrial policy needs to be founded on clear principles. The following are critical:

- Firstly: it is the people, not Governments, that create successful businesses. The primary role of Government is to help create the environment in which people want to start new businesses, to grow those businesses and to explore new directions when entrepreneurial ideas fail, as some inevitably must.
- Secondly: Government must respond to the dynamic inherent in business. For too long, Irish industrial policy has been dominated by a

protectionist tendency, propping up and protecting businesses which have no inherent competitive advantage or long-term prospects of survival. The plain truth is that Ireland's economy is constantly changing and our industrial base must undergo a similar process of transformation and upgrading.

- Finally: we need to recognise that not all companies want, or have the potential, to grow. Many firms are lifestyle businesses which will not grow beyond a certain point. Such businesses are a normal healthy part of any market economy. However, their existence serves to underscore the point that State assistance, if it is provided at all, must necessarily be limited. The risks of deadweight and displacement are ever present, threatening to dissipate government's development efforts and waste taxpayers money.

'On coming into Office, I directed my Department to undertake a root and branch review of industrial policy. That review of policy started from a zero base: nothing was ruled in or out. Indeed, the first option considered was the abolition of all direct State supports to industry and the consequent dissolution of the agencies providing those supports. This option was considered on the basis of the following potential benefits:

- One – the Exchequer resources freed up by this approach could be used to improve the enterprise environment through, for example, investment in infrastructure or tax reductions;
- Two – the elimination of direct supports would effectively end the "grant mentality" and leave companies free to focus on their competitive strategy instead of trying to exploit complex and unwieldy agency structures; and
- Thirdly, market forces would promote the survival of companies fit to compete in the global free market.

'I decided not to pursue this option because of the clear evidence that Irish industry has still not reached the stage where it is fully self-sufficient. Various market failures and other barriers to development still exist. Some examples are in the areas of:

- Finance, where the key market failure is in the provision of affordable equity and working capital to developing firms, especially those competing in international services and technologically intensive sectors.
- Lack of scale is also a major issue. Eighty-four percent of Irish-owned manufacturing firms are SMEs employing less than 250 people, and fifty-three per cent employ between eleven and one hundred employees.
- Related to the lack of scale are issues of accumulated experience and depth of infrastructure. Virtually all advanced economies display strong groupings of firms in specific sectors or in related and supporting industries. Such groupings create a positive mix of competition and cooperation which strengthens the industry as a whole.

- Because of Ireland's late industrialisation we have yet to develop such mutually reinforcing groupings of firms and the associated depth of infrastructure (in areas such as technology and logistics, for example) to support them.
- These deficiencies in scale and experience give rise to information deficits at firm level. Many small or developing firms are not in a position to undertake strategic analysis and to identify their strengths and weaknesses or to take the necessary steps to address them.
- Key information deficits at firm level involve research, development and design; knowledge of and access to markets; and training and human resource development, generally.

'I am convinced, therefore, that a role exists for the continued provision of some direct State supports to industry. However, I am far from satisfied that the existing structures, programmes and approaches are delivering optimum results.

'I therefore propose to put in place a new strategy. That strategy will be built around the key elements of:

- One – Sustainable Competitive Advantage; and
- Two – the Business Development Model (BDM)

'What is Sustainable Competitive Advantage? Quite simply, it is "the ability to consistently and profitably deliver products and services which customers are willing to choose in preference to those of competitors". The definition may be simple, but for the individual firm or entrepreneur, developing and sustaining a competitive advantage is by no means a trivial issue.

'Success or failure at firm level is determined by a complex interaction of forces that run across the firm's value chain from its suppliers to its final customers.

'Out of these forces come the inescapable facts that:

- with the advent of global free trade, input prices are considerably more volatile than in a sheltered domestic market;
- customer needs and tastes are constantly changing;
- new technologies emerge which give rise to new products and processes and render existing products obsolete; and
- new markets are opening up, while others are declining as a result of globalisation.

'To prosper and grow, firms need to constantly evolve to meet the needs of this changing environment. Failure to do so is evidenced by the fact that, to take just one random example, every single one of the one hundred and thirteen manufacturing firms which started in the year 1974 are now closed.

'It is no surprise then that there is a general perception that we are strong when it comes to creating businesses, but weak when it comes to sustaining them. Why should this be the case?

'We can certainly gain some insights from an assessment of the performance of indigenous industry which identifies some significant strategic weaknesses. For example:

- There is an excessive dependence on traditional sectors. Many firms are
  located in traditional industrial sectors where growth prospects are poor
  and competition from low cost producers is intense. Such competition
  will intensify further with increasing globalisation and free trade.
- Average profitability is poor. While average profitability (defined as return
  on sales) has increased in recent years, it remains low in absolute terms
  at 4.3 per cent for the food sector and 9.2 per cent for general manufacturing (according to Forfás surveys). This restricts the funds available
  for investment and growth.
- There is a low propensity to conduct R&D. In 1996, 55 per cent of
  indigenous companies undertook no R&D. And of those companies that
  did, only 19 per cent spent more than £100,000.
- There is insufficient investment in human resources. There is evidence
  that, overall, Irish business does not invest sufficiently to upgrade the
  skills of workers and management. This is particularly the case for smaller
  firms; and finally,
- Continuing reliance on home and UK markets is a cause for concern.
  Only 44 per cent of Irish SMEs export compared to an EU average of
  54 per cent. 65 per cent of indigenous manufacturing output is sold on
  the home market. Of the balance that is exported, 43 per cent is sold in
  the UK market.

'These problems have persisted despite an interventionist industrial policy
which has featured widespread availability of grants. In this decade alone,
almost 70 per cent of the firms recorded on my Department's Industrial
Database received a grant of some kind.

'These deficiencies paint a bleak picture. However, they should be taken in
context. On the positive side, the Irish enterprise sector as a whole is thriving. Employment in the Foreign Direct Investment sector has grown by
32 per cent and 32,000 jobs since 1992, while employment in indigenous
manufacturing companies has grown by 13.5 per cent and 16,000 jobs in
the same period. Even more striking has been the growth in the services
sector where employment has grown by 142,000 since 1992.

'This growth, and Ireland's very rapid economic progress in the 1990s
generally, has been underpinned by a commitment to getting the climate
right. Prudent management of the public finances, coupled with the contribution of successive partnership agreements, has created a virtuous circle of
rapidly growing productivity and real wage increases.

'The European Union has also played a major part both through the
contribution of the Structural Funds, and in the liberalisation of markets in
the run up to EMU.

'We are therefore faced with a conundrum. Overall, enterprise is booming. In particular, we now have a thriving domestic services sector which is capable of further significant growth as living standards continue to rise. In addition, we have now arrived at the point where it is no longer necessary to grant-aid firms simply to offset the effects of a dysfunctional cost and taxation environment.

'But in the midst of all of these positives the fact remains that the indigenous traded sector displays significant performance weaknesses which the traditional industrial policy model is failing to address.

'The policy review which I initiated identified specific weaknesses in that model which I will now outline to the House.

'The traditional approach can be characterised as supply driven. Under this approach, the development agencies channel their cash into a wide range of schemes which they have established, and the onus is largely on the firm to match its needs to those schemes.

'The effect of this supply driven approach is that there are too many schemes and too little focus on the real needs of the client firm. At best, this gives rise to a scattergun approach in the hope that if enough clients get support across enough categories at least some of it will hit the mark.

'This approach is wasteful, inefficient and less than optimally effective. Moving away from it requires a much greater focus on identifying the real needs of client firms and addressing those needs in a streamlined, flexible way. Such a move will result in better value for money, better targeting of supports and better performance from the assisted companies.

'The key to fulfilling client needs is to first establish what those needs are. Historically, the industrial development agencies have tended to concentrate on grant administration based on "paper" plans rather than on taking a hands-on approach and spending time with the client to develop an in-depth knowledge of their business and the strategic issues facing it.

'This approach works well in the Foreign Direct Investment context where the majority of firms are well established successful firms who are essentially negotiating the level of cash subsidy which will be paid to secure the location of their project in Ireland. By definition, the majority of these firms should already have the necessary internal competencies in R&D, marketing and strategy.

'As I have already indicated, however, indigenous firms tend to be less well developed and their needs are more complex, ranging across the entire spectrum of business functions. At present, firms are faced with the prospect of having to deal with three independent agencies which are administering in excess of 45 different schemes.

'There are, of course, some firms which profit from the current system. Those firms that have a clear idea of their needs and the resources to exploit the system will be more successful than other less well developed firms and may thus capture a greater proportion of agency resources. In addition, the existence of three separate agencies: FÁS, Forbairt and An Bord Tráchtála, offers firms the opportunity of using a positive decision on funding by one agency to leverage funding from the other agency.

'The ability of firms to "grant shop" among the agencies reinforces the "grant mentality" which has been strongly criticised for its negative impact on entrepreneurship and risk-taking in enterprise. It also diverts scarce resources from the areas of most need.

'The Culliton Report summarised the problem, and I quote: "Industrial firms are integrated business entities. The different functional areas operate together in a cohesive way. State support for the functional activities of firms, whether in marketing, training or finance should be provided in an integrated package."

'The Culliton Group's key insight was to recognise that State supports relate directly to the key strategic business functions performed by firms.

'My Department has built upon the Culliton view by formulating a Business Development Model (BDM) which provides the basis for assessing existing agency schemes and programmes and for streamlining them into a format which is clear, simple and directly related to developmental needs of firms in the areas of:

- strategy assessment and formulation;
- research development and design;
- production and operations;
- marketing;
- human resources; and
- finance.

'Simple support structures meeting real business needs and efficient client-friendly delivery – these are the goals. Self evidently, three separate agencies operating in excess of 45 different schemes is not the way to achieve this. If we want to continue with a policy which is unfocused and which fails to target the State's resources at the real developmental needs of firms then, clearly, we should leave the existing agency structures as they are.

'If, on the other hand, we intend to take an integrated, holistic approach to the development of enterprise and to make a real impact on industrial performance, we need to have an integrated agency; hence the creation of Enterprise Ireland.'

Source: Press release from the Department of Enterprise and Employment, Dublin. Reproduced with the kind permission of the Department of Enterprise and Employment.

Points raised

This statement by a government minister presents the rationale behind a real example of the creation of a revamped enterprise support structure. It presents an analysis of the situation, including references to, or aspects of, a summary of the issues in the economy, a review of past intervention efforts, an appreciation of the option of ending intervention and a summary of the problem.

QUESTIONS, EXERCISES, ESSAY AND DISCUSSION TOPICS

- Comment on the social and economic benefits which SMEs deliver to communities.
- Examine the barriers which prevent small firms from making a full contribution to the development of modern economies.
- 'Intervening to assist SME owners is a misguided activity.' Discuss.
- 'You can take a horse to water but you cannot make it drink.' Do psychological barriers (see Case 10.1) mean that intervention to support small businesses will be unproductive?
- Why do almost all governments ignore the arguments of neo-liberal market economists and intervene to support small firms?
- How might a government strategy for promoting wealth differ from one designed to promote employment?
- Is it possible to separate the economic and social benefits provided by small businesses?
- Is market failure a good reason for intervening to support small businesses, or is it only advanced as a justification?
- Is intervention only justified when there are market failures?
- Identify the failures, whether market, governmental or systemic, quoted by the Tánaiste in Case 10.2.
- What arguments for not intervening do you think should have been considered in the analysis behind Case 10.2?
- Identify and compare the arguments for and against intervention to promote small business formation and development.

SUGGESTIONS FOR FURTHER READING

J. Curran, 'What is Small Business Policy In the UK For? Evaluation and Assessing Small Business Policies', *International Small Business Journal* 2000; 18(3): 43–5.

D. J. Storey, *Understanding the Small Business Sector* (London: Routledge, 1994), Chapter 8, 'Public Policy'.

OECD, *The Role of SMEs: Findings and Issues* (Paris: OECD/DSTI/IND, 2000).

REFERENCES

1   D. Birch, cited in D. J. Storey, *Understanding the Small Business Sector* (London: Routledge, 1994), p. 161.
2   C. Gallagher, cited in Storey, *op. cit.*, p. 165.
3   From the back cover of A. Westall and M. Cowling, *Agenda for Growth* (London: Institute for Public Policy Research, 1999).
4   Storey, *op. cit.*, p. 253.
5   DTI, *Our Competitive Future: Building the Knowledge Driven Economy* (London: HMSO, CM4176, 1998), pp. 14–15.
6   Z. J. Acs and S. Gifford, 'Innovation of Entrepreneurial Firms', *Small Business Economics* 1996; 8: 203–18.
7   OECD, *The Role of SMEs: Findings and Issues* (Paris: OECD/DSTI/IND, 2000), pp. 1–20, at p. 11.
8   D. Pugh, 'Understanding and Managing Organisational Change', in C. Mabey and B. Mayon-White (eds), *Managing Change* (London: Paul Chapman, 1994), pp. 108–12.
9   OECD, *op. cit.*, p. 7.
10 See H. Mintzberg, *Power In and Around Organizations* (Englewood Cliffs, NJ: Prentice-Hall, 1983), p. 636, for a discussion of the fallacy of economic markets.
11 See W. R. Scott, *Organizations* (Englewood Cliffs, NJ: Prentice-Hall, 1992), Chapter 10, for a discussion of the impact of size on organisations.
12 C. Mason, R. Harrison and J. Chaloner, *Informal Risk Capital In the UK* (Southampton: Venture Finance Research Project, 1991).
13 M. B. Slovin and J. E. Young, 'The Entrepreneurial Search for Capital: An Investment in Finance', *Entrepreneurship, Innovation and Change* 1992; 1: 177–94.
14 G. Bannock and A. Peacock, *Governments and Small Business* (London: Paul Chapman, 1989).
15 OECD, *Regulatory Reform for Smaller Firms* (Paris: OECD, 1999).
16 J. Curran, 'What is Small Business Policy In the UK For? Evaluation and Assessing Small Business Policies', *International Small Business Journal*, Vol. 2000; 18(3): 43–5.
17 G. Lightfoot, *Financial Management and Small Firm Owner-Managers*, unpublished PhD thesis, quoted by Curran, *op. cit.*
18 A. A. Gibb, 'SME Policy, Academic Research and the Growth of Ignorance: Mythical Concepts, Myths, Assumptions, Rituals and Confusions', *International Small Business Journal* 2000; 18(3): 13–35.
19 Bannock and Peacock, *op. cit.*
20 OECD (2000), *op. cit.*, p. 2.
21 F. Delmar, 'The Psychology of the Entrepreneur', in S. Carter and D. Jones-Evans (eds), *Enterprise and Small Business* (London: Pearson Education, 2000), pp. 132–54, at p. 148.
22 Mintzberg, *op. cit.*, p. 636.

23 A. A. Gibb, 'Enterprise Culture and Education: Understanding Enterprise Education and its Links with Small Business, Entrepreneurship and Wider Educational Goals', *International Small Business Journal* 1993; 11: 11–34.

24 A. A. Gibb, *op.cit.*: 15.

25 C. C. Chen, P. G. Greene and A. Crick, 'Does Entrepreneurial Self-Efficacy Distinguish Entrepreneurs from Managers?', *Journal of Business Venturing* 1998; 13: 295–316.

26 Chen *et al., op. cit.*: 303

27 A. Phizacklea and M. Ram, 'Ethnic Entrepreneurship In Comparative Perspective', *International Journal of Entrepreneurial Behaviour and Research* 1995; 1: 48–58.

28 A. Fadahunsi, D. Smallbone and S. Supri, 'Networking and Ethnic Minority Enterprise Development: Insights from a North London Study', *Journal of Small Business and Enterprise Development* 2000; 7: 228–40.

29 M. Ram, 'Unravelling Social Networks In Ethnic Minority Firms', *International Small Business Journal* 1994; 12: 42–53.

30 S. Carter and P. Rosa, 'The Financing of Male- and Female-Owned Businesses,' *Entrepreneurship and Regional Development* 1998; 10: 225–41.

31 D. Walker and B. E. Joyner, ' Female Entrepreneurship and the Market Process: Gender-Based Policy Considerations', *Journal of Developmental Entrepreneurship* 1999; 4: 95–116.

32 Curran, *op. cit.*, pp. 38, 42.

33 R. J. Bennett, 'SMEs and Public Policy: Present Day Dilemmas, Future Priorities and the Case of Business Links', Paper presented at the *19th ISBA National Small Firms Policy and Research Conference*, Birmingham, 1996, p. 6.

34 Curran, *op. cit.*: 36, 38.

35 *Business Week* Editors, *The Reindustrialization of America* (New York: McGraw-Hill, 1982), cited in K. Vesper, *Entrepreneurship and National Policy* (Chicago: Heller Institute for Small Business Policy Papers, 1983), p. 74.

36 A. C. P. de Koning, J. A. H. Snijders and J. G. Vianen, 'SME Policy In the European Community', Paper presented at conference *Gateways to Growth: Opportunities for Smaller Firms in the EC* (1992); cited in Storey, *op. cit.*, p. 258.

37 See Mintzberg, *op. cit.*, pp. 171–83 for a discussion of the conditions that favour political behaviour in organisations.

11

THEORIES, MODELS AND ASSUMPTIONS (THAT MIGHT GUIDE INTERVENTION)

CONTENTS

KEY CONCEPTS

. . . .

This chapter covers:
- theories, models and assumptions about enterprise, including both entrepreneurship and small business development, that might help to guide interventions to promote more or better enterprise;
- a possible hierarchy of enterprise needs model;
- the difference between hard and soft intervention;
- the need for insight in understanding enterprise and in interpreting research.

LEARNING OBJECTIVES

··

By the end of this chapter the reader should:
- have an understanding of some of the main theories and models of enter-prise and how they might be used to suggest intervention methods;
- appreciate the different theories and models that might apply to entre-preneurship and to small business development;
- appreciate the possibility of a hierarchy of enterprise needs, which could explain why different needs may be apparent at different times or to different people;
- understand the difference between hard and soft intervention;
- understand the possible limitations of research results and the need for insight in interpreting them.

INTRODUCTION

Chapter Ten considered some of the arguments for and against intervening to try to promote more enterprise. If, for whatever reason, the decision has been made to intervene, however, then on what basis might it be done? What theories and models are there to guide that intervention?

This chapter looks at some of the assumptions that have been made about enterprise, and the theories and models of it which have been advanced, that might indicate where intervention could be effective and what form it might take. Examples of specific areas and types of intervention are given in the next chapter (Chapter 12), but before they are discussed it may be helpful to have some ideas about how enterprise can be influenced. This will not only indicate the theory which underlies some of the intervention methods currently practised but also provide the basis for new approaches.

Some of these ideas have been described in previous chapters but are referred to again here, in order to show a comparative selection of these ideas without the need to refer back frequently. There is however no guarantee that all the theories are correct. Like any theory in science, they are useful, not for explaining the past, but to model behaviour in a way which predicts what will happen in the future as a result of any action taken. The theories do not have to conform to some absolute level of truth to be helpful, nor do they all have to be consistent one with another. Newton's proposals for laws of gravity may have been proved to be less accurate than Einstein's ideas on the behaviour of space, but they are still good enough for many predictions about the movement of objects in space. The wave theory of light may help to explain light interference, although it is apparently inconsistent with particle theory, which can better explain other observable phenomena.

APPROACH

There are a variety of theories and models about how entrepreneurs and businesses behave and, because they have to be described in some sort of order, they are presented here in the sequence in which they might apply to the emergence and development of an enterprise, from the culture in which the initial idea may be sown through to the establishment and growth of a subsequent business, or other venture. This therefore follows broadly the stages of development of a business which were outlined in Chapter Six.

The earlier stages in this sequence cover the readiness of people to display enterprise and the development of their ideas to the stage where they put them into action. The subsequent stages concern the development of the businesses that may be started as a result of that enterprise. This division is consistent with the distinction which is drawn between an entrepreneurship policy, which is aimed primarily at increasing the business start-up rate, and a small business policy, which is aimed primarily at assisting those small businesses which have been established.

The early, or 'entrepreneurship', stages therefore focus primarily on the behaviour and development of people and the later or 'small business' stages on the behaviour and development of any businesses which those people may start. This distinction can also be seen to follow to some extent the different perspectives on enterprise, mentioned in Chapter Six, which are obtained when the unit of analysis is taken to be the person or the business.

Taken together, these stages and their relevant policies can be given the label 'enterprise'. This book has looked at both the broad and narrow definitions of enterprise and this label conforms to the broad definition, while the stages and policies to which the label 'small business' is applied conform to the narrow definition.

EARLY STAGES – ENTREPRENEURSHIP DEVELOPMENT

The development of a readiness to display enterprise, or of enterprise culture, may be a particularly appropriate starting point because of the belief, which conforms to many observations, that enterprising people are 'made not born'. The exercise of enterprising behaviour is not, it is suggested, something that depends solely, or largely, on inherited characteristics but instead is, to a very considerable extent, something that can be developed by learning and experience. If that is so then intervention to promote more of it may be both possible and practical. Promoting awareness of it may be the start.

Awareness

The pursuit of entrepreneurship can be likened to choosing an occupation. To be successful it requires an initial awareness of it, an interest in it, a desire to try it and the decision and action to do it, followed by a sufficient degree of attainment in it. That process must start with an awareness of the possibility of doing it.

It would be wrong to assume that everyone is aware of the possibility that he or she might be entrepreneurial, or that entrepreneurship might have potential for him or her. Research by Curran and Blackburn indicates that sixth-form pupils in Britain, unless they have a parent or a close relative in their own business, are unlikely to be interested in entrepreneurship as a career.[1] People may not want to try entrepreneurship, either because it is not, for them, desirable, or because they don't think that they would be able to do it, or because the possibility has never occurred to them. A first intervention step therefore may be an act of social persuasion to raise awareness of entrepreneurship and its potential benefits: a process of encouraging people to want to be entrepreneurs.

A time when awareness might most appropriately be raised by or with young people is during the time they are in school. Interventions at this stage are generally based on communicating enterprise awareness through the consideration of entrepreneurship. There are programmes that try to introduce young people to the notion of small business and the possibility of setting up a new business. However, Gibb suggests that many of these programmes are not themselves delivered in an enterprising manner.[2] They focus on the technical aspects of managing a small firm, and fail to provide participants with insights into the dynamic and ultimately enterprising nature of small business management. Instead it is important to incorporate the 'essence of small enterprise' into the learning method. If this is done then participants will acquire useful technical knowledge but will also learn how to cope with the complex, variable and ambiguous world of the small business.

The small scale of operation in an SME renders the owner vulnerable to environmental uncertainties and a reliance on outside stakeholders. In addition, owners and their staff must complete numerous tasks and develop a holistic view of their work. The ensuing task environment is complex and changeable, and the fact that owners are in charge means that they cannot walk away from problems – they must see tasks through to completion. As a result, owners experience a strange mixture of freedom and flexibility coupled with customer-led demands to meet their wants. Myriad demands create a need to develop problem-solving skills and a capacity to obtain requisite information and resources through networks of personal contacts. To survive in this environment, owner managers in small businesses must be adaptable and able to learn from experience. They learn by doing, by taking risks, by problem-solving, by interacting with others and by tolerating ambiguity. They also initiate more than they react to situations. If the essence of entrepreneurship is to be inculcated into potential entrepreneurs then the essential elements of a small business environment must be created in the learning situation. It is important to create an uncertain task environment and to encourage learning by 'self-discovery'. Teachers must be facilitators rather than fonts of knowledge, and must create an effective learning environment that uses a project of suitable complexity as a learning vehicle. Table 2.4 in Chapter

Two summarises some key differences between an educational and an entrepreneurial focus.

As well as school-based programmes, other means can be employed to raise enterprise awareness. Again, Gibb has indicated some of them in his illustration of the components of an enterprise culture shown in Figure 2.1 in Chapter Two.

However, there may be dangers in being too positive in promoting enterprise. Creating a rosy picture of the entrepreneurial world and ignoring the difficulties that can arise may not help; and neither may talking about 'the enterprise culture' for apparently political reasons without any attempt to explain what it means and to acknowledge what might be the emotional, psychological, social and financial costs of unsuccessful participation (see Chapter Five for some of the disadvantages of enterprise).

Developing a preference for enterprise

Raising the level of awareness may stimulate interest in enterprise, but if entrepreneurial behaviour is to be increased then more individuals must develop a preference for it.

Krueger believes 'perceptions of the entrepreneurial climate are critical ... To encourage new business founders, communities must cultivate an environment that they will perceive as being favourable.'[3] To do this it is helpful to understand the process underlying the intention to become an entrepreneur. Krueger, like many others, notes that intentions have antecedents that are derived from a person's experiences and the meaning an individual ascribes to them. His intentions model and cognitive psychological theories (summarised in Chapter Three) suggest that the act of creating a venture must be considered to be desirable and feasible by would-be entrepreneurs. Interventions should therefore aim to reinforce these perceptions.

Perceived desirability

Potential entrepreneurs should perceive that a new venture can deliver what they want. They must believe that the experience will be rewarding and enjoyable. Research on the motivation of entrepreneurs reveals that they have multiple motives and that economic ones rarely predominate. Highlighting the potential autonomy and sense of achievement that can be gained may therefore be more important than the potential financial rewards. Research has also revealed that many people consider entrepreneurship when they are experiencing dissatisfaction with other jobs or careers. This finding may indicate when it might be most appropriate to reinforce an entrepreneurial message and those at whom it might most effectively be targeted.

The personal desirability of entrepreneurship is important, but if the entrepreneurial act is also perceived as socially desirable then this is likely to encourage prospective entrepreneurs. A positive community attitude to enterprise is important, because often the capacity for enterprise is embedded in a community. Markets, resources, information and support, both practical and psychological, all originate there and, if that community is perceived as hostile, many potential entrepreneurs may be deterred. The absence of entrepreneurial role models or of a positive encouragement to enter one of the 'professions', while not actually being hostile towards enterprise, nevertheless act counter to it.

Perceived feasibility

In developing a preference for an occupation, as well as evaluating the attractiveness of the potential outcomes, individuals generally assess their chances of attaining those outcomes. To do this they consider whether they can obtain:

- the necessary knowledge and skill;
- the resources required;
- the means to overcome any shortfall.

If individuals have the opportunity to develop and manage enterprising projects in their existing employment, or to practise entrepreneurship on a part-time or temporary basis, they will have an appreciation of what is involved and can assess their attributes against the perceived requirements. As it has been put by Delmar: 'What stands out … is whether people feel that entrepreneurship is a feasible option for themselves. In other words a person will try to start a business if he or she can do it in terms of possessing the ability and knowledge required to carry it out.'[4] Entrepreneurial counselling can also help people to assess their competence in this area. Krueger believes that if the process of review is carried out sensitively, and if the emphasis is on positive steps to develop skills and overcome environmental obstacles, then this can be effective in building confidence and enhancing a person's perceived self-efficacy.[5]

Preparation

> Success = Idea + Know-how + Know-who
> Rein Peterson and Robert Rondstadt[6]

Building an appropriate culture does not itself create more enterprise. It does however provide an important precondition, like preparing a seedbed before sowing seeds: seeds sown on rocky ground will not find any sustenance and the energy in them will be wasted. But, given a seedbed of sorts, the formula for success given above can also be interpreted to indicate that entrepreneurial success starts with the idea: both the idea of starting a business in the first place and the idea of what business to start. Technical know-how appropriate to that business idea will be needed as well as business know-how to guide the establishment and running of the venture as a business. Know-who is also highlighted to indicate the importance of developing and using a network of contacts to obtain resources, advice, guidance and other forms of assistance.

The early stages of development can be seen as preparation for the possibility of a business at some time, before any decision may have been made about start-up. The later stages can be preparation for a venture that has already been decided upon. Chapter Three included a view of enterprise based on self-efficacy or the attributes and resources which an individual may possess (see Table 3.2). If these attributes and resources are appropriate for an entrepreneurial venture then it makes it more likely that the individual will engage in such a venture, given the right opportunity or 'trigger'. Therefore if the individual thinks that entrepreneurship is something that he or she might like to try at some time then he or she might endeavour to acquire the appropriate attributes and resources.

Acquiring and developing such attributes and resources in preparation for the possibility of enterprise can be seen as necessary foundation work. Preparing to start an enterprise, once the decision has been made to do it, is to prepare to build a structure on those foundations. Actually the distinction is not hard and fast. If the necessary foundations are not in place when the decision is made to build, it means that it will be necessary to address them at that time. Nevertheless, the analogy does help to separate the general preparation from the specific.

LATER STAGES – BUSINESS DEVELOPMENT

At this stage in the development of a business the focus for intervention starts to shift from the person to the business. It becomes less about helping a person to develop than about helping an enterprise to overcome specific barriers.

The barrier analogy may be a helpful one. Realising an idea or starting a business inevitably means encountering a number of difficulties and obstacles. To get to the desired destination it will be necessary to reduce them, cross them, avoid them or find ways through and around them as appropriate. Intervention can help by signposting pitfalls, by removing obstacles, by lowering barriers, and also by improving jumping capability, by raising the take-off point for jumping fences, and by raising confidence: showing that in general it is possible to complete the course.

Start-up

There are numerous barriers which can impede the launch of new businesses or other enterprising projects. Interventions in support of them can try to remove or reduce the tangible restrictions or to enhance the capacity of the actors to overcome the constraints. These can be addressed in both the short and the long term. (See Table 11.1.)

Table 11.1   Schema of small business intervention strategies

Time frame	Type of problem	
	Barriers to overcome	Capability to be acquired
Shorter	The direct provision of help to entrepreneurs to overcome obstacles, for example by offering grants, loans, advice, consultancy, and so on	Provide basic knowledge and skills training and lay the foundations for future development
Longer	Reduce or remove obstacles by addressing market failures, by improving the infrastructure, by changing regulations, and so on	Develop owner-manager and in-company capacity for learning, for analysis and for accessing appropriate assistance

In the short term, intervention to remove barriers is usually one-off help to overcome problems, and intervention to improve competence is mainly basic training in issues such as business plans, cash flow management and selling. Sometimes the training may be tied to a grant to ensure that it is taken up by making its completion a condition of the grant. This is the equivalent of providing fish to feed the hungry, and possibly combining pills with it to provide some medication.

In the longer term, barriers can be addressed by effective management of the economy to increase aggregate demand, increase financial stability, meet changing labour market and educational needs, and improve the context within which business development takes place. In the longer term, competence can be enhanced by increasing the organisation's own capacity to learn through skills in accessing information, in analysis, in planning, and in using appropriate outside sources of advice without the need for 'hand-holding'. In essence, owners and businesses are assisted to develop the attributes, knowledge and skills that are needed for sustainable development.

The latter is the equivalent of teaching the hungry to fish, but can have its problems when free fish are readily available without the need to learn how to catch them. Grant regimes can result in an attitude of dependency, including examples of a refusal to contemplate action without a grant, even when the action concerned would most likely be profitable without one.

Growth

Up to start-up the focus for intervention has been on the individual, the development of his or her entrepreneurship, and the minimisation of barriers. As the business comes closer to reality, different issues such as the securing of markets and the marshalling of resources become critical and, at start-up, a new range of problems can emerge. Once trading commences, however, intervention typically switches from entrepreneurship to business development with the focus being on the firm, not the individual. The aim of intervention becomes the growth of the business, for which business and management knowledge and skill become crucial, so it is important to consider how small business managers are to acquire them. Individual owner-managers are responsible for their own self-development. However, as their ventures move from owner-managed to owner-directed status they will have to develop a management structure and delegate key roles. The changing roles for self and others will bring a requirement to master new skills. Some of these skills can be learned on the job, but a lack of previous relevant experience is likely to be a handicap. Help in this area would therefore seem to be particularly beneficial.

Like start-up businesses, growing businesses also face external barriers, especially those associated with finance and employment. For instance, an important source of finance for growth is the venture capital sector. However, only a small proportion of formal venture capital tends to find its way to small businesses. In contrast to the formal venture capital industry, 'business angels' do seem to make a significant contribution to the development of small businesses. Nevertheless, there are still considered to be some funding gaps in the private financial market that intervention might try to address.[7]

Another popular target for intervention is the promotion of innovative and high-technology businesses. Innovation is widely regarded as a key factor in business survival, development, growth and competitiveness, and high-technology businesses are thought to offer the potential for greater growth, higher returns or longer life than 'low'-technology businesses, which are easier for others to copy. The apparent link between innovation and economic prowess in the USA is often cited as an example in making this point.

For small businesses to become innovative, or to remain so, they will need to have access to new ideas developed by others and/or to develop and protect their own ideas. In addition they will need financial resources to tide them over the non-revenue-generating phases of research and development. Other suggestions for intervention in this field include addressing the system for registering and protecting intellectual property, either by making it easier for small businesses to take out patents and other protection or, alternatively, by making it more difficult for large firms to defend their patent rights. This would encourage small businesses to adapt and develop technological ideas developed by others.

Decline and termination

One stage of business development not often considered for intervention is that of decline and ultimately termination. Nevertheless, there could be economic benefits to intervention here also. The benefits of reversing a decline may seem more obvious, but there may be benefits to be gained even in termination. If a business is going to terminate then it is better for its owners, its staff, its customers and its creditors if it does so in an orderly and controlled way, rather than trading beyond the point of insolvency and subsequently collapsing in debt. Adverse knock-on effects on creditor businesses will be avoided or reduced, and the business proprietors may even be prepared to learn from their experience and try again, instead of being discouraged, perhaps permanently, from developing further business ventures. The medical profession acknowledges that, while a terminally ill patient is by definition past the stage when medicine can effect a cure, there are still three things that can be offered to help at such times: support, information and choices. Similarly, there may be forms of intervention that provide benefits even in the termination stage of a business.

A HIERARCHY-OF-NEEDS MODEL

It has been observed that, if people involved in the process of starting new enterprises are asked what they need to help that process, the answer is very often 'money'; whereas, if people seeking to help that process are asked, they will often mention other areas of assistance such as premises, training, advice and mentoring, and some people go as far as to say that money is not the issue. However, frequently there appears to be a connection between the assistance that those seeking to help are best able to supply and what they claim is the main need: trainers for instance often seem to see skills as the key issue.

So is the main need money or not? What explains this apparent difference of opinion? How is it that different people, each of whom ought to be in a position to know, can provide different answers? Is it like the case of three blind people each seeking to identify an elephant by what they could feel, and who therefore variously described it as a rubbery hose, a tree, or an unravelled rope, depending on whether they felt the trunk, a leg or the tail?

One model (shown in Figure 11.1) developed to explain the variety of answers obtained to this question borrows a concept from Maslow in his analysis of human needs. He postulated that those needs could be placed in a hierarchy in which lower-order needs are dominant until they are satisfied, whereupon the higher-order needs start to be felt. The higher-order needs are there, but may not reveal themselves until the lower-order needs are satisfied. It has been suggested that a similar hierarchy could apply to enterprise needs, which would explain why they appear differently to different observers. Thus, without an idea, no need is felt for the resources to develop it and, until those resources are provided, no need is often apparent for any extra enterprise skills. Ultimately, if the enterprise is to be a success, it needs an environment which, given a sound approach by the enterprise, is capable of sustaining it.

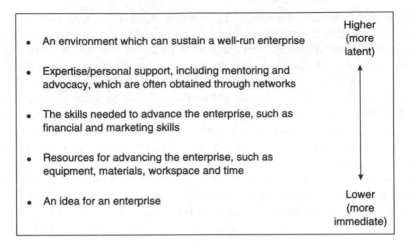

Figure 11.1 A hierarchy of enterprise needs

An enterprise, in this context, can be any form of human endeavour in which enterprising attributes might assist. This definition would include artistic and social endeavour as well as business entrepreneurship. A successful enterprise is considered to be one which has gone from the idea stage to implementation on a basis which is sustainable because the income attracted by that enterprise; whether earned income from sales, income from investments, sponsorship attracted from patrons, or charitable donations; is consistently high enough to pay for the outgoings of the enterprise.

The model appears, for instance, to work for artistic as well as for business enterprise. For example there is a need for pump-priming support for the artist until he or she can become established, and becoming established can mean earning enough to support the art from direct sales or through some sort of benefaction. Given artistic skill there is still a need for skill in marketing and in money control if the venture is to succeed.

In this presentation, money is often a complicating factor. It has not been included in the hierarchy because it is not a direct need but is sought because it can be used to buy what is needed. It is a means not an end. Money is needed at an early stage to buy the resources required for start-up and then it is needed at a later stage to sustain the venture once it is launched. At the later stage however the money required should be found from the earnings of the venture itself. These two types of funding can be likened to the flight of a glider. At its launch a glider needs external help to get into the air, but then, if it is successfully launched and piloted, it should itself be able to find enough lift to sustain its flight. But if the glider pilot does not have sufficient skills to do this, the glider will descend and will once again need external help if it is to rise again. It is however only when the glider has been launched that such a lack of skills will be apparent. Similarly in enterprise, if some of the higher-order needs are not then satisfied, the enterprise will not be operated viably and will need more 'pump-priming' money as a result. Therefore, given an initial idea and then some form of start-up finance, failure to meet higher-level needs can appear as a further need for finance, just as if it were still a lower level start-up finance need. This can be further complicated when higher level needs are combined with some, but inadequate, start-up finance.

Given an idea, which is often the starting-point without which the needs issue will not arise, the lowest, and therefore the most obvious, need is likely to be resources, to which money appears to be the obvious answer. Therefore this hierarchy-of-needs hypothesis explains why the needs of enterprise are, at an early stage, often expressed as a need for money, and why the other needs are hidden until that need is apparently satisfied. Hence it explains why there can be confusion and disagreement about what is the most appropriate assistance to offer. It also explains why, when asked, most people will say that money is the key issue, yet there are other people who will talk, not about money, but about training and mentoring needs for example. It also explains why providing more money often does not solve the problem.

The model can also be expanded and explained further. A level below the idea might be added, which is the need for a culture in which ideas for enterprise can arise and which encourages people to be enterprising. Further explanation could also be added of the sorts of needs at the various levels.

The model also highlights the reason for a not-infrequent temptation to use money as the tool with which to help enterprise. Often bodies which are created to help enterprises are given a budget with which to operate. Then, when they ask people engaged in enterprise what would most help them, they are told it is money. In such circumstances it is very easy for them to believe that money is the tool to use, instead of seeing that it has to be converted into something else if it is actually to achieve the desired effect. The model also indicates that anyone seeking to assist the enterprise process should not believe that it is possible to intervene at one stage only and succeed in addressing in one way all the main needs of enterprise development.

Advocacy

One further explanation might also help. In the hierarchy model 'advocacy' has been included as a possible source of advice which is a separate requirement from that of mentoring. The concept of 'advocacy' has been borrowed from the legal world. In that area lawyers are hired to argue cases, not because they know the case better than the litigants, but because they know the system and how to present the case so that the system can best understand it and recognise its good points. Similarly when making applications for support for ideas it can help to know how those who might provide the support think and act.

The issue of advocacy is recognised in legal circles, even though all are equal before the law. It is often not recognised amongst funders, however, where those who administer the funding like to believe that they can judge a case on its merits without some third party explaining it to them. Some of those who have worked in the funding system may recognise that the way a case is presented can influence the funding decision and that, because those making the decision work in a different culture to those making the applications, good communication between them may only be possible with the help of interpreters who can understand the concerns of both sides.

Advocacy, in the sense in which it is used in the model, is not the same as mentoring. In this context advocacy is taken to mean help with the presentation of a proposal or venture to those who are being asked to make a decision on it, whereas mentoring is taken to mean one-to-one personal help with different aspects of the business or idea development process (although not all uses of the words 'mentoring' and 'advocacy' conform to these definitions).

HARD AND SOFT

One category of initiatives to promote small businesses is one which, instead of offering direct help to the individual entrepreneur or business, attempts to create conditions in which businesses can better germinate and grow. A clear example of this sort of initiative is the creation of science parks and business incubators. These have been called 'hard' assistance, in comparison with 'soft' assistance such as training provision and mentoring, presumably because they involve the creation of 'hard' physical structures (buildings) rather like the physical hardware of computers.

There are a number of places including, in the USA, Silicon Valley in California and Route 128 in Massachusetts, and around Cambridge in England (sometimes referred to as Silicon Fen), where there has been an extraordinary growth of productive clusters of high-technology firms. In these clusters the conditions which produce innovative business communities, with significant outputs of patents and innovations and new businesses, are thought to include a university or other technological research facility; the close proximity of other innovative firms, which encourages the spread of ideas and helps small businesses to access the expertise of other businesses around them; and informal networks incorporating business angels, venture capitalists, professional firms including accountants and lawyers, and a business school. Providing help with these conditions is soft assistance.

Science parks seek to replicate at least some of these conditions. As well as science parks there are also research parks, technology parks and innovation parks but, whatever the name used, they all generally share a number of common components, which include:

- a property base which provides suitable business premises;
- close links with a source of technology expertise and possible spin-off ideas. Often these are formal and operational links with a university or other higher education body or major centre of research;
- assisted access to finance and advice;
- a management function which is actively engaged in the transfer of technology and business skills to the organisations on-site and in encouraging the formation and growth of knowledge-based businesses.

This list highlights the university or other research links and the transfer of technology as key components in a science park and it is this link that distinguishes science parks from many business incubators. Science parks may be business incubators but business incubators are not necessarily science parks. Incubators may concentrate more on providing nursery space, often at subsidised rents, and access to support services such as word-processing, copying, telephone-answering and telecommunications. The theory behind the creation of this environment is that it provides services which might otherwise be beyond the means of the small start-up business, but it also provides what it is possible and, once premises are available, easy to provide.

However, there appears to be little convincing evidence yet that a science park, or other form of business park, necessarily has a significant impact on the innovative performance of its tenant firms. In England it was Segal, Quince, Wicksteed[8] who did most to highlight the spin-off from technical developments at Cambridge University facilitated by the Cambridge Science Park, now known as the 'Cambridge Phenomenon'. Some other studies of individual parks and incubators have also indicated that they can be successful but Deakins, in reviewing this area,[9] finds that the overall picture is less certain. He reports on a study for the DTI[10] which found that there was little difference in performance between firms on and off science parks and indicates that other studies based on incubator facilities also contain similarly equivocal findings.

ILLUSTRATION 11.1
Does location matter in Israel and Ireland?

Innovation activities of Israeli firms are found to be much more locationally sensitive than those of Irish companies. In other words in Israel, a metropolitan location gives firms an advantage in terms of the probability of innovating. Locations in Belfast and Dublin, however, are no more propitious for innovation than other areas of Northern Ireland or the Republic of Ireland. One plausible explanation is that the more R&D-intensive activities of Israeli high-tech firms mean that these firms benefit more from a metropolitan location than their Irish counterparts.

In terms of policy, the implication is that dispersing high-tech industry in Israel is likely to be more 'costly' in terms of its negative impact on innovation than in Ireland. For policy-makers in Ireland this is a heartening conclusion, suggesting that the policy of dispersing high-tech activity over the last three decades is likely to have had little detrimental effect on the overall level of innovative activity. For Israel, however, more tension is evident between industrial and regional policy. The pattern of industrial incentives, and particularly high levels of public support for R&D, have stimulated investment in highly R&D-intensive sectors which are unlikely to fare well in more peripheral areas. For these areas offering high levels of R&D support may actually be an inappropriate policy, at least in the absence of measures designed to improve other aspects of the operating environment for R&D-intensive businesses (such as by developing local higher education institutions).

Source: Northern Ireland Economic Research Centre, *Does Location Matter for Innovation? A Comparison of High-Tech Firms In Israel and Ireland*, Research briefing (Belfast: NIERC, 2001).

RESEARCH AND INSIGHT

It ain't what you don't know that gets you into trouble, it's what you know for sure that ain't so.

Mark Twain

It might be expected that guidance for intervention to promote more enterprise might come from research and, in the last two decades of the 20th century, there was an 'explosion of research into entrepreneurship and the small and medium enterprise'.[11] However Gibb points out that, despite the resultant increase in academic knowledge, or even perhaps because of it, there has also been a growth in ignorance about entrepreneurship and small and medium enterprises.[12]

Earlier Gibb[13] had looked at the problem of trying to ensure that small firms research was relevant to policy-makers. He highlighted issues such as the relationship between academic knowledge and insight, showing, for instance, that insight into small businesses was needed if research findings were to be interpreted in a meaningful way. The assumption that objectivity was a prerequisite for good research could, he suggested, mean that the need for insight was often overlooked on the grounds that those who knew enough about small businesses to have insight might be too close to their subject to be fully objective.

Gibb has identified a number of 'mythical concepts' which he describes as important policy development areas around which there is an expanding mass of literature but also a considerable degree of confusion and ignorance. These include entrepreneurship and the enterprise culture, network development, the 'growth' company, local 'bottom-up' development, and competency and learning. He has also highlighted 'a number of more straightforward myths which have influenced key policy objectives in the 1990s and continue to do so'. These are:[14]

- That three out of every five new businesses started fail within the first three years.
- That growth companies are the major job creators.
- That in the USA failure is regarded positively by banks and other stakeholders compared with the UK.
- That there is a major gap in bank finance for SMEs in the UK.

CASE 11.1
The start-up failure myth
....

'Among the more straightforward myths which have influenced key policy objectives in the 1990s and continue to do so is the myth that three out of every five new businesses started fail within the first three years.

'Much has been written about the failure of new business starts. All these studies indicate that of all business exits (as measured by VAT de-registrations, exits from self-employment or from the companies register), only a small fraction are due (in the case of individuals) to bankruptcy and (in the case of companies) to compulsory involuntary liquidation ... It is evident, however, that a useful distinction can be made between the legal entity, the business activity and the entrepreneur. Casual observations would indicate that even in apparently stable business conditions there can be a great deal of 'churning' in respect of registration with little else changing.

'[Table 11.2] demonstrates the movement into and out of various forms of business registration in 'Brigadoon', a 'mythical' village (known well to the author). It indicates that there were, in the space of six years, fourteen 'starts', twelve 'failures', and eight 'new entrepreneurs'; [but overall there was only] one business activity loss and one business activity gain. The explanation mainly lies in changes in legal status arrangements. For example the architect resident in the village went into two partnerships, each of which lasted only a short time, before resuming independent status.

Table 11.2 The Brigadoon economy: change over six years

Business	De-registration	New registration	Persons change	Activity change
Architect	4	4	0	0
Pub	2	2	2	0
Post Office	3	3	3	1
Bus	1	1	1	0
Electrical contractor	1	1	1	0
Plumber (informal)	0	1	0	0
Garage/caravan site	0	1	1	0
House cleaner (informal)	0	1	0	0
Weaving	1	0	0	−1

'Other changes related to marital arrangements, to deaths and, perhaps not uncommon in the rural community, to (in the case of the Post Office) families running this community service, adding a small store, for a short period of time as a duty before transferring it to someone else. Other explanations related to the movement from the informal to the more formal economy, and to a wife's ambition to run part of an existing business and subsequently to register it. The economic life of the village looks extremely turbulent if a business registration approach is taken to describe it. In practice, little has changed in terms of activity.

'The start-up failure myth needs to be more clearly exposed as it is frequently quoted by politicians and easily leads into other policy assumptions, for example that investment in training in start-ups is undesirable because such training is written off with failure; that the majority of those who start businesses are poor managers; and that start-ups are not a source of employment growth which is untrue. It also lends credence to the belief that microenterprises are not entrepreneurial or in dynamic sectors of the economy.

'An alternative view, coloured by the notion that individuals may move into and out of self-employment, is that starting a business can be seen as an intrinsic part of the flexible labour market, and that start-up might be one of the best ways of experiencing, learning and practising enterprise. When combined with the notion that the learning curve during the start-up process, particularly for the novice start-up, is probably greater than any other time during the life of the small business then the potential for reconsideration of the rate of return to the training investment is considerable.'

Sources: A. A. Gibb, 'SME Policy, Academic Research and the Growth of Ignorance, Mythical Concepts, Myths, Assumptions, Rituals and Confusions', *International Small Business Journal* 2000; 18(3): 22–3; A. A. Gibb, 'SME Policy, Mythical Concepts, Myths, Assumptions, Rituals and Confusions', *21st ISBA National Small Firms Conference*, Durham, 1998, p. 12.

Points raised

This example is extracted from a longer paper by Allan Gibb. It illustrates how the statistics of business registration, and de-registration, can give a very misleading impression of what is actually happening to those engaged in business and can appear to suggest a much higher failure rate than is actually the case.

Each myth, Gibb indicates, is shared in different ways by different groups and each has influenced policy, being treated as a 'fact' rather than as an assumption with little or questionable supporting evidence. If there is this 'growth of ignorance' then, Gibb argues, there are three contributory factors:[15]

- The first factor is that of the nature of the relationship and involvement between SMEs, policy-makers, other stakeholders and academics. Between and within these groups there are substantial differences concerning beliefs, values and assumptions about the ways that things work, and these differences influence the processes by which the groups learn from each other.
- The second factor relates to understanding of the way that governance works and the kinds of assumptions made in establishing priorities for policy action as well as assumptions concerning the process by which these priorities are met. If academics do not understand the process of governance, and believe, for instance, that it pursues a rational discovery and problem-solving model, then their contribution is likely to be marginalised.
- The third factor arises in respect of the way in which academics approach their policy-related work. There is a need for researchers to attach greater value to insight into the way that others see and feel things and to distinguish data, descriptions of empirical results, constructs and hypotheses from useful theory.

THE OTHER VIEW–THE PERSPECTIVE OF THE INDIVIDUAL

In considering intervention in enterprise it is important not to see it only from the point of view of the intervener, but also to consider the view of the individuals engaging in it. In making their occupational choice, individuals will, at least to some extent, conduct appraisals although, as in other 'consumption' decisions, issues of 'fantasy, feeling and fun'[16] also play a part. Macro-economic issues such as the general health of the economy will be considered, along with the personal attributes deemed necessary for occupational success. If the potential outcomes of an endeavour are valued, and if individuals consider that their efforts in that endeavour will lead to the requisite performance and associated rewards, then they are likely to expend energy in its pursuit.[17] That applies both to enterprise in a business context and to enterprise applied in other situations.

At an early stage, perceptions are all-important, and there are possibilities of misconceptions because appraisals are conducted on the basis of suppositions. While entrepreneurial choice has quite a lot in common with occupational choice in general, it has some unique features that should be borne in mind when considering intervention. As individuals move through life, their career choices are moulded by 'the opportunity structures to which individuals are exposed, first in education, and subsequently in employment. Individuals' ambitions in turn, can be treated as reflecting the influence of the structures through which they pass.'[18] However, education and work opportunities do not normally expose people to the realities of entrepreneurship. Few educational courses delve into the nature of enterprise/entrepreneurship, and most individuals experience employment through the eyes of the employee. If they learn anything about work, they learn the skills of job-readiness and successful employment. They will be 'job-takers' not 'job-makers'. People generally choose occupations that they know something about, and in the absence of a conception of entrepreneurship this may not be a realistic option for many.

Furthermore, enterprise is a somewhat heterogeneous occupation. Entrepreneurs run manufacturing firms and service organisations. Similarly enterprising individuals may display their talents in healthcare, education or the church. These individuals are responsible for the technological aspects of their ventures, and the socio-economic tasks of administration, coordination and leadership. A range of technical and managerial abilities is needed, and previous education and work will rarely prepare individuals fully for these tasks.

In addition, entrepreneurs must develop a viable business idea and marshal appropriate resources to create a business venture. The multiple technical and management skills, coupled with the need for ideas and resources, contribute to the complexity of entrepreneurship as an occupation and the need to consider many leverage points for intervention. Entrepreneurship also differs from normal employment, in that potential entrepreneurs are not screened in the way that potential employees are. In many countries there are no formal entry qualifications, there is no formal selection and interview process, and there is no appointment and review procedure.[19] Business counsellors, bankers and other advisers may proffer advice, but no one can prevent a person starting a business if he or she decides so to do whatever his or her abilities. Further, when it is done, there is no compulsory process for identifying and rectifying any deficiencies in relevant skills and knowledge.

The absence of selectors and the complexities of entrepreneurial choice should indicate the need for wariness about prescribing simple solutions to the problem of attracting and developing entrepreneurs. This complexity is confirmed by the fact that many business founders tend to choose entrepreneurship only after trying other jobs or career paths. By their mid-thirties, potential entrepreneurs will tend to have been exposed to a selection of jobs or roles, and while they may not have had direct experience of entrepreneurship, they may have had an opportunity to assess interests, values, abilities and opportunities. This being so, intervention in this area may need to address a number of issues experienced by people at different stages of entrepreneurial development. Since each individual is unique, a very wide range of interventions would be needed to reach all of them in an appropriate way.

It is also relevant to remember that intervention can be direct or indirect. It can seek to target the individual or business directly, or it may seek to change the context or conditions in which they operate, which will in turn influence the individuals or businesses concerned. Gibb's diagram presented in Chapter Seven (Figure 7.1) helps to make this point by showing that the purposive support network, through which much of the intervention might come, may in reality have much less direct influence on entrepreneurs and small businesses than many of their other layers of contacts. It may be more effective for organisations in that network to try to work through some of the other layers than to try to go directly to the business owners concerned.

THE KEY POINTS OF CHAPTER 11

- As entrepreneurs and businesses go through different stages of their development their influences and needs change, and so therefore do the opportunities for intervention.
- Intervention in the early stages of development may be referred to as entrepreneurship policy, and intervention in the later stages, after a business has started trading, as small business policy.
- The first stage is the development of an enterprise culture, which can both provide an awareness of the possibility of enterprise and the development of a preference for it. The society in which individuals live, the education they receive, and the environment in which they work can all be very influential in this and are therefore possible targets for intervention.
- Preparation for enterprise involves the identification of an idea or opportunity to pursue, the building of experience, skills and other attributes relevant to its pursuit, and the acquisition of the finances, networks and other resources necessary for it. Intervention might help in all these areas.
- Start-up is a common focus for intervention, in particular to help those wishing to start businesses to overcome the barriers they face. Such intervention may attempt to reduce the barriers or to raise ability to overcome them. It can use measures with short-term or immediate effects, such as grants to overcome financial difficulties, or it may seek longer-lasting effects by seeking to address market failures or by developing a capacity

to learn. However entrepreneurship is a heterogeneous occupation and the requisite resources, knowledge and skills will be diverse.

- Intervention to assist declining, or even terminating, businesses may also produce benefits, and should not therefore be discounted automatically.
- Simplistic, direct solutions to intervention should be suspect however. There are no formal selectors for entrepreneurship that can prevent occupational entry to those who are unsuited to it. The variety of people trying it is therefore considerable, and so are the influences on them. Direct intervention may be considered, but it may also be effective to seek to influence people through others.
- Entrepreneurs starting businesses also have a variety of needs, not all of which will be equally apparent at any one time. It will therefore rarely be possible to help them significantly by meeting just one need.
- One vehicle for help has been the provision of physical facilities, such as premises, which are designed to stimulate the conditions in which at least some businesses seem to thrive. This is 'hard' assistance, in contrast with the 'soft' assistance such as training and mentoring provided directly to improve individual businesses.
- Research into small businesses has not necessarily led to increased understanding of them to the degree that might have been expected. In this area ignorance, not least in the form of false concepts and myths about small businesses and their behaviour, still persists.
- The perspective of the individual engaged in enterprise is also of relevance when considering intervention.

QUESTIONS, EXERCISES, ESSAY AND DISCUSSION TOPICS

- Is it true that intervention is often based more on what can be provided than on what is needed?
- What interventions might be desirable, but impractical?
- Is it always a good thing to get more people to start their own businesses?
- 'Backing winners' was a popular small business development strategy in the 1990s. What was the theory behind it, and was it valid?
- 'Don't worry too much about why. It's more important to start something. Then we will be able to see if it really works.' Is that a good basis for introducing new enterprise initiatives?

- It will always be possible to find a theory to support any strategy you want to adopt. Is this true of enterprise support?

SUGGESTIONS FOR FURTHER READING

J. Curran and R. A. Blackburn, *Researching the Small Enterprise* (London: Sage, 2001).

A. A. Gibb, 'SME Policy, Academic Research and the Growth of Ignorance: Mythical Concepts, Myths, Assumptions, Rituals and Confusions', *International Small Business Journal* 2000; 18(3): 13–35.

REFERENCES

1   J. Curran and R. Blackburn, *Young People and Enterprise: A National Survey*, Occasional paper No. 11 (Kingston: Kingston Business School, 1989).
2   A. A. Gibb, 'Enterprise Culture and Education: Understanding Enterprise Education and Its Links With Small Business, Entrepreneurship and Wider Educational Goals', *International Small Business Journal* 1993; 11: 11–34.
3   N. F. Krueger Jr., *Prescriptions for Opportunity: How Communities Can Create Potential for Entrepreneurs*, Working paper 90-03 (Washington, DC: The Small Business Foundation of America, 1995).
4   F. Delmar, 'The Psychology of the Entrepreneur', in S. Carter and D. Jones-Evans (eds), *Enterprise and Small Business* (London: Pearson Education, 2000), pp. 132–154, at p. 148.
5   Krueger, *op. cit.*
6   R. Peterson and R. Rondstadt, 'A Silent Strength: Entrepreneurial Know-Who', *The 16th ESBS/efmd /IMD Report* (86/4), pp. 11–15. at p. 11.
7   See R. T. Harrison and C. M. Mason, 'Finance for the Growing Business: The Role of Informal Investment', *National Westminster Bank Review* May 1993: 17–29 for a discussion of business angels.
8   Segal, Quince, Wicksteed, *The Cambridge Phenomenon*, (London: Segal, Quince, Wicksteed, 1985).
9   D. Deakins, *Entrepreneurship and Small Firms* (London: McGraw-Hill, 1999), pp. 150, 156–8.
10 P. Westhead and D. J. Storey, *An Assessment of Firms Located on and off Science Parks: Main Report* (London: DTI / HMSO, 1994).
11 A. A. Gibb, 'SME Policy, Academic Research and the Growth of Ignorance, Mythical Concepts, Myths, Assumptions, Rituals and Confusions', *International Small Business Journal* 2000; 18(3): 13–35, at 13.
12 *Ibid.*: 13.
13 A. A. Gibb, 'Can Academe Achieve Quality In Small Firms Policy Research?', *Entrepreneurship and Regional Development* 1992; 4: 127–144.
14 Gibb (2000), *op. cit.*: 22.

15 Gibb (2000), *ibid.*: 24–31.
16 M. B. Holbrook and E. C. Hirschman, 'The Experiential Aspects of Consumption: Consumer Fantasies, Feeling and Fun', *Journal of Consumer Research* 1982; 9: 132–40.
17 P. M. Blau, J. W. Gustad, R. Jessor, H. S. Parnes and R. C. Wilcox, 'Occupational Choice: A Conceptual Framework', *Industrial and Labour Review* 1956; 19: 531–43.
18 K. Roberts, 'The Social Conditions, Consequences and Limitations of Careers Guidance', *British Journal of Guidance and Counselling* 1977; 5: 3.
19 V. H. Vroom, *Work and Motivation* (New York: Wiley, 1964).

12 INTERVENTION METHODS (OBJECTIVES, STRUCTURES AND APPROACHES)

CONTENTS

KEY CONCEPTS

This chapter covers:

- the reasons why governments feel the need to intervene to promote aspects of enterprise, but often do so without an overall strategy;
- the frequent lack of clarity of intervention objectives;
- the very wide variety of possible structures for, and methods of, intervention;
- developments in enterprise policy and delivery systems in the UK and the evolution of EU policy towards enterprise development;

- typical instruments for intervention in the UK and other EU countries.

LEARNING OBJECTIVES
....

By the end of this chapter the reader should:
- understand the reasons why governments intervene to support entrepreneurship and small business;
- appreciate that governments do intervene but often do not have clear objectives or overall strategies;
- appreciate the range of possible areas and methods for intervention in the UK and other EU countries;
- understand the main developments in policy towards entrepreneurship and small business and how it is being delivered in the UK;
- be aware of the major developments in EU policy for entrepreneurship and small business;
- understand the range of forms of assistance and their application in specific fields.

INTRODUCTION

Because of the growth in the perceived importance of smaller firms for economic development, virtually every country in the developed and developing world is now intervening in some way to promote enterprise skills, to encourage more entrepreneurs and the development of more self-employment, and to grow more indigenous businesses.

Some of the motivations and justifications for these interventions have been described in Chapter Ten and some of the theories, models and assumptions behind them in Chapter 11. This chapter describes the array of objectives, structures and approaches used for intervention. These are the methods, not the strategies, used for the promotion of entrepreneurship and small business, and indeed often the strategies appear to be missing. In the UK, despite apparently hundreds of initiatives since the end of the 1970s, an overall strategy, in the sense of a coherent set of objectives and associated means of achieving them, has been lacking. The last real attempt in the UK to articulate a coherent SME policy in a single document, some claim, was the *Bolton Report On Small Firms* in 1971. At least part of the reason for this gap lies in the fact that the small business sector is characterised by very considerable diversity with competing interests, making the prioritisation of needs very difficult for politicians and policy-makers. This has led Bennett among others to suggest that 'Fragmentation of government programmes for SMEs appears to reflect the fragmentation and variety of the problems that

SMEs confront.'[1] On the other hand the Audit Commission saw the situation just as 'a patchwork quilt of complexity and idiosyncrasy'.[2]

In this the UK is not alone. An OECD paper[3] reviews the experience of its member countries in encouraging entrepreneurship and their contribution to job creation. Amongst its observations are:

- Member governments lack the presence of a comprehensive strategy towards entrepreneurship and job creation.
- The explicit promotion of entrepreneurship as a source of job creation is scarce in policy formulation.
- Better policy coordination is needed to exploit more fully the potential of entrepreneurship and new business in order to help start-ups and existing firms in the creation of new jobs.

Lundström and Stevenson reflect that:

> [because] entrepreneurship itself is still not a well defined concept and the differences between SME and entrepreneurship policies are unclear, efforts to become a more 'entrepreneurial economy' are somewhat impeded. Instead of assuming an integrated approach to stimulating a higher level of entrepreneurial activity, governments currently tend to add on projects and activities in a piecemeal incremental fashion.[4]

ENTERPRISE, ENTREPRENEURSHIP AND SMALL BUSINESS POLICIES

One consequence of the lack of clear definitions of words such as 'enterprise' and 'entrepreneurship' is that there is also confusion about what is meant by enterprise, entrepreneurship and small business policies. They can be perceived as interchangeable, overlapping or quite separate and, as a result, important policy differences can often be obscured or ignored.

There can be at least three distinct policy areas which some people now distinguish with the labels 'small business', 'entrepreneurship' and 'enterprise', although those labels have also been used with less discrimination. These policy areas are:

- *Small business policies.* these are policies for stimulating growth of already established small business, variations of which have also been called a 'growth' or 'business growth' policy and a 'backing winners' policy. This sort of policy tends to focus on the businesses and what will help them to grow, not the entrepreneurs behind them.
- *Entrepreneurship policies.* these are policies for encouraging and facilitating more people to take up self-employment. These policies are centred on people and on what will persuade or help them to start businesses, although they can be referred to as 'business start' or 'business birthrate' policies.

- *Enterprise policies*. these are policies for encouraging enterprise in its broad sense, much, but not all, of which may be manifest as new business starts. These policies are clearly focused on people, both as individuals and in groups, and seek to develop skills and attitudes likely to assist people to be more successful in any chosen career or endeavour. However the description 'enterprise' may also be applied to policies which try to incorporate the promotion of both entrepreneurship and small business growth, or the term 'enterprise policy' may be used to describe a combination of both entrepreneurship and small business policies.

This terminology, because it can at least separate entrepreneurship from small business policy, facilitates a distinction which is important because these policies require very different approaches. A small business policy should be about business development while policies for entrepreneurship and enterprise should be about wider social and economic development. Unfortunately however this distinction is often not appreciated, with the result that even those who formulate the policies sometimes mix them up and therefore mix different objectives or fail to select appropriate means for achieving them. Different words can mean the same or different things depending upon who is using them and in what context. In this chapter the labels used are generally those applied by the policy originators or 'owners', but an explanation is offered where this is thought to be necessary.

Linking entrepreneurship to economic growth

It is important, one might even say necessary, when viewing the role of policy and how it might influence the achievement of objectives, to have some kind of picture of how key components and elements in the system relate to one another. GEM (see Chapter Four) is one example of a project which has established and is exploring a correlation between entrepreneurship and economic growth but it has not yet established just what the link between them is. Nevertheless, if economic growth is an objective, an apparent relationship between entrepreneurship and economic growth might suggest that an entrepreneurship policy should at least be tried. Having a theory tried and tested in terms of a working model of this relationship would be ideal. It is evident, however, that there is still some way to go before there is such an understanding of how our economic systems operate. Specifically the nature and functioning of the link between individuals, entrepreneurship and economic growth is not yet adequately understood. It is not surprising, therefore, that there is also a general lack of clarity about whether and how to develop integrated entrepreneurship and small business development policies. Lundström and Stevenson have proposed however an illustrative model of the linkages between entrepreneurship and economic growth (shown in Figure 12.1) which highlights some areas where more research is required to establish, *inter alia*, the nature of any linkages, their causal relationships, their magnitudes and the lead times.

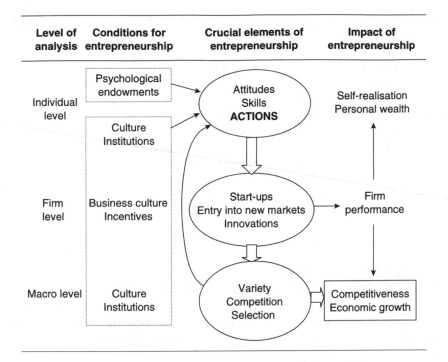

Level of analysis	Conditions for entrepreneurship	Crucial elements of entrepreneurship	Impact of entrepreneurship

Individual level — Psychological endowments / Culture Institutions → Attitudes, Skills, **ACTIONS** → Self-realisation, Personal wealth

Firm level — Business culture, Incentives → Start-ups, Entry into new markets, Innovations → Firm performance

Macro level — Culture Institutions → Variety, Competition, Selection → Competitiveness, Economic growth

Source: A. Lundström and L. Stevenson, *Entrepreneurship Policy For the Future*, Vol. 1 of the 'Entrepreneurship for the Future' series (Stockholm: Swedish Foundation for Small Business Research, 2001), p. 70.

Figure 12.1   Linking Entrepreneurship and Economic Growth

OBJECTIVES

Having a strategy implies having objectives and targets, and therein lies a problem for policy-makers. The objectives of entrepreneurship or small business strategies are often not explicit. European Union publications (such as the White Paper *Growth, Competitiveness, Employment: The Challenge and Ways Forward in the 21st Century,* 1993) have emphasised the objectives of employment growth, economic growth and competitiveness of enterprises, and these appear to have had some impact on member states' policies. Nevertheless, to be able to understand and evaluate strategies, the objectives must be explicit. Often they are not.

Storey claims that the objectives of public policies to assist small firms are rarely specified directly.[5] Instead, it is necessary for analysts to infer objectives by observing the policies in operation, rather than by finding them being clearly stated as a coherent response to an agreed role that government plays. According to de Koning, Snijders and Vianen[6] this is true of most European countries. Inferring objectives is made harder by the frequent failure of policy-makers to distinguish between means and ends. However, the following objectives appear to be generally agreed:

- increased wealth through economic growth;
- job creation;
- increased competition;
- promotion of and spread of innovation and technology;
- greater diversification and choice;
- revitalisation of traditional sectors/international competitiveness;
- expanding and strengthening the production chain;
- more efficient markets;
- greater social cohesion (including removal of discrimination).

ILLUSTRATION 12.1
The common objectives of 'small firm'* policy
···

The objectives of government SME policies – intermediate and final, stated and unstated – are likely to be one or more of the following:

1   Increase employment
2   Increase number of start-ups
3   Promote use of advisors
4   Increase competition
5   Promote 'efficient' markets
6   Promote technology diffusion
7   Increase wealth
8   Get elected

David Storey[7]

* Here the term 'small firm policy' covers the full range of policies including both those for entrepreneurship and those for small business.

Organisation, confusion and churn

Another problem which, at least in the UK, can make it hard to identify objectives is articulated by Perren *et al.*[8] as:

> a plethora of organisations and initiatives that have been identified as having some part to play in this area … The continuing churn and name changes adds to the challenge.
>
> The majority of the organisations identified and many of the initiatives are funded through the public purse, either fully or through part subsidy. Therefore the government

is largely responsible for the volume and fragmentation of organisations and initiatives in the area. Indeed the inflexibility of funding regimes often appears to encourage the development of new initiatives even if there are similar schemes already in operation. The aim may have been to respond to perceived needs, but instead it appears to have resulted in a tangled and confusing assortment of dislocated organisations and initiatives ... Many organisations in the area appear to be driven by government agendas and funding rather than any direct demand from SMEs themselves.

Informants, and by implication their organisations, appear to have a relatively narrow sphere of knowledge and relationships ... They can be seen as occupying micro-worlds that are embedded within a wider system of which they have partial knowledge. No single organisation emerges as providing a central bridge between the various ... worlds. The inevitable consequence is that any new initiatives run the risk of being developed in isolation from what presently exists.

While it might seem surprising to some people that apparently little regard should be paid in this way to the consumers' needs, this is yet another example of market forces. If the government is funding the initiatives, then the government is the customer. It is not surprising therefore that the organisations delivering initiatives pursue the money and follow the customer's agenda, not that of the consumers.

The result however is a small firms policy (and it is still largely about small businesses) that has been described as 'a patchwork quilt'[9] and 'an excess of loosely connected and apparently uncoordinated policy initiatives shooting off in all directions, generating noise and interest, but not commensurate light'.[10]

Targets

> Too often the target is anything you happen to hit.
>
> David Storey[11]

While there may be a range of objectives which are generally agreed, it is unusual for governments to set targets for their (enterprise) policies in the sense of measured outputs to be achieved within a given time frame. Some would argue the need for such targets if governmental attention is to be adequately focused on what it is trying to achieve and how it expects to do so. On the other hand it is problematical to argue for targets for interventions when it is not known whether they will work, how they work, within what time scales they will achieve what outputs, or how those outputs will in turn lead to the desired outcomes. To be able to predict outcomes in a system requires knowledge not just of its inputs but also of the process which links them to outputs and in turn to the outcomes. This process, as previously noted, is often not sufficiently understood in the field of enterprise development for it to be possible to predict outcomes accurately.

Nevertheless governments have been attracted occasionally to setting targets for programmes as, without them, it is argued that 'If you don't know were you are trying to go, any road will take you there.' Intermediate targets, or 'milestones' can also provide a form of progress measurement. A recent example of the problems inherent in setting targets was in Scotland when, early in the 1990s, Scottish Enterprise embarked on a 'business birthrate strategy'.

This strategy reflected what was felt to be an entrepreneurial deficit in Scotland compared to the most prosperous areas of the UK and sought an increase in the country's historic rate of new firm formation. The target set was that this rate should be increased by a factor of 3.5, which was not, in the event, achieved. This failure to achieve the predetermined target led many people to regard the strategy itself as a failure, whereas an alternative view was that it appeared to have been more successful in changing attitudes to enterprise and entrepreneurship in a positive direction than in increasing the business birthrate within the relatively short time scale originally set. (See also Case 12.1.)

CASE 12.1
Scotland's birthrate strategy

In Scotland, at the beginning of the 1990s, Scottish Enterprise introduced its 'Birthrate Strategy'. This initiative derived from the knowledge that Scotland's business start-up rate was considerably below that of the most prosperous regions of the UK. The target set was to increase the start-up rate by a factor of 3.5. It was recognised subsequently that setting such an ambitious target (higher than the prosperous South East of England) was counter-productive in that failure to achieve it induced some to view the strategy overall as a failure. A review of the strategy in 2001 concluded that its impact on new firm formation was an increase of around three per cent. In reality, whatever the pressures to achieve an explicit definition of success, it needs to be recognised that creating a more entrepreneurial economy, the real aim of the strategy, requires a focus on the longer term. Moreover an entrepreneurial economy exhibits itself in more than the rate of business start-ups which is only one expression of enterprise.

Nevertheless the Welsh Development Agency has set itself a target of a 65 per cent increase in the rate of new firm formation, and Northern Ireland appears to be setting a target of bringing its start-up rate up to the UK average. These regions seek to overcome what they regard as an 'entrepreneurial deficit' in similar ways to Scotland, including developing processes for, *inter alia*:

- changing attitudes to enterprise and business success;
- assisting careers advisers to articulate self-employment and other business career options;
- altering the National Curriculum to support enterprising attitudes and behaviour;
- promoting business spin-outs and exploitation of intellectual property rights (IPR) from further and higher education;
- supporting social entrepreneurs;
- introducing a business birthrate strategy;
- encouraging entrepreneurship in growth businesses.

Points raised

Scotland's experience showed a downside of setting targets when the socio-economic dynamics are not fully appreciated and of setting a too ambitious time scale for achieving them. Nevertheless the public sector environment is such that similar targets are still being set by others.

It should be recognised that seeking a more entrepreneurial economy requires the changing of attitudes to entrepreneurship and other fundamental changes which themselves are long-term and will not be apparent solely in the number of new firms (or jobs) created and that even these may take many years to be realised. Inevitably measurement of deeper changes will take time and involve other indicators. When setting performance targets, governments and agencies appear to rely often on short-term indicators to measure what is inevitably long-term change. There is therefore a danger that policy and programme implementation become 'target driven' to achieve an easily measurable definition of success in the shorter term. (The possible counterproductive/dysfunctional side effects of such an approach were evident in the UK in the health sector in the year 2001 when the length of hospital waiting lists was seen as a key indicator of the success of its National Health Service. The result however was that patients where taken off the lists by a variety of means, many of which did not actually involve treating them. This had the effect of reducing the numbers on the lists but had nothing to do with providing a better service.) Thus:

adoption of a set of intermediate targets employing traditional measures does not accurately reflect an agency's contribution towards improving the entrepreneurial culture. Such targets do not show the nature of change within an economy and offer little scope for subtlety of focus.[12]

409

ILLUSTRATION 12.2
Government policies are not adequately promoting entrepreneurship[13]

Overall, Danish experts do not believe that government policies are aimed at, or give priority to, entrepreneurship. Entrepreneurship, according to the experts, is subject to political whim (according to ideology) and is used as a regulating means to other ends rather than being an issue of self-standing interest. The experts were also highly critical of those government policies which are aimed at promoting entrepreneurship, claiming that they are short sighted and produce equally short-term initiatives which lack continuity and therefore have less effect. Accordingly, there is a need for a long-term strategy that provides a sense of stability in this area. Further criticism was levelled at the government's lack of concern about the administrative burden faced by small firms, the taxation system, a lack of coordination between ministries and a general lack of understanding of entrepreneurship on the part of politicians.

STRUCTURES FOR INTERVENTION

The following description of organisational arrangements focuses primarily on aspects of small business support in the UK, as it serves to highlight the relevant problems and principles which have a wider relevance for the formulation and implementation of entrepreneurship and small business policy in many other countries.

The inability to formulate a coherent policy agenda in the UK is undoubtedly compounded by the fact that policies directly and/or indirectly affecting small business and enterprise are dispersed over several ministries, although this situation is not unique to the UK. It has a special small business office, the Small Firms Division within the Department of Trade and Industry (DTI) and a junior minister with, *inter alia*, a small business responsibility. The division has a role in the formulation of small business policy and a coordination role on small business issues that are the responsibility of other ministries. Small business is however also influenced and affected by the actions of the Department for Education and Skills and the Department of the Environment, Transport and the Regions, not to mention the Treasury (finance and taxation). Guaranteeing consistent and coherent treatment of the sector is made difficult by this dispersal of policies across ministries. As a result, support schemes have tended to grow piecemeal.

An important distinction also has to be made between the formulation of small business policy and its implementation. In the UK, as in many EU countries, the formulation of such policy is very largely determined at the level of central government, while the implementation of measures is achieved through a network of regional agencies. Within the overall framework of policy, these agencies can, and indeed are often expected to, alter the emphasis and priorities of implementation according to local needs and circumstances. Indeed this change towards decentralisation of the delivery of support services has been a significant trend in many countries over recent years. In the UK, for the most part, the public sector business support structure has been undergoing yet further restructuring and refocusing as described below. This constant process of change, which is intended to produce greater effectiveness and efficiency in support, is viewed by some as self-defeating in that structures are not allowed to settle. Until April 2001 the situation which prevailed was one which included such agencies as the Training and Enterprise Councils (TECs) in England and Wales and the Local Enterprise Companies (LECs) in Scotland. In addition regional and local authorities contribute a network of support services while Scottish Enterprise (SE) in Scotland and the Welsh Development Agency (WDA) in Wales have countrywide jurisdictions like their Northern Ireland counterpart: Invest Northern Ireland, which now includes the former Local Enterprise Development Unit (LEDU), Industrial Development Board (IDB) and Industrial Research and Technology Unit (IRTU).

The TECs and LECs were complemented in Great Britain by the establishment of the DTI-initiated Business Links in England, by Business Connect in Wales and by Business Shops in Scotland. Business Links are funded by the DTI, but this funding came through the TEC network, which was the responsibility of the then Department for Education and Employment. TECs and Business Links therefore found themselves under the direction of two different government departments.

The UK government announced in its 1999 budget its intention to establish a new Small Business Service (SBS). The SBS was subsequently launched in April 2000 to provide a single organisation within government dedicated to promoting the interests of small firms. Its chief executive reports to the Secretary of State for Trade and Industry. In addition, the chief executive is supported by a Small Business Council and a Small Business Investment Task Force (and see Illustration 12.3).

ILLUSTRATION 12.3
The UK Small Business Service (SBS)

The objectives of the SBS are:
- to provide a strong voice for small firms at the heart of Government;
- to simplify and improve the quality and coherence of public support for small businesses;
- to help small firms deal with regulation, compliance, and to ensure that small firms' interests are properly considered in future regulation.

In addition, the SBS aims to 'promote enterprise across society and particularly in under-represented and disadvantaged groups'.[14] It will develop a single gateway for business advice, enabling businesses to access an extensive range of information via the internet or the telephone.

In March 2001 a new Business Links network was launched, reducing the number of Business Links from 81 to 45 as part of the SBS's drive to streamline and improve the network of organisations running business support services.

In January 2001 the SBS launched its strategy paper *Think Small First* outlining a framework for Government support for UK SMEs. It highlighted three priority areas:

- the prevailing culture and environment, including macro-economic stability and the policy environment;
- the regulatory framework for business;
- support for business at each stage of the business life cycle, including people, skills, advice, workspace, IT, finance and international trade.

Its overall aim is that by 2005, 'the UK should be the best place in the world to start and grow a business'. The SBS also runs national initiatives to help small firms, such as the Small Firms Loan Guarantee Scheme (SFLGS) and grants for technology transfer.

Business support in Scotland, Wales and Northern Ireland

The SBS's services are largely offered only in England, unless it is responsible for delivering specific schemes which it is agreed should continue on a UK-wide basis.

Scotland has its own business support structure in place through Scottish Enterprise and Highlands and Islands Enterprise. The Scottish Parliament and Executive are trying to create a simpler and more cohesive structure and to improve support for small businesses. For example, the Enterprise Networks are being reviewed, Local Enterprise Fora are being established, services are being brought together under the Small Business Gateway brand, and a Business Growth Unit and Business Growth Fund have been established.

In Wales, the Business Connect network is a single gateway to business support for small firms. The management has recently been strengthened by the establishment of a business led Management Board, Business Connect Wales Ltd. This development is one part of the agenda to improve the existing support network.

In Northern Ireland, the Local Enterprise Development Unit (LEDU) within the Department of Enterprise, Trade and Investment was the dedicated agency for small business development. It had a network of local offices providing advice to new and existing businesses. LEDU also offered financial assistance to businesses and to a range of other organisations which had an enterprise agenda within Northern Ireland. Since April 2002 LEDU has merged with both the Industrial Development Board of Northern Ireland, which provided support for bigger businesses and inward investment, and the Industrial Research and Technology Unit to provide one comprehensive business support network. The new body is known as Invest Northern Ireland and is a company limited by guarantee which is intended to give it greater flexibility than if it were part of the Civil Service.

Source: Based on *Finance for Small Firms: An Eighth Report* (London: Bank of England, 2001), pp. 21–2.

The SBS, although at an early stage of its life, is to be the subject of further restructuring due to a review of the Department of Trade and Industry to which it reports. The main aim appears to be the desire to separate its policy and regulatory functions from its business support functions. Illustration 12.4 highlights some of the key issues inherent in developing a strategy in this field (and see also Case 12.2).

ILLUSTRATION 12.4
Letter from the Chief Executive of the Small Business Service to the Business Links Network

20 November 2001
THE DTI REVIEWS: IMPLICATIONS FOR THE SBS
Patricia Hewitt [Secretary of State for Trade and Industry] has announced today the main outcome of the DTI Review. It will have significant implications for the SBS – hence this note.

Overview
1   The key points are:
* Overall the structure within the DTI will be streamlined with four mainline Directorates General (DGs).
* Ministers wish in future to draw a clearer distinction between the SBS function of providing world class business support, and the SBS function of lobbying within Government for a better deal for SMEs on regulation and policy issues. The first is essentially a service provided to individual customers; and the second is a service on behalf of the generality of SMEs.

413

- The SBS will continue to be an agency but reflecting the two functions above will have two reporting lines within a restructured DTI. The 'business support' function will report to the new DG Business Relationship Management & Business Support and form a key part of that group. The 'policy and regulation' function, in contrast, will report into the DG for Competitive Frameworks.
- There will also be some operational changes within both functions. On business support, Ministers have decided that they do not wish Government Offices to be engaged in the delivery of business support. The SBS will, therefore, be taking over from the Government Offices the responsibility for Enterprise grants and the regional delivery of SMART [a grant scheme for SME technology development].
- On the policy and regulation function, Ministers want to see us making more use of the Small Business Council and its Chair in particular – with the latter becoming the personal embodiment of the 'strong voice' role. This is a recognition of the dilemma in which we have found ourselves – trying on the one hand to work within Government to achieve a change in behaviour whilst also being expected to shout publicly about our success.

Why are these changes being made?

2   Ministers' starting point has been their wish to build on the achievements of the SBS to date and strengthen it further. They want to see improved delivery of small business support as well as engaging DTI more widely in 'Think Small First' principles.

3   We will therefore continue to develop our range of services under the Business Link brand. In addition, Ministers wish Government Offices (GOs) to concentrate on more policy-focussed activities, so it no longer makes sense for them to have service delivery functions. With the exception of Regional Selective Assistance cases (which are going to the RDAs [Regional Development Agencies]), the logical home for GO business support activity is the SBS. There are personnel issues here for the Government Offices and David Higham of the Government Office North West is leading a working group to take this forward, with SBS representation. We are unlikely to be talking about large numbers of people joining the SBS – perhaps a handful in each region – but we will need to consider carefully how best to integrate this with what we are doing already.

4   The development of the Whitehall-facing work of the SBS, together with the SBC, are potentially more complex. On this side, DTI Ministers themselves wish to play an active role in handling both policy and casework in support of Think Small First. They also wish to see the SBC Chair used in the strong voice role, much as Lord Haskins operates on regulation generally, carrying the confidence of business, in that they know he is

not subject to the constraints of being a civil servant. We will be working up this model as it develops to see how it can best be taken forward.

Implications for the way we work

5   The implications for SBS staff will vary – but we will all still be part of one organisation with a single vision to make the UK the best place in the world to start and grow a business.

6   But there will, in essence, be in future two reporting lines. For business support issues, including issues about the service delivery of regulations, the business support reporting line will clearly dominate. Equally, promoting Think Small First to government departments is clearly a policy and regulation function as part of the DTI's work on competitive frameworks.

7   A number of individuals may find they use both lines – for example the Investment Directorate may well want to lobby Treasury Ministers on new tax breaks for SMEs, while simultaneously be developing new services for our SME customers. But this sort of approach is essential if 'joined-up Government' is to work – and I have no hesitations about the SBS staff being able to cope effectively with the challenges of the new structure. I certainly do not rule out internal organisational changes as we work up the detail of the new approach but I doubt those changes need be extensive.

My own position

8   Given the proposed changes in reporting arrangements and the strong desire within DTI to reduce the number of DGs, I have decided not to seek an extension of my contract when it expires in March. As you all know, I retain a strong commitment to my previous work and to my family base in Newcastle and I have never seen myself as having a long-term career in London. So I always knew I would be leaving at some point.

9   I have not achieved everything I would have wished in the two years but, with your enthusiastic support, we have achieved a great deal in fighting off some of the wilder new ideas for regulation, and I think that the restructured Business Link Service has the potential to be the world class service that we have been seeking. I shall certainly want to keep closely in touch!

Final comments

There is still an important job to do for SBS and its stakeholders. I hope that we can continue to work together to build on the achievements of the last 18 months.

With best wishes

David Irwin

Source: Letter written by David Irwin, chief executive of the Small Business Service, dated 20 November 2001. Reproduced with permission from the Small Business Service.

The business support landscape was further altered in England by the creation of business-led Regional Development Agencies (RDAs) and the Learning and Skills Council for England (LSC). The RDAs are an attempt to give greater influence at a regional level to economic policy. The LSC, effective from April 2001, is the leading body in post 16 years learning and skills development and operates through 47 local arms known as local LSCs. They have a key role in human resource development for small businesses and replace the Training and Enterprise Councils (TECs)

The role of Business Links, and their counterparts, is to create partnerships of providers of small business services in their region. Such providers include LSCs, chambers of commerce, local authorities and enterprises agencies. The aim is to ensure that the small business consumer is presented with a seamless collection of services accessed through 'one-stop shops', or through 'first-stop shops'.

Although greater efficiency, professionalism, and quality of impact are believed to be possible where services are concentrated, bringing together individuals and organisations offering support services into close physical proximity is difficult to achieve and very unusual. Mostly, what is achieved or sought is in fact a 'first-stop shop' where users can receive advice and information from a range of services immediately available and can be signposted to those others believed to be most useful to them.

Ideally, of course, the aim of Business Links and similar organisations should be to create a service based upon effective networking amongst each other. Ultimately what is envisaged by some is technologically linked service providers that can 'link clients with overseas trade partners, help them find full- or part-time staff, introduce them to business "angels" offering equity investments or furnish them with whatever else the company of 2001 might require'.[15] However, they have some way to go before such an ideal can be realistically tackled and for the moment the expected benefits of Business Links and their equivalents would appear to focus on:

- bringing the main suppliers of enterprise support together in partnership arrangements so as to bring about their meaningful integration and coherence and for the client, a single point of contact;
- upgrading the quality of services and support;
- having a strong and visible network across Britain with a high degree of physical concentration of supply partners in each location.

Two different approaches have been evolved for such networking: Business Links in England aim to be 'one-stop shops', while Business Shops in Scotland are based on a 'first-stop shop' approach. The distinction between the concept of a 'one-stop shop' and a 'first-stop shop' is however often missed. While both derive from a desire to reduce proliferation and dispersal of support services and to make accessing them easier and less confusing for the potential user, the 'one-stop-shop' approach aims to concentrate them, or at least their representatives, into one location. On the other hand the 'first-stop shop' concept assumes that it will often not be feasible to concentrate all the relevant sources of support in this way. Instead it is suggested that there should be initial contact points, the 'first-step shops', which will either offer assistance directly if they can, or will be able to signpost the inquirer to the right place for specific assistance. The aim is that the knowledge throughout the network about the other organisations in it should be such that an inquirer to one, if he or she doesn't get the right place initially, will be so directed that his or her second stop will be correct. (The right place might therefore be the second place to be contacted which is why this approach is also sometimes referred to as the 'second-stop shop' concept.) This is a different approach from a 'one-stop shop' and indeed it has been further observed that one does not get a 'second-stop shop' by aiming at a 'one-stop shop' and missing.

Part of the problem for the 'one stop-shop' is that, while government-organised or government-controlled organisations can be instructed by government to behave in a particular way, others cannot. Because of the potential social and other benefits of enterprise and small business, many other organisations have sought to offer support or assistance. They are more likely to want to maintain their independence and sense of identity and are therefore more likely to resist conforming to the mould of a 'one-stop shop'. Indeed there would seem to be an element of incongruity in requiring organisations, whose aim is essentially to support enterprise and its associated varieties, themselves to conform to an externally determined strategy or mode of operation.

> The notion of a one-stop shop is, for serious entrepreneurial regions, simply untenable.
>
> Ron Botham[16]

APPROACHES

There are essentially two broad approaches to achieving entrepreneurship or small business policy objectives, however ambiguously those objectives are stated:

- The first approach is the one that concentrates on the creation of a favourable environment for business creation and growth. This policy approach results in measures to liberalise trade, to deregulate, to privatise, and to reform legal and taxation regimes as well as to create a positive climate to reinforce a culture of enterprise. Not all these measures are designed with only, or even mainly, small businesses in mind, but a number are aimed at addressing distortions or areas of market failure that are believed to harm smaller businesses specifically.
- The second approach is that of supporting the actual start-up and growth of individual businesses by providing direct assistance to the individuals or businesses concerned.

417

These two approaches are not mutually exclusive, and in nearly all countries they are adopted simultaneously. This was for instance specifically acknowledged in the UK by the former Department of Employment, which stated:

> There are three strands in the Government's approach to small firms. First, and of most importance, the role of the Government is to ensure that small firms can flourish in conditions of fair competition and to create space and incentives for enterprise by minimising taxation regulations and red tape. Second, the Government strongly supports and reinforces the change to more positive social attitudes towards the small business sector. Third, the Government helps to fill gaps in the supply side by providing commercial services for small firms, largely to improve their access to finance, information, professional advice and training. Wherever possible the Government's approach is provided in partnership with the private sector.[17]

A multi-strand approach is not however universally accepted. It has for instance been argued by many, on the basis of numerous surveys, that the main factors which restrict the growth of businesses relate to the macro-economy. Accordingly the Confederation of British Industry's (CBI's) SME Council has claimed:

> It is through the creation of a healthy economy and conditions for growth that employment will be generated ... the CBI therefore believes that Governments should focus on creating the right conditions for SMEs to start and grow rather than introducing individual policy objectives aimed at market distortions.[18]

Policies and instruments

To achieve the objective of intervention, policies and instruments are adopted. The main UK government small business policies have been categorised as shown in Table 12.1.

The annual reports of the European Observatory for SMEs have distinguished between policy fields and instruments. To quote one of them:

> Although the instrumental design of schemes aiming at the same target can differ by Member State, the fields SME policy measures focus on tend to converge towards a set of nine fields of activity. These are:

Start-ups and growth	Research and Development	Capital and finance
Investment	Exports	Cooperation
Sub-contracting	Education	Job creation[19]

Table 12.5, later in this chapter, provides an overview of actual and planned new developments in the national SME policies of many European countries in the period 1997 to 1999.

Table 12.1 UK government SME policies

Macro policies
- Interest rates
- Taxation
- Public spending
- Inflation

Deregulation and simplification
- Cutting 'red tape'
- Legislative exemptions
- Legal form

Sectoral and problem-specific policies
- High-tech firms
- Rural enterprises
- Community enterprises
- Cooperatives
- Ethnic businesses
- Women-owned businesses

Finance assistance
- Business Expansion Scheme / Enterprise Investment Scheme
- Small Firms Loan Guarantee Scheme
- Venture Capital Funds
- Grants

Indirect assistance
- Information and advice (including the High Growth Start-up Programme)
- Training
- Consultancy initiative / mentoring
- Network development (for example for owners and business angels)

Relationships
- DTI Small Firms division
- Lobbyist / policy formulation

Source: Adapted from D. J. Storey, *Understanding the Small Business Sector* (London: Routledge, 1994), p. 269.

The instruments of intervention identified, each of which can be applied to one or more fields, are:

- direct subsidies or grants;
- subsidised loans;
- loan guarantee / participation;
- tax relief;
- service;
- export guarantees;
- subsidised start-up for unemployed;

419

- subsidised personnel;
- subsidised buildings, power, communication networks, sites.

All the instruments of intervention listed above are geared towards the second of the two approaches described earlier: intervention at the level of specific businesses or individuals. The Observatory report also indicates that, of these instruments, financial inducements are the most popular form of intervention in support of many policy fields. Inducements commonly take the form of direct subsidies, grants or loan guarantees, and subsidies are used to reduce the cost of loans, employees, premises and various services.

Van Wijngaarden and Van der Horst offer a similar framework. They identify the most important 'fields' and 'instruments' (measures taken in the different policy fields to achieve the objectives)[20] as shown in Table 12.2. Again, the fields are a mix of more general and specific areas, and combine market segments and functions with processes. Indeed, information and counselling appear both as a policy field and as an instrument!

Table 12.2   Policy fields and instruments

Field	Instrument(s)
General tax facilities	
Regional development	Financial means (guarantees on loans, venture capital,
Technology and R & D	insurance)
Export	
Employment	Fiscal regulations (tariffs, exemptions)
Start-ups	
Information and counselling	Information and counselling
Finance	
Education	Training
Business licensing	
Administrative simplification	Others (programmes and legislation)
Environment / energy	

Source: Adapted from K. de Lind Van Wijngaarden and R. Van der Horst, 'A Comparison of SME Policy In the EU Member States', *Business Growth and Profitability* 1996; 2(1): 40.

The above frameworks make no real attempt to relate intervention measures to the stages in the growth of a business, as described in Chapter Seven, or to the pre-start-up stage, which influences the number of new businesses created. Therefore the framework shown in Table 12.3 is offered in an attempt to categorise fields and instruments according to a stages-of-development model of business formation and growth. It suffers from the limitations associated with such modelling, summarised in Chapter Six, but it is intended to assist by providing greater coherence across target markets, ends and means.

While instruments (support measures) are general in description, the table outlines a representative range of the very many variations that apply. It is apparent that certain measures, such as information and counselling, finance and training, are available throughout most or all of the development stages of a business. However, both the nature and extent of delivery mechanisms can change at each stage.

Table 12.3 A taxonomy of enterprise initiatives

Stage of business	Policy field or need	Instrument
Culture	A positive, encouraging and supportive environment	Community programmes Capacity-building Role models Enterprise in education
Pre-start	Ideas	Spin-off ideas Technology transfer Ideas generation workshops and publications
	Small business know-how (accounts, finance, selling, marketing and so on)	Small business skills training Training trainers
	'Know-who' networks	Networking advice Network access points, for both business and technical assistance
	Advice	Pre-start counselling/mentoring
Start-up: external	Customers	Purchasing initiatives
	Suppliers	Local sourcing initiatives Trade directories
	Advice / consultancy: business	Business expertise available Coordination of third party provision (Business Links) Training, counselling and mentoring Websites
	Advice / consultancy: technical	Technical advice, research and so on
	Networks	Business clubs Export clubs
	Information	Databases Internet portals
	Producing the business plan	Business plan services
	Premises	Incubation centres Managed workspaces Business/science parks
Start-up: internal	Finance	Grants, loans, loan guarantee schemes Business angel networks
	Market expertise Administration expertise Financial management Employment expertise Company formation	Training services Advice/counselling Mentors

Table 12.3 *continued*

Stage of business	Policy field or need	Instrument
Established	Ideas	Ideas generation workshops Spin-off ideas Technology transfer programmes
	Encouragement	Guidance services, including 'one-stop shops'
	Specialist guidance	Banks, accountants
	Investment	Solicitors
Growth	Market opportunities, including exports	Trade missions Market visits Export development advisers Export credit insurance Market information: trends, contacts and so on
	Product development	Technical advice / support for product development
	Strategic approach	Development courses
	Management skills	Salary support Subsidised staff attachment programmes Benchmarking
	Finance	Grants, loans, and so on Business angel networks
Decline	Confidence Customers Money	Mentors
	Strategic review and planning	Advice and guidance
Termination	Legal and other advice	Provision of advice and counselling
Other dimensions	Business sector	Sector initiatives, including sector-based training
	Business support environment	Information and education
All	Information on small business needs and behaviour	Research coordination Research databases Research centres
	General information and advice	Internet portals and other online assistance
	Legislative and other administrative developments	

A comprehensive framework

To provide a more comprehensive framework, elements of these various illustrations have been combined into the model shown in Table 12.3 to illustrate the fields of intervention for enterprise policy (in its broad sense). Such a model provides a categorisation mechanism with which to analyse and describe small business policy fields, and on which to plot intervention measures. In so doing, no attempt is made at this stage to be prescriptive but merely to describe. Indeed, prescription would require, as already noted, some agreed objectives based on what sort of economy is wanted and the desired role of small business therein (see Chapter 13).

AREAS OF INTERVENTION

The analysis framework in Figure 12.2 is an attempt to highlight the main fields of public policy in enterprise (including entrepreneurship and small business) support, and it includes the broad elements indicated below, which are considered in more detail on the following pages.

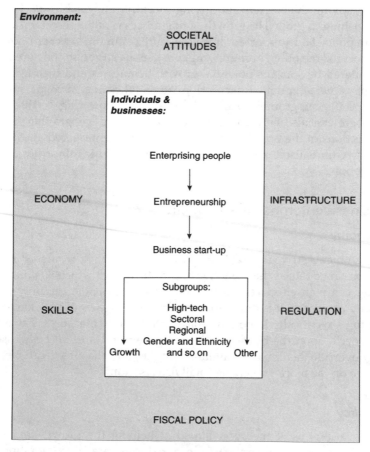

Figure 12.2   Enterprise policy analysis framework

1   The business environment is included. It affects the performance of all firms, not just small businesses, but it is nevertheless crucial to a healthy small business sector, regardless of firm size, motivation or stage of development. Improvement of the business environment, the first of the two broad approaches to small business support, as described above, is defined as comprising six broad categories: the economy, skills, infrastructure, regulations, fiscal policy and societal attitudes.

2   Individuals and their businesses are also included. This field embraces:

(a)   the development of enterprising people (in the broad sense) and the supply of entrepreneurs who start businesses are other areas of intervention (see Illustration 12.5);

(b)   assisting the start-up business in its birth stages and subsequent aftercare. Such assistance can be viewed as critical not only to survival rates but also to the quality and quantity of the subsequent growers;

(c)   removing the barriers and giving incentives to established businesses wishing to grow. The growth of businesses is often perceived as central to policy and support for it is now quite common. Less common is support for the other, non-growing, businesses although they are still considered by some as potential growth businesses and therefore worthy of some attention. Intervention often takes the form of support of specific subgroups such as high-tech or exporting businesses and there can also be a focus on selected sectors, geographic regions or sections of the population which are under-represented and/or which have unrealised potential such as women, ethnic minorities and older people.

The business/enterprise environment

The economy

Most governments strive for stable growth, low inflation, low interest rates, and a steady exchange rate as the economic backcloth against which it is thought that businesses can plan effectively in the context of reasonable certainty of future trading circumstances. It is thus supposed that the impacts of taxation and public spending are critically important policy intervention measures. The effects of the trade cycle upon the birth-, death- and growth-rates of all businesses may generally override the impact of all interventions, and the effects can be particularly severe on the more vulnerable small firms sector.

Fiscal policy

There are various fiscal measures aimed at helping the growth and survival of small businesses. These range from a reduced rate of corporation tax to

ILLUSTRATION 12.5
Issues relevant to an entrepreneurship policy, according to
the Global Entrepreneurship Monitor

1   Promoting entrepreneurship and enhancing the entrepreneurial dynamic of a country should be an integral element of any government's commitment to improving economic well-being.

2   Government policies and programmes targeted specifically on the entrepreneurial sector will have a more significant, direct impact than programmes simply aimed at improving the national business context.

3   To be effective, government programmes designed to encourage and support entrepreneurial activity must be carefully coordinated and harmonised so as to avoid confusion and to enhance their utilisation by those for whom such programmes are designed.

4   Increasing entrepreneurial activity in any country will entail raising the participation level of those outside the most active age group of 25–45 years old.

5   For most GEM countries, the greatest and most rapid gain in firm start-ups will be achieved by increasing the participation of women in the entrepreneurial process.

6   Long-term, sustained enhancement of entrepreneurial activity requires a substantial commitment to and investment in education at the third level.

7   Developing the skills and capabilities required to start a business should be integrated into specific educational and vocational training programmes at all educational levels.

8   Regardless of education level, emphasis should be placed on developing an individual's capacity to recognise and pursue new opportunities.

9   The capacity of a society to accommodate the higher levels of income disparity associated with entrepreneurial activity is a defining feature of a strong entrepreneurial culture.

10 Government and public policy officials and opinion leaders from all spheres have a key role to play in creating a culture that validates and promotes entrepreneurship throughout society.

Source: Authors' interpretation, developed from various reports from the Global Entrepreneurship Monitor (Kansas City, MO: Kauffman Centre for Entrepreneurial Leadership at the Ewing Marion Kauffman Foundation, various years).

inheritance tax concessions and extended value added tax (VAT) exemption thresholds, as well as tax incentives for business angels and investors.

Although, when asked, small business owners will say that they want lower taxes to allow them to keep more of the rewards for enterprise, the relationship between lower taxes (more disposable income) and economic activity does not however appear to be straightforward. For example, Rees and Shah investigated the hours worked by self-employed persons and found that personal and family factors like age and number of children were key determinants.[21] However, when these variables were controlled, they found that the number of hours worked fell when personal taxation rates fell.

Skills

The business need for labour market skills is apparent at all levels from management to operative. The ability to access appropriate skills at affordable prices is an essential ingredient in any supportive economic environment. Small businesses, especially growing ones, would appear to have more acute difficulties in accessing skills. Indeed, small firms would appear to experience genuine problems in dealing with the formalities and legalities of recruitment in an increasingly sophisticated environment. In particular, there is evidence that the small business sector both is reluctant to recruit graduate labour and has difficulty in doing so. Recent changes have however taken place in the UK in the tax treatment of share options, allowing many more firms, and particularly small high-growth companies, to use them as a carrot to attract key staff.

Infrastructure

An efficient and effective infrastructure is needed, including appropriate transportation systems and networks, communication networks and an adequate supply of business premises, appropriately located. Indeed with the knowledge economy becoming all-pervasive, speedy and reliable transfer of more and more information has put increasing pressure on regions and nations to ensure that they are abreast of the latest developments in information and communication technology (ICT) and have the infrastructure to support it.

(De)regulation and administrative simplification

It is noticeable that regulation, and the volume, complexity, rate of change and interpretation of it, or, more colloquially, of 'red tape and bureaucracy', tend to come at or near the top of any list when surveys are made either of the problems of small businesses, or of the constraints on their growth. Clearly, a certain level of regulation is needed to create a healthy business environment; adequate

Table 12.4   The Dirty Dozen

The 12 regulatory provisions which hit UK small firms hardest are reported to be:

- the EU Working Time Directive;
- provisions for parental leave;
- provisions for trade union recognition;
- other aspects of the Employment Relations Act;
- unfair dismissal rules;
- the Disability Discrimination Act;
- the National Minimum Wage;
- time off for study or training for 16 to 18 year olds;
- the Working Families Tax Credit;
- the Asylum and Immigration Act;
- the EU Part-Time Workers Directive;
- tax and payroll burdens.

Source: 'The Dirty Dozen' from by 'Help for Small Firms to Beat Bureaucrats', Clare Oldfield, *The Sunday Times*, 14 November 1999. © Times Newspapers Limited

standards are needed in the areas of health and safety, employment rights, environmental protection and reducing anti-competitive practices, and, as is often claimed, one man's right is another man's burden. Nevertheless, it has been argued that statutory regulations in the above areas and in taxation, statistical reporting and company registration are disproportionately burdensome for small businesses. It is asserted that employment legislation prevents small businesses from employing more labour, and that requirements such as the statutory audit for incorporated businesses discourages them from availing themselves of this legal form of business. VAT compliance, data protection legislation and other statutory requirements have also been listed as barriers. However, it has been suggested that, while these and other burdens have been identified by lobby groups as barriers to small business development, they are not necessarily perceived as such by all small businesses. (See also Table 12.4.)

Governments across the world pay at least lip service to reducing the burdens on small business. In the UK there has been increasing emphasis on deregulation since the publication of the White Paper *Lifting the Burden* in 1985. The OECD and the EU also have task forces or equivalents examining the issue. The UK established the Deregulation Unit within the DTI in 1985, and in 1994 the Deregulation Task Force was set up. In 1997 it was renamed the 'Better Regulation Task Force'. In November 2001, the DTI announced 'the appointment of a small business equivalent of Lord Haskins [who was the chair of the government's Better Regulation Task Force] with the responsibility to look into regulations impacting significantly on small and medium-sized enterprises'.[22] The results of these and other initiatives suggest that increasing attention will be paid to:

- measuring the impact of new regulations on small businesses;
- critically examining existing legislative measures affecting business with a view to eliminating many of them;
- increasing emphasis on making regulations 'goal-based' and not over-prescriptive (that is, emphasising outcomes, not processes, in enforcement procedures).

There is a history, nevertheless, of slow and doubtful progress in these areas which is reflected in reports such as:

One proposal is a crackdown on enforcing strict rules on consultation over proposed legislation. This would introduce a new transparency to policy-making that is likely to be uncomfortable for ministers and civil servants. Regulatory impact assessments have been ignored by several departments, a failure which is being investigated by the National Audit Office.[23]

Actions currently proposed in the UK include offering payroll services for new and small businesses, extending the lower turnover limit for VAT registration and making it more difficult for disgruntled employees to take firms to tribunals.[24] In the European Union efforts are being made to cut start-up costs for new businesses. Contrasts are being drawn between the United States where it 'takes about a week and costs $500 to set up a business' and Europe where 'on average it takes 12 weeks and costs $2000'.[25] Illustration 12.6 elaborates further on this issue.

ILLUSTRATION 12.6
Setting up a private limited liability company
....

In the Netherlands, setting up a private limited liability company takes three to four times as long as it does in the United Kingdom or the United States. These disparities can to some extent be explained by differences between Anglo-Saxon and Dutch Law systems. But apart from this, a study of international laws and regulations reveals a number of differences which in the Netherlands present bigger obstacles to entrepreneurs wanting to start a new company. For example, the Netherlands requires a mandatory minimum capital of NLG 40,000 (before conversion to Euros). Countries such as Australia, Ireland and the United Kingdom apply only a symbolic amount. In the US, there is no minimum capital requirement at all. It is striking that some branch organisations in the Netherlands impose added requirements with regard to operational activities. In the transport sector, for example, this NLG 40,000 is imposed per existing truck rather than per new private limited liability company.[26]

> The time authorities need for processing other applications highlights additional aspects of the administrative burden in the European Union. Lundström and Stevenson[27] note that this particularly holds for the permits companies often need for types of machinery and other capital items. The longer authorities take to issue these permits, the longer the investments are delayed. They point out that the French Government took a bold step on this issue and decided that any application not answered within three months shall be considered granted. On the other hand, the United Kingdom abolished some regulations related to permits while the Belgian and Danish governments have passed acts according to which any proposed legislation must be checked regarding its administrative impact on business before passing through parliament (with an attachment which indicates the impact).

It is not the purpose of this chapter to argue for or against regulation; however, it is worth noting the opinion that 'there needs to be a more coherent and systematic investigation of the precise nature of the disadvantages facing small firms in this domain as the basis for a policy thrust',[28] the aim of which is to remove or at least reduce the disadvantages affecting small businesses as against large ones.

Societal attitudes

A government's position is usually that it supports and encourages more positive attitudes in society to enterprise, entrepreneurship and the small business sector. The phrase most commonly used to describe the approach is 'creating an enterprise culture'. Certainly, the language of enterprise has never been more popular in politics, economics and business. Critics, however, say it has simply become a synonym for success or a political slogan or is a searching for a Heffalump – a creature of supposed vast importance that no one has ever actually seen.

The different interpretations of the word 'enterprise' and aspects of its development have already been described in earlier chapters. It is true to say, nevertheless, that governmental efforts in this area have concentrated generally on the 'narrow' approach of business entrepreneurialism. The broad 'educational' interpretations have not been ignored, but little of significance has been done. A notable exception in the UK was the 'Enterprise in Higher Education' initiative of 1990–1995 in the universities and, while an Enterprise Bill was introduced in November 2001, it cannot be said to address many of the aspects which underpin an entrepreneurial culture, especially amongst the young.

The lack of an enterprise culture has been variously identified through, for example, low business start-up and growth rates, significant external ownership of businesses, an over large public sector and high unemployment rates. Specifically, policy in this area would seek to create a climate that enhances perceptions of the feasibility and desirability of entrepreneurship. Overall, it is accepted that the image of enterprise in a community will impact on the perception of enterprise on the part of potentially enterprising people within it. The instruments used in fostering such a policy include publicity campaigns, highlighting successful role models, business start-up and awareness programmes, and seminars, information and advice.

ILLUSTRATION 12.7
Enterprise education

The view is often articulated that the supply of entrepreneurs will ultimately be increased more if awareness of the feasibility and desirability of starting a business is established at a young age. Thus the education system is assisted in fostering, supporting and encouraging those interested in knowing what it is like to run a business. Young Enterprise, a mostly privately funded charity, is the leading UK organisation engaged in this process. Its aim is to develop 'enterprise skills' and currently its major programme involves setting up and running mini-businesses.

Similarly, government and others have assisted entrepreneurship programmes for final year undergraduates. In 1999 the UK's Office for Science and Technology (part of the DTI) funded selected universities through a competitive tendering process, to expand entrepreneurship education across their courses especially among students of science and technology. The UK government is also carrying out a review into how to nurture an enterprise culture through schools and colleges.

The perceived potential role for education to develop enterprise is being increasingly stressed. The Enterprise Directorate General of the EU claims that general knowledge about business and entrepreneurship needs to be taught right through primary, secondary and tertiary education, 'Yet many of them (school leavers) know little of enterprise and almost nothing of the opportunities offered by entrepreneurship'.[29] A Danish report[30] sums up the views of many as follows:

> The experts in each one of the 21 GEM (Global Entrepreneurship Monitor) nations consistently placed the provision of individuals with high quality entrepreneurship education as a high priority. Danish experts do not believe that the current education system provides adequately for the promotion of entrepreneurship. They believe that the education system does

not focus sharply enough on entrepreneurship and that there is a paucity of formal courses in the subject. Furthermore, they were of the opinion that the quality of both teachers and the material taught in entrepreneurship is low. According to the experts, there are more opportunities for entrepreneurship in Denmark than there are people equipped and skilled to take advantage of them. Other programmes have targeted youth, the unemployed, corporate employees, women and the disabled.

There have also been examples of programmes that have attempted to improve a community's or society's self-image and self-confidence, and to change it from a 'can't do' to a 'can do' attitude. This has been done on the grounds that such an improvement will in turn make it easier for other enterprise ideas to take root. To use a horticultural analogy (see also Figure 12.3) such schemes aim to prepare the soil so that seeds are more likely to germinate in it and so that it is better able to support and sustain any seedlings that may then appear.

Individuals and businesses: the enterprise process

The second broad approach to policy described earlier in this chapter is that of promoting the enterprise process by interventions targeted at the level of the individual business or at the person preparing to start a business. This is in contrast to the interventions just considered which are at the meso- or macro-economic level – albeit there is no clear division between where one approach ends and the other begins.

These interventions, aimed either at individual people or at individual businesses, generally target segments or subgroups of this population categorised by age, by stage of development, by business sector, by geographic region, by market area, or by type of ownership: categories where unique sets of problems and/or opportunities are perceived to exist. Some of these categories are described further below.

Pre-start-up

The pre-start-up stage could be perceived as including all those who have not even considered self-employment or business creation as a career option. However enterprise policies addressing this issue are considered under the earlier heading of 'Societal attitudes'. Instead attention is focused here on those disposed to become entrepreneurs. There are interventions to help people who are

Figure 12.3 Where to apply limited resources to maximise the benefits returned

thinking about, or preparing for, business start-up. The most common form of intervention in this area is probably business skills training in its various forms, but there are also interventions to assist and guide market research, and schemes to help with early product/service development. Included in the latter are initiatives that try to assist inventors to meet business people capable of understanding the potential of new ideas. In the field of ideas, however, a phenomenon encountered by many who offer assistance is the 'mad inventor', someone who believes that his or her invention is wonderful and the basis for certain commercial success. He or she believes that the 'hard' bit has been done, so all that is needed is help with the 'easy' bit of turning the invention into a thriving business. In this situation the appropriate intervention can be to disillusion the inventor and to reduce his or her unrealistic expectations.

There are also variations of intervention that help with the sourcing, identification and development of business ideas, and with the formation of enterprise teams to combine the different strengths of individuals in order to promote one successful venture. The Welsh Development Agency in its national business start-up programme seeks to use:

'a realistic approach based on 'the escalator principle', i.e. working with individuals in the process of developing an idea, starting the business and providing the necessary support needed for that business to achieve its full potential. It is intended to move away (from) a purely programmatic approach and instead to focus on continuity of service for new starts through a National Business Centre Network which is to be created under the aegis of Business Connect which will deliver the 'Gateway' service.[31]

Start-ups

It has been noted that, while a healthy level of start-ups is essential for new ideas, innovation, competitiveness and the overall vibrancy of the economy, policy emphasis through most of the 1990s was increasingly placed on the perceived quality of start-ups, such as their potential for growth or for exporting. It has been argued that non-discriminating support to start-ups is counter-productive, because many will fail, and that this implies that a more selective approach to business support should be adopted. (The arguments for and against this were described in Chapter Eight.) Thus in Britain the role of the Business Links and the TECs and LECs was to offer, as the 1990s progressed, most support to firms with the motivation to grow (and to target companies with between ten and 200 employees). Under the Business Start-up Scheme (formerly the Enterprise Allowance Scheme), support for start-ups was delivered uniformly across all areas, but under the Single Regeneration Budget (and more recently with the Government's proposals for 'Challenge Budgets') support for start-ups was not guaranteed. Since the creation of the Small Business Service, however, there is evidence of a more balanced approach as the attention of political leaders becomes more focused on the volume of start-ups as well as their 'quality'. Government policy has reverted to its previous position, offering practical support (in the form of advice and training) to all start-ups.

Interventions in the field of start-ups have included financial assistance, training, networking, information, advice and counselling. They have also included the provision of workspace geared specifically to meet the needs of small businesses. This has taken the form of managed workspace ('MWS'— premises with easy leasing terms and, typically, with the availability of central services such as secretarial support and business advice), often on attractive leasing terms. In addition, there have been variations on the business incubator concept. Special attention has also been paid to enabling the small business sector to take advantage of the information and communication technology revolution.

High-tech businesses

Probably the greatest and most salient shift in SME policy over the last 15 years has been a shift from trying to preserve SMEs that are confronted with a cost disadvantage due to size inherent scale disadvantages, towards promoting the start-up and viability of small entrepreneurial firms involved in the commercialisation of knowledge, or knowledge-based SMEs.

Zoltan Acs and David Audretsch[32]

Businesses in the high-tech category are believed to have particular problems needing tailored solutions. Specific support for them is now a strong feature in many countries because of their contribution to innovation and their potential for growth, and because they are likely to be the seeds for the new industry sectors of the future. Their particular needs are seen to arise from the relatively high cost of research and development and its associated risks, which makes them unattractive to conservative or risk-averse lending institutions. High-tech businesses can also have the potential for fast growth, which means that the need for finance will be even greater. Such problems are frequently compounded by other aspects of these businesses: for example

- a value which is often linked primarily to longer-term growth, based on scientific knowledge and intellectual property;
- a lack of tangible assets in their initial development to use as collateral when significant up-front investment may be needed (and little evidence that the businesses can trade profitably);
- products with little or no track record, untested in the marketplace and possibly subject to a high rate of obsolescence;
- the funders' lack of understanding of the potential of the products or processes, which is due very often to their specialist nature; and
- their owners' frequent failure to pay enough attention to communicating meaningfully in a non-technical way.

The overall result is that funders have difficulties in assessing the viability of the proposals, particularly in terms of judging the technology, estimating prospective demand and quantifying the risks.

Since the 1980s, therefore, a range of schemes have been introduced to help high-tech businesses financially and in other ways. Examples of such help are shown in Illustration 12.8.

ILLUSTRATION 12.8
Public sector initiatives for high-tech businesses

Various public sector initiatives and fiscal incentives have been provided in the UK in recent years to encourage greater investment in high-tech small firms. These include initiatives aimed specifically at improving the provision of small amounts of risk capital at the seed and start-up stages, and at tackling both demand- and supply-side constraints. Examples are given below.

- Clustering – US high-tech companies are believed to have benefited greatly from the clustering of firms and finance providers together, in for example Silicon Valley. The DTI is developing plans to use a regional innovation fund to facilitate the formation of local clusters of high-technology companies. RDAs (Regional Development Agencies) are also being encouraged by government to continue developing existing and embryonic clusters.

- Business incubators – these are viewed as an effective means of encouraging innovation and the wider dissemination of technology. UK Business Incubation (UKBI) was established in 1998, jointly funded by the public and private sectors.
- Business Links and innovation and technology counsellors – all Business Links offer an innovation and technology counselling service and most employ experienced independent counsellors.
- Enterprise Centres – in November 1998 the creation of the Science Enterprise Challenge was announced, targeted on developing entrepreneurial skills among university scientists and engineers. Eight enterprise centres were established in universities around the country, with the help of a £25 million contribution from the Government. A further public sector allocation has added to the number of centres and a special allocation was made towards the cost of a joint institute to be established by the Massachusetts Institute of Technology and Cambridge University. This is designed to stimulate, *inter alia*, spin-outs from the University's academic base.
- The Small Firms Merit Award for Research and Technology (SMART)—this provides grants of amounts varying from around £2500 to £150,000 to help SMEs to access technology and research, and develop innovative products and processes.
- The Enterprise Fund – with public funds worth £180 million over three years, this has been developed to stimulate the provision of both debt and equity finance to UK SMEs with growth potential. The Fund expects to lever in significant amounts of private sector funding. The Fund, which is administered by the SBS, has four main elements: the UK High-Tech Venture Capital Fund, Regional Venture Capital Funds, the Small Firms Loan Guarantee Scheme (see text) and the National Business Angel Network (NBAN).
- The UK High-Tech Venture Capital Fund is a public/private partnership designed to encourage institutional investors currently not active in this market to invest in the early stage high-technology sector. The Fund Manager, Westport Private Equity, has already secured £105 million from the private sector to go alongside the £20 million from government. Commitments to invest in the early stage high-technology venture capital market have begun.
- Regional Venture Capital Funds – these are another joint public/private partnership initiative. The Government aims to establish at least one Venture Capital Fund, with a minimum fund size of £10 million (both public and private investors), in each English region. The Fund will not be restricted to high-technology investments but they are likely to feature to a considerable extent in their activities. The aim is to increase the supply of equity in amounts of less than £500,000 available to SMEs with growth

potential, whilst stimulating the creation of venture capital funds that will address the 'equity gap'.

- University Challenge Fund – intended to encourage the transfer of science, engineering and technology from the universities into the commercial world and to demonstrate that very early stage investments can be profitable. In conjunction with major charities, the Government is providing £65 million for seedcorn venture capital funds, enabling the universities to develop their business proposals and start-up companies.
- The Enterprise Management Incentive (EMI) Scheme – intended to promote and improve the supply of labour to SMEs in general and technology-based small firms in particular, as well as facilitating the flow of finance to such companies. Since 2000, the EMI Scheme permits tax-advantaged share options up to a total value of £2.5 million to be given in small higher risk companies.
- Taxation of corporate venturing – the Chancellor's 2000 Budget introduced up-front corporation tax relief at 20 per cent on investments by corporate venturers in small higher risk trading companies. The Corporate Venturing Tax Relief Scheme provides tax incentives for corporate equity investment in the same types of companies as are eligible under the Enterprise Investment Scheme (EIS) and Venture Capital Trusts (VCT).
- Tax credit for R&D – an R&D tax credit for SMEs based on the total cost of their R&D expenditure was introduced in 2000.
- EU initiatives – there are a range of European-funded initiatives which will work to increase the supply of funds to high-tech small firms. These include: the European Investment Bank's (EIB's) European Technology Facility, which will support business through business incubators and seed funds; I-TEC, which covers 50 per cent of the costs of administering funds making early stage investments in technologically innovative SMEs; and the EIB's Innovation 2000 Initiative (i2i) which is reorientating lending resources towards the dissemination of innovation, SME development and information and communication technologies. Furthermore, by the end of 2000, the EIB/EIF had invested £20 million in the UK High-Technology Venture Capital Fund. In addition, the EU has adopted a new Multi-Annual Programme for Enterprise and Entrepreneurship (see also Case 12.3).

Source: Based on *Finance for Small Firms: An Eighth Report* (London: Bank of England, 2001), pp. 71–2. With kind permission of the Bank of England.

Geographical areas of disadvantage

Policies have been adopted to assist in the regeneration, through enterprise and small business development, of areas of special disadvantage. Deprivation is a complex issue and the nature and extent of its impact vary, not least between urban and rural areas:

> Deprived areas have particular features which include high mortality rates, poor physical environment, low levels of educational attainment and participation, high crime rates, and poor housing. The promotion of enterprise can play an important role in addressing social exclusion ... It should not, however, be viewed as a panacea for social and financial exclusion. High levels of displacement of existing businesses, the risks involved in setting up in business and the propensity to create marginal businesses are potential limitations to the contribution of small firms in deprived areas.[33]

On the other hand, run down inner cities and depressed rural areas have benefited from initiatives designed to promote 'community enterprises' and cooperatives. In addition, managed workspace has been publicly funded in whole or in part in an attempt to provide localised support that is relevant and real (and visible).

This provision often takes the form of local enterprise agencies, which can become the centrepiece of policies to create a focus for urban or rural regeneration involving local people in their management and activities. Such local roots can greatly strengthen the ability of local agencies to be true centres and role models for stimulating a local enterprise culture. As well as premises, they can offer various other forms of business support – particularly training, advice and information – and can be vehicles for moulding regional programmes to meet local needs. Recent UK initiatives are described in the next section.

Population subgroups

ILLUSTRATION 12.9
Population subgroups
··

A variety of (usually business start-up) programmes have targeted graduates, youth, the unemployed, corporate employees, ethnic minorities, women and the disabled. Across Europe, it is recognised that an effective enterprise policy will seek to improve the start-up rate among some or all of such subgroups. It will for instance aim at 'improving the start-up rate among women, young people and unemployed'.[34] Indeed, the Global Entrepreneurship Monitor (see Chapter Four) identified three main demographic characteristics as impacting on entrepreneurship, of which one was 'the level of female participation in entrepreneurial activity',[35] women being the largest 'subgroup' in the population.

Efforts to encourage the population in general, and certain subgroups in particular, to become more aware of and receptive to the possibilities of enterprise have already been referred to in earlier chapters.

Many such interventions begin with young people when they are in school. Schools have cross-curricular themes to pursue such as 'economic awareness', which create an opportunity to develop a positive culture, attitude and motivation towards enterprise and business. In most instances they are used to give an introduction to what is loosely referred to as the 'world of work'. In the UK, Young Enterprise's Company Programme (an initiative, described in Chapter Two, for teams of students in secondary and tertiary education to run their own businesses) applies from the age of 16. Other Young Enterprise programmes are aimed at younger age groups. The Shell Livewire Scheme and the Prince's Youth Business Trust are both aimed specifically at young people who wish to start a business.

Special programmes, usually awareness-raising or start-up seminars and training, have, as already noted, been targeted on groups that are believed to be underrepresented in entrepreneurship or that may share common problems or disadvantages. Barriers to the potential for women, for example, to run their own businesses has led to special funding from the European Union and a range of national and transnational programmes to enable that potential to be realised. In Northern Ireland a portfolio of training programmes has also been developed ('target programmes') for subgroups of the population deemed to have particular disadvantages or potential. They have covered women, youth, the unemployed, the employed, the disabled and graduates. In Great Britain the danger of some members of ethnic minorities being economically and socially marginalised by a vicious cycle of dependency is well recognised. It derives from the lack of a business tradition, the shortage of entrepreneurs, the dearth of enterprise, the absence of role models, and institutional barriers, all of which reinforce lack of confidence. As a result, special funds and initiatives to break that cycle have been created.

Exporters

There is a danger that support for specific small businesses will result in displacement of other local small business activity and will not therefore result in net local benefits. However, if the businesses assisted are exporting then this danger will be largely avoided. Because of this there has been a variety of incentives to encourage greater export performance by the small firm sector, mainly through financial subsidies and information-based assistance (such as travel and trade show subsidies, export credit guarantees, subsidised market research, free access to databases, and information on trends, market requirements and potential contacts). Growth has become associated, in the minds of many, with the need to export, and such businesses are finding an increasing amount of support from the private sector (particularly the banks), as well as from the public sector.

FORMS OF ASSISTANCE

Where assistance is directed at filling perceived gaps on the supply side, it usually takes the form of providing various services to small businesses. Such services are not necessarily available to all small firms, but, as indicated above, may often be targeted on specific groupings that apparently share a number of common needs. Some examples of such assistance are described below.

Financial assistance

Since 1931, when the Macmillan Committee reported and identified what has since been known as the 'Macmillan Gap', shortage of finance has been one of the central issues in discussions of the support needs of small firms. This need was reiterated in the Bolton Report (1971) and in numerous other reports and papers since. Burns[36] presents the problem thus:

> The question remains as to whether there is a funding gap (defined as an unwillingness on the part of suppliers of finance to supply it on terms and conditions that owner-managers need). Owner-managers who are unsuccessful in obtaining finance will always say that there is. Survey after survey of owner-managers will reveal this to be a major 'barrier to growth'. However, just because the owner-manager might want finance, on specific terms, does not necessarily mean that it should be provided, either for the good of the owner-manager, the financier or the economy as a whole.
>
> Economists would criticise the use of the word 'gap' and prefer to use the term 'market failure' or 'credit rationing' because there may be a 'gap' even in a perfect market simply because, for example, an owner-manager is unwilling to pay higher rates of interest or investors judge a project to be too risky ... 'Gaps' can easily arise, largely as a result of information asymmetry, the fixed costs of providing small amounts of capital, and the requirement of bankers for collateral. Also there is the inherent reluctance of the owner-manager to share equity in their business. The question is, however, whether there is evidence that the gap actually exists.
>
> On the other hand there is the evidence of numerous surveys which ask owner-managers what they perceive to be barriers to the growth of their firm. Almost inevitably lack of appropriately priced finance will be cited as a major constraint, particularly for fast-growing and newer firms. However this proves nothing: perception is one thing and reality another. Even if accurate, the lack of appropriately priced finance for certain projects may actually indicate that the market is working perfectly well.

Burns goes on to claim that numerous surveys 'have been unable to objectively establish that a "gap" exists in any systematic way'.[37]

Despite Burns's conclusions and the availability of other sources of finance, the issue continues to be central to many intervention strategies. There is, at least in some economies, a strongly held view that the major problem now for the funding of small businesses lies not in an overall shortage of finance, but in the appropriate means of focusing that finance, and, for instance, avoiding an over-reliance on overdrafts and security-based lending. As a result, in the UK, the relationship between banks and small businesses has been under strain and scrutiny for some time, and the subject has probably been the single most prominent issue in the small business literature over many years. It led in part in 1998 to the commissioning of a review in the UK which resulted in the publication of *Competition in UK Banking* in

March 2000. Key elements of this report (called the Cruickshank Review after the review body's chairman) are shown in Illustration 12.10.

ILLUSTRATION 12.10
The Cruickshank Review
....

The Cruickshank Review posed two main questions relating to SMEs:
- whether they have access to appropriate external finance;
- whether there is effective competition in the provision of banking services to SMEs.

As part of this, three banking services for SMEs were examined in detail: money transmission, debt and savings.

On banking services, Cruickshank concluded that:
- there was no evidence to suggest that SMEs currently have difficulty accessing debt finance from banks;
- there were a limited number of suppliers;
- the banks were making excess profits in the SME market;
- there was almost no new entry into the SME banking services market.

As far as equity finance was concerned, the Review:
- highlighted some key barriers to entry in the SME equity markets, including asymmetric information;
- confirmed the existence of an equity gap for firms who seek to raise between £100,000 and £500,000;
- criticised the Small Firms Loan Guarantee Scheme for not addressing these market imperfections.

Source: Bank of England, *Finance for Small Firms: An Eighth Report* (London: Bank of England, 2001), pp. 63–4, with kind permission of the Bank of England.

Cruickshank's findings triggered a Competition Commission inquiry which found 'a complex monopoly' which distorted price competition in banking services to small businesses from within the 'Big Four' (clearing banks) which control 90 per cent of the market.[38] The Competition Commission's report, which went to the Secretary of State for Trade and Industry in October 2001, estimated that 'excessive charges' of £725 million had been imposed on the sector and recommended that 'price controls are temporarily imposed', believing that excessive prices and profits 'arise from failure of the banks to pay interest on business current accounts'.[39] In March 2002, in anticipation of government action, 'the British Bankers' Association issued a voluntary code of conduct for the treatment of small business customers, which was widely seen as an attempt to head off moves by the government'[40] and, at the time of writing, no government action had been announced.

To help in the area of small business finance a number of initiatives have been developed over the years in the UK, most of which are quite common in many other countries. Governments are tending to focus on both the demand and supply sides of the issue, promoting both the knowledge of and ability to access finance, and the availability of finance. Descriptions of some of the different types of such initiatives are given in the following paragraphs.

Reducing late payment of debts

Late payment by customers can be a severe handicap to small businesses, and the consequent adverse effect on cash flow and viability has been a constant complaint by small firms and their representative organisations. Various initiatives have been identified to address this. In the UK the legal procedures for recovery of debts through the courts have been simplified and a statutory right to claim interest on late-paid commercial debts now exists. Under the Late Payments of Commercial Debts (Interest) Act (1998), small businesses (up to 50 employees) may charge interest to all businesses and public sector debtors. (The final phase of the staggered legislation, effective from November 2002, gives the right to statutory interest to all firms – see also Chapter 13). The EC adopted a Directive on Combating Late Payment in Commercial Transactions in February 2001, to be implemented by all EU member states by August 2004. In addition, the CBI has promoted a Prompt Payment Code, which encourages organisations to adhere to agreed payment terms and to publish details of their payment performance, and a British Standard for payment performance (Achieving Good Payment and Performance in Commercial Transactions, BS 7890) is in existence.

Small Firms Loan Guarantee Scheme (SFLGS)

A Small Firms Loan Guarantee Scheme was introduced in the UK as a pilot. It was based on the commonly held belief that the ability of small firms to borrow for expansion was limited by the lack of security or lack of a track record they could offer lenders, in particular the banks. Under the scheme, the government, through its Small Business Service, provides a guarantee to the banks (or other approved institutions) of a percentage (variously between 70 per cent and 85 per cent) of specified loans. The lending however must still be justified on normal commercial criteria, and the borrowers must pay an interest rate premium on the loans provided. Loans extend from two to ten years on amounts from £5000 to £250,000 (with a ceiling of £100,000 for those trading less than two years). The Cruickshank Review has recommended that the government should, over time, switch the financial support for the scheme to the provision of small scale risk capital to those segments of the SME market where it perceives that there is a market failure.

Enterprise Investment Scheme (EIS) and
Venture Capital Trusts (VCT)

The Enterprise Investment Scheme and its precursors, the Business Start-Up Scheme (BSUS) and Business Expansion Scheme (BES), were introduced in the

UK to increase the supply of relatively small amounts of equity capital to mainly manufacturing and tradeable service businesses. EIS, introduced in 1993, provides tax relief to individuals (business angels) investing in qualifying unquoted companies. Unlike its predecessors, EIS allows the investor to be a manager or director of the businesses concerned. The Venture Capital Trusts (VCTs) introduced in 1995 are a pooled investment mechanism to enable private investors to spread the risk of investing in private companies. They aim to increase the supply of risk capital for businesses with growth potential. As with EIS, tax relief (on income and capital gains tax) is a prime incentive, but the investors are also expected to benefit from the greater marketability of their shares as VCTs are quoted companies.

Alternative Investment Market (AIM)

Replacing the Unlisted Securities Market (USM) in the UK, the Alternative Investment Market was introduced by the Stock Exchange, in 1995, as a second tier market to target small or young companies whose shares are not publicly traded. It provides easier entry requirements and less rigorous continuing obligations than the main market, thereby encouraging smaller companies to access public equity. However 'costs are considered by some companies to be not much lower than those required for a full listing'.[41]

Business angel networks

'Business angels' is the term often used for informal investors in small businesses, who tend to operate on the basis of personal knowledge and contacts rather than through formal equity markets. These high net worth individuals invest risk capital in small unquoted companies. They provide not only capital but often experience and advice to assist the company also. In the UK pools of potential business angels are being developed by Business Links, banks and others through a variety of local and regional networks. However, many business angels wish to remain anonymous making it difficult to measure their overall impact. The British Venture Capital Association, in its 1999/2000 directory *Sources of Business Angel Capital*, listed 48 business angel networks.[42]

It has been estimated that there are approximately 18,000 business angels in the UK investing up to £500 million annually, mostly for start-up and early stage finance (many will use the Enterprise Investment Scheme as a tax-efficient vehicle for their investments). The government seeks to strengthen the UK informal investment market by offering financial support to enable the Small Business Service to develop, with the banks, the National Business Angel Network (NBAN) as a national conduit for matching investors and investees. Such initiatives aim to promote more investment, cut the costs of finding suitable partners and make the process speedier and more efficient.

Grants and loans

As well as schemes of the kinds considered above, there is a wide variety offering direct grant aid to encourage business development. Often such support is targeted on increases in competitiveness through improvements in key areas of the business such as management, marketing, design, production, research and development, quality systems and training. Grants may also be available to assist with the cost of capital acquisitions such as premises, machines and equipment.

Instead of grants, assistance may sometimes be provided in the form of subsidised low-interest loans ('seedcorn' loans). The costs of administering such funds may be subsidised, but usually interest and repayments are expected to provide a continuing source of revolving support without the need for additional capital injections.

Grants have been suspected of developing further dependence on them. There is an impression that in many cases grants were introduced because government wanted to assist small businesses, and a financial budget was the facility it could most easily make available to the relevant agencies. However, not perceiving a hierarchy of needs (see Figure 11.1 in Chapter 11), the agencies often in effect took that money as the tool they were to use, especially because money was what small businesses frequently said they wanted. Agencies therefore gave out money in the form of grants, instead of asking what tool would be most effective for achieving their purpose and then considering how to convert the money into it. (See Illustration 12.8 which includes a summary of some UK and EU financial initiatives to help small firms and especially those with a strong emphasis on technological innovation.)

Exporters

Small exporting businesses have had difficulty in acquiring attractive credit insurance from the private sector. The causes of this were noted in a Bank of England report[43] and, while new products have been introduced, take-up is low. In 2000 the DTI's Export Credit Guarantee Department announced a new export credit package for SMEs and indicated that it intended to work with the Small Business Service and other government agencies to give export advice to SMEs.

Support for particular subgroups

Support for ethnic minority businesses (EMB): There is a recognition that ethnic minority businesses have special financing needs given that they can face 'difficulties in raising external finance (which) can be more acute'[44] than for small businesses as a whole. Any real problems of discriminatory practice become mixed up with issues such as the disproportionately high representation of EMBs in inner city areas, and in rented accommodation, and a tendency towards concentration in sectors with above-average failure rates (such as catering and retail). Recent evidence suggests that 'as a group EMBs are not disadvantaged in terms of start-up capital from banks and other formal sources' and that there is more variation 'within EMBs (as a group) than with white-owned firms'.[45]

Many EMBs have benefited from their own community finance schemes used instead of, or in addition to, bank finance. For example, 'partnering schemes' which involve members paying an agreed amount of savings into a mutual savings fund are important for African-Caribbean businesses.

There is also concern that the take-up of official business support by EMBs is lower than for other businesses with both demand- and supply-side factors being used as explanations. An Ethnic Minority Business Forum was set up in 2000 to highlight issues of concern to EMBs and to consider how government policies might meet them.

Support for women-owned businesses. Women-owned businesses are another subgroup which may need special forms of support (see also Chapters Three and Seven). Despite the significant recent growth in women-owned businesses in the UK:

> ... the absolute rise in female self-employment appears to have been largely caused by an increase in the number of women in the labour market as a whole. The rate of female self-employment has increased less, but is still a substantial growth, from approximately 3.12 per cent of total females economically active in 1979 to 6.76 per cent in 1997. During the same period the rate of male self-employment increased from 9.27 per cent of total males economically active to 15.43 per cent in 1997.[46]

Similar trends have been seen in many other Northern European countries. In the USA however there has been strong growth in the number of women starting in business. There women account for about 38 per cent of business owners. Within the EU generally and the UK in particular there exist a range of initiatives seeking actively to promote women entrepreneurs. The importance attached in the Global Entrepreneurship Monitor to the role of women as entrepreneurs has already been noted and is believed to be enhanced as information technology and the internet cause changes in how business is structured and operated. The UK Government has a Women's Unit at the Cabinet Office while the Small Business Services (SBS) strategy document *Think Small First* states that the government 'will seek to increase the number of women entrepreneurs to levels in comparable economies such as the US by researching and understanding their needs. The SBS is also developing an online women's business advice centre.'[47] As with EMBs, issues of discrimination in relation to bank finance become intermingled with 'factors such as lower expected, and actual, turnover and a greater desire to work part-time which might reduce the ability of women-owned businesses to raise finance'.[48]

Deprived areas

Following the establishment of the UK Government's Social Exclusion Unit in 1997, a report was published entitled *Enterprise and Social Exclusion* focusing on access to finance and support services by small firms in deprived areas. It called upon the Bank of England to report on a regular basis on finance for business in these areas. The Bank accepted this remit citing several factors that may limit lending by external agents such as a 'lack of business experience, lack of collateral and personal equity; concentration in business sectors subject to higher failure rates; remoteness; small and localised markets and high crime rates'.[49]

Recognising the potential of a strong community development sector to promote enterprise in deprived areas, a Social Investment Task Force was established in 2000 to explore suitable ways in which social investment and financing might be developed. (Its recommendations are summarised in Illustration 12.11.) In addition the Phoenix Fund has been in operation since 1999 to further assist businesses in deprived communities (see Illustration 12.12).

ILLUSTRATION 12.11
The Social Investment Task Force

Set up in February 2000, the Social Investment Task Force is independently managed by the UK Social Investment Forum in partnership with the New Economics Foundation and the Development Trusts Association (the Treasury has an observer role).

The Task Force aims to find out how entrepreneurial practices can be applied to obtain higher social and financial returns from social investment and financing in regeneration and community economic development. It seeks also to unleash new sources of private and institutional investment in low income areas.

The Task Force has made five recommendations that it suggests would create the environment in which a 'vibrant, entrepreneurial community development sector' could emerge. The proposals were for:

- a community investment tax credit – the Chancellor announced in his November 2000 Pre-Budget Report that he would consult regarding this proposal which would provide an incentive for private investment in community development;
- Community Development Venture Funds – the Chancellor has welcomed this recommendation and committed £10 million of matched funding to the first Community Development Venture Fund;
- disclosure of individual bank lending activities in under-invested communities – this proposal was welcomed in the Chancellor's November 2000 pre-budget speech, and the banks are currently in dialogue with the Treasury;
- greater latitude and encouragement for charitable trusts and foundations to invest in community development initiatives;
- support for Community Development Financial Institutions (CDFIs)— initiatives such as a trade body for CDFIs, and the appointment of a community finance champion are currently under review.

Source: *Finance for Small Firms: An Eighth Report* (London: Bank of England, 2001), p. 66. Reproduced with kind permission of the Bank of England.

ILLUSTRATION 12.12
Government initiatives for deprived areas
••

Government support for businesses in deprived communities includes the Small Business Service's increased focus on providing advice to such businesses; and the establishment of the Phoenix Fund to encourage entrepreneurship in disadvantaged areas and within disadvantaged groups. This fund is, however, part of a much wider regeneration programme, outlined below.

- The Phoenix Fund – this fund, designed specifically to encourage entrepreneurship in disadvantaged areas and within disadvantaged groups, was launched in 1999. The Fund, initially worth £30 million and trebled in the 2000 Budget, currently has four key elements, which together aim to assist businesses in deprived communities indirectly by providing assistance to intermediaries, most notably business support providers and Community Finance Initiatives (CFIs).
- The Challenge Fund – this helps resource CFIs in England and to provide capital for on-lending.
- Loan guarantees – these encourage commercial and charitable lending to CFIs in the UK. Under the proposals a CFI would borrow money for on-lending within the community, servicing the bank loan with the funds obtained from their clients' repayments. A proportion of the lending by the CFI could be covered by guarantees from the Phoenix Fund in the event of default, in order to assist the CFI with the repayment of its bank borrowings. The first round of support for CFIs, encompassing both the Challenge Fund and the loan guarantee support, has been completed.
- The Development Fund – this is designed to support innovative ideas on how to promote enterprise in deprived areas and under-represented groups in England. Fifty projects totalling £15 million were approved from over 250 proposals submitted in the first bidding round.
- Business Volunteer Mentors Association—£3 million was allocated in 2000 from the Phoenix Fund to support such an association. As with the pilot initiative, it is being run by the National Federation of Enterprise Agencies for delivery through local enterprise agencies and other local partnerships. It is based on a core of volunteers drawn from all sections of the business community, who provide mentoring advice aimed at pre- and early start-up businesses and micro-businesses, including those in disadvantaged communities.

Source: Based on *Finance for Small Firms: A Special Report* (London: Bank of England, 2001), pp. 67–8. Reproduced with kind permission of the Bank of England.

Additional developments include the Government's Inner City 100 initiative, a scheme to profile the fastest-growing unquoted companies in the most disadvantaged areas of ten major cities to serve as role models; and Enterprise Insight, launched in 2000 (as a joint initiative amongst the British Chambers of Commerce, the Institute of Directors, the Confederation of British Industry, Young Enterprise, Shell Livewire, and the Prince's Trust), to promote a culture of enterprise among young people across the UK.

Community and group self-help schemes

An alternative to externally supplied grants or loans for small businesses may, in various parts of Europe, be found in community or group self-help financing schemes such as credit unions and mutual credit guarantee schemes. The logic behind such schemes is that each individual in a community may be able to save a small amount, and if these amounts are pooled they are together much more effective than they would be separately. Alternatively, shared resources can be used together to guarantee a bigger loan than any one person could manage alone. Mutual credit guarantee schemes apply the same principle to small businesses, which combine into self-help groups to pool their financial resources in order to fund, or secure credit for, significant projects for the member businesses as appropriate. Thus, one or two at a time, the members can afford to undertake projects they could not have afforded on their own. Such schemes apply ideas similar to those on which the early building societies were based. Intervention may help to get them started by providing encouragement and by making available information on how to set up and run them.

Summary

Governments are thus tending to focus on both the demand and supply sides of the financing issue. On the demand side, the major approaches seek to improve the information flow between SMEs and investors and to provide counselling services to SMEs to improve their willingness and ability to find and secure debt and equity financing. On the supply side the major approaches have been to encourage banks to do more small business lending and make them accountable (through loan guarantees, statistical reporting and setting minimum targets for SME loans); to provide tax incentives for equity investments, and to provide government financial assistance programmes (such as micro-loans, subsidised interest rate loans, and R & D funds).

This is how Lundström and Stevenson sum up international trends in financing:[50]

> With the growing understanding of 'gaps' in small business financing and the differences in financing needs, governments are ensuring that multiple sources and types of financing are available (such as micro-loans, seed capital, venture capital and informal investment capital) to different types of entrepreneurs (such as women, ethnic minorities) and firms (such as high-growth firms, technology firms) at different stages of development (such as R&D stage, start-up stage, growth stage).

ILLUSTRATION 12.13
LETS (Local Exchange Trading Systems)

A further form of self-help scheme is one that uses no money at all. Strictly it is not a small business funding system, but a means of facilitating micro-business trading in a local area. A LETS will provide a local currency based on credits and debits that permit and facilitate trading within a local area without the need for money to pay for transactions.

LETS generally need a central body to administer the recording of credits and debits. When a newcomer joins the scheme then he or she will be given an initial credit of local exchange units, which are often given a particular name. As a member supplies products or services to other members, or consumes products or services provided by others, his or her account will be credited or debited accordingly. It thus helps those with low incomes, or who are otherwise short of money, to engage in local economic activity and it ensures that the credits for products or services supplied will be retained and re-used in that local area.

Other assistance

Although financial assistance may be the most obvious kind, there are many other types of assistance measures. Subsidised provision of a variety of forms of information, advice, training and counselling is a very large and fast-growing part of attempts to improve the internal efficiency of small businesses. Some such forms of assistance are described below.

Information and advice

Small businesses are believed to be at a disadvantage relative to larger ones because of their limited ability to scan the environment and filter for information relevant to their progress. Indeed it can be argued that a lack of relevant and timely information, delivered in a manner which can be quickly and easily absorbed and used, is a critical problem for most small businesses and that this example of market failure in access to information needs to be addressed if small businesses are to realise their growth potential. Consequently, the major part of the remit of the network of business support agencies is to remedy this information gap.

With the huge expansion of the internet as a means of communicating vast amounts of data, this medium has assumed a significant role in providing information for SMEs. International, national, regional and local agencies as well as private sector organisations are developing websites and knowledge portals dedicated to supplying information believed to be useful for SMEs. *Business in the Information Age* (2000), commissioned by the DTI, found that '81 per cent of all businesses were online in 2000' (compared with 63 per cent in 1999) and for micro-businesses (fewer than 10 employees) 'the proportion had risen from 15 per cent to 55 per cent'.[51] Such rapid growth in connectivity reveals the potential for reaching SMEs.

Another method, employed by Business Links and their equivalent, is the use of personal business advisers (PBAs) offering person-to-person and face-to-face communication, which is an approach preferred by many business owners. Subsidised consultancy also can enable businesses to engage professional specialists to help them to analyse their situations and prescribe improvement actions. Another type of special initiative relies on experienced business people acting as 'mentors' to selected local businesses. Working typically only for expenses, the mentors assist owner-managers with information, advice and counselling, usually over a six- to twelve-month period. The UK recently initiated a Business Volunteers Mentors Association and in the Republic of Ireland, the government's business support agency, Enterprise Ireland, has delivered the Mentor Programme nationally to SMEs for over ten years. Examples can be found in many other countries, often using retired business people. In the UK the High Growth Start-Up Programme which began in 1999 and links advice, mentoring and training, is the first new national start-up initiative there since the Enterprise Allowance Scheme. The programme endeavours to provide a high-quality advice service and targeted 10,000 growth start-ups a year by 2002.

Management development and training

Support for management development in small businesses has developed significantly over recent years, as both the private and the public sectors have identified a gap in the market. It is well known that the right mix of management skills is important for any business and is critical if a business is to grow successfully. Yet a consistent finding of research on training provision in developed countries is that workers in small firms are less likely to be in receipt of formal training than those in larger enterprises.[52] For instance the Council for Excellence in Management and Leadership[53] reported (see also Chapter Six):

Joyce *et al.*[54] found that only 43 per cent of businesses with under five employees provided training compared with 92 per cent of businesses with over 200 employees, while Hankinson's[55] interviews with key personnel from engineering firms with under 100 employees found that 'Hardly any firms had specific policies of staff training by in-house seminars, conferences, short courses, etc.' Matlay[56] found that only two per cent of micro-businesses (under ten employees) provided 'formal or mixed learning' opportunities compared with 60 per cent of medium-sized businesses (50 to 250 employees).

In addition Sargent[57] found that, on average, 'Small businesses spent £103 per annum per employee on staff development, compared to £182 from a previous study of medium- and large-sized businesses.' Extracts from Hankinson's[58] interviews with owner-managers provide further evidence: ' ... small firms would find it costly to provide training over and above a minimum level'; '... training beyond a "hands-on" approach would be too expensive for us'.

While there is a proliferation of providers of training and development opportunities, there is strong evidence that amongst the reasons for low uptake is dissatisfaction with much of the current offering. Sargent suggests from his survey of 77 'small businesses' in Devon that 'Many small business owners feel that management courses lack practicality and are too academic in terms of their style of delivery.' This evidence is supported by Gibb's suggestion[59] that education and training will need to move away from 'detached provision' based around abstract/functional knowledge, towards 'embedded provision' based around 'context and processes'. Perren *et al.*'s[60] exploratory case studies provide support for Gibb suggesting that owner-managers' learning is often problem-focused and motivated by dealing with current concerns. There is also evidence that 'on-the-job' learning is preferred to 'off-the-job' courses, perhaps as a means of overcoming *inter alia* problems of cost and relevance.

Government intervention over many years has been designed to enhance management and workforce training in small businesses (perceiving a market failure to exist in that small businesses do not see the benefits of training). In the UK Small Firms Training Loans were introduced in 1994 to help pay for training by subsidising the interest payments on bank loans which small firms took out to invest in training. The scheme is administered by LSCs in England, which consider applications before they are sent to the lending bank, and offer help and advice where necessary. In the 1980s Business Growth Training offered a consultant paid from public funds to train and develop management in small firms. More recently there has been strong encouragement for smaller firms to engage in Investors in People (IiP) while, in 2000, the DfEE (now DES)/DTI in a joint initiative established a Council for Excellence in Management and Leadership. It aimed 'to develop a strategy to ensure that the UK has the managers and leaders of the future to match the best in the world'. It further sought, in the context of SMEs, 'to establish a coherent approach to the confusing plethora of management and leadership development initiatives' and to introduce schemes which offer entrepreneurs 'a range of solutions which work with the grain and mimic their informal processes (eg self-managed mentorship, entrepreneurial networking and skills sharing)'.[61]

ILLUSTRATION 12.14
Graduates and small businesses
....

Both business and graduates each perceive the other as a high risk, though they have much to offer each other. Small businesses can benefit from the abilities of graduates, yet many small businesses have a resistance to the perceived cost of employing them, requiring immediate added value from the extra cost of a graduate's salary. Graduates, in particular those who might want a business of their own eventually, have much to gain from working for small businesses, but do not want to find that they are working for employers who will not value their skills. Moreover, graduates tend to perceive that larger employers offer more formalised development programmes, greater opportunities for advancement and greater security of employment.

Specific schemes have therefore been devised aimed at encouraging the recruitment of graduates by small businesses. They include measures such as match-making between individual graduates and businesses, training for graduates in small business issues, and subsidies for graduate salaries for an initial settling-in period or longer.

Market, product and process development

Small businesses may have difficulty finding and researching new markets, especially export markets. Equally in the longer term the survival and growth of businesses will require the constant development of new or improved products or services. Various programmes of support to help businesses in these areas have been devised. They include R&D assistance, export marketing grants, trade missions and shows, market intelligence reports, and export credit guarantee schemes, as well as assistance with the development and production of sales literature and advertising materials. Productivity increases through, for example, process development are encouraged by assisting benchmarking studies, quality initiatives and best practice visits. The linking of markets and products or services, suppliers and customers, has also been facilitated by the internet and e-commerce and therefore there are also initiatives to promote and assist increased small business connectivity.

Technology

The importance of technology in stimulating innovation, competitiveness and growth of businesses is well understood. It is believed, however, that the potential of many smaller businesses to identify and exploit new and existing technologies is limited by lack of information on their availability and potential, or by cost factors (another example of 'market failure'?). A wide range of schemes exist to ensure that the process of technology transfer is enhanced. Additionally, all Business Links offer an Innovation and Technology Counselling Service using independent counsellors, and the DTI offers the Technology Transfer Initiative (formerly the Teaching Company Scheme): a scheme which brings SMEs and universities into cooperative alliances through two-year placements for highly qualified graduates.

Networking

If 'Success = Idea + Know-how + Know-who' (see Chapter 11) then intervention to help networking to provide the 'know-who' is clearly appropriate. Generally however it appears not to be addressed nearly as often as 'idea' and 'know-how'. As noted by Bennett and Smith,[62] 'Cluster theory developed from the work of Porter[63] suggests that local interactions ... improve the competitive position of the SME.' Also, 'Local networks allow SMEs to gain advantage from being embedded in local institutions that can offer knowledge pools of advice and support.' Networking can be promoted by highlighting its usefulness, and thus legitimising it by giving pointers in how to do it best, and by providing opportunities for it. The latter, for instance, can be achieved through enterprise and business clubs, and through trade fairs. One major example of an intervention to promote networking was the EU's Europartenariat Programme to stimulate the development of less favoured European regions through international fairs to promote the development of business relationships.

UK and European small business support: a summary

UK

Overall the characteristics of the UK approach to small business support may be summarised as:

- creating a healthy business environment, with increasing emphasis on deregulation and reduced and simplified administrative burdens;
- selective intervention where market failure can be demonstrated;
- developing forms of support geared to improving the competitiveness and export performance of small firms, emphasising marketing, quality, productivity, benchmarking, product development, management and workforce skills;
- encouraging greater private sector involvement in the delivery of services through 'partnership' arrangements;
- decentralised delivery combined with variations in the priorities and scope of support services to cater for differences in local and/or regional needs.

The reality however is that UK governments have not usually looked to small business for a significant contribution to economic renewal and development. Attracting inward investment has been seen as a much more fruitful focus for support.

European Union

Within the EU as a whole, policy towards small businesses may be summarised as focusing on two approaches (as in the UK): first, addressing the economic

Table 12.5 Implemented and planned national actions in Europe to support SMEs, 1997–1999

Country	Business environment administrative burdens	Financial environment		Internationalisation and information		Labour, training and innovation		
		Late payment	Finance	Internationalisation	Information	Labour training	R&D innovation	Fostering entrepreneurship
Austria	X		X	X	X	X	X	X
Belgium	X		X	X	X	X	X	
Denmark	X		X	X	X	X	X	X
Finland	X		X	X	X	X	X	X
France	X		X	X	X	X	X	X
Germany	X	X	X	X	X		X	X
Holland	X		X	X	X	X	X	X
Ireland	X	X	X	X	X	X	X	X
Italy	X	X	X	X	X	X	X	X
Luxembourg	X		X	X	X	X	X	
Norway	X	X	X	X	X	X	X	
Portugal	X		X	X	X	X	X	X
Spain	X		X	X	X	X	X	X
Sweden	X		X	X	X	X	X	X
Switzerland	X		X	X	X	X	X	X
UK	X	X	X	X	X	X	X	X

Source: Based on the *Sixth Report of the European Observatory for SMEs* (Luxembourg: OOPEC, 2001), Table 8.1. Reproduced with the permission of the Office for Official Publications of the European Communities.

environment with the emphasis on fiscal measures and increasing labour market flexibility; and second, developing additional enterprise support schemes, with the emphasis on R&D, internationalisation and the supply of finance. (See Table 12.5 and Case 12.3.)

In fact, the majority of measures in the EU countries are concentrated on three instruments:

- grants and tax reliefs;
- counselling and information services;
- subsidised loans.

There is little evidence of tension between support for new enterprises as opposed to established and growing ones. In the EU the two approaches are considered to be complementary. A noticeable trend in a number of EU countries and in the European Commission itself is an increasing emphasis on 'the entrepreneurial economy' and internationalisation. Indeed, it is interesting to note that 38 countries are now participating in the Global Entrepreneurship Monitor project to benchmark themselves according to their total entrepreneurial activity (see Chapter Four).

Small business policy in most countries of the EU is closely linked to regional policy. The UK has tended to be an exception with most policies being national in coverage. However with the establishment of a Parliament in Scotland, Assemblies in Wales and Northern Ireland and Regional Development Agencies in England, there is growing evidence of greater regionalisation within the constraints of the UK-wide regulatory and fiscal regime.

Recent research indicates that, while policy fields and instruments may be similar from country to country, their implementation and delivery mechanisms can vary considerably, resulting in significant differences in the perception of their effectiveness. It is further contended that European Commission programmes, while providing a useful range of funds for SMEs and their support organisations, 'can prove very difficult to access, and in some cases the costs of advice, and time, required to put forward a satisfactory application can outweigh the benefits'.[64] Overall, however, there has undoubtedly been a fundamental shift in many countries over recent years with the locus of enabling policies being increasingly at the local or regional level, as opposed to the federal or national level.

ILLUSTRATION 12.15
New developments in SME policy in Europe

- New policy developments for SMEs are correlated with what is widely acknowledged as that group of enterprises' ability to create growth and employment. Even more than in the past there seems to be widespread attention to SME problems with specific policies in administrative

---

simplification, finance, internationalisation, promotion of technological innovation, and dissemination of enterprise culture.

- Administrative modernisation in most countries is one of the key elements for promoting SME development. Measures have been taken to reduce administrative overheads for fiscal, social security, and statistical requirements and to simplify the bureaucratic structure for creating and expanding businesses. This process also comprises measures to decentralise and rationalise the administrative apparatus and to develop one-stop shops for service to businesses.
- The difficulty SMEs have in access to financial markets entails the adoption of policies for promoting the start-up of new businesses and increasing the capital of existing ones through recourse to financial tools (venture capital, seed capital, and so on) and tax incentives.
- The internationalisation of SMEs has been accompanied by specific measures to provide information services and market research assistance as well as subsidies and support services (often provided by specialist agencies) to promote products and businesses, the search for foreign partners, and outward investment.
- The new scenario of competition arising from globalisation has affected action in support of R&D and the dissemination of innovation among SMEs, although very often the programmes in this sector are not specifically keyed to small businesses. There are instruments to foster the creation of innovative SMEs (financial tools and incubators) as well as direct incentives (subsidies) and indirect ones (programmes for cooperation and technology transfer, giving new energy to national systems of innovation), and the acquisition of innovative technology. Also there is much effort to enhance the quality of human capital alongside legislative changes concerning the use and cost of the labour factor.
- To foster the competitiveness of small companies and to reduce unemployment by favouring the self-employed, many countries have been promoting enterprise knowledge and culture in the school system by introducing specific courses as well as fostering new business in areas of society that are particularly subject to exclusion (young people, women, and the jobless).

Source: *Sixth Report of the European Observatory for SMEs* (Luxembourg: OOPEC, 2001). Reproduced with the permission of the Office for Official Publications of the European Communities.

MAKING A CHOICE

This chapter has indicated that there is a wide range of possibilities for intervention and therefore some choice will inevitably have to be made between them. That choice will depend on many factors, including local policies and priorities, but a key influence will be the perceived effectiveness of the different options. Evaluation of the results of intervention is therefore the subject of the next chapter.

Comparing methods is not easy, however. Not only, as the next chapter indicates, is the evidence of effectiveness not clear, but different methods can apply at different stages of the process. It is not therefore usually a choice among alternatives where the decision is for one or the other, but among approaches which can work together, which means that the choice is among a whole range of possible combinations. Figure 12.3 illustrates this dilemma using a horticultural analogy.

THE KEY POINTS OF CHAPTER 12

- Because of the perceived importance of smaller firms for economic development, virtually every country in the developed and developing world is now intervening in some way to promote more enterprise. However, such interventions often lack an overall strategy in the sense of a coherent set of objectives and the coordinated means of achieving them. Aspects of enterprise, entrepreneurship or small business policy and intervention are often dispersed across different government departments and, as a result, support schemes have tended to grow piecemeal. Their objectives appear to include increased wealth and economic growth, job creation, and other benefits including greater social cohesion.
- Agencies are often established to deliver much of the direct intervention, but the dispersal of policy and the involvement of different organisations can result in a confusing variety of apparent sources of help. Attempts to coordinate this and give it some form of structure can follow the 'one-stop-shop' approach of trying to concentrate services into one location, or the 'first-stop-shop' approach of ensuring that different sources of support are well signposted from single access points.
- The means of achieving enterprise, entrepreneurship or small business policy objectives include two broad approaches, which are not mutually exclusive: They are:
  - creating a favourable environment for enterprise, which can involve actions in the areas of the economy, fiscal policy, skills, infrastructure, regulations and societal attitudes;
  - intervening to support the enterprise process, by direct and indirect support to individuals and businesses. This is often tailored to specific stages of development and to subgroups such as pre-start and start-up, high-tech businesses, geographic areas of disadvantage, population subgroups and exporters. The forms of assistance used include

> financial assistance (such as grants, loan guarantees, business angel and venture finance), information and advice, management development and training, marketing, R&D, networking, and technology transfer.
> * While differences in delivery systems and policy emphasis exist, there is, across Europe, much more that is common than is different.

CASE 12.2
A Letter from David Irwin, Chief Executive of the Small Business Service, to the Institute of Business Advisers and others
....

The Small Business Service
1 Victoria Street, London SW1H OET

9 May 2001
ONE YEAR ON
The Small Business Service came into being on 3 April 2000. It started in a blaze of publicity and with ambitious plans. What has it achieved in its first year? And what are its future plans?

Encouraging government to think small first
A major role for the Small Business Service, particularly in relation to regulation, is to ensure that government departments really are thinking about the effects of their actions on small businesses. To promote this objective, the government published *Think Small First* on 15 January. This document, developed by the SBS, sets out for the first time a national framework for business support for all government departments. *Think Small First* is intended to encourage departments to consider all alternatives to regulation, before deciding to regulate, and then, if they really need to regulate, adopting the principles of better regulation promulgated by the Better Regulation Taskforce. Not only do I sit on the ministerial panel for regulatory accountability, but also the SBS's Regulatory Action Team has been developing good bilateral relationships with all other government departments. SBS has recently represented small businesses on childcare standards, passive smoking in the workplace, environmental legislation, care standards, the private security industry, company merger fees and the interception of employees' electronic communications. We pushed hard for the changes to the rules governing Employment Tribunals to make it harder to bring frivolous and

vexatious cases. SBS is organising focus groups of small businesses in order to secure qualitative feedback. Recent focus groups have concentrated on the timescale for the introduction of requirements for the employment of people with disabilities, the Green Paper on parental leave and the proposed regulation for waste electrical and electronic equipment.

Think Small First also encourages departments, when they want to initiate schemes to help small businesses, to do so in partnership with the Small Business Service and the Business Link network. A good example of this during the year was MAFF [Ministry of Agriculture, Fisheries and Food] and SBS working together to launch the Farm Business Advisory Service, giving all Business Link operators additional resource to enable them to provide specialist support to farms.

The government has also agreed to introduce a minimum period of twelve weeks for consultation regarding possible new regulations and a twelve-week period of grace after regulations are finally agreed, before they are enforced, in order to give small businesses an opportunity to consider the implications and make changes if required, to personnel policies or to procedures.

We have been successful in persuading DETR [Department of Environment, Transport and the Regions] that they should replace their proposal for a supplementary rate with the concept of Business Improvement Districts, which has the support of all parties including businesses.

Developing a world class business support service

At end of March, we launched the new Business Link network. We have reduced the number of Business Link contracts from 81 to 45. Following an intensive competitive contracting process, we are confident that all Business Link partners will have the needs of small businesses uppermost in their minds. This is being reinforced by a commitment to improve the quality of all those working in the Business Link network. We are adopting revised standards for business advisers and other staff. All staff will be assessed against those standards. We have ambitious plans to launch the SBS'U' to provide appropriate professional development to every one of the staff working within the Small Business Service and the Business Link network. We have been engaged in a major exercise to offer every member of staff at the Business Link contractors and their key partners the opportunity to participate in Imagine – a vision-and-values event designed to ensure that everyone understands and shares our purpose. We estimate that the Business Link operators helped over 300,000 businesses and individuals last year and distributed over eight million leaflets and publications.

In October 2000 we launched the Farm Business Advisory Service as part of an action plan for farming which includes the use of our Benchmark Index, CONNECT and Inside UK Enterprise services. Our national contact centre started on 2 April, though an emergency call centre had been running for a couple of weeks before that to deal with calls relating to problems caused by Foot and Mouth [disease]. The centre is currently dealing with about 300 calls per day, and currently has the capacity to deal with more than three times this number. There has been some limited advertising recently focusing on help for businesses affected by Foot and Mouth and we are planning a major campaign to begin later this year which will promote the SBS Gateway more generally.

The SBS has brought the benefits of benchmarking to 1600 businesses, up by over 600 over 1999's total. 9800 business visitors have learnt about good management practices through our company visit programme, Inside UK Enterprise, up 3000 on 1999. 10,000 participants have viewed one of our CONNECT programmes on good management practice, with about 80 per cent going on to further work in their business.

The UK online business adviser network will be fully integrated as part of the new Business Link network in England. We will be spending an additional £15 million over the period 2000/03 to provide additional UK online for business front-line advisers and services to help small companies to take advantage of information and communications technologies.

We helped 1200 undergraduate students gain a work placement in a small business through the STEP programme jointly supported by Shell.

We increased the number of companies working with universities on technology and knowledge transfer via the TCS programme from 703 to around 800.

We are working with DfEE's [now DES's] new National & Local Learning & Skills Councils on workforce and management development, and also with managing the transition of IiP [Investors in People] delivery to small businesses from the TECs to the local Business Link operators.

The website, www.businesslink.org will be launched at the end of this month, though we will continue to add new functionality and services over the next few months.

Improving access to finance

The SBS inherited the responsibility for the Small Firms Loan Guarantee Scheme and the SMART Awards. Last year we guaranteed over 4300 loans worth £240 million. Our long-term net loss rate is 18 per cent. For SMART, we made 590 commitments worth nearly £29 million. In July, we launched a high-tech Venture Capital Fund providing £20 million which levered £106 million from the private sector to invest in a number of venture funds which are themselves investing in technology-based businesses. We intend to launch Regional Venture Capital Funds in every region of England as soon as we receive clearance from the EU, which we now anticipate within the next couple of months. We have plans to create catalyst funds that will invest small amounts of equity finance to support businesses in their early stage of development. The SBS has teamed up with the clearing banks and other organisations to support the National Business Angel Network in an effort to increase the level of angel finance provided to small businesses. The SBS is also exploring ways to encourage corporate venturing.

Reaching the parts other schemes fail to reach

SBS is investing in deprived areas and among groups who are under-represented in business. Earlier this year, we agreed to award £15 million to 50 community and business support organisations to launch innovative projects to encourage and support entrepreneurship in disadvantaged areas. In March we launched a second round, inviting more proposals. In addition, the Phoenix Fund has agreed to provide financial support to 15 community finance initiatives, in an effort to increase the availability of non-bank finance to small businesses primarily in disadvantaged areas. The first year of the Business Volunteer Mentors Association appears to have been a success and we will be continuing to support that initiative.

Changing the culture

If the UK is genuinely to become an enterprising society, there is no doubt that more needs to be done to encourage everyone in society to believe that they can really make it in business. It is also important that failure is seen as a learning experience and that people are encouraged to try again. The SBS wants to see a culture that respects and values entrepreneurs and enterprise in the same way that it values pop stars and footballers. That is why we are supporting Enterprise Insight, launched by the Prime Minister at Number 10 [Downing Street], and which will initially concentrate on promoting enterprise in schools and amongst young people.

Future priorities

The White Paper on enterprise, skills and innovation (*Opportunity for All In a World of Change*) published in February announced a new £75 million fund to support the development of many more incubator and managed work-spaces. This will be managed in partnership with the RDAs [Regional Development Agencies].

We are working with the Treasury to develop the concept of City Growth Strategies which will build on the work of Professor Michael Porter's US-based Initiative for a Competitive Inner City.

We are looking forward to the results of the consultation on tax credits for Community Development Venture Funds.

We are intending to strengthen our work in Brussels by setting up a UK SME liaison point to help build up the voice of small business in Europe. This will be operational from June.

We expect to publish our three-year strategy and one-year business plan within the next month or so and will ensure that you are sent a copy.

I believe that we are making a difference – but perhaps more importantly we have laid some excellent foundations for our work over the next few years. With best wishes
David Irwin

Source: Letter from David Irwin, chief executive of the Small Business Service, to the Institute of Business Advisers, dated 9 May 2001. Reproduced with the permission of the Small Business Service.

Note
On 23 November 2001 the *Financial Times* reported that, following a DTI reorganisation, changes were to be made to the Small Business Service. The SBS was to continue to deliver its core services, but the role of advising on the impact of new regulations was to be separated – see Illustration 12.4.

Points raised
This real example shows how the Small Business Service interpreted its remit and approached its task in its first year of existence.

CASE 12.3
EU and OECD perspectives

The perspective of the European Union on enterprise and small business is presented briefly below.

When the Rome Treaty was signed in 1957, unsurprisingly nothing was said about either issue, the focus being on the establishment and growth of large-scale enterprises (with particular attention being paid to the industries of shipbuilding, coal and steel and textiles where the workforces were under threat or in decline).

As evidence of the probably important role of SMEs, a first Community programme in their support was adopted in 1983 by the European Parliament and the Economic and Social Committee.[65] The same year was designated the European Year of SMEs and Craft Industries. In the following couple of years moves were made to emphasise the importance of improving the environment for SMEs.

A Commission working party reported in 1985 leading to the establishment of an independent SME Task Force the following year. Also in 1986 the Community launched an Action Programme for SMEs,[66] the first occasion on which a coherent framework for a Community business support policy was defined.

The Action Programme focused on what were regarded as areas of identified need:[67]
- a simple and open administrative and regulatory environment;
- availability of capital;
- increased and efficient information flows and networks;
- tailored training.

Following on from the Action Programme, the Council of Ministers adopted a decision in 1989[68] 'on the improvement of the business environment and the promotion of the development of enterprises, and in particular small and medium-sized enterprises, in the Community'.

The essence of the Community Enterprise Policy was similar to the content of the Action Programme (the ensuing programme was to be implemented from 1991 to 1993).

Also in 1989 the SME Task Force in the Commission was transferred to the Directorate-General XXIII (DGXXIII) responsible for Enterprise Policy, Distributive Trades, Tourism and Cooperatives (which in turn was integrated into DG Enterprise in 1999, starting its work in January 2000 – see below).

A second and subsequent programmes were developed as follows:
- the Multi-Annual Programme on Community Measures, covering the period 1993–96, to identify priority areas and to ensure the continuation and consolidation of policy for enterprises, in particular SMEs, in the Community;[69]
- the Third Multi-Annual Programme for Small and Medium Sized Enterprises in the European Union 1997–2000;[70]
- the Multi-Annual Programme for Enterprise and Entrepreneurship and in particular for Small and Medium-sized Enterprises (SMEs) (2001–2005).[71]

The latest programme was influenced by external evaluation of the Third Multi-Annual Programme. The evaluation concluded, *inter alia*, that 'There is a need for an active voice in favour of SMEs within the Commission and the policy work is important and appreciated.' It stressed, however, that this work demands substantial resources to ensure that all research is followed up and that concerted actions are well prepared and targeted. It also argues that policy development should be more integrated and perhaps more measured, with priority target themes developed every one or two years (*sic*).

It also found that, with respect to pilot projects, there were too many small pilot projects and actions, there was too much fragmentation and there was insufficient dissemination of outcomes and experiences.[72]

Not only has the latest Multi-Annual Programme been influenced by the above evaluation outcomes and the experience of previous programmes but it also takes account of the European Charter for Small Enterprises and the Bologna Charter on SME Policies[73] (see below).

The new Programme is seen as instrumental in fulfilling the objectives of the European Charter. The five main goals of the Programme are:

- enhancing the growth and competitiveness of business in a knowledge-based internationalised economy of entrepreneurship;
- promotion of entrepreneurship;
- simplification and improvement of the administrative and regulatory framework enabling research, innovation and business creation to flourish;
- improvement of the financial environment;
- easier access for business to Community support services, programmes and networks and improvement in the coordination of such facilities.

Unlike earlier Programmes, this one discusses performance indicators including cost-benefit analysis of measures applied.

In addition to the Multi-Annual SME Programmes, the European Commission proposed an Integrated Programme for SMEs and the Craft Sector in 1994,[74] revised in 1996.[75] The aim was 'to establish a framework for all actions for the benefit of SMEs within the European Union and to achieve closer coordination between all parties involved in SME development'. That included national, regional and local authorities, the social partners and community institutions. It also aimed to bring together Community Enterprise Policy, those elements of other Community policies such as the Structural Funds, R&D and training and certain aspects of member states' enterprise policies.

One of the important new measures presented was the Concerted Actions approach, based on identifying and promoting the exchange of best practice between the Member States.[76]

DG Enterprise

As noted above, DGXXIII, formed in 1989 with responsibility for Enterprise Policy, Distributive Trades, Tourism and Cooperatives, has become part of the new DG Enterprise having merged with DGIII (Industry) and Directorate D of the former DGXIII (Information Society) in 1999.

The mission of DG Enterprise is 'to address the entire business environment to enable enterprises to strengthen their competitiveness, growth and development in a way that is compatible with the overall EU goal of sustainable development'.

OECD and the Bologna Charter

SMEs and entrepreneurship are receiving increasing attention as OECD member countries are concerned about ways to strengthen long-term growth performance. The Bologna Conference for Industry Ministers and Ministers Responsible for SMEs (June 2000) has contributed to putting 'SMEs at the forefront of the international policy agenda'.[77] The Bologna Charter on SME Policies has developed from the conference. It articulates certain principles and calls for greater dialogue and cooperation amongst countries and international institutions.

The Bologna Charter articulates certain principles shared by OECD member and participating non-member countries regarding SME policies. It considers implicitly that business challenges have to be addressed on the basis of the firm itself, the entrepreneur (including women and young entrepreneurs) and the business life cycle. Therefore, in addition to fostering market liberalisation and securing appropriate framework conditions that affect firm creation and expansion, governments should:

- promote entrepreneurship;
- facilitate firm start-up and expansion (and not hinder exit);
- improve access to venture capital and other types of financing;
- improve access of new firms and SMEs to information, innovation networks and business services;
- reduce the regulatory burden on smaller firms; and
- promote enterprise partnerships, networks, and clusters which can enhance SME performance and competitiveness.

The Bologna Charter also calls for intensified dialogue and cooperation between OECD member and non-member countries in this area, as well as between international institutions. It implies a willingness on the part of governments to redesign SME policies and insert them into a coherent and integrated approach to economic growth and social development both in OECD countries and in the rest of the world. The Bologna Charter provides a framework of reference for countries concerned that more could be done to improve the efficacy of policies and programmes directed at fostering entrepreneurship and assisting the development of smaller firms. To promote the potential of SMEs and their contribution to growth, there is a need for policy-makers to identify and take into account the opportunities as well as the problems facing SMEs in this new context.[78]

Points raised
These examples indicate how the EU and OECD have approached the needs they perceived for promotion of, and support for, SMEs.

QUESTIONS, EXERCISES, ESSAY AND DISCUSSION TOPICS

- How do the things that small businesses want from intervention compare with the objectives of that intervention?
- Compare the advantages and disadvantages of intervention to create a favourable environment for business creation and growth with intervention directly to support actual start-up and growth.
- It has been said that 'SME intervention methods are as fragmented as SME needs.' Should they be?
- Why is there an absence of coherent national strategies for entrepreneurship and small business?
- Describe the structure for small business support in your region.
- Might it be possible to set meaningful targets and avoid the problems identified in Case 12.1?
- Identify the main policy fields and instruments being used to support entrepreneurship and small business in your region.
- What are the relative roles of the public and private sectors in support of entrepreneurship and small business in the UK or in your region?
- What approach should be taken to expand entrepreneurship education in the schools or outside the formal schooling system?
- Is there too much or too little public support being offered to small businesses nationally or in your region?
- Compare the EU and OECD approaches (see Case 12.3) to the perceived needs for promotion of, and support for, SMEs.
- Have the remit and policies of the Small Business Service been consistent with the distinction that can be drawn between entrepreneurship and small business policy. Which direction has it taken (see Illustrations 12.3 and 12.4 and Case 12.2)?

SUGGESTIONS FOR FURTHER READING

R. Aernoudt, 'European Policy Towards Venture Capital: Myth or Reality?', *Venture Capital* 1999; 1(7).

Department of Trade and Industry, *Opportunity for All in a World of Change*, White Paper on Enterprise, Skills and Innovation (London: DTI, 2001).

European Observatory for SMEs Sixth Report, L-2985 (Luxembourg: Office for Official Publications of the European Communities, 2001).

A. Lundström and L. Stevenson, *Entrepreneurship Policy for the Future*, Volumes 1 and 2 of the 'Entrepreneurship for the Future' Series, (Stockholm: Swedish Foundation for Small Business Research, 2001).

Social Investment Task Force, *Enterprising Communities: Wealth Beyond Welfare* (London: DTI, 2000).

WEBSITES

Note: Website information presented here was correct at the time of finalising the material for this book, but is of course subject to change.

A site for online advice	www.businesseurope.com
Business Link	www.businesslink.org
	www.businessadviceonline.org
Chambers of Commerce	www.britishchambers.org.uk
Companies House	www.companies-house.gov.uk
Confederation of British Industry	www.cbi.org.uk
Quarterly SME Trends Report	
Confidential free advice through	www.smallbusinessadvice.org.uk
the National Federation of	
Enterprise Agencies	
Connecting entrepreneurs to	www.e-start.com
venture capital and	
service providers	
Details of The Mentor	www.enterprise-ireland.com
Programme Ltd	
DTI services and reports	www.dti.gov.uk
Global Entrepreneurship	www.entreworld.org
Monitor reports	
Lloyds TSB/Small Business	www.sbrt.co.uk
Research Trust	
Mentoring	www.mentorsforum.co.uk
	www.smallbusiness.info.au
Networking	www.enterpriseforum.co.uk
	www.firsttuesday.com
Review of Scottish Enterprise's	www.newbusiness.org.uk
'Business Birth-rate Strategy'	
Scottish Enterprise	www.scotent.co.uk

Scottish Enterprise's services	www.scottish-enterprise.com
Small Business Research Portal (an overall resource on small firms with useful links for advisers)	www.smallbusinessportal.co.uk
Small Business Service	www.sbs.gov.uk
Small Business Service research reports	www.sbs.gov/research
The Institute of Business Advisers	www.iba.org.uk
UK Business Barometer Monthly Survey	www.ukbb.ac
UK Government response to the Cruickshank Review	www.hm-treasury.gov.uk
USA's Small Business Administration site	www.sba.gov
Welsh Development Agency services	www.wda.co.uk

REFERENCES

1   R. J. Bennett, 'SMEs and Public Policy: Present Dilemmas, Future Priorities and the Case of Business Links', Paper presented to *19th ISBA National Small Firms Policy and Research Conference*, November 1996, p. 3.
2   Quoted in J. Curran, 'What Is Small Business Policy in the UK For? Evaluating and Assessing Small Business Policies', *International Small Business Journal* 2000; 18(3): 36–50, at 43.
3   L. Stevenson, *Lessons Learned From the Implementation of Entrepreneurship Development Strategy in Canada: The Case of the Atlantic Region* (Moncton, NB: Atlantic Canada Entrepreneurship Agency, April 1996, unpublished), p. 2.
4   A. Lundström and L. Stevenson, *Entrepreneurship Policy for the Future: Final Report*, eu2001.se (Brussels: European Commission, Directorate General Enterprise, 2001), pp. 34–5.
5   D. Storey, *Understanding the Small Business Sector* (London: Routledge, 1994), p. 258.
6   A. C. p. de Koning, J. A. H. Snijders and J. G. Vianen, 'Policies On Small and Medium Enterprises in Countries of the European Community', *International Small Business Journal* 1992; 10(3): 25–39.
7   D. Storey, 'Six Steps to Heaven: Evaluating the Impact of SME Policies', Paper presented to *23rd ISBA Small Firms Conference*, Leeds, 1999; also published in D. L. Sexton and H. Landstrom (eds), *Handbook of Entrepreneurship* (Oxford: Blackwell, 2000), pp. 176–94.
8   L. Perren, M. Davis and R. Kroessin, *Mapping the UK SME Management and Leadership Development Provision* (London: Council for Excellence in Management Leadership, 2001), p. 14.
9   Storey (1994), *op. cit.*, p. 304.
10 J. Curran and D. Storey, *Small Business Policy: Past Experiences and Future Directions*, The Small Business Service and Kingston University Small Business Research Centre SME Seminar Series 'Linking Research and Policy', DTI Conference Centre, December 2000, p. 2.
11 Storey (1999/2000), *op. cit.*
12 Scottish Enterprise and Paisley Business School, 'Discussion paper for "A Celtic Comparison" ', distributed at the *UK Evaluation Society Symposium*, Belfast, 6–8 Dec 2001.
13 M. Hancock, K. Klyver and T. Bager, *Global Entrepreneurship Monitor: Danish National Executive Report* (Prepared at the University of Southern Denmark, for the Danish Agency for Trade and Industry, Danish Ministry for Trade and Industry, 2000), p. 22.
14 SBS promotional leaflet, *Small Business Service: The Vision* (London: SBS, 2000).
15 CBI SME Council, Internal working paper (unpublished).
16 R. Botham of the Training and Employment Unit, University of Glasgow, speaking at a *Scott Policy Seminar* in Belfast, 12 November 2001.
17 J. Stanworth and C. Gray, *Bolton 20 Years On: The Small Firm in the 1990s* (London: PCP, 1991), p. 20.
18 CBI SME Council, *op. cit.*
19 European Network for SME Research, *The European Observatory for SMEs Second Annual Report* (Zoetermeer, The Netherlands: EIM Small Business Research and Consultancy, 1994).

20 K. de Lind van Wijngaarden and R. van der Horst, 'A Comparison of SME Policy in the EU Member States', *Business, Growth and Profitability* 1996; 2(1): 36–48, at 40.

21 H. Rees and A. Shah, 'The Characteristics of the Self-Employed: The Supply of Labour', in J. Atkinson and D. J. Storey (eds), *Employment, The Small Firm and the Labour Market* (Routledge: London, 1993), pp. 317–27.

22 Department of Trade and Industry on www.dti.gov.uk/dti reviews/16/07/44

23 H. Arnold, extract from 'Police Castigation from the Voice of Small Business Owners', from *The Financial Times* © 13 July 2001.

24 D. Smith, extract from 'Brown to End Banks' Abuse of Small Firms' from *The Sunday Times* © Times Newspapers Limited, 10 March 2002.

25 Extract from DTI news release, *Byers Calls For a European Charter for Small Firms*, 8 Feb 2000.

26 *Entrepreneurship In the Netherlands: New Economy: New Entrepreneurs* (Zoetermeer, The Netherlands: EIM Business and Policy Research, 2000), p. 37.

27 A. Lundström and L. Stevenson, *Entrepreneurship Policy for the Future* (Stockholm: Swedish Foundation for Small Business Research, 2001), pp. 124–6.

28 Stanworth and Gray, *op. cit.*, p. 20.

29 Commission of the European Communities, *Towards Enterprise Europe: Work Programme for Enterprise Policy 2000–2005*, Commission Staff working paper, Brussels 08.05.2000, SEC(2000)771, p. 7.

30 Hancock *et al.*, *op.cit.*, p. 22.

31 Scottish Enterprise and Paisley Business School, *op.cit.*, p. 3.

32 Z. J. Acs and D. B. Audretsch, *The Emergence of the Entrepreneurial Society*, Presentation for the acceptance of the 2001 International Award for Entrepreneurship and Small Business Research (Stockholm: Swedish Foundation for Small Business Research, April 2001), p. 23.

33 Bank of England, *Finance for Small Firms: An Eighth Report* (London: Bank of England, March 2001), pp. 63–4.

34 Commission of the European Communities (2000), *op.cit.*, p. 7.

35 Hancock *et al.*, *op.cit.*, p. 59.

36 P. Burns, *Entrepreneurship and Small Business* (Basingstoke: Palgrave (now Palgrave Macmillan, 2001)) pp. 347–8.

37 Burns, *op. cit.*, p. 348.

38 Patrick Tooher, *Financial Mail On Sunday*, 27 January 2002.

39 J. Moore, 'Banks Face Price Controls Aimed At Curbing Charges', *Times*©, 15 March 2002.

40 D. Smith, 'Brown to End Banks' Abuse of Small Firms', *Sunday Times*©, 10 March 2002.

41 Bank of England, *op. cit.*, p. 54

42 Bank of England, *ibid.*, p. 51.

43 Bank of England, *Small Exporters: A Special Report* (London: Bank of England, January 1998).

44 D. Smallbone, R. Baldock, M. Ram and D. Deakins, 'Access to Finance by Ethnic Minority Businesses: Some Results from a National Study', *Proceedings of the 24th ISBA National Small Firms Policy and Research Conference*, Nov 2001, pp. 1115–36, at p. 1134.

45 Bank of England (March 2001), *op. cit.*, p. 76.

46 S. Carter, 'Improving the Numbers and Performance of Women-Owned Businesses: Some Implications for Training and Advisory Services', *Education and Training* 2000; 42(4): 326–34.

47   Bank of England (March 2001), *op. cit.*, p. 76.
48   *Ibid.*, p. 2.
49   *Ibid.*, p. 64.
50   Lundström and Stevenson, *op. cit.*, p. 185.
51   Bank of England (March 2001), *op. cit.*, p. 8.
52   S. Fraser, D. Storey, J. Frankish and R. Roberts 'The Relationship Between Training and Small Business Performance: An Analysis of the Barclays Bank Small Firms Training Loans Scheme', 20 July 2001, version of paper presented to the *23rd ISBA National Small Firms Policy and Research Conference*, Aberdeen, November 2000, made available to the present authors by personal communication.
53   Council for Excellence In Management and Leadership, *Excellent Managers and Leaders: Meeting the Need: A Consultation Paper* (London, CEML, 2001), p. 24.
54   P. Joyce, T. McNulty and A. Woods, 'Workforce Training: Are Small Firms Different?', *Journal of European Industrial Training* 1995; 19(5): 19–25.
55   A. Hankinson, 'Small Firms' Training: The Reluctance Prevails', *Industrial and Commercial Training* 1994; 26(9): 28–30.
56   H. Matlay, 'The Learning Small Business: Myth or Reality?', Paper presented to the *21st ISBA National Small Firms Policy and Research Conference*, Durham, November 1998.
57   A. Sargent and R. Matheson, 'Management Training: Are Business Schools Out of Touch With Their Market?', *The Thornlea Papers*, University of Exeter, 1995, cited in A. Sargent, 'Training For Growth: How Can Education Assist In the Development Of Small Businesses?', *Industrial and Commercial Training* 1996; 28(2): 3–9.
58   Hankinson, *op. cit.*
59   A. A. Gibb, 'Small Firms' Training and Competitiveness. Building Upon the Small Business as a Learning Organisation', *International Small Business Journal* 1997; 15(3): 13–29.
60   L. J. Perren, A. Berry and M. Partridge, 'The Evolution of Management Information, Control and Decision-Making Processes In Small Growth Oriented Service Sector Businesses: Exploratory Lessons From Four Cases of Success" *Journal of Small Business Enterprise and Development* 1998; 5(4): 351–62.
61   Council for Excellence In Management and Leadership, *op. cit.*, p. 2.
62   R. J. Bennett and C. Smith, 'The Influences of Location and Distance On the Supply of Business Advice', *Proceedings of the 24th ISBA National Small Firms Policy and Research Conference*, Hinckley, November 2001, pp. 487–507, at p. 489.
63   M. E. Porter, 'On Competition', *Harvard Business Review* 1998; November–December: 72ff.
64   Bank of England (March 2001), *op. cit.*, p. 62.
65   Commission of the European Communities, *Action Programme for a Community Policy on SMEs* (Strasbourg: The Commission, 9 December 1983).
66   COM (86) 445, 1986.
67   EEC Commission, *Problems of SMEs: National and Community Policies* (Brussels: The Commission, March 1986).
68   89/490/EEC, 28 July 1989; *OJL* 239, p. 33.
69   Council Decision 93/397/EEC; *OJL* 161, 2 July 1993, p. 68 (based on COM (92) 470).
70   Council Decision 97/15.EC; *OJL* 006, 10 January 1997, p. 25.
71   Council Decision 2000/819/EC; *OJL* 333, 29 December 2000, p. 84.
72   A. Lundström and L. Stevenson, *Entrepreneurship Policy for the Future*, Special edition (Stockholm: Swedish Foundation for Small Business Research, 2001), p. 95.

73   OECD, *Bologna Charter On SME Policies: Followup To the Bologna Conference for Ministers Responsible for SMEs and Industry Ministers On Enhancing the Competitiveness of SMEs In the Global Economy: Strategies and Policies* (Paris: OECD, 2000), p. 135.

74   COM (94) 207, 3 June 1994.

75   COM (96) 329, 10 July 1996.

76   Lundström and Stevenson (2001), *op. cit.*, p. 96.

77   OECD, *The Role of SMEs: Findings and Issues* (Paris: OECD Directorate for Science, Technology and Industry, Industry Committee DSTVIND (2000) 1S/REV1, December 2000), p. 5.

78   OECD, *ibid.*, pp. 5–6.

chapter 13

INTERVENTION EVALUATION AND RESULTS

CONTENTS

Introduction
Requirements
Methods
Problems
   National trends
   Strategic implications
   Key policy questions
Results: the current state of knowledge
   High-tech firms
   Rural/urban businesses
   Financial assistance
   Counselling and advisory services
   Management training and development
   Impact of interventions
In conclusion

KEY CONCEPTS

This chapter covers:
- the need for evaluation of interventions;
- the need for rigorous and comprehensive evaluation criteria and methods;
- the distinction between monitoring and evaluation;
- the principles of evaluation studies;
- theoretical and practical problems inherent in evaluation studies including issues of deadweight, displacement, multiplier effects, effectiveness, efficiency and economy;
- the strategic implications of inadequate evaluation;
- current trends, practices and measures adopted in monitoring and evaluation studies of enterprise development policies;
- current understanding of the impact of various policy interventions and instruments on small businesses.

LEARNING OBJECTIVES

By the end of this chapter the reader should:
- understand the various objectives of evaluations and the different stake-holder requirements;
- have an appreciation of the differences between monitoring and evaluation;
- understand the general principles underlying evaluation studies;
- understand the problems of carrying out evaluations;
- be able to identify some of the key policy issues, the application and impact of which require evaluation;
- appreciate some of the results of evaluation studies of enterprise programmes;
- recognise where more effort is needed to improve understanding of the efficacy of enterprise policy interventions.

INTRODUCTION

It would be expected that intervention would be justified, or not justified, as the case may be, by the results it achieves. While there may be some circumstances where being seen to intervene is itself thought to be important, most people would expect that, if intervention is to continue, then there should be clear evidence that it achieves its purpose. If that is so then the fact that many governments across the world, including that of the UK, devote substantial resources to assist enterprise and small business development suggests that the results are indeed positive.

However the evidence for positive results is not as clear as might be expected. Relevant results are frequently hard to measure or to ascribe to any particular intervention. Unambiguous evidence of direct positive outcomes appears to be sparse. It is also recognised that there is ambiguity, inconsistency and even confusion in the thoughts and words of those who influence policy-makers, as well as in the actions of those policy-makers themselves. This has produced a spreading belief that there may be too many policies and/or programmes of uncertain effectiveness.

As a result, it is not surprising that increasing attention is being paid to evaluating the efficacy of policies in the whole area of enterprise. Measuring the results of the substantial resource investments in promoting and pursuing enterprise development is climbing up the agenda, not just for the public sector, but also for private sector investors in this process. Issues of efficiency, economy and effectiveness are becoming an integral part of the formulas that determine priorities, and monitoring and evaluation are being called for and are becoming a required component to be built into new initiatives at the planning stage.

Consequently, the requirements for the measurement and assessment of results, the development of rigorous and comprehensive evaluation criteria, the methods available, and the problems that these entail, all need to be considered. The results already obtained need to be examined, along with any conclusions that can be drawn from them. These issues form the subject of this chapter.

ILLUSTRATION 13.1
The difference between appraisal and evaluation

Appraisal is the process of defining objectives, examining options and weighing up the costs and benefits and risks and uncertainties before a decision is made.

Evaluation is the retrospective analysis of a project, programme, or policy to assess how successful or otherwise it has been, and what lessons can be learnt for the future. The terms 'policy evaluation' and 'post-project evaluation' are often used to describe evaluation in those two areas.

Source: H. M. Treasury, *Appraisal and Evaluation In Central Government: 'The Green Book'*, (London: The Stationery Office, 1997), pp. 96–7.

REQUIREMENTS

Many people would like to know the results of intervention programmes, not least those responsible for their design and implementation. Providing meaningful information about results is not however just a simple matter of measurement. Before that can be done a number of issues have to be considered.

Who are interested in the results, and what do they want, or need, to know? The stakeholders in intervention include the consumers, or recipients of the intervention, who are often considered to be the customers of intervention but who rarely pay more than a small portion of its costs. If the customer is the one who pays, then government is frequently the customer as it often pays the major share of the cost and therefore has a legitimate interest in knowing what it is getting for its money. Then there are other stakeholders, including the deliverers of the intervention and in the case of public sector-funded interventions, the voters and taxpayers in whose name it is done.

What do these stakeholders want to know? For government, at least in the UK, there is a desire for evaluations to provide answers to major policy questions, some of which are listed in Table 13.1. For other stakeholders the position is less clear, although they will generally share the same concerns.

Table 13.1 Major UK small business policy questions

- What is the appropriate balance to be accorded to assisting start-ups, existing businesses and growing businesses? Is there a case for a selective targeting and, if so, then on what basis should it be undertaken?
- How can the business birthrate be increased, especially that of fast growing, technology-based businesses?
- To what extent can more firms be encouraged to grow beyond the 20 employee threshold?
- Will the restructured Business Link delivery system prove effective in generating meaningful demand for and supply of services to small business?
- Is the current analysis of the financial needs of new and growing firms correct?
- How critical is the role of management training and development in the small firm sector?
- How can the sector be facilitated to expand its exports and keep abreast of technological developments?
- Should policy-making and its delivery be more, or less, centralised?
- Which interventions 'work' (however defined) and which don't?
- Who should pay, the client or the provider/government?

Answering the questions in Table 13.1 requires rigorous and comprehensive evaluation criteria and methods: the 'what' and the 'how' of measurement. The question of what to measure itself raises a number of other questions, however:

- What are the links between enterprise, jobs and other benefits?
- With what should the results be compared? What results might be expected (benchmarks) and how does this compare with the results required?
- Over what time scale is it reasonable to expect and measure results?
- What value could or should be attached to results which cannot easily be measured (due to their intangibility or difficulties in isolating cause and effect relationships)?
- To whom do the benefits, or the drawbacks, accrue (the 'stakeholders') and who bears the costs?

Of the two main aims of evaluation indicated in Illustration 13.2 it is that of proving, or examining the difference made by an intervention, that is often the trickier. Seeking to examine the impact of a policy requires knowing what would have happened in the absence of the specific initiative in question and then determining what has changed as a result of the initiative. The changes considered should not be restricted to the direct recipients of assistance only (for instance a small business being assisted), but should also embrace the effects on the wider economy, community and society (for instance on the other businesses that did not receive assistance). This implies clearly identifying the stakeholders interested in changes or, more importantly, affected by them.

Different individuals, groups or organisations in society may well seek different outputs or combinations of outputs from policy interventions. These outputs

---

ILLUSTRATION 13.2
Monitoring and evaluation

In his work in this area, R. Scott[1] emphasised the distinction between monitoring and evaluation, because these concepts are often confused with each other.

Monitoring has narrower objectives than evaluation. It is limited to observing and recording partial indicators of inputs and outputs. Typical inputs would be that conditions of assistance have been met, a description of the programme of assistance and the scope, level and types of activity undertaken. These findings would usually be rounded off with some partial indicators of outputs such as jobs created or qualifications gained.

Evaluation is broader and usually has two primary aims:

- an improving and learning aim, to provide information that will help those involved to learn and so improve the design, operation and outcomes of policy initiatives;
- a proving aim, to examine what difference the policy initiative has made to the individuals or firms or to the wider economic and social parameters it seeks to influence.

Evaluation studies will have additional benefits if they also indicate how and why initiatives have their effects. Such learning enables initiatives to be enhanced in an informed way. This can be particularly valuable when more than one initiative is aimed at a particular objective. In this case, it may be important to analyse not only individual impacts but also whether the combined effects are greater than the sum of those individual impacts.

---

can range broadly across economic, social and political aspirations, with the different stakeholder interests not infrequently being incompatible or in conflict.

In short, society is made up of many and varied customer groupings with different requirements. Thus a conclusion, such as 'the policy worked', often begs the question, 'in whose terms?'. The need to take a wide view of the effects is reinforced by current emphasis on the concepts of *social accounting* and the *social audit*. Traditionally, recorded effects have tended to be limited to the direct and easily measurable effects, especially those that could be expressed in money terms. Now, with increasing concern for the environmental and social impact of policies and the functioning of organisations generally, wider measures, new measures and new measuring techniques are becoming imperative. Traditional accounting systems are too narrow in scope to deal with many of the complexities and interest groups in the modern world. Even if financial assessments of some effects were possible, such an assessment might be too costly, too uncertain or could take too long. Projects which target social need, for example, will have a number of objectives, the achievement of which will be evidenced not only in some economic measurements but also in other qualities or values that cannot be added together and then scientifically compared. If a project produces apples and pears they cannot all be considered to be apples. Assuming that they could, or alternatively ignoring the pears, does not help!

ILLUSTRATION 13.3
The Macnamara fallacy
....

The first step is to measure whatever can be easily measured. That is OK as far as it goes. The second step is to disregard that which can't easily be measured or give it an arbitrary quantitative value. This is artificial and misleading. The third step is to presume that what can't be measured really isn't important. This is blindness. The fourth step is to say that what can't be easily measured really doesn't exist. This is suicide.

Daniel Yankelovich, 1972[2]

METHODS

CASE 13.1
Two guides to evaluation
....

From the UK Government 'Green Book'[3]
Evaluation examines the outturn of a project or policy. When carried out it adds value by providing lessons from experience to help future project management or development of a specific policy. It may also contribute to the quality of wider policy debate ... The evaluation itself should normally follow this sequence:

1   Establish exactly what is to be evaluated and how the past outturns can be measured.
2   Choose alternative states of the world and/or alternative management decisions as counterfactuals. (The decision on exactly what should be compared with what needs clear thinking ... The outturn of any complex activity will never be exactly as projected in advance. However the reasons for the outturn being in some respects better or worse than

---

expected may be attributable to the 'state of the world'. Or it may be attributable to actions under the control of the responsible body.)

3   Compare the outturn with the target outturn, and with the effects of the chosen alternative states of the world and/or management decisions.

4   Present the results and recommendations.

5   Disseminate and use the results and recommendations.

From David Storey's 'Six Steps to Heaven'[4]

The six steps of increasing level of sophistication of evaluation (of small-business support programmes) are:

Step 1 The take-up (numbers)?

Step 2 Do they like it (happy sheets)?

Step 3 What difference did it make?

Step 4 Compare assisted firms with 'typical' firms (but assisted firms are not typical).

Step 5 Compare assisted firms with 'match' firms (but there is still selection bias).

Step 6 Compare assisted firms with 'match' firms taking account of selection bias.

Note

In most OECD countries evaluation rarely passes Step 3 and in many instances does not pass Step 1.

Points raised

The results of evaluations are often quoted but the process of evaluation is rarely written about, and its limitations are not highlighted. These extracts summarise two approaches.

Some general principles of evaluation studies can be enunciated:

1   Clearly understand the objectives of the initiative, so that evaluation can be related as closely as possible to them. (But, as noted in Chapter 12, determining the objectives of policy initiatives is often very difficult, because they may not be made explicit.)

2   Look for and record not just intended effects but other effects as well, both direct and indirect. This may mean broadening the scope of the evaluation study. Policy initiatives can have effects beyond those intended, both positive and negative. For instance, will an increase in business start-ups reduce the growth prospects of some existing businesses? Moreover, as already noted, the scope of an evaluation may need to embrace social and environmental as well as economic effects.

3 Record the effects as they impact on the various stakeholders.
4 Have common measures of the effect, so that comparisons can be made across different initiatives.
5 Decide upon the basis on which the effect of any initiative is to be judged. Is it to be compared with the situation in the absence of that initiative, or against the effect of a previous initiative, or a (future) alternative initiative, or of the effects of the best parallel initiative elsewhere (a benchmark)? In short, it is necessary to determine whether there are better ways to achieve similar results.
6 Determine what the effects of more, or less, expenditure on the initiative might be, not just the effect of all or nothing.
7 Determine whether the policy initiative would be more effective if it were implemented within a different institutional framework and delivery mechanism.

The core of an evaluation should be the extent of the net benefit, or *additionality*, attributable to the intervention in question. Implicit in the foregoing however are two concepts that are often ignored in evaluation studies of small business policies: the *deadweight* and *displacement* effects. They have the effect of reducing the net benefit of interventions. *Multiplier* effects have the opposite effect. They enhance the benefits and should also be considered. *Effectiveness, efficiency* and *economy* are measures of different aspects of the process.

- *Additionality*. This is the measure of the net benefit: the benefit which accrued as a result of the measure, whether intended or not, which would not otherwise have accrued.
- *Deadweight*. This is a measure of 'what would have happened anyway' without the measure. Because of deadweight, even the direct effects alone of intervention are often not easy to ascertain. It may be possible to show that a business has received assistance and has subsequently improved, but to what extent is that improvement due to other factors and would therefore have happened anyway, even had there been no intervention?
- *Displacement*. This is a measure of 'how much of the gain in one area is offset by losses elsewhere'. It may be that a business directly benefits from intervention and increases its employment as a result. However if the employment in a rival business is reduced because the first business takes its market, the total employment between the two may not increase and therefore overall there may be no benefit. The increase in activity in one business merely displaces activity in another, albeit the quality of the jobs may change. While, superficially, improved small business creation and growth may appear to be beneficial, this is so only if there is net growth and wealth creation as opposed to redistributing existing wealth, and no adverse effects on non-economic benefits. (In addition the benefits of a measure should exceed the cost of the measure.)
- *Multiplier effects*. There can be additional benefits from the indirect or side effects of intervention. If an increase in activity in a directly affected business

results in an increase in activity in another business, for instance because it is a subcontractor, that is a beneficial *multiplier* effect, which increases the extent of the additionality.

- *Effectiveness, efficiency and economy.* This is a trio of measures concerned with value for money. *Effectiveness* is the extent to which an intervention achieved its aims; *efficiency* measures the amount of direct output that the inputs achieved; and *economy* is concerned with the cost of those inputs.

Observance of the principles described above, coupled with a practical and useful evaluation method, would provide a sound basis for determining the value for money of an economy's (or region's) support programmes. It strongly suggests that the implications of enterprise development polices have to be examined in a wider framework than has traditionally been the case.

ILLUSTRATION 13.4
Economic appraisals

Although a prior appraisal of a project is not an evaluation of its eventual results, there is a connection in that the issues raised in the appraisal are likely to influence the agenda for a subsequent evaluation.

In the UK at least the established government system for the prior appraisal of projects is essentially an economic one. The 'Green Book'[5] produced by H. M. Treasury to guide government departments in project appraisal describes a method of economic appraisal based on a comparison of net present values.* Those values can only include items to which a monetary value can be assigned. The book does acknowledge that, in making a choice among options, there will frequently be a need to consider factors that cannot usefully be valued in money terms. However, by concentrating primarily, and in some detail, on the more easily appraised economic aspects, it can have the result of encouraging appraisers to ignore the other factors, or at least to treat them as if they were less important. This is particularly serious when the other factors are the main point of the project, or where they could be the deciding factor in prioritising projects.

It is only to be expected that the issues raised by the appraisal are then likely to feature in the requirements set for monitoring during the project, which will in turn influence the subsequent evaluation. A limited, and biased, agenda will have been set, even if only subconsciously.

* The net present value of a project is defined as the difference between the present value of its stream of benefits and of its stream of costs. The present value of a stream of benefits (or costs) is the projected values at the time when the benefits (or costs) will occur, discounted at an appropriate rate.

PROBLEMS

It is unusual to find evaluation studies that observe the principles of evaluation fully. There are a number of possible reasons for this:

- The cost of a rigorous study may be viewed as too expensive. To fully establish all the results might cost more than the original initiative.
- Studies may be deliberately circumscribed so as to 'prove' a desired outcome. This is, for instance, particularly possible when the researchers are reliant on the policy-makers or deliverers for some or all of their funding.
- In some situations it is argued that there are so many variables at work that it is not possible in practice to isolate the effects of one or two.
- Even if a correlation can be demonstrated between inputs and outputs, it does not necessarily imply causation, or clarify its direction. Research is often supposed to be better if done impartially, but someone who is impartial is often not involved, and without involvement it is hard to get the insight needed to understand cause and effect.
- It is argued that many of the effects of an initiative can be intangible and therefore difficult or impossible to measure.
- It is not easy to determine over what period results should be measured.

Some of these notions have been brought into focus by, *inter alia*, R. Bennett,[6] who argues that ' "Scientific" evaluation methods as normally applied will be unlikely to offer much useful assessment of SME policy effectiveness.' He suggests that evaluation of intervention measures can only effectively be made by the business owners and managers affected.

ILLUSTRATION 13.5
Two types of evaluation

According to Curran, the evaluation of small business policies in the UK has been of two main kinds:

- evaluations sponsored by government funding departments and/or agencies delivering the policy, conducted by private sector for-profit bodies. Most small business support evaluation in the UK is probably of this type and often the results never enter the public domain;
- evaluations by independent (usually academic) researchers on a not-for-profit basis, sponsored by others than those funding or delivering the initiative ... The results are normally made public with the aim of promoting constructive discussion.

> The distinction between the two is important ... The first kind is much more likely to be favourable to the policy or programme than the second kind. Where those conducting the evaluation are dependent on the initiator or deliverer for their fees and future similar work, there will be pressures to be less critical. This is less likely if evaluation is by researchers not reliant on policy-makers or deliverers for their funding and the results are open to peer scrutiny. One result of such a poor record is that overall small business initiatives receive more favourable recognition for promoting small businesses, employment and economic performance than they merit.
>
> Source: J. Curran, 'What is Small Business Policy in the UK For? Evaluation and Assessing Small Business Policies', *International Small Business Journal* 2000; 18(3): 38–9.

Notwithstanding the genuine nature of some of the above problems and issues, they do not explain the poor record of evaluation work, not only in the UK but internationally also.

National trends

It is to be expected that the move to a relatively new policy area like that of enterprise development will require new thinking about how progress will be measured. Lundström & Stevenson[7] review what they call 'interesting transitions' in measuring performance in entrepreneurship development in their review of ten economies. In the more established area of 'SME policy', they identify four levels of measurement:

- at the sector level, for instance:
  - the net increase in number/share of SMEs;
  - the SME share of employment and value added output;
  - survival and growth rates;
- at the firm level:
  - how are individual firms performing in terms of sales, exports, productivity, and employment (especially if in receipt of government assistance)?
- at the customer service level:
  - the number of clients served and degree of satisfaction;
- at the programme level:
  - the cost-effectiveness of public programmes.

They note that 'evaluation approaches in this area have been subject to considerable criticism', with evaluation measures tending to focus 'either on numbers of clients reached and satisfaction ratings or the impact on assisted firms compared to a control group of non-assisted firms'.[8]

They note certain emerging trends in measuring performance and provide a comprehensive list of specific indicators being used across a number of countries and claim that 'Driving forces making these developments possible are current research linking entrepreneurial activity to economic growth, attempts to define the intervening variables and development of methodologies and instruments to collect data over time.' (Their summary of these trends can be found in Case 13.4 at the end of this chapter.)

Strategic implications

It has already been pointed out that, in the UK as elsewhere, there is an absence of explicit statements of objectives and targets to guide the development of policies to encourage and support small business. This situation has led, *inter alia*, to a piecemeal development of policies. Moreover, the review and evaluation of existing support measures has often been narrow in scope, lacking in rigour and superficial. The explanations for the latter state of affairs are often complex and include reactions which range from 'it is very difficult', 'the data aren't there', and 'lack of resources' to 'the political will is lacking'. Certainly much more can be done and, until it is, our knowledge of policy effects will be limited and policy itself will be 'hit and miss'.

Thus the combination of these two strands, lack of objectives and inadequate review, has led to a situation where policy is formulated, and support maintained, too often on the basis of 'pressure from small business lobby groups, short-term fluctuations in macro-economic conditions and political expediency'.[9]

This same problem is further highlighted by Stevenson in explaining the difficulties of formulating and implementing an Entrepreneurship Development Strategy in the Atlantic Region of Canada.[10] She listed the following obstacles:

- *Lack of existing comprehensive models.* It is argued, in essence, that few if any models of entrepreneurship development exist that are based on a comprehensive, integrated and well researched strategy. Because of this, 'there was a great deal of risk in the initiative'.
- *Lack of clarity about what entrepreneurship development is.* It is claimed that 'there is confusion in the minds of policy-makers and practitioners alike' about the meaning of entrepreneurship development, about its relationship with small business, about how to stimulate new ventures and growth of existing ones, and about how to determine priorities.
- *Prevailing myths.* Attention is drawn to the 'born not made' ('nature vs nurture') argument about entrepreneurs. 'There are still a number of government officials, policy-makers and business leaders who do not accept that the supply of entrepreneurs can be increased ...'
- *Adapting to the paradigm shift in regional development policy.* It is argued that entrepreneurship development requires a different approach to economic development: that the emphasis needs to be on 'community animation' rather

than on the traditional 'industrial development' approaches of developing economic infrastructure, undertaking macro-economic planning or evaluating investment projects.

The above themes are reinforced by an OECD study,[11] which concluded that member governments lacked a comprehensive strategy towards entrepreneurship and job creation; that there was scope for more to be done in promoting the entrepreneurial culture and business start-up; that organisational arrangements and delivery systems could be improved. It also noted that few of the programmes which presently exist in member countries have been rigorously evaluated. The evaluation of the EU's Third Multi-Annual Programme for SMEs notes that: 'policy development should be more integrated and perhaps more measured with priority target themes developed ... '; and 'there was too much fragmentation and insufficient dissemination of outcomes and experiences'.[12] The latest programme (see Chapter 12) proposes a cost-benefit analysis of the different measures implemented.

Key policy questions

In summary, the key questions for governments seeking to support an enterprise development policy may be posed as follows:

1 Why do enterprise and small business development warrant policies of support?
2 If support is justified, what outcomes are sought and how will they be measured? This requires setting objectives and targets.
3 What are the policies and programmes for achieving the objectives set? Subsidiary questions might include:
   • What can be done to stimulate a stronger enterprise culture and entrepreneurial vitality?
   • What can be done to influence and support the process by which people decide to start their own business so as to know how to vary the number and quality of such businesses?
   • What is needed to improve the survival and growth rates of new and existing businesses and their international competitiveness?
4 What are the most effective delivery mechanisms for chosen forms of support? Subsidiary questions might include:
   • What is the appropriate balance between private and public sector delivery?
   • What is the appropriate balance between national as opposed to local initiatives?
   • To what extent is targeting relevant or necessary?
   • How can delivery be made more effective?

5   What forms of evaluation frameworks/methods are needed to evaluate the impacts of policies and programmes?

6   What works and what doesn't? Why does it work and how?

7   Is it capable of transference to another place, if so, with what adjustments?

RESULTS: THE CURRENT STATE OF KNOWLEDGE

Despite the difficulties described there has been much research into the effectiveness of the various methods of enterprise intervention. As a result some indications are available of the results they have achieved.

In the UK a significant research programme took place largely over the period 1989–1992. It was commissioned by the Economic and Social Research Council (ESRC) and coordinated by Storey. Some of the published results[13] of the programme have already been widely referred to in this book. There have also been many other assessments which have sometimes produced contrary evidence. The following summary of some of these has therefore to be selective, but it seeks to give a flavour of the results reported in a variety of areas. Unless otherwise indicated, its source is the ESRC work.

High-tech firms

It appears that high-tech businesses have benefited from government grants in their ability to survive and grow. Not only did the grant amount matter, but the credibility associated with its receipt eased the problem of levering in additional external monies. Science parks also appear to meet at least some of the needs of those wishing to start high-tech businesses. The Bank of England, in concluding that there is no evidence of a major market failure as far as finance is concerned, acknowledges an improvement in the financing environment for these firms. Nevertheless it does perceive a financing gap in the provision of early stage finance. It makes two suggestions in this regard:

> greater focus on the role of business angels; and further measures on the part of both the public and private sectors to assist (these firms) to become investment-ready and therefore better understand the expectations and requirements of investors.[14]

Rural/urban businesses

Some evidence exists that small manufacturing businesses in rural environments (but not 'remote' rural ones) outperform similar firms in urban locations. However, there is no suggestion that such a differential is attributable to government intervention, but rather to issues of owner motivation.

Enterprise policies in inner urban areas of main cities do reveal some interesting results in the context of managed workspace and community enterprises. Managed workspace was found, in terms of job creation, to be a more efficient use of public funds than community enterprises. Jobs in the community enterprises however were more likely to be taken by persons from the locality and thus more likely to give the long-term unemployed a 'taste of enterprise'. Such results beg questions about the objectives of public policy.

Financial assistance

Enterprise Allowance Scheme/Business Start-up Scheme

The Enterprise Allowance Scheme (EAS) was introduced as a pilot initiative in 1982 and later became the Business Start-up Scheme (BSUS). It offered financial inducement for unemployed people to become self-employed and was arguably one of the better researched public policy initiatives. Almost 700,000 people started the scheme in the ten-year period 1982/83 to 1992/93.

The scheme could be evaluated against three criteria: job creation for the recipients (that is, the recipients leaving the unemployment register); creation of employment (for others); and net reduction in the numbers of unemployed (for example, after allowing for persons being employed who were not registered unemployed, or reduced outward migration).

The results indicated that the scheme was cost-effective. It is estimated that the scheme cost £2000 for each individual removed from the unemployment register. However, the scheme has been subject to some criticisms. For instance, a study in Cleveland in the North East of England found that the net effect in terms of job creation was negligible, with, it is argued, many of the new businesses (in areas such as hairdressing) merely displacing existing ones. Others have argued that instead of creating a 'culture of enterprise' it has merely created a culture of 'survival', with too many self-employed, low-income businesses operating at the margin. However a further argument is that, even if the businesses eventually ceased trading, there would still be lasting personal development benefits, such as gains in knowledge, skills and confidence.

Grants

Grants are, at least in the eyes of many recipients, a popular way of intervening to promote small business development and the resultant job creation. The job creation aspect is frequently seen, by those awarding the grants, to be crucial to the extent that the amount of grant awarded in total was often reported in terms of grant cost per job. Frequently this is specified as the cost per job promoted, because what is known at the time the grant is awarded is the number of jobs planned, or at least indicated in the business plan on which the grant award is based. If the plan works, which it does not always, the jobs will be created later. The number of jobs promoted can therefore be recorded at the time the grant award is made. The number of jobs actually created will not be known until some time later.

As well as the cost per job, therefore, evaluations have also considered the difference between the jobs planned (promoted) and the number of jobs eventually created, as well as issues concerned with the 'quality' of the jobs. Summarising the results is not very helpful, because the range of answers is so large. Costs per job can range from zero (a job which was created with no grants) to many tens of thousands of pounds. Job creation rates, for programmes in Northern Ireland, appear to have varied from only 40 per cent of jobs promised being realised to a success rate of between 70 per cent and 80 per cent. Job quality is particularly problematic. One measure of it is taken to be job duration, but this cannot actually be measured until the job ends, which may take many years.

ILLUSTRATION 13.6
A negative effect of grants

One way in which grants can lead directly to a reduction in productivity concerns capital grants. If a business can get a 50 per cent capital grant for the purchase of a new machine then it may be tempted to buy a better (faster, higher quality, greater capacity) machine than was originally envisaged. If however the business did not need the extra speed, quality or throughput, then it would not make full use of the machine and output would not in consequence increase above that which a cheaper machine might have produced. The more expensive machine would, however, probably be more complex and have higher depreciation and maintenance costs (which would not be grant-assisted). Thus the business would, as a direct result of the grant, have higher production costs and no increase in output, which means higher unit costs.

The evidence for the success of grants is mixed. Owen, who examined state aid to small businesses in three areas of Europe[15] (South Yorkshire in England, Nord-Pas-de-Calais in France and the Hainault region of Belgium), found that in all three areas the provision of grants led to additional economic activity. A report however by Hitchens, Wagner and Birnie on Northern Ireland's industrial productivity compared with West Germany's[16] found that Northern Ireland firms, despite lower productivity, were at least as profitable as their German counterparts. This was attributed in a large part to lower wages and to the level of government financial assistance. It was suggested that the level and nature of such assistance (which in the 1980s amounted to about 20 per cent of manufacturing GDP) impeded the efficient operation of some local businesses by reducing their incentive to carry out essential research and development, training and product innovation and design. In effect, the grant tended to become almost a straight addition to the firm's profit (although, it is argued, it has sometimes led to lower, and therefore subsidised, pricing).

This work was instrumental in triggering a change in the emphasis of Northern Ireland's grant strategy away from capital grants towards assistance with planning, product development, marketing, strengthening management, and applying quality standards as well as training and development of staff.

A subsequent study in Northern Ireland appeared to be much more positive about the effectiveness of grants. Scott's work[17] has used control groups in Leicestershire in England and in the Republic of Ireland to demonstrate the effect of the work of the government-funded Northern Ireland small business agency LEDU (which was subsequently absorbed into Invest Northern Ireland). He found that LEDU-assisted businesses had higher employment growth rates than comparable but non-assisted businesses and that the cost per job year was estimated at between three per cent and five per cent below the estimate for the Regional Investment Grant in Great Britain.

It is worth noting, however, that the additional employment creation by grant-assisted small firms was due more to a higher survival rate 'than to variations in subsequent employment growth'. It may also be relevant that LEDU engaged in a variety of interventions in addition to grants, including work to promote a more positive enterprise culture. The employment growth benefits may not therefore be due solely to grants. They may be more likely to be an indication of the overall effectiveness of LEDU than simply the result of a single intervention.

Trade credit and late payment

The Late Payment of Commercial Debts (Interest) Act (described in Chapter 12) took effect in the UK in 1998 and introduced, on a three-phase basis, the statutory right to interest on late payments of debt. Recent research claims to show, nevertheless, that:

> over 90 per cent of small businesses have not noticed any improvement in late payment since the introduction of the Act ... Many small businesses are reluctant to pursue their customers in the courts. The CRMC (Credit Management Research Centre) found that over 90 per cent were aware of the first phase of the Act and 80 per cent were aware of the second phase. Although only four per cent of respondents indicated that they had seen an improvement in payment times, 22 per cent stated that they thought the legislation would have an advantage in the long term.[18]

Small Firms Loan Guarantee Scheme

A rigorous assessment of the impact of the Small Firms Loan Guarantee Scheme (SFLGS) was carried out by National Economic Research Associates in 1990.

Overall, it concluded that the impact of the scheme on the small business sector was negligible, although it may have had some initial effect 'in providing a demonstration to the clearing banks that there were opportunities for profitable lending in the small business sector'.[19]

More recently independent evaluations of the scheme (for example that by KPMG in December 1998) have suggested that it continues to play an important role in businesses that lack a track record or collateral. Another study[20] found evidence that the scheme did help to meet genuine market gaps in the provision of finance to SMEs. Nevertheless the Cruickshank Review recommended that the government 'should progressively switch financial support away from the Scheme and instead focus on market imperfections in the provision of small scale risk capital to certain segments of the SME population'.[21]

In so recommending, it is reasonable to conclude that it was not a case of the scheme failing to meet a need, but rather that Cruickshank thought that the financial resources could be put to a more focused and, presumably, more rewarding use in meeting equity gaps.

Business Expansion Scheme

A 1986 review by Peat Marwick judged that the Business Expansion Scheme (BES) was 'effective in terms of generating additional jobs, at a cost to the Exchequer of between £8000 and £10,000'.[22]

However, as investments moved into non-productive areas and as the amounts invested became larger, the scheme failed to add value by assisting businesses needing small amounts of equity, which was the original purpose of BES. Again, while the scheme probably had some clear demonstration or 'symbolic' benefits, those benefits were that it 'encouraged financial institutions to take an interest in … small firms, encouraged private investment in small firms … and educated some small business owners in the benefits of external equity'.[23] For both investors and small business owners, its measurable impact appeared to be minimal. It was replaced in 1993 by the Enterprise Investment Scheme, which allows investors to play a role in their investee companies.

As noted in Chapter 12, changes to this scheme and to Venture Capital Trusts have been made to improve their effectiveness and to benefit small, higher-risk companies. It has not yet been possible to make a judgement on the scale of the impact of these changes.

Counselling and advisory services

Counselling has been one of the fastest growing areas of small business support. Evaluation of these services tends to typify the superficial nature of studies in this area. Such studies concentrate on headcounts (how many use the service) and satisfaction indicators (how many clients say they find it useful). The critical question, however, is how the service affects the performance of the business in terms of turnover, profitability or other measures.

On the issue of satisfaction indicators it would appear that reaction is largely positive from clients of these services. However, some studies reveal that small businesses found greater satisfaction with their banks and accountants than with public support services.[24]

The evaluation of improved business performance appears to be inconclusive. Relatively little research has been done in this area, and most of what has been done does not stand up to rigorous critical analysis. A comprehensive evaluation of the High Growth Business Start-Up Programme, described as a high quality advice service to new start-ups, has yet to be completed (see Chapter 12) so it is hard to make meaningful comment on it. The conclusion of Storey is that 'We are not aware of any studies which demonstrate that the provision of information and advice is a significant factor influencing the survival of the business.'[25] It must be remembered, however, that the absence of proof does not mean that the influence of this form of support is not positive in terms of business performance; it has merely yet to be demonstrated!

To the extent that advisory services provide some genuine benefits, a recent study by Bennett and Smith highlights a potential public policy issue. It analyses the influence of location and distance on the supply of external business advice. It focuses on the demand side and the supply side of such services, confirming that it is the supply structure which is often most influential on the choice of adviser. Amongst its conclusions is the finding that some locations offer SMEs a better market in which to find the best advisers than others do:

> In weaker markets, which are generally those which are smaller and more peripheral, an SME may suffer disadvantage in the ability to choose advisers. These locations may therefore be the main ones in which a public policy support may be most useful.[26]

Indeed the issue of the relatively low take-up of external advice by SMEs (evidence suggests less than ten per cent) has been a cause for concern. The European Observatory in its Fifth Annual Report[27] identified three main factors which affect the use of external advice (see Table 13.2) while classifying such advice into three groups according to the life cycle of the enterprise:

- external advice related to the start-up phase;
- advice connected to growth and change;
- external advice linked to crisis.

In various phases of the business life cycle, the type of advice and the reasons for usage differ accordingly. The report identifies what hampers the use of external advice as follows:

- barriers related to resources;
- barriers related to content;

- barriers related to the availability of information;
- barriers related to implementation.

Table 13.2 Profile of entrepreneurs and enterprises using external advice

Enterprise-related factors	Entrepreneur-related factors	Life cycle phase-related factors
• Size of the enterprise: less use of external advice the smaller the enterprise is. Additionally, small enterprises mainly use advice related to finance, whereas large enterprises request advice on a wider scope of fields. • Sector: manufacturing enterprises make more use of external advice than their tertiary counterparts. • Age of the enterprise: with the exception of start-ups, external advice is more in demand in mature enterprises. • Internationalisation and international orientation of an enterprise increases the use of external advice. • Enterprises 'challenged' by the EU internal market use more advice than those not 'challenged'.	• Highly educated, growth-oriented and opportunistic entrepreneurs use more external advice.	• Start-up phase: search for advice relates to the development and screening of business ideas or to help over administrative problems. • Growth phase: active users of various external advice • Mature phase: selective users of external advice

Source: *Fifth Report of the European Observatory for SMEs* (Luxembourg: OOPEC, 2001), p. 8. Reproduced with the permission of the Office for Official Publications of the European Communities.

It continues:

The ENSR Enterprise Survey 1997 provides some insight into the importance of such barriers affecting the use of external advice by SMEs. They are resource-related (high cost of external advice, 40 per cent of respondents), content-related (advice is not geared towards needs, 26 per cent of respondents, nature of advice too general, 22 per cent of respondents) and information-related (insufficient information on external advice, 17 per cent of respondents). Interestingly, the ENSR Enterprise Survey 1997 shows that information-related barriers are more frequently quoted by very small and small enterprises and by enterprises in services, whereas manufacturing enterprises seem to be more affected by content-related barriers.

Management training and development

The conclusion reached in relation to advice and information applies equally to another area of considerable investment by the public sector: management training development. Improving the quality of management is self-evidently the *sine qua non* of improved business performance. The question posed is 'To what extent does management development lead to improved management and therefore to improved business performance?'

While a great deal of research has been carried out in the field of management development (and to a lesser extent of consultancy), its value is limited. What research there is confirms the importance of developing management, especially in the growing firm, but it does not isolate the benefits either of management development in general or of different types of management development appropriate to the particular circumstances of groups of businesses.

Storey and Westhead[28] concluded that there was 'little evidence that management training programmes clearly led directly to better performance amongst participating SMEs', and also criticised most studies as methodologically flawed. More recently, however, an analysis by Fraser *et al.*[29] of the impact of the Small Firms Training Loans Scheme did find that it enhanced business performance. This latter finding was not supported in the major study undertaken by Cambridge University *et al.*[30] of training for the British Bankers' Association (the Golden Key Package). While reaction to the scheme by the parties involved was positive, there was no statistically significant impact on business performance.

Overall this is clearly a cause for concern, which applies also to the role of consultancy in the small business. The DTI's 'Consultancy Initiative' was designed to encourage small businesses to use commercial management consultants. However, little is known of what benefit was achieved and under what circumstances. Official evaluations concentrated mainly on take-up and subsequent use of consultants and were inconclusive as regards the impact on the businesses.

The reasons for the lack of useful research evidence in the areas of advice, information, training and consultancy, and indeed other areas, are essentially twofold:

- A lack of rigour exists in much of the research, and the methodology adopted is inappropriate to the objectives of the research (in so far as the objectives are genuinely to assess impact). There are various reasons for this, including a failure to distinguish between the training of managers and that of other employees, the time scales not being adequate, the sample sizes being too small, the impact of multiple variables not being allowed for, and the absence of control groups for comparisons.

- The area of training and advice is a very complex one. It can be difficult even for rigorous research to clearly demonstrate the benefits of management development. Distinguishing between correlation and causality, and knowing the direction of causality, is particularly problematical. Moreover, the effectiveness of management development activity in any business is subject to many influences, not least the size and structure of the management team itself, the nature of its products or services, its stage of development and, of course, the quality of the management development input provided.

CASE 13.2
Why workers in smaller businesses are less likely to receive training

A consistent finding in research on training provision in developed countries is that workers in small firms are less likely to be in receipt of formal training than those in larger enterprises.[31]

Two explanations can be provided for this. The first is that small firm owners are unaware of the benefits to their enterprise of the provision of training. This, Storey and Westhead[32] refer to as the Ignorance Explanation: that is, small firm owners are, for some reason, less aware than those managing large firms of the benefits which training provides for their enterprise. There is evidence that government certainly appears to believe small firm owners underestimate (are ignorant of) the benefits of training. Thus the official Investors in People (IiP) literature highlights the benefits which firms themselves will gain from enhanced workforce procedures. It seeks to show that firms, which have participated in the past, have obtained 'bottom line' benefits. A similar pattern is observed in the promotional literature on Small Firms Training Loans (SFTL).

Government support for these initiatives, which focused on smaller firms, appears to be based on persuading firms that there are tangible benefits from the firm's training provision and, by implication, that the small firm owner is imperfectly aware of these benefits.

In contrast, the second explanation does not imply imperfect knowledge on the part of the small firm owner. Instead it assumes the small firm owner-manager makes a (fully) informed judgement but is more likely than a large firm counterpart to conclude that the benefits of training are insufficient to offset the costs.

To some extent these explanations are open to empirical assessment. It is possible to assess whether small firms which provide training, in some sense, perform better than otherwise compatible firms which do not. If there is no evidence of enhanced performance on the part of the firm providing training then this would favour the second explanation over the first.

This issue is of central policy importance, at least in the UK. Here there has been a major effort, for many years, to enhance management and workforce training in smaller enterprises. For example in the late 1980s government introduced Business Growth Training (BGT) Option 3, under which a consultant was paid from public funds to train and develop management in small firms. More recently there has been a drive to encourage smaller firms to participate in Investors in People. There have also been pilot schemes, initially developed at the City of Norwich College, in which the Nat West Bank provided financial inducements to start-up and pre-start firms to seek training with the college.

A final example is the Small Firms Training Loans Scheme (SFTLS) through which government subsidised the interest payments on bank loans which small firms took out to invest in training.

Source: Based on: S. Fraser, D. Storey, J. Frankish and R. Roberts, 'The Relationship Between Training and Small Business Performance: An Analysis of the Barclays Bank Small Firms Training Loans Scheme', Paper presented at the *23rd ISBA National Small Firms Policy and Research Conference*, Aberdeen, 2000, pp. 1–2.

Points raised

Because there is a diagnosed need for training it does not mean that training will be consumed if it is supplied, even when it is subsidised. This extract explores some of the issues behind the observed lack of training up-take.

Impact of interventions

The main impression is that the case for many forms of assistance in the UK is 'not proven'. Clearly the government, LSCs and Business Links will need to make greater efforts to determine the value added from these schemes. Also, the research community will need to adopt a more rigorous approach to the 'proving' element of evaluation studies (as opposed to the 'learning' and 'improving' elements).

CASE 13.3
A view on Training and Enterprise Councils

Training and Enterprise Councils (TECs) were introduced in England and Wales in 1990, with the aim of fostering economic growth and contributing to regeneration by strengthening the skill base and assisting local enterprise to expand and compete effectively. They have now been replaced by Learning and Skills Councils (LSCs).

An evaluation of TEC services in 1995 on behalf of the DTI concluded that 'Information, advice and business skills training services provided by TECs to existing SMEs generate benefits to those firms that take them up, to the local economies in which they are situated, and to the national economy as a whole.'[33] According to this report, there are likely to be supply side gains for the national economy as a result of these activities.

However, TECs have been frequently criticised. Smallbone[34] lists some of the main objections:

- Their funding was inadequate for them to be really effective.
- They lacked democratic accountability.
- They were run for SMEs, but by representatives of large businesses.
- They were failing to reach the majority of small businesses.

For such reasons TECs have been seen by some people as at least partial failures. While the new LSCs may not be exempt from some of the same criticisms, it is too early to evaluate the impact of their new remit.

Points raised

It might be argued that the TECs did as well as could have been expected. This commentary however suggests that their achievement was not good enough.

If interventions are to be successful both in rates of take-up and ultimately in impact, more attention will need to paid to why so many business owners decline help despite '20 years of substantial government funding, the setting up of hundreds of dedicated local support agencies and ... at least 200 initiatives'.[35]

Common reasons as noted previously may lie in the owner's desire for personal autonomy and 'doing it my way'; the large company mindset of some advisers; the delay factor in delivery and other bureaucratic implications of government administered schemes; compounded by general confusion as to what is available, to whom, on what conditions and how it can be accessed readily.

Curran, in questioning the need for and cost-effectiveness of, at least national (if not regional) small business policies comments:

Despite the strong consensus among policy-makers that policies are needed to promote the small firm and its role in the economy ... it is difficult to see how the large and growing support for the small enterprise could be having any great impact. Too few small businesses appear willing to accept the support and, among those that do, the evidence of any significant impact on the performance on the business appears to be scant.[36]

Bannock[37] questions why governments ('and not just in the UK – Germany spends far more than the UK does') persist with support services of the present kind. The answer he suggests is that:

> There is a paternalistic view that, whether SMEs want these services or not, they need them. The underlying assumptions are that SME owners, or many of them, are not very competent and need educating. There may be some truth in this though ... on the whole, small business owners are rational and are forced to be rational and realistic by their circumstances ... There is no doubt a further reason for the continuing emphasis on the first strand of SME policy (support services): the second strand (that of offsetting discrimination against SMEs or improving the enabling environment) is difficult, and potentially politically painful, though there are encouraging signs that nettles are being grasped.

Ultimately, the recipients of these support services should engage in a more systematic approach to gauging the benefits for their investment of time and money and/or clearly articulate their own specific requirements. The recipient businesses could and should have an important role in shaping provision. It is regularly argued and generally agreed that small businesses lack management skills and information and advice, as noted above. However, the recognition of need does not define intervention to meet it. This dilemma derives from the unique nature of each business: while they have many generic and common features, each has its own internal characteristics and relationship to various stakeholders (customers, suppliers and funders, for example).

This theme is also taken up by Westall and Cowling of the Institute for Public Policy Research who comment that recent studies show that the 'take-up of services is significantly biased towards manufacturing'; that 'support is too heavily focused on manufacturing and influenced by its models of growth and business practice'; and that 'small business owners might be more receptive to advice being offered by people who know their industry'. They further contend that:

> policy initiatives ... seem to be aimed at a manufacturing model of business and fail to recognise the heterogeneity of small business. Policy solutions have tended to adopt a 'one-size-fits-all' approach and have not taken into account the impact of differences in small firms – for example, sector, size, age or business models.[38]

This approach, it is argued, adversely affects the implementation of policies.

In short, identifying an appropriate management training, counselling or information supply response means determining, for each business, what its deficiency in the area is, what form of assistance is required, who needs it and how best to meet the need. Even when such questions are answered for a business, the opportunity cost of meeting the need has to be assessed. As the circumstances of each business are often so unique, generalised solutions, such as offering more management training or information and counselling, will ignore the specifics of each business's market, trading situation and internal characteristics. Hence, it is often argued that there is a need to put more onus on the individual business to identify and seek out provision appropriate to its own circumstances.

This need is recognised by the DfEE (now DES)/DTI-initiated Council for Excellence in Management and Leadership which states that:

> Support agencies have tried it all but have failed to engage with the world of the entrepreneur. They have tried to encourage the entrepreneur to come out of his or her world and engage in initiatives created by providers supported by public funds.[39]

The Council argues for a new approach to be 'based on joining entrepreneurs in their world and tapping seamlessly into the activities undertaken as a normal part of running the business'.[40] It recommends that a flexible diagnostic tool should be made available to business professionals with whom owner-managers come into regular contact. The tool is intended to help the owner-manager, with the assistance of his or her chosen 'professional', to identify his or her own development needs, to be followed by signposting to a range of solutions. It is anticipated that the most sought-for solutions will be those which 'mimic the informal development opportunities which many entrepreneurs experience'.[41] Examples offered of such solutions include self-managed mentorship, entrepreneurial shadowing, skill sharing and action-centred networking opportunities.

IN CONCLUSION

It would appear therefore that some interventions are having, or have had, a positive effect. The evidence is, however, generally inconclusive. While some of the research into interventions has been criticised for its methodology, the lack of clear findings is probably due more to the complexity of the subject area than to avoidable shortcomings in the evaluations.

Policy-makers would like to know how effective the possible forms of intervention are in order to select the ones that will be most cost-effective in achieving their purposes. The evidence available to them however is often imperfect, ambiguous and even contradictory. There appears to be no strong body of evidence to say that intervention works, but also there is no clear evidence that it doesn't.

ILLUSTRATION 13.7
The evidence of businesses

Most surveys of business opinion in the UK point to a number of simple conclusions, similar to those already articulated by a number of other commentators. Based on what businesses say their needs are, these surveys have suggested that:

- A key role for government should be to create a stable and positive economic environment, and encourage an enterprise culture.

- The needs of small businesses for government support do not differ significantly from those of bigger firms (except in the special cases of the impact of regulations and diseconomies of scale).
- There is no strong case for a large array of firm- or sector-specific policies.
- Where services are required and supplied, the most common need is not for more but for better. Moreover, the case for public, as opposed to private, provision is often highly questionable.

Evaluating enterprise policy interventions is not easy. In commenting on this Bennett notes:

> Thus for small businesses we have the general conclusion that age, size, sector and location are crucial distinctions of small business characteristics (e.g. Storey 1994) but beyond that we know that a multiplicity of other variables is also important in different combinations for each business.[42]

Thus, he argues, in researching small businesses to assess policy interventions, there are two possible courses of action. The first, typified by 'matched pairs' research, involves so subdividing the population by careful sampling that any conclusions relate only to very constrained circumstances from which generalisations are difficult or impossible. The second involves taking large samples that include businesses from a wide range of different ages, sectors, locations and other distinguishing factors. The problem with such approaches is that 'It is usually impossible to obtain the sample size necessary to say anything useful about specific business problems: generalisation to the population is emphasised at the expense of detailed or specific assessments.' The range of different business circumstances is however such that even surveys with samples of up to two thousand can focus only 'on a restricted range of issues that does not allow each business to be put in a proper context'.[43] This view is also articulated by Curran, claiming that:

> a serious problem with quantitatively based aggregate evaluations of small business policies (by far the most common) is that they offer little on how individual firms respond to policies. Given the heterogeneity of small firms the asymmetrical impact of policy is likely to be great. How owner-managers integrate any support with their business goals, how it impacts on operational procedures and relates with those outside the firm, is hidden where evaluation offers aggregate findings only. Yet without knowing how a policy goes through 'the black box' which is the firm and its activities, no evaluation can properly estimate impact on business performance.[44]

Bennett contends that it is in 'the area of evaluation of SME programmes that there is also one of the greatest methodological challenges'.[45]

The extent of the challenge facing governments can be summed up in the following extracts from recent publications, the first applying to the UK and the second to OECD countries in general:

In recognising growing pressures on limited government revenues, Curran asks:[46]

Is public support for small enterprise value for money? To what extent has it helped to promote the increase in small business since 1979? Even if it can be shown to have been effective, is it still justified in the late 1990s?

He argues that the reason why evaluation of policies and initiatives has

lagged behind their growth and proliferation ... is the consensus that supporting small enterprise undoubtedly promotes entrepreneurship, employment and national economic performance.

In the 1990s, however, concerns have emerged. In 2000 the OECD commented:[47]

In most OECD countries, there is a need to deal with a maze of SME-specific programmes, which have tended to proliferate over the years with inadequate rationale or evaluation. Just the cost of administering these programmes is becoming a burden to governments which need to streamline their activities in cost-cutting efforts ... Governments need to engage in more systematic evaluation of these programmes to ensure they are justified and efficient. They need to avoid incoherence and contradictions in existing or future policies while ensuring transparency and 'value-for-money'. As yet, most OECD countries have not acquired an 'evaluation culture'.

CASE 13.4
Measuring performance: the trends, indicators and outcomes observed by Anders Lundström and Lois Stevenson
....

The move to any new policy area, like that of entrepreneurship, demands new thinking about how progress will be measured. What performance indicators are needed? What types of evaluation should be undertaken? What are the appropriate benchmarks against which to monitor developments over time or in relationship to other regions or nations? This section focuses on some of the emerging developments in this area of entrepreneurship policy based on the insights gained from a study of ten economies.

First of all, we see some interesting transitions. In the more established area of SME policy, there appear to be at least four levels of measurement:

1   At the level of the sector: how well is the SME sector doing in terms of net increases in the number/share of SMEs, growth in SME share of

employment, increased SME value added output, aggregate SME survival and growth rates?

2   At the level of the firm: how well are individual firms performing in terms of growth in productivity, employment, and sales, particularly if they have accessed government assistance programmes?

3   At the customer service level: how many clients have been served, how satisfied have they been?

4   At the programme level: how effective are government programmes on a cost-benefit basis?

Evaluation approaches in this area have been subject to considerable criticism. Because a lot of measures are targeted towards individual firms or sectors and the majority of support is in the form of direct assistance programmes (of a financial or non-financial nature), evaluation measures have tended to focus either on reach (numbers of clients) and client satisfaction or the impact of assistance on the firms of assisted clients versus a control group of non-assisted firms.

In the area of measuring performance, a number of emerging trends are worth highlighting. First of all, with the increasing emphasis on the 'entrepreneurial economy', we notice less interest in measures motivated from a neo-classical point of view, for instance less about external effects or imperfections in the market, and less interest in individual firms such as measuring the impacts of 'picking the winner' strategies. Instead a whole new category of performance indicators is emerging. These are referred to as measurements of 'general entrepreneurship trends' and of the entrepreneurship climate/culture.

From our case studies, it is evident that Finland and the Netherlands are particularly focused on articulating these measures. Indicators to measure increases in the entrepreneurial climate/culture include things like increases in the entrepreneurial potential of the population, increases in the preconditions for becoming an entrepreneur and decreases in obstacles, and changes in social attitudes towards entrepreneurship. Finland proposes to track, at the community level, changes in entrepreneurial attitude, role identity, motivation level and intent to start a business, changes in the self-employment level, and changes in the level of entrepreneurial activity among women, youth, immigrants and academics. These could be classified as measures of the environment for entrepreneurship.

In the Netherlands, the government has established a set of performance indicators which include the level of business start-ups, exits and growth firms (measures of 'dynamism'), increases in the number of sole traders (measure of social value attached to entrepreneurship), reduced cost and time needed to start a business/reduced barriers to hiring the 'first' employee (measure of reduced administrative burden), the number of professors who teach entrepreneurship and the attitudes of students towards entrepreneurship (measures of impact of entrepreneurship education inputs), and business entry, exit and turbulence rates in each of 25 cities.

In the UK, changes in social attitudes towards entrepreneurship and the number of nascent entrepreneurs are being used to measure increases in the entrepreneurship climate/culture and reduced burden to comply with government regulation to measure reductions in obstacles to business entry. In Atlantic Canada, the government is tracking increases in the intent to start a business by asking the question 'How likely is it that you will start a business within the next two years?' on regular omnibus household surveys.

We also observe a trend to develop performance indicators for specific entrepreneurship policy/programme areas like entrepreneurship education, entrepreneurship promotion, entrepreneurship network activity, start-up financing, and administrative obstacles to business entry. The measures themselves, the outputs being measured, and the longer-term orientation of many of these measures are also apparent. In addition we see the development of new categories of entrepreneurs (even people who are not yet entrepreneurs as in the nascent entrepreneur category) and the use of new indices like 'business formations per capita' (a measure of the business start-up propensity in the population), 'enterprises per capita' (a measure of density of entrepreneurs in the population), the Total Entrepreneurial Index (used by the Global Entrepreneurship Monitor to measure the prevalence rate of entrepreneurial activity in a region/country) and business 'turbulence' (measurement of the business dynamics of entries and exits).

These new indices are being used as indicators of the level of entrepreneurial vitality in a country or region. Static and dynamic measures like this allow international comparisons on a country-by-country basis which in turn is leading to international benchmarking of entrepreneurship levels. This capability mirrors the existing capability and practice of countries to benchmark their SME sector against that of others (a pattern we also see in many of the cases in this study). Governments are benchmarking them-selves against the performance of other countries in a number of SME/entrepreneurship-related areas: this is particularly evident in Taiwan, the Netherlands, Ireland and the UK. They are tracking their performance against that of other countries on such indicators as SME share of businesses, SME share of employment, SME share of value added and exports, new business entry and exit rates, net increases in SME population, SME survival rates over time, percentage of high-growth SMEs, self-employment rates, attitudes of the population towards entrepreneurship, and more recently, the rate of nascent entrepreneurship.

At this point, the development and adoption of these sorts of performance indicators and measures are in very early stages and certainly not widespread.

Only a few of the economies in this study have made progress in this area, and then only recently. What may be most important here is that what gets measured gets attended to and what is attended to tends to get measured. Either way, the importance of entrepreneurship in a government's policy mix is being raised as a result of the ability to identify and quantify inputs, outputs and outcomes in the area.

Points raised

This case reviews the measurement of the performance of entrepreneurship policy and summarises the different approaches taken in different countries.

Source: A. Lundström and L. Stevenson, *Entrepreneurship Policy for the Future* (Stockholm: Swedish Foundation for Small Business Research, 2001), pp. 144–6. Reproduced with the permission of the Swedish Foundation for Small Business Research.

THE KEY POINTS OF CHAPTER 13

- There are a number of stakeholders in the process of intervention to promote more enterprise. They include the initiator(s) of the intervention, which is often government, those who deliver it and those who receive it. They all have an interest in knowing how effective it is or what its impact is on its recipients.
- To answer their questions, rigorous and comprehensive evaluation criteria and methods are needed. Evaluation can have a number of aims including both an 'improving' and 'learning' aim to provide information which will help to improve policy initiatives, and a 'proving' aim to examine what difference the policy initiative has made to the individuals or firms or to the wider economic and social parameters it seeks to influence. Evaluations also have to contend with issues such as 'In whose terms is success to be measured?' and 'How can both economic and social benefits be assessed?'
- The methods employed should be carefully considered and should address issues such as additionality, deadweight, displacement, and multiplier effects as well as effectiveness, efficiency and economy.
- The problems of doing this are considerable. For instance, they include a lack of clear objectives, a lack of existing comprehensive models, a lack of clarity about what entrepreneurship development is, prevailing myths, and adapting to paradigm shifts in regional development policy.

- There are some indications that interventions can work, but overall the evidence for positive results is not as clear as might be expected. There appears to be ambiguity, inconsistency and even confusion in the thoughts and words of policy-makers, as well as in their actions. Relevant results are frequently hard to measure or to ascribe to any particular intervention, and clear evidence of direct positive outcomes appears to be sparse.
- Overall there appears therefore to be no strong body of evidence to say that intervention works, but equally there is no clear evidence that it doesn't.
- There is increasing recognition of the need to determine the efficacy of enterprise policies and initiatives.

QUESTIONS, EXERCISES, ESSAY AND DISCUSSION TOPICS

- What would the various stakeholders of an entrepreneurship or small business support initiative hope to learn from an evaluation of it?
- Outline the key steps involved in a rigorous evaluation of policy.
- Are the two guides to evaluation presented in Case 13.1 contradictory or complementary?
- Identify the main problems associated with assessment of policy and support for small businesses.
- If an evaluation of small business support measures finds evidence of a low take-up, what might be the explanation(s) and how should that be tested in order to learn from the problem?
- How could the impact of management training on business performance be evaluated?
- If the overall verdict on the effectiveness of small business intervention is still undecided, should small business intervention still continue?
- Are SME policies and programmes satisfactory? Are they critically evaluated? Are bad policies phased out or refocused? Illustrate your answer with examples.
- If the aim of the TECs (Training and Enterprise Councils – see Case 13.3) was to foster economic growth and contribute to regeneration by strengthening the skill base and assisting local enterprise to expand and compete effectively, what steps might they have taken? Are the Learning and Skills Councils likely to be able to take those steps?

- Which are the most important policy instruments for improving SME performance and what should change in government policies if more favourable conditions are to be obtained?
- If workers in small businesses are less likely to be in receipt of formal training than those in larger enterprises (see Case 13.2), what might be the implications and how might they be addressed?
- Case 13.4 summarises the different approaches being taken in different countries to measure the performance of entrepreneurship policy. What do you conclude should be included in a perfect approach, and why?

SUGGESTIONS FOR FURTHER READING

J. Curran, 'What Is Small Business Policy In the UK For? Evaluating and Assessing Small Business Policies', *International Small Business Journal* 2000; 18(3): 43–5.

J. Curran and R. A. Blackburn, *Researching the Small Enterprise* (London: Sage, 2001).

A. A. Gibb, 'SME Policy, Academic Research and the Growth of Ignorance, Mythical Concepts, Myths, Assumptions, Rituals and Confusions', *International Small Business Journal* 2000; 18(3): 13–35.

H. M. Treasury, *Appraisal and Evaluation in Central Government: 'The Green Book'* (London: The Stationery Office, 1997), for its small section on evaluation.

REFERENCES

1   R. Scott, personal correspondence based on work for Northern Ireland's Department of Economic Development.
2   D. Yankelovich, *Corporate Priorities: A Continuing Study of the New Demands on Business* (Stanford, CN: Daurer Yankelovich Inc., 1972).
3   H. M. Treasury, *Appraisal and Evaluation in Central Government: 'The Green Book'* (London: The Stationery Office, 1997), p. 12.
4   D. J. Storey, 'Six Steps to Heaven', presented to the *22nd ISBA National Small Firms Policy and Research Conference*, Leeds, 1999; also published in D. L. Sexton and H. Landström (eds) *Handbook of Entrepreneurship* (Oxford: Blackwell, 2000). pp.176–94.
5   H. M. Treasury, *op. cit.*
6   R. J. Bennett, 'SMEs and Public Policy: Present Dilemmas, Future Priorities and the Case of Business Links', Keynote address to the *19th ISBA National Small Firms Policy and Research Conference*, Birmingham, November 1996, at p. 20 of paper handed out.

7 A. Lundström and L. Stevenson, *Entrepreneurship Policy for the Future*, Volume 1 of the 'Entrepreneurship Policy for the Future' series, (Stockholm: Swedish Foundation for Small Business Research, 2001).

8 *Ibid.*, p. 144.

9 D. Storey, quoted in D. Smallbone, 'Policies to Support SME Development: The UK Experience', Paper presented at a conference in Novara, Italy, June 1995, p. 3.

10 L. Stevenson, *Lessons Learned From the Implementation of an Entrepreneurship Development Strategy In Canada: The Case of the Atlantic Region*, April 1996 (unpublished), p. 2.

11 OECD, *Jobs Study Followup: Thematic Review of Entrepreneurship and Job Creation Policies* (Paris: OECD, 1996).

12 Lundström and Stevenson, *op. cit.*, p. 98.

13 D. Storey, *Understanding the Small Business Sector* (London: Routledge, 1994).

14 Bank of England, *Finance for Small Firms: An Eighth Report* (London: Bank of England, March 2001), p. 73.

15 G. Owen, *Aid Regimes and Small Business In the UK France and Belgium*, efmd report to ESRC (Brussels: efmd, 1992).

16 D. M. W. N. Hitchens, K. Wagner and J. E. Birnie, *Northern Ireland Manufacturing Productivity Compared With West Germany* (Belfast: Northern Ireland Economic Research Centre, 1989).

17 R. Scott, 'Does a Regime of Intensive Grant Assistance to Small Firms Create Jobs?', Paper presented to the *23rd efmd European Small Business Seminar*, N. Ireland, September 1993.

18 Bank of England, *op. cit.*, pp. 30–1.

19 Storey (1994), *op. cit.*, p. 227.

20 M. Cowling and P. Mitchell, *Is the Small Firms Loan Guarantee Scheme Hazardous for Banks or Helpful to Small Businesses?* (Birmingham: Birmingham Business School Research Centre for Industrial Strategy, March 2000).

21 Bank of England, *op. cit.*, p. 29.

22 Storey (1994), *op. cit.*, p. 229.

23 *Ibid.*, p. 229.

24 Bennett, *op. cit.*, pp. 3–4.

25 Storey (1994), *op. cit.*, p. 291.

26 R. J. Bennett and C. Smith, 'The Influence of Location and Distance on the Supply of Business Advice', Paper presented at the *24th ISBA National Small Firms Policy and Research Conference*, Hinkley, November 2001.

27 The European Observatory for SMEs, *Fifth Annual Report*, Report submitted to DGXXIII by European Network for SME Research, October 1997.

28 D. J. Storey and P. Westhead, *Management Training and Small Firm Performance: A Critical Review*, Working paper No. 18 (Coventry: Warwick University Centre for Small and Medium-Sized Enterprises, 1997), p. 1.

29 S. Fraser, D. Storey, J. Prankish and R. Roberts, 'The Relationship Between Training and Small Business Performance: An Analysis of the Barclays Bank Small Firms Training Loans Scheme', Paper presented to the *24th ISBA National Small Firms Policy and Research Conference*, Hinkley, November 2001.

30 Cambridge University *et al.* for The British Bankers' Association, *The Evaluation of the Golden Key Package Component of the Small Business Initiative*, (London: The Association, April 2001).

31 For the US: L. M. Lynch and S. E. Black, 'Beyond the Incidence of Employer Provided Training', *Industrial and Labour Relations Review* 1998; 52(1): 64–81. For the UK: A. L. Booth,

'Job Related Formal Training: Who Receives It and What Is It Worth?', *Oxford Bulletin of Economics and Statistics* 1991; 53(3): 281–94.

32 D. J. Storey and P. Westhead, 'Management Training In Small Firms: A Case of Market Failure?', *Human Resource Management Journal* 1997; 7(2): 61–71.

33 Department of Trade and Industry, *Evaluation of DTI Funded TEC Services In Support of Small and Medium Sized Enterprises*, Report prepared by PA Economic Consultants on behalf of the DTI (London: HMSO, 1995).

34 Smallbone, *op. cit.* in reference 9.

35 J. Curran, 'What is Small Business Policy in the UK For? Evaluation and Assessing Small Business Policies', *International Small Business Journal* 2000; 18(3): 36–50, at 43.

36 Curran, *ibid.*: 45.

37 G. Bannock, 'Letter: A Comment on Gibb and Curran', *International Small Business Journal*, Vol. 2000; 18(4): 85–6.

38 M. Westall and M, Cowling, *Agenda for Growth* (London, Institute for Public Policy Research, 1999), pp. 5–6 and back cover.

39 Council for Excellence in Management and Leadership, *Excellent Managers and Leaders: Meeting the Need: A Consultation Paper* (London: CEML, 2001), p. 10.

40 *Ibid.*, p. 10.

41 *Ibid.*, p. 10.

42 Bennett, *op. cit.*, p. 3.

43 Bennett, *ibid.*, p. 4.

44 Curran, *op. cit.*: 41.

45 Bennett, *op. cit.*, p. 20.

46 Curran, *op. cit.*: 38.

47 OECD, *The Role of SMEs: Findings and Issues* (Paris: OECD, Directorate for Science, Technology and Industry/Industry Committee, December 2000), p. 16.

AFTERWORD

14

SCIENCE, ART OR MAGIC?

> It is time for change. Time to realise that Governments on their own cannot provide us with permanent secure jobs and a growing standard of living ... Time to accept that the solutions to our problems lie in our own hands. We need to foster a spirit of self-reliance and determination to take charge of our future. The next decade will provide greater opportunities for enterprise and initiative than we have ever seen before. The extent to which our community will accept this challenge will determine our future levels of employment and national wealth.
>
> The Culliton Report, Ireland, 1992[1]

Who should provide opportunities in our lives, and particularly in our economic lives? Is a job something which is a right and which should therefore be provided for us? If there is a problem is it someone else's task to sort it out, and is that someone usually the government? Many people alive today were brought up in a culture where lifetime employment was seen as being both available and the norm, and therefore as the desired and natural state for individual economic activity, even though in reality it had not been the norm for very long, if at all. Many of the large businesses, which earlier last century seemed to provide the core employment in most economies, are dying, or are at least in decline. Like human beings, businesses are born, live and then die, and generally they die at an earlier age than humans. Lifetime employment is not to be expected in those circumstances. Should we instead view employment rather as Buddhists view life? Should we expect that after our present life ends we will be reborn into a different existence; that when one form of employment ends there can be another? If there is continuity it will be seen in the life of the individual person and in its progression, not in his or her employment which must be expected to change. Who though will provide the other forms of employment?

We have, in recent years, seen the re-emergence of the small business. That is not to say that it ever went away. There have always been small businesses in the form of farms, shops and many personal services such as those provided by hairdressers, restaurateurs, plumbers and window-cleaners. What is now recognised is the distinctiveness and the contribution of small businesses. Small businesses are understood to have particular features which distinguish them from larger businesses and to have a distinct role to play in a modern economy; whereas it used to be the case that, while it was recognised that many businesses were small, their size was not thought to be a crucial distinction and the business population was thought in effect to be relatively homogeneous.

It is small businesses which are providing many of the new jobs, but it takes enterprising people to start those small businesses. Even for those being employed in them, the new small businesses do not offer the same employment prospects as used to be offered by the declining big businesses. For both employers and employees economic security will increasingly depend on skills, ideas, and the ability to learn and to adapt to meet changing requirements. That means having people who are enterprising. There is therefore an interest in building an enterprise culture in which people feel that they can and should use their own initiative to secure their economic future.

This represents a challenge that is social as well as economic. It has been observed that in the USA, 'the nature of work has changed, but the nature of education has not ... Global competition and new technology are overthrowing the assumptions behind mass production and, simultaneously, the lessons taught in American classrooms.'[2] People need a different approach: an enterprising approach.

Enterprising behaviour, however, is not something just limited to, or reserved for, a business context. Being enterprising and seeking to contribute in that way can impact on many of aspects of our lives. Enterprise is a mode of behaviour that can have a wide application, and the results of that application can themselves have a range of consequences, including both social and economic impacts:

> A close-knit social fabric can be good for democracy and the economy. A study of Italian regions ... suggested that membership of choral societies is one of the three best predictors of a robust and effective local democracy and economy.[3]

If private sector small business enterprise is growing, so too is social enterprise. Examples of social economic actions now include community businesses, development trusts, telecottages, credit unions, country markets, managed workspace, community recycling schemes, city farms and local exchange trading schemes (LETS).

It is one thing, however, to see the potential for such initiatives and another thing to achieve them. There are many obstacles between potential and achievement, including habits, attitudes, beliefs and expectations. If people are used to seeing the economic cake as essentially fixed in size, where every gain by one person means a corresponding loss by another, they are likely to be concerned primarily with the distribution of that cake. If, however, they can see that a bigger cake is possible then they might look for creative ways of enlarging it.

If European politics in the 19th century was about dividing up the cake, Marxism was supposed to make the reallocation permanent. To the astonished Virginian in his buckskins, the idea must have seemed absurd. Everything you could possibly want or need was there, waiting for you, only provided you were prepared to cut it down, dig it out or plough it. That was the deal God had offered: you could have it, but only if you did the work.

Simon Hoggart[4]

Getting more enterprise involves addressing obstacles: obstacles to enterprising behaviour such as belief, individual and society values and attitudes, and obstacles to its application to (small) business such as a shortage of ideas, finance and advice.

If we want more enterprise then it helps to have some idea of what it is. Is enterprise a science? Are there theories about enterprise that can be used to predict accurately how it will behave in specific circumstances? Is enterprise an art? Is it something that is hard to define, but that can be recognised when it is seen, that can be followed by many or demonstrated only by a few, and that, while it has rules, often appears to succeed by breaking the rules? Or is enterprise a magic, because it is a mystery to us, because it is unpredictable and because we have no control over it?

In this book some of the issues relevant to such a debate have been presented. There is no one single accepted view on enterprise, on what it means, what gives rise to it, what its implications are, or how it can be promoted. However, 'One of the commonplace yet probably essential characteristics in the development of any new body of knowledge is the competing values of those who generate and use that knowledge.'[5] The authors hope that this book helps to present the emerging body of knowledge on enterprise.

REFERENCES

1 Industrial Policy Review Group, *A Time For Change: Industrial Policy for the 1990s* (Dublin: Stationery Office, 1992), p. 7.
2 M. Penrose, 'Is America In Decline?', *Harvard Business Review* 1992; July–August: 34–45, at 44.
3 S. Zadek and E. Mayo, 'Ten Reasons Why Society Does Count', *New Economics Magazine* 1997; 41(Spring): 5.
4 S. Hoggart, *America: A User's Guide* (London: Fontana, 1991), p. 6.
5 A. Pettigrew in the Foreword to C. B. Handy, *Understanding Organisations* (Harmondsworth: Penguin, 1976), p. 7.

INDEX